Vision and Mind

Vision and Mind

Selected Readings in the Philosophy of Perception

edited by
Alva Noë and Evan Thompson

A Bradford Book

The MIT Press
Cambridge, Massachusetts
London, England

This book was set in Sabon by SNP Best-set Typesetter Ltd., Hong Kong.

Printed and bound in the United States of America.

Library of Congress Cataloging-in-Publication Data

Vision and mind : selected readings in the philosophy of perception / edited by Alva Noë and Evan Thompson.
    p. cm.
  Includes bibliographical references and index.
  ISBN 0-262-14078-0 (alk. paper)—ISBN 0-262-64047-3 (pbk. : alk. paper)
  ISBN-13 978-0-262-14078-2 (hc. : alk. paper)—
  ISBN-13 978-0-262-64047-3 (pbk. : alk. paper)
  1. Perception (Philosophy) I. Noë, Alva. II. Thompson, Evan.

B828.45 .V565 2002
121′.34—dc21   2002023533

10 9 8 7 6 5 4 3

Contents

Preface

The writings in this volume investigate the nature of visual perception. Our goal has been to produce a collection that can serve as a starting point for the philosophy of perception. These writings provide, we believe, a clear statement of the central issues confronting the philosophical study of perception today. It is our hope that this volume will make a contribution to their ongoing study.

All the works collected here, except for one, have been previously published. Many are classics; most have been important for philosophical discussion of perception; all serve, we hope, to indicate clearly an important family of problems. In order to make the book as useful as possible, we have resisted (in all but a few instances) reprinting materials that are easily available elsewhere or that are excerpted from larger works.

Vision and Mind has been long in the making. Through several incarnations, it has grown leaner and more focused. We are grateful to many people for advice, criticism, and encouragement. We would like to express our thanks to Ned Block, Justin Broakes, Alex Byrne, Dave Chalmers, Dan Dennett, Sean Kelly, Erik Myin, Luiz Pessoa, Susanna Siegel, and Francisco Varela. We are grateful to the authors and to their original publishers for granting us permission to include their works here. We offer special thanks to Carolyn Gray Anderson and to her predecessor at The MIT Press, Amy Yeager, for their strong support of this project. We also wish to thank Diane Zorn for her help in preparing the manuscript. Finally, A. N. gratefully acknowledges the support of faculty research funds from the Humanities Division of the University of California, Santa Cruz.

Sources

Maurice Merleau-Ponty. Selections from *Phenomenology of Perception*. Trans. Colin Smith. London: Routledge & Kegan Paul, [1945] 1962. Reprinted by permission of the publisher. "The 'sensation' as a unit of experience." (pp. 3–12) "Experience and objective thought: The problem of the body." (pp. 67–72) "The theory of the body is already a theory of perception." (pp. 203–206)

H. P. Grice. "Some remarks about the senses." In R. J. Butler, ed., *Analytic Philosophy*, 15–153. Oxford: Basil Blackwell, 1962. Reprinted by permission of the publisher.

G. E. M. Anscombe. "The intentionality of sensation: A grammatical feature." In *Metaphysics and the Philosophy of Mind: Collected Philosophical Papers, Vol. III*, 3–20. Oxford: Blackwell, 1965. Reprinted by permission of the publisher.

James J. Gibson. "A theory of direct visual perception." In J. R. Royce and W. W. Rozeboom, eds., *The Psychology of Knowing*, 215–240. New York: Gordon & Breach, 1972. Reprinted by permission of the publisher.

P. F. Strawson. "Perception and its objects." In G. F. Macdonald, ed., *Perception and Identity: Essays Presented to A. J. Ayer with His Replies*, 41–60. London: Macmillan, 1979. Reprinted by permission of the author and the publisher.

Richard L. Gregory. "Perceptions as hypotheses." *Philosophical Transactions of the Royal Society* B 290 (1980): 181–197. Reprinted by permission of the author and the Royal Society.

David Lewis. "Veridical hallucination and prosthetic perception." In *Australasian Journal of Philosophy* 58 (1980): 239–249. Reprinted by permission of the author and the Australasion Journal of Philosophy. D. Lewis, "Postscript." In *Philosophical Papers Volume 2*, 287–290. Reprinted by permission of the author. Oxford: Oxford University Press, 1986.

Paul Snowdon. "Perception, vision and causation." *Aristotelian Society Proceedings New Series* 81 (1980–1981): 175–192. Reprinted by courtesy of the Editor of the Aristotelian Society: © [1981] and by permission of the author.

Jerry A. Fodor and Zenon W. Pylyshyn. "How direct is visual perception?: Some reflections on Gibson's 'Ecological Approach.'" *Cognition* 9 (1981): 139–196. Reprinted with permission from Elsevier Science.

David Marr. "Part I: Introduction and Philosophical Preliminaries." Selections from *Vision: A Computational Investigation into the Human Representation and Processing of Visual Information*. New York: W. H. Freeman and Company, 1982. Used with permission.
"General introduction." (pp. 3–7)
"The philosophy and the approach." (pp. 8–38)

Christopher Peacocke. "Sensation and the content of experience: A distinction." In Christopher Peacocke, *Sense and Content*, 4–26. Oxford: Oxford University Press, 1983. Reprinted by permission of Oxford University Press.

Davida Y. Teller. "Linking propositions." *Vision Research* 24, no. 10 (1984): 1233–1246. Reprinted with permission from Elsevier Science.

Gareth Evans. "Molyneux's question." In Gareth Evans, *Collected Papers*, ed. John McDowell, 364–399. Oxford: Oxford University Press, 1985. © Antonia Phillips 1985. Reprinted by permission of Oxford University Press.

Evan Thompson, Adrian Palacios, and Francisco J. Varela. "Ways of coloring: Comparative color vision as a case study for cognitive science." *Behavioral and Brain Sciences* 15 (1992): 1–26. Reprinted with the permission of the authors and Cambridge University Press.

Fred Dretske. "Conscious experience." *Mind* 102, no. 406 (1993): 263–283. Reprinted by permission of Oxford University Press.

John McDowell. "The content of perceptual experience." *The Philosophical Quarterly* 44, no. 175 (1994): 190–205. Reprinted by permission of the editors of The Philosophical Quarterly.

Dana H. Ballard. "On the function of visual representation." In Kathleen Akins, ed., *Perception*, 111–131. *Vancouver Studies in Cognitive Science*, vol. 5. Oxford: Oxford University Press, 1996. Used by permission of Oxford University Press, Inc.

Daniel C. Dennett. "Seeing is believing—or is it?" In Kathleen Akins, ed., *Perception*, 158–172. Vancouver Studies in Cognitive Science, vol. 5. Oxford: Oxford University Press, 1996. Used by permission of Oxford University Press, Inc., and by permission of the author.

Paul Bach-y-Rita. "Substitution sensorielle et qualia" [Sensory substitution and qualia]. In J. Proust, ed., *Perception et Intermodalité*, 81–100. Paris: Presses Universitaires de France, 1996. Reprinted by permission of the author.

A. David Milner and Melvyn A. Goodale. "The visual brain in action." *Psyche: An Interdisciplinary Journal of Research on Consciousness*. Available at ⟨http://psyche.cs.monash.edu/au/v4/psyche-4-12-milner.html⟩. 1998. Reprinted by permission of the authors.

David J. Chalmers. "What is a neural correlate of consciousness?" In T. Metzinger, ed., *Neural Correlates of Consciousness: Empirical and Conceptual Questions*, 17–39. Cambridge, MA: The MIT Press, 2000. Reprinted by permission of the authors and MIT.

1

Introduction

Alva Noë and Evan Thompson

The philosophy of perception is a microcosm of the metaphysics of mind. Its central problems—*What is perception? What is the nature of perceptual consciousness? How can one fit an account of perceptual experience into a broader account of the nature of the mind and the world?*—are problems at the heart of metaphysics. It is often justifiably said that the theory of perception (and especially vision) is the area of psychology and neuroscience that has made the greatest progress in recent years. Despite this progress, or perhaps because of it, philosophical problems about perception retain a great urgency, both for philosophy and for science.

Beyond these general remarks, however, it is difficult to state precisely what the philosophy of perception comprises, and hence which topics, issues, and viewpoints should be included in a book such as this one. Numerous philosophical problems about perception and many different strands in the philosophy of perception exist. For this reason, we have not tried to make this book a comprehensive collection of philosophical writings on perception. Our aim, instead, has been more focused.

The works collected in this volume target a distinct philosophical and scientific orthodoxy about the nature of perception. Some of the papers defend the orthodoxy; most criticize it; and some set forth positive alternatives to it. Each selection provides, we believe, a crucial moment in the articulation of an important family of problems for contemporary philosophy of perception. Our purpose in this brief introduction is to sketch the philosophical and scientific setting of this family of problems.

1 The Orthodox View

The defining problem of traditional visual theory is that of understanding how we come to enjoy such rich, apparently world-representing visual impressions. You open your eyes and you take in an environment of meaningful objects and events and of colors, forms, and movements. What makes such perceptual experience so difficult to explain is the fact—if it is a fact—that when we open our eyes and contemplate a scene, we make no *direct contact* with that which we seem to see. What is given to us, one might suppose, is not the world itself, but the pattern of light on the retina, and *that* pattern does not supply enough information to determine how things are in the environment. For example, from the retinal image of a table alone, it may not be possible to tell whether it is large and far away, or small and nearby.

Visual scientists are quick to add that the problem is really even more baffling than we have indicated. The eye is in nearly constant motion; the resolving power (spatial and chromatic) of the retina is limited and nonuniform; passage to the retina is blocked by blood vessels and nerve fibers; there is a large "blind spot" on the retina where there are no photoreceptors; there are two retinal images, each of which is upside down. Given this impoverished basis, how do we manage to enjoy such richly detailed visual experiences of the environment? The central puzzle for traditional visual science has been to explain how the brain bridges the gap between what is given to the visual system and what is actually experienced by the perceiver.

In the face of this puzzle, an orthodox or "Establishment View" of perception (Fodor and Pylyshyn, chapter 10) has taken shape over the last fifty years. According to this orthodoxy, perception is a process whereby the brain, or a functionally dedicated subsystem of the brain, builds up representations of relevant features of the environment on the basis of information encoded by the sensory receptors. As David Marr (chapter 11) surmises: "Vision is the *process* of discovering from images what is present in the world, and where it is." Because the patterns on the retina are not sufficient by themselves to determine the layout of the surrounding environment, perception must be thought of as a process of inductive inference. Perceptions are, as Richard L. Gregory (chapter 7) suggests, hypotheses concerning the distal causes of proximal stimulation. In the famous phrase of Helmholtz, perception is unconscious inference.

The orthodox view, in its modern computational form, treats perception as a "subpersonal" process carried out by functional subsystems or modules instantiated in the person's or animal's brain. For this reason, among others, it is often held that much of perception—specifically "early vision," in which a model of the surface layout is supposed to be produced—is "cognitively impenetrable," that is, impervious to the direct influence of cognition or thought. In other words, the beliefs and expectations of the perceiver are thought to have no influence on the character of the subpersonal computations that constitute perception. Thus, on the orthodox approach, perception is thought-independent (see Pylyshyn 1999 for a recent statement of this position).

Most adherents of the orthodox view also believe that for every conscious perceptual state of the subject, a particular set of neurons exists whose activities are sufficient, as a matter of scientific law, for the occurrence of that state. Davida Teller (chapter 13) calls such neurons "the bridge locus" of visual perception; others, like David J. Chalmers (chapter 22), call them the "neural correlate of consciousness" (NCC) for visual perception. According to this viewpoint, to suppose that there is no bridge locus or neural correlate of consciousness would be to give up all hope of securing a scientific explanation of perceptual experience.

2 Heterodox Views

Although the orthodox view has dominated perceptual psychology, visual neuroscience, and artificial vision and robotics, important alternative research programs have existed for many decades. Collectively these alternatives constitute a significant heterodoxy in visual science (and cognitive science more generally), one whose influence seems to be felt increasingly in mainstream cognitive science and philosophy. Important differences exist among these alternative research programs, but what unites them is their convergence on certain fundamental criticisms of the orthodox view and their insistence on the inseparability of perception and action.

The Ecological Approach
The theoretical and empirical research on vision undertaken by the perceptual psychologist James J. Gibson (1966; 1979; chapter 5) marks an important break with the orthodox view. Perception, Gibson argues, is not an occurrence that takes place in the brain of the perceiver, but rather is an act of the whole animal, the act of perceptually guided exploration of the environment. One misdescribes vision if one thinks of it as a subpersonal process whereby the brain builds up an internal model of the environment on the basis of impoverished sensory images. Such a conception of vision is pitched at the wrong level, namely, that of the internal enabling conditions for vision rather than that of vision itself as an achievement of the whole animal. Put another way, the function of vision is to keep the perceiver in touch with the environment and to guide action, not to produce inner experiences and representations.

According to this animal-level account, the information directly available to the perceiver in vision is not to be found in the pattern of irradiation on the retinal surface, but rather in the world or environment that the animal itself explores. In other words, Gibson denies the assumption of the orthodox view—and of representational theories in general—that one makes no direct contact with that which one sees. For Gibson, perception is direct: It is not mediated by sensations or images that serve as the basis for reconstructing a representation of the things that we see. Perception, one might say, is direct inspection, not *re*-presentation.

If perception does not operate according to mechanisms of inferential reconstruction on the basis of internal representations, then how does it operate, according to Gibson? The central working hypothesis of this *ecological* approach is that the perceiver makes direct contact with the environment thanks to the animal's sensitivity to invariant structures in the ambient light. Two points are important here. First, perception is active: the animal moves its eyes, head, and body to scan the layout visually, while simultaneously moving through the environment. Thus visual perception occurs not as a series of snapshots corresponding to stationary retinal images, but as a dynamic visual flow. Second, there are lawful correlations between the structure of this flow and visible properties of the environment. Because perceivers are implicitly familiar with these lawful correlations, they are able to "pick up" content from the environment as specified in the light without having to reconstruct the environment from impoverished images through information processing.

The ecological approach remains highly controversial. Perhaps the most well-known criticism is that of Jerry A. Fodor and Zenon W. Pylyshyn (chapter 10). They defend the Establishment View, and they insist that Gibson failed to make a serious break with this view. At the end of the day, they suggest, the only significant contact one makes with the world in perception is through the stimulation of one's sensory receptors by patterns of energy. Perception, therefore, must be indirect: It must be a process of representation on the basis of that peripheral sensory contact. According to this way of thinking, perception remains, from a scientific viewpoint, a subpersonal process of computational representation, and accordingly is not usefully thought of as an animal-level achievement. On the other hand, John McDowell (chapter 17) scrutinizes the conceptual and epistemological coherence of this Establishment position in the context of philosophical issues about the content of perceptual experience and knowledge; he argues that the nature of perception will continue to be misunderstood as long as perception is cast as an internal, subpersonal process.

The Enactive Approach

Another alternative approach to perception has emerged from the work of the neuroscientists Humberto R. Maturana and Francisco J. Varela. They argue that it is a mistake to think of the nervous system as an input-output system that encodes an internal representation of the outside world (Maturana and Varela 1980, 1987; Varela 1979, 1995, 1997). Rather than representing an independent, external world, the nervous system generates or brings forth, on the basis of its own self-organized activity, the perceptuo-motor domain of the animal. (A similar viewpoint has also been put forward by the neuroscientist Walter Freeman: See Freeman and Skarda 1995; Skarda and Freeman 1987; Freeman 1999). On the basis of this reappraisal, Varela has presented an enactive approach to perception (Varela 1991; Thompson, Palacios, and Varela, chapter 15), as one component of a comprehensive *enactive* or *embodied* view in cognitive science (Varela, Thompson, and Rosch 1991; see also Clark 1997). According to this view, meaningful perceptual items, rather than being internally represented in the form of a world-model inside the head, are enacted or brought forth as a result of the structural coupling of the organism and its environment (see also Noë forthcoming).

A good example of the enactive approach is the account of color vision provided by Evan Thompson, Adrian Palacios, and Francisco J. Varela (chapter 15). They reject the orthodox view, as exemplified in computational color vision research (e.g., Maloney and Wandell 1986) and functionalist philosophy of mind (e.g., Matthen 1988; Hilbert 1992), according to which the function of color vision is to recover from the retinal image reliable estimates of the invariant distal property of surface spectral reflectance (the percentage of light at each wavelength that a surface reflects). On the basis of cross-species comparisons of color vision, Thompson, Palacios, and Varela argue that different animals have different phenomenal color spaces, and that color vision does not have the function of detecting any single type of environmental property. They then use these arguments to motivate an enactive account of color, according to which color properties are enacted by the perceptuo-motor coupling of animals with their environments (see also Thompson 1995, 2000).

Animate Vision

The research program of *animate vision* has emerged at the interface of computational vision, artificial intelligence, and robotics (Ballard, chapter 18; see also Ballard 1991; Ballard et al. 1997). Instead of abstracting perceptual processes from their bodily context, animate vision proposes what Ballard calls a distinct *embodiment level* of explanation, which specifies how the facts of sensorimotor embodiment shape perception. For example, the orthodox view starts from the abstraction of a stationary retinal image and asks how the visual system manages to derive a model of the objective world; in so doing, it decomposes visual processes into modules that are passive in the sense of not being interconnected with motor processes. Animate vision, however, starts from the sensorimotor cycles of saccadic eye movement and gaze fixation, and asks how the perceiver is able to fixate points in the environment; in so doing, it decomposes visual processes into visuomotor modules that guide action and exploration. Such an embodied, action-based analysis reduces the need for certain kinds of representations in vision, in particular for an online, moment-to-moment, detailed world-model.

The Sensorimotor Contingency Theory

According to this theory, put forward by J. Kevin O'Regan and Alva Noë (see O'Regan 1992; O'Regan and Noë 2001; Noë and O'Regan, chapter 23; Noë 2001, 2002, forthcoming), it is a mistake to think of vision as a process taking place in the brain. Although the brain is necessary for vision, neural processes are not, in themselves, sufficient to produce seeing. Instead, seeing is an exploratory activity mediated by the animal's mastery of *sensorimotor contingencies*. That is, seeing is a skill-based activity of environmental exploration. Visual experience is not something that happens *in* an individual. It is something he or she *does*. This sensorimotor conception forms the basis of Noë and O'Regan's challenge (chapter 23) to the widespread view, articulated in this volume by Teller (chapter 13) and Chalmers (chapter 22), that the content of visual experience is represented at some specific stage of neural processing (the "bridge locus" or the "neural correlate of consciousness").

3   The Importance of Action and Embodiment

If one common theme emerges from the heterodoxy, it is that perception must be understood in the context of action and embodiment. This theme is echoed by other chapters in this book.

Chapter 21 by the neuropsychologists A. David Milner and Melvyn A. Goodale provides an example from recent neuroscience that draws attention to the importance of perception-action linkages. Milner and Goodale argue that two visual systems exist, one of which is dedicated to the visual guidance of action (chapter

21; see also Milner and Goodale 1995). In support of this finding they adduce clinical studies in which the reports that perceivers make indicate *misperception* even though their motor responses seem to be based on accurate visual assessments of the environment.

Paul Bach-y-Rita (chapter 20) discusses his work on tactile-vision substitution systems. This research suggests that it is possible to "see" by means of tactile sensations, if these sensations are appropriately embedded within a sensorimotor framework.

In a different vein, Gareth Evans (chapter 14) emphasizes the importance of skillful capacities of bodily movement for perception, in his philosophical analysis of the classic "Molyneux Question" posed by William Molyneux to John Locke—whether a man blind from birth, who is able to distinguish a sphere and a cube by touch, would be able to tell, upon having his sight restored, which is which by sight alone before touching them. Evans argues that mastery, by the perceiver, of a set of perceptuo-motor skills is a condition on the perceiver's ability to experience space.

Finally, the importance of action and embodiment has long been emphasized by philosophers and psychologists working in the tradition of phenomenology derived from Edmund Husserl; for this reason, there is significant convergence between the concerns and analyses of this tradition and action-oriented approaches to perception in recent cognitive science (see Petitot et al. 1999). Husserl, in his groundbreaking and extensive analyses of the phenomenology of perceptual experience, delineated the intricate functional interdependencies of perception and kinaesthesis (Husserl 1997; see also Mulligan 1995), and these analyses were taken up and developed by Maurice Merleau-Ponty in his 1945 book, *Phenomenology of Perception*, selections of which are reprinted here.

4 Perceptual Experience and the New Skepticism

We now turn to another recent topic of discussion in philosophy and visual science that also brings critical pressure to bear upon the orthodox view. The issue concerns the kind of experience one takes oneself to have in seeing: Does one enjoy the sort of richly detailed visual impressions that perceptual scientists and philosophers have typically assumed one does? A growing number of philosophers and scientists challenge this basic presupposition of the orthodox stance (see Dennett 1991, chapter 19; Ballard, chapter 18; O'Regan 1992; Mack and Rock 1998). As Dana H. Ballard (chapter 18) puts it: "You Don't See What You Think You See." This challenge has given rise to a new form of skepticism about perceptual experience. Whereas traditional skepticism challenged whether we can know, on the basis of experience, that things are as we experience them as being, the new skepticism questions whether we even have the perceptual experience we think we have. Perceptual consciousness, according to the new skepticism, is a kind of false consciousness. Perceptual experience is a "grand illusion."

The skeptical reasoning goes as follows. It seems to us as if we enjoy picturelike visual experiences that capture everything before us in sharp focus and uniform detail. You open your eyes and *there it all is*. This idea about the character of visual experience is beautifully captured by Ernst Mach, who represented his (monocular) visual field in a now famous drawing (see figure 1.1). In Mach's drawing, the visual field is in sharp focus and uniform detail from the center out to the periphery where

Figure 1.1
From *The Visual Field* (Mach 1959).

it suddenly fades to white. Yet there is ample reason to believe that visual experience is not as Mach's picture would have us believe.

First, because of the relatively limited number of photoreceptors at the periphery of the visual field, humans have very poor parafoveal vision. Hold a playing card at arm's length just within your field of view. You will not be able to tell its color. The visual field is *not* sharply focused from the center out to the periphery, contrary to what Mach's drawing suggests.

Second, there is in each eye a stretch of the retina—the optic disk—where there are no photoreceptors. As a result, one is in fact blind to what falls on this region (the "blind spot"). One does not normally notice the gap, even in monocular vision. If you fix your gaze at a wall of uniform color, with one eye shut, you will not notice a gap in your impression of the wall corresponding to the part of the wall you cannot see because of the blind spot. Your perceptual experience, so runs the skeptical reasoning, deceives you as to its true character. The visual field is not continuous and gap free, as Mach's picture would suggest.

Third, psychologists have recently demonstrated the attention-dependent character of perception. Unless you actively attend to detail in your environment, you do not perceive that detail. In one demonstration, you are asked to watch a videotape of a basketball game and to attend to some aspect of play. A person in a gorilla suit walks onto the court, stops in the middle to do a little jig, and then continues his way across the court (Simons and Chabris 1999). Very few people watching the tape will report seeing the gorilla! In another series of demonstrations, changes are made to the scene before you, and you are asked to report the change. It is very difficult to do this because, unless you attended to the change when it happened, you are unlikely to be able to tell. What makes these experiments striking is that they seem to challenge Mach's conception of what seeing is like. Despite the impression of seeing everything, people see only very little of what is there before them.

From these facts, one can conclude that the way of thinking about perceptual experience captured by Mach in his drawing is, in fact, a mischaracterization of what experience is really like. It may seem to you as if your perceptual experience is detailed, continuous, and gap-free. In fact, it is fragmentary, discontinuous, and sparsely detailed. You have false beliefs about the character of experience. You do not actually enjoy the experience you think you do.

This rejection of the phenomenological assumptions implicit in the orthodox approach to perception has important implications for framing the key problems of perceptual science. As we have seen, the central problem for traditional visual science is that of understanding how you see so much given such limited perceptual contact with the world. A new approach, taking its start from the new skepticism, seeks to understand instead why it seems to you as if you see so much, when in fact you see so very little!

Is perceptual experience a grand illusion? What is the character of perceptual experience? The chapters in this volume by Daniel C. Dennett, Dana H. Ballard, and Alva Noë and J. K. O'Regan all touch on these questions.

Finally, it bears mentioning that these questions about the nature of visual experience are relevant to another long-standing issue in the philosophy of perception— that of how to understand the differences between the sensory modalities. One way to appreciate this issue is to notice that there is nothing about the character of the neural impulses in the brain that indicates whether they are caused by stimulation of the retina, cochlea, or other sensory membranes. Many scientists seem satisfied with some variant of Mueller's (1838) idea of "specific nerve energy," according to which the senses are differentiated by the different pathways along which they propagate neural activity. An alternative and widely influential philosophical proposal is advanced by H. P. Grice (chapter 3), who argues that the senses can be individuated by their distinct qualitative characters. O'Regan and Noë (2001) and Noë and O'Regan (chapter 23) have challenged these proposals, arguing instead that the senses are to be distinguished by the different patterns of sensorimotor contingency by which they are governed. Their position is compatible with Bach-y-Rita's work on tactile-vision substitution systems (chapter 20), which suggests that it is possible to "see" or experience the world "visually" through sensory systems other than vision. *INCLUDING COLOR?*

5   The Argument from Illusion

In a different context from that of the foregoing discussion, some philosophers have attacked the conception of perceptual experience implicit in the orthodox approach. J. L. Austin, and then after him Paul Snowdon and John McDowell, have attacked the well-known *Argument from Illusion*. According to this argument, it is not possible to tell the difference between a veridical visual experience and a corresponding hallucinatory one. That's why hallucinations can fool you. Therefore, it must be that there is no difference in what you are aware of when you undergo a perceptual experience and what you are aware of when you undergo the corresponding hallucination. You know, in the hallucinatory case, that what you are aware of is a mental figment. It follows, then, that what you are aware of in the veridical case is also, at least in the first instance, a mental figment. The conclusion of the argument is that the direct objects of perceptual awareness are not things in the world, but mental items called "sense data."

Snowdon (chapter 9) and McDowell (1982, 1986), building on ideas of Austin (1962) and Hinton (1973), reject the claim that there is a common experiential content to perceptual experiences and the corresponding hallucinations. There is all the difference in the world between something's looking a certain way to one, and its merely seeming to one as if something looks a certain way to one. In the first case, one's experience involves an object in the world. In the second, it does not. Because there is no common content to veridical and hallucinatory experiences, the idea that an individual is aware of one and the same thing when he or she perceives/hallucinates can be rejected.

Philosophers have explored the further implications of this way of thinking about perceptual experience (the so-called disjunctive view of experience). One important further implication concerns the status of what is known as the causal theory of perception. On one natural interpretation, this theory rests on the idea that cases of genuine perception and some cases of misperception turn only on the absence of an appropriate causal dependence between the experience and what the experience is of. It might seem, however, that this cannot be right, at least on the disjunctive conception. After all, on the disjunctive conception, there is no one experiential content common to both the hallucinatory and the veridical episodes. This issue is explored by Snowdon (chapter 9). David Lewis (chapter 8) provides a now classic presentation of the causal theory of perception.

6   Thought and Experience

The thought-independence of perceptual experience is another important theme in recent philosophy of perception. It has been defended and elaborated, over the years, by both Fred Dretske (1969; chapter 16) and by Peacocke (1992). It is rejected, however, by some of the philosophers collected in this volume—G. E. M. Anscombe (chapter 4), Grice (chapter 3), Strawson (chapter 6), Peacocke (chapter 12)—and also by Sellars (1963). The central idea of these writers—central also to the phenomenological tradition—is that perceptual experience has *intentional content*— that is, it purports to represent the world as being this way or that. For experience to have perceptual content in this way, the perceiver must have some grasp, however primitive, of how the experience represents the world as being. The intentional, world-referring character of perceptual experience has a further important consequence. It is a common claim that perceptual judgments made on the basis of perceptual experience—such as, for example, that there's a tomato on the table—go beyond what is, strictly speaking, given in the experience itself. The experience itself, is after all, compatible with there being no tomato on the table at all, but merely a tomato likeness of one kind or another. A strictly accurate description of experience, so runs this line of reasoning, must abjure all mention of the stuff of the mind-independent world and confine itself to the raw sensory data the presence of which is guaranteed by the mere occurrence of the experience itself. This argument falters, however, because, as Strawson (chapter 6) insists, it utterly misdescribes the character of our perceptual experience, which presents itself to us precisely in the terms needed to frame the relevant judgment. It would be impossible to describe accurately the experience in question, so the rebuttal runs, without mentioning tomatoes. The concept *tomato* enters immediately into the content of the experience.

7   Conclusion

It would be difficult to overstate the degree to which the problems dealt with by the writers in this book are alive and unresolved. Insofar as these problems are empirical, much work remains to be done. But what is at stake is not merely the correct empirical account of the workings of perception, and hence the standing of various approaches in visual science. Rather, because perception is such a pervasive feature of one's conscious life, what is at stake is ultimately one's understanding of consciousness itself and one's conception of one's place in the natural world.

References

Austin, J. L. 1962. *Sense and Sensibilia*. Oxford: The Clarendon Press.

Ballard, D. H. 1991. Animate vision. *Artificial Intelligence* 48: 57–86.

Ballard, D. H., M. M. Hayhoe, P. K. Pook, and R. P. N. Rao. 1997. Deictic codes for the embodiment of cognition. *Behavioral and Brain Sciences* 20: 723–767.

Clark, A. 1997. *Being There: Putting Brain, Body, and World Together Again*. Cambridge, MA: The MIT Press.

Dennett, D. C. 1991. *Consciousness Explained*. Boston: Little Brown.

Dretske, F. I. 1969. *Seeing and Knowing*. London: Routledge.

Freeman, W. J. 1999. *How Brains Make Up Their Minds*. London: Weidenfeld and Nicholson.

Freeman, W. J., and C. Skarda. 1995. Spatial EEG patterns, nonlinear dynamics, and perception: The neo-Sherringtonian view. *Brain Research Reviews* 10: 145–175.

Gibson, J. J. 1966. *The Senses Considered as Perceptual Systems.* Boston: Houghton Mifflin.

Gibson, J. J. 1979. *The Ecological Approach to Visual Perception.* Boston: Houghton Mifflin.

Hilbert, D. R. 1992. What is color vision? *Philosophical Studies* 68: 351–370.

Hinton, J. M. 1973. *Experiences: An Inquiry into Some Ambiguities.* Oxford: Clarendon Press.

Husserl, E. 1997. *Thing and Space: Lectures of 1907.* Trans. Richard Rojcewicz. Dordrecht: Kluwer Academic Publishers.

Mach, E. 1959. *The Analysis of Sensations and the Relation of the Physical to the Psychical.* Trans. C. M. Williams. New York: Dover Publications.

Mack, A., and I. Rock. 1998. *Inattentional Blindness.* Cambridge, MA: The MIT Press.

Maloney, L. T., and B. A. Wandell. 1986. Color constancy: A method for recovering surface spectral reflectance. *Journal of the Optical Society of America* A3: 29–33.

Matthen, M. 1988. Biological functions and perceptual content. *Journal of Philosophy* 85: 5–27.

Maturana, H. R., and F. J. Varela. 1980. *Autopoiesis and Cognition: The Realization of the Living.* Boston Studies in the Philosophy of Science, Volume 42. Dordrecht: Kluwer Academic Publishers.

Maturana, H. R., and F. J. Varela. 1987. *The Tree of Knowledge: The Biological Roots of Human Understanding.* Boston: Shambala/New Science Library.

McDowell, J. 1982. Criteria, defeasibility and knowledge. *Proceedings of the British Academy* 68: 455–479.

McDowell, J. 1986. Singular thought and the extent of inner space. In P. Pettit and J. McDowell, eds., *Subject, Thought, and Context,* 137–180. Oxford: Oxford University Press.

Milner, A. D., and M. A. Goodale. 1995. *The Visual Brain in Action.* Oxford: Oxford University Press.

Mueller, J. 1838. *Handbuch der Physiologie des Menschen.* Coblenz: Hoelscher.

Mulligan, K. 1995. Perception. In Barry Smith and David Woodruff Smith, eds., *The Cambridge Companion to Husserl,* 168–238. Cambridge: Cambridge University Press.

Noë, A. 2001. Experience and the active mind. *Synthese* 129: 41–60.

Noë, A. 2002. On what we see. *Pacific Philosophial Quarterly* 83(1).

Noë, A. Forthcoming. *Action in Perception.* Cambridge, MA: The MIT Press.

O'Regan, J. K. 1992. Solving the "real" mysteries of visual perception: The world as an outside memory. *Canadian Journal of Psychology* 46: 461–488.

O'Regan, J. K., and A. Noë. 2001. A sensorimotor account of vision and visual consciousness. *Behavioral and Brain Sciences* 24(5).

Peacocke, C. 1992. *A Study of Concepts.* Cambridge, MA: The MIT Press.

Petitot, J., F. J. Varela, B. Pachoud, and J.-M. Roy. 1999. *Naturalizing Phenomenology: Issues in Contemporary Phenomenology and Cognitive Science*. Stanford, CA: Stanford University Press.

Pylyshyn, Z. 1999. Is vision continuous with cognition? The case for cognitive impenetrability of visual perception. *Behavioral and Brain Sciences* 3: 341–423.

Sellars, W. 1956. Empiricism and the philosophy of mind. In Herbert Feigl and Michael Scriven, eds., *Minnesota Studies in the Philosophy of Science, Volume I: The Foundations of Science and the Concepts of Psychology and Psychoanalysis*, 253–329. Minnesota: University of Minnesota Press.

Simons, D. J., and C. F. Chabris. 1999. Gorillas in our midst: Sustained inattentional blindness for dynamic events. *Perception* 28: 1059–1074.

Skarda, C., and W. Freeman. 1987. How brains make chaos in order to make sense of the world. *Behavioral and Brain Sciences* 10: 161–195.

Thompson, E. 1995. *Colour Vision: A Study in Cognitive Science and the Philosophy of Perception*. London: Routledge Press.

Thompson, E. 2000. Comparative color vision: quality space and visual ecology. In Steven Davis, ed., *Color Perception: Philosophical, Psychological, Artistic and Computational Perspectives*, 163–186. Vancouver Studies in Cognitive Science, Volume 9. Oxford: Oxford University Press.

Varela, F. J. 1979. *Principles of Biological Autonomy*. New Jersey: Elsevier North-Holland.

Varela, F. J. 1991. Perception and the origin of cognition: A cartography of current ideas. In F. J. Varela and J.-P. Dupuy, eds., *Understanding Origins: Contemporary Ideas on the Origin of Life, Mind, and Society*. Boston Studies in the Philosophy of Science, Vol. 130. Dordrecht: Kluwer Academic Publishers.

Varela, F. J. 1995. Resonant cell assemblies: A new approach to cognitive functions and neural synchrony. *Biological Research* 28: 81–95.

Varela, F. J. 1997. Patterns of life: Intertwining identity and cognition. *Brain and Cognition* 34: 72–87.

Varela, F. J., E. Thompson, and E. Rosch. 1991. *The Embodied Mind: Cognitive Science and Human Experience*. Cambridge, MA: The MIT Press.

2

Selections from *Phenomenology of Perception*

Maurice Merleau-Ponty

The "Sensation" as a Unit of Experience

At the outset of the study of perception, we find in language the notion of sensation, which seems immediate and obvious: I have a sensation of redness, of blueness, of hot or cold. It will, however, be seen that nothing could in fact be more confused, and that because they accepted it readily, traditional analyses missed the phenomenon of perception.

I might in the first place understand by sensation the way in which I am affected and the experiencing of a state of myself. The greyness which, when I close my eyes, surrounds me, leaving no distance between me and it, the sounds that encroach on my drowsiness and hum "in my head" perhaps give some indication of what pure sensation might be. I might be said to have sense-experience (*sentir*) precisely to the extent that I coincide with the sensed, that the latter ceases to have any place in the objective world, and that it signifies nothing for me. This entails recognizing that sensation should be sought on the hither side of any qualified content, since red and blue, in order to be distinguishable as two colours, must already form some picture before me, even though no precise place be assigned to them, and thus cease to be part of myself. Pure sensation will be the experience of an undifferentiated, instantaneous, dotlike impact. It is unnecessary to show, since authors are agreed on it, that this notion corresponds to nothing in our experience, and that the most rudimentary *factual perceptions* that we are acquainted with, in creatures such as the ape or the hen, have a bearing on relationships and not on any absolute terms.[1] But this does not dispose of the question as to why we feel justified *in theory* in distinguishing within experience a layer of "impressions." Let us imagine a white patch on a homogeneous background. All the points in the patch have a certain "function" in common, that of forming themselves into a "shape." The colour of the shape is more intense, and as it were more resistent than that of the background; the edges of the white patch "belong" to it, and are not part of the background although they adjoin it: the patch appears to be placed on the background and does not break it up. Each part arouses the expectation of more than it contains, and this elementary perception is therefore already charged with a *meaning*. But if the shape and the background, as a whole, are not sensed, they must be sensed, one may object, in each of their points. To say this is to forget that each point in its turn can be perceived only as a figure on a background. When Gestalt theory informs us that a figure on a background is the simplest sense-given available to us, we reply that this is not a contingent characteristic of factual perception, which leaves us free, in an ideal analysis, to bring in the notion of impressions. It is the very definition of the phenomenon of perception, that without which a phenomenon cannot be said to be perception at all. The perceptual "something" is always in the middle of something else, it always forms part of a "field." A really homogeneous area offering *nothing to be* cannot be given to *any perception.* The structure of actual perception alone can teach us what perception is. The pure impression is, therefore, not only undiscoverable, but also imperceptible and so inconceivable as an instant of perception. If it is introduced, it is because instead of attending to the experience of perception, we overlook it in favour of the object perceived. A visual field is not made up of limited views. But an object seen is made up of bits of matter, and spatial points are external to each other. An isolated datum of perception is inconceivable, at least if we do the mental experiment of attempting to perceive such a thing. But in the world there are either isolated objects or a physical void.

I shall therefore give up any attempt to define sensation as pure impression. Rather, to see is to have colours or lights, to hear is to have sounds, to sense (*sentir*) is to have qualities. To know what sense-experience is, then, is it not enough to have seen a red or to have heard an A? But red and green are not sensations, they are the sensed (*sensibles*), and quality is not an element of consciousness, but a property of the object. Instead of providing a simple means of delimiting sensations, if we consider it in the experience itself which evinces it, the quality is as rich and mysterious as the object, or indeed the whole spectacle, perceived. This red patch which I see on the carpet is red only in virtue of a shadow which lies across it, its quality is apparent only in relation to the play of light upon it, and hence as an element in a spatial configuration. Moreover the colour can be said to be there only if it occupies an area of a certain size, too small an area not being describable in these terms. Finally this red would literally not be the same if it were not the "woolly red" of a carpet.[2] Analysis, then, discovers in each quality meanings which reside in it. It may be objected that this is true only of the qualities which form part of our actual experience, which are overlaid with a body of knowledge, and that we are still justified in conceiving a "pure quality" which would set limits to a pure sensation. But as we have just seen, this pure sensation would amount to no sensation, and thus to not feeling at all. The alleged self-evidence of sensation is not based on any testimony of consciousness, but on widely held prejudice. We think we know perfectly well what "seeing," "hearing," "feeling" are, because perception has long provided us with objects which are coloured or which emit sounds. When we try to analyse it, we transpose these objects into consciousness. We commit what psychologists call "the experience error," which means that what we know to be in things themselves we immediately take as being in our consciousness of them. We make perception out of things perceived. And since perceived things themselves are obviously accessible only through perception, we end by understanding neither. We are caught up in the world and we do not succeed in extricating ourselves from it in order to achieve consciousness of the world. If we did we should see that the quality is never experienced immediately, and that all consciousness is consciousness of something. Nor is this "something" necessarily an identifiable object. There are two ways of being mistaken about quality: one is to make it into an element of consciousness, when in fact it is an object *for* consciousness, to treat it as an incommunicable impression, whereas it always has a meaning; the other is to think that this meaning and this object, at the level of quality, are fully developed and determinate. The second error, like the first, springs from our prejudice about the world. Suppose we construct, by the use of optics and geometry, that bit of the world which can at any moment throw its image on our retina. Everything outside its perimeter, since it does not reflect upon any sensitive area, no more affects our vision than does light falling on our closed eyes. We ought, then, to perceive a segment of the world precisely delimited, surrounded by a zone of blackness, packed full of qualities with no interval between them, held together by definite relationships of size similar to those lying on the retina. The fact is that experience offers nothing like this, and we shall never, using the world as our starting-point, understand what a field of vision is. Even if it is possible to trace out a perimeter of vision by gradually approaching the centre of the lateral stimuli, the results of such measurement vary from one moment to another, and one never manages to determine the instant when a stimulus once seen is seen no longer. The region surrounding the visual field is not easy to describe, but what is certain is that it is neither black nor grey. There

Handwritten margin notes:

APPARENTLY SO!

IMAGINATION OR RECOLLECTION C/N/P SENSATION OR PERCEPTION

2 MISTAKES ABOUT Quality 1. FOR NOT OF CONSCIOUSNESS 2.

NOT OUR VISION, PERHAPS, BUT WE STILL PERCEIVE LIGHT ON CLOSED EYELIDS, + ALSO PERIPHERAL VISION.

BUT THE IMAGE ON THE RETINA IS REVERSED.

TIME FOR THE LAST PHOTON OR LIGHT FROM THE OBJECT, THEN TIME FOR THE REALIZATION THAT PERCEPTION HAS CEASED TO CATCH UP.

* WHY SHOULD A FIELD OF VISION BE STATIC?

Figure 2.1

occurs here an *indeterminate vision*, a *vision of something or other*, and, to take the extreme case, what is behind my back is not without some element of visual presence. The two straight lines in Müller-Lyer's optical illusion (figure 2.1) are neither of equal nor unequal length; it is only in the objective world that this question arises.[3] The visual field is that strange zone in which contradictory notions jostle each other because the objects—the straight lines of Müller-Lyer—are not, in that field, assigned to the realm of being, in which a comparison would be possible, but each is taken in its private context as if it did not belong to the same universe as the other. Psychologists have for a long time taken great care to overlook these phenomena. In the world taken in itself everything is determined. There are many unclear sights, as for example a landscape on a misty day, but then we always say that no real landscape is in itself unclear. It is so only for us. The object, psychologists would assert, is never ambiguous, but becomes so only through our inattention. The bounds of the visual field are not themselves variable, and there is a moment when the approaching object begins absolutely to be seen, but we do not "notice" it. But the notion of attention, as we shall show more fully, is supported by no evidence provided by consciousness. It is no more than an auxiliary hypothesis, evolved to save the prejudice in favour of an objective world. We must recognize the indeterminate as a positive phenomenon. It is in this atmosphere that quality arises. Its meaning is an equivocal meaning; we are concerned with an expressive value rather than with logical signification. The determinate quality by which empiricism tried to define sensation is an object, not an element, of consciousness, indeed it is the very lately developed object of scientific consciousness. For these two reasons, it conceals rather than reveals subjectivity.

The two definitions of sensation which we have just tried out were only apparently direct. We have seen that they were based on the object perceived. In this they were in agreement with common sense, which also identifies the sensible by the objective conditions which govern it. The visible is what is seized upon *with* the eyes, the sensible is what is seized on *by* the senses. Let us follow up the idea of sensation on this basis,[4] and see what becomes of this "by" and this "with," and the notion of sense-organ, in the first-order thinking constituted by science. [Having shown that there is no experience of sensation,] do we at least find, in its causes and objective origins, any reasons for retaining it as an explanatory concept? Physiology, to which the psychologist turns as to a higher court of appeal, is in the same predicament as psychology. It too first situates its object in the world and treats it as a bit of extension. *Behaviour* is thus hidden by the reflex, the elaboration and patterning of stimuli, by a longitudinal theory of nervous functioning, which establishes a theoretical correspondence between each element of the situation and an element of the reaction.[5] As in the case of the reflex arc theory, physiology of perception begins by recognizing an anatomical path leading from a *receiver* through a definite *transmitter* to a recording station,[6] equally specialized. The objective world being given, it is assumed that it passes on to the sense-organs messages which must be registered, then deciphered in such a way as to reproduce in us the original text. Hence we have in principle a point-by-point correspondence and constant connection between the stimulus and the elementary perception. But this "constancy hypothesis"[7] conflicts with the data of consciousness, and the very psychologists who accept it recognize its purely theoretical character.[8] For example, the intensity of a sound under certain circumstances lowers its pitch; the addition of auxiliary lines makes two figures unequal which are objectively equal;[9] a coloured area appears to be the same colour over the whole of its surface, whereas the chromatic thresholds of the different parts of the retina ought to make it red in one place, orange somewhere else, and in certain cases colourless.[10] Should these cases in which the phenomenon does not correspond to the stimulus be retained within the framework of the law of constancy, and explained by additional factors—attention and judgement—or must the law itself be jettisoned? When red and green, presented together, give the result grey, it is conceded that the central combination of stimuli can immediately give rise to a different sensation from what the objective stimuli would lead us to expect. When the apparent size of an object varies with its apparent distance, or its apparent colour with our recollections of the object, it is recognized that "the sensory processes are not immune to central influences."[11] In this case, therefore, the "sensible" cannot be defined as the immediate effect of an external stimulus. Cannot the same conclusion be drawn from the first three examples we have mentioned? If attention, more precise instructions, rest or prolonged practice finally bring perception into line with the law of constancy, this does not prove the law's universal validity, for, in the examples quoted, the first appearance possessed a sensory character just as incontestable as the final results obtained. So the question is whether attentive perception, the subject's concentration on one point of the visual field—for example, the "analytic perception" of the two main lines in Müller-Lyer's optical illusion—do not, instead of revealing the "normal sensation," substitute a special set-up for the original phenomenon.[12] The law of constancy cannot avail itself, against the testimony of consciousness, of any crucial experience in which it is not already implied, and wherever we believe that we are establishing it, it is already presupposed.[13] If we turn back to the phenomena, they show us that the apprehension of a quality, just as that of size, is bound up with a whole perceptual context, and that the stimuli no longer furnish us with the indirect means we were seeking of isolating a layer of immediate impressions. But when we look for an "objective" definition of sensation, it is not only the physical stimulus which slips through our fingers. The sensory apparatus, as conceived by modern physiology, is no longer fitted for the role of "transmitter" cast for it by traditional science. Non-cortical lesions of the apparatus of touch no doubt lessen the concentration of points sensitive to heat and cold, or pressure, and diminish the sensitivity of those that remain. But if, to the injured system, a sufficiently extensive stimulus be applied, the specific sensations reappear. The raising of the thresholds is compensated by a more vigorous movement of the hand.[14]

One can discern, at the rudimentary stage of sensibility, a working together on the part of partial stimuli and a collaboration of the sensory with the motor system which, in a variable physiological constellation, keeps sensation constant, and rules out any definition of the nervous process as the simple transmission of a given message. The destruction of sight, wherever the injuries be sustained, follows the same law: all colours are affected in the first place,[15] and lose their saturation. Then the spectrum is simplified, being reduced to four and soon to two colours; finally a grey monochrome stage is reached, although the pathological colour is never identifiable with any normal one. Thus in central as in peripheral lesions "the loss of nervous substance results not only in a deficiency of certain qualities, but in the change to a less differentiated and more primitive structure."[16] Conversely, normal functioning must be understood as a process of integration in which the text of the external world is not so much copied, as composed. And if we try to seize "sensation" within the perspective of the bodily phenomena which pave the way to it, we find not a psychic individual, a function of certain known variables, but a formation already bound up with a larger whole, already endowed with a meaning, distinguishable only in degree from the more complex perceptions, and which therefore gets us no further in our attempt to delimit pure sensation. There is no physiological definition of sensation, and more generally there is no physiological psychology which is autonomous, because the physiological event itself obeys biological and psychological laws. For a long time it was thought that peripheral conditioning was the surest method of identifying "elementary" psychic functions, and of distinguishing them from "superior" functions less strictly bound up with the bodily substructure. A closer analysis, however, reveals that the two kinds of function overlap. The elementary is no longer that which by addition will cumulatively constitute the whole, nor is it a mere occasion for the whole to constitute itself. The elementary event is already invested with meaning, and the higher function will bring into being only a more integrated mode of existence or a more valid adaptation, by using and sublimating the subordinate operations. Conversely, "the experience of feeling is a vital process, no less than procreation, breathing or growth."[17] Psychology and physiology are no longer, then, two parallel sciences, but two accounts of behaviour, the first concrete, the second abstract.[18] We said that when the psychologist asks the physiologist for a definition of sensation "in causal terms," he encounters once more on this new ground his familiar difficulties, and now we can see why. The physiologist for his part has to rid himself of the realistic prejudice which all the sciences borrow from common sense, and which hampers them in their development. The changed meaning of the terms "elementary" and "more advanced" in modern physiology proclaims a changed philosophy.[19] The scientist too must learn to criticize the idea of an external world in itself, since the facts themselves prompt him to abandon that of the body as a transmitter of messages. The sensible is what is apprehended *with* the senses, but now we know that this "with" is not merely instrumental, that the sensory apparatus is not a conductor, that even on the periphery the physiological impression is involved in relations formerly considered central.

Once more, reflection—even the second-order reflection of science—obscures what we thought was clear. We believed we knew what feeling, seeing and hearing were, and now these words raise problems. We are invited to go back to the experiences to which they refer in order to redefine them. The traditional notion of sensation was not a concept born of reflection, but a late product of thought directed towards objects, the last element in the representation of the world, the furthest removed from its original source, and therefore the most unclear. Inevitably science, in its general effort towards objectification, evolved a picture of the human organism as a physical system undergoing stimuli which were themselves identified by their physico-chemical properties, and tried to reconstitute actual perception[20] on this basis, and to close the circle of scientific knowledge by discovering the laws governing the production of knowledge itself, by establishing an objective science of subjectivity.[21] But it is also inevitable that this attempt should fail. If we return to the objective investigations themselves, we first of all discover that the conditions external to the sensory field do not govern it part for part, and that they exert an effect only to the extent of making possible a basic pattern—which is what Gestalt theory makes clear. Then we see that within the organism the structure depends on variables such as the biological meaning of the situation, which are no longer physical variables, with the result that the whole eludes the well-known instruments of physico-mathematical analysis, and opens the way to another type of intelligibility.[22] If we now turn back, as is done here, towards perceptual experience, we notice that science succeeds in constructing only a semblance of subjectivity: it introduces sensations which are things, just where experience shows that there are meaningful patterns; it forces the phenomenal universe into categories which make sense only in the universe of science. It requires that two perceived lines, like two real lines, should be equal or unequal, that a perceived crystal should have a definite number of sides,[23] without realizing that the perceived, by its nature, admits of the ambiguous, the shifting, and is shaped by its context. In Müller-Lyer's illusion, one of the lines ceases to be equal to the other without becoming "unequal": it becomes "different." That is to say, an isolated, objective line, and the same line taken in a figure, cease to be, for perception, "the same." It is identifiable in these two functions only by analytic perception, which is not natural. In the same way the perceived contains gaps which are not mere "failures to perceive." I may, through sight or touch, recognize a crystal as having a "regular" shape without having, even tacitly, counted its sides. I may be familiar with a face without ever having perceived the colour of the eyes in themselves. The theory of sensation, which builds up all knowledge out of determinate qualities, offers us objects purged of all ambiguity, pure and absolute, the ideal rather than the real themes of knowledge: in short, it is compatible only with the lately developed superstructure of consciousness. That is where "the idea of sensation is approximately realized."[24]

The images which instinct projects before it, those which tradition recreates in each generation, or simply dreams, are in the first place presented on an equal footing with genuine perceptions, and gradually, by critical labour, the true, present and explicit perception is distinguished from phantasms. The word perception indicates a *direction* rather than a primitive function.[25] It is known that the uniformity of apparent size of objects at different distances, or of their colour in different lights, is more perfect in children than in adults.[26] It follows that perception is more strictly bound up with the local stimulus in its developed than in its undeveloped state, and more in conformity with the theory of sensation in the adult than in the child. It is like a net with its knots showing up more and more clearly.[27] "Primitive thought" has been pictured in a way which can be understood only if the responses of primitive people, their pronouncements and the sociologists' interpretations are related to the fund of perceptual experience which they are all trying to translate.[28] It is sometimes the adherence of the perceived object to its context, and, as it were, its viscosity, sometimes the presence in it of a positive indeterminate which prevents the spatial, temporal and numerical wholes from becoming articulated into manageable, distinct and identifiable terms. And it is this pre-objective realm that we have to explore in ourselves if we wish to understand sense experience.

Experience and Objective Thought: The Problem of the Body

Our perception ends in objects, and the object once constituted, appears as the reason for all the experiences of it which we have had or could have. For example, I see the next-door house from a certain angle, but it would be seen differently from the right bank of the Seine, or from the inside, or again from an aeroplane: the house *itself* is none of these appearances; it is, as Leibnitz said, the flat projection of these perspectives and of all possible perspectives, that is, the perspectiveless position from which all can be derived, the house seen from nowhere. But what do these words mean? Is not to see always to see from somewhere? To say that the house itself is seen from nowhere is surely to say that it is invisible! Yet when I say that I see the house with my own eyes, I am saying something that cannot be challenged: I do not mean that my retina and crystalline lens, my eyes as material organs, go into action and cause me to see it: with only myself to consult, I can know nothing about this. I am trying to express in this way a certain manner of approaching the object, the "gaze" in short, which is as indubitable as my own thought, as directly known by me. We must try to understand how vision can be brought into being from somewhere without being enclosed in its perspective.

To see an object is either to have it on the fringe of the visual field and be able to concentrate on it, or else respond to this summons by actually concentrating upon it. When I do concentrate my eyes on it, I become anchored in it, but this coming to rest of the gaze is merely a modality of its movement: I continue inside one object the exploration which earlier hovered over them all, and in one movement I close up the landscape and open the object. The two operations do not fortuitously coincide: it is not the contingent aspects of my bodily make-up, for example the retinal structure, which force me to see my surroundings vaguely if I want to see the object clearly. Even if I knew nothing of rods and cones, I should realize that it is necessary to put the surroundings in abeyance the better to see the object, and to lose in background what one gains in focal figure, because to look at the object is to plunge oneself into it, and because objects form a system in which one cannot show itself without concealing others. More precisely, the inner horizon of an object cannot become an object without the surrounding objects' becoming a horizon, and so vision is an act with two facets. For I do not identify the detailed object which I now have with that over which my gaze ran a few minutes ago, by expressly comparing these details with a memory of my first general view. When, in a film, the camera is trained on an object and moves nearer to it to give a close-up view, we can *remember* that we are being shown the ash tray or an actor's hand, we do not actually identify it. This is because the screen has no horizons. In normal vision, on the other hand, I direct my gaze upon a sector of the landscape, which comes to life and is disclosed, while the other objects recede into the periphery and become dormant, while, however, not ceasing to be there. Now, with them, I have at my disposal their horizons, in which there is implied, as a marginal view, the object on which my eyes at present fall. The horizon, then, is what guarantees the identity of the object throughout the exploration: it is the correlative of the impending power which my gaze retains over the objects which it has just surveyed, and which it already has over the fresh details which it is about to discover. No distinct memory and no explicit conjecture could fill this rôle: they would give only a probable synthesis, whereas my perception presents itself as actual. The object-horizon structure, or the perspective, is no obstacle to me when I want to see the object: for just as it is the means whereby objects are distinguished from each other, it is also the means whereby they are disclosed. To see is to enter a universe of beings which *display themselves*, and they would not do this if they could not be hidden behind each other or behind me. In other words: to look at an object is to inhabit it, and from this habitation to grasp all things in terms of the aspect which they present to it. But in so far as I see those things too, they remain abodes open to my gaze, and, being potentially lodged in them, I already perceive from various angles the central object of my present vision. Thus every object is the mirror of all others. When I look at the lamp on my table, I attribute to it not only the qualities visible from where I am, but also those which the chimney, the walls, the table can "see"; but back of my lamp is nothing but the face which it "shows" to the chimney. I can therefore see an object in so far as objects form a system or a world, and in so far as each one treats the others round it as spectators of its hidden aspects and as guarantee of the permanence of those aspects. Any seeing of an object by me is instantaneously reiterated among all those objects in the world which are apprehended as co-existent, because each of them is all that the others "see" of it. Our previous formula must therefore be modified; the house itself is not the house seen from nowhere, but the house seen from everywhere. The completed object is translucent, being shot through from all sides by an infinite number of present scrutinies which intersect in its depths leaving nothing hidden.

What we have just said about the spatial perspective could equally be said about the temporal. If I contemplate the house attentively and with no thought in my mind, it has something eternal about it, and an atmosphere of torpor seems to be generated by it. It is true that I see it from a certain point in my "duration," but it is the same house that I saw yesterday when it was a day younger; it is the same house that either an old man or a child might behold. It is true, moreover, that age and change affect it, but even if it should collapse tomorrow, it will remain for ever true that it existed today: each moment of time calls all the others to witness; it shows by its advent "how things were meant to turn out" and "how it will all finish"; each present permanently underpins a point of time which calls for recognition from all the others, so that the object is seen at all times as it is seen from all directions and by the same means, namely the structure imposed by a horizon. The present still holds on to the immediate past without positing it as an object, and since the immediate past similarly holds its immediate predecessor, past time is wholly collected up and grasped in the present. The same is true of the imminent future which will also have its horizon of imminence. But with my immediate past I have also the horizon of futurity which surrounded it, and thus I have my actual present seen as the future of that past. With the imminent future, I have the horizon of past which will surround it, and therefore my actual present as the past of that future. Thus, through the double horizon of retention and protention, my present may cease to be a factual present quickly carried away and abolished by the flow of duration, and become a fixed and identifiable point in objective time.

But, once more, my human gaze never *posits* more than one facet of the object, even though by means of horizons it is directed towards all the others. It can never come up against previous appearances or those presented to other people otherwise than through the intermediary of time and language. If I conceive in the image of my own gaze those others which, converging from all directions, explore every corner of the house and define it, I have still only a harmonious and indefinite set of views of the object, but not the object in its plenitude. In the same way, although my present draws into itself time past and time to come, it possesses them only in intention, and even if, for example, the consciousness of my past which I now have seems to me to cover exactly the past as it was, the past which I claim to recapture is not the real past, but my past as I now see it, perhaps after altering it. Similarly in the future I may have a mistaken idea about the present which I now experience. Thus the synthesis of horizons is no more than a presumptive synthesis, operating with certainty and precision only in the immediate vicinity of the object. The remoter surrounding is no longer within my grasp; it is no longer composed of still discernible objects or memories; it is an anonymous horizon now incapable of bringing any precise testimony, and leaving the object as incomplete and open as it is indeed, in perceptual experience. Through this opening, indeed, the substantiality of the object slips away. If it is to reach perfect density, in other words if there is to be an absolute object, it will have to consist of an infinite number of different perspectives compressed into a strict co-existence, and to be presented as it were to a host of eyes all engaged in one concerted act of seeing. The house *has its* water pipes, *its* floor, perhaps its cracks which are insidiously spreading in the thickness of its ceilings. We never see them, but it *has them* along with its chimneys and windows which we can see. We shall forget our present perception of the house: every time we are able to compare our memories with the objects to which they refer, we are surprised, even allowing for other sources of error, at the changes which they owe to their own duration. But we still believe that there is a truth about the past; we base our memory on the world's vast Memory, in which the house has its place as it really was on that day, and which guarantees its *being* at this moment. Taken in itself—and as an object it demands to be taken thus—the object has nothing cryptic about it; it is completely displayed and its parts co-exist while our gaze runs from one to another, its present does not cancel its past, nor will its future cancel its present. The positing of the object, therefore makes us go beyond the limits of our actual experience which is brought up against and halted by an alien being, with the result that finally experience believes that it extracts all its own teaching from the object. It is this *ek-stase* [Active transcendence of the subject in relation to the world. The author uses either the French word *extase*, or Heidegger's form *ek-stase*. The latter is the one used throughout this translation (Translator's note).] of experience which causes all perception to be perception of something.

ONE'S OWN REPRESENTATION OF THE OBJECT.

Obsessed with being, and forgetful of the perspectivism of my experience, I henceforth treat it as an object and deduce it from a relationship between objects. I regard my body, which is my point of view upon the world, as one of the objects of that world. My recent awareness of my gaze as a means of knowledge I now repress, and treat my eyes as bits of matter. They then take their place in the same objective space in which I am trying to situate the external object and I believe that I am producing the perceived perspective by the projection of the objects on my retina. In the same way I treat my own perceptual history as a result of my relationships with the objective world; my present, which is my point of view on time, becomes one moment of time among all the others, my duration a reflection or abstract aspect of universal time, as my body is a mode of objective space. In the same way, finally, if the objects which surround the house or which are found in it remained what they are in perceptual experience, that is, acts of seeing conditioned by a certain perspective, the house would not be posited as an autonomous being. Thus the positing of one single object, in the full sense, demands the compositive bringing into being of all these experiences in one act of manifold creation. Therein it exceeds perceptual experience and the synthesis of horizons—as the notion of a *universe*, that is to say, a completed and explicit totality, in which the relationships are those of reciprocal determination, exceeds that of a *world*, or an open and indefinite multiplicity of relationships which are of reciprocal implication.[29] I detach myself from my experience and pass to the *idea*. Like the object, the idea purports to be the same for everybody, valid in all times and places, and the individuation of an object in an objective point of time and space finally appears as the expression of a universal positing power.[30] I am no longer concerned with my body, nor with time, nor with the world, as I experience them in antepredicative knowledge, in the inner communion that I have with them. I now refer to my body only as an idea, to the universe as idea, to the idea of space and the idea of time. Thus "objective" thought (in Kierkegaard's sense) is formed—being that of common sense and of science—which finally causes us to lose contact with perceptual experience, of which it is nevertheless the outcome and the natural sequel. The whole life of consciousness is characterized by the tendency to posit objects, since it is consciousness, that is to say self-knowledge, only in so far as it takes hold of itself and draws itself together in an identifiable object. And yet the absolute positing of a single object is the death of consciousness, since it congeals the whole of existence, as a crystal placed in a solution suddenly crystallizes it.

We cannot remain in this dilemma of having to fail to understand either the subject or the object. We must discover the origin of the object at the very centre of our experience; we must describe the emergence of being and we must understand how, paradoxically, there is *for us* an *in-itself*. In order not to prejudge the issue, we shall take objective thought on its own terms and not ask it any questions which it does not ask itself. If we are led to rediscover experience behind it, this shift of ground will be attributable only to the difficulties which objective thought itself raises. Let us consider it then at work in the constitution of our body as object, since this is a crucial moment in the genesis of the objective world. It will be seen that one's own body evades, even within science itself, the treatment to which it is intended to subject it. And since the genesis of the objective body is only a moment in the constitution of the object, the body, by withdrawing from the objective world, will carry with it the intentional threads linking it to its surrounding and finally reveal to us the perceiving subject as the perceived world.

The Theory of the Body is Already a Theory of Perception

Our own body is in the world as the heart is in the organism: it keeps the visible spectacle constantly alive, it breathes life into it and sustains it inwardly, and with it forms a system. When I walk round my flat, the various aspects in which it presents itself to me could not possibly appear as views of one and the same thing if I did not know that each of them represents the flat seen from one spot or another, and if I were unaware of my own movements, and of my body as retaining its identity through the stages of those movements. I can of course take a mental bird's eye view of the flat, visualize it or draw a plan of it on paper, but in that case too I could not grasp the unity of the object without the mediation of bodily experience, for what I call a plan is only a more comprehensive perspective: it is the flat "seen from above," and the fact that I am able to draw together in it all habitual perspectives is dependent on my knowing that one and the same embodied subject can view successively *from* various positions. It will perhaps be objected that by restoring the object to bodily experience as one of the poles of that experience, we deprive it of precisely that which constitutes its objectivity. From the point of view of my body I never see as equal the six sides of the cube, even if it is made of glass, and yet the word "cube" has a meaning; the cube itself, the cube in reality, beyond its sensible appearances, has *its* six equal sides. As I move round it, I see the front face, hitherto a square, change its shape, then disappear, while the other sides come into view and one by one become squares. But the successive stages of this experience are for me merely the opportunity of conceiving the whole cube with its six equal and simultaneous faces, the intelligible structure which provides the explanation of it. And it is even necessary, for my tour of inspection of the cube to warrant the judgement: "here is a cube," that my movements themselves be located in objective space and, far from its being the case that the experience of my own movement conditions the position of an object, it is, on the contrary, by conceiving my body itself as a mobile object that I am able to interpret perceptual appearance and construct the cube as it truly is. The experience of my own movement would therefore appear to be no more than a psychological circumstance of perception and to make no contribution to determining the significance of the object. The object and my body would certainly form a system, but we would then have a nexus of objective correlations and not, as we were saying earlier, a collection of lived-through correspondences. The unity of the object is thus conceived, and not experienced as the correlate of our body's unity.

But can the object be thus detached from the actual conditions under which it is presented to us? One can bring together discursively the notion of the number six, the notion of "side" and that of equality, and link them together in a formula which is the definition of the cube. But this definition rather puts a question to us than offers us something to conceive. One emerges from blind, symbolic thought only by perceiving the particular spatial entity which bears these predicates all together. It is a question of tracing in thought that particular form which encloses a fragment of space between six equal faces. Now, if the words "enclose" and "between" have a meaning for us, it is because they derive it from our experience as embodied subjects. In space *itself* independently of the presence of a psycho-physical subject, there is no direction, no inside and no outside. A space is "enclosed" between the sides of a cube as we are enclosed between the walls of our room. In order to be able to conceive the cube, we take up a position in space, now on its surface, now in it, now outside it, and from that moment we see it in perspective. The cube with six equal sides is not only invisible, but inconceivable; it is the cube as it would be for itself; but the cube is not for itself, since it is an object. There is a first order dogmatism, of which analytical reflection rids us, and which consists in asserting that the object is in itself, or absolutely, without wondering what it is. But there is another, which consists in affirming the ostensible significance of the object, without wondering how it enters into our experience. Analytical reflection puts forward, instead of the absolute existence of the object, the thought of an absolute object, and, through trying to dominate the object and think of it from no point of view, it destroys the object's internal structure. If there is, for me, a cube with six equal sides, and if I can link up with the object, this is not because I constitute it from the inside: it is because I delve into the thickness of the world by perceptual experience. The cube with six equal sides is the limiting idea whereby I express the material presence of the cube which is there before my eyes, under my hands, in its perceptual self-evidence. The sides of the cube are not projections of it, but precisely sides. When I perceive them successively, with the appearance they present in different perspectives, I do not construct the idea of the flat projection which accounts for these perspectives; the cube is already there in front of me and reveals itself through them. I do not need to take an objective view of my own movement, or take it into account, in order to reconstitute the true form of the object behind its appearance; the account is already taken, and already the new appearance has compounded itself with the lived-through movement and presented itself as an appearance of a cube. The thing, and the world, are given to me along with the parts of my body, not by any "natural geometry," but in a living connection comparable, or rather identical, with that existing between the parts of my body itself.

External perception and the perception of one's own body vary in conjunction because they are the two facets of one and the same act. The attempt has long been made to explain Aristotle's celebrated illusion by allowing that the unaccustomed position of the fingers makes the synthesis of their perceptions impossible: the right side of the middle finger and the left side of the index do not ordinarily "work" together, and if both are touched at once, then there must be two marbles. In reality, the perceptions of the two fingers are not only disjoined, they are inverted: the subject attributes to the index what is touched by the middle finger and vice versa, as can be shown by applying two distinct stimuli to the fingers, a point and a ball, for example.[31] Aristotle's illusion is primarily a disturbance of the body image. What makes the synthesis of the two tactile perceptions in one single object impossible, is not so much that the position of the fingers is unaccustomed or statistically rare, it is that the right face of the middle finger and the left face of the index cannot combine in a joint exploration of the object, that the crossing of the fingers, being a movement which has to be imposed on them, lies outside the motor possibilities of the fingers themselves and cannot be aimed at in a project towards movement. The synthesis of the object is here effected, then, through the synthesis of one's own body, it is the reply or correlative to it, and it is literally the same thing to perceive one single marble, and to use two fingers as one single organ. The disturbance of the body image may even be directly translated into the external world without the intervention of any stimulus. In heautoscopy, before seeing himself, the subject always passes through a state akin to dreaming, musing or disquiet, and the image of himself which appears outside him is merely the counterpart of this depersonalization.[32] The patient has the feeling of being in the double outside himself, just as, in a lift which goes upwards and suddenly stops, I feel the substance of my body escaping from me through my head and overrunning the boundaries of my objective body. It is in his own body that the patient feels the approach of this Other whom he has never seen with his eyes, as the normal person is aware, through a certain burning feeling in the nape of the neck, that someone is watching him from behind.[33] Conversely, a certain form of external experience implies and produces a certain consciousness of one's own body. Many patients speak of a "sixth sense" which seems to produce their hallucinations. Stratton's subject, whose visual field has been objectively inverted, at first sees everything upside down; on the third day of the experiment, when things are beginning to regain their upright position, he is filled with "the strange impression of looking at the fire out of the back of his head."[34] This is because there is an immediate equivalence between the orientation of the visual field and the awareness of one's own body as the potentiality of that field, so that any upheaval experimentally brought about can appear indifferently either as the inversion of phenomenal objects or as a redistribution of sensory functions in the body. If a subject focuses for long-distance vision, he has a double image of his own finger as indeed of all objects near to him. If he is touched or pricked, he is aware of being touched or pricked in two places.[35] Diplopia is thus extended into a bodily duplication. Every external perception is immediately synonymous with a certain perception of my body, just as every perception of my body is made explicit in the language of external perception. If, then, as we have seen to be the case, the body is not a transparent object, and is not presented to us in virtue of the law of its constitution, as the circle is to the geometer, if it is an expressive unity which we can learn to know only by actively taking it up, this structure will be passed on to the sensible world. The theory of the body image is, implicitly, a theory of perception. We have relearned to feel our body; we have found underneath the objective and detached knowledge of the body that other knowledge which we have of it in virtue of its always being with us and of the fact that we are our body. In the same way we shall need to reawaken our experience of the world as it appears to us in so far as we are in the world through our body, and in so far as we perceive the world with our body. But by thus remaking contact with the body and with the world, we shall also rediscover ourself, since, perceiving as we do with our body, the body is a natural self and, as it were, the subject of perception.

Notes

1. See *La Structure du Comportement*, pp. 142ff.

2. J. P. Sartre, *L'Imaginaire*, p. 241.

3. Koffka, *Psychologie*, p. 530.

4. There is no justification for dodging the issue, as does Jaspers, for example (*Zur Analyse der Trugwahrnehmungen*) by setting up in opposition, on the one hand a descriptive psychology which "understands" phenomena, and on the other an explanatory psychology, which concerns itself with their origin. The psychologist always sees consciousness as placed in the body in the midst of the world, and for him the series stimulus-impression-perception is a sequence of events at the end of which perception begins. Each consciousness is born in the world and each perception is a new birth of consciousness. In this perspective the "immediate" data of perception can always be challenged as mere appearances and as complex products of an origin. The descriptive method can acquire a genuine claim only from the transcendental point of view. But, even from this point of view, the problem remains as to how consciousness perceives itself or appears to itself as inserted in a nature. For the philosopher, as for the psychologist, there is therefore always a problem of origins, and the only method possible is to follow, in its scientific development, the causal explanation in order to make its meaning quite clear, and assign to it its proper place in the body of truth. That is why there will be found no *refutation*, but only an effort to understand the difficulties peculiar to causal thinking.

5. See *La Structure du Comportement*, Chap. I.

6. We are translating roughly the series Empfänger-Übermittler-Empfinder spoken of by J. Stein, *Über die Veränderung der Sinnesleistungen und die Entstehung von Trugwahrnehmungen*, p. 351.

7. Koehler, *Über unbemerkte Empfindungen und Urteilstäuschungen*.

8. Stumpf does so explicitly. Cf. Koehler, ibid., p. 54.

9. Koehler, ibid., pp. 57–8, cf. pp. 58–66.

10. R. Déjean, *Les Conditions objectives de la Perception visuelle*, pp. 60 and 83.

11. Stumpf, quoted by Koehler, ibid., p. 58.

12. Koehler, ibid., pp. 58–63.

13. It is only fair to add that this is true of all theories, and that nowhere is there a crucial experience. For the same reason the constancy hypothesis cannot be completely refuted on the basis of induction. It is discredited because it overlooks phenomena and does not permit any understanding of them. To discern them and to pass judgement on the hypothesis, indeed, one must "suspend" it.

14. Stein, op. cit., pp. 357–9.

15. Even daltonism does not prove that certain systems are, and are alone in being, entrusted with "seeing" red and green, since a colour-blind person manages to distinguish red if a large area in that colour is put before him, or if the presentation of the colour is made to last a long time. Id. ibid., p. 365.

16. Weizsäcker, quoted by Stein, ibid., p. 364.

17. Weizsäcker, quoted by Stein, ibid., p. 354.

18. On all these points see *La Structure du Comportement*, in particular pp. 52 and ff., 65 and ff.

19. Gelb, *Die Farbenkonstanz der Sehdinge*, p. 595.

20. "The sensations are certainly artificial products, but not arbitrary ones, they are the last component wholes into which the natural structures can be decomposed by the 'analytical attitude.' Seen from this point of view, they contribute to the knowledge of structures, and consequently the results of the study of sensations, correctly interpreted, are an important element in the psychology of perception." Koffka, *psychologie*, p. 548.

21. Cf. Guillaume, *L'Objectivité en Psychologie*.

22. Cf. *La Structure du Comportement*, Chap. III.

23. Koffka, *Psychologie*, pp. 530 and 549.

24. M. Scheler, *Die Wissenformen und die Gesellschaft*, p. 412.

25. M. Scheler, *Die Wissenformen und die Gesellschaft*, p. 397. "Man approaches ideal and exact images better than the animal, the adult better than the child, men better than women, the individual better than the member of a group, the man who thinks historically and systematically better than the man impelled by tradition, 'imprisoned' in it and incapable of objectivizing, by building up recollection, the environment in which he is involved, of localizing it in time and possessing it by setting it away from himself in a past context."

26. Hering, Jaensch.

27. Scheler, *Die Wissenformen und die Gesellschaft*, p. 412.

28. Cf. Wertheimer, *Über das Denken der Naturvölker*, in *Drei Abhandlungen zur Gestalttheorie*.

29. Husserl, *Umsturz der kopernikanischen Lehre: die Erde als Ur-Arche bewegt sich nicht* (unpublished).

30. "I understand by the sole power of judging, which resides in my mind, what I thought I saw with my eyes." *2nd Meditation*, AT, IX, p. 25.

31. Tastevin, Czermak, Schilder, quoted by Lhermitte, *L'Image de notre Corps*, pp. 36 and ff.

32. Lhermitte, *L'Image de notre Corps*, pp. 136–88, cf. p. 191: "During the period of autoscopy the subject is overcome by a feeling of profound sadness which spreads outwards and into the very image of the double, which seems to be filled with effective vibrations identical with those experienced by the original person"; "his consciousness seems to have moved wholly outside himself." And Menninger-Lerchenthal, *Das Truggebilde der eigenen Gestalt*, p. 180: "I suddenly had the impression of being outside my body."

33. Jaspers, quoted by Menninger-Lerchenthal, op. cit., p. 76.

34. Stratton, *Vision without Inversion of the Retinal Image*, p. 350.

35. Lhermitte, *L'Image de notre Corps*, p. 39.

Bibliography

Déjean, *Les Conditions objectives de la Perception visuelle*, Paris, Presses Universitaires de France.

Gelb, *Die Farbenkonstanz der Sehdinge*, in *Handbuch der normalen und pathologischen Physiologie*, Bethe, XII/1, Berlin, Springer, 1927 and ff.

Guillaume (P.), *L'Objectivité en Psychologie*, Journal de Psychologie, 1932.

Husserl, *Umsturz der kopernikanischen Lehre: die Erde als Ur-Arche bewegt sich nicht* (unpublished).

Koehler, *Über unbemerkte Empfindungen und Urteilstäuschungen*, Ztschr. f. Psychologie, 1913.

Koffka, *Psychologie*, in *Lehrbuch der Philosophie*, edited by M. Dessoir, Part II, *Die Philosophie in ihren Einzelgebieten*, Berlin, Ullstein, 1925.

Lhermitte, *L'Image de notre corps*, Nouvelle Revue critique, 1939.

Menninger-Lerchenthal, *Das Truggebilde der eigenen Gestalt*, Berlin, Karger, 1934.

Merleau-Ponty, *La Structure du Comportement*, Paris, Presses Universitaires de France, 1942.

Sartre, *L'Imagination*, Paris, Alcan, 1936.

————*Esquisse d'une théorie de l'émotion*, Paris, Hermann, 1939.

————*L'Imaginaire*, Paris, Gallimard, 1940.

————*L'Être et le Néant*, Paris, Gallimard, 1943.

Scheler, *Die Wissenformen und die Gesellschaft*, Leipzig, der Neue Geist. 1926.

Stein (J.), *Über die Veränderung der Sinnesleistungen und die Entstehung von Trugwahrnehmungen*, in *Pathologie der Wahrnehmung, Handbuch der Geisteskrankheiten*, edited by O. Bumke, Bd. I, Allgemeiner Teil I, Berlin, Springer, 1928.

Stratton, *Vision without inversion of the retinal image*, Psychological Review, 1897.

Wertheimer, *Über das Denken der Naturvölker* and *Die Schlussprozesse im produktiven Denken*, in *Drei Abhandlungen zur Gestalttheorie*, Erlangen, 1925.

3

Some Remarks about the Senses

H. P. Grice

A claim to the effect that certain creatures possess a faculty which should be counted as a sense, different from any of those with which we are familiar, might be met in more than one way, without actual repudiation of the alleged facts on which the claim is based.[1] It might be said that this faculty, though possibly in some way informative about the world, was not a faculty of perceiving; or it might be admitted that the exercise of the faculty constituted perception, and maintained that no new sense was involved, but only one of the familiar ones operating, perhaps, in some unfamiliar way.

About the first alternative I shall not say a great deal. It embraces a number of subalternatives:

(1) The faculty might be assimilated to such things as a moral sense, or a sense of humor. These are dubiously informative; and even if treated as informative, could not be regarded as telling (in the first instance) only about conditions of the world spatially and temporally present to the creature who is exercising them.

(2) The faculty might be held to be some kind of power of divination. This line might be adopted if the creature seemed to have direct (noninferential) knowledge of certain contemporary states or events in the material world, though this knowledge was not connected with the operation of any sense-organ. We should, of course, be very reluctant to accept this subalternative. We should so far as possible cling to the idea that such knowledge must be connected with the operation of a sense-organ, even if we could not identify it.

(3) The exercise of the faculty—let us call it x-ing—might be denied the title of perception because of its analogy with the having of sensations. It might be held that x-ing consisted in having some sort of experience generated by material things or events in the x-er's environment by way of some effect on his nervous system, though it did not qualify as perceiving the things or events in question. The kind of

situation in which this view might be taken may perhaps be indicated if we consider the assaults made by physiologists and psychologists on the so-called "sense
of touch." They wish, I think on neurological grounds, to distinguish three senses:
a pressure-sense, a warm-and-cold sense, and a pain-sense. Would we be happy to
accept their pain-sense as a sense in the way in which sight or smell is a sense? I
think not; for to do so would involve regarding the fact that we do not "external-
ize" pains as a mere linguistic accident. That is to say, it would involve considering
as unimportant the following facts: (a) that we are ready to regard "malodorous,"
as distinct from "painful" or "sharply painful," as the name of a relatively abiding
characteristic which material things in general either possess or do not possess; we
are as a general rule prepared to regard questions of the form 'Is M (a material
thing) malodorous?' as being at least in principle answerable either affirmatively or
negatively, whereas we should very often wish to reject questions of the form "Is
M painful?" or "Is M sharply painful?"; and (b) that we speak of smells but not of
pains as being in the kitchen.

Very briefly, the salient points here seem to me as follows:

(a) Pains are not greatly variegated, except in intensity and location. Smells are.

(b) There is no standard procedure for getting a pain: one can be cut, bumped,
burned, scraped, and so on. There is a standard procedure for smelling, namely,
inhaling.

(c) Almost any type of object can inflict pain upon us, often in more than one
way.

In consequence of these facts, our pains are on the whole very poor guides to the
character of the things that hurt us. Particular kinds of smells, on the other hand,
are in general characteristic of this or that type of object. These considerations I
hope constitute a partial explanation of the fact that we do not, in general, attribute pain-qualities to things: we may in a special case speak of a thumbscrew, for
example, as being a painful instrument, but this is because there is a standard way
of applying thumbscrews to people.

We do not speak of pains as being in (say) the kitchen; and the reason for this is,
I think, that if a source of pain moves away from a given place, persons arriving in
this place after the removal do not get hurt. Smells, on the other hand, do linger
in places, and so are "detachable" from the material objects which are their source.
Though pains do not linger in places, they do linger with individuals after the source
of pain has been removed. In this again they are unlike smells.

I shall now turn to discussion of the second possible way of meeting the claim of x-ing to be the exercise of a new sense. This, you will remember, took the form of arguing that x-ing, though perceiving, is merely perceiving by one of the familiar senses, perhaps through an unfamiliar kind of sense-organ. At this point we need to ask by what criteria senses are to be distinguished from one another. The answer to this question, if obtainable, would tell us how x-ing must differ from the exercise of familiar senses in order to count as the operation of a distinct sense. Four seemingly independent ideas might be involved:

I. It might be suggested that the senses are to be distinguished by the differing features that we become aware of by means of them: that is to say, seeing might be characterized as perceiving (or seeming to perceive) things as having certain colors, shapes, and sizes; hearing as perceiving things (or better, in this case, events) as having certain degrees of loudness, certain determinates of pitch, certain tone-qualities; and so on for the other senses.

II. It might be suggested that two senses, for example, seeing and smelling, are to be distinguished by the special introspectible character of the experiences of seeing and smelling; that is, disregarding the differences between the characteristics we learn about by sight and smell, we are entitled to say that seeing is itself different in character from smelling.

III. Our attention might be drawn to the differing general features of the external physical conditions on which the various modes of perceiving depend, to differences in the "stimuli" connected with different senses: the sense of touch is activated by contact, sight by light rays, hearing by sound waves, and so on.

IV. Reference might be made to the internal mechanisms associated with the various senses—the character of the sense-organs, and their mode of connection with the brain. (These suggestions need not of course be regarded as mutually exclusive. It is possible—perhaps indeed likely—that there is no one essential criterion for distinguishing the senses; that there is, rather, a multiplicity of criteria.)

One procedure at this point (perhaps the most desirable one) would be to consider, in relation to difficult cases, the applicability of the suggested criteria and their relative weights. But a combination of ignorance of zoology with poverty of invention diverts me to perhaps not uninteresting questions concerning the independence of these criteria, and in particular to the relation between the first and the second. The first suggestion (that differing senses are to be distinguished by the differing features which we perceive by means of them) may seem at first sight attractive and unmystifying; but difficulties seem to arise if we attempt to make it the sole basis of distinction between the senses. It looks as if, when we try to work out suggestion (I) in detail we are brought round to some version of the second suggestion (that the senses are to be distinguished by the special introspectible characters of their exercise).

There is a danger that suggestion (I) may incorporate from the start, in a concealed way, suggestion (II): for instance, to adopt it might amount to saying "Seeing is the sort of experience that we have when we perceive things as having certain colors, shapes, etc." If we are to eliminate this danger, I think we must treat suggestion (I) as advancing the idea that, starting with such sense-neutral verbs as "perceive," "seem," we can elucidate the notion of seeing in terms of the notion of perceiving things to have such-and-such features, smelling in terms of perceiving things to have such-and-such other features, and so on. In general, special perceptual verbs are to be explained in terms of general perceptual verbs together with names of special generic features which material things or events may be perceived to have. At this point an obvious difficulty arises: among the features which would presumably figure in the list of tactual qualities (which are to be used to distinguish feeling from other modes of perceiving) is that of warmth; but to say that someone perceives something to have a certain degree of warmth does not entail that he is *feeling* anything at all, for we can *see* that things are warm, and things can *look* warm.

To extricate the suggestion from this objection, it looks as if it would be necessary to introduce some such term as "directly perceive" (and perhaps also the term "directly seem," the two terms being no doubt definitionally linked). How precisely these terms would have to be defined I do not propose to inquire, but the definition would have to be such as to ensure that someone who saw that something was blue might be directly perceiving that it was blue, while someone who saw that something was warm could not be directly perceiving that it was warm. We then might try to define "see" and its congeners (and primary uses of "look" and its congeners) in terms of these specially introduced verbs. We might put up the following as samples of rough equivalences, without troubling ourselves too much about details, since all we require for present purposes is to see the general lines on which the initial suggestion will have to be developed:

(1) X sees M (material object) = X directly perceives M to have some color and some spatial property.

(2) X feels M = X directly perceives M to have some spatial property and degrees of one or more of such properties as warmth (coldness), hardness (softness), etc.

(3) M looks (primary sense) φ to X = M directly seems to X to have certain spatial and color properties, one of which is φ.

(4) M looks (secondary sense) φ to X = M directly seems to X to have certain spatial and color properties, one or more of which indicate to X that M is or may be φ.

Analogous definitions could be provided for primary and secondary uses of "feel" (with a nonpersonal subject).

This maneuver fails, I think, to put suggestion (I) in the clear. Some might object to the definitions of verbs like "see" (used with a direct object) in terms of "perceive that"; and there would remain the question of defining the special terms "directly perceive" and "directly seem." But a more immediately serious difficulty seems to me to be one connected with the seemingly unquestionable acceptability of the proposition that spatial properties may be directly perceived to belong to things both by sight and by touch. Suppose a man to be resting a half-crown on the palm of one hand and a penny on the palm of the other: he might (perhaps truthfully) say, "The half-crown looks to me larger than the penny, though they feel the same size." If we apply the rough translations indicated above, this statement comes out thus: "The half-crown and the penny directly seem to me to have certain spatial and color properties, including (in the case of the half-crown) that of being larger than the penny: but they also directly seem to me to have certain properties, such as certain degrees of roughness, warmth, etc., and spatial properties which include that of being equal in size."

The facts stated by this rigmarole seem to be (differently ordered) as follows:

(1) The coins directly seem to have certain spatial and color properties.

(2) The coins directly seem to have certain properties drawn from the "tactual" list.

(3) The half-crown directly seems larger than the penny.

(4) The coins directly seem to be of the same size.

But there is nothing in this statement of the facts to tell us whether the coins *look* different in size but *feel* the same size, or alternatively *feel* different in size but *look* the same size.

At this point two somewhat heroic courses suggest themselves. The first is to proclaim an ambiguity in the expression "size," distinguishing between visual size and tactual size, thus denying that spatial properties are really accessible to more than one sense. This more or less Berkeleian position is perhaps unattractive independently of the current argument; in any case the introduction of the qualifications "visual" and "tactual," in the course of an attempt to distinguish the senses from one another without invoking the special character of the various modes of perceiving, is open to the gravest suspicion. The second course is to amend the accounts of looking and feeling in such a way that, for example, "A looks larger than B" is re-expressible more or less as follows: "A directly seems larger than B in the kind of way which entails that A and B directly seem to have certain color-properties." But this seems to introduce a reference to special kinds or varieties of "direct seeming," and this brings in what seems to be only a variant version of suggestion (II).

But there is a rather more subtle course to be considered.[2] In addition to the link (whatever that may be) which may join certain *generic* properties (e.g., color, shape, size) so as to constitute them as members of a group of properties associated with a particular sense (e.g., as visual properties), another kind of link may be indicated which holds between specific properties (e.g., specific colors and shapes, etc.), and which might be of use in dealing with the difficulty raised by this current example. Suppose that A_1 is a specific form of some generic property which occurs only in the visual list (e.g., a particular color), that B_1 is a specific form of some generic property occurring in only the tactual list (e.g., a particular degree of warmth), and that X_1 and X_2 are specific forms of a generic property occurring in both the visual and the tactual lists (e.g., are particular shapes). Suppose further that someone simultaneously detects or seems to detect the presence of all these properties (A_1, B_1, X_1, X_2) in a given object. Now the percipient might find that he could continue to detect or seem to detect A_1 and X_1 while no longer detecting or seeming to detect B_1 and X_2; and equally that he could detect or seem to detect B_1 and X_2 while no longer detecting or seeming to detect A_1 and X_1; but on the other hand that he could not retain A_1 and X_2 while eliminating B_1 and X_1, or retain B_1 and X_1 while eliminating A_1 and X_2. There would thus be what might be called a "detection-link" between A_1 and X_1, and another such link between B_1 and X_2. On the basis of this link between X_1 and a purely visual property it might be decided that X_1 was being visually detected, and analogously it might be decided that X_2 was being tactually detected. Similarly in the example of the coins one might say that there is a detection-link between inequality of size and certain purely visual properties the coins have or seem to have (e.g., their real or apparent colors) and a detection-link between equality of size and certain purely tactual properties the coins have or seem to have (e.g., their coldness): and thus the difficulty may be resolved.

There are three considerations which prevent me from being satisfied with this attempt to make suggestion (I) serviceable. I put them in what I regard as the order of increasing importance:

(1) Consider the possible case of a percipient to whom the two coins *look* equal in size when only seen, *feel* equal in size when only felt, but look unequal and feel equal when *both* seen *and* felt. This case is no doubt fantastic, but nevertheless it *seems* just an empirical matter whether or not the way things appear to one sense is affected in this sort of way by the operation or inoperation of another sense. If such a case were to occur, then the method adumbrated in my previous paragraph would be quite inadequate to deal with it : for equality of size would be codetectable *both* with visual properties alone *and* with tactual properties alone, whereas inequality in size would be codetectable neither with visual properties alone nor with tactual properties alone. So the percipient would, so far as this test goes, be at a loss to decide by which sense he detected (or seemed to detect) inequality. But I doubt whether this conclusion is acceptable.

(2) If it were possible for a creature to have two different senses by each of which he detected just the same generic properties, then the test suggested could not be applied in the case of those senses; for it depends on these being properties accessible to one but not both of two senses with regard to which it is invoked. It is far from clear to me that it is inconceivable that just the same set of generic properties should be detectable by either one of two different senses. (I touch again on this question later.)

(3) Whether or not the suggested test, if applied, would always rightly answer the question whether a given spatial property is on a given occasion being detected by sight or touch, it seems quite certain that we never do employ this method of deciding such a question. Indeed there seems something peculiar about the idea of using *any* method, for the answer to such a question, asked about ourselves, never seems in the slightest doubt. And it seems rather strange to make the difference between detecting (or seeming to detect) a given property by sight and detecting (or seeming to detect) it by touch turn on what would be the result of an experiment which we should never in any circumstances perform.

Suggestion (I) has a further unattractive feature. According to it, certain properties are listed as visual properties, certain others as tactual properties, and so forth; and to say that color is a visual property would seem to amount to no more than saying that color is a member of a group of properties the others of which are . . .

This leaves membership of the group as an apparently arbitrary matter. I now wish to see if some general account of the notion of a visual (tactual, etc.) property could be given if (as suggestion (II) would allow) we make unhampered use of special perceptual verbs like "see" and "look." I shall go into this question perhaps rather more fully than the immediate purposes of the discussion demand, since it seems to me to be of some intrinsic interest. I doubt if such expressions as "visual property" and "tactual property," have any clear-cut accepted use, so what follows should be regarded as a preliminary to deciding upon a use, rather than as the analysis of an existing one. I shall confine myself to the notion of a visual property, hoping that the discussion of this could be adapted to deal with the other senses (not, of course, necessarily in the same way in each case).

First, I suggest that we take it to be a necessary (though not a sufficient) condition of a property P being a visual property that it should be linguistically correct to speak of someone as *seeing* that some material thing M is P, and also (with one qualification to be mentioned later) of some thing M as *looking* P to someone. Within the class of properties which satisfy this condition I want to make some distinctions which belong to two nonindependent dimensions, one of which I shall call "determinability," the other "complexity":

(1) There are certain properties (for example, that of being blue) such that if P is one of them there is no better way (though there may be an equally good way) for me to make sure that a thing M is P than to satisfy myself that, observational conditions being optimal, M looks P to me. Such properties I shall label "directly visually determinable."

(2) It seems to me that there might be a case for labeling some properties as visually determinable, though indirectly so. I have in mind two possible kinds of indirectness. First, it might be the case that a primary (noninferior) test for determining whether M is P would be not just to ensure that M looked P in the most favorable conditions for observation, but to ensure, by scrutiny, that certain parts (in a wide sense) or elements of M had certain characteristics and were interrelated in certain ways; it being understood that the characteristics and relations in question are to be themselves *directly* visually determinable. For me, though no doubt not for a Chinese, the property of being inscribed with a certain Chinese character might be of this kind; and for everyone no doubt the property of having a chiliagonal surface would be of this kind. Second, a characteristic might be such that its primary test involved comparison of M (or its elements) with some standard specimen. Under this head I mean to take in both such properties as being apple-green, for which the

primary test involves comparison with a color chart, and such a property as that of being two feet seven inches long, the primary test for which is measurement by a ruler. It is to be understood that the results of such comparison or measurement are to be describable in terms of properties which are directly visually determinable.

It seems to me possible that "visual characteristic" might be used in such a way that P would qualify as a visual characteristic only if it were directly visually determinable, or in such a way that it would so qualify if it were visually determinable either directly or indirectly. But there also seems to be a different, though I think linked, basis of classification, which might also be employed to fix the sense of the expression "visual characteristic." There will be some values of P such that an object M may be said to look P, with regard to which the question, "What is it about the way that M looks that makes it look P?" has no answer. More generally, it will be impossible to specify anything about the way things look, when they look P, which will account for or determine their looking P. One cannot, for example, specify anything about the way things look when they look blue, which makes them look blue. Characteristics for which this rough condition is satisfied I will call "visually simple." But with regard to those values of P which are such that a thing may look P, but which are not visually simple, there are various possibilities:

(1) The specification of what it is about the way a thing looks which makes it look P, or determines it to look P, may consist in specifying certain characteristics (of the visually determinable kind) which M has or looks to have, the presence of which indicates more or less reliably that M is P. Warmth is such a characteristic. In this kind of case P will not be visually determinable, and I should like to say that P is not a visual characteristic, and is neither visually simple nor visually complex. P will be merely "visually indicable."

(2) The specification of what it is about the way a thing M looks which makes it look P or determines it to look P might take the form of specifying certain properties (of a visually determinable or visually simple kind or both) the possession of which constitutes a logically sufficient condition for being P. The property of being lopsided might be of this kind. A man's face could perhaps be said to be made to look lopsided by his looking as if he had (and perhaps indeed his actually having) one ear set lower than the other; and his actually having one ear set lower than the other would perhaps be a logically sufficient condition of his face's being lopsided. Characteristics belonging to this class I will label "visually tightly complex."

(3) Consider such examples as "X's face looks friendly" or "X looks tough." Certainly friendliness and toughness are not themselves visually determinable: and

certainly the questions "What is there about the way his face looks that makes it look friendly?" and "What is there about the way he looks that makes him look tough?" are in order. Nevertheless there may be considerable difficulty in answering such questions; and when the answer or partial answer comes, it may not amount to saying what it is about the look of X's face (or of X) which indicates more or less reliably that X is friendly (or tough). In such cases one might be inclined to say that though toughness is not a visual characteristic, being tough-looking is. The following remarks seem in point:

(4) It might be thought necessary, for this type of characteristic, to relax the initial condition which visual characteristics were required to satisfy, on the grounds that one cannot speak of someone as "looking tough-looking." But as Albritton has pointed out to me, it does not seem linguistically improper to say of someone that (for example) he looked tough-looking when he stood in the dim light of the passage, but as soon as he moved into the room it could be seen that really he looked quite gentle.

(a) Being tough-looking is in some way dependent on the possession of visually determinable characteristics: there would be a logical absurdity in saying that two people were identical in respect of all visually determinable characteristics, and yet that one person was tough-looking and the other was not.

(b) Even if one has specified to one's full satisfaction what it is about the way X looks that make him look tough, one has not given a logically sufficient condition for being tough-looking. If I just produced a list of X's visually determinable characteristics, the possession of which does *in fact* make him look tough, no one could strictly *deduce* from the information given that X looks tough; to make quite sure, he would have to look at X himself.

(c) Though the primary test for determining whether X is tough-looking is to see how he looks in the most favorable observational conditions, this test may not (perhaps cannot) be absolutely decisive. If, after examination of X, I and my friends say that X is tough-looking, and someone else says that he is not, it need not be the case that the last-mentioned person is wrong or does not know the language; he may for example be impressed by some dissimilarity between X and standard tough customers, by which I and my friends are not impressed, in which case the dissident judgment may perhaps be described as eccentric, but not as wrong. In the light of this discussion one might say that such characteristics as being tough-looking are "visually near-determinable"; and they might also be ranked as visually complex (in view of their dependence on visually determinable characteristics), though "loosely complex" (in view of the nonexistence of logically sufficient conditions of their presence).

(5) The logical relations between the different sections of the determinability range and those of the simplicity-complexity range may need detailed examination. For instance, consider the statement "The sound of the explosion came from my right" (or "The explosion sounded as if it were on my right"). It may be impossible to specify anything about the way the explosion sounded which determined its sounding as if it were on my right, in which case by my criterion being on my right will qualify as an auditory simple property. Yet certainly the explosion's sounding, even in the most favorable observational conditions, as if it were on my right is a secondary (inferior) test for the location of the explosion. So we would have an example of a property which is auditorily simple without being auditorily determinable. This may be of interest in view of the hesitation we may feel when asked if spatial characteristics can be auditory.

I should like to emphasize that I have not been trying to legislate upon the scope to be given to the notion of a visual characteristic, but have only been trying to provide materials for such legislation on the assumption that the special character of visual experience may be used to distinguish the sense of sight, thus allowing a relatively unguarded use of such words as "look."

Let us now for a moment turn our attention to suggestion (II), the idea that senses are to be distinguished by the special character of the experiences which their exercise involves. Two fairly obvious difficulties might be raised. First, that such experiences (if experiences they be) as seeing and feeling seem to be, as it were, diaphanous: if we were asked to pay close attention, on a given occasion, to our seeing or feeling as distinct from what was being seen or felt, we should not know how to proceed; and the attempt to describe the differences between seeing and feeling seems to dissolve into a description of what we see and what we feel. How then can seeing and feeling have the special character which suggestion (II) requires them to have, if this character resists both inspection and description? The second difficulty is perhaps even more serious. If to see is to detect by means of a special kind of experience, will it not be just a contingent matter that the characteristics we detect by means of this kind of experience are such things as color and shape? Might it not have been the case that we thus detected characteristic smells, either instead of or as well as colors and shapes? But it does not seem to be just a contingent fact that we do not see the smells of things. Suggestion (I), on the other hand, seems to avoid both these difficulties; the first because the special character of the experiences connected with the various senses is not invoked, and the second because since the smell of a thing is not listed among the properties the (direct) detection of which counts as seeing, on this view it emerges as tautological that smells cannot be seen.

We seem now to have reached an impasse. Any attempt to make suggestion (I) work leads to difficulties which seem soluble only if we bring in suggestion (II), and suggestion (II) in its turn involves difficulties which seem avoidable only by adopting suggestion (I). Is it the case, then, that the two criteria should be combined; that is, is the right answer that, for anything to count as a case of seeing, two conditions must be fulfilled: first, that the properties detected should belong to a certain group, and second, that the detection should involve a certain kind of experience? But this does not seem to be a satisfactory way out; for if it were, then it will be logically possible to detect smells by means of the type of experience characteristically involved in seeing, yet only to do this would not be to *see* smells, since a further condition (the property qualification) would be unfulfilled. But surely we object on logical grounds no less to the idea that we might detect smells through visual experiences than to the idea that we might see the smells of things: indeed, the ideas seem to be the same. So perhaps the criteria mentioned in suggestions (I) and (II) are not distinguishable; yet they *seem* to be distinct.

Maybe all is not yet lost, for there still remains the possibility that something may be achieved by bringing into the discussion the third and fourth suggestions. Perhaps we might save suggestion (I), and thus eliminate suggestion (II), by combining the former with one or both of the last two suggestions. For if to see is to detect certain properties (from the visual list) by means of a certain sort of mechanism (internal or external or both), then the arguments previously advanced to show the need for importing suggestion (II) seem to lose their force. We can now differentiate between the case in which two coins look different in size but feel the same size and the case in which they feel different in size but look the same size: we shall say that in the first case by mechanism A (eyes and affection by light waves) we detect or seem to detect difference in size while by mechanism B (hands and pressure) we detect or seem to detect equality of size: whereas in the second case the mechanisms are transposed. We can also characterize the visual list of properties as those detectable by mechanism A, and deal analogously with other lists of properties. In this way the need to invoke suggestion (II) seems to be eliminated.

Promising as this approach may appear, I very much doubt if it succeeds in eliminating the need to appeal to the special character of experiences in order to distinguish the senses. Suppose that long-awaited invasion of the Martians takes place, that they turn out to be friendly creatures and teach us their language. We get on all right, except that we find no verb in their language which unquestionably corresponds to our verb "see." Instead we find two verbs which we decide to render as "x" and "y": we find that (in their tongue) they speak of themselves as x-ing, and also as y-ing, things to be of this and that color, size, and shape. Further, in physical appearance they are more or less like ourselves, except that in their heads they have, one above the other, two pairs of organs, not perhaps exactly like one another, but each pair more or less like our eyes: each pair of organs is found to be sensitive to light waves. It turns out that for them x-ing is dependent on the operation of the upper organs, and y-ing on that of the lower organs. The question which it seems natural to ask is this: Are x-ing and y-ing both cases of seeing, the difference between them being that x-ing is seeing with the upper organs, and y-ing is seeing with the lower organs? Or alternatively, do one or both of these accomplishments constitute the exercise of a new sense, other than that of sight? If we adopt, to distinguish the senses, a combination of suggestion (I) with one or both of suggestions (III) or (IV), the answer seems clear: both x-ing and y-ing are seeing, with different pairs of organs. But *is* the question really to be settled so easily? Would we not in fact want to ask whether x-ing something to be round was like y-ing it to be round, or whether when something x-ed blue to them this was like or unlike its y-ing blue to them? If in answer to such questions as these they said, "Oh no, there's all the difference in the world!" then I think we should be inclined to say that either x-ing or y-ing (if not both) must be something other than seeing: we might of course be quite unable to decide *which* (if either) was seeing.

(I am aware that here those whose approach is more Wittgensteinian than my own might complain that unless something more can be said about how the difference between x-ing and y-ing might "come out" or show itself in publicly observable phenomena, then the claim by the supposed Martians that x-ing and y-ing are different would be one of which nothing could be made, which would leave one at a loss how to understand it. *First*, I am not convinced of the need for "introspectible" differences to show themselves in the way this approach demands (I shall not discuss this point further); *second*, I think that if I *have* to meet this demand, I can. One can suppose that one or more of these Martians acquired the use of the lower y-ing organs at some comparatively late date in their careers, and that at the same time (perhaps for experimental purposes) the operation of the upper x-ing organs was inhibited. One might now be ready to allow that a difference between x-ing and y-ing would have shown itself if in such a situation the creatures using their y-ing organs for the first time were unable straightaway, without any learning process, to use their "color"-words fluently and correctly to describe what they detected through the use of those organs.)

It might be argued at this point that we have not yet disposed of the idea that the senses can be distinguished by an amalgam of suggestions (I), (III), and (IV); for it is not clear that in the example of the Martians the condition imposed by suggestion (I) is fulfilled. The thesis, it might be said, is only upset if x-ing and y-ing are accepted as being the exercise of different senses; and if they are, then the Martians' color-words could be said to have a concealed ambiguity. Much as "sweet" in English may mean "sweet-smelling" or "sweet-tasting," so "blue" in Martian may mean "blue-x-ing" or "blue-y-ing." But if this is so, then the Martians after all do not detect by x-ing just those properties of things which they detect by y-ing. To this line of argument there are two replies:

(1) The defender of the thesis is in no position to use this argument; for he cannot start by making the question whether x-ing and y-ing are exercises of the same sense turn on the question (*inter alia*) whether or not a single group of characteristics is detected by both, and then make the question of individuation of the group turn on the question whether putative members of the group are detected by one, or by more than one, sense. He would be saying in effect, "Whether, in x-ing and y-ing, different senses are exercised depends (*inter alia*) on whether the same properties are detected by x-ing as by y-ing; but whether a certain x-ed property is the same as a certain y-ed property depends on whether x-ing and y-ing are or are not the exercise of a single sense." This reply seems fatal. For the circularity could only be avoided by making the question whether "blue" in Martian names a single property depend *either* on whether the kinds of experience involved in x-ing and y-ing are different, which would be to reintroduce suggestion (II), *or* on whether the mechanisms involved in x-ing and y-ing are different (in this case whether the upper organs are importantly unlike the lower organs): and to adopt this alternative would, I think, lead to treating the differentiation of the senses as being solely a matter of their mechanisms, thereby making suggestion (I) otiose.

(2) Independently of its legitimacy or illegitimacy in the present context, we must reject the idea that if it is accepted that in x-ing and y-ing different senses are being exercised, then Martian color-words will be ambiguous. For *ex hypothesi* there will be a very close correlation between things x-ing blue and their y-ing blue, far closer

than that between things smelling sweet and their tasting sweet. This being so, it is only to be expected that x-ing and y-ing should share the position of arbiters concerning the color of things: that is, "blue" would be the name of a single property, determinable equally by x-ing and y-ing. After all, is this not just like the actual position with regard to shape, which is doubly determinable, by sight and by touch?

While I would not wish to quarrel with the main terms of this second reply, I should like briefly to indicate why I think that this final quite natural comparison with the case of shape will not do. It is quite conceivable that the correlation between x-ing and y-ing , in the case supposed, might be close enough to ensure that Martian color-words designated doubly determinable properties, and yet that this correlation should break down in a limited class of cases: for instance, owing to some differences between the two pairs of organs, objects which transmitted light of a particular wavelength might (in standard conditions) x blue but y black. If this were so, then for these cases the conflict would render decision about the real color of the objects in question impossible. (I ignore the possibility that the real color might be made to depend on the wavelength of the light transmitted, which would involve depriving color of its status as a purely sensibly determinable property.)

I am, however, very much inclined to think that a corresponding limited breakdown in the correlation between sight and touch with regard to shape is not conceivable. The nature of the correlation between sight and touch is far too complicated a question to be adequately treated within the compass of this essay; so I shall attempt only to indicate, in relation to two comparatively simple imaginary cases, the special intimacy of this correlation. Both cases involve medium-sized objects, which are those with regard to which we are most willing to accept the equality of the arbitraments of sight and touch. The question at issue in each case is whether we can coherently suppose both (a) that, in a world which in general exhibits the normal correlation between sight and touch, some isolated object should standardly feel round but standardly look square, and also (b) that it should be undecidable, as regards that object, whether preference should be given to the deliverance of sight or to that of touch.

Case A. In this case I do not attribute to the divergent object the power of temporarily upsetting the correlation of sight and touch with regard to other normal objects while they are in its vicinity. Suppose that, feeling in my pocket, I were to find an object which felt as if it were round and flat like a penny, I take it out of my pocket and throw it on the table, and am astonished to see what looks like a square flat object: I find, moreover, that when surveyed by myself (and others) from various points, it continues to look as a square object should look. I now shut my eyes and "frame" the object by running my finger round its edge; my finger feels to me as if it were moving in a circle. I then open my eyes, and, since we are supposing that other objects are not affected by the divergent one, my finger also feels to me as if it were tracing a circular path, but not, of course, as if it were "framing" the visible outline of the object. One possibility is that my finger is seen to cut through the corners of the visible outline of the divergent object; and I think that such a lack of "visual solidity" would be enough to make us say that the object is really round, in spite of its visual appearance. Another possibility is that the visible path of my finger should be a circle within which the visible outline of the object is inscribed, and that, if I try, I fail to establish visible contact between my finger and the object's outline, except at the corners of that outline. I suggest that if the object's outline were visually unapproachable in this kind of way, this would very strongly incline us to say that the object was really round; and I suspect that this inclination could be decisively reinforced by the application of further tests of a kind to be mentioned in connection with the second case.

Case B. In this case I do attribute to the object the power of "infecting" at least some other objects, in particular my finger or (more strictly) the path traced by my finger. Suppose that, as before, when I trace the felt outline of the divergent object, it feels to me as if my finger were describing a circle, and also that, as before, the object looks square; now, however, the visible path of my moving finger is not circular but square, framing the visible outline of the object. Suppose also that I find a further object which is indisputably round, the size of which feels equal to the size which the divergent object is felt as having, and which (we will suppose) is not infected by proximity to the divergent object; if I place this unproblematic object behind the divergent one, as I move my finger around the pair of objects, it *feels* as if I am continuously in contact with the edges of both objects, but it *looks* as if I am in continuous contact with the divergent object, but in only occasional contact with the normal object. (I am taking the case in which the corners of the visible outline of the divergent object overlap the visible outline of the normal object.) Given this information alone, I think that it cannot be decided what the real shape of the divergent object is; but there are various further tests which I can make. One of these would be to put the two objects on the table, the divergent object being on top, to place my finger and thumb so that they are in felt contact with both objects but are visually in contact only with opposed corners of the visible outline of the divergent object, and then raise my hand; if thereby I lift both objects, the divergent object is really round; if I lift only the divergent object, it is really square.

A test closely related to the foregoing would be to discover through what sorts of aperture the divergent object could be made to pass, on the general principle that it is square pegs which fit into square holes and round pegs which fit into round holes. For example, suppose I find an aperture the real shape and size of which is such that, according to tactual comparison, it ought to accommodate the divergent object, while according to visual comparison it ought not to do so; then (roughly speaking) if the object can be made to pass through the aperture it is really round; if it cannot, it is really square. It seems to me that the decisiveness of this test can be averted only if we make one of two suppositions. We might suppose our fantasy-world to be such that apertures of a suitable real shape are not available to us; for this supposition, however, to be of interest, it would have to amount to the supposition of a *general* breakdown of the correlation of sight and touch as regards shape, which is contrary to the terms of our discussion, which is concerned only with the possibility of a limited breakdown in this respect. Alternatively, we might suppose that when we attempt to make the divergent object pass through a suitably chosen aperture which is really round, it feels as if the object passes through, but it looks as if the object fails to pass through. On this supposition there is some prospect that the real shape of the divergent object should remain undecidable. But we must consider the consequences of this supposition. What, for example, happens to my finger when it is pushing the divergent object tactually, though not visually, through the aperture? In order to keep the question of the real shape undecidable, I think we shall have to suppose that the finger tactually moves into the aperture, but visually remains outside. Given this assumption, it seems reasonable to conclude that it will have become a practical possibility, with regard to any object whatsoever, or at least any movable object, to divorce its tactual location from its visual location. Imagine, for example, that the divergent object is just outside one end of a suitably selected cylinder, and is attached to my waist by a string which passes through the cylinder; now I set myself the task of drawing the object through the cylinder by walking away. If I do not tug too hard, I can ensure that tactually my body, together with any objects attached to it, will move away from the cylinder, while visually it will not. And one might add, where shall *I* be then?

I suggest, then, that given the existence of an object which, for the Martians, standardly x-ed blue but y-ed black (its real color being undecidable), no conclusion could be drawn to the effect that other objects do, or could as a matter of practical possibility be made to, x one way and y another way either in respect of color or in respect of some other feature within the joint province of x-ing and y-ing; given, on the other hand, the existence of an object which, for us, standardly felt one shape and looked another, then *either* its real shape would be nonetheless decidable, *or* it would be practically possible to disrupt in the case of at least some other objects the correlation between sight and touch as regards at least one feature falling within their joint domain, namely spatial location; at least some objects could be made standardly to feel as if they were in one place and standardly to look as if they were in another. Whether such notions as those of a material object, of a person, and of human action could apply, without radical revision, to such a world, and whether such a world could be coherently supposed to be governed by any system of natural laws, however bizarre, are questions which I shall not here pursue.

(6) Compare the Molyneux problem. It has been properly objected against me that, in comparing the possibility of a limited breakdown in the correlation between x-ing and y-ing with the possibility of a corresponding limited breakdown in the correlation between sight and touch, I have cheated. For whereas I consider the possibility that a certain *class* of objects might x blue but y black, I consider only the possibility that a certain *isolated* object should standardly feel round but look square: I have failed to consider the possibility that, for example, objects of a particular felt size which feel round should look square and that there should therefore be no normal holes to use for testing divergent objects.

I can here do no more than indicate the lines on which this objection should be met. (1) The supposed limited breakdown cannot be restricted to objects of particular shapes, since the dimensions of objects and of holes can be measured both tactually and visually by measuring rods: and what happens when a divergent measuring rod is bent double? (2) Any shape-divergent object would be tolerated tactually but not visually (or vice versa) by normal holes (if available) of more than one specifically different size. Consequently, since we are ruling out a *general* breakdown of the correlation between sight and touch as regards the shapes in question, there must be *at least some* normal holes which will tolerate tactually but not visually (or visually but not tactually) *at least some* divergent objects: and this is enough for my purpose.

To return to the main topic, I hope that I have put up a fair case for supposing that suggestion (II) cannot be eliminated. How then, are we to deal with the difficulties which seemed to lead us back from suggestion (II) to suggestion (I), with a consequent impasse? The first of these was that such an alleged special experience as that supposedly involved in seeing eluded inspection and description. I think that this objection conceals an illegitimate demand. We are being asked to examine and describe the experience we have when we see, quite without reference to the properties we detect or think we detect when we see. But this is impossible, for the description of the experiences we have when we see involves the mention of properties we detect or seem to detect. More fully, the way to describe our visual experiences is in terms of how things look to us, and such a description obviously involves the employment of property-words. But in addition to the specific differences between visual experiences, signalized by the various property-words employed, there is a generic resemblance signalized by the use of the word "look," which differentiates visual from nonvisual sense-experience. This resemblance can be noticed and labeled, but perhaps not further described. To object that one cannot focus one's attention, in a given case, on the experience of seeing, as distinct from the properties detected, is perhaps like complaining that one cannot focus one's attention on the color of an object, ignoring its particular color. So the initial assumption of the independence of suggestions (I) and (II) has broken down: how extensive the breakdown is could be determined only by going on to consider how far differences in character between things reduce to differences between the experiences which people have or would have in certain circumstances. This would involve a discussion of traditional theories of perception for which at the moment I have neither time nor heart.

The second difficulty is that of explaining why, if sight is to be distinguished from other senses by the special character of the experiences involved in seeing, there is a logical objection to the idea that we might detect (say) the smells of things by means of experience of the visual type. Why can we not see the smell of a rose? Well, in a sense we can; a rose can (or at any rate conceivably might) look fragrant. But perhaps the objector wants us to explain why a rose cannot look fragrant in the same sense of "look" in which it may look red. The answer here is presumably that had nature provided a closer correlation between the senses of sight and smell than in fact obtains, the word "fragrant" might have been used to denote a doubly determinable property: in which case roses could have been said to look fragrant in just the sense of "look" in which they now look red. But of course the current rules for the word "fragrant" are adapted to the situation actually obtaining. If, however, the objector is asking us to explain why, on our view, given that fragrance is *merely* an olfactorily determinable property, it is not also at the same time a visually determinable property, then perhaps we may be excused from replying.

Notes

1. I am indebted to Rogers Albritton for a number of extremely helpful criticisms and suggestions concerning this essay.
2. This idea was suggested to me by O. P. Wood.

4

The Intentionality of Sensation: A Grammatical Feature

G. E. M. Anscombe

I Intentional Objects

Berkeley calls "colours with their variations and different proportions of light and shade" the "proper" and also the "immediate" objects of sight.[1] The first at any rate long seemed obvious to everyone, both before Berkeley and since his time. But Berkeley's whole view is now in some disrepute. Sense-data, a thoroughly Berkeleyan conception given that name by Russell, have become objects of ridicule and contempt among many present-day philosophers.

That word "object" which comes in the phrase "object of sight" has suffered a certain reversal of meaning in the history of philosophy, and so has the connected word "subject," though the two reversals aren't historically connected. The subject used to be what the proposition, say, is about: the thing itself as it is in reality—unprocessed by being conceived, as we might say (in case there is some sort of processing there); objects on the other hand were formerly always objects *of* ———. Objects of desire, objects of thought, are not objects in one common modern sense, not indivdual things, such as *the objects found in the accused man's pockets*.

I might illustrate the double reversal by a true sentence constructed to accord with the *old* meanings: subjectively there must be some definite number of leaves on a spray that I see, but objectively there need not: that is, there need not be some number such that I *see* that number of leaves on the spray.

When Descartes said that the cause of an idea must have at least as much formal reality as the idea had objective reality, he meant that the cause must have at least as much to it as what the idea was of would have, if what the idea was of actually existed. The "*realitas objectiva*" of an idea thus meant what we should call its "content"—namely what it is of, but considered as belonging purely to the idea. "What a picture is of" can easily be seen to have two meanings: what served as a model, what the picture was taken from—and what is to be seen in the picture itself, which may not even have had an original.

Thus formerly if something was called an object that would have raised the question "object of what?" It is hardly possible to use the word "object" in this way nowadays unless it actually occurs in such a phrase as "object of desire" or "object of thought." Suppose somebody says that the object of desire, or desired object, need not exist, and so there need not be any object which one desires. He is obviously switching from one use of the word "object" to another. If, however, we speak of objects of sight, or seen objects, it will usually be assumed that "objects" has the more modern sense: these will be objects, things, entities, which one sees. Now to prevent confusion I will introduce the phrase "intentional object" to mean "object" in the older sense which still occurs in "object of desire."

"Intentional" in these contexts is often spelt with an *s*. This was an idea of Sir William Hamilton's; he wanted to turn the old logical word "intention" into one that looked more like "extension." I prefer to keep the older spelling with two *t*s. For the word is the same as the one in common use in connection with action. The concept of intention which we use there of course occurs also in connection with *saying*. That makes the bridge to the logician's use.

There are three salient things about intention which are relevant for my subject. First, not any true description of what you do describes it as the action you intended: only under certain of its descriptions will it be intentional. ("Do you mean to be using that pen?"—"Why, what about this pen?"—"It's Smith's pen."—"Oh Lord, no!") Second, the descriptions under which you intend what you do can be vague, indeterminate. (You mean to put the book down on the table all right, and you do so, but you do not mean to put it down anywhere in particular on the table—though you do put it down somewhere in particular.) Third, descriptions under which you intend to do what you do may not come true, as when you make a slip of the tongue or pen. You act, but your intended act does not happen.

Intentionality, whose name is taken from intention and expresses these characteristics of the concept *intention*, is found also in connection with many other concepts. I shall argue that among these are concepts of sensation. Like many concepts marked by intentionality, though unlike intention itself, these are expressed by verbs commonly taking direct objects. I shall speak of intentional verbs, taking intentional objects. I have mentioned the history of the word "object" to forestall any impression that "an intentional object" means "an intentional entity."

Obvious examples of intentional verbs are "to think of," "to worship," "to shoot at." (The verb "to intend" comes by metaphor from the last—"*intendere arcum in*," leading to "*intendere animum in*.") Where we have such a verb taking an object, features analogous to the three features of intentionalness in action relate to some descriptions occurring as object-phrases after the verb.

The possible non-existence of the object, which is the analogue of the possible non-occurrence of the *intended* action, is what has excited most attention about this sort of verb. "Thinking of" is a verb for which the topic of the non-existent object is full of traps and temptations; "worshipping" is less dangerous and may help us to keep our heads. Consider the expression "object of thought." If I am thinking of Winston Churchill then he is the object of my thought. This is like "What is the object of these people's worship?" Answer: "The moon." But now suppose the object of my thought is Mr Pickwick, or a unicorn; and the object of my worship is Zeus, or unicorns. With the proper names I named no man and no god, since they name a fictitious man and a false god. Moreover Mr Pickwick and Zeus are nothing but a fictitious man and a false god (contrast the moon, which, though a false god, is a perfectly good heavenly body). All the same it is clear that "The Greeks worshipped Zeus" is true. Thus "X worshipped ———" and "X thought of ———" are not to be assimilated to "X bit ———." For, supposing "X" to be the name of a real person, the name of something real has to be put in the blank space in "X bit ———" if the completed sentence is to have so much as a chance of being true. Whereas in "X worshipped ———" and "X thought of ———" that is not so.

This fact is readily obscured for us because with "X thought of ———" the more frequent filling-in of the blank is a name or description of something real; for when the blank is filled in so in a true sentence, it is the real thing itself, not some intermediary, that X thought of. This makes it look as if the reality of the object mattered, as it does for biting. Nevertheless, it is obvious that vacuous names can complete such sentence-frames. So perhaps they stand in such frames for something with a *sort* of reality. That is the hazy state of mind one may be in about the matter.

A not very happy move to clarify it is to say, "Well, X had his idea of Zeus, or unicorns, or Mr Pickwick, and that gives you the object you want." This is an unhappy move on several counts. First, it makes it seem that the *idea* is what X was worshipping or thinking of. Second, the mere fact of real existence (is this now beginning to be opposed to existence of some other kind?) can't make so very much difference to the analysis of a sentence like "X thought of ———." So if the idea is to be brought in when the object doesn't exist, then equally it should be brought in when the object does exist. Yet one is thinking, surely, of Winston Churchill, not of the idea of him, and just that fact started us off. When one reads Locke, one wants to protest: "The mind is not employed about ideas, but about things—unless ideas are what we happen to be thinking about." Whatever purpose is served by introducing ideas, by saying, "Well, they had an idea of Zeus," we cannot say that the idea is the object of thought, or worship. It will not be right to say X worshipped an idea. It is rather that the subject's having an idea is what is needed to give the proposition a chance of being true. This may seem helpful for "worshipping," but not for "thinking of"; "thinking of" and "having an idea of" are too similar; if the one is problematic, then so is the other.

Let us concentrate on the fact that many propositions containing intentional verbs are true, and let us not be hypnotized by the possible non-existence of the object. There are other features too: non-substitutability of different descriptions of the object, where it does exist; and possible indeterminacy of the object. In fact all three features are connected. I can think of a man without thinking of a man of any particular height; I cannot hit a man without hitting a man of some particular height, because there is no such thing as a man of no particular height. And the possibility of this indeterminacy makes it possible that when I am thinking of a particular man, not every true description of him is one under which I am thinking of him.

I will now define an intentional verb as a verb taking an intentional object; intentional objects are the sub-class of direct objects characterized by these three connected features. By this definition, "to believe" and "to intend" are not themselves intentional verbs, which may seem paradoxical. But, say, "to believe—to be a scoundrel" will accord with the definition, so that it is not so paradoxical as to leave out belief and intention altogether.

But now comes a question: ought we really to say that the intentional object is a bit of language, or may we speak as if it were what the bit of language stands for? As grammarians and linguists use the words nowadays "direct object" and "indirect object" stand for parts of sentences. So if I call intentional objects a sub-class of direct objects, that may seem already to determine that an intentional object is a bit of language.

However, the matter is not so easily settled. Of course I do not want to oppose the practice of grammarians. But it is clear that the concept of a direct object—and hence the identification of the sentence-part now called the direct object—is learned somewhat as follows: the teacher takes a sentence, say "John sent Mary a book" and says: "What did John send Mary?" Getting the answer "A book" he says: "That's the direct object." Now the question does not really suppose, and the pupil, if he goes along with the teacher, does not take it, that any particular people, of whom the sentence is true, are in question, and so we may say that when the teaching is successful the question is understood as equivalent to "What does the sentence 'John sent Mary a book' say John sent Mary?" The grammatical concept of a direct object is acquired by one who can answer any such question. The correct answer to such a question gives (in older usage) or itself is (in more recent usage) the direct object. Now suppose that someone were to ask: "What is communicated to us by the phrase that we get in a correct answer? Is the phrase being used or mentioned?" It is clear that nothing is settled about *this* question by a choice whether to say, following older usage, that the phrase *gives* the direct object or, following more modern usage, that "direct object" is a name for a sentence-part.

I propose—for a purpose which will appear—to adopt the older usage. Then the question "What is the direct object of the verb in this sentence?" is the same as "What does the sentence say John sent Mary?" and the question "What does the phrase which is the answer to that question communicate to us, i.e. is it being used or mentioned?" can be asked in the form "Is the direct object a bit of language or rather what the bit of language stands for?"—and *this* is now not a mere question of terminology, but a substantive-seeming question of curious perplexity. For someone pondering it may argue as follows: It won't do to say that in this example a book is the direct object. For if we say that we can be asked: "Which book?"; but the sentence isn't being considered as true, and there is no answer to the question "Which book?" except "No book"; and yet without doubt the verb has a direct object, given by the answer "A book." So it must be *wrong*, and not just a matter of terminology, to say that the grammatical phrase "direct object" stands for, not a bit of language, but rather what the bit of language stands for. And, if intentional objects are a sub-class of direct objects, the phrase "intentional object" too will stand for a bit of language rather than what the language stands for; we are evidently not going to have to plunge into the bog made by the fact that in the most important and straightforward sense the phrase giving the intentional object may stand for nothing.

But wait—in that case *must* we not say, "the phrase which *is* the intentional object" rather than "the phrase giving the intentional object"? This is indeed a difficulty. For the intentional object is told in answer to a question "What?" But the answer to "What do they worship?" cannot be that they worship a phrase any more than that they worship an idea. A similar point holds, of course, for direct (and indirect) objects in general.

It may be argued that this is no argument.[2] Perhaps we cannot say "What John is said to have sent is a phrase." But then no more can we say "What John is said to have sent is a direct object"—for the sentence did not say John sent Mary a direct object.

What this shows is that there is a way of taking "The direct object is not a direct object" which makes this true; namely, by assimilating this sentence to "The direct object is not a girl." (One could imagine explaining to a child: "The girl isn't the direct object, but the *book* that John sent.")

Frege's conclusion "The concept horse is not a concept" was based on the same sort of trouble about different uses of expressions. What "*cheval*" stands for is a concept, and what "*cheval*" stands for is a horse; these premises do not, however, yield the result that if Bucephalus is a horse he is a concept. Similarly, what John is said to have sent Mary is a book, and what John is said to have sent Mary is a direct object; these premises do not yield the result that if John gave Mary a book, he gave her a direct object.

Frege eventually proposed to deal with the trouble by stipulating that such a phrase as "What 'cheval' stands for" should *only* be used predicatively. A parallel stipulation in our case: "What John is said to have sent Mary is . . ." may only be completed with such expressions as could fill the blank in "John sent Mary. . . ."

The stipulation, while harmless, would be based on failure of ear for the different use of the phrase "What John is said to have sent Mary" in the explanation "What John is said to have sent Mary is the direct object of the sentence." But an ear for a different use cannot be dispensed with, as the further course of the argument shows.

The argument began with stating reasons why a direct object can't be something that the direct-object phrase stands for. Yet one can, one correctly does, say "A book" in answer to the question "What does the sentence 'John sent Mary a book' say John sent Mary?" which asks the same thing as "What is the direct object in that sentence?" Nevertheless the way the phrase "a book" is being used is such that one can't sensibly ask "Which book?"

We must conclude of "objects" (direct, indirect and likewise intentional) that the object is neither the phrase nor what the phrase stands for. What then is it? The question is based on a mistake, namely that an explanatory answer running say "An intentional (direct, indirect) object is such-and-such" is possible and requisite. But this need not be so. Indeed the only reasonable candidates to be answers are the ones we have failed. But what is the actual use of the term? Given a sentence in which a verb takes an object, one procedure for replying to the question: "What is the object in this sentence?" is to recite the object phrase.

If putting the object phrase in quotes implies that the object—i.e. what John is said to have sent Mary, what the Greeks worshipped—is a piece of language, that is wrong; if its not being in quotes implies that something referred to by the object phrase is the object, that is wrong too. To avoid the latter suggestion one might insist on putting in quotes; to avoid the former one might want to leave them out. One is inclined to invent a special sort of quotes; but the question is how the phrase within such new quotes would function—and if we understand that, we don't need a new sign. So ends the argument.

To repeat, I am not opposing the practice of grammarians and linguists for whom the expression "direct object" is defined as an expression for a phrase; they use that as I use the expression "direct-object phrase." But, as I have argued, the question "What does the sentence say John gave?" is fundamental for understanding either "direct object" or "direct-object phrase" as I am using those expressions; and hence for understanding "direct object" when it is used for a phrase. And though the question is answered (like many questions) by uttering a phrase—in this case "a book"— the phrase has *a special use* in answer to that question "What does the sentence say John gave?" *It* can name neither a piece of language, nor anything that the piece of language names or otherwise relates to, nor indeed anything else. The interest of the question and answer is the rather special interest of getting grammatical understanding. Grammatical understanding and grammatical concepts, even the most familiar ones like sentence, verb, noun, are not so straightforward and down-to-earth a matter of plain physical realities as I believe people sometimes suppose. The concept of a noun, for example, is far less of a physical concept than that of a coin; for someone might be trained to recognize coins with fair success though he knew nothing of money, but no one could be trained to recognize nouns without a great familiarity with language; and yet the concept of a noun is not one which he will automatically have through that familiarity, as he will have that of a coin if he operates with coined money. Indeed the explanations of grammatical terms are only hints at what is really grasped from examples. Thus no one should think that by merely adopting the usage of modern grammarians, for whom the direct object is a word or words, he has avoided handling difficult concepts and remained in a plain man's world of plain thing.

"The direct object is what John sent" (= "what the sentence says John sent").

"The intentional object is what X was thinking of."

These two sentences are parallel. It is for the sake of parallelism that we opted for the old fashioned usage of "direct object." For even in that usage, no one will be tempted to think that direct objects as such are a special type of entity. Just this temptation exists very strongly for objects of thought and sensation; that is, for intentional objects, which appear as entities under the names "idea" and "impression."

It may be objected: the context "The sentence says John sent Mary ———" is itself intentional. How, then, can my considerations about direct objects throw light on intentional objects? Fully spelled out they are themselves merely examples of sentences whose objects are intentional objects.[3]

The answer is that what is said in the objection is true. But these examples, where we talk about direct objects, are harmless and profitable because certain sorts of suggestion about direct objects are patent nonsense. For example no one would think that if a sentence says John sent Mary a book, what it immediately and directly says he sent her was a direct object, and only in some indirect fashion, via this immediate object, does it say he sent her a book. I want, that is, to use a comparison with patent nonsense about direct objects in order to expose as latent nonsense of just the same kind some very persuasive views about ideas and impression. Not that ideas and impressions are to be excluded from consideration; but as they enter into epistemology they will be rightly regarded as grammatical notions, whose role is readily misunderstood. And "grammatical" is here being used in its ordinary sense.

We must now ask: does any phrase that gives the direct object of an intentional verb in a sentence necessarily give an intentional object? No. Consider: "These people worship Ombola; that is to say, they worship a mere hunk of wood." (cf. "They worship sticks and stones.") Or "They worship the sun, that is, they worship what is nothing but a great mass of frightfully hot stuff." The worshippers themselves will not acknowledge the descriptions. Their idol is for them a divinized piece of wood, one that is somehow also a god; and similarly for the sun.

An intentional object is given by a word or phrase which gives a *description under which*.

It will help if we consider shooting at, aiming. A man aims at a stag; but the thing he took for a stag was his father, and he shoots his father. A witness reports: "He aimed at his father." Now this is ambiguous. In the sense in which given the situation as we have described it, this report is true, the phrase "his father" does not give an intentional object. Let us introduce the term "material object": "his father" gives, we shall say, the *material* object of the verb in the sentence "He aimed at his father" in the sense in which this was true. Not because he hit his father—he might after all merely have gone wide of the mark. But because the thing he took for a stag actually was his father. We can ask what he was doing—what he was aiming at—*in that* he was aiming at a stag: this is to ask for another description "*X*" such that in "He was aiming at *X*" we still have an intentional object, but the description "*X*" gives us something that exists in the situation. For example, he was aiming at that dark patch against the foliage. The dark patch against the foliage was in fact his father's hat with his father's head in it.

Thus, the given intentional object (the stag) being nonexistent in the situation, we looked for another intentional object until we found one that did exist. Then the phrase giving that intentional object, and any other true description of the existent thing in question, gives the *material* object of "He aimed at. . . ."

Does this account depend on the report's being true? No; but if the witness lies or is quite mistaken, all the same he can be questioned about what his report meant. Does he mean the phrase "his father" to give the intentional, or only the material, object? If only the material object, what does he mean by "He aimed at . . ."? That you could see that the man was taking aim, and where his target lay? There might not be true answers to these questions, but the witness has got to pretend there are or be confounded.

And now, for greater ease of expression, I will speak, as is natural, of the material and intentional objects of aiming, of worshipping, of thinking. This should always be interpretable in terms of the verbs and their objects.

There need not be a material object of aiming. If a man were totally hallucinated, and, shooting at something in his hallucinatory scene, hit his father, that would not make his father the *material* object of his aiming. Similarly, if there is no description, still giving the intentional object of worship, which describes anything actual, the worshippers, materially speaking, worship a nothing, something that does not exist.

Not that it will then do to say "They worship nothing," but only: "What they worship is nothing." For "They worship nothing" would imply that no sentence

"They worship such-and-such" will be true; and in the case supposed some such sentence is true.

Questions about the identity of an intentional object, when this cannot be reduced to the identity of a *material* object, are obviously of some interest. How do we decide that two people or peoples worship or do not worship the same god? Again, when a proper name is obscure and remote in its historical reference, like "Arthur," the question may arise whether two people are thinking of the same man—if they have different, incompatible, pictures of him.

But I perceive that my saying "when this cannot be reduced to the identity of a *material* object" may mislead: for by *material* objects I do not mean what are now called "material objects"—tables, planets, lumps of butter and so on. To give a clear instance: a debt of five dollars is not a material object in this latter sense; but given that someone had contracted such a debt, my thought "that debt of five dollars" would have as its material object something described and indicated by the phrase giving the intentional object of my thought. When it is beyond question that the phrase giving an intentional object does describe and indicate a material object in this sense, then the question as to the identity of the intentional object reduces to the question as to the identity of the material object. Are we referring to the same debt? That is, perhaps, not too difficult to establish. But when either there is no real debt or it is very obscure whether there is, the case is altered.

The fact that we can use the concept of identity in connection with intentional objects should not lead us to think there is any sense in questions as to the kind of existence—the ontological status—of intentional objects as such. All such questions are nonsensical. Once more we can clear our heads by thinking of direct objects. The answer to "What is the direct object in 'John sent Mary a book'?" is "A book." This is the right answer as much when the sentence is false as when it is true, and also when it is only made up, as it is in this case, to illustrate a point. It is evident nonsense to ask about the mode of existence or ontological status of the direct object as such: or to ask what kind of thing *a book* is, as it is thought of in answer to the question about the direct object.

II Sensation

In the philosophy of sense-perception there are two opposing positions. One says that what we are immediately aware of in sensation is sense-impressions, called "ideas" by Berkeley and "sense-data" by Russell. The other, taken up nowadays by "ordinary language" philosophy, says that on the contrary we at any rate *see* objects (in the *wide* modern sense which would include, e.g. shadows) without any such intermediaries. It is usually part of this position to insist that I can't see (or, perhaps, feel, hear, taste or smell) something that is not here, any more than I can hit something that is not there: I can only *think* I see (etc.) something if it isn't there, or only in some extended usage of "see" do I see what isn't there. I shall say most about seeing, as most people do in discussing this topic. The other verbs are for good reasons (which aren't very relevant to my topic) often treated rather differently, especially by ordinary language philosophy.

I wish to say that both these positions are wrong; that both misunderstand verbs of sense-perception, because these verbs are intentional or essentially have an intentional aspect. The first position misconstrues intentional objects as material objects of sensation; the other allows only *material* objects of sensation; or at any rate does not allow for a description of what is seen which is e.g. neutral as between its being a real spot (a stain) or an after-image, giving only the content of an experience of seeing concerning which one does not yet know whether one is seeing a real spot or an after-image.[4]

To see the intentionality of sensation it is only necessary to look at a few examples which bring it out.

(1) "When you screw up your eyes looking at a light, you see rays shooting out from it."

(2) "I see the print very blurred: is it blurred, or is it my eyes?"

(3) "Move these handles until you see the bird in the nest." (Squint-testing apparatus; the bird and the nest are on separate cards.)

(4) "I see six buttons on that man's coat, I merely see a lot of snow flakes framed by this window-frame—no definite number."

(5) ". . . a mirage. An approaching pedestrian may have no feet (they are replaced by a bit of sky)."[5]

(6) "With this hearing aid, when you talk I hear some screeching noises; no low tones and the consonants are very indistinct."

(7) "I hear a ringing in my ears."

(8) "I heard a tremendous roaring noise outside, and wondered with alarm for a moment what great machine or floodwater could be making it. And then I realized that it was only my little dog snoring close at hand."[6]

(9) "Do you know how a taste can sometimes be quite indeterminate until you know what you are eating?"

(10) "I keep on smelling the smell of burning rubber when, as I find out, there is no such thing."

Someone who wishes to say that the verbs of sense are used right in normal cases *only* with real things as objects, and even with real things correctly characterized, may say that these are exceptional uses. Either the context (eye-testing apparatus) or what is said, with the tone of voice and special emphasis appropriate to it, shows this. There was presumably a definite number of snowflakes falling so as to be seen from a certain position, and that was the number seen; only the subject did not know how many there were, was not able to tell by looking as he could tell the number of buttons on the coat. He expressed this by saying he did not *see* a definite number of snowflakes; but this is an odd use of "see," different from the more normal use we get in the following example:

(11) "I saw someone in the study just now." "Nonsense! You can't have, because there isn't anyone there." "Well, I wonder what I saw, then."

Now this may be; on the other hand the oculist testing the degree of a squint does not have to teach a new use of "see" or of "I see a (picture of a) bird in a nest" before he can ask "Do you see the bird in the nest?"—the bird-picture and the nest-picture being in fact spatially separated. To call such a use "new" simply means that some difference between it and what is being called the old use strikes us as important.

There is indeed an important difference; though it is wrong to regard the uses which it marks as, so to speak, *deviant*, for our concepts of sensation are built up by our having *all* these uses. The difference we are attending to is that in these cases, object phrases are used giving objects which are, wholly or in part, merely intentional. This comes out in two features: neither possible non-existence (in the situation), nor indeterminacy, of the object is any objection to the truth of what is said.

Now "ordinary language" views and "sense-datum" views make the same mistake, that of failing to recognize the intentionality of sensation, though they take opposite positions in consequence. This failure comes out clearly on the part of an ordinary-language philosopher if he insists that what I say I see must really be there if I am not lying, mistaken, or using language in a "queer," extended (and therefore discountable) way.

The Berkeleyan sense-datum philosopher makes the same mistake in his insistence that, e.g., one sees visual impressions, visual data. I would say that such a philosopher makes an incorrect inference from the truth of the grammatical statement that the intentional object, the impression, the visual object, is what you see. He takes the expression "what you see" materially. "The visual impression is what you see," which is a proposition like "The direct object is what he sent," is misconstrued so as to lead to "You see an impression," as the other never would be misconstrued so as to lead to "He sent her a direct object."

This is a more interesting and permanently tempting mistake than the other, whose appeal is merely that of a common-sense revolt against a Berkeleyan type of view. But both doctrines have a great deal of point. To take the "ordinary language" doctrine:

First, what I shall call the material use of verbs of sense exists. The material use of "see" is a use which demands a *material* object of the verb. "You can't have seen a unicorn, unicorns don't exist." "You can't have seen a lion, there wasn't any lion there to see." These uses are quite commonplace. It is not merely that the object-phrase is taken materially—as we have seen, that may be the case with an intentional verb without reflecting on its intentionality. Here the verb "to see" is not allowed to take a *merely* intentional object; non-existence of the object (absolutely, or in the situation) is an objection to the truth of the sentence. We see the double use of the verb "see" by contrasting it with "worship." No one would ever say: "They cannot have worshipped unicorns, because there are no such things."

Second, the words giving the object of a verb of sense are necessarily most often intended as giving *material* objects of sense: for this is their primary application. To see this, consider the following. Suppose a bright red plastic toy elephant looks greyish-brown to me in a certain light. Only if I do not know that the greyish-brown colour is mere appearance do I say without any special context (e.g. that of describing impressions), or apology, or humour: " I see a greyish-brown plastic toy elephant." This is because we understand the description-of-an-appearance "greyish-brown" by understanding the description "greyish-brown": this describes what the appearance is of. To do that, it must in the first instance be a description of such a thing as it would be true of (for the appearance is an appearance of that)— really, and not merely in appearance: this will be its primary application. But, being a description of a sensible property, it must also in its primary application enter into the object phrases for the appropriate verbs of sense, since we get to know sensible properties by the appropriate senses.

Further, we ought to say, not: "Being red is looking red in normal light to the normal-sighted," but rather "Looking red is looking as a thing that *is* red looks in normal light to the normal-sighted." For if we ought rather to say the first, then how do we understand "looking red"? Not by understanding "red" and "looking." It would have to be explained as a simple idea; and so would looking any other colour. It may be replied: These all are simple ideas; "looking yellow" and "looking red" are the *right* expressions for what you show someone when you show him yellow and red, for he will only learn "yellow" and "red" from the examples if they look yellow and look red; so it is *looking-yellow* and *looking-red* that he really gets hold of and has been introduced to, even though you *say* you are explaining "yellow" and "red." This would come to saying that in strictness "looking" should be part of every colour word in reports of perception: it will then cease to perform the actual function of the word "looking." It was plausible to say: Only if it looks red to him will he learn what is meant; but wrong to infer: What he then grasps as the correlate of the word "red" is a red look. Even granted that he knows he is to learn the name of a colour, still it invites misunderstanding to rely on something that only *looks* red to teach him the word; if he notices that it only looks red, how natural for him to suppose that "red" was the name of the colour that it actually *is*. If you tell him: "It's the colour that this 'looks,'" this presupposes that "looks C" and "C" are originally, and not just subsequently, distinct: that, in short, "being red" is not after all to be explained as a certain looking-red.

Again, things do not always look the same shape, colour, size and so on, but we commonly look at and describe them, saying, e.g., "It's rectangular, black and about six foot in height," without paying attention to how they look—indeed we might say that often things *look* to us, strike us, not as they look but as they are! (Conviction that *only* so is "looks" used rightly was the cause of confusion to an over-confident ordinary-language philosopher on an occasion famous in Oxford: F. Cioffi brought in a glass vessel of water with a stick in it. "Do you mean to say," he asked, "that this stick does not look bent?" "No," said the other bravely: "It looks like a straight stick in water." So Cioffi took it out and it *was* bent.)

So much at least there is to be said on the side of the "ordinary-language" philosopher. But, turning to the sense-impression philosophy, how much it points out and can investigate which often gets querulously dismissed by the other side! There is such a thing as simply describing impressions, simply describing the sensible appearances that present themselves to one situated thus and thus—or to *myself*.

Second, the sense-impression philosophy will be right in its way of taking the Platonic dictum: "He who sees must see something." Plato compared this to "He who thinks must think something," and has sometimes been criticized on the ground that "seeing" is a relation of a subject to an object in the modern sense of that last word, while thinking is different: that such-and-such is the case isn't a thing. But "He who sees must see something" is being wrongly taken if taken as meaning: "Whenever anyone can rightly be said to see, there must be something there, which is what he sees." Taken in that sense, it is not true; to say it is true is to legislate against all except the material use of "see." The sense in which it is true is that if someone is seeing, there is some content of his visual experience. If he says he can see ("can see" is English idiom for "is seeing") we can ask him "What can you see?" He may say "I don't know." Perhaps that means that he doesn't know what the material object of his seeing is; perhaps simply that he is at a loss to make out *what* what he (in any sense) sees *looks like*. But then we can say: well, at any rate, describe what colours, what variation of light and dark you see. He may say: "It's frightfully difficult, it all changes so fast, so many colours shifting all the time, I can't describe it, it doesn't stay long enough"—and that's a description. But he cannot say: "how do you mean, what I see? I only said I could see, I didn't say I could see something—there's no need of a '*what*' that I see." That would be unintelligible.

This brings out the third point in favour of the sense-impression philosophy, which offers it some support even in its strict Berkeleyan form. The minimum description that must be possible if someone can see, will be of colours with their variations of light and darkness. One cannot say "Colour, light and dark? No question of any such things," in response to a *present* enquiry about what one sees.

That is to say, it is so with us. Perhaps we could imagine people whose language has no colour vocabulary, though they are sighted, i.e. they use eyes and need light to get about successfully, etc. A man of such a people, taught to read by sight, learns names of letters, could read out words which were black on white, but could not understand the words "black" and "white." We'd say we do not know "how he tells" the words, the shapes. But is that to say anything but that for us appeal to colours is used in an account of how we tell shapes? Whereas perhaps for him there is in this sense no such thing as a "how he tells"—any more than there is for us with the colours themselves. We don't ask for a "how we tell" it's red, as we ask for a "how we tell" it's the word "red" and accept as part of the answer "by seeing these shapes, i.e. colour patches of these shapes". We may wonder "How could there be such recognition of a thing like the pattern of a word—*unmediated* recognition? How could it but be mediated by perception of colour?" (One of the origins of the notion of simple ideas, elements.) But although in this case we have an account of the perception of the pattern as mediated by the perception of colour, think of our recognition of human expressions. We feel that this is the *kind* of thing to be mediated, but fail in our attempts to describe the elements and their arrangements, seeing which we recognize a cheerful or ironical expression. But, one may say, optically speaking he must be being affected by light of the wavelengths belonging to the different colours. Yes—but does that show that, so to speak, the content of a colour concept is pushed into him, so that all he has to do is utter it in a name, whose use he will later make to fit with other people's in its range of application? I believe this is thought. (cf. Quine about "square" and each man's retinal projection of a square tile.)[7] Formulated, this loses its plausibility. For one thing, the optical process does not exhibit anything to the man in whom it takes place. For another, no concept is simply given; every one involves a complicated technique of application of the word for it, which could not just be presented by an experience-content. The fact that there is no "how we tell" about colour-recognition does not mean that training in practices—most strikingly the practices comprising that technique of application—is not as necessary for the acquisition of colour concepts as those of substances or square roots.

Pursuant to this false conception of the primitively given, Berkeley—and Russell—thought that all else in description of the seen, all besides the arrangement of colour patches in the visual field, was inference and construction. This is not acceptable. There are impressions of distance and size, for example, independent of assumptions about what a thing is. One may be utterly perplexed what a thing is just because one is seeing it as at a different distance from the right one, and hence as the wrong size. Or vice versa. I once opened my eyes and saw the black striking surface of a matchbox which was standing on one end; the other sides of the box were not visible. This was a few inches from my eye and I gazed at it in astonishment wondering what it could be. Asked to describe the impression as I remember it, I say: "Something black and rectangular, on end, some feet away, and some feet high." I took it for three or four feet distant, and it looked, if anything, like a thick post, but I knew there could be no such thing in my bedroom. Or I have taken a small black prayer book for a great family Bible sort of volume, judging that it lay on a footrest some feet away instead of a nearby ledge nearer eye-level. These were not judgements of distance based on identifications of things—the supposition of what thing it might be was based on an impression of size which went with a false impression of distance.

Departing, then, from Berkeley, we can note that descriptions of visual impressions can be very rich and various. There can be impressions of depth and distance and relative positions and size; of kinds of things and kinds of stuff and texture and even temperature; of facial expression and emotion and mood and thought and character; of action and movement (in the *stationary* impression) and life and death. Even within the compass of the description "colours with their variations of light and shade" there are diverse kinds of impression.

It remains to sort out the relations between the intentional and material objects of sensation; as I have done most of the time, I will concentrate on seeing.

While there must be an intentional object of seeing, there need not always be a material object. That is to say "X saw A" where "saw" is used materially, implies some proposition "X saw ———" where "saw" is used intentionally; but the converse does not hold. This leads to the feeling that the intentional use is somehow prior to the material use. The feeling seems to run contrary to the recognition, the feeling, that for descriptions of objects of sight the material application is the prior one. Both feelings are—legitimately—satisfied by allowing that an intentional object is necessarily involved in seeing, while granting that this does not confer epistemological priority on purely intentional sentences, which indeed, in a host of the most ordinary cases of reported seeing, are never formulated or considered.

John Austin, who opposed the view that there are two senses of "see" according as the seeing has to be veridical or not, remarked casually that there were perhaps two senses of "object of sight." I think it was in this connection that he contrasted "Today I saw a man born in Jerusalem" and "Today I saw a man shaved in Oxford"—both said in Oxford. At any rate, one says, you didn't *see* him born today; perhaps you did see someone being shaved. So the one description, while true of what you saw, in a sense does not give what you saw. A description which is true of a material object of the verb "to see," but which states something that absolutely or in the circumstances "you can't have *seen*," necessarily gives *only* a material object of seeing.

In speaking of the material object of aiming, I said that if a man aimed at that dark patch against the foliage, and that patch was his father's hat with his father's head in it, then his father was a material object of his aim; but if he aimed at some patch in a totally hallucinatory scene, and hit his father, you could not say that.

Now if we try to apply this explanation to the case of seeing we run into difficulties which reflect back on the case of aiming. But in the case considered the material object of aiming was arguably an *intentional* object of seeing. For what else— it might be asked—is a dark patch against the foliage?

This may seem to plunge us into confusion. For surely what is *only* an intentional object of seeing can't be a material object of aiming? Then when does a description give a material object of sight? One kind of case we have seen: when a description is true of what is seen, but does *not* give an intentional object. "I see a man whose great uncle died in a lunatic asylum"—the relative clause gives an absolutely non-intentional description. "I see a girl who has a mole between her shoulder-blades"—in the circumstances it gives a non-intentional description. For she is facing me, etc. "You can't have *seen* that," one says.

But why? If I can't see that, why can I see Professor Price's tomato? It has a back-side that I don't see. Mr Thompson Clarke draws our attention to the fact that a view of a tomato and a half-tomato may be exactly the same. That is so; but it is not like the fact that a view of someone with and without a mole between his shoulder blades may be exactly the same. If you look at a tomato and take only a single view, you *must* see what *might* be only a half tomato: that is what seeing a tomato is. Whereas there is a view of the mole; and no front view *is* a view of a mole between the shoulder blades. Such a mole does not stamp the front view as may approaching death or a load of troubles, and so there is no impression of it—just as there is no "born-in-Jerusalem" look about a man.

But a material object of seeing is not necessarily given by a description of what is before my eyes when they are open and I am seeing; if I am totally hallucinated, then in no sense do I see what is before my eyes. Thus it is essential to a material object of seeing that it is given by a description which is true of *what is seen*; and we have to enquire into the significance here of this phrase "*What is seen.*"

The problem is this: there is a material object of φ-ing if there is a phrase giving an intentional object of φ-ing which is also a description of what exists in a suitable relation to the φ-er. Now this can't be a description of what exists merely by describing the intentional object of some *other* act (he aims at the dark patch that he sees); if simply describing an intentional object of φ-ing will not—as of course it will not—guarantee that we have described a material object of φ-ing, then how can it give a material object of some other verb, φ-ing?

All would be plain sailing if we could say: we have a material object of sight only if *some* intentional description is also true of what really—physically—exists. And perhaps we can say that the dark patch against the foliage is not merely an intentional object of seeing; there really is a dark object or a region of darkness there.

But this is not always the case when we see. Suppose I have defective sight: all I see is a shiny blur over there. That blur, we say, is my watch. We therefore say I see my watch, though very indistinctly; and I want to say that my watch is the material object of seeing. But I may not be able to see it as a watch; all I see is a shiny blur. But the description "a shiny blur" is not true of anything that physically exists in the context. Supposing the father had a dark hat on, it would follow that, to mention the puzzle that perplexed Moore for so long, the dark patch against the foliage was *part of the surface of a material object (modern sense)*; but certainly "a blur" is no part of the surface of my watch. But it may be I have no other description of what I see than "a shiny blur over there." So is there any intentional description which is also a description of a material object of sight?

Yes; for even if my watch is not a blur, it is a shiny thing and it is over there. Suppose I had said: I see a roughly triangular red blur here, and some causal connection via the visual centres in the brain could have been discovered between that and the presence of my watch over there—would it have been right to say: 'What I am seeing is my watch"? I believe not.

An interesting case is that of *muscae volitantes*, as they are called. You go to the doctor and you say: "I wonder if there is something wrong with my eyes or my brain? I see"—or perhaps you say "I *seem* to see"—"floating specks before my eyes." The doctor says: "That's not very serious. They're there all right" (or: "You see them all right")—"they are just the floating debris in the fluids of the eye. You are a bit tired and so your brain doesn't knock them out, that's all." The things he says you see are not *out there* where you say you see them—*that* part of your intentional description is not true of anything relevant; but he does not say that what you are seeing is that debris *only* because the debris is the cause. There really are floating specks. If they caused you to see a little red devil or figure of eight, we should not say you saw them. It may be possible to think of cases where there is nothing in the intentional object that suggests a description of what is materially being seen. I doubt whether this could be so except in cases of very confused perception—how could a very definite intentional description be connected with a quite different material object of seeing? In such cases, if we are in doubt, we resort to moving the supposed material object to see if the blurred, not colour-true and misplaced image of it moves.

When you said: "I see"—believing that the objects were quite illusory—you *intended* your description purely as an intentional one; you were giving the words "floating specks" a secondary application. It came as a surprise to you that you would have had the right to intend the words materially. In the well-known case of H. H. Price's mescaline illusion, when without any derangement of his judgement he was able to describe what he saw—a great pile of leaves on his counterpane, which he knew not to be there—we again have a secondary application: the words "a pile of leaves" were intended *only* as a description of an impression.

It is important to notice that very often there is no answer to the question whether people intend the word "see" in its *material* use or not: that is, whether they are so using the word "see" that they would have to take it back supposing that what they said they saw was not there. If they were mis-seeing something that was there, they would usually want to correct themselves, finding out "what they really saw." But what if the seeing were hallucinatory?

The question would be: supposing that turned out to be the case, would you claim that you mean "see" in such a away that all you have to do is alter your intentions for the description of the object, from intending it in its *primary* application as a description of the *material* object of sight to intending it in a *secondary* application as a description of a mere *impression*?

Faced with such a question, we have in general the right to reject it, saying like Tommy Traddles: But it isn't so, you know, so we won't suppose it if you don't mind. And even if we have not this right, we generally entertain no such supposition and *therefore* are unprepared with an answer. We need not have determinately meant the word "see" one way or the other.

We may make a similar point about "phantom limb." I take the part of the body where pain is felt to be the object of a transitive verb-like expression "to feel pain in ———." Then when there is, e.g., no foot, but X, not knowing this, says he feels pain in his foot, he may say he was wrong ("I did not see a lion there, for there was no lion") or he may alter his understanding of the phrase "my foot" so that it becomes a purely intentional object of the verb-like expression. But it need not be determined in advance, in the normal case of feeling pain, whether one so intends the expression "I feel pain in ———" as to withdraw it, or merely alters one's intentions for the description of the place of the pain, if one should learn that the place was missing.

Notes

1. Throughout this paper I use double quotes for ordinary quotations (and so singles for quotes within quotes) and singles I use as scare quotes.
2. This was argued to me by Mr G. Harman, for which I am obliged to him.

3. I am indebted for this objection and the discussion of it to Professors Bernard Williams and Arthur Prior and Mr P. T. Geach.

4. I am obliged to Professor Frank Ebersole for telling me of an experience of his which supplied this example.

5. Example from M. Luckiesh.

6. Example from W. James.

7. *Word and Object* (Cambridge, Mass., 1960), p. 7.

5

A Theory of Direct Visual Perception

James J. Gibson

The theory to be outlined is partly developed in *The Senses Considered as Perceptual Systems* (Gibson, 1966), especially in chapters 9–12 on vision. It is related to, although a considerable departure from, the theory presented in *The Perception of the Visual World* (Gibson, 1950). Some of its postulates go back 20 years to that book, but many are new.

What is "direct" visual perception? I argue that the seeing of an environment by an observer existing in that environment is direct in that it is not mediated by visual sensations or sense data. The phenomenal visual world of surfaces, objects, and the ground under one's feet is quite different from the phenomenal visual field of color–patches (Gibson, 1950, Ch. 3). I assert that the latter experience, the array of visual sensations, is not entailed in the former. Direct perception is not based on the having of sensations. The suggestion will be that it is based on the pickup of information.

So far, all theories have assumed that the visual perception of a stable, unbounded, and permanent *world* can only be explained by a process of correcting or compensating for the unstable, bounded, and fleeting sensations coming to the brain from the retinal images. That is to say, all extant theories are sensation-based. But the theory here advanced assumes the existence of stable, unbounded, and permanent stimulus-information in the ambient optic array. And it supposes that the visual system can explore and detect this information. The theory is information-based, not sensation-based.

Perception and Proprioception

Simplifying a distinction made by Sherrington, the term *perception* will be used to refer to any experience of the environment surrounding the body of an animal, and the term *proprioception* for any experience of the body itself (including what Sherrington called *interoception*). Far from being one of the senses, then, proprioception is a kind of experience cognate with perception. Proprioception *accompanies* perception but it is not the same thing as perception.

An awareness of the body, however dim, does in fact seem to go along with an awareness of the world. Conversely, an awareness of the body, however intense, even an experience of pain, is never wholly without some awareness of the environment. And this reciprocity is only to be expected since the very term "environment" implies something that is surrounded, and the term "observer" implies a surrounding world.

The difference between perception and proprioception, then, is one of function, not a difference between the receptors stimulated as Sherrington assumed, that is, the exteroceptors and the proprioceptors. Perception and proprioception both depend on stimulation, but the visual system, for example, can isolate from the flux of stimulation that which is extero-specific (specifies the world) from that which is propriospecific (specifies the body). Vision, in other words, serves not only awareness of the environment but also awareness of self.

For example, the motion of an object relative to the stationary environment can be detected by vision, and this is a case of *perception*. Likewise the motion of one's body relative to the stationary environment, whether active or passive, can be detected by vision, and this is a case of *proprioception*. Locomotion, as distinguished from object motion, is specified by transformation of the ambient optic array as a whole. An observer can ordinarily distinguish the two cases with no difficulty, and so can animals, even species with very simple eyes.

Note that proprioception, as here defined, it not to be confuse with *feedback* in the modern usage of the word, that is, a return input to the nervous system from a motor action. The movements and postures of the body are detected (in several independent ways) whether they are imposed by outside forces or are obtained by an action of the observer himself. Proprioception can be passive or active, just as perception can be passive or active. The above hypothesis is elaborated in Chapter 2 of *The Senses Considered as Perceptual Systems*. The classical doctrine that proprioception is one of the sense modalities is familiar, and is still taught, but it simply will not work. The evidence is against it.

It should already be evident that this theory of perception does not accept the usual analogy between the brain and a computer, and rejects the idea that perception is a matter of processing the information fed into a computer. No one has suggested that a computer has the experience of being "here."

Optical Stimulation and Optical Information

The theory distinguishes between stimulation by light and the information in light. The difference is between light that is seen and the light by which *things* are seen. Light as energy is treated by physical optics. Light as information is treated by an unfamiliar discipline called ecological optics (Gibson, 1961; 1966, Ch. 10). The facts of physical optics are sufficient for a psychophysics of the light sense, and of the elementary visual sensations. But the facts of ecological optics are required for an understanding of direct visual perception.

The relation between optical stimulation and optical information seems to be as follows. The stimulation of photoreceptors by light is a necessary condition for visual perception. The activity of the visual system depends on ambient light; there is no vision in darkness. But *another* necessary condition for visual perception is an *array* of ambient light. It must be structured or differentiated, not homogeneous. With homogeneous ambient light, perception fails although the sensation of light remains. Such is the case in dense fog, empty sky, or in the experiment of wearing plastic diffusing eye-caps, an experiment that we repeat every year at Cornell. In homogeneous darkness, perception fails because stimulation is absent. In homogeneous light, perception fails because stimulus *information* is absent although stimulation is present. We conclude that stimulus energy is a necessary but by no means sufficient condition of stimulus information.

The meaning of the term "information." There are currently two radically different usages of the word "information" in psychology. One I will call *afferent-input information* and the other *optic-array information*. The former is familiar; it is information conceived as impulses in the fibers of the optic nerve. Information is assumed to consist of *signals*, and to be *transmitted* from receptors to the brain. Perception is a process that is supposed to occur *in* the brain, and the only information for perception must therefore consist of neural inputs *to* the brain.

Optic-array information is something entirely different. It is information in light, not in nervous impulses. It involves geometrical projection to a point of observation, not transmission between a sender and a receiver. It is outside the observer and available to him, not inside his head. In my theory, perception is *not* supposed to occur in the brain but to arise in the retino-neuro-muscular system as an activity of the whole system. The information does not consist of signals to be interpreted but of structural invariants which need only be attended to.

It has long been assumed by empiricists that the only information for perception was "sensory" information. But this assumption can mean different things. If it means that the information for perception must come through the senses and not through extrasensory intuition, this is the doctrine of John Locke, and I agree with it, as most of us would agree with it. But the assumption might mean (and has been taken to mean) that the information for perception must come over the sensory nerves. This is a different doctrine, that of Johannes Müller, and with this we need *not* agree. To assume that visual information comes through the visual sense is not to assume that it comes over the optic nerve, for a sense may be considered as an active system with a capacity to extract information from obtained stimulation. The visual system in fact does this. Retinal inputs lead to ocular adjustments, and then to altered retinal inputs, and so on. It is an exploratory, circular process, not a one-way delivery of messages to the brain. This hypothesis is elaborated in Chapters 2 and 3 of *The Senses Considered as Perceptual Systems*.

The Main Principles of Ecological Optics

The term *ecological optics* was introduced in a paper (Gibson, 1961) and the subject was further developed in a chapter on environmental information (Gibson, 1966, Ch. 10). But the concepts and postulates are not yet wholly established, and what follows must be regarded as tentative.

Ecological optics attempts to escape the reductionism of physical and geometrical optics. It introduces a new concept, *ambient light*, which goes beyond the physicist's conception of radiant light, and it postulates a notion of space-filling illumination that extends the classical meaning of illuminance.

The Unlimited Reflecting of Light Waves

In a medium of water or air, in which animals live and move and have evolved, light not only propagates as it does in empty space but also reverberates. It is rapidly reflected back and forth between earth and sky, and also between the facing surfaces of semi-enclosed spaces. Given the speed of light and the fact of sunlight, it almost instantly reaches an equilibrium in the medium, that is, a steady state. The light moves in all directions at once. This steady state of multiply reflected light has very interesting properties. First, at every point in the medium there is ambient light and, second, the ambient light at every such point will be structured by the reflecting surfaces facing that point.

Projection to a Point

At any point in a medium there will exist a bundle of *visual solid angles* corresponding to components or parts of the illuminated environment. The *faces* and *facets* of reflecting surfaces are such components; what we call *objects* are others; and the *patches of pigment* on a flat surface are still others. Note that the bundle of *solid angles* postulated above is not the same as a pencil of rays, which is concept of *geometrical* optics. The cross section of a solid angle always has a "form," no matter how small, whereas the cross section of a ray is a formless point. And the cross section of a *bundle* of solid angles always has a pattern whereas the cross section of a pencil of rays does not.

The Ambient Optic Array

A bundle of visual solid angles at a point (a point of observation) is called an *ambient optic array*. Such an array is invariant under changes in the illumination from noon to sunset. It is an arrangement of components, not an assemblage of points, and the components are nested within others of larger size. It is analyzed by topology or perspective geometry, not by analytic geometry. The array can be said to exist at a point of observation whether or not an eye is stationed at that point. In this respect the array is quite unlike a retinal image, which occurs only if a chambered (vertebrate) eye is put there and aimed in a certain direction. The array is also unlike an image inasmuch as the image is usually said to be an assemblage of focus points each corresponding to a luminous radiating point (presumably an atom) in the environment.

Projected Surfaces and Occluded Surfaces at a Point of Observation

Given that surfaces are in general *opaque*, not transparent, some of the surfaces of the world will be hidden at a given point of observation (occluded) and the remainder will be unhidden (projected at the point). This holds for any layout of surfaces other than a flat plane unobscured to its horizon. But any hidden surface may become unhidden by a change of the point of observation. The occlusion of one surface by another entails an *occluding edge*.

Connected Sets of Observation Points

A path of locomotion in ecological space consists of a connected set of observation points. To each connected set of observation points there corresponds a unique family of perspective transformations in the ambient optic array. In short the changing optic array at a moving point of observation specifies the movement of the point (i.e., the path of locomotion of the observer).

The optical transition between what I call two "vistas" of the world (as when an observer goes from one room to another) entails the progressive occlusion of some parts of the world and the disocclusion of others. The transition, however, arises from a path of locomotion which is reversible, and the transition is itself reversible. What went out of sight in going comes back into sight on returning. This reversible optical transition is to be distinguished from an *irreversible* transition such as occurs when an object is melted or dissolved or destroyed. The study of the two different ways in which an object can go out of sight, by being hidden or by being destroyed, suggests that they are clearly distinguishable on the basis of optical information.

The Family of Perspectives for an Object

Given an illuminated object with several faces (a polyhedron for example) it will be surrounded by an unlimited set of points of observation. Each *perspective* of the object (its projection in each optic array) is unique at each point of observation. The family of perspectives is unique to the object. An observer who walked around the object (looked at it "from all sides") would obtain the whole family.

The features of the object that make it different from other objects have corresponding features in the family of perspectives that are *invariant* under perspective transformations. These invariants constitute information about the object. Although the observer gets a different form-sensation at each moment of his tour, his information-based perception can be of the same object. This hypothesis provides new reasons for realism in epistemology (Gibson, 1967).

Correspondence of Structure between an Ambient Optic Array and the Environment

There is evidently some correspondence between the structure of the environment and the structure of the ambient light at a stationary point of observation. It is by no means a simple correspondence. It is not point-to-point but component-to-component. There are subordinate and superordinate components of the world and corresponding subordinate and superordinate forms in the array, each level of units being nested within larger units. But some components of the environment are missing from a frozen array, because of occlusion. All components of the environment, however, could be included in the changing array over time at a moving point of observation.

Invariant Information in an Ambient Optic Array

A list of the *invariants* in an array as the amount of illumination changes, as the type of illumination changes, as the direction of the prevailing illumination changes, and (above all) as the point of observation changes cannot yet be drawn up with any assurance. But a few facts seem to be clear. The *contours* in an array are invariant with most of the changes in illumination. The *textures* of an array are reliably invariant with change of observation-point. The property of a contour being *closed* or *unclosed* is always invariant. The *form* of a closed contour in the array is independent of lighting but highly variant with change of observation point. A great many properties of the array are *lawfully* or *regularly* variant with change of observation point, and this means that in each case a property defined by the law is *invariant*.

Summary

Eight main principles of ecological optics have been outlined. They are perhaps enough to show that the new optics is not just an application of the accepted laws of physical and geometrical optics, inasmuch as different laws emerge at the new level. And it should now be clear why ecological optics is required for a theory of direct visual perception instead of what is taught in the physics textbooks.

The Sampling Process in Visual Perception

The theories of sensation-based perception presuppose the formation of a retinal image and the transmission of it to the brain. The theory of direct perception presupposes the sampling of the ambient array by the ocular system. What is this sampling process?

No animal has wholly panoramic vision (although some approximate to having it) and therefore no animal can perceive the whole environment at once. The successive sampling of the ambient array is carried out by head-movements, the eyes being stabilized to the structure of the array by compensatory eye-movements (see Gibson, 1996, Ch. 12, for an explanation of head-movements and compensatory eye-movements). The point to be noted is that vertebrate animals with chambered eyes must perform *sample-taking* in order to perceive the environment. Invertebrates with compound eyes probably do the same, although very little is known about visual perception in arthropods. The sampling of the optical environment is a more general process than the fixating of details. The latter arises in evolution only when the eyes develop concentrated foveas.

Along with the taking of stabilized samples of the spherical array there goes a process of optimizing the pickup of information in the sample. Accommodation of the lens, the centering of the retinal fovea on an item of the sample, and the adjustment of the pupil for an optimal level of intensity, together with the adaptation of the retina, are all cases of the adjustment of the ocular system to the requirements of clear vision.

From the earliest stage of evolution, therefore, vision has been a process of exploration in time, not a photographic process of image registration and image transmission. We have been misled about vision by the analogy between eye and camera. Physical optics, and the physiological optics that depends on it, do not now conceive the eye in any way except as a camera. But a camera is not a device with which one can perceive the whole environment by means of sampling, whereas an eye does perceive the environment by sampling it.

If the visual system is exploratory we can assume that it extracts the information in successive samples; we do not have to speculate about how the brain could "store" the sequence of images transmitted to it and combine them into a total image of the world. The experience of the visual world is not compounded of a series of visual fields; no one is aware of the *sequence* but only of the total *scene*. Presumably this is because the ocular system detects the invariants over time that specify the scene.

I once assumed (Gibson, 1950) that the only way one can be aware of the environment behind one's back is to remember it, in the sense of having *a memory image* of it. Similarly, I supposed that, when I look out of the window, my lawn, only part of which is projected through the window to my eyes, must be filled out by images of the remainder. But I no longer believe this theory. Awareness of the room behind my back and the lawn outside my window cannot depend on imagery. I doubt if it depends on *memory*. I apprehend part of the room as *occluded by my head*, and part of the lawn as *occluded by the edges of the window*. And the perception of occlusion, it seems to me, entails the perception of *something* which is *occluded*.

A memory image of a room or of a lawn is something quite different from the perception of surfaces that are temporarily hidden from sight. I can summon up a memory image of the house and the lawn where I lived as a child. This is not at all like the awareness I have of the room behind my back and the lawn outside my window. The theory of information-based perception differs from the theory of sensation-based perception in many ways but in none more radical than this: it does not require the assumption that memories of the past must somehow be mixed with sensations of the present.

The False Problem of Depth Perception and the True Problem of Environment Perception

For centuries, the problem of space perception has been stated as the puzzle of how "depth" or the "third dimension" could be seen when the sensations for the perception were depthless or two-dimensional. Three kinds of solution have been offered, one by nativism (intuition), one by empiricism (past experience), and a third by Gestalt theory (spontaneous orgainzation in the brain). But none of them has been convincing. In the light of the present theory the puzzle of depth perception is insoluble because the problem is false; we perceive the layout of the environment, not the third dimension of space. There is nothing special about "depth" in the environment. As Merleau-Ponty somewhere pointed out, "depth is nothing but breadth seen from the side." We have been misled by taking the third dimension of the Cartesian coordinate system to be a phenomenal fact of perception. And if the flat patchwork of visual sensation is not the basis of visual perception in any case, a third dimension does not *have* to be added to the two dimensions they already possess.

Perception of the *environment* differs from a perception of *space*. An environment implies points of observation in the medium, whereas a space does not. The points of geometrical space are abstract fictions, whereas the points of observation in an environment are the positions where an observer might be stationed. Perception of the environment is thus accompanied by an awareness of the perceiver's existence in the environment (and this is what I call proprioception) whereas a perception of space in its purest form need not be accompanied by any awareness of the thinker's existence in that space.

Geometrical optics is based, of course, on geometrical space. This is everywhere transparent, and it is composed of ghostly points, lines, and planes. It is impersonal and lifeless. Ecologocal optics is based on a space of solid opaque surfaces with a transparent medium in which living animals get about, and which permits the reverberation of reflected light. The surfaces are textured and pigmented. They are flat or curved. They have corners and occluding edges. There are objects and the interspaces between objects. In short, the environment has a layout.

The so-called *cues* for the perception of depth are not the same as the *information* for the perception of layout. The former are called *signs* or *indicators* of depth, or *clues* for an inference that depth exists in the world. Their meaning has to be learned by association. They are sensations in the visual field of the observer, noticeable when he introspects. The latter, the available kinds of information, are *specifiers* of layout, not signs or indicators or clues. They have to be distinguished or discriminated, but their meaning does not have to be learned by association. They are not sense impressions or sense data. When the information for occlusion of one surface by another is picked up there is no sensation for the occluded surface but it is nevertheless perceived. And the information for the occlusion of one surface by another *is* picked up by vision.

The surface layout of the world is thus perceived *directly* when the information is available and when the cycle of action from retina to brain to eye to retina again is attuned to this information. The information must be *attended to*, of course, and this may depend on the maturation of the system, and on practice in looking, and even on the education or training of attention. But the meanings of an edge, of a falling-off-place, of an obstacle in one's path, or of the solid ground under one's feet are given in the ambient optic array and do not have to be memories of past experience attached to present sense-data, or memories of touching aroused by sensations of seeing.

False Questions in the Perception of the Environment

We have seen that the old question of why the phenomenal environment has depth whereas the retinal images are depthless is a false question. There are other false questions of this same sort. One is the question made famous by Stratton's experiment in 1897, *why is the phenomenal world upright whereas the retinal image is inverted on the retina?* Another, going back at least to Helmholtz, is *why is the phenomenal world stationary when the retinal image continually moves with respect to the retina?* Still another (connected with the fact of sampling) is, *why is the phenomenal environment unbounded when each retinal image is bounded by the margins of the retina?* In another form, this is the question, *why does the phenomenal world seem to persist when the retinal images are impermanent?* The answer to all the above questions is this: we do not *see* our retinal images. We see the environment. The doctrine of Müller that all we can see is our retinal images (or at least all we can ever see *directly*) is quite false. If we saw our retinal images we would perceive two worlds, not one, since there is a separate image of it in each eye.

The False Puzzle of the Constancy of Phenomenal Object

The so-called "constancy" of objects in perception despite changing stimulation and changing sensation has long been considered a puzzle. For the past century, experimenters have studied the perceived size of an object with retinal size variant, the perceived form of an object with retinal form variant, and the perceived surface-color of an object with variation of the intensity and wavelength of the light in the retinal image. There is always some tendency to perceive the "real" size, form, and color of the surface of the object, the amount of constancy depending on experimental conditions. Explanations of this result differ with different theorists but they all begin with one assumption, namely, that the perceived size, form, and color are based on retinal size, form, and color respectively—that the process of perception must *start with* these stimulus variables of the image.

According to the present theory this assumption is mistaken. There is information in the optic array for the size, shape, and color of a surface in a layout of other surfaces. The information is a matter of complex invariant ratios and relations; it is not easy to isolate experimentally. But the size, the form, and the color of the image impressed on the retina, when they are experienced at all, are not relevant to and not commensurable with the dimensions and slant and pigmentation of the surface. If I am right, a whole century of experimental research on the *amount* of constancy obtained by an observer is pointless. Insofar as these laboratory experiments have impoverished the stimulus information for perception they are not relevant to perception.

The Effect on Perception of Impoverishing the Stimulus Information

If perception is a process of operation on the deliverances of sense, it has seemed obvious that one way of investigating the process is to *impoverish* the stimulation, to *minimize* the cues, and observe what happens. Visual perception is supposed to come into its own when the input is reduced. Perception then has more work to do. Experiments with a tachistoscope, or with blurred pictures, or with very faint images on a screen are therefore common in the psychology laboratory.

According to the present theory, however, this is not the best way of investigating the process, for perception is frustrated when the stimulus information is impoverished. If the visual system is not allowed to "hunt" for the external specifying information, all sorts of internal processes begin to occur. They are very interesting processes, worthy of investigation, but they should not be confused with the normal process of perceiving.

The situation is similar when contradictory information in the same display is presented to an observer, "conflicting cues." The ambiguous figures and reversible perspectives that have been so frequently studied are of this sort. Ink blots are a combination of impoverished and inconsistent information. I argue that the *guessing* that goes on in these experiments, the attempt to fill out or complete a perception by supplementing the almost meaningless data, is not indicative of what goes on in ordinary perception. The process does not reach an equilibrium state of *clarity* as it does in ordinary perception. And the achieving of precise awareness is the aim of perception.

Orthodox theories assume that there is always an "objective contribution" to perception (the sensations) and a "subjective contribution" to perception (innate ideas, or memories, or field-forces in the brain), the two contributions being combined in various proportions. I reject this assumption. If unequivocal stimulus information is made available to an observer in an experiment, his perception will be determined by it and by nothing else. When *ambient* stimulus information is available to an observer outside the laboratory he can *select* the information that interests him; he can give attention to one part instead of another, but his perception will be determined by the information he attends to.

When *no* stimulus information is allowed to reach the eyes of an observer, as when the eyes are covered by diffusing plastic caps (which can be made of halved ping-pong balls) he is *deprived* of visual perception, although not of sensation. The subject does not like the situation; it is worse than being blindfolded. The only visual experience is that of "nothing." His perceptual system acts a little like a motor running without a load. If he is not allowed to go to sleep, experiences resembling hallucinations may arise.

Summary and Conclusions

This theory of vision asserts that perception is direct and is not mediated by retinal images transmitted to the brain. Most theories assume that perception of the world is *indirect*, and that all we ever *directly* perceive is our retinal images.

Now it is perfectly true that when an observer looks at a painting, photograph, sculpture, or model, he gets an *indirect* visual perception, a *mediated* experience, an awareness at *second hand*, of whatever is represented. A human artifact of this sort is an *image* in the original meaning of the term. It is a light-reflecting object in its own right but it displays *information* to specify a quite different object (Gibson, 1966, Ch. 11). An image in this straightforward meaning of the term is something to be looked at, and it has to be looked at, of course, with eyes. Thus there can be a direct perception of a man's portrait accompanied by an indirect perception of the man himself.

The fallacy of the standard theories of perception consists of taking as a model for vision the kind of indirect visual perception that uses pictures as substitutes for things. The false analogy should now be evident. Direct perception of a retinal image implies an eye inside the head, in the brain, with which to look at the image. But there is no little man anywhere in the brain who can do this. We do not look at our retinal images and perceive the world in the way that we look at a portrait and perceive the sitter. Putting the objection another way, the so-called image on the retina is not an image at all, properly speaking, since it cannot be looked at, as a picture can be looked at, and cannot therefore mediate perception. The famous experiment of looking at the back of the excised eye of a slaughtered ox and observing an image is profoundly misleading. The eye is a biological device for sampling the information available in an ambient optic array. The vertebrate eye does it in one way and the insect eye does it in another way but both register differences of light in different direction at a point of observation.

The availability of information in ambient light and the possibility that it can be picked up directly have implications for epistemology. They lend sophisticated support to the naive belief that we have direct knowledge of the world around us. They support direct realism (Gibson, 1967). If these hypotheses prove correct, they justify our deep feeling that *the senses can be trusted*. At the same time they explain the seemingly contrary conviction *that the senses cannot be trusted*. For a distinction has been drawn between what might be called the *useful* senses, the perceptual systems, and the *useless* senses, the channels of sensation.

Bibliography

Gibson, J. J., *The perception of the visual world*. Boston: Houghton Mifflin, 1950.

Gibson, J. J., Ecological optics. *Vision research*, 1961, 1, 253–262.

Gibson, J. J., *The senses considered as perceptual systems*. Boston: Houghton Mifflin, 1966.

Gibson, J. J., New reasons for realism. *Synthese*, 1967, 17, 162–172.

6

Perception and Its Objects

P. F. Strawson

I

Ayer has always given the problem of perception a central place in his thinking. Reasonably so; for a philosopher's views on this question are a key both to his theory of knowledge in general and to his metaphysics. The movement of Ayer's own thought has been from phenomenalism to what he describes in his latest treatment of the topic as "a sophisticated form of realism."[1] The epithet is doubly apt. No adequate account of the matter can be simple; and Ayer's account, while distinguished by his accustomed lucidity and economy of style, is notably and subtly responsive to all the complexities inherent in the subject itself and to all the pressures of more or less persuasive argument which have marked the course of its treatment by philosophers. Yet the form of realism he defends has another kind of sophistication about which it is possible to have reservations and doubts; and, though I am conscious of being far from clear on the matter myself, I shall try to make some of my own doubts and reservations as clear as I can. I shall take as my text chapters 4 and 5 of *The Central Questions of Philosophy*; and I shall also consider a different kind of realism—that advocated by J. L. Mackie in his book on Locke.[2] There are points of contact as well as of contrast between Ayer's and Mackie's views. A comparison between them will help to bring out the nature of my reservations about both.

According to Ayer, the starting point of serious thought on the matter of perception consists in the fact that our normal perceptual judgements always "go beyond" the sensible experience which gives rise to them; for those judgements carry implications which would not be carried by any "strict account" of that experience.[3] Ayer sees ordinary perceptual judgements as reflecting or embodying what he calls the common-sense view of the physical world, which is, among other things, a realist view; and he sees that view itself as having the character of "a theory with respect to the immediate data of perception."[4] He devotes some space to an account of how the theory might be seen as capable of being developed by an individual observer on the basis of the data available to him; though he disavows any intention of giving an actual history of the theory's development. The purpose of the account is, rather, to bring out those features of sensible experience which make it possible to employ the theory successfully and which, indeed, justify acceptance of it. For it is, he holds, by and large an acceptable theory, even though the discoveries of physical science may require us to modify it in certain respects.

Evidently no infant is delivered into the world already equipped with what Ayer calls the common-sense view of it. That view has to be acquired; and it is open to the psychologist of infant learning to produce at least a speculative account of the stages of its acquisition. Ayer insists, as I have remarked, that his own account of a possible line of development or construction of the common-sense view is not intended as a speculative contribution to the theory of infant learning. It is intended, rather, as an analysis of the nature of mature or adult perceptual experience, an analysis designed to show just how certain features of mature sensible experience vindicate or sustain the common-sense view which is embodied or reflected in mature perceptual judgements. Clearly the two aims here distinguished—the genetic-psychological and the analytic-philosophical—are very different indeed, and it will be of great importance not to confuse them. In particular it will be important to run no risk of characterising mature sensible experience in terms adequate at best only for the characterisation of some stage of infantile experience. It is not clear that Ayer entirely avoids this danger.

What is clear is that if we accept Ayer's starting point, if we agree that our ordinary perceptual judgements carry implications not carried by a "strict account" of the sensible experience which gives rise to them, then we must make absolutely sure that our account of that experience, in the form it takes in our mature life, is indeed strict—in the sense of strictly correct. Only so can we have any prospect of making a correct estimate of the further doctrines that the common-sense view of the world has the status of a *theory* with respect to a type of sensible experience which provides *data* for the theory; that this experience supplies the *evidence* on which the theory is based;[5] that the common-sense view can be regarded as *inferred* or at least inferrable from this evidence; and that our ordinary perceptual judgements have the character of *interpretations*,[6] in the light of theory, of what sensible experience actually presents us with.

But can we—and should we—accept Ayer's starting point? I think that, suitably interpreted, we both can, and should, accept it. Two things will be required of a strict account of our sensible experience or of any particular episode or slice of sensible experience: first, as I have just remarked, that it should in no way distort or misrepresent the character of that experience as we actually enjoy it, i.e. that it should be a true or faithful account; secondly, that its truth, in any particular case, should be independent of the truth of the associated perceptual judgement, i.e. that it should remain true even if the associated perceptual judgement is false. It is the second requirement on which Ayer lays stress when he remarks that those judgements carry implications which would not be carried by any strict account of sensible experience; or, less happily in my opinion, that in making such judgements we take a step beyond what our sensible experience actually presents us with. But it is the first requirement to which I now wish to give some attention.

Suppose a non-philosophical observer gazing idly through a window. To him we address the request, "Give us a description of your current visual experience," or "How is it with you, visually, at the moment?" Uncautioned as to exactly what we want, he might reply in some such terms as these: "I see the red light of the setting sun filtering through the black and thickly clustered branches of the elms; I see the dappled deer grazing in groups on the vivid green grass . . . "and so on. So we explain to him. We explain that we want him to amend his account so that, without any sacrifice of fidelity to the experience as actually enjoyed, it nevertheless sheds all that heavy load of commitment to propositions about the world which was carried by the description he gave. We want an account which confines itself strictly within the limits of the subjective episode, an account which would remain true even if he had seen nothing of what he claimed to see, even if he had been subject to total illusion.

Our observer is quick in the uptake. He does not start talking about lights and colours, patches and patterns. For he sees that to do so would be to falsify the character of the experience he actually enjoyed. He says, instead, "I understand. I've got to cut out of my report all commitment to propositions about independently existing objects. Well, the simplest way to do this, while remaining faithful to the character of the experience as actually enjoyed, is to put my previous report in inverted commas or oratio obliqua and describe my visual experience as such as it would have been natural to describe in these terms, had I not received this additional instruction. Thus: 'I had a visual experience such as it would have been natural to describe by saying that I saw, etc. . . . [or, to describe in these words, "I saw . . .

etc."] were it not for the obligation to exclude commitment to propositions about independently existing objects.' In this way [continues the observer] I *use* the perceptual claim—the claim it was natural to make in the circumstances—in order to characterise my experience, without actually making the claim. I render the perceptual judgement internal to the characterisation of the experience without actually asserting the content of the judgement. And this is really the best possible way of characterising the experience. There are perhaps alternative locutions which might serve the purpose, so long as they are understood as being to the same effect—on the whole, the more artificial the better, since their artificiality will help to make it clearer just to what effect they are intended to be. Thus we might have: 'It sensibly seemed to me just as if I were seeing such-and-such a scene' or 'My visual experience can be characterised by saying that I saw what I saw, supposing I saw anything, *as* a scene of the following character. . . .' "

If my observer is right in this—and I think he is—then certain general conclusions follow. Our perceptual judgements, as Ayer remarks, embody or reflect a certain view of the world, as containing objects, variously propertied, located in a common space and continuing in their existence independently of our interrupted and relatively fleeting perceptions of them. Our making of such judgements implies our possession and application of concepts of such objects. But now it appears that we cannot give a veridical characterisation even of the sensible experience which these judgements, as Ayer expresses it, "go beyond," without reference to those judgements themselves; that our sensible experience itself is thoroughly permeated with those concepts of objects which figure in such judgements. This does not mean, i.e., it does not follow directly from this feature of sensible experience, that the general view of the world which those judgements reflect must be true. That would be too short a way with scepticism. But it does follow, I think, that our sensible experience could not have the character it does have unless—at least before philosophical reflection sets in—we unquestioningly *took* that general view of the world to be true. The concepts of the objective which we see to be indispensable to the veridical characterisation of sensible experience simply would not be in this way indispensable unless those whose experience it was initially and unreflectively took such concepts to have application in the world.

This has a further consequence: the consequence that it is quite inappropriate to represent the general, realist view of the world which is reflected in our ordinary perceptual judgements as having the status of a *theory* with respect to sensible experience; that it is inappropriate to represent that experience as supplying the *data* for such a theory or the *evidence* on which it is based or from which it is *inferred* or *inferrable*; that it is inappropriate to speak of our ordinary perceptual judgements as having the character of an *interpretation*, in the light of theory, of the content of our sensible experience. The reason for this is simple. In order for some belief or set of beliefs to be correctly described as a theory in respect of certain data, it must be possible to describe the data on the basis of which the theory is held in terms which do not presuppose the acceptance of the theory on the part of those for whom the data *are* data. But this is just the condition we have seen not to be satisfied in the case where the so-called data are the contents of sensible experience and the so-called theory is a general realist view of the world. The "data" are laden with the "theory." Sensible experience is permeated by concepts unreflective acceptance of the general applicability of which is a condition of its being so permeated, a condition of that experience being what it is; and these concepts are of realistically conceived objects.

I must make it quite clear what I am saying and what I am not saying here. I am talking of the ordinary non-philosophical man. I am talking of us all before we felt, if ever we did feel, any inclination to respond to the solicitations of a general scepticism, to regard it as raising a problem. I am saying that it follows from the character of sensible experience as we all actually enjoy it that a common-sense realist view of the world does not in general have the status of a theory in respect of that experience; while Ayer, as I understand him, holds that it does. But I am not denying that to one who has seen, or thinks he has seen, that sensible experience might have the character it does have and *yet* a realist view of the world be false, to *him* the idea may well present itself that the best way of accounting for sensible experience as having that character is to accept the common realist view of the world or some variant of it. *He* might be said to adopt, as a theory, the doctrine that the common realist view of the world is, at least in some basic essentials, true. But this will be a philosopher's theory, designed to deal with a philosopher's problem. (I shall not here discuss its merits as such.) What I am concerned to dispute is the doctrine that a realist view of the world has, for any man, the status of a theory in relation to his sensible experience, a theory in the light of which he interprets that experience in making his perceptual judgements.

To put the point summarily, whereas Ayer says we take a step beyond our sensible experience in making our perceptual judgements, I say rather that we take a step back (in general) from our perceptual judgements in framing accounts of our sensible experience; for we have (in general) to include a reference to the former in framing a veridical description of the latter.

It may seem, on a superficial reading, that Ayer had anticipated and answered this objection. He introduces, as necessary for the characterisation of our sensible experience, certain concepts of types of pattern, the names for which are borrowed from the names of ordinary physical objects. Thus he speaks of visual leaf patterns, chair patterns, cat patterns, and so on.[7] At the same time, he is careful, if I read him rightly, to guard against the impression that the use of this terminology commits him to the view that the employment of the corresponding physical-object concepts themselves is necessary to the characterisation of our sensible experience.[8] The terminology is appropriate (he holds) simply because those features of sensible experience to which the terminology is applied are the features which govern our identifications of the physical objects we think we see. They are the features, "implicitly noticed,"[9] which provide the main clues on which our everyday judgements of perception are based.

This is ingenious, but I do not think it will do. This we can see more clearly if we use an invented, rather than a derived, terminology for these supposed features and then draw up a table of explicit correlations between the invented names and the physical-object names. Each artificial feature name is set against the name of a type of physical object: our perceptual identifications of seen objects as of that type are held to be governed by implicit noticings of that feature. The nature and significance of the feature names is now quite clearly explained and we have to ask ourselves whether it is these rather than the associated physical-object terms that we ought to use if we are to give a quite strict and faithful account of our sensible experience. I think it is clear that this is not so; that the idea of our ordinary perceptual judgements as being invariably based upon, or invariably issuing from, awareness of such features is a myth. The situation is rather, as I have already argued, that the employment of our ordinary, full-blooded concepts of physical objects is indispensable to a strict, and strictly veridical, account of our sensible experience.

Once again, I must make it clear what I am, and what I am not, saying. I have been speaking of the typical or standard case of mature sensible and perceptual experience. I have no interest at all in denying the thesis that there also occur cases of sensible experience such that the employment of full-blooded concepts of physical objects would not be indispensable, and may be inappropriate, to giving a strict account of the experience. Such cases are of different types, and there is one in particular which is of interest in the present connexion. An observer, gazing through his window, may perhaps, by an effort of will, bring himself to see, or even willessly find himself seeing, what he knows to be the branches of the trees no longer *as* branches at all, but as an intricate pattern of dark lines of complex directions and shapes and various sizes against a background of varying shades of grey. The frame of mind in which we enjoy, if we ever do enjoy, this kind of experience is a rare and sophisticated, not a standard or normal, frame of mind. Perhaps the fact, if it is a fact, that we can bring ourselves into this frame of mind when we choose may be held to give a sense to the idea of our "implicitly noticing" such patterns even when we are not in this frame of mind. If so, it is a sense very far removed from that which Ayer's thesis requires. For that thesis requires not simply the possibility, but the actual occurrence, in all cases of perception, of sensible experience of this kind. One line of retreat may seem to lie open at this point: a retreat to the position of saying that the occurrence of such experiences may be *inferred*, even though we do not, in the hurry of life, generally notice or recall their occurrence. But such a retreat would be the final irony. The items in question would have changed their status radically: instead of data for a common-sense theory of the world, they would appear as consequences of a sophisticated theory of the mind.

This concludes the first stage of my argument. I have argued that mature sensible experience (in general) presents itself as, in Kantian phrase, an *immediate* consciousness of the existence of things outside us. (*Immediate*, of course, does not mean *infallible*.) Hence, the common realist conception of the world does not have the character of a "theory" in relation to the "data of sense." I have not claimed that this fact is of itself sufficient to "refute" scepticism or to provide a philosophical "demonstration" of the truth of some form of realism; though I think it does provide the right starting point for reflection upon these enterprises. But that is another story and I shall not try to tell it here. My point so far is that the ordinary human commitment to a conceptual scheme of a realist character is not properly described, even in a stretched sense of the words, as a theoretical commitment. It is, rather, something given with the given.

II

But we are philosophers as well as men; and so must examine more closely the nature of the realist scheme to which we are pre-theoretically committed and then consider whether we are not rationally constrained, as Locke and Mackie would maintain we are, to modify it quite radically in the light of our knowledge of physics and physiology. Should we not also, as philosophers, consider the question of whether we can rationally maintain any form of realism at all? Perhaps we should; but, as already remarked, that is a question I shall not consider here. My main object, in the present section, is to get a clear view of the main features of our pretheoretical scheme before considering whether it is defensible, as it stands, or not. I go in a somewhat roundabout way to work.

I have spoken of our pre-theoretical scheme as realist in character. Philosophers who treat of these questions commonly distinguish different forms of realism. So do both Ayer and Mackie. They both mention, at one extreme, a form of realism which Mackie calls "naïve" and even "very naïve," but which might more appropriately be called "confused realism." A sufferer from confused realism fails to draw any distinction between sensible experiences (or "perceptions") and independently existing things (or "objects perceived") but is said (by Mackie expounding Hume) to credit the former with persistent unobserved existence.[10] It should be remarked that, if this is an accurate way of describing the naïve realist's conception of the matter, he must be very confused indeed, since the expression "unobserved" already implies the distinction which he is said to fail to make. Speaking in his own person, Mackie gives no positive account of the naïve realist's view of things, but simply says that there is, historically, in the thought of each of us, a phase in which we fail to make the distinction in question.[11] It may indeed be so. The point is one to be referred to the experts on infantile development. But in any case the matter is not here of any consequence. For we are concerned with mature perceptual experience and with the character of the scheme to which those who enjoy such experience are pre-theoretically committed. And it seems to me as certain as anything can be that, as an integral part of that scheme, we distinguish, naturally and unreflectively, between our seeings and hearings and feelings—our perceivings—of objects and the objects we see and hear and feel; and hence quite consistently accept both the interruptedness of the former and the continuance in existence, unobserved, of the latter.

At the opposite extreme from naïve realism stands what may be called scientific or Lockian realism. This form of realism credits physical objects only with those of their properties which are mentioned in physical theory and physical explanation, including the causal explanation of our enjoyment of the kind of perceptual experience we in fact enjoy. It has the consequence that we do not, and indeed cannot, perceive objects as they really are. It might be said that this consequence does not hold in an unqualified form. For we perceive (or seem to perceive) objects as having shape, size and position; and they really do have shape, size and position and more or less such shape, size and position as we seem to perceive them as having. But this reply misconstrues the intended force of the alleged consequence. We cannot in sense perception—the point is an old one—become aware of the shape, size and position of physical objects except by way of awareness of boundaries defined in some sensory mode—for example, by visual and tactile qualities such as scientific realism denies to the objects themselves; and no change in, or addition to, our sensory equipment could alter this fact. To perceive physical objects as, according to scientific realism, they really are would be to perceive them as lacking any such qualities. But this notion is self-contradictory. So it is a necessary consequence of this form of realism that we do not perceive objects as they really are. Indeed, in the sense of the pre-theoretical notion of perceiving—that is, of immediate awareness of things outside us—we do not, on the scientific—realist view, perceive physical objects at all. We are, rather, the victims of a systematic illusion which obstinately clings to us even if we embrace scientific realism. For we continue to enjoy experience *as of* physical objects in space, objects of which the spatial characteristics and relations are defined by the sensible qualities we perceive them as having; but there are no such physical objects as these. The only true physical objects are items systematically correlated with and causally responsible for that experience; and the only sense in which we *can* be said to perceive them is just that they cause us to enjoy that experience.

These remarks are intended only as a *description* of scientific realism. I do not claim that they show it to be untenable. I shall return to the topic later.

In between the "naïve" and the "scientific" varieties, Ayer and Mackie each recognise another form of realism, which they each ascribe to "common sense." But there is a difference between Ayer's version of common-sense realism and Mackie's. For Mackie's version, unlike Ayer's, shares one crucial feature with scientific realism.

The theory of perception associated with scientific or Lockian realism is commonly and reasonably described as a representative theory. Each of us seems to himself to be perceptually aware of objects of a certain kind: objects in space outside us with visual and tactile qualities. There are in fact, on this view, no such objects; but these object appearances can in a broad sense be said to be representative of those actual objects in space outside us which are systematically correlated with the appearances and causally responsible for them. The interesting feature of Mackie's version of common-sense realism is that the theory of perception associated with it is no less a representative theory than that associated with Lockian realism. The difference is simply that common sense, according to Mackie, views object appearances as more faithful representatives of actual physical objects than the Lockian allows: in that common sense, gratuitously by scientific standards, credits actual objects in space outside us with visual and tactile as well as primary qualities. As Mackie puts it, common sense allows "colours-as-we-see-them to be *resemblances* of qualities actually in the things."[12] On both views, sensible experience has its own, sensible objects; but the common-sense view, according to Mackie, allows a kind of resemblance between sensible and physical objects which the scientific view does not.

I hope it is already clear that this version of common-sense realism is quite different from what I have called our pre-theoretical scheme. What we ordinarily take ourselves to be aware of in perception are not resemblances of physical things but the physical things themselves. This does not mean, as already remarked, that we have any difficulty in distinguishing between our experiences of seeing, hearing and feeling objects and the objects themselves. That distinction is as firmly a part of our pre-theoretical scheme as is our taking ourselves, in general, to be immediately aware of those objects. Nor does it mean that we take ourselves to be immune from illusion, hallucination or mistake. We can, and do, perfectly adequately describe such cases without what is, from the point of view of the pre-theoretical scheme, the quite gratuitous introduction of sensible objects interposed between us and the actual physical objects they are supposed to represent.

The odd thing about Mackie's presentation is that at one point he shows himself to be perfectly well aware of this feature of the real realism of common sense; for he writes, "What we seem to see, feel, hear and so on . . . *are seen as real things without us*—that is, outside us. We just see things as being simply there, of such-and-such sorts, in such-and-such relations. . . ."[13] He goes on, of course, to say that "our seeing them so is logically distinct from their being so," that we might be, and indeed are, wrong. But he would scarcely dispute that what is thus *seen as* real and outside us is also *seen as* coloured, as possessing visual qualities; that what is *felt as* a real thing outside us is also felt as hard or soft, smooth or rough-surfaced—as possessing tactile qualities. The real realism of common sense, then, does indeed credit physical things with visual and tactile properties; but it does so not in the spirit of a notion of representative perception, but in the spirit of a notion of direct or immediate perception.

Mackie's version of common-sense realism is, then, I maintain, a distortion of the actual pre-theoretical realism of common sense, a distortion which wrongly assimilates it, in a fundamental respect, to the Lockian realism he espouses. I do not find any comparable distortion in Ayer's version. He aptly describes the physical objects we seem to ourselves, and take ourselves, to perceive as "visuo-tactual continents." The scheme as he presents it allows for the distinction between these items and the experiences of perceiving them and for the causal dependence of the latter on the former; and does so, as far as I can see, without introducing the alien features I have discerned in Mackie's account. It is perhaps debatable whether Ayer can consistently maintain the scheme's freedom from such alien elements while continuing to represent it as having the status of a "theory" in relation to the "data" of sensible experience. But, having already set out my objections to that doctrine, I shall not pursue the point.

Something more must be said, however, about the position, in the common-sense scheme, of the causal relation between physical object and the experience of perceiving it. Although Ayer admits the relation to a place in the scheme, he seems to regard it as a somewhat sophisticated addition to the latter, a latecomer, as it were, for which room has to be made in an already settled arrangement.[14] This seems to me wrong. The idea of the presence of the thing as accounting for, or being responsible for, our perceptual awareness of it is implicit in the pre-theoretical scheme from the very start. For we think of perception as a way, indeed the basic way, of informing ourselves about the world of independently existing things: we assume, that is to say, the general reliability of our perceptual experiences; and that assumption is the same as the assumption of a general causal dependence of our perceptual experiences on the independently existing things we take them to be of. The thought of my fleeting perception as a *perception* of a continuously and independently existing thing implicitly contains the thought that if the thing had not been there, I should not even have *seemed* to perceive it. It really should be obvious that with the distinction between independently existing objects and perceptual awareness of objects we already have the general notion of causal dependence of the latter on the former, even if this is not a matter to which we give much reflective attention in our pre-theoretical days.

Two things seem to have impeded recognition of this point. One is the fact that the correctness of the description of a perceptual experience as the perception of a certain physical thing *logically* requires the existence of that thing; and the *logical* is thought to exclude the *causal* connection, since only logically distinct existences can be causally related. This is not a serious difficulty. The situation has many parallels. Gibbon would not be the historian of the decline and fall of the Roman Empire unless there had occurred some actual sequence of events more or less corresponding to his narrative. But it is not enough, for him to merit that description, that such a sequence of events should have occurred and he should have written the sentences he did write. For him to qualify as the *historian* of these events, there must be a causal chain connecting them with the writing of the sentences. Similarly, the memory of an event's occurrence does not count as such unless it has its causal origin in that event. And the recently much canvassed "causal theory of reference" merely calls attention to another instance of the causal link which obtains between thought and independently (and anteriorly) existing thing when the former is rightly said to have the latter as its object.

The second impediment is slightly more subtle. We are philosophically accustomed—it is a Humian legacy—to thinking of the simplest and most obvious kind of causal relation as holding between types of item such that items of both types are observable or experienceable and such that observation or experience of either term of the relation is distinct from observation or experience of the other: i.e., the causally related items are not only distinct existences, but also the objects of distinct observations or experiences. We may then come to think of these conditions as constituting a requirement on all primitive belief in causal relations, a requirement which could be modified or abandoned only in the interests of theory. Since we obviously cannot distinguish the observation of a physical object from the experience of observing it—for they are the same thing—we shall then be led to conclude that the idea of the causal dependence of perceptual experience on the perceived object cannot be even an implicit part of our pre-theoretical scheme, but must be at best an essentially theoretical addition to it.

But the difficulty is spurious. By directing our attention to causal relations between *objects* of perception, we have simply been led to overlook the special character of perception itself. Of course, the requirement holds for causal relations between distinct objects of perception; but not for the relation between perception and its object. When x is a physical object and y is a perception of x, then x is *observed* and y is *enjoyed*. And in taking the enjoyment of y to be a perception of x, we *are* implicitly taking it to be caused by x.

This concludes the second phase of my argument. I have tried to bring out some main features of the real realism of common sense and of the associated notion of perception. From the standpoint of common-sense realism we take ourselves to be immediately aware of real, enduring physical things in space, things endowed with visual and tactile properties; and we take it for granted that these enduring things are causally responsible for our interrupted perceptions of them. The immediacy which common sense attributes to perceptual awareness is in no way inconsistent either with the distinction between perceptual experience and thing perceived or with the causal dependence of the former on the latter or the existence of other causally necessary conditions of its occurrence. Neither is it inconsistent with the occurrence of perceptual mistake or illusion—a point, like so many others of importance, which is explicitly made by Kant.[15] Both Ayer and Mackie, explicitly or implicitly, acknowledge that the common-sense scheme includes this assumption of immediacy—Mackie in a passage I have quoted, Ayer in his description of the common-sense scheme. Unfortunately, Mackie's acknowledgment of the fact is belied by his describing common-sense realism as representative in character and Ayer's acknowledgment of it is put in doubt by his describing the common-sense scheme as having the status of a theory in relation to sensible experience.

III

It is one thing to describe the scheme of common sense; it is another to subject it to critical examination. This is the third and most difficult part of my task. The main question to be considered, as already indicated, is whether we are rationally bound to abandon, or radically to modify, the scheme in the light of scientific knowledge.

Before addressing ourselves directly to this question, it is worth stressing—indeed, it is essential to stress—the grip that common-sense non-representative realism has on our ordinary thinking. It is a view of the world which so thoroughly permeates our consciousness that even those who are intellectually convinced of its falsity remain subject to its power. Mackie admits as much, saying that, even when we are trying to entertain a Lockian or scientific realism, "our language and our natural ways of thinking keep pulling us back" to a more primitive view.[16] Consider the character of those ordinary concepts of objects on the employment of which our lives, our transactions with each other and the world, depend: our concepts of cabbages, roads, tweed coats, horses, the lips and hair of the beloved. In using these terms we certainly intend to be talking of independent existences and we certainly intend to be talking of immediately perceptible things, bearers of phenomenal (visuo-tactile) properties. If scientific or Lockian realism is correct, we cannot be doing both at once; it is confusion or illusion to suppose we can. If the things we talk of really have phenomenal properties, then they cannot, on this view, be physical things continuously existing in physical space. Nothing perceptible—I here drop the qualification "immediately," for my use of it should now be clear—is a physically real, independent existence. No two persons can ever, in this sense, perceive the same item: nothing at all is publicly perceptible.

But how deep the confusion or the illusion must go! How radically it infects our concepts! Surely we mean by a cabbage a kind of thing of which most of the specimens we have encountered have a characteristic range of colours and visual shapes and felt textures; and not something unobservable, mentally represented by a complex of sensible experiences which it causes. The common consciousness is not to be fobbed off with the concession that, after all, the physical thing has—in a way—a shape. The way in which scientific realism concedes a shape is altogether the wrong way for the common consciousness. The lover who admires the curve of his mistress's lips or the lover of architecture who admires the lines of a building takes himself to be admiring features of those very objects themselves; but it is the visual shape, the visually defined shape, that he admires. Mackie suggests that there is a genuine *resemblance* between subjective representation and objective reality as far as shape is concerned;[17] but this suggestion is quite unacceptable. It makes no sense to speak of a phenomenal property as *resembling* a non-phenomenal, abstract property such as physical shape is conceived to be by scientific realism. The property of looking square or round can no more resemble the property, so conceived, of being physically square or round than the property of looking intelligent to looking ill can resemble the property of being intelligent or being ill. If it seems to make sense to speak of a resemblance between phenomenal properties and physical properties, so conceived, it is only because we give ourselves pictures—phenomenal pictures—of the latter. The resemblance is with the picture, not the pictured.

So, then, the common consciousness lives, or has the illusion of living, in a phenomenally propertied world of perceptible things in space. We might call it the lived world. It is also the public world, accessible to observation by all: the world in which one man, following another's pointing finger, can see the very thing that the other sees. (Even in our philosophical moments we habitually contrast the colours and visual shapes of things, as being publicly observable, with the subjective contents of consciousness, private to each of us, though not thereby unknowable to others.)

Such a reminder of the depth and reality of our habitual commitment to the common-sense scheme does not, by itself, amount to a demonstration of that scheme's immunity from philosophical criticism. The scientific realist, though no Kantian, may be ready, by way of making his maximum concession, with a reply modelled on Kant's combination of empirical realism with transcendental idealism. He may distinguish between the uncritical standpoint of ordinary living and the critical standpoint of philosophy informed by science. We are humanly, or naturally—he may say—constrained to "see the world" in one way (i.e., to think of it as we seem to perceive it) and rationally, or critically, constrained to think of it in quite another. The first way (being itself a causal product of physical reality) has a kind of validity at its own level; but it is, critically and rationally speaking, an inferior level. The second way really is a correction of the first.

The authentically Kantian combination is open to objection in many ways; but, by reason of its very extravagance, it escapes one specific form of difficulty to which the scientific realist's soberer variant remains exposed. Kant uncompromisingly declares that space is in us; that it is "solely from the human standpoint that we can speak of space, of extended things etc.";[18] that things as they are in themselves are not spatial at all. This will not do for the scientific realist. The phenomenally propertied items which we take ourselves to perceive and the apparent relations between which yield (or contribute vitally to yielding) our notion of space, are indeed declared to have no independent reality; but, when they are banished from the realm of the real, they are supposed to leave behind them—as occupants, so to speak, of the evacuated territory—those spatially related items which, though necessarily unobservable, nevertheless constitute the whole of physical reality. Ayer refers in several places to this consequence; and questions its coherence.[19] He writes, for example, "I doubt whether the notion of a spatial system of which none of the elements can be observed is even intelligible."

It is not clear that this difficulty is insuperable. The scientific realist will claim to be able to abstract the notion of a position in physical space from the phenomenal integuments with which it is originally and deceptively associated; and it is hard to think of a conclusive reason for denying him this power. He will say that the places where the phenomenally propertied things we seem to perceive seem to be are, often enough, places at which the correlated physically real items really are. Such a claim may make us uneasy; but it is not obvious nonsense.

Still, to say that a difficulty is not clearly insuperable is not to say that it is clearly not insuperable. It would be better to avoid it if we can. We cannot avoid it if we embrace unadulterated scientific realism and incidentally announce ourselves thereby as the sufferers from persistent illusion, however natural. We can avoid it, perhaps, if we can succeed in combining elements of the scientific story with our common-sense scheme without downgrading the latter. This is the course that Ayer recommends[20] and, I suspect, the course that most of us semi-reflectively follow. The question is whether it is a consistent or coherent course. And at bottom this question is one of identity. Can we coherently identify the phenomenally propertied, immediately perceptible things which common sense supposes to occupy physical space with the configurations of unobservable ultimate particulars by which an unqualified scientific realism purports to replace them?

I approach the question indirectly, by considering once again Mackie's version of common-sense realism. According to this version, it will be remembered, physical things, though not directly perceived, really possess visual and tactile qualities which resemble those we seem to perceive them as possessing; so that if, *per impossibile*, the veil of perception were drawn aside and we saw things in their true colours, these would turn out to be colours indeed and, on the whole, just the colours with which we were naïvely inclined to credit them. Mackie does not represent this view as absurd or incoherent. He just thinks that it is, as a matter of fact, false. Things *could* really be coloured; but, since there is no scientific reason for supposing they are, it is gratuitous to make any such supposition.

Mackie is surely too lenient to his version of common-sense realism. That version effects a complete logical divorce between a thing's being red and its being red-looking. Although it is a part of the theory that a thing which is, in itself, red has the power to cause us to seem to see a red thing, the logical divorce between these two properties is absolute. And, as far as I can see, that divorce really produces nonsense. The ascription of colours to things becomes not merely gratuitous, but senseless. Whatever may be the case with shape and position, colours are visibilia or they are nothing. I have already pointed out that this version of common-sense realism is not the real realism of common sense: *that* realism effects no logical divorce between being red and being red-looking; for it is a perceptually direct and not a perceptually representative realism. The things seen as coloured are the things themselves. There is no "veil past which we cannot see"; for there is no veil.

But this does not mean that a thing which is red, i.e. red-looking, has to look red all the time and in all circumstances and to all observers. There is an irreducible relativity, a relativity to what in the broadest sense may be called the perceptual point of view, built in to our ascriptions of particular visual properties to things. The mountains are red-looking at this distance in this light; blue-looking at that distance at that light; and, when we are clambering up them, perhaps neither. Such-and-such a surface looks pink and smooth from a distance; mottled and grainy when closely examined; different again, perhaps, under the microscope.

We absorb this relativity easily enough for ordinary purposes in our ordinary talk, tacitly taking some range of perceptual conditions, some perceptual point of view (in the broad sense) as standard or normal, and introducing an explicit acknowledgement of relativity only in cases which deviate from the standard. "It looks purple in this light," we say, "but take it to the door and you will see that it's really green." But sometimes we do something else. We shift the standard. Magnified, the fabric appears as printed with tiny blue and yellow dots. So those are the colours it really is. Does this ascription contradict "it's really green"? No; for the standard has shifted. Looking at photographs, in journals of popular science, of patches of human skin, vastly magnified, we say, "How fantastically uneven and ridgy it really is." We study a sample of blood through a microscope and say, "It's mostly colourless." But skin can still be smooth and blood be red; for in another context we shift our standard back. Such shifts do not convict us of volatility or condemn us to internal conflict. The appearance of both volatility and conflict vanishes when we acknowledge the relativity of our "reallys."

My examples are banal. But perhaps they suggest a way of resolving the apparent conflict between scientific and common-sense realism. We can shift our point of view within the general framework of perception, whether aided or unaided by artificial means; and the different sensible-quality ascriptions we then make to the same object are not seen as conflicting once their relativity is recognised. Can we not see the adoption of the viewpoint of scientific realism as simply a more radical shift— a shift to a viewpoint from which no characteristics are to be ascribed to things except those which figure in the physical theories of science and in "the explanation of what goes on in the physical world in the processes which lead to our having the sensations and perceptions that we have"?[21] We can say that this is how things really are so long as the relativity of this "really" is recognised as well; and, when it is recognised, the scientific account will no more conflict with the ascription to things of visual and tactile qualities than the assertion that blood is really a mainly colourless fluid conflicts with the assertion that it is bright red in colour. Of course, the scientific point of view is not, in one sense, a point of *view* at all. It is an intellectual, not a perceptual, standpoint. We could not occupy it at all, did we not first occupy the other. But we can perfectly well occupy both at once, so long as we realise what we are doing.

This method of reconciling scientific and common-sense realism requires us to recognise a certain relativity in our conception of the real properties of physical objects. Relative to the human perceptual standpoint the grosser physical objects are visuo-tactile continuants (and within that standpoint the phenomenal properties they possess are relative to particular perceptual viewpoints, taken as standard). Relative to the scientific standpoint, they have no properties but those which figure in the physical theories of science. Such a relativistic conception will not please the absolute-minded. Ayer recommends a different procedure. He suggests that we should conceive of perceptible objects (i.e. objects perceptible in the sense of the common-sense scheme) as being literally composed of the ultimate particles of physical theory, the latter being imperceptible, not in principle, but only empirically, as a consequence of their being so minute.[22] I doubt, however, whether this proposal, which Ayer rightly describes as an attempt to *blend* the two schemes can be regarded as satisfactory. If the impossibility of perceiving the ultimate components is to be viewed as merely empirical, we can sensibly ask what the conceptual consequences would be of supposing that impossibility not to exist. The answer is clear. Even if there were something which we counted as perceiving the ultimate particles, this would still not, from the point of view of scientific realism, count as perceiving them as they really are. And nothing could so count; for no phenomenal properties we seemed to perceive them as having would figure in the physical explanation of the causal mechanisms of our success. But, so long as we stay at this point of view, what goes for the parts goes for any wholes they compose. However gross those wholes, they remain, from this point of view, imperceptible in the sense of common sense.

Ayer attempts to form one viewpoint out of two discrepant viewpoints; to form a single, unified description of physical reality by blending features of two discrepant descriptions, each valid from its own viewpoint. He can seem to succeed only by doing violence to one of the two viewpoints, the scientific. I acknowledge the discrepancy of the two descriptions, but claim that, once we recognise the relativity in our conception of the real, they need not be seen as in contradiction with each other. Those very things which from one standpoint we conceive as phenomenally propertied we conceive from another as constituted in a way which can only be described in what are, from the phenomenal point of view, abstract terms. "This smooth, green, leather table-top," we say, "is, considered scientifically, nothing but a congeries of electric charges widely separated and in rapid motion." Thus we combine the two standpoints in a single sentence. The standpoint of common-sense realism, not explicitly signalled as such, is reflected in the sentence's grammatical subject phrase, of which the words are employed in no esoteric sense. The standpoint of physical science, explicitly signalled as such, is reflected in the predicate. Once relativity of description to standpoint is recognised, the sentence is seen to contain no contradiction; and, if it contains no contradiction, the problem of identification is solved.

I recognise that this position is unlikely to satisfy the determined scientific realist. If he is only moderately determined, he may be partially satisfied, and may content himself with saying that the scientific viewpoint is *superior* to that of common sense. He will then simply be expressing a preference, which he will not expect the artist, for example, to share. But, if he is a hard-liner, he will insist that the common-sense view is wholly undermined by science; that it is shown to be false; that the visual and tactile properties we ascribe to things are nowhere but in our minds; that we do not live in a world of perceptible objects, as understood by common sense, at all. He must then accept the consequence that each of us is a sufferer from a persistent and inescapable illusion and that it is fortunate that this is so, since, if it were not, we should be unable to pursue the scientific enterprise itself. Without the illusion of perceiving objects as bearers of sensible qualities, we should not have the illusion of perceiving them as space-occupiers at all; and without that we should have no concept of space and no power to pursue our researches into the nature of its occupants. Science is not only the offspring of common sense; it remains its dependant. For this reason, and for others touched on earlier, the scientific realist must, however ruefully, admit that the ascription to objects of sensible qualities, the standard of correctness of such ascription being (what we take to be) intersubjective agreement, is something quite securely rooted in our conceptual scheme. If this means, as he must maintain it does, that our thought is condemned to incoherence, then we can only conclude that incoherence is something we can perfectly well live with and could not perfectly well live without.

Notes

1. A. J. Ayer, *The Central Questions of Philosophy* (London: Weidenfeld and Nicolson, 1973) chs. 4 and 5, pp. 68–111.

2. J. L. Mackie, *Problems from Locke* (Oxford: Clarendon Press, 1976) chs. 1 and 2, pp. 7–71.

3. Ayer, *Central Questions*, pp. 81, 89.

4. Ibid., p. 88.

5. Ibid., p. 89.

6. Ibid., p. 81.

7. Ibid., p. 91.

8. Ibid., p. 96.

9. Ibid., p. 91.

10. Mackie, *Problems*, p. 67.

11. Ibid., p. 68.

12. Ibid., p. 64.

13. Ibid., p. 61.

14. Ayer, *Central Questions*, pp. 87–8.

15. Kant, "The Refutation of Idealism," in *Critique of Pure Reason*, B274–9.

16. Mackie, *Problems*, p. 68.

17. Ibid., chs. 1 and 2, *passim*.

18. Kant, "Refutation of Idealism," in *Critique*, B42.

19. Ayer, *Central Questions*, pp. 84, 86–7, 110.

20. Ibid., pp. 110–11.

21. Mackie, *Problems*, p. 18.

22. Ayer, *Central Questions*, p. 110.

7

Perceptions as Hypotheses

Richard L. Gregory

I Introduction

Are perceptions like hypotheses of science? This is the question that I propose to examine; but there is an immediate difficulty, for there is no general agreement on the nature of scientific hypotheses. It may be said that hypotheses *structure* our accepted reality. More specifically, it may be said that hypotheses allow limited data to be used with remarkable effect, by allowing interpolations through data-gaps, and extrapolations to be made to new situations for which data are not available. These include the future. (They also include inventions and indeed the whole of applied science, which apart from cases of pure trial and error, are surely created by the predictive power of hypotheses.)

I shall hold that all of these statements are true, and that they apply to perception. In addition, both the hypotheses of science and the perceptual processes of the nervous system allow recognition of familiar situations or objects from strictly inadequate clues, as signalled by the transducer-instruments of science and the transducer-senses of organisms. This is at least true for typical situations: in atypical situations the hypotheses of both science and perception may be dangerously and systematically misleading. Errors and illusions can be highly revealing for appreciating the similarities—and the differences—between perceptions and the conceptual hypotheses of science.

It is not always allowed that hypotheses are predictive, or have all or even any of the powers that I have credited them with. I take Sir Karl Popper to hold that hypotheses do not have predictive power, and that they do not have a priori probabilities. This is part of his rejection of induction as a way of gaining knowledge. Here I shall not follow Popper's notion of "objective knowledge" (Popper 1972), for my theme is what happens to observers when they observe and when they learn.

On this account much of learning is induction and behaviour is set very largely by probabilities based on past experience and so is predictive. Probable objects are more readily seen than improbable objects, so "subjective" probability seems to apply, both for selecting perceptions and for perceptions to have the predictive power evident in much behaviour and all skills.

To suggest that perceptions are like hypotheses is to suppose that the instruments and the procedures of science parallel essential characteristics of the sense organs and their neural channels, regarded as transducers transmitting coded data; and the data-handling procedures of science may be essentially the same as cognitive procedures carried out by perceptual neural processes of the brain. There will clearly be surface differences between science and perception, and we may expect some deeper differences, but for the suggestion to be interesting there should be more than overall *similarities*: there should be significant conceptual *identities*.

I shall start by setting out three claims, which I hope to justify, and no doubt qualify.

Claims:

(1) that perceptions are essentially like predictive hypotheses in science;

(2) that the procedures of science are a guide for discovering processes of perception;

(3) that many perceptual illusions correspond to and may receive explanations from understanding systematic errors occurring in science.

It is hoped that by exploring this analogy (or perhaps deep identity) between science and perception, we may develop an effective epistemology related to how the brain works. I shall attempt to indicate concepts and processes that seem important for the opening moves towards the end play of this understanding.

The approach is based on regarding perception and science as *constructing hypotheses* by "fiction-generators" which may hit upon truth by producing symbolic structures matching physical reality.

II Steps to Perception

In the first place we regard the sense organs (eyes, ears, touch receptors, and so on) as transducers essentially like photocells, microphones, and strain guages. The important similarity, indeed identity, is that the sense organs and detecting instruments convert patterns of received energy into signals, which may be read according to a code. As a signal, the neural activity is fully described in physical terms and measurable in physical units; but the code must be known in order to use or appreciate it as data. We suppose that the coded data are—in perception and science—used for generating hypotheses. For perception we may call them "perceptual hypotheses." These are what are usually called "perceptions." Here are the three stages of perception, in these terms.

A   Signals
Patterns of neural events, related to input stimulus patterns according to the transducer characteristics of sense organs.

For the eye, for example, there is a roughly logarithmic relation between intensity of light and the firing rate of the action potentials at the initial stage of the visual channel. Colour is coded by the proportion of rates of firing from the three spectrally distinct kinds of cone receptor cell, and so on. These transducer characteristics must be understood before the physiologist can appreciate what is going on. He can then (with other knowledge or assumptions) describe the neural signals as data representing states of affairs.

B   Data
Neural events are accepted as *representing* variables or states, according to a code which must be known for signals to be read or appreciated as data.

This necessity of knowing the code is surely clear from examples such as signals conveying data in Morse code. The dots and dashes have no significance, and may not even be recognized as signals conveying data when the code is not known. The same holds for the words on this page: we must know the rules of the English language, and a great deal more, to see them as more than patterns of ink on paper.

It is generally true that a lot more than the code must be known before signals can be read as data. For a detecting instrument (such as a radio-telescope, magnetometer, or voltmeter) it is essential to know something of the source, whether it is a star, a given region of the Earth, or just which part of the circuit a voltmeter is connected to. The outputs of some instruments (such as optical telescopes, microscopes, and X-ray machines as used in medicine) may give sufficient structure for the source to be identified without extra information. This is especially so when the structure of the output matches our normal perceptual inputs. This is, however, somewhat rare for instruments. A voltmeter provides no such structured output by which we can recognize its source of signals without collateral knowledge. Some sense organs (especially the eye) provide highly structured signals allowing identification of the source; but visual and any other sensory data can be ambiguous (including touch, hence the game of trying to identify by touch objects in a bag), and indeed all sensory and instrumental data are, strictly speaking, ambiguous. The fact that vision is usually sufficient for immediate object identification distracts us from realizing the immense importance of contextual knowledge for reading data from signals. Scientific data from instruments are almost always presented with explicit collateral information, on how the instrument was used, what source it was directed to, its calibration corrections and scale settings. The gain setting of oscilloscopes and the magnification scale of photographs and optical instruments of all kinds are essential for scientific use. If the scale is given incorrectly, serious misinterpretation can result, even to confusing the surface of a planet with biological structures. So, not only the signal code must be known, but also a great deal of context knowledge is required for signals to be read as data. This holds for perception as it does for the use of scientific instruments, though for perception the context knowledge is generally implicit and so its contribution may not be recognized.

It is important to note that signals can be fully described and measured with physical concepts and physical units, but this is not so for data. Data are highly peculiar, being (it is not too fanciful to say) in this way outside the physical world, though essential for describing the physical world.

The codes necessary for reading signals as data are not laws of physics. They are, rather, essentially arbitrary and held conventionally. Some may be more convenient or efficient than others, but in no case are they part of the physical world as laws of physics are, or reflect, "deep structures" of reality. Further, data are used to select between *hypothetical* possibilities, only one of which (if indeed any) exists. The greater the number of alternatives available for the selection (or rather the greater their combined probability) the greater the quantity of information in the data (Shannon and Weaver 1949). The information content thus depends not only on what *is* but on the hypothetical stored alternatives of what *may be*. But these are not in the (physical) reality of the situation, so data cannot be equated with what (physically) *is*; neither can they be equated with signals, for data are *read from* signals by following the conventional rules (which are not physical laws) of a code.

C Hypotheses

There is, unfortunately, no general agreement as to just what hypotheses are or what characterizes them. This, it must be confessed, is a weakness in our position. If there is no agreement on what are hypotheses, how can it be argued cogently that perceptions are hypotheses? Just what is being claimed? With the present lack of agreement, one must either be vague or stick out for a particular account, which may be arbitrary, of the nature of hypotheses. Current accounts range from Popper's view that they have no prior probabilities and no predictive power (and that they cannot be confirmed but only disconfirmed) to very different accounts, such as that they can be in part predicted; that they can be used for prediction; and that they can be confirmed (though not with certainty) as well as disconfirmed by observations. I shall not entirely follow Popper's account of hypotheses (Popper 1972), but hold, rather, an alternative account: that they have *predictive power*, and that they can be suggested by observation and induction, and can be confirmed or disconfirmed though not with logical certainty.

It may be objected here that if perceptions are themselves hypotheses, they cannot be evoked to confirm or disconfirm the explicit hypotheses of science. This is, however, no objection, for it is common experience that a perception can confirm or disconfirm other perceptions. And one scientific hypothesis may (it is usually held) confirm or disconfirm other hypotheses in science. So there is no clear distinction between hypotheses and perception here to make my argument invalid.

There is, however, this problem of the lack of agreement of what constitutes hypothesis. The notion of hypothesis has grown in importance with the rejection of hopes of certainty in science like the supposed certainty of geometrical knowledge before non-Euclidian geometries, and with Kuhn's (1962) paradigms. Perhaps all scientific knowledge is now regarded as hypothesis. But if Popper is right, would we have any wish to associate perception with hypotheses? For in his view they have none of the power we attribute to perception. What, then, are hypotheses?

I suggest that *hypotheses are selections of signalled and postulated data organized to be effective in typical (and some novel) situations*. Hypotheses are effective in having powers to predict future events, unsensed characteristics, and further hypotheses. They may also predict what is *not* true. I shall assume that we accept that these are important characteristics of scientific hypotheses and perception.

To amplify this, we may now consider in some detail similarities—and also differences, for there clearly *are* differences—between hypotheses and perceptions. We shall look first at similarities when perceptions and scientific hypotheses are appropriate. We shall then go on to compare them when they are inappropriate, or "false," and finally we shall consider ways in which perceptions clearly differ from hypotheses of science.

III Perception and Scientific Hypotheses Compared

A Results of Appropriate Uses of Perception and Science

1 Interpolation across Gaps in Signals or Data This allows continuous behaviour and control with only intermittent signals, which is typical of organisms and important in science, though rare in machines.

Interpolations may be little more than inertial or may be highly sophisticated and daring constructs. Let us first consider interpolation in a graph, such as figure 7.1. The curve is derived according to two very different kinds of processes. It is generated from the readings by following procedures, which are easy to state and to carry out automatically without particular external considerations. The most common procedure here is fitting by least squares. The curve may not touch any of the points representing the readings and yet it is accepted as the "best" curve. It is an idealization—a hypothesis of what should occur in the absence of irrelevant disturbances and an infinite set of readings with no gaps.

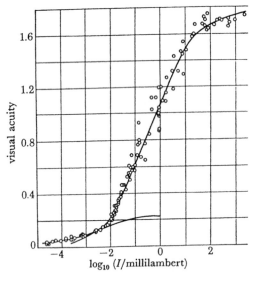

Figure 7.1
A typical graph of experimental reading with a fitted curve. The fitting may be done both "upwards," by a routine procedure such as by "least-mean" squares; and "downwards," from which (generally theoretical) function is most likely. The fitted curve may be regarded as a predictive hypothesis. Contour perception seems similar.

Any graph of experimental or observational data has some *scatter* in the readings through which the curve is drawn. The scatter may be due to random disturbances of the measuring device, or to variation in what is being measured, such as quantal fluctuations. These kinds of scatter have very different statuses, though for some purposes they may be treated alike and there may be a mixture of the two. In any case the curve may not touch any of the points indicating the readings. So it is a kind of fiction, accepted as the fact of the situation.

The second kind of procedure for obtaining the curve and for gap-filling is selecting a *preferred* curve, on theoretical or other general grounds, which may be aesthetic. The first kind of procedure is "bottom-upwards" from the readings, by following procedures without reference to contextual considerations; the second is "top-downwards," from stored knowledge or assumptions suggesting what is a likely curve. This may be set by a general preference (or prejudice) for example for a linear, or a logarithmic, or some other favoured type of function; or it may be set by particular considerations. Both have their dangers: the first biases towards the accepted, and the second tends to perpetuate false theories by bending the data in their direction.

The example of a graph illustrates that hypotheses—for the accepted curve or function may *be* a predictive hypothesis—can be *non-propositional*. Perhaps hypotheses are generally thought of as sets of propositions, but there seems no reason to restrict hypotheses to propositions as expressed in language. An equation such as $E = \frac{1}{2}mv^2$ is a hypothesis, in this case concerning quite abstract concepts (energy, mass and velocity), believed to represent something of the deep structure of physics, but it is not propositional in form. It could be written in language as a set of sentences expressing propositions but this would be relatively clumsy. It could also be expressed as a graph, and this could be adequate for some purposes. Analogue computers, indeed, work from this kind of non-propositional representation.

There seems no reason to hold that "perceptual hypotheses" require a propositional brain language, underlying spoken and written language, though this might be so. The merits of this notion need not be considered here, as we are free to regard hypotheses as not *necessarily* being in propositional form.

Perhaps interpolations are generally regarded as gap-filling in situations for which we do not have complete or strictly adequate readings, but interpolation can be far more elaborate than this, for example postulating unknown species to fill gaps in evolutionary sequences. For a visual example, consider figure 7.2. Perhaps "illusory contours" are edges of objects postulated to account for gaps in available sensory

Figure 7.2
Illusory contours and regions of modified brightness seem to be postulates of nearer eclipsing objects, to "explain" unlikely gaps. It seems that an essentially Bayesian strategy is responsible.

signals or data. They take more or less ideal forms, and they are (generally useful) fictions joining data. This indeed defines interpolation in perception and science.

2 Extrapolation from Signals and Data, to Future States and Unsensed Features

Extrapolation allows hypotheses to take off from what is given or accepted, into the unknown. Going beyond accepted data is not very different from filling gaps, except that interpolations are limited to the next accepted data point; extrapolations, however, have no endpoint in what is known or assumed, so extrapolations may be infinitely daring, and so may be dramatically wrong.

Extrapolation beyond the end of graphs of functions supported by data is sometimes essential (as for determining "absolute zero" temperature by extrapolating beyond the range through which measures can, even in principle, be made). Extrapolations can leap from spectral lines to stars, and from past to future. With interpolation and extrapolation, data become stepping stones and springboards for science and perception. This is to say that perceptions are not confined to stimuli, just as science is not limited to signals or available data; neither, of course, is confined to fact.

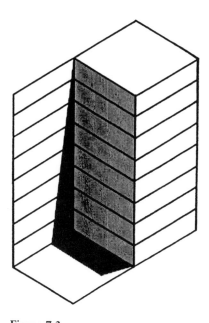

Figure 7.3
In this depth-ambiguous figure the grey rectangular region changes in brightness for most observers according to whether this area is a probable shadow. The systematic brightness change with depth-reversal is, clearly, centrally initiated and is a "downwards" effect.

3   Discovery and Creation of Objects, in Perceptual and Conceptual Space   The perceptual selection of sensed characteristics may create *objects*. There is also strong evidence for creating visual *characteristics* from what is accepted as objects (cf. figure 7.3).

We know too little about the criteria for *assigning* data to objects, and *creating* object-hypotheses from data. What science describes as an object may or may not correspond to what appears to the senses as an object; different instruments reveal the world as differently structured. Further, general theories change what are regarded as objects. There is evidently a complex multi-way traffic here by which the world is parcelled out into objects; it seems that here again we have "upwards" and "downwards" procedures operating. The various rules of "closure," "common fate" and so on, emphasized by the Gestalt psychologists such as Wertheimer (1923), reflect features typical of the vast majority of objects as we see them. Most objects are closed in form, and their parts move together. These common object characteristics become identifying principles—and may structure random patterns to *create* object forms, even from noise. More recently, the work in artificial intelligence on object recognition makes use of typical features—especially the intersections of lines at corners of various kinds—to describe objects and their forms in depth (Guzman 1968). The effectiveness of these classifications and rules depends on what objects are generally like (cf. Guzman 1971). For exceptional objects, the rules mislead, as we see in the Ames demonstrations (Ittelson 1952) and in distortion figures (Gregory 1968). The object-recognizing and object-creating rules are applied *upwards* to filter and structure the input. (It is, however, interesting to note that they may have been *developed* downwards, by generalized experience of what are, through the development of perception, taken as objects. For the Gestalt writers this is largely innate; but our similar experience and needs might well generate common object-criteria through experience.)

Knowledge can work downwards to parcel signals and data into objects; as knowledge changes, the parcelling into objects may change, both for science and perception, We see this most clearly when examining machines: the criteria for recognizing and naming the various features as separate depend very much on our knowledge of functions. Thus the pallets on the anchor of a clock escapement are seen and described as objects in their own right once the mechanism is understood, though they are but shapes in one piece of metal, which happens also to look like an anchor. So we see here again the importance of *upward* and *downward* processing in perception and science—the complex interplay of signals, data and hypotheses. Unravelling this is surely essential for understanding the strategies and procedures of perception and science. It is also important for appreciating the status of objects. How far are objects *recognized* and how much are they *created* by perception and science? This is a deep question at the heart of empiricism.

What may be a profound difference between perceptual and conceptual objects is that perceptual objects are always, as Frege put it (Dummett 1978) *concrete objects*, while the conceptual objects of science may be *abstract objects*. The point is that objects as perceived have spatial extension, and may change in time, while conceptual objects (such as numbers, the centre of gravity of concrete objects, and the deep structure of the world as described by laws of physics) cannot be sensed, may be unchanging and spaceless, and yet have the status of objects in that they are *public* though not sensed. We all agree that the number 13 is a prime number, that it is greater than 12 and less than 14, that it is odd and not even, and that *all* prime numbers except 2 are odd numbers. This kind of agreement is characteristic of the agreement and public ownership of objects as known by the senses (tables, stones, and so on), yet numbers cannot be sensed, though they are as "public" as tables and stones.

This situation is rendered even more difficult by the consideration that, clearly, *concrete* objects have some features that are abstract, as we believe especially from scientific knowledge. Take, as an example, centre of gravity: stones have centres of gravity, which is useful as a scientific concept, and are indeed what Newton took to be the "objects" of the solar system for his astronomy. Centres of gravity may indeed lie not *in* but *between* concrete objects, such as between Earth and Sun, or between binary stars. Does the centre of gravity exist, as stones and stars exist? Or is it a useful fiction created as a tool for scientific description?

Even within what is clearly perception, we can be uncertain of what is "concrete" and what is "abstract." We see that a triangle has three sides, and yet number is regarded, at least by Frege, as "abstract." Are shadows "concrete objects"? The trouble here is that they are known by only one sense (if we except differences of sensed temperature) and they have few causal properties. Also, they are always attached to what is clearly a concrete object (which may be the ground) and by contrast they seem far less concrete, almost abstract though we see them.

These are exceedingly difficult issues, which can hardly be resolved without deeper understanding of hypothesis-generation, and further analysis of the similarities and differences between perceptual and conceptual hypotheses.

If we consider such "objects" as electrons, which are clearly inferred indirectly from observational evidence, how do they compare with concrete objects of perception? If we believe that normal perception of concrete objects such as tables and stones requires a great deal of inference ("unconscious inference," to use Helmholtz's term), then the difference may not be great. The more perception depends on inference the more similar we may suppose is the status of perceptual and conceptual objects.

We shall now consider inappropriate or "false" hypotheses and perceptions. Here I describe certain phenomena of perception, such as various kinds of illusions, as our actually *seeing* what are *described* when occurring in science as errors; various kinds of ambiguities, distortions, paradoxes and fictitious features. The claim is that these categories, which are normally applied to arguments and descriptions, appear in perceptions as experiences of recognizable kinds, which can be investigated much as the phenomena of physics can be investigated; though for some of these perceptual phenomena rather different kinds of explanations from those of physics may be required.

B   Results of Inappropriate Uses of Perception and Science

1   Ambiguity, Sometimes with Spontaneous Alternations and Disagreements   The point here is that alternative hypotheses can be elicited by the same signals. There are many examples of visual ambiguity in which a figure (or sometimes an object) is seen to switch from one orientation to another, or transform into another design or object. This has been attributed to bi-stable (or multi-stable) brain circuits (Attneave 1971) and, very differently, to putative hypotheses in rivalry for acceptance when their probabilities on the available evidence are nearly equal. The first would be an account in terms of *signals*, the second in terms of *data*. Inspection suggests strongly that the second is what is going on in most cases, for the stimulus pattern can be immensely varied, but what it *represents* matters a great deal. There are, however, many examples of the first kind: retinal rivalry, from different colours presented to the eyes producing spontaneous alternations, and lines of different orientation presented binocularly, producing rivalry. Here it is purely the stimulus characteristics that matter. On the other hand, figures such as the Necker cube, the Schroeder staircase or the Boring wife-mistress figure, present equal evidence for example for two very different faces, which gives the ambiguity. For the Necker cube there is no evidence favouring either of two or more orientations. For both figures the ambiguity no doubt depends on our knowledge of faces and cubes. (We studied the case of a man blind from infancy and allowed to see by corneal graft when in his fifties: when we showed him ambiguous figures such as Necker cubes he saw no depth and no reversals. He made nothing of pictures of faces [Gregory and Wallace 1963].) It is likely that different experience might change the bias of ambiguous alternations in cases such as the Boring figure.

That science can be ambiguous is shown by the frequent changes of opinion and the occasional disputes which give it light and heat. For a current example of scientific ambiguity: are quasars astronomically near objects with abnormal red shifts, perhaps due to their powerful gravitational fields (and thus not obeying the Hubble law of increasing red shift with distance), or are they very distant, but of enormous intrinsic brightness? Here is a clear case of an important ambiguity which is not yet quite resolved. It might de resolved by further data derived by instrumental signals, or by a change in the general theoretical position, for which this is a central question. In short, the change that resolves the paradox might be "upwards" or "downwards"—both in science and in perception.

2 Distortion, Especially Spatial Distortions Distortions can occur at the *signal* level by loss of calibration (as by sensory adaptation), by inappropriate calibration corrections, by mismatch of the instrument or sense organ "transducer" to the input (or affecting the input, as by loading with a voltmeter of low internal resistance, or detecting temperature by touch of thin metal, which rapidly adopts the skin temperature).

Distortions may also occur in the *data* and stored knowledge level, as when knowledge is transferred inappropriately to the current situation, so that signals are misread.

Signal errors are to be understood through physics and physiology; data errors (which are cognitive errors) are understood by appreciating what knowledge or strategies are being brought to bear, and in what ways they are inappropriate to the current problem or situation.

Visual distortions can occur with: (i) mirrors, mirages, sticks bent in water, or astigmatic lenses giving optical distortion of the input; (ii) astigmatic lenses of the eyes (physiological optical distortion); (iii) inappropriate neural correction of optical astigmatism (a calibration correction error); (iv) neural signal distortion (which may be pathological or may be due to other signals interfering by cross-talk, or neural lateral inhibition, or some such); (v) signals being misread as data (especially by "negative transfer" of knowledge: generally from typical to similar but atypical situations).

I shall not expand on these, except the last, and that only briefly. Here again we find the distinction between processing *upwards* and *downwards* important. To take an example of misreading data that has received a great deal of attention, though explanations are still controversial, we may consider visual distortion illusions.

Since the perceived size of things is ambiguously represented by retinal image size, size must be *scaled*. Visual scale is set by what I have called (Gregory 1970) "constancy scaling." It seems that scaling can set *upwards*, from stimulus patterns normally accepted as data for distances (especially converging lines and corners normally indicating depth by perspective). When these stimulus shapes occur without their normal depth—as when perspective is presented on a picture plane—they may be accepted as though they correctly represented depth, there to set the scaling inappropriately. Features represented as distant on a picture plane are perceptually expanded, for normally expansion with increased object distance is required to compensate for the shrinking of retinal images with object distance; but this is not appropriate for the flat-perspective drawings. Scale-setting is essential for maintaining perceived size independently of object distance (giving "size constancy"), but when scale-setting by perspective features occurs other than by the retinal projection of parallel lines, etc., lying in the three dimensions of normal space, then the scale is set inappropriately, to generate distortion "upwards" from the misleading perspective features.

"Downwards" distortions occur when an incorrect depth hypothesis is adopted. This is clear from depth-ambiguous objects, such as wire cubes, which change shape with each depth reversal, though the retinal input and neural signals from the eye remain unchanged. Ambiguous objects and figures are extremely useful in this way for separating upward from downward perceptual processes (Gregory 1968, 1970).

Astronomy is rich in examples of scales set *upwards* from instrumental readings (with fewest assumptions by heliocentric parallax) and also *downwards* from considerations such as the mass–luminosity relation applied to a certain class of variable star, so that their observed periodicity can be used, together with their apparent luminosity, to infer distance. This involves a great deal of stored knowledge and associated assumptions. When these change, the Universe may be rescaled.

There seems to be a remarkable similarity in the setting of scale for perceptual and for scientific hypotheses. Perceptual space is not, however, Euclidian, except for near objects. Consider the perception of an engine driver: the rails appear parallel only for a few hundred metres, then they converge alarmingly. The driver can use his *perceptual* Euclidian near-space, in which parallel lines never meet, with confidence; but for greater distances he must reject his non-Euclidian perceptual space in favour of his Euclidian *conceptual* space, to drive his train further without a certainty of disaster. If, now, the driver reads Einstein in his spare time, he will adopt still another space: then what he relies upon professionally will become for him a parochialism, adequate for the job but not for fuller understanding. Each view— perceptual or conceptual—which seems undistorted will appear distorted from the spaces of his other views.

3 Paradoxes, Especially Spatial Paradoxes   Paradoxes can be generated by conflicting inputs, or by generating hypotheses from false or inappropriate assumptions. A well known conflicting-input perceptual paradox is given by adapting one hand to hot water and the other to cold, and then placing both hands in a dish of warm water. To one hand this will be cold and to the other hot. The adaptation has produced (or rather *is*) mis-calibration, which gives incompatible signals to produce a paradox, since we do not allow that an object can be both hot and cold at the same time.

In recent science there has been a relaxing of the strictures of paradox, such that what now seems paradoxical to common sense may, sometimes, be accepted as scientifically true. An example is light accepted as both waves and particles. Also, what *appears* paradoxical may be *understood* as non-paradoxical—as indeed for the "impossible triangle" object or drawing (figures 7.4 and 7.5). Here we discover that conceptual understanding is sometimes powerless to correct or modify even clearly bizarre perceptions. We can, at the same time, hold incompatible perceptual and conceptual hypotheses: so we can *see* a paradox.

The "impossible triangle" is clearly a cognitive illusion, for there is nothing special about this as a *stimulus* to disturb the physiology or signals of the visual channel. By making a model (figure 7.5), it may be seen and understood that this occurs with a special view of a normal object. When viewed from the critical position, the perceptual system assumes that two ends of what appear to be sides of a triangle are joined and lie at the same distance, though they are separated in distance. Even when we know this we still experience the visual paradox. It is very interesting that

Figure 7.4
The Penrose "impossible triangle" drawing. This appears paradoxical; but it can be an object lying in normal three-dimensional space as viewed from a critical position, as shown in figure 7.5.

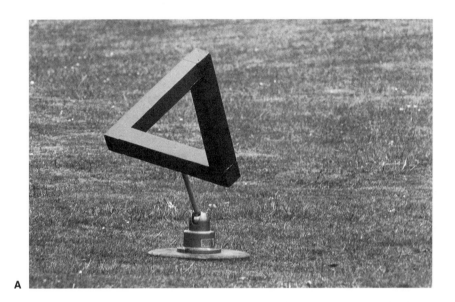

A

B

Figure 7.5
This wooden object appears paradoxical when viewed from a critical position. This is as true
of the object itself as of the photograph.

this false visual assumption—that the ends are at the same distance though they are separated—can generate a perception which is clearly extremely unlikely, and recognized as unlikely or even impossible. This shows convincingly that perceptions are built up by following rules from assumptions. Since perceptions can be extremely improbable and even impossible, it follows that perceiving is not *merely* a matter of accepting the most likely hypotheses. Figures and objects of this kind present useful opportunities for discovering perceptual assumptions and rules by which perceptual hypotheses that may conflict with high level knowledge are generated "upwards" from assumptions by rule-following.

Our ability to generate and accept extremely unlikely perceptions must be important for survival, for occasionally highly unlikely events and situations do occur and need to be appreciated. Indeed, perceptual learning would be impossible if only the probable were accepted. At the same time, though, there is marked probability biasing in favour of the likely against the unlikely; as in the difficulty, indeed the impossibility, of seeing a hollow mask as hollow, without full stereoscopic vision (figure 7.6). So there are, again, the two opposed principles—processing upwards and downwards—the first generating hypotheses which may be highly unlikely and

Figure 7.6
The "face" on the right is in fact the hollow mould of the face on the left. Though hollow, the mould appears as a normal face. Texture and even stereoscopic counter-information are rejected to maintain this highly probable (but incorrect) hypothesis.

even clearly impossible, the second offering checks "downwards" from stored knowledge, and filling gaps which may be fictional and false.

4   Fictions, Sometimes to Fit and Sometimes to Depart from Fact   We can see perceptual fictions in phenomena such as the illusory contours (figure 7.2). These were described by Schuman (1904) and have recently become well known with the beautiful examples due to Kanizsa (1966). If we are right in thinking (Gregory 1972) that they are postulated masking objects to "explain" the surprising gaps in these figures, we at once assign to them a cognitive status. Related examples are shadows of writing: letters that would cast such shadows are seen though there is no stimulus pattern of letters. The letters are evidently fictions to "explain" what are accepted as shadows by postulating letter-shaped objects (Gombrich 1960).

It is reasonable to suppose that a very great deal of perception is in this sense fictional: generally useful but occasionally clearly wrong, when it can be an extremely powerful deception. No doubt this holds also for science.

It is particularly interesting that the *absence* of signals can be accepted as data. This is so for the discovery of the van Allen radiation belts, when the space probes' sensors were overloaded so that they failed to provide signals; and the gaps of the illusory contours figures which provide data for an eclipsing (though non-existent) object. These examples indicate ways by which the hypotheses of science and perception become richer than signalled data. They show also that we cannot equate neural signals with experience.

5   Causes and Inferences Link Hypotheses and Perception to the World   Hypotheses of science and perceptions are, I believe, linked to reality very indirectly. What kind of relations do they have? There are two important questions here: (a) Are they *causally* linked? (b) Are they linked by *inference*? We should allow the possibilities that either or both may be true or false. Let us consider these.

(a)   That hypotheses are *causally* linked to reality would be held, if there are what we have called *signal* links between reality and hypotheses. We accept this for transducers and signal channels, but what of the signals when read as *data*? There can be gaps in signals. These are often filled by interpolating processes (see section 7.3), so here science and perception clearly maintain hypotheses (and maintain continuous control from hypotheses) through signal gaps. Nevertheless, we do not want to say that this gap-filling requires processes outside causal explanation. Part of the aim of theories of perception and accounts of science is indeed to explain gap-filling, and these explanations, if they are to be like most explanations, should preferably be causal. We may, however, expect to find some deep conceptual difficulties over *data*, though not signals, as causes.

What of *data* distortions? Are they breaks in causal sequences? One can see cases of data errors (rather than signal errors) in which there clearly are no causal breaks in the signals, and it is possible to understand why the signals are read as misleading data. This occurs when signals are read normally as though occurring in a typical situation, when in fact the situation is atypical. Particular perceptual examples are, on this account, many of the distortion illusions (cf. Gregory 1963). Here the scaling is supposed to be set quite normally by signalled features, but these features do not have their usual significance in these figures. For example, converging lines on a picture plane are read as perspective, as though the convergence were produced as in normal three-dimensional space when parallel lines lying in depth are imaged on the retina. Picture perspective misleads not by distorting neural signals, but by providing signals that are read as depth data although the picture is flat. There is no break in the usual causation of perception, but there is marked distortion, and the distortion is of data, not of signals.

To understand why this happens we always need to know what knowledge (in this case that convergence of lines is associated with depth) has been transferred to the current situation, and why in this situation it is inappropriate.

What of paradoxical hypotheses? Since we do not accept that reality can be paradoxical, we cannot accept that paradoxical hypotheses or perceptions can match or represent reality. There is therefore some kind of gap—but is this a causal gap? We can think of signal distortion paradoxes where there clearly is no causal gap, for example the hands sensing hot and cold for the same bowl of water, when one hand has been adopted to hot and the other to cold. Here we have incompatible signals owing to adaptation of one of more channels, combining to form a paradox—but without any causal break.

Figures such as the Penrose impossible triangle drawing (figure 7.4) or our impossible model (figure 7.5) are very different from signal distortions. We attribute these perceptual paradoxes not to signal errors, but to false assumptions. So these are top-down errors.

The question is: Do top-down injections of data or assumptions produce causal gaps in signal processing? They certainly introduce considerations that may be very far removed from the current situation, and for quite displaced assumptions it may be very difficult indeed to see how they have come into play. If we give them a "mental" status, then we may be tempted to say that they are caused mentally; it seems better, however, to say that the situation is something like a filling card index, in that references are sought by criteria of relevance and so on, as formulated within a physical search system. This may go wrong by misreading of signals or by indexing errors, and it may also produce misleading data because what is generally relevant is not appropriate in the particular situation. These mistakes are very different, but they can be explained in terms of the logic of the procedures plus the mechanical steps used to carry out the procedures.

(b) If probabilities can affect reasoning and acceptance or rejection of hypotheses, then just how can we hold that signals though not data are causal? To maintain a causal account we must allow that assessed probabilities have causal effects. We may, however, translate this into: *Signals have causal effects according to the significance in the situation of the data that they convey.*

If the distinction between signals and data is seen as a dualism, at least this dualism does not apply uniquely to mind and brain. As argued earlier, it applies with equal force in the case of instruments supplying signals and data for science. So the activity of science becomes a test-tube—indeed a laboratory—for appreciating the mind-brain problem.

We may now consider some *differences* between scientific and perceptual hypotheses.

C   Differences between Scientific and Perceptual Hypotheses, When They Are Appropriate or Inappropriate

1   Perceptions Are from One Vantage-Point and Run in Real Time; Science Is Not Based on an Observer's View   Perceptions differ from conceptions by being related to events in real time from a local region of space, while conceptions have no locale and are essentially timeless. They not only lack any locale in the three-dimensional space of the physical world, but they may express variables and relations in all manner of conceptual spaces, which are not claimed to exist though they are useful fictions for descriptive purposes.

So perception is far more limited in range and application than conception. The basis of empiricism is that all conception depends upon perception. But conception can break away from perception, to create new worlds—though perhaps always using as building blocks the objects of perception.

2   Perceptions Are of Instances; Science Is of Generalizations   We perceive individual objects, but we can conceive, also, generalizations and abstractions. Thus we can see *a* triangle, but we can conceive general properties of *all* triangles—triangularity. Is this difference absolute or, rather, a matter of degree? A chess player may claim that he *sees* the situation rather than the pieces; and when reading, one is more aware of the meaning of the words than their form, and this can hold when the words express generalizations. This is a tricky issue requiring investigation. I incline to think that there is not a sharp distinction here between perceiving and conceiving.

3   Perceptions Are Limited to "Concrete Objects"; Science Has Also "Abstract Objects"   This distinction is due to the logician Frege, and is discussed above (section 7.3). Again, this is a tricky issue, closely bound up with the deepest problems of perception and epistemology. The distinction is not clear-cut.

Concrete objects are what are (or are believed to be) sensed. They may be simple or complex. Thus a magnetic field may be simple and a table is complex. It is not, however, at all clear that sensing is *ever* free from inference: for example, perceiving a table is far more than sensing various parts, and sensing a magnetic field requires all manner of inferences about the transducer and how it is placed and used. The contribution of inferences and assumptions to sensing even simple objects makes the distinction between concrete and abstract objects difficult and perhaps impossible to make clearly, for abstract objects—such as numbers and centres of gravity—are or at least may be known via sense experience, and perhaps nothing is sensed "directly." If nothing is sensed or perceived directly—if *all* perception and all scientific observation, however instrumented, involve inference—then it seems that there are no purely concrete objects. This is indeed a major conclusion from the thesis that perceptions are hypotheses. This conclusion applies equally to perception and to science.

4   Perceptions Are Not Explanations, but Conceptions Can Be Explanatory   Scientific hypotheses are closely linked to explanation: it is an explanation that the tides are caused by the pull of the Moon. Perceptions certainly have far less explanatory power, but perhaps they do have some. One understands social situations, or mechanisms, through looking: is this understanding part of the *perception*? I incline to think that it is. This difference is rather of degree than kind.

5   Perception Includes Awareness; the Physical Sciences Exclude Awareness   This is by far the most striking difference between hypotheses of science and perceptions: sensations are involved in perception (though not all perceptions) but awareness, or consciousness, has no place in the hypotheses of physics.

The scientist may be aware that he is working on a hypothesis; but the hypothesis is not itself aware—or so we assume! On the other hand, we do want to say that awareness is an integral part of many perceptual hypotheses, so here we have a clear distinction between scientific hypotheses and some perceptions.

Returning to our distinctions between signals and data: a traditional view was that perceptions are made up of sensations, but this we have rejected. It must, however, be confessed that the role, if any, of awareness or consciousness in perception is totally mysterious. Much of human behaviour controlled by perception can occur without awareness: consciousness is seldom, if ever, necessary. Perhaps consciousness is particularly associated with mismatch between expectation and signalled events; but if this is so, its purpose remains obscure, because it is not clearly causal.

Popper and Eccles (1977) argue from phenomena of visual ambiguity—especially maintaining or changing visual orientations by will—that mind, as associated with consciousness, has some control over brain. This argument was also suggested by William James (1890), but, as he points out, it could be *other brain processes* affecting reversal rates, or whatever. There seems no good reason to suppose that consciousness, at least in this situation, is causal.

Is consciousness so difficult to understand and describe, just because it is *not* part of scientific hypotheses about the physical world? It is these, only, that provide conceptual understanding? If so, we must be careful with our suggestion that perceptions are hypotheses: for if *all* we can know are hypotheses of physics, then perceptions are *bound* to look like hypotheses of physics. This is an impasse for which I have no ready answer. I can only hope that further consideration will unravel or cut these Gordian knots of knowing.

We may conclude that, all in all, there are marked similarities and important identities between hypotheses of science and perceptions. It is these that justify calling perceptions "hypotheses." The differences are, however, extremely interesting, and I fear that I have not done them justice. This is not through any desire to minimize them, but rather that I do not know what to add. Possibly this is because we think in terms of the hypotheses of science so that when something crops up that departs from them drastically, we are lost. We are lost for consciousness. It is very curious that we can think conceptually with such effect "outwards" but not "inwards." It may be that developments in artificial intelligence will provide concepts by which we shall see ourselves.

References

Attneave, F. 1971 Multistability in perception. *Scient. Am.* 225 (6), 62–71.

Dummett, M. 1978 *Frege.* London: Duckworth.

Gibson, J. J. 1950 *Perception of the visual world.* London: Allen & Unwin.

Gregory, R. L. 1963 Distortion of visual space as inappropriate constancy scaling. *Nature, Lond.* 119, 678.

Gregory, R. L. 1968 Perceptual illusions and brain models. *Proc. R. Soc. Lond.* B 171, 279–296.

Gregory, R. L. 1970 *The intelligent eye.* London and New York: Weidenfeld and Nicolson.

Gregory, R. L. 1972 Cognitive contours. *Nature, Lond.* 238, 51–52.

Gregory, R. L. and Wallace, J. G. 1963 Recovery from early blindness: A case study. *Monogr. Suppl.* no. 2, *Q. Jl exp. Psychol.* Cambridge: Heffers. (Reprinted in Gregory, R. L. 1974 *Concepts and mechanisms of perception.* London: Duckworth).

Gombrich, E. H. 1960 *Art and illusion.* London: Phaidon.

Guzman, A. 1968 Decomposition of a visual scene into three-dimensional bodies. In *Proc. of the Fall Joint Computer Conference*, pp. 291-304.

Guzman, A. 1971 Analysis of curved line drawings using context and global information. In *Machine intelligence*, vol. 6 (ed. B. Meltzer and D. Michie), pp. 325–375. University of Edinburgh Press.

Ittelson, W. H. 1952 *The Ames demonstrations in perception.* Princeton University Press.

James, W. 1890 *Principles of psychology.* Macmillan.

Kanizsa, G. 1966 Margini quasi-percettivi in campi con stimulazioni omogenea. *Riv. Psicol.* 49, 7.

Kuhn, T. 1962 *The structure of scientific revolutions.* University of Chicago Press.

Penrose, L. S. and Penrose, R. 1958 Impossible objects: A special type of illusion. *Br. J. Psychol.* 49, 31.

Popper, K. R. 1972 *Objective knowledge: An evolutionary approach.* Oxford: Clarendon Press.

Popper, K. R. and Eccles, J. C. 1977 *The self and its brain.* Springer International.

Shannon, C. E. and Weaver, W. 1949 *The mathematical theory of communication.* Urbana: University of Illinois Press.

Schumann, F. 1904 Einige Beobachtungen uber die Zusammenfassung von Gesichtseindrucken zu Einheiten. *Psychol. Stud., Lpz.* 1, 1.

Wertheimer, M. 1938 Laws of organisation of perceptual forms. In *Source book of Gestalt psychology* (ed. W. H. Ellis), pp. 71–88. New York: Routledge Kegan Paul.

8

Veridical Hallucination and Prosthetic Vision

David Lewis

I

I see. Before my eyes various things are present and various things are going on. The scene before my eyes causes a certain sort of visual experience in me, thanks to a causal process involving light, the retina, the optic nerve, and the brain. The visual experience so caused more or less matches the scene before my eyes. All this goes on in much the same way in my case as in the case of other people who see. And it goes on in much the same way that it would have if the scene before my eyes had been visibly different, though in that case the visual experience produced would have been different.

How much of all this is essential to seeing?

II

It is not far wrong to say simply that someone sees if and only if the scene before his eyes causes matching visual experience. So far as I know, there are no counterexamples to this in our ordinary life. Shortly we shall consider some that arise under extraordinary circumstances.

But first, what do we mean by "matching visual experience"? What goes on in the brain (or perhaps the soul) is not very much like what goes on before the eyes. They cannot match in the way that a scale model matches its prototype, or anything like that. Rather, visual experience has informational content about the scene before the eyes, and it matches the scene to the extent that its content is correct.

Visual experience is a state characterised by its typical causal role, and its role is to participate in a double causal dependence. Visual experience depends on the scene before the eyes,[1] and the subject's beliefs about that scene depend in turn partly on his visual experience. The content of the experience is, roughly, the content of the belief it tends to produce.

The matter is more complicated, however. The same visual experience will have a different impact on the beliefs of different subjects, depending on what they believed beforehand. (And on other differences between them, e.g. differences of intelligence.) Holmes will believe more on the basis of a given visual experience than Watson; and Watson in turn will believe more than someone will who suspects that he has fallen victim to a field linguist no less powerful than deceitful.[2] We should take the range of prior states that actually exist among us, and ask what is common to the impact of a given visual experience on all these states. Only if a certain belief would be produced in almost every case may we take its content as part of the content of the visual experience. (The more stringently we take "almost every," the more we cut down the content of the visual experience and the more of its impact we attribute to unconscious inference; for our purposes, we need not consider how that line ought to be drawn.)

Beliefs produced by visual experience are in large part self-ascriptive: the subject believes not only that the world is a certain way but also that he himself is situated in the world in a certain way. To believe that the scene before my eyes is stormy is the same as to believe that I am facing a stormy part of the world. Elsewhere[3] I have argued that the objects of such beliefs should be taken, and that the objects of all beliefs may be taken, as properties which the subject self-ascribes. Hence the content of visual experience likewise consists of properties—properties which the subject will self-ascribe if the visual experience produces its characteristic sort of belief. The content is correct, and the visual experience matches the scene before the eyes, to the extent that the subject has the properties that comprise the content of his visual experience.

Equivalently we might follow Hintikka's scheme and take the content of visual experience as a set of alternative possibilities.[4] A modification is desirable, however, in view of the self-ascriptive character of visually produced belief. We should take these visual alternatives not as possible worlds but as possible individuals-situated-in-worlds. The visual experience characteristically produces in the subject the belief that he himself belongs to this set of alternative possible individuals. Matching then means that the subject is, or at least closely resembles, a member of his alternative set.

Not all of the content of visual experience can be characterised in terms of the beliefs it tends to produce. It is part of the content that the duck-rabbit look like a duck or a rabbit, but the belief produced is that there is no duck and no rabbit but only paper and ink. However, aspects of the content that do not show up in the produced belief also are irrelevant to our task of saying what it is for visual experience to match the scene before the eyes. We can therefore ignore them.

III

I shall not dwell on the question whether it is possible to see even if the scene before the eyes does not cause matching visual experience. Three sorts of examples come to mind. (1) Perhaps someone could see without having visual experience. He would need something that more or less played the role of visual experience; but this substitute might not be visual experience, either because it played the role quite imperfectly[5] or because it is not what normally plays the role in human beings (or in some other natural kind to which the subject in question belongs).[6] (2) Perhaps someone could see in whom the scene before the eyes causes non-matching visual experience, provided that the failure of match is systematic and that the subject knows how to infer information about the scene before the eyes from this non-matching visual experience. (3) Perhaps someone could see in whom the scene elsewhere than before the eyes causes visual experience matching that scene, but not matching the scene before the eyes (if such there be). I do not find these examples clear one way or the other, and therefore I shall consider them no further. They will not meet the conditions for seeing that follow, wherefore I claim only sufficiency and not necessity for those conditions.

Two further preliminaries. (1) My analysandum is seeing in a strong sense that requires a relation to the external scene. Someone whose visual experience is entirely hallucinatory does not see in this strong sense. I take it that he can be said to see in a weaker, phenomenal sense—he sees what isn't there—and this is to say just that he has visual experience. (2) My analysandum is seeing in the intransitive sense, not seeing such-and-such particular thing. The latter analysandum poses all the problems of the former, and more besides: it raises the questions whether something is seen if it makes a suitable causal contribution to visual experience but it is not noticed separately from its background, and whether something is seen when part of it—for instance, its front surface—makes a causal contribution to visual experience.[7]

IV

My first stab is good enough to deal with some familiar counterexamples to causal analyses of seeing: they are not cases of seeing because they are not cases in which the scene before the eyes causes matching visual experience.[8]

Example 1: The Brain. I hallucinate at random; by chance I seem to see a brain floating before my eyes; my own brain happens to look just like the one I seem to see; my brain is causing my visual experience, which matches it. I do not see. No problem: my brain is no part of the scene before my eyes.

Example 2: The Memory. I hallucinate not at random; visual memory influences the process; thus I seem to see again a scene from long ago; this past scene causes visual experience which matches it. I do not see. No problem: the past scene is not part of the scene before my eyes.[9]

However, more difficult cases are possible. They are cases of *veridical hallucination*, in which the scene before the eyes causes matching visual experience, and still one does not see. They show that what I have said so far does not provide a sufficient condition for seeing.

Example 3: The Brain before the Eyes. As in example 1, I hallucinate at random, I seem to see a brain before my eyes, my own brain looks just like the one I seem to see, and my brain is causing my visual experience. But this time my brain is before my eyes. It has been carefully removed from my skull. The nerves and blood vessels that connect it to the rest of me have been stretched somehow, not severed. It is still working and still hallucinating.

Example 4: The Wizard. The scene before my eyes consists mostly of a wizard casting a spell. His spell causes me to hallucinate at random, and the hallucination so caused happens to match the scene before my eyes.

Example 5: The Light Meter. I am blind; but electrodes have been implanted in my brain in such a way that when turned on they will cause me to have visual experience of a certain sort of landscape. A light meter is on my head. It is connected to the electrodes in such a way that they are turned on if and only if the average illumination of the scene before my eyes exceeds a certain threshold. By chance, just such a landscape is before my eyes, and its illumination is enough to turn on the electrodes.

V

Ordinarily, when the scene before the eyes causes matching visual experience, it happens as follows. Parts of the scene reflect or emit light in a certain pattern; this light travels to the eye by a more or less straight path, and is focused by the lens to form an image on the retina; the retinal cells are stimulated in proportion to the intensity and spectral distribution of the light that falls on them; these stimulated cells stimulate other cells in turn, and so on, and stimulations comprise a signal which propagates up the optic nerve into the brain; and finally there is a pattern of stimulation in the brain cells which either is or else causes the subject's visual experience.

That is not at all what goes on in our three examples of veridical hallucination. Rather, the scene before the eyes causes matching visual experience by peculiar, non-standard causal processes. Perhaps, as has been proposed by Grice[10] and others, seeing requires the standard causal process. That would explain why Examples 3, 4, and 5 do not qualify as cases of seeing.

(The proposal faces a technical dilemma. If the standard process is defined as the process in which light is reflected or emitted, etc. (as above), then it seems to follow that few of us now (and none in the not-too-distant past) know enough to have the concept of seeing; whereas if the standard process is defined as the most common process by which the scene before the eyes causes matching visual experience, whatever that may be, then it seems to follow that any of our examples of veridical hallucination might have been a case of seeing, and what I am doing now might not have been, if only the frequencies had been a bit different. Either conclusion would be absurd. However, the dilemma can be avoided by appeal to the recent idea of fixing reference by rigidified descriptions.)[11]

Unfortunately, requiring the standard process would disqualify good cases along with the bad. Some cases in which the scene before the eyes causes matching visual experience by a non-standard process seem fairly clearly to be cases of genuine seeing, not veridical hallucination.

Example 6: The Minority. It might be found that a few of us have visual systems that work on different principles from other people's. The differences might be as extreme as the difference between AM versus FM transmission of signals; analogue versus digital processing; or point-by-point measurement of light versus edge detection. If so, would we be prepared to say that the minority don't really see? Would those who belong to the minority be prepared to say it? Surely not.

I anticipate the reply that the abnormal process in the minority is not different enough; the boundaries of the standard process should be drawn widely enough to include it. But I think this puts the cart before the horse. We know which processes to include just because somehow we already know which processes are ones by which someone might see.

Example 7: The Prosthetic Eye.   A prosthetic eye consists of a miniature television camera mounted in, or on, the front of the head; a computer; and an array of electrodes in the brain. The computer receives input from the camera and sends signals to the electrodes in such a way as to produce visual experience that matches the scene before the eyes. When prosthetic eyes are perfected, the blind will see. The standard process will be absent, unless by "standard process" we just mean one that permits seeing; but they will see by a non-standard process.

Some prosthetic eyes are more convincing than others as means for genuine seeing. (1) It seems better if the computer is surgically implanted rather than carried in a knapsack, but better if it's carried in a knapsack rather than stationary and linked by radio to the camera and electrodes. (2) It seems better if the prosthetic eye contains no parts which can be regarded as having wills of their own and cooperating because they want to. (3) It seems better if the prosthetic eye works in some uniform way, rather than dealing with different sorts of inputs by significantly different means. (4) It seems better if it does not use processes which also figure in the standard processes by which we sometimes hallucinate. But if these considerations influence us, presumably it is because they make the prosthetic eye seem a little more like the natural eye. (Or so we think—but we just might be wrong about the natural eye, and these properties of a prosthetic eye just might detract from the resemblance.) Why should that matter, once we grant that the standard process is not required? I see no real need for any limits on how a prosthetic eye might work. Even the least convincing cases of prosthetic vision are quite convincing enough.

If you insist that "strictly speaking" prosthetic vision isn't really seeing, then I'm prepared to concede you this much. Often we do leave semantic questions unsettled when we have no practical need to settle them. Perhaps this is such a case, and you are resolving a genuine indeterminacy in the way you prefer. But if you are within your rights, so, I insist, am I. I do not really think my favoured usage is at all idiosyncratic. But it scarcely matters: I would like to understand it whether it is idiosyncratic or not.

VI

The trouble with veridical hallucination is not that it involves a non-standard causal process. Is it perhaps this: that the process involved produces matching visual experience only seldom, perhaps only this once?

No; someone might go on having veridical hallucinations for a long time. Veridical hallucinations are improbable, and a long run of them is still more improbable, but that doesn't make it impossible. No matter how long they go on, the sorts of occurrences I've classified as cases of veridical hallucination still are that and not seeing.

On the other hand, a process that permits genuine seeing might work only seldom, perhaps only this once.

Example 8: The Deathbed Cure. God might cure a blind man on his deathbed, granting him an instant of sight by means of some suitable non-standard process. For an instant he sees exactly as others do. Then he is dead. The scene before his eyes produces matching visual experience by a suitable process, but only this once.

Example 9: The Loose Wire. A prosthetic eye has a loose wire. Mostly it flops around; and when it does the eye malfunctions and the subject's visual experience consists of splotches unrelated to the scene before the eyes. But sometimes it touches the contact it ought to be bonded to; and as long as it does, the eye functions perfectly and the subject sees. Whether he sees has nothing to do with whether the wire touches the contact often, or seldom, or only this once.

The proposal isn't far wrong. It asks almost the right question: when the scene before the eyes causes matching visual experience this time, is that an isolated case or is it part of a range of such cases? The mistake is in asking for a range of actual cases, spread out in time. Rather, we need a range of counterfactual alternatives to the case under consideration.

VII

What distinguishes our cases of veridical hallucination from genuine seeing—natural or prosthetic, lasting or momentary—is that there is no proper counterfactual dependence of visual experience on the scene before the eyes. If the scene had been different, it would not have caused correspondingly different visual experience to match that different scene. Any match that occurs is a lucky accident. It depends on the scene being just right. In genuine seeing, the fact of match is independent of the scene. Just as the actual scene causes matching visual experience, so likewise would alternative scenes. Different scenes would have produced different visual experience, and thus the subject is in a position to discriminate between the alternatives.

This is my proposal: if the scene before the eyes causes matching visual experience as part of a suitable pattern of counterfactual dependence, then the subject sees; if the scene before the eyes causes matching visual experience without a suitable pattern of counterfactual dependence, then the subject does not see.

An ideal pattern of dependence would be one such that any scene whatever would produce perfectly matching visual experience. But that is too much to require. Certainly one can see even if the match, actual and counterfactual, is close but imperfect and the content of visual experience is mostly, but not entirely, correct. Perhaps indeed this is our common lot. Further, one can see even if there are some alternative scenes that would fail altogether to produce matching visual experience, so long as the actual scene is not one of those ones.

Example 10: The Laser Beam.   I see now; but if the scene before my eyes had included a powerful laser beam straight into my eyes, I would have been instantly struck blind and would not have had matching visual experience even for a moment.

Example 11: The Hypnotic Suggestion.   I must do business with Martians and I can't stand the sight of them. The remedy is hypnotic suggestion: when a Martian is before my eyes I will seem to see not a Martian but a nice black cat. Thus when there are Martians around, the scene before my eyes causes visual experience that does not match the scene very closely. But when there are no Martians, I see perfectly well.[12]

We cannot require that any two different scenes would produce different visual experience; for they might differ in some invisible respect, in which case the same visual experience would match both equally well. Its content would concern only those aspects of the scene in which both are alike. For one who sees, *visibly* different scenes would (for the most part) produce different visual experience; but that is unhelpful unless we say which differences are the visible ones, and that seems to be an empirical matter rather than part of the analysis of seeing. What can be required analytically is that there be plenty of visible differences of some sort or other; that is, plenty of different alternative scenes that would produce different visual experience and thus be visually discriminable.

That would almost follow from a requirement of match over a wide range of alternative scenes. But not quite. Most of our visual experience is rich in content; but some is poor in content and would match a wide range of alternative scenes equally well. Any pitch-dark scene would produce matching visual experience—what content there is would be entirely correct—but it would be the same in every case. Seeing is a capacity to discriminate, so this sort of match over a wide range of alternatives will not suffice.

I conclude that the required pattern of counterfactual dependence may be specified as follows. There is a large class of alternative possible scenes before the subject's eyes, and there are many mutually exclusive and jointly exhaustive subclasses thereof, such that (1) any scene in the large class would cause visual experience closely matching that scene, and (2) any two scenes in different subclasses would cause different visual experience.

The requirement admits of degree in three ways. How large a class? How many subclasses? How close a match? The difference between veridical hallucination and genuine seeing is not sharp, on my analysis. It is fuzzy; when the requirement of suitable counterfactual dependence is met to some degree, but to a degree that falls short of the standard set by normal seeing, we may expect borderline cases. And indeed it is easy to imagine cases of partial blindness, or of rudimentary prosthetic vision, in which the counterfactual dependence is unsatisfactory and it is therefore doubtful whether the subject may be said to see.

VIII

A further condition might also be imposed: that in the actual case the subject's visual experience must be rich in content, that it must not be the sort of visual experience that would match a wide range of scenes equally well. For instance, it must not be the sort of visual experience that we have when it is pitch dark. This condition of rich content is needed to explain why we do not see in the dark, even though the scene before the eyes causes matching visual experience as part of a suitable pattern of counterfactual dependence.

But we are of two minds on the matter. We think we do not see in the dark; but also we think we find things out by sight only when we see; and in the pitch dark, we find out by sight that it is dark. How else—by smell? By the very fact that we do not see?—No, for we also do not see in dazzling light or thick fog, and it is by sight that we distinguish various situations in which we do not see.

In a sense, we do see in the dark when we see that it is dark. In a more common sense, we never see in the dark. There is an ambiguity in our concept of seeing, and the condition of rich content is often but not always required. When it is, it admits of degree and thus permits still another sort of borderline case of seeing.

IX

Given a suitable pattern of counterfactual dependence of visual experience on the scene before the eyes (including both the actual case and its counterfactual alternatives) it is redundant to say as I did that the scene causes, or would cause, the visual experience. To make the explicit mention of causation redundant, according to my counterfactual analysis of causation, we need not only a suitable battery of scene-to-visual-experience counterfactuals but also some further counterfactuals. Along with each counterfactual saying that if the scene were S the visual experience would be E, we need another saying that if the scene S were entirely absent, the visual experience would not be E. Counterfactuals of the latter sort may follow from the battery of scene-to-visual-experience counterfactuals in some cases, but they do not do so generally. According to the counterfactual analysis of causation that I have defended elsewhere,[13] any such counterfactual dependence among distinct occurrences is causal dependence, and implies causation of the dependent occurrences by those on which they depend. It would suffice if our counterfactuals said just that if the scene before the eyes were so-and-so, then the visual experience would be such-and-such.

If we leave the causation implicit, however, then we must take care that the counterfactuals from scene to visual experience are of the proper sort to comprise a causal dependence. We must avoid back-trackers: those counterfactuals that we would support by arguing that different effects would have to have been produced by different causes.[14] Backtracking counterfactual dependence does not imply causal dependence and does not suffice for seeing.

Example 12: The Screen.   I am hallucinating at random. My hallucinations at any moment are determined by my precursor brain states a few seconds before. My brain states are monitored, and my hallucinations are predicted by a fast computer. It controls a battery of lights focused on a screen before my eyes in such a way that the scene before my eyes is made to match my predicted visual experience at the time. It is true in a sense—in the backtracking sense—that whatever might be on the screen, my visual experience would match it. But my visual experience does not depend causally on the scene before my eyes. Rather, they are independent effects of a common cause, namely my precursor brain states. Therefore I do not see.

The same example shows that it would not suffice just to require that the laws of nature and the prevailing conditions imply a suitable correspondence between visual experience and the scene before the eyes. That could be so without the proper sort of counterfactual, and hence causal, dependence; in which case one would not see.

X

The following case (example 11 carried to extremes) is a hard one. It closely resembles cases of genuine seeing, and we might well be tempted to classify it as such. According to my analysis, however, it is a case of veridical hallucination. The scene before the eyes causes matching visual experience without any pattern of counterfactual dependence whatever, suitable or otherwise.

Example 13: The Censor.   My natural or prosthetic eye is in perfect condition and functioning normally, and by means of it the scene before my eyes causes matching visual experience. But if the scene were any different my visual experience would be just the same. For there is a censor standing by, ready to see to it that I have precisely that visual experience and no other, whatever the scene may be. (Perhaps the censor is external, perhaps it is something in my own brain.) So long as the scene is such as to cause the right experience, the censor does nothing. But if the scene were any different, the censor would intervene and cause the same experience by other means. If so, my eye would not function normally and the scene before my eyes would not cause matching visual experience.

The case is one of causal preemption.[15] The scene before my eyes is the actual cause of my visual experience: the censor is an alternative potential cause of the same effect. The actual cause preempts the potential cause, stopping the alternative causal chain that would otherwise have gone to completion.

The argument for classifying the case as seeing is that it is just like a clear case of seeing except for the presence of the censor; and, after all, the censor doesn't actually do anything; and if the scene before the eyes were different and the censor nevertheless stood idly by—as in actuality—then the different scene would indeed cause suitably different visual experience.

My reply is that the case is really not so very much like the clear case of seeing to which it is compared. The censor's idleness is an essential factor in the causal process by which matching visual experience is produced, just as the censor's intervention would be in the alternative process. No such factor is present in the comparison case. If the scene were different this factor would not be there, so it is wrong to hold it fixed in asking what would happen if the scene were different. We cannot uniformly ignore or hold fixed those causal factors which are absences of interventions. The standard process might be riddled with them. (Think of a circuit built up from exclusive-or-gates: every output signal from such a gate is caused partly by the absence of a second input signal.) Who knows what would happen in an ordinary case of natural (or prosthetic) vision if the scene were different and all absences of interventions were held fixed? Who cares? We do not in general hold fixed the absences of intervention, and I see no good reason to give the censor's idleness special treatment.

The decisive consideration, despite the misleading resemblance of this case to genuine cases of seeing, is that the censor's potential victim has no capacity at all to discriminate by sight. Just as in any other case of veridical hallucination, the match that occurs is a lucky accident.[16]

Postscript to "Veridical Hallucination and Prosthetic Vision"

Further Considerations on "Suitability"

As I noted, it is in several ways a matter of degree whether my condition for "a suitable pattern of counterfactual dependence" is satisfied. That leaves room for borderline cases of seeing. Among these borderline cases, some may be better than others. I think there are further considerations that never—or hardly ever—make the difference between a clear negative case and a clear positive, but that do influence our judgments that one unclear case is more of a case of seeing than another. The general principle is simple: we know what happens in the ideal or normal case, and differences from that tend to detract from the claim of other cases to be judged positive.

It is in this way, if at all, that considerations of mechanism are relevant. I do not think they are ever decisive, or close to decisive, by themselves. But they may tend to incline us one way or another in otherwise doubtful cases.

A second consideration that might have some weight, but I think much less than decisive weight, comes if we have a probabilistic kind of causal dependence. Suppose that what we have are not counterfactuals saying that if there were such-and-such scene then there would definitely be such-and-such matching experience; but rather that there would be a chance distribution over experiences giving significant probability (and much more than there would have been without the scene) to matching experience. Other things being equal, the better the chances of matching experience, the better case of seeing. Here I have in mind the actual chance given the actual scene, as well as the chances there would be given other scenes. *Ex hypothesi* the actual experience does match the actual scene. And that is enough, if I am right that a counterfactual with a true antecedent is true iff its consequent is, to give us a non-probabilistic counterfactual for that one, actual scene: if there were that scene, there would be that matching experience. But there will be a probabilistic counterfactual as well: if there were that scene, there would be so-and-so chance of that matching experience, and maybe also some chance of various other experiences. If the actual chance of match is substantially below one, then despite the non-probabilistic counterfactual, we have a consideration that detracts somewhat from the claim of the case to be judged positive.

John Bigelow has suggested (in discussion, 1980) a third consideration: call it the *Island Effect*. There are good scenes that would produce matching experience, and bad scenes that would not. An ideal pattern would have no bad scenes, but that is too much to demand; so I settled for the requirement that there be a wide range of good scenes. Note that scenes may be close together or far apart; they may differ from one another more or less. So a good scene might be surrounded by other good scenes, with no bad ones nearby. The nearest bad scene to it might differ quite substantially. Or at the opposite extreme it might be a tiny island, surrounded by a sea of bad scenes. Suppose the actual good scene is such an island. My requirement that there be a wide range of good scenes may be satisfied only in virtue of some distant continent. (Or in virtue of many other islands, widely scattered.) It's a narrow escape: the subject sees, on my analysis, but had the scene been just a little different then he wouldn't have done. For any scene just a little different would have been a bad scene. To make matters still worse, Bigelow considers the case that any nearby scene not only would have been bad, but also would have produced just the same experience that the actual good scene produces. Within limits—the distance to the next land—a different scene would have made no difference to visual experience. Then does the subject see?

One might go so far as to think that extreme cases of the Island Effect are clear cases of not seeing, even if there is nothing else wrong with them. I disagree; but I certainly think that the Island Effect influences comparative judgements about unclear cases, even that it suffices to turn what would otherwise be clearly positive cases into doubtful ones.

I said that these secondary considerations would never turn a clear positive into a clear negative—or hardly ever. What if all three of the secondary considerations were present to an extreme degree, working together? What if there is an abnormal mechanism; and in addition the chance of matching experience given the actual scene is quite low, though as it happens there is matching experience; and in addition the actual scene is a tiny island, and my requirement of counterfactual dependence through a wide range of scenes is satisfied only by means of scenes quite different from the actual one? How would we judge that case? It satisfies my main conditions; but the secondary considerations go against it as powerfully as can be.

I know how I *did* judge such a case: I judged it negative. And so perhaps did you, if you read my paper before reading this postscript. For it is none other than my example of the wizard. I thought it a clear negative case, and cited it in my favor, without ever noticing that my own conditions classified it as positive![17] For the actual scene with the hallucinogenic wizard *does* cause matching experience;[18] and we *do* have a wide range of alternative scenes—namely, ordinary scenes without the wizard—that would cause matching experience in a normal way. (Compare scenes without Martians in my example of the hypnotic suggestion.)

So the secondary considerations *can* have decisive weight, if they all push together as hard as they can. Nothing less would do, I think. I would not judge the example of the wizard negative if the spell left the normal mechanism in operation but increased its rate of random errors and thus drastically lowered its probability of success; or if the wizard's presence produced matching experience for that particular scene with high probability, though not by the standard mechanism; or if the scene with the wizard were in the midst of other scenes that would somehow, with significant probability, also produce matching experience.

Bruce LeCatt[19] has suggested a consideration that tends in the positive direction: *Stepwise Dependence.* Take some intermediate stage in the causal process that leads from scene to visual experience. It may be that there is a good pattern of counterfactual dependence whereby what goes on at the intermediate stage depends on the scene; and also a good pattern of counterfactual dependence whereby visual experience depends on what goes on at the intermediate stage. Further, this two-fold pattern might link scenes indirectly with matching experience, over a suitably wide and varied range of scenes. Even more indirectly, there might be linkage via a threefold pattern of counterfactual dependence involving two intermediate stages; and so on. Then we have a suitable pattern of stepwise counterfactual dependence of visual experience on the scene before the eyes. It does not follow that we have a suitable pattern of counterfactual dependence *simpliciter*, because counterfactuals are not necessarily transitive.[20] In fact my case of the censor is a case of excellent stepwise dependence and no dependence *simpliciter* at all. LeCatt suggests, and I agree, that it is the stepwise dependence that accounts for any inclinations we have to judge the case of the censor as a positive case of seeing. He further claims that this judgment is correct; but there I do not agree, and I insist that the essential feature of seeing is altogether missing.

But there are mixed cases: partial or conditional censorship, some dependence *simpliciter* but not much compared with normal cases. Then indeed the presence of stepwise dependence might make the difference between better cases and worse.

Notes

1. I shall have more to say about this dependence in what follows. So although my concern here is with the analysis of seeing in terms of visual experience, what I say would also figure in a prior analysis of visual experience in terms of its definitive causal role.

2. The problem of the suspicious subject is raised in Frank Jackson, *Perception: A Representative Theory* (Cambridge: Cambridge University Press, 1977), pp. 37–42.

3. "Attitudes *De Dicto* and *De Se*," *The Philosophical Review*, LXXXVIII (1979), pp. 513–543.

4. Jaakko Hintikka, "On the Logic of Perception," in his *Models for Modalities: Selected Essays* (Dordrecht: Reidel, 1969). The proposed modification solves (by theft rather than toil) a problem for Hintikka's important idea of perceptual cross-identification: where do we get the cross-identification of the perceiving subject himself, in relation to whom we perceptually cross-identify the things that surround him?

5. As in cases of "blind sight" in which the subject claims to have no visual experience and yet acquires information about the scene before his eyes just as if he did.

6. See my "Mad Pain and Martian Pain," in Ned Block, ed., *Readings in the Philosophy of Psychology* Vol. 1 (Cambridge, Massachusetts: Harvard University Press, 1980).

7. Alvin Goldman considers transitive seeing in his "Discrimination and Perceptual Knowledge," *Journal of Philosophy*, LXXIII (1976), pp. 771—791. Despite the difference of analysandum, I have followed his treatment to a considerable extent.

8. Example 1 and an auditory version of Example 2 are due to P. F. Strawson, "Causation in Perception," in his *Freedom and Resentment and other essays* (London: Methuen, 1974), pp. 77–78.

9. However, it seems that some past things are part of the scene now before my eyes: distant stars as they were long ago, to take an extreme case. It would be circular to say that they, unlike the past scene in example 2, are visible now. Perhaps the best answer is that the stars, as I now see them, are not straighforwardly past; for lightlike connection has as good a claim as simultaneity-in-my-rest-frame to be the legitimate heir to our defunct concept of absolute simultaneity. (I owe the problem to D. M. Armstrong and the answer to Eric Melum.)

10. H. P. Grice, "The Causal Theory of Perception," *Proceedings of the Aristotelian Society*, Supplementary Volume XXXV (1961), pp. 121–152.

11. See the discussion of the metre and the metre bar in Saul A. Kripke, "Naming and Necessity," in Donald Davidson and Gilbert Harman, *Semantics of Natural Language* (Dordrecht: Reidel, 1972), pp. 274–275 and 288–289.

12. Adapted from an olfactory example in Robert A. Heinlein, *Double Star* (Garden City, New York: Doubleday, 1956), Ch. 3.

13. "Causation," *Journal of Philosophy*, LXX (1973), pp. 556–567.

14. This is circular in the context of a counterfactual analysis of causation; but in "Counterfactual Dependence and Time's Arrow," *Noûs*, XIII (1979), pp. 455–476, I have proposed a way to distinguish backtrackers without the circular reference to causation, at least under determinism.

15. See my discussion of preemption in "Causation" (publication information in note 13).

16. I am grateful to seminar audiences at the University of Auckland, Victoria University of Wellington, the University of Sydney, and Monash University for valuable comments on earlier versions of this paper; and to the New Zealand-United States Educational Foundation and Monash University for making those seminars possible.

17. My mistake was pointed out to me by Cliff Landesman in 1984.

18. You might wonder whether the presence of the spell-casting wizard really *causes* the matching experience, when the probability of matching experience would have been much better without him. Yes, the probability that there would somehow have been a match would have been much better. But the probability of *this* experience would have been much lower; and that is what makes it so that the scene causes this experience, an experience which is in fact matching. Do not say: the scene causes the experience *qua* experience of such-and-such, but not *qua* matching; no such distinction is part of our concept of causation. I take it that causation relative to descriptions is a philosophers' invention, motivated by a misguided deductive-nomological analysis of causation.

19. "Censored Vision," *Australasian Journal of Philosophy* 60 (1982): 158–162.

20. See "Counterfactuals and Comparative Possibility," *Journal of Philosophical Logic*, 2 (1973), pp. 418–446, and "Causation" (publication information in note 13).

9

Perception, Vision and Causation

Paul Snowdon

It is believed by some that reflection on many of our psychological notions reveals that they can be instantiated by an object only if some sort of causal condition is fulfilled. Notions to which it has been supposed this applies include those of remembering, knowing, acting for a reason and perception.[1] I wish here to discuss the application of such a view to this last case, an application which is, I think, often believed to be more or less obviously correct, or at least to be as obviously correct as it ever is.[2] Although the present discussion is primarily of causal theories of perception (or more accurately, of one case of perception, namely vision), some elements in it may be relevant to the assessment, or understanding, of causal theories for some other psychological notions. The reason this may be so is that the principal argument used to support a causal theory of perception of this sort exhibits a similar form to arguments used to support some causal theories elsewhere and involved in any consideration of how strongly causal theories of perception are supported is the task of getting clear about the force of arguments with that structure.

I

I want to begin by characterising the causalist viewpoint—a viewpoint first propounded by Grice, and endorsed and added to in an impressive tradition, containing Strawson, Pears, and Peacocke (and, of course, many others).[3] In contrast to this assenting tradition, there has also been a dissenting one, but the points raised in it have seemed to most people not strong enough to threaten the causal theory.[4]

The view is defined by three claims. I shall specify them for the visual case, rather than for the more general case of perception itself.

The first claim is this: it is necessarily true that if a subject (S) sees a public object (O) then O causally affects S. I shall call this the causal thesis. Different theorists may (and do) disagree about how to explain the required relation of causal dependence and may (and do) differ about quite what sort of objects the claim should be formulated for. I want to ignore these variations.

The causal claim says nothing about what effect O must have on S. The second claim fills that gap and asserts: (II) O must produce in S a state reportable in a sentence beginning "It looks to S as if . . . ," where those words are interpreted both phenomenologically (rather than as ascribing, say, a tentative judgement by S) and, in Quine's terms, notionally rather relationally. I shall call this the effect thesis, and refer to the alleged effects as looks-states (or L-states).

The third thesis amounts to a comment on the status of the other two. It says (III) theses (I) and (II) represent requirements of our ordinary concept, or notion, of vision. It is thus asserting, notably, that the causal thesis is, in some sense, a conceptual truth. I shall call this the conceptual thesis.[5]

It is, of course, very hard to say precisely what the conceptual thesis is claiming, but it seems reasonable to suggest that part of what is involved in a truth's being a conceptual one is that it is supportable (but not necessarily only supportable) in a distinctive way. And at least part of what is distinctive about the way is that there is a restriction on the data to which appeal can be made in the supporting argument. A somewhat rough way of specifying the restriction is that the data must be relatively immediately acknowledgable by any person, whatever their education, who can count as having the concept in question. The aim of the restriction is to exclude any facts of which we can become aware only in the context of certain activities (for example, carrying out experiments, or becoming acquainted with the results of experiments, or reading psychological textbooks) which need not be indulged in by just anyone who has the concept. It has to be asked, therefore, whether any good argument satisfying this constraint exists for the causal thesis.

Now, that the causal thesis is true is something which most educated people would accept, and it is fair to suppose that its truth is a matter of relatively common knowledge. In this it resembles, say, the claim that the earth goes round the sun, or the claim that there has been evolution. It should, though, be clear that its having this status is no ground for accepting that the conceptual thesis is correct. For it is obvious that, despite there being widespread acquaintance with the conclusion, the fundamental justification of the causal thesis may rely on data outside the restricted class.

Theses I to III constitute the theory the support and correctness of which I wish to assess, but, of course, there is another claim, which anyone subscribing to this position would accept. It is that it is not sufficient for a subject to see an item that the item relate to the subject in accordance with the requirements of the first two theses. The problem then is to isolate the further conditions which will rule out deviant ways in which an object can fulfil the earlier two. Contributions to the assenting tradition, as I have called it, are mainly attempts to refute earlier purported solutions, combined with suggestions as to better ones.

The theory which has been specified is a causal theory of vision. There are, of course, structurally parallel theories about the other actual senses, but there is also a parallel thesis about perception itself, which is, probably, the one which is most often explicitly endorsed. There is, though, a reason for concentrating on the more specific visual claim, namely that it is possible thereby to avoid discussing a lacuna in the standard argument for the more general thesis. Thus the usual (although not invariable) procedure is to provide an argument for (say) the visual thesis, but to draw as a further immediate consequence the general thesis about perception. However, the more specific claim does not entail the general conclusion and something needs to be said in support of the move.

II

The main argument for the described position which was originally propounded by H. P. Grice, I shall consider in the next section. But before taking that up, there are some recent remarks of Professor *Strawson* which are, I think, aimed at providing support for the causal and conceptual thesis (at least, I shall interpret them that way) and on which I wish very briefly to comment.

Strawson says this:

The idea of the presence of the thing as accounting for, or being responsible for, our perceptual awareness of it is implicit in the pre-theoretical scheme from the very start. For we think of perception as a way ... of informing ourselves about the world of independently existing things: we assume, that is to say, the general reliability of our perceptual experiences; and that assumption is the same as the assumption of a general causal dependence of our perceptual experiences on the independently existing things we take them to be of. The thought of my fleeting perception as a perception of a continuously and independently existing thing implicitly contains the thought that if the thing had not been there, I should not even have seemed to perceive it. It really should be obvious that with the distinction between independently existing objects and perceptual awareness of objects we already have the general notion of causal dependence of the latter on the former, even if this is not a matter to which we give much reflective attention in our pre-theoretical days.[6]

Now this is a very suggestive but also a very concise passage, in which it seems possible to detect three, no doubt intended to be interlocking, considerations. The first is as follows. Perception (of objects) is thought to be a way of acquiring information about the world. This amounts to (or at least involves) the assumption that experiences which are perceptual are, in general, reliable. This assumption is the same as the belief that if an experience is perceptual of object *O* it is causally dependent on that object.

To assess this we need to explain what the assumption of the reliability of perceptual experience is supposed to be. One plausible way to view it is this: we treat experiences which we take to be perceptual as reliable in the sense that how it seems in these experiences to us to be is, by and large (in general), the way our environment actually is. If that, however, is the correct interpretation then it seems wrong to suppose that the reliability assumption is equivalent to the causal claim. In the first place, the mere assumption that if an experience is perceptual then it is causally dependent on the object it is a perception of, does not have as a consequence that appearances in these cases are even more or less accurate. This point, though, is unimportant, since all that is needed by the line of thought is that the reliability assumption requires the causal one, not that there is an equivalence. There is, however, no logical requirement here, since this sort of reliability could be present, if, say, our perceptions and the states of the world were joint effects of some other cause which produced the match. The reply is possible that it is excessively rigid to interpret "requires" as "entails," but it needs then to be explained what kind of transition between the assumptions is involved. There is, I think, a reason for doubting that any transition of a sufficiently interesting sort can be made here. Thus, we can re-express the reliability assumption (on the present interpretation, and limiting it to vision for convenience) as follows: if our experience is a case of an object *O* looking certain ways to us (that is, is visually perceptual of object *O*) then (by and large) *O* is how *O* looks. In so far as a causal assumption is implicit in this claim it would be that how an object looks is causally dependent on (amongst other things) how the object otherwise is. To unearth this causal assumption, though, is not to unearth a commitment to the causal thesis, for what if anything has been revealed is the assumption that when an object is seen, its being seen a certain way (that is, how it looks) causally depends on the nature of the object, which amounts in no way to the view that what it is for the object to be seen (a certain way) is for it to affect the viewer. An analogy is this: it is one thing to admit that whether *A* is heavier than *B* is, in part, causally determined by (say) *A*'s previous history, another to hold that *A*'s being heavier than *B* is a matter of *A* (or *A*'s previous history) having an effect on *B*.

The second consideration in favour of the theory is the claim that to think of someone as perceiving an object implies that if the item perceived had not been there then the subject would not have even seemed to perceive it. To avoid triviality here we must treat "seem to perceive it" as equivalent to "seem to perceive something of its character." Now, taken that way, it does not seem that this claim is unrestrictedly true. There are two sorts of counter example (which I shall specify for the visual case). The first is where a subject sees an object in an environment which would have appeared the same to him even if that object had not been present in it. For example, a man can see a coin immediately behind which is an identical coin, removal of the front coin would not alter the scene. The second is when a subject sees an object in circumstances which would have given him an hallucination of just such an object if the item had not been present. For example, a man can see a clock the noise from which is the only thing preventing a drug he has already taken from giving him the hallucination of a clock. Suppose, however, that the counterfactual is true. The belief that it implies the causal thesis relies on the assumption that the claim "If *S* sees *O* at *t* then if *O* had not been present things would have seemed a different way to *S*" implies "If *S* sees *O* at *t* then (the presence of) *O* causally accounts for how it seems to *S*," an assumption which would be correct if the consequent of the first of these conditionals (itself a conditional) entailed the consequent of the second (a causal claim). It is unobvious that there is any such entailment, for the first consequent merely records a dependence of one fact on another, and there can, surely, be dependencies where the relation is not causal dependence. (An example would be: if I had not parked on those yellow lines I would not have broken the law.) The causal thesis is not, therefore, an immediate implication of the remark under discussion.

Finally, it is true that we draw a distinction between (say) sighting an object and the object sighted, and that means that for there to be a sighting more must obtain than presence of the object, but it is not obvious that this extra is the object's having an effect on the sighter.

The causal thesis remains, therefore, to be supported, and I want next to determine how good the main argument is.

III

The main argument[7] relies on the acceptance of something implied by (but not implying) the looks-thesis, namely, the claim that if *S* sees *O* then *S* is in an L-state. This is, surely, highly plausible, and not something I wish to question.[8] The argument also assumes that if *S* sees *O* then *O* exists. (Rather than calling that an assumption we might say—the theory just deals with sightings of actual objects.)

The argument itself (sometimes expressed with extreme brevity) has three stages. The first consists in the presentation of certain interesting possible cases of visual experience. The second consists in judging of these that they are cases where certain, what we might call, candidate objects involved are not seen. The third stage is simply an inference to the correctness of the causal thesis.

Now, the following are examples of the sort which are given. (a) Lady Macbeth has the hallucination that there is blood on her hands, there in fact being none. Her nurse then smears on some blood. (b) A man is facing a pillar of a certain character and it looks to him as if there is in front of him an object of that character. However between him and the pillar is a mirror in which is reflected another pillar. (c) A man is facing a clock, it looks to him as if there is a clock, but his experience is the result of a scientist's direct simulation of his cortex in a way which would have yielded experience of that character even if there had been no clock.

The intention is to specify possible cases fulfilling three conditions. First, the two basic necessary requirements for an object-sighting are met. Second, they are cases where there is no sighting of the "candidate" object. Third, there is an absence of any sort of causal dependence of the looks-state on that object.

Now, it is dubious that the descriptions of the cases necessitate the fulfilment of the last two features. For example, to consider the second requirement and case (a), it may be that smearing blood on Lady Macbeth stops the hallucination and enables her to see the blood. Again, considering the third requirement, and (b), it may be that the pillar behind the mirror is depressing a light-switch which controls the illumination of the reflected pillar. However, it seems clear that there are possible cases matching the descriptions and fulfilling these features, and it is very natural to interpret the description of the examples as introducing cases of this sort. When taken this way, I shall call them *U*-cases ("*U*" for unseen).

If, then, we allow such cases are possible, we must agree that it is not enough for a subject to see an object that the object be present and it looks as if there is an object of that character present. That much is established, but it is not conclusively established that the causal thesis is correct. All we have is the claim that there are possible cases where (i) S is in an L-state appropriate to seeing O, (ii) O is in his environment, (iii) the L-state is not causally dependent on O; and (iv) O is not seen. That such cases are possible does not entail that there are no cases where S and O are so related as to fulfil (i) to (iii) but in which O is seen by S.

If there is no entailment, how should we think of the move from accepting that in the described cases the object is not seen to accepting the causal thesis? We should, I want to propose, view it as a suggested inference to the best explanation. The issue raised is: why, in U-cases, are the mentioned objects not sighted? The causal theorist is suggesting that they are not sightings because of the lack of causal connexion. It is a plausible suggestion because the absence of such a causal connexion is a prominent element in the cases, and there is no other obvious explanation.

A question that arises at this point is where this interpretation leaves the conceptual thesis. Plainly, if the argument given is to be, not only a good reason for accepting the causal thesis, but, as well, a reason of a sort which licenses the conceptual thesis as a gloss on the status of its conclusion, then, in line with the elucidation of that gloss proposed earlier, the "data" it relies on should be acknowledgable by (more or less) anyone who has mastered the concept (of vision). The data in our case consists of the supposed facts reported in the judgements about the specified examples to the effect that they are not cases of (appropriate) vision. Now, it seems that these facts are of the right sort, for they are ones which are recognised by people who have no specialist information about vision at all. Hence, if the argument is a good one the conceptual thesis is warranted.

Now treating the argument in the way suggested leaves the causal thesis with the status of an attractive explanatory hypothesis. It would seem incautious, though, to be confident of its correctness without giving some consideration to other hypotheses, of which we can, I think envisage two sorts. The first sort of alternative which we might call non-radical, stays fairly close to the causal theory in structure, in that it allows that it makes sense to regard the looks-state as something causally produced by the seen object, but it claims that, nonetheless, we can best explain why the U-cases are not cases of vision by adding to our theory of vision an extra condition (or set of conditions) which requires less than the full causal connexion proposed by the causalist.

There is no argument demonstrating that this strategy is in principle wrong, but it is hard to see how it can work. If different U-cases are explained by different features, then (i) a sense, which it is hard to resist, that there is a unified explanation is not satisfied, and (ii) there will be a suspicion that either the various features do not cover all *U*-cases or they do but at the cost of turning out to be equivalent to the causalist's explanation. If, in contrast, there is a single, non-causal but non-radical, explanation, what is it? The reason I do not wish to pursue this idea further is really that there is what I call a radical alternative which has the advantage that it can, at least, be specified and developed.

IV

To introduce the radical idea, in the form in which I shall develop it, consider this line of thought which bears some formal resemblance to the main argument. Its aim is to support a theory of what it is for A to be married to B. We agree, surely, that if A is married to B then A is a spouse. But it is clear that A could be a spouse and B also be around when A became a spouse without A being married to B. For example, suppose that when A became a spouse the ceremony at which it happened was one to which B's presence was completely irrelevant. It would have gone ahead exactly as it did whether B had been there or not. However, this case suggests something else that is needed: not only must A be a spouse, with B around when A became a spouse, but B's presence must have been causally relevant to A's becoming a spouse. Of course, this is still not sufficient, since the residing clergyman (or what have you) also fulfils this condition. So we might consider adding that for A to be married to B is for B to be causally relevant to A's being a spouse in the way in which . . . etc.

There is, of course, the analogue of the non-radical reply even here; "it is rather strong to require causal dependence, let us, instead, rule out certain ways for B to be involved."

Plainly both the argument and this reply lack plausibility. But why? A shot at explaining why this theory moves in the wrong direction, an explanation having two stages, is as follows: (i) the best theory we could offer of what it is to be a spouse is simply that it is to be married to someone or other; (ii) so, replacing in the original theory the notion of being a spouse by its explanation, we see that the original is trying to add conditions to the requirement that A be married to someone, which guarantee that A is married to B. But this is absurd, in that if we could explain what must apply to someone in order to be married to A, all we need to do to explain what it is for B to be married to A is to say that the someone to whom those conditions apply is B. Now, the more radical non-causalist response to the main argument is to allege that to draw a causal conclusion on its basis is similarly absurd.

We have, so far, then, an analogy and a general suggestion, and what is needed is a specific proposal to carry out the general suggestion. Pursuing the analogy, what is needed is a suggested theory about the supposed effect-end in the causal theory which renders its treatment in the causal theory, as the effect, absurd.

Such a suggestion can be extracted from J. M. Hinton's article (*Mind*, 1967) "Visual Experience." Hinton's idea is that the best theory for the state of affairs reported by "I seem to see a flash of light" (or "I seem to see an *F*") is that it is a case of either my seeing a flash of light or my having the illusion of a flash of light (or my seeing an *F* or my having the illusion of an *F*). The claim, then, is that the best theory of seeming to see is disjunctive. For our purposes, the suggestion becomes that a theory of the same structure and content applies to the state of affairs reported by "It looks to *S* as if there is . . .

But this suggestion as it stands is mistaken, for far from being the best theory, the explaining disjunction is not even coextensive with the state it is offered as explaining. There are at least two sorts of counter examples. (i) The disjunction is true if *S* sees an *F*. But *S* might see an *F* which does not look like an *F*, in which case it might well not look to *S* as if there is an *F*. For example, *S* might be seeing a rabbit which had been shaved and painted to look like a cat. (ii) It seems we can have illusions which are not visual—e.g. auditory or tactile ones. Consider a kind of thing—say an explosion—which is both sightable and can be felt. Then *S* might be having the illusion of such a thing in virtue of how it feels to him. It would not follow that it looked to him as if there was an explosion. Hinton's example—of a flash of light—masks the second difficulty, in that it is only sensible to treat an illusion of it as visual.

We can avoid these objections by offering the following revised disjunction:

it looks to *S* as if there is an *F*; (there is something which looks to *S* to be *F*) v (it is to *S* as if there is something which looks to him (*S*) to be *F*).

Let us assume that it is correct. Now, if we make this assumption it seems that the visual case does resemble the spouse-example. Thus, we replace the supposed effect, by what it is best explained to be. We are given, that is, that there is some way (*F*) such that either something looks that way to *S* or it is to *S* as if something looked that way. How can we add to this to guarantee that *O* is seen? The answer, surely, is that *O* is seen so long as it is overall a case of something's looking *F* to *S*, rather than its being to *S* as if something looked that way, and *O* is the something that looks that way. But for *O* to be that something is not for *O* to bring about the separate state of affairs of something's looking *F*, it is, evidently, simply for *O* to be the something, i.e. for *O* to look that way.

On the assumption that this theory is correct, we can provide an alternative explanation for the status of the *U*-cases. This explanation relies on the claim that an object is seen only if it looks some way to the subject and on noticing that we are given in the description of the *U*-cases information which makes it likely that the cases are not ones where the specified objects look some way. The information is precisely that what *actually* went on *would have gone on* whether the objects were present or not. But if that is true they could not have been cases in which the objects were looking some way to the subject, since that could not have obtained in the absence of the object.[9]

A comment that it would be natural to make at this stage is that if the discussion so far is tenable, the main argument is rejectable if a disjunctive theory is correct, but little has been said as to quite what a disjunctive theory is claiming, and even less as to precisely what a non-disjunctive account would be. The request in this comment for further elucidation is totally reasonable, but difficult to respond to adequately.

The phrase so far used to explain the disjunctive approach has been that the disjunct gives "the best theory." Something like this is needed because even someone who accepts the picture involved in the casual theory could agree that the claim resulting from a bi-conditional between "it looks to *S* as if . . ." and the disjunction expresses a truth, hence the contrasting (disjunctive) theory cannot be identified as the requirement that such a bi-conditional be true. Further, I see no help, in an account of the dispute, in saying that for the disjunctive theorist the disjunct *"gives the meaning"* of "It looks to *S* as if . . ." whereas for the causalist it does not, since the fairly superficial factors which might make a remark about meaning appropriate in the case of the phrase "is a spouse," are not present in our case. Without these factors, such a remark fails to illuminate what is in dispute.

But we are able to add vividness to the contrast by expressing it this way. The non-disjunctive theorist espouses a picture in which there is in all cases a single sort of state of affairs whose obtaining makes "looks"-ascriptions true. This sort of state of affairs is common to such diverse cases as seeing a cricket ball and having an after-image with one's eyes shut tight. This obtaining of such states is intrinsically independent of the arrayed objects surrounding a subject, but will, so long as it is suitably produced by them, constitute a sighting of them. If it is not suitably caused it is not a sighting.

The disjunctive picture divides what makes looks ascriptions true into two classes. In cases where there is no sighting they are made true by a state of affairs intrinsically independent of surrounding objects; but in cases of sightings the truth-conferring state of affairs involves the surrounding objects.

It is this picture, rather than the claim that the *actual* formula given to express the disjunctive theory adequately does so, which constitutes the core-idea, on the basis of which radical alternative explanation can be given.

V

If the present suggestion is correct, the next question to settle is whether a disjunctive theory is correct. If it is, then the main argument fails and the theory it is supposed to support is incorrect; if it is not, it is still possible that the non-radical rejection of the argument is the right response, but it cannot be said that the structure of the causalist theory is absurd.

It is, of course, impossible to settle this question now, but what I want to do instead is to propose a sketchy line of thought which relies on claims which seem intuitively plausible and which favours the disjunctive approach. In this line of thought an important role is initially played by demonstrative judgements—i.e. those expressible in the words "that is an F."

Let us suppose that the visual scene you are scanning contains only what appears or looks to be a single feint light. If you hold, there and then, that you can actually see a real feint light-bulb, you will also hold of the thing which looks to be a feint light that it (that thing) is a light bulb. You will hold a judgement that you could express to yourself in the words "That is a light bulb." We can put the same point this way: if you are in doubt as to whether the judgement expressed by "that is a light bulb" is correct, then, in these circumstances, you will, also, be in doubt as to whether you are seeing a light bulb.

It is tempting to generalise this by saying: if S holds that he can see an F then he must accept that there is a certain item of which he is correct in demonstratively identifying it as an F. This would be a mistake since the direct tie between the self-ascribed perceptual claim and the demonstrative identification present in the first case derives from its extremely simple character. Thus it is consistent and possible for me to hold in a case where there are three distinct objects apparently seen that

I can see Boycott's bat even though I am not prepared to make of any of them the identification of it as the bat, simply because I do not know which it is. Still, it is evident in this sort of case that if I do not hold a disjunction of identificatory judgements correct, I will not hold that I see the bat.

So far, the tie between demonstratives and judgements about seeing has been presented in terms of a tie between perceptual judgements about yourself that you would make and demonstrative identifications you would make. But surely the tie is more general and, as a first shot, we might express it this way:

(S) (O) (If S sees O and O is an F then there is some object to which S is so related that if he were to demonstratively identify it as an F the judgement would be correct.)

Now, we can add to this, I suggest, a further principle which we are inclined to hold; let us restrict ourselves to the visual case; consider a scene that you can see and the public objects in it; now we can imagine a list of all the true identificatory demonstrative judgements you could have there and then made of the elements in the public scene. The second principle claims that if you encounter such a scene and are not at that time having after-images, a partial hallucination or undergoing any experiences of that sort, then the previously specified set of true identificatory demonstrative judgements contains all the true demonstrative judgements you could there and then have made on the basis of your current *visual* experience. The best support for this is contained in the challenge; try to specify an extra demonstrative judgement.

Holding this in mind, we can return to the contrast between the disjunctive and non-disjunctive theories of looks-states. This time I want to concentrate on the non-disjunctive picture (theory) and to link it with the preceding claims.

The picture of perception it involves can be explained as follows: when we have an after-image (say) there is an L-state produced in a certain way, a way which rules out its being a perception of an object. Further what we are talking about when we speak of the image itself is, as it were, an element in the visual impression (or L-state) in this case. When we see (say) a feint light there is also such a state produced, but this time it is produced by the feint light, which is therefore, not in the same way an element in it. However the sort of element produced in both types of case is the same; that the instance of the sort in the first case is an after-image whereas the instance in the second is not, is due entirely to the difference in how the elements are produced. It seems to be carried by this that the subject is related in the same way in both cases to the elements in the impression (= the effect).

I want now to assume that we can make (true and false) demonstrative-type judgements about what I am calling the elements in the L-state. To recognise that this is plausible (though not, I hope, certain) consider the following case. It looks to you as if there is a feint light before you. You are not, however, sure whether you are seeing a feint light or having an after-image. Now you might pose the question thus: what is that—an after-image or a feint light? In fact you are having an image and you persuade yourself that you are; the question then receives the answer: *that* is an after-image. Prima facie, this is a (true) instance of the kind of demonstrative judgement which I am assuming can be made.

Consider next, a related but different example. S is in fact seeing a feint light. Initially he believes (wrongly) that he is having an after-image. Granting the previous assumption, we can ascribe to him the demonstrative judgement—that is an after-image—supposed true by him of what it is he takes to be the image. However, he subsequently realises he is not having an after-image but rather seeing a feint light; he comes to hold of that that it is a feint light. The problem to be faced is: what relation obtains between his initial, incorrect, demonstrative judgement and his subsequent one?

Now, on the present picture (and given our assumption) there are two possible erroneous judgements the man might have been making at the beginning. Either he judged of what was the feint light that it was an after-image or he judged of an element in the impression (produced in fact by the feint light) that it was an after-image. The latter demonstrative judgement was also of course erroneous. But the new demonstrative judgement as well, on this picture, has two possible interpretations. Either he is judging (correctly) of what is the feint light that it is a feint light; or (incorrectly) of an element in the L-state that it is a feint light. He should, on this picture, be able, however, to make a new and correct demonstrative judgement about the elements in the *L*-state, viz. that it (that) is an element of an L-state produced by a feint light in a certain way. So there are two possible truth-accruing changes S could make in his demonstrative judgements. He could move from "that is an after-image" to "that is a feint light," where his demonstrative picks out the feint light; or he could move from "that is an after-image" to "that is an element in an *L*-state caused in a certain way by a feint light" given that he was identifying an element in the impression. But it seems plain, now, that this is incompatible with the second principle which most of us accept, for it requires the existence of true identificatory judgements outside the class the principle claims are exhaustive. This theory as to what the effect in perception is, allied to our assumption about the permissibility of demonstrative judgements, is committed to the possibility of a "language-game" which cannot be played.

So, to sustain the picture of the effect as a common visual element whose presence constitutes the truth of a looks-claim, it seems we must either (i) modify the assumption that demonstrative judgements are possible of "elements" in "impressions" or (ii) abandon the principle. Two modifications of the first assumption seem possible. The first tries to accommodate the case which made the initial assumption plausible, by claiming (i) where the visual effect is produced in a way that means it is not a case of perception, demonstrative judgements can be made about its elements, but (ii) where it is produced in a perception-making way, demonstrative identifications are not possible in respect of its elements but only in respect of the influencing object. Now, this may be a correct result, but it is impossible, I think, for this picture to explain why it is correct. For, why should ancestry affect identifiability? The second modification is more radical; (i) no elements in the L-state can be demonstratively identified, only objects, so to speak, in the world can be so identified; (ii) a subject who when actually having an after-image thinks he is seeing a feint light and thinks to himself "that is a feint light" really makes no mistaken judgement with those words at all; his mistake is to suppose that he has made a judgement; (iii) a person seeing a light but believing that he is having an after-image may be allowed to make a demonstrative judgement to the effect that that is an after-image, but, of course, it can only be corrected in one way. I leave undecided whether such a view is acceptable.

However, even if it is, a difficulty still remains. For if we cannot demonstratively identify elements in impressions, there are certain psychological attitudes we can have towards the visual states which we are, in some sense, aware of when we have after-images. We can be interested by, concentrate on, be distracted by, scrutinize and attempt to describe them. Now, on the present interpretation of the causal theory with L-states as visual effects it is committed to there being in cases of vision features of this sort (though distinctly brought about). This seems to amount to supposing that in ordinary cases of vision we can have the cited psychological attitudes to features quite distinct from the object which produces them (i.e. the object seen). But, this is not at all obviously true; certainly it is not a supposition we are commonly inclined to make.[10]

VI

There is nothing in the previous discussion which amounts to a disproof of the causalist viewpoint (that is, of the conjunction of theses I to III). If the disjunctive account of looks-states is correct, then thesis II is incorrect, hence the overall position also is. Even if the disjunctive theory is not acceptable, and theses I and II are admissible, the overall position may still be wrong if the refutation of the disjunctive theory involves considerations external to those permitted by the conceptual thesis. (So an assertion of the disjunctive theory is not needed for a rejection of the present causalist view). However, what I hope to have made some sort of case for is not so much a rejection of the causalist viewpoint as non-acceptance of it.

The issue of the proper attitude to the overall position should be sharply distinguished from the issue of the proper attitude to the causal thesis (thesis I). There are, I think, good empirical reasons for believing that to see an object is for it to have, in a certain sort of way, a certain sort of effect. Thus, (i) it seems physically necessary for S to see O that O have an effect on S, and we can either think of the affecting as a de facto necessary condition for another relation's obtaining (viz. seeing) or treat the seeing *as* the affecting. The parsimonious naturalist will incline to the latter. (ii) There are things about us (for example, certain capacities for avoiding, if we want to, or hitting, if we want to, objects) which we hold vision explains; I assume that these capacities can, in fact, also be traced to the ways in which the objects affect us. This seems to support an identity and with it thesis I. If this is correct, the question that emerges is: given thesis I is true, why does it matter that there is no proof of it which licenses its status as a "conceptual" truth? But that, like much else, I propose to leave hanging in the air.

Notes

1. See Martin and Deutscher, "Remembering," *Philosophical Review* (1966), Goldman, "A Causal Theory of Knowing," *Journal of Philosophy* (1967), Davidson, "Actions, Reasons, and Causes," *Journal of Philosophy* (1963) and Grice, "The Causal Theory of Perception," *Aristotelian Society, Supp. Vol. 35* (1961), reprinted in Warnock, *The Philosophy of Perception* (Oxford, 1967). Hereafter, page references to Grice's article will be to the reprint.

2. David Wiggins, for example, talks of "the finality of Grice's argument about perception," "Freedom, Knowledge, Belief and Causality" in G. N. A. Vesey (ed.), *Knowledge and Necessity* (1970), p. 137. P. F. Strawson describes the view as "obvious," Perception and its Objects," in G. F. Macdonald (ed.), *Perception and Identity* (1979), p. 51.

3. See P. F. Strawson, "Causation in Perception" in *Freedom and Resentment* (1974), D. F. Pears, "The Causal Conditions of Perception," *Synthese 33* (1976), and Christopher Peacocke, *Holistic Explanation* (1979).

4. The "dissenting tradition" includes A. R. White, "The Causal Theory of Perception," *Aristotelian Society, Supp. Vol. 35* (1961), Jenny Teichmann, "Perception and Causation," *Proceedings of the Aristotelian Society, LXXI* (1970–1971), Jaegwon Kim, "Perception and Reference without Causality," *Journal of Philosophy* (1977), and (perhaps) Michael Dummett, "Common Sense and Physics," pp. 35–36, in G. F. Macdonald (ed.) *op. cit.*

5. Grice describes himself as "characterising the ordinary notion of perceiving," in Grice *op. cit.* p. 105. Strawson talks of "the general idea" of "causal dependence" being "implicit" in "the concept of perception," in "Causation in Perception," p. 83.

6. Strawson, "Perception and its Objects," p. 51.

7. For expositions see Grice *op. cit.* pp. 103–4, Strawson, "Causation in Perception," p. 83, Wiggins *op. cit.* p. 137.

8. It should be clear that the claim I am here accepting just means; if *S* sees *O* then it is true to say of *S* that it looks to him to be some way. The talk of *L*-states is merely abbreviatory of that. I am not, as will emerge, granting the ontological picture the causalist has in mind when formulating it this way (i.e., in terms of states).

9. It may be objected, "you are still left with an unexplained distinction between an object's looking F to S and it merely being to S as if something looks F to him, and you have not shown that the best account of this is not a causal theory for the former." These remarks are true, but that the alternative explanation to the normal one relies on distinctions for which no explanation is provided does not discredit it as an explanation. How could it avoid this feature? Since it remains a possible explanation, its role in the present argument is not affected. So if the best account of the distinction involves a casual theory of the relational disjunct, another argument than the main one is needed.

10. I intend the argument here as a challenge to supporters of the causal theory to explain where it goes wrong, rather than as a serious attempt to show they have gone wrong. There are three lines of reply available: (i) to agree that in ordinary perception we cannot have the cited attitudes to anything but the perceived objects, but to deny the claim that in (for example) after-imaging there are "elements" we can have the attitudes to; (ii) to agree that we can have such attitudes in cases like after-imagings, but to claim we also have them to "elements" distinct from the perceived objects in perceptual cases; (iii) to agree that there is a prima facie puzzle about what we are able to attend to but to allege that our inability in the ordinary perception case does not show that there is no common visual element shared by it and (say) after-imaging. I have said nothing to block any of these options.

10

How Direct Is Visual Perception?: Some Reflections on Gibson's "Ecological Approach"

Jerry A. Fodor and Zenon W. Pylyshyn

1 Introduction

There is always a scientific Establishment, and what it believes is always more or less untrue. Even in the respectable sciences empirical knowledge is forever undergoing reformulation, and any generation's pet theories are likely to look naive when viewed from the perspective of thirty or forty years on. In psychology, however, reformulation tends to be radical. When the dominant paradigm goes, the whole picture of the mind may shift; and, often enough, the scientific consensus about what constitutes a psychological explanation changes too. At such times, to use a phrase of Gibson's, the "old puzzles disappear"[1] (p. 304), and one may be hard put to understand what on earth one's predecessors thought that they were up to. This has happened so often in the history of psychology that it would surely be unwise to assume that it is not going to happen again; in particular, it would be unwise to assume that it is not going to happen to *us*. Gibson thinks that it has already, and it seems that a substantial minority of the cognitive science community is inclined to agree with him. The purpose of this essay is to examine whether there is anything to that claim. In particular, we will examine the thesis that the postulation of mental processing is unnecessary to account for our perceptual relationship with the world; that if we describe the environment in the appropriate terms we see that visual perception is *direct* and requires only a selection from information present in the ambient light.

The current Establishment theory (sometimes referred to as the "information processing" view) is that perception depends, in several respects presently to be discussed, upon *inferences*. Since inference is a process in which premises are displayed and consequences derived, and since that takes time, it is part and parcel of the information processing view that there is an intrinsic connection between perception and memory. And since, finally, the Establishment holds that the psychological mechanism of inference is the transformation of mental representations, it follows that perception is in relevant respects a computational process.

What makes Gibson's position seem outrageous from the Establishment perspective is that it is presented as an outright denial of every aspect of the computational account, not merely as a reformulation of parts of it. According to Gibson, the right way of describing perception is as the "direct pickup" of "invariant properties." (More precisely, we are taking Gibson to be claiming this: for any object or event x, there is some property P such that the direct pickup of P is necessary and sufficient for the perception of x.) Now, what is "direct" is ipso facto not mediated; in particular, according to Gibson, perception is not mediated by memory, nor by inference, nor by any other psychological processes in which mental representations are deployed. Moreover, Gibson insists upon the radical consequences of his unorthodoxy: "The ecological theory of direct perception ... implies a new theory of cognition in general" (p. 263).

In his last book, which will serve as the basis for our discussion, Gibson elaborates on the views he has arrived at after thirty years of research on perception, and on the bases of his disagreement with the Establishment position. The tone of the book, when it comes to Gibson's relation to received psychological theorizing is pretty intransigent:

The simple assumption that the perception of the world is caused by stimuli from the world will not do. The more sophisticated assumption that perceptions of the world are caused when sensations triggered by stimuli are supplemented by memories will not do ... Not even the current theory that the inputs of the sensory channels are subject to "cognitive processing" will do. The inputs are described in terms of information theory, but the processes are described in terms of old-fashioned mental acts: recognition, interpretation, inference, concepts, ideas and storage and retrieval of ideas. These are still the operations of the mind upon the deliverances of the senses, and there are too many perplexities entailed by this theory. It will not do, and the approach should be abandoned ... What sort of theory, then, will explain perception? Nothing less than one based on the pickup of information ... (p. 238)

The theory of information pickup differs radically from the traditional theories of perception. First, it involves a new notion of perception, not just a new theory of the process. Second, it involves a new assumption about what there is to be perceived. Third, it involves a new concept of the information for perception ... Fourth, it requires the new assumption of perceptual systems with overlapping functions ... Finally, fifth, optical information pickup entails an activity of the system not heretofore imagined by any visual scientist ... (p. 239). Such is the ecological approach to perception. It promises to simplify psychology by making old puzzles disappear. (p. 304)

We will suggest that there is a way of reading Gibson which permits the assimilation of many of his insights into the general framework of Establishment psychological theorizing. Moreover, given this conciliatory reading, much that Gibson says is seen to be both true and important; and it does indeed differ in significant respects from what has generally been assumed by psychologists who accept the information processing framework. But, as should be clear from the preceding quotes, Gibson *does not want* to be read in a conciliatory way. And for good reason: if the program as he presents it were to succeed, it would constitute a conceptual revolution on the grand scale. Many of the deepest problems on cognitive psychology and the philosophy of mind would be bypassed, and the future of research in both disciplines would be dramatically altered. Such a possibility may seem particularly attractive to those who believe that our current understanding of psychological processes has been too much influenced by the achievements of computer technology. And it will appeal, too, to those who feel that the anti-behaviorist revolution in cognitive psychology has gone too far; a sentiment with which Gibson is by no means unsympathetic.

We will argue, however, that Gibson's claim to have achieved, or even to have initiated, such a fundamental reformulation of the theory of mind simply cannot be sustained. The main line of our argument will go like this: Gibson's account of perception is empty *unless* the notions of "direct pickup" and of "invariant" are suitably constrained. For, patently, if *any* property can count as an invariant, and if any psychological process can count as the pickup of an invariant, then the identification of perception with the pickup of invariants excludes nothing. We will show, however, that Gibson has no workable way of imposing the required constraints consonant with his assumption that perception is direct. To put the same point the other way around, our argument will be that the notion of "invariant" and "pickup" can be appropriately constrained only on the assumption that perception is inferentially mediated. This is hardly surprising: Gibson and the Establishment agree that pickup and inference exhaust the psychological processes that could produce perceptual knowledge; hence, the more pickup is constrained, the more there is left for inference to do.

It will turn out, in the case of visual perception, that at least two constraints upon pickup are required. First, nothing can be picked up except a certain restricted class of properties of the ambient light. Second, spatio-temporal bounds on the properties that are picked up are determined by what stimuli turn out to be "effective"; i.e., sufficient to cause perceptual judgements. The consequence of the first restriction is that all visual perception must involve inferences based upon those properties of the light that are directly detected; in particular, all visual perception of features of objects in the environment requires such inferences. The consequence of the second restriction is that visual perception typically involves inference from the properties of the environment that are (to use Gibson's term) "specified" by the sample of the light that one has actually encountered to those properties that would be specified by a more extensive sample. This sort of inference is required because the causally effective stimulus for perception very often underdetermines what is seen. These two kinds of inference are, however, precisely the ones that information processing theories have traditionally assumed must mediate visual perception. We will therefore conclude that Gibson has not offered a coherent alternative to the Establishment view; indeed, that the Establishment view falls out as a consequence of the attempt to appropriately constrain Gibson's basic theoretical apparatus.

2   The Trivialization Problem

The easiest way to see that constraints on the notion of invariant and pickup are required is to notice that, in the absence of such constraints, the claim that perception is direct is *bound* to be true simply because it is empty. Suppose that under certain circumstances people can correctly perceive that some of the things in their environment are of the type P. Since you cannot correctly perceive that something is P unless the thing is P, it will always be trivially true that the things that can be perceived to be P share an invariant property: namely, *being* P. And since, according to Gibson, what people do in perceiving is directly pick up an appropriate invariant, the following pseudoexplanation of any perceptual achievement is always available: to perceive that something is P is to pick up the (invariant) property P which things of that kind have. So, for example, we can give the following disarmingly simple answer to the question: how do people perceive that something is a shoe? There is a certain (invariant) property that all and only shoes have—namely, the property of being a shoe. Perceiving that something *is* a shoe consists in the pickup of this property.

It is quite true that if you do psychology this way, the old puzzles tend to disappear. For example many psychologists have wondered how somebody like Bernard Berenson managed to be so good at perceiving (i.e., telling just by looking) that some painting was an authentic Da Vinci. This problem is one of those that disappears under the new dispensation, since there is obviously some property that all and only genuine Da Vincis share; namely, the property, *having been painted by Da Vinci.* What Berenson did was simply to pick up this invariant.[2]

Clearly this will not do, and we do not suppose that Gibson thinks it will. Although he never discusses the issues in quite these terms, it is reasonably evident from Gibson's practice that he wishes to distinguish between what is *picked up* and what is *directly perceived.* In fact, Gibson ultimately accepts something like our first constraint—that what is picked up in visual perception is only certain properties of the ambient light array. Gibson is thus faced with the problem of how, if not by inferential mediation, the pickup of such properties of light could lead to perceptual knowledge of properties of the environment. That is: how, if not by inference, do you get from what you pick up about the light to what you perceive about the environmental object that the light is coming from? If Gibson fails to face this difficulty, it is because of a curious and characteristic turn in his theorizing: when he is being most careful, Gibson says that what is picked up is the *information* about the environment which is contained in the ambient array. We shall see that it is close to the heart of Gibson's problems that he has no way of construing the notion *the information in the ambient array* that will allow it to do the job that is required.

Pursuing the main course of Gibson's attempt to constrain the notion of pickup will thus bring us, eventually, to the notion of the "information in the light." There are, however, other passages in Gibson's writings that can also plausibly be viewed as attempts to impose constraints on the notions of pickup and invariance. We will discuss several of these proposals, but we want to emphasize that it is not clear which, if any, of them Gibson would endorse. This deserves emphasis because the constraints are not only non-coextensive, they are not even mutually consistent; and none of them is consistent with *all* of the things that Gibson describes as being directly perceived. So this is very much a matter of our reconstruction of Gibson's text. The reason it is worth doing is that we will argue that there is, in fact, *no* satisfactory way of constraining the notions of invariant and of pickup so as both to exclude the sort of trivialization discussed above and at the same time to sustain the thesis of unmediated perception; and to make such an argument one has to consider all the possible ways of interpreting Gibson's views.

2.1   First Gambit: Only the Ecological Properties of the Environment Are Directly Perceived

Gibson's last book starts with the observation that "Physics, optics, anatomy and physiololgy describe facts, but not facts at the level appropriate for the study of perception" (p. xiii). The first section of the book is then devoted to sketching an alternative taxonomy in terms of *ecological* properties of environmental objects and events. Gibson provides many examples of properties that are to count as ecological and some examples of properties that are not. The former include some properties of objects (for example, texture, shape, illumination, reflectance, and resistance to deformation are mentioned). There are also ecological properties of arrangements of objects and of surfaces. For example, being *open* or *cluttered* are ecological properties of what Gibson calls the "layout" of an environment (an open layout is one which consists of just a ground, horizon and sky; a cluttered layout is one that has objects scattered on the ground). Similarly, containing a hollow or an enclosure is to count as an ecological property of a layout.

This list by no means exhausts the examples that Gibson provides, nor are we to assume that the examples he provides exhaust the category of ecological properties. There is, however, one class of ecological properties which requires special mention: the "affordances." Affordances are certain properties of objects which somehow concern the goals and utilities of an organism. So, being edible is an affordance of certain objects, as is being capable of being used as a weapon or tool, being an obstacle, being a shelter, being dangerous or being a potential mate. Roughly, affordances are *dispositional* properties (because they concern what an organism *could* do with an object); and they are *relational* properties (because different organisms can do different things with objects of a given kind).

According to Gibson then, "the environment of any animal (and of all animals) contains substances, surfaces, and their layouts, enclosures, objects, places, events and other animals . . . The total environment is too vast for description even by the ecologist, and we should select those features of it that are perceptible by animals like ourselves" (p. 36). When, by contrast, Gibson gives examples of properties that are *not* ecological, they tend also to be properties that things *cannot be perceived to have*. "Perceiving" here means something like telling-by-looking. (Perceiving by the use of instruments does not count as a core case for Gibson.) So, properties like being made of atoms, or being a thousand light years away are offered as instances of *non*-ecological properties. This makes it seem as though Gibson has it in mind that "ecological" and "directly perceivable" should be interdefined, as is also suggested by the quotation just cited.

But, of course, that will not work. If the notion of an ecological property is to serve to constrain the notion of direct perception, then it cannot be stipulated to embrace all properties that are "perceptible by animals like ourselves." Consider again the property of being a shoe. This is clearly a property that we can perceive things to have, hence it is a property we can *directly* perceive, assuming that being ecological is a sufficient condition for being perceptible. But this means that introducing the construct "ecological property" has not succeeded in constraining the notion of direct perception in such a way as to rule out vacuous explanations like "the way that you perceive a shoe is by picking up the property it has of *being a shoe.*" If all properties that can be perceived are ipso facto ecological, then the claim that perception is the pickup of ecological properties is vacuously true. What we need, of course, is some criterion for being ecological *other than perceptibility.* This, however, Gibson fails to provide.

2.2   Second Gambit: Only the Projectible Properties of Ecological Optics Are Directly Perceived

We have just seen that if by "ecological properties" Gibson means *all* perceptible properties, then the notion of an ecological property will not serve to constrain the notion of direct pickup. Perhaps, then, only some independently specifiable subset of the ecological properties should count as directly perceptible. In particular, the directly perceptible properties might be the ones that figure in the laws of the science of "ecological optics."

There are, according to Gibson, *laws* about ecological properties of the environment. The laws that get discussed most in Gibson's text are the ones which connect ecological properties with features of the light that objects in the environment emit or reflect. For example, such laws connect certain sorts of discontinuities in the light array with the spatial overlap of surfaces of environmental objects; and they connect flow patterns in the light array with characteristic alterations of the relative spatial position of the observer and the object being observed. Similarly, Gibson presents the following "tentative hypothesis." "Whenever a perspective transformation of form or texture in the optic array goes to its limit and when a series of forms or textures are progressively foreshortened to this limit, a continuation of that surface of an object is specified as an occluding edge." Presumably, if this hypothesis is true, then the relation between the occlusion and the transformation of the textures is lawful, and the generalization that the hypothesis expresses is a law of ecological optics.

Now, it is generally held that laws of a science are distinguished by, among other things, characteristic features of their vocabulary (see Goodman 1954). Only certain sorts of predicates can appear in a law, those being the ones which pick out natural kinds in the domain that the law subsumes. We need such a notion of "natural kind" in order to explain a striking difference between laws and mere true generalizations: the former hold in counterfactual cases (hence, they apply to unexamined instances) and the latter do not.

Consider, for example, the following two generalizations: *all mammals have hearts* and *all mammals are born before 1982*. The point is that (as of this writing) *both generalizations hold for all the observed cases*. To date there have been no observations of mammals without hearts, and there have been no observations of mammals born after 1982. The difference between the cases is that, whereas the observation of a large number of mammals with hearts (and none without) is grounds for believing that there *could be* no mammals without hearts, the observation of a large number of mammals born before 1982 (and none born after) provides no reason at all for believing that there could be no mammals born in 1983. The idea, then, is that the property *being born before 1982* fails to subsume a natural kind; it is not the sort of property in virtue of which things enter into lawful relations. Since generalizations about things which happen to have that property are not laws, there is no reason for believing that they will hold in *new* cases. The inductive "confirmation" of such generalizations provides no rational basis for making predictions.

We will borrow a term from the philosophy of science and refer to predicates that appear in laws as "projectible predicates," and we will say that projectible predicates express "projectible properties." To say that a predicate is *not* projectible is thus to say that there are no laws about the property that it expresses. For example, the predicate "is my grandmother's favorite metal" is nonprojectible since, presumably, there are no laws that apply to things in virtue of their being metal of my grandmother's favorite kind. Notice that this is still true even on the assumption that my grandmother's favorite metal is gold and that there *are* laws about gold. This is because *being my grandmother's favorite metal* and *being gold* are different properties, and the laws about gold would continue to hold even if my grandmother's taste in metals were to change. Coextensive properties may differ in projectability (see also note 8).

To return to Gibson: the projectible ecological properties would be the ones which are connected, in a lawful way, with properties of the ambient light. It would thus be in the spirit of much of Gibson's text to suggest that it is the projectible ecological properties, and only those, that are the possible objects of direct visual perception. This would at least rule out the direct perception of such properties as having been painted by Da Vinci since, presumably, there are no laws, ecological or oth- erwise, which subsume objects in virtue of their possession of that property (whereas, on Gibson's assumptions, there *are* laws which subsume objects in virtue of such of their properties as their surface texture—see earlier).

As will presently become clear, we think that there is much to be said for expli- cating the notion of a directly detected property by reference to the notion of pro- jectibility. Nevertheless, this move will not do much for Gibson, for the following reasons:

a. Not all projectible properties are directly perceived on Gibson's view. For example, the projectible properties of classical optics are not; that is why you need *ecological* optics to construct a theory of visual perception. That classical optics fails to taxonomize properties in the ways that a theory of direct visual perception requires is, in fact, among Gibson's favorite themes. So, then, if the distinction between directly perceptible properties and others is to be explicated by reference to the projectible *ecological* properties, and if the explication is to be noncircular, we need a principled way of distinguishing between ecological laws and laws of other kinds. This, however, Gibson does not provide. Rather, insofar as Gibson is explicit about the matter at all, the notion of an ecological law is introduced by ref- erence to the notion of an ecological property (e.g., ecological laws connect eco- logical properties to properties of the ambient light). But, as we have seen, the notion of an ecological property appears to be characterizable only by reference to the notion of a property that is directly perceivable (e.g., by "animals like ourselves"). And, of course, it was precisely the notion of direct perception that needed expli- cation in the first place.

b. Not all of the properties that Gibson wants to be directly perceptible are plau- sibly considered to be projectible; in particular, affordances usually are not pro- jectible. There are, for example, presumably no laws about the ways that light is structured by the class of things that can be eaten, or by the class of writing imple- ments, though being edible or being a writing implement are just the sorts of prop- erties that Gibson talks of objects as affording. The best one can do in this area is to say that things which share their affordances often (though, surely, not always) have a characteristic shape (color, texture, size, etc.) and that there are laws which connect *the shape* (etc.) with properties of the light that the object reflects. But, of course, this consideration does Gibson no good, since it is supposed to be the affor- dances of objects, not just their shapes, that are directly perceived. In particular, Gibson is explicit in denying that the perception of the affordances of objects is mediated by inference from prior detection of their shape, color, texture, or other such "qualities."

In short, if we assume (as we should) that being a Da Vinci (or a pencil, or a shoe) is *not* projectible, we are in need of an explanation of how people perceive that some paintings are Da Vincis (or that some objects are shoes). The natural view would be: the Da Vincihood of an object (or its shoehood) is inferred from those of its (projectible) properties that are directly perceived. But this is the Establishment solution, precisely the one that Gibson is pledged to avoid.

As is customary with dilemmas, Gibson's has two horns. Either you trivialize the notion of a projectible property by stipulating that all perceptible properties are projectible; or you assume that some perceptible properties are not projectible, in which case you need to say how the perception of these nonprojectible properties is possible. The Establishment story is that the detection of nonprojectible properties is inferential, but that is the route that Gibson has eschewed. In either case, projectibility is not doing the job that Gibson needs done: viz., to provide a notion of direct perception that is simultaneously nonvacuous and compatible with the doctrine that perception is immediate.

2.3   Third Gambit: Only Phenomenological Properties Are Directly Perceived

Introspection suggests that the world is perceptibly accessible under some descriptions but less so under others. A landscape, for example, is readily seen as containing fields, trees, sky, clouds, houses, shrubs, and stones. But it takes special training to see those properties of a landscape which a convincing *trompe l'oeil* painting would have to duplicate; typically, properties which depend on a fixed locus of observation. It is a matter of considerable significance that properties of the world that seem to be perceptually accessible are generally ones that children learn early to recognize and to name.

Suppose we call these relatively accessible properties of things their *phenomenological* properties. Then much of what Gibson says can be construed as suggesting that it is phenomenological properties, and only those, that are directly perceived. This may be what is at issue in Gibson's injunction that the environment must be described in *meaningful* terms: ". . . the qualities of the world in relation to the needs of the observer are experienced directly," whereas "sensations triggered by light, sound, pressure and chemicals are merely incidental" (p. 246).

Phenomenological properties are accorded a similarly central role in Gibson's discussion of ontogenesis. ". . . the infant does not begin by first discriminating the qualities of objects and then learning the combinations of qualities that specify them. Phenomenological objects are not built up of qualities; it is the other way around. The affordance of an object is what the infant begins by noticing. The meaning is observed before the substance and the surface, the color and the form, are seen as such" (p. 134).

If we go by introspection alone, the identification of the perceptually accessible properties with those that are directly perceived certainly seems plausible: phenomenological properties are precisely the ones which strike one as "given" rather than inferred. Gibson says such things as that "the perceiving of the world entails the coperceiving of where one is in the world and of being in the world at that place" (p. 200) and "the environment seen-at-this-moment does not constitute the environment that is seen" (p.195). And these remarks (with which, by the way, Husserl would have been entirely comfortable) seem true enough in light of introspections of perceptual salience. There is a scale of phenomenological accessibility, and locations, objects, and affordances are high on this scale. Contrariwise, the "sensory properties" which function as the bases of perceptual inference in, for example, Helmholtzian versions of the Establishment theory, do seem to be very low in phenomenological accessibility.

There are, however three objections to the proposal that we take the phenomenological properties to be directly perceived. The first is internal: the proposal fails to include some of Gibson's own favorite examples of ecological invariants. For example, the slant of surfaces, the gradients and flows of textures, the amount of texture occluded by interposing objects, the moving occluding texture edge, etc., are *not* phenomenologically accessible. Witness the fact that it requires delicate experimentation to discover the central role that the detection of such properties plays in perception. Roughly, the present proposal has difficulties complementary to those of the suggestion that the object of direct perception is the projectible properties of ecological optics (see earlier); whereas the projectibility criterion leaves the affordances out, the phenomenological criterion lets almost only the affordances in. This is not surprising; you would not really expect the properties in virtue of which objects satisfy laws to be coextensive, in the general case, with those which are phenomenologically accessible. If such a general coextension held, doing science would be a lot easier than it has turned out to be.

Second, it seems at best a dubious strategy to infer direct perception from phenomenological salience: perhaps the latter is *solely* a phenomenon of conscious access and tells us nothing about the nature of perception per se. This is, in any event, a familiar claim of Establishment theories, and it is often rendered persuasive by experimental demonstrations that the perception of phenomenologically salient properties of the stimulus is causally dependent upon the detection of features whose phenomenological accessibility is negligible; properties of the stimulus which may, in fact, entirely escape the conscious notice of the subject. For example, Hess (1975) has shown that a variety of highly accessible perceived properties of faces—including their relative attractiveness—depends on the detection of the relatively *in*accessible property of pupilary diameter. In the light of such findings, Gibson cannot, in any event, establish the identification of directly perceived properties with phenomenologically salient ones by fiat; he cannot simply assume that what is most readily reported is what is noninferentially perceived.

Finally, we are going to need a *mechanism* for the direct perception of phenomenological properties, and it is hard to imagine one that will work in the case of properties like the affordances. It is, for example, not good enough merely to *say* that we directly perceive that a rock can be used as a weapon; we need an account of how the apprehension of such a property *could* be noninferential. We will see, presently, that Establishment theories do propose mechanisms for the direct pickup of certain sorts of stimulus properties; but it is a consequence of the Establishment proposal that affordances (and, indeed, most phenomenologically salient properties) are inferred rather than directly perceived. Gibson sometimes speaks of the perceptual mechanism as "resonating" to the values of ecological parameters that they are "tuned" to. But since a more detailed account does not appear to be forthcoming, the resonance metaphor amounts to little more than whistling in the dark. We shall return to this issue further on.

2.4   Fourth Gambit: What Is Directly Perceived Is Whatever "Perceptual Systems" Respond To

It is a point that we will presently make much of—and that Gibson is reasonably clear about—that *all* theories of perception must acknowledge the direct pickup of *some* properties. In Establishment theories, what is directly picked up is often taken to be the properties to which *transducers* respond. There is a circle of interdefined notions here, a directly detected property being one to which a transducer responds, and a transducer being a mechanism that responds directly to the properties that it detects. One way that Establishment theories have of breaking out of this circle is by specifying—typically by enumeration—which organs are to count as transducers; for example, the retina in the case of vision and the tympanic membrane in the case of audition.

We shall have more to say about how the notion of transduction can be constrained presently, and we will argue that such specification by anatomical enumeration is inadequate. The present point is that Gibson recognizes that to specify what is to count as a perceptual organ is implicitly to constrain what a theory says is directly picked up. For example, if you think that the organ of visual transduction is the retina, and if you can show that the retina responds only to such properties as the wavelength and intensity of light, then you are committed to the view that only those properties are directly detected. Consequently, other properties of the light (and, a fortiori, all visual properties of distal objects) are apprehended only *indirectly*, presumably via processes that involve inference.

Gibson believes that the perceptual organs have been misidentified by Establishment theorists. Correspondingly, he claims that if one individuates the perceptual organs correctly, one gets a new and better census of the immediately perceived properties. So, "Helmholtz argued that we must deduce the causes of our sensations because we cannot detect them . . . The alternative is to assume that sensations triggered by light, sound pressure, and chemicals are merely incidental, that *information* is available to *perceptual systems*, and that the qualities of the world in relation to the needs of the observer are experienced directly" (p. 246, emphasis added). It is a moral of *The Ecological Approach to Visual Perception*, and it is the main point of *The Senses Considered as Perceptual Systems* (Gibson, 1966) that the "perceptual system" for vision is the entire complex consisting of "first, the lens, pupil, chamber, and the retina . . . Second, the eye with its muscles in the orbit . . . Third, the two eyes in the head . . . Fourth, the eyes in a mobile head that can turn . . . Fifth, the eyes in a head on a body . . ." (p. 245). It is the discriminative capacity of this system—*and not the discriminative capacity of the retina*—which determines what vision can, in principle, detect.

We can certainly grant that the class of properties to which this complex system is specifically "tuned"—the class of properties it can "directly respond to"—may not be the class of properties that Establishment theories have usually taken to be visually transduced. (It is far from clear that it will be the class of ecological properties either. But as we remarked above, the criteria we are ascribing to Gibson for selecting candidate objects of direct visual perception are not, in general, coextensive.) So, Gibson is right to claim that reparsing the system of perceptual organs provides for, or at least permits, a new census of directly detected properties. It follows that *if* Gibson had a motivated criterion for deciding what is to count as a perceptual system, he would ipso facto have a principled way of constraining the notion of direct pickup.

But Gibson provides *no* criterion for identifying perceptual systems, or even for circumscribing which organs can in general be regarded as parts of the same perceptual system. For example, it is notable that Gibson's enumeration of the parts of the visual system does not include the brain. Inasmuch as Gibson emphasizes that perceptual systems can overlap (different such systems may share anatomically individuated organs) this exclusion seems, to put it mildly, unmotivated. If, however, the brain *is* included as a component of the visual system, then presumably the properties that the visual system can pick up would ipso facto be coextensive with the properties that people can visually perceive and we are back where we started. We still want independent characterizations of "perceive" and "pick up directly" if the identification of perception with direct pickup is to amount to an empirical hypothesis.

It is clear from Gibson's discussion of perceptual systems that he intends to individuate them functionally rather than anatomically, a decision which we applaud. The problem is that the proposed criteria of individuation are so flexible that the notion of "perceptual system" actually provides *no* constraint on what might count as a "directly detected" invariant. According to Gibson, there are five overlapping perceptual systems, each of which can ". . . orient, explore, investigate, adjust, optimize, and come to an equilibrium. . . ." The functioning of these systems is explicitly *not* limited to the transduction of impinging stimulation. Rather, the responses of perceptual systems are "specific to the qualities of things in the world, especially affordances" (p. 246). Furthermore, the nature of the information which such systems can pick up "becomes more and more subtle, elaborate and precise with practice." Given the unbounded scope of the activities that perceptual systems can perform, there would seem to be nothing in the notion that prevents the detection of shoes, grandmothers, genuine Da Vincis, performances of Beethoven's Kreutzer Sonata, or authentic autographs of George Washington all being possible "achievements of perceptual systems." It looks as though whatever is perceived is ipso facto the proper object of a perceptual system, and whatever is the proper object of a perceptual system is ipso facto perceived directly; we have, in particular, no independent constraints on the individuation of perceptual systems that will permit us to break into this chain of interdefinitions.

The moral of all this is that to define the directly perceivable in terms of what perceptual systems respond to is merely to shift the locus of trivialization from the former notion to the latter. It puts the same pea under a different shell. We believe that there *are* ways of constraining the notion of a perceptual mechanism—via an independent characterization of transduction—but the price you pay is that many perceptual processes turn out to be *non*transductive, hence presumably inferential. This is Gibson's characteristic dilemma, and we claim that he has no way out of it.

2.5   The Problem of Misperception

In much of the preceding discussion we have emphasized the undesirable consequences of interdefining "pick up," "invariant," "ecological property," and "directly perceive," but that is not the only difficulty with Gibson's approach. Part of an adequate theory of perception ought to be an account of perceptual *errors*, and it is hard to see how this requirement can be squared with the claim that perception is direct on *any* of the interpretations that Gibson's text suggests.

People who have tried to understand the nature of the mind, at least since Plato, have been particularly worried about the problem of false belief. In the present context, this is the problem of explaining how *misperception* is possible. The standard approach to this problem within Establishment theories is to connect misperception with failed inference. Your perception that something is edible, for example, is said to depend upon inferences from the appearance of the thing (e.g., from its smell, taste, texture, shape, color, and so forth). These inferences depend upon generalizations gleaned from past experience, and the generalizations are themselves nondemonstrative, and hence fallible. So, for these and other reasons, the (perceptual) inference from appearance to edibility sometimes goes wrong, with consequences that are typically painful and occasionally fatal.

Now consider how a noninferential story about misperception might go. Here we get a first glimpse of a dilemma that emerges, in various guises, throughout Gibson's text. If "directly perceive that" is taken to be factive, then by stipulation "x directly perceives that y is edible" will entail that y is edible. It follows that what goes on when one misperceives something as edible cannot be the direct perception of edibility. If, on the other hand, "directly perceive that" is *not* taken to be factive, then it is logically possible to, as it were, directly *misperceive* that something is edible. But Gibson will then need an account of what has gone wrong when misperception is direct. Notice, in particular, that he *cannot* account for such cases by saying that what you pick up when you directly misperceive the edibility of a thing is the property of *apparent* edibility. For, things that are misperceived to be edible *do* have the property of being *apparently* edible, and the problem for a theory of misperception is to explain how things could be taken to have properties that in fact they do *not* have. (A way out would be to say that you pick up the apparent edibility and *infer* the edibility from that; but this just *is* the Establishment way out and, of course, it is closed to Gibson.)

Probably the line that Gibson wants to take is that *if* an affordance is correctly perceived, *then* it is perceived directly; and that is, of course compatible with the factivity of "directly perceive." Notice, however, that such an approach does not help with the problem of misperception, since it does not tell us how we are to describe the cases where the antecedent of the hypothetical is *false*. We will return to this sort of difficulty. Suffice it at present to say that the problem of constraining "directly perceive" so as to provide a nonvacuous construal of the claim that perception is noninferential, and the problem of providing a coherent account of misperception without recourse to the notion of perceptual inference, are two sides of the same coin. No wonder Gibson is so unhappy about the role that appeals to illusions have played in the confirmation of Establishment theories of perception.

If a theory of perception is to be tenable it must not only address the most common (veridical) cases, but also the ones in which perception fails to be veridical and leads to false beliefs. The relative infrequency of the latter sorts of cases does not alter this principle (and, in fact, they are arguably not all that infrequent; only they tend to escape our notice except when the consequences are serious). Gibsonians sometimes urge that we should take very seriously the fact that perception works most of the time (see Reed and Jones, 1978), and it is true that this fact is of central importance for epistemology. But the goal of psychological theory construction is not to predict most (or even all) of the variance; it is to explicate the underlying mechanisms upon whose operation the variance depends. It seems quite inconceivable that the psychological mechanisms of perception and the psychological mechanisms of misperception are different *in kind*.

This problem is such a serious one that it sometimes drives Gibsonians to truly desperate recourses. For example, Turvey and Shaw (1979) suggest that we should cope with the issue of perceptual error by "tak(ing) perception out of the propositional domain in which it can be said to be either right or wrong . . . and relocat(ing) it in a nonpropositional domain in which the question of whether perception is right or wrong would be nonsensical" (p. 182). Apparently, this means either that we should stop thinking of perception as eventuating in beliefs, or that we should stop thinking of beliefs as having truth values. Turvey and Shaw describe this proposal as "radical," but "suicidal" might be the more appropriate term.

Perhaps the most characteristic Gibsonian move in this area is to identify misperception with failure to pick up 'all the relevant information" (the bird flies into the window because it failed to pick up the ambient information that specifies *window*). But, of course, pick up of the very light structures which failed to specify *window* for the bird might be adequate to specify *window* for *us*. From a mentalistic point of view, this is not surprising; we know a lot more about windows than birds do. So, the form of the problem for Gibson is to explain how pick up of the very same state of affairs that constitutes an adequate sample of information for one organism could constitute an inadequate sample for another. The Establishment account has an answer: *viz.* that what you perceive depends not only on the ambient information picked up, but also on the mental processes deployed in processing that information. It is far from clear what alternative the Gibsonian position could propose.

3   The Problem of Direct Detection in Establishment Theories

Our argument thus far has been that unless the notions of pickup and invariant are constrained, it will always be trivially true that there is an invariant property whose pickup is necessary and sufficient for the perception of any object: viz., the property of being that object. We have also argued that some doctrines of Gibson's which can plausibly be construed as attempts to provide the relevant constraints do not succeed in doing so.

Though these considerations raise problems for Gibson's theory, it is important to understand that all other theories, including Establishment theories, have problems of a corresponding sort. This is because even theories that hold that the perception of many properties is inferentially mediated must assume that the detection of *some* properties is direct (in the sense of *not* inferentially mediated). Fundamentally, this is because inferences are processes in which one belief causes another. Unless some beliefs are fixed in some way other than by inference, it is hard to see how the inferential processes could get started. Inferences need premises.[3]

To admit this is not, however, to endorse any "foundationalist" view of epistemology: to say that the pickup of some properties must be noninferential is not to say that our knowledge of these properties is infallible, or that the justification of perceptual beliefs depends upon assuming that the mechanisms of direct pickup are epistemologically privileged. Many philosophers have held that the deliverances of direct perception must figure centrally in the arguments which justify our perceptually based knowledge claims, but it is quite unnecessary to read this sort of moral from Establishment perceptual psychology.

The psychologist's topic is the causation of perceptual judgements, not the establishment of epistemic warrant in justificatory arguments. One can perfectly well hold—as in fact we are inclined to do—*both* that matters of epistemic warrant are typically determined by "inference to the best explanation" *and* that the causation of perceptual judgements typically involves inferences from premises which are not themselves inferred. The causal chain in perception typically flows "inward" from the detection of those properties to which peripheral transducers respond. But the flow of epistemic justification typically goes in every which way since the justification of perceptual knowledge claims is heavily constrained by principles of conservatism, parsimony, and coherence. In what follows, then, the epistemological issues will be put completely to one side: we make no assumptions about the epistemological role of whatever is directly detected[4]; for us, "direct" means only "noninferential."

One can distinguish at least two proposals that Establishment theories have made about how to draw the line between what is directly detected and what is inferentially mediated. On some views, especially the older, epistemologically based theories, the distinction between direct detection and inferential mediation is taken to be coextensive with the distinction between "sensory" properties and the rest. Typically, the sensory properties are characterized by introspective availability, and often enough it is assumed that the deliverances of introspection are infallible; hence the putative connection between perceptual immediacy and epistemic warrant that we noted in the preceding paragraph. Gibson holds, and we think that he is right about this, that the appeal to introspection will not do the job. In fact, as we saw when we discussed the "phenomenological" criterion for direct detection, what is introspectively accessible is typically not the traditional sensory properties (color, two-dimensional form, etc.) but rather "meaningful" properties like the affordances. When Gibson says that "phenomenological objects are not built up of qualities; it is the other way around" (p. 134) he is quite right about the deliverances of introspection. Since, however, traditional theorizing is precisely concerned to treat properties that are on the level of the affordances as *inferred*, it very early abandoned the identification of what is directly detected with what is introspectively available. If, however, the sensory properties are *not* identifiable with the ones that are introspectively available, it does not help much to say that sensory properties are what we detect directly, the former notion being as unclear as the latter.

Recent versions of the Establishment theory have sought to constrain the notion of direct detection by identifying the properties that are available without inferential mediation with those to which transducer mechanisms are sensitive. This transfers the problem of constraining "directly detectible property" to the problem of constraining "mechanism of transduction" and, contrary to assumptions that appear to be widely made, specifying what is allowed to count as a transducer for the purposes of cognitive theory is a nontrivial problem. For example, transducers are technically defined as mechanisms which convert information from one physical form to another. But this definition is entirely compatible with there being transducers for *any* pattern of stimulation to which the organism can respond selectively since *whole organisms* are, in that sense, transducers for any category to which they can reliably assign things; e.g., for sentences, or shoes, or, in Berenson's case, for Da Vincis. This is precisely Gibson's problem as it arises in the context of Establishment theories, and to fail to grasp its seriousness is to fail to understand the challenge that Gibson poses to the Establishment. The theory that perception is typically direct is empty barring an independent construal of pickup; *but so too is the theory that perception is typically inferential.* On the other hand, it should be borne in mind that the Establishment does not accept Gibson's condition on the solution of this problem; viz., that the objects of direct detection (transduction) must be so specified that no perceptual judgements turn out to be inferentially mediated. We think that Gibson's position is hopeless precisely because pickup can be constrained only if that condition is abandoned.

Some theorists in the Establishment tradition hold that the way to decide what transducers we have is by appealing to neurophysiology—for example, by finding out what biological mechanisms serve to convert ambient stimulation into the electrical energy of nerve impulses. There are, however, several difficulties with this sort of approach. In the first place, it fails to rule out the whole nervous system as a transducer since, after all, converting ambient energies into neural excitations is a good part of what the nervous system does. Moreover, the class of mechanisms that would count as transducers by this criterion involves many which perform no function that is of significance for the theory of perception. This is because not all stimulus events that affect the character of nerve impulses are ipso facto available for the causation of perceptual judgements. Uttal (1967) refers to those neural events that are functionally relevant as *signals* and those that are not as *signs*, precisely in order to emphasize this distinction. This consideration suggests that the identification of transducers will have to advert not, in the first instance, to their neurological structure but to their role in the cognitive processes that they subserve. Like Gibson, we assume that the individuation of perceptual mechanisms is primarily functional rather than physiological.

Finally, it might be argued that whether a device (including a neurophysiological mechanism) counts as a transducer depends, at least in part, on its psychophysical characteristics; on the way that its output depends upon its input. As will become clear, we think that some proposal of this general kind is probably correct. Notice, however, that it does not follow that the sort of evidence that is collected in standard psychophysical experiments will resolve the issue. This is because such evidence does not, in the general case, directly reflect the behavior of isolated components of the perceptual system. Psychophysical curves reflect patterns of judgements produced by *whole organisms*, and are typically affected not only by stimulus parameters, but by the utilities, expectations, and beliefs that the organism entertains.

We will assume, in what follows, the identification of what is "picked up" with those properties that transducers respond to. Our problem will thus be to find some satisfactory alternative to the ways of constraining transduction that we have just discussed.

4   The First Constraint on Pickup: What Is Picked Up in (Visual) Perception Is Certain Properties of the Ambient Light

We begin by considering a fundamental construct in Gibson's theory, the notion that states of affairs can *contain information about* one another. The basic idea is that the state of affairs S1 contains information about the state of affairs S2 if and only if S1 and S2 have correlated properties. Suppose that S1 consists of a's having property F and S2 consists of b's having property G. Then if, in general, x's having property F is correlated with y's having property G, then S1 contains information about S2.

As Gibson repeatedly remarks, this is an entirely "objective," nonpsychological notion of information. Information in this sense is something "in the world," just as correlation is. In particular, information-cum-correlation is not something that is encoded, or transmitted, or stored; though it is, according to Gibson, "picked up" whenever anything is perceived.

But, whereas information is an ontological category, *specification* is an episte-mological one. The idea is basically that when two states of affairs are correlated, the organism can use the occurrence of one to find out about the other. Under such circumstances, the first state of affairs is said to *specify* the second (for that organ-ism). Correlation (hence information) is presumably a necessary condition for specification: when S1 specifies S2, S1 and S2 are correlated,[5] and S1 contains infor-mation about S2. Gibson's favorite example is the relation of specification that holds between features of the ambient light and features of the distal environmental layout. Features of the light are correlated with features of the layout in virtue of the regularities expressed by laws of ecological optics. The structure of the light therefore contains information about the character of the layout; and, since organ-isms actually use that information in the perceptual identification of layout features, the structure of the light is said to specify the character of the layout.

Now, the relation of *containing information about* is symmetrical, but, in the general case, the relation of *specifying* is not. Suppose that the state of the layout is correlated in a certain way with the state of the light. While it is then true that the properties of the light contain information about the properties of the layout, it is equally true that the properties of the layout contain information about the properties of the light. However, for no organism that we know of—barring, perhaps, the occasional ecological optician—does the structure of the layout specify the light. Organisms just do not use the properties of the layout to find out how the light is arranged. Notice that that is not because the information is not here. Since the two are correlated you could, in principle, determine the structure of the light given the facts about the layout (and about the correlations) just as you can, in principle, determine the structure of the layout given the facts about the light (and about the correlations). And this raises a problem, though not one that Gibson discusses in these terms: viz., *What determines the direction of specification?*

As soon as the problem is put this way, the principle at issue seems clear enough. What determines the direction of specification is the nature of the detectors (trans-ducers) available to the organism. Light specifies layout and not vice versa precisely because we have transducers for light and no transducers for layout. If we had trans-ducers for layout and no transducers for light, then any specification relation that held between the two would have to go in the opposite direction. The moral is: if we are in a position to say what the direction of specification is for a given or-ganism, then that fact constrains our attribution of transducer mechanisms to the organism. The attribution of transducers must serve (*inter alia*) to explain the facts about the direction of specification for the organism.

So we have a constraint on transduction. But how is this constraint to be applied? In particular, how do you tell which sorts of states of affairs serve as specifiers for a given organism? Given correlated states of affairs, how do you tell which specifies which? The answer is sufficiently obvious. What you do is, you break the correlation experimentally (you set up a case in which the correlation fails) and then you see what happens.[6]

Consider the following simple examples. How do we know that the light specifies the layout and not *vice versa*? Well, we can create paired situations in one of which we preserve the features of the light without the corresponding layout, and in the other of which we preserve the features of the layout without the corresponding light. The presentation of a hologram would be an example of the first kind; turning out the lights would be an example of the second kind. There is no dispute about what would happen in such experiments. You can vary the layout as much as you like; so long as the properties of the light are unaffected, the perceptual judgements of the organism are unaffected too. On the other hand, leaving the layout intact does you no good if the structure of the light is changed. In the extreme case, take the light away, and the organism cannot see.

In short, the way you determine which of a pair of correlated states of affairs specifies the other is by applying the "method of differences," in which one determines which of two factors is the cause of some effect by setting up a situation in which only one of the factors is operative. In the present case, we have a pair of correlated states of affairs and a perceptual judgement in which they eventuate. We assume that the light contains information about the layout, but we have still to show that the information in the light serves to *specify* the layout; viz., that the perception of layout features is causally dependent upon the detection of the information in the light. The hypothesis that the light does specify the layout implies two predictions corresponding to the two ways of breaking the correlation between light features and layout features: since the detection of the light is causally *necessary* for the (visual) perception of the layout, we predict that the organism sees nothing in the layout-without-light setup. Since the detection of the light is causally *sufficient* for the perception of the layout, we predict *layout illusions* in the light-without-layout setup.

It is the latter consideration which accounts for the centrality, in perceptual psychology, of experiments which turn on the creation of perceptual illusions. An illusion is simply a case in which the specifying state of affairs is brought about without the occurrence of the correlated state of affairs that it normally serves to specify. To produce an illusion is thus to demonstrate a direction of specification. It is characteristic of Gibson's break with the tradition that he disapproves of psychological theories which appeal to perceptual illusions as data, Gibson's point being that the laboratory illusion is an "ecologically invalid" happening. So it is—by definition—since, as we have seen, you construct an illusion precisely by breaking a correlation that holds *in rerum natura*. Our point is, however, that the theoretical pertinence of facts about illusions is an immediate consequence of taking the specification relation seriously. If saying that S1 specifies S2 implies that the perception of S2 is causally dependent upon the detection of S1, and if causal dependence implies causal sufficiency, then one is committed by the logic of the case to the prediction that S1 presentations can engender S2 illusions. It is notable that Gibson himself (tacitly) accepts this form of argument. When he cites evidence in support of particular empirical claims regarding the identity of specifying stimuli, he frequently appeals to the standard kinds of experimental data about illusions; e.g., cases where one can produce illusions of motion by providing subjects with simulations of optical flow patterns. It seems that some illusions are ecologically more valid than others.

The state of the argument is now as follows: when S1 specifies S2, the perception of S2 is causally dependent upon the detection of S1. Since the direction of specification is determined by the transductive capacities of the organism, it follows that S1 specifies S2 only if the organism has transducers for S1. The notion that the facts about transduction determine the direction of specification thus serves simultaneously to constrain the notion "object of detection" (only specifiers are directly detected) and the notion "mechanism of transduction" (only mechanisms which respond to specifiers are transducers). The method of differences gives us a way out of the threatened interdefinition of "transducer" with "object of direct detection" since we have *empirical* tests for whether a stimulus is a specifier.

Here, then, is the proposal in a nutshell. We say that the system S is a detector (transducer) for a property P only if (a) there is a state S_i of the system that is correlated with P (i.e., such that if P occurs, then S_i occurs); and (b) the generalization *if P then* S_i is counterfactual supporting—i.e., would hold across relevant employments of the method of differences.[7] It is, of course, condition (b) that does the work. For, if a state of a system is correlated with a property, then it will typically also be correlated with any property with which that property correlates. Specifically, if there is a subsystem of the organism whose states are correlated with properties of the light, then the states of that subsystem will also be correlated with the properties of the layout that the light specifies. However, only the former correlation will be counterfactual supporting in the required way; visual transducers are unaffected by manipulation of the layout unless the manipulations affect the properties of the light. Hence, by our criterion, *only* properties of the light are transduced in visual perception.

Another way of stating this condition is to say that a system which is functioning as a detector of P is in a certain sense illusion-free with respect to P. This is not, however, because detection is, in some puzzling way, infallible; it is only because, by assumption, the validity of P-*perception* depends upon situational correlations in a way that the validity of P-*detection*, by assumption, does not. To say that a property is detected is to say that the property would continue to have its psychological effect in circumstances in which correlated properties were suppressed. But P-illusions are possible only where the perception of P is mediated by the detection of one of its correlates, the illusion occurring when the correlation fails. Since, however, transduction is, by assumption, direct—i.e., *not* dependent on specification—failure-of-correlation illusions cannot, by definition, arise in the case of transduced properties.

We have seen that the counterfactual-support condition on transducers has the consequence that only properties of the light are transduced in visual perception. It should be emphasized, however, that not *all* properties of the light can be so transduced if that condition is to be honored. Consider, for example, the (relational) property that the light has if and only if it is caused by the layout being arranged in a certain way. This is a perfectly good property of the light, but it is not one that can be directly detected according to the present view. For, this property has its effect on perception only via the effects of such correlated light features as wavelength, intensity, color discontinuities, etc. That is, the perceptual effects of the former property are preserved only in those circumstances in which the latter properties are detected. (We make this claim on empirical rather than a priori grounds; we assume that it is what the relevant employments of the method of differences would show to be true.) The property of having-been-caused-by-such-and-such-a-layout-feature is thus a property that the light may have, but it is not a detectable property of the light.

Because the counterfactual support condition is not satisfiable by such properties, the illusion freedom condition is not either. It will always be possible, at least in principle, to construct minimal pairs of light arrays such that one of them has the property and the other does not; and the organism will be unable to distinguish between such pairs within the limits of the experimental procedure. That is what happens when we construct an object that looks like a shoe but isn't one; if it structures the light in a way sufficiently like the way that a shoe does, the subject cannot tell by looking that the light structure lacks the property of having been caused by a shoe. Similarly, mutatis mutandis, when one fakes a Da Vinci. So, then, on the one hand, nothing but the properties of the light can be directly detected in visual perception; and, on the other hand, there are (infinitely) many properties of light that cannot be so detected.

We shall presently return to the bearing of all this upon the main question of whether perception ought to be considered to be an inferential process. First, however, it may be worth considering some further implications of the counterfactual-support condition. We believe that the tacit acceptance of this condition upon detection explains a number of intuitions theorists have had concerning what can count as a transducer.

For example, it is frequently assumed that detectors are sensitive only to *physical* properties (i.e., to such properties of states of affairs as can be expressed in the vocabulary of the physical sciences). On this view, we could, in principle, have detectors for wavelength, intensity, pressure, or even chemical composition, but not, say, for being expensive, being nutritious, being causally related to some past event (e.g., being a genuine Da Vinci), or being a sentence of English. We suggest that these intuitions about which properties are transducible are shaped by the theorist's implicit allegiance to the counterfactual support condition via the following considerations.

It is usually assumed that the only empirical generalizations which support counterfactuals are laws. This is practically tautological since a law just is a generalization that holds in all physically possible worlds in which the relevant background conditions are satisfied; i.e., across all relevant employments of the method of differences. Suppose that this assumption is correct. Then, since generalizations which specify the relation between detector output states and detected properties must be counterfactual supporting, it follows that such generalizations must be lawful. However, as we have seen, the vocabulary of laws is restricted to predicates which express projectible properties. In short, then, the following theoretical decisions ought to go together: (a) the decision as to whether a property is detectible; (b) the decision as to whether the property is projectible; (c) the decision as to whether a generalization which involves that property is a law; (d) the decision as to whether the generalization is counterfactual-supporting; (e) the decision as to whether a mechanism which is sensitive to the property can count as a detector for that property.

Now, many theorists have held, more or less explicitly, that the only laws there are laws of the physical sciences, hence that the only properties that can be subsumed by counterfactual supporting generalizations are physical properties. If you believe this, then given the considerations just reviewed, you ought also to hold that there can be detectors only for physical magnitudes. And, whether or not you believe that all laws are laws of physics, there is presumably nobody who believes that there are laws about, say, grandmothers qua grandmothers or about genuine Da Vincis qua genuine Da Vincis, though there may, of course, be laws about coextensive kinds. (Remember that coextensive properties may nevertheless differ in projectibility.)[8] The suggestion is that the intuition that there are no laws about the property *grandmother* is what explains the intuition that there cannot be grandmother detectors. The moral is: the decision about what detectors there are is linked to the decision about what laws there are. A world in which there were laws about the property *shoe* would be a world in which there could be detectors for shoes. After all, a law about *shoe* would, presumably, connect the shoe property to other sorts of properties, and then things which have properties of these other sorts would ipso facto be available for service as shoe detectors.

In the light of these considerations, we can now understand at least one of the moves that Gibson makes. The fact that Gibson holds *both* that there is detection of ecological parameters and that there are *laws* of ecological optics are seen to be linked decisions. If you hold that nonphysical parameters can be detected, and if, by definition, the states of detectors are lawfully connected with the properties they detect, then you must also hold that there are laws which involve nonphysical magnitudes. In this respect, at least, Gibson's doctrines are mutually consistent.

5   The "Information in the Light"

The main point of our discussion was to establish some conditions on the notion *detection* (transduction). We needed to do this because we doubted that the notion *could* be appropriately constrained consonant with the doctrine that perception is, in the general case, not inferentially mediated. We are now in a position to see one of the ways in which the conflict arises; indeed, one of the respects in which the

Gibsonian model of visual perception is after all committed to inferential mediation, just as Establishment models are.

The first point to notice is that Gibson actually agrees with much of what we have been saying, although the terminology he employs sometimes obscures the consensus. Gibson makes a distinction (largely implicit, and not invariably honored) between what he describes as "directly perceived" and what he describes as "picked up." The latter locution is usually reserved for features of the light, while the former is usually used for features of the layout. Moreover, Gibson seems to agree that picking up features of the light is causally necessary for "directly perceiving" features of the layout. Notice that, in this respect, Gibson's view is simply indistinguishable from the Establishment theory. Where Gibson speaks of directly perceiving features of the layout in consequence of picking up features of the light, the Establishment theory speaks of perceiving features of the layout in consequence of transducing features of the light. Thus far, the differences are merely terminological. The important fact is the agreement that the subject's epistemic relation to the structure of the light is different from his epistemic relation to the layout of the environment, and that the former relation is causally dependent upon the latter.

There is, however, this difference: the classical theory has a story about *how you get from detected properties of the light to perceived properties of the layout.* The story is that you infer the latter from the former on the basis of (usually implicit) knowledge of the correlations that connect them. Gibson clearly does not like this story, but it is quite unclear how he is going to get along without it. It is all very well to call your epistemic relation to layout features "direct perception," but if it is agreed that that relation is dependent upon an epistemic relation to properties of the light, "direct" certainly cannot be taken to mean "unmediated." The basic problem for Gibson is that picking up the fact that the light is so-and-so is ipso facto a *different* state of mind from perceiving that the layout is so-and-so. In the normal case, states of mind like the first are causally necessary to bring about states of mind like the second (and they are normally causally sufficient for organisms which have had appropriate experience of the ways in which light states and layout states are correlated). Some process *must* be postulated to account for the transition from one of these states of mind to the other, and it certainly looks as though the appropriate mechanism is inference. The point is that Gibson has done nothing to avoid the need to postulate such a process; it arises as soon as "direct detection" is appropriately constrained. And he has suggested no alternative to the proposal that the process comes down to one of drawing perceptual inferences from transducer outputs; in the present state of the art that proposal is, literally, the only one in the field.

What obscures this problem in Gibson's presentation is that, instead of speaking of picking up properties of the light, he talks about picking up *the information about the layout* that the light contains. This certainly appears to be an alternative to the Establishment idea that layout features are inferred from light features. But, in fact, if one bears in mind the character of the theory of information that Gibson has actually provided, one sees that the appearance is illusory. Remember that "information" is a defined construct for Gibson; S1 contains information about S2 if, and only if, they are correlated states of affairs. The problem is that while Gibson gives no hint of any notion of information other than this one, it is hard to see how this account can sustain talk of information pickup.

Given that "contains information about" just means "is correlated with," what could it mean to say that an organism picks up the information that S1 contains about S2? The obvious suggestion is that you pick up some property of S1 that you know to be correlated with some property of S2, and you use your knowledge of the correlation to infer from the former property to the latter. But this cannot be what Gibson has in mind, since this is just the Establishment picture; we learn about the layout by inference from the detected properties of the light. That is, what we detect is not the information *in* S1 but rather the informative properties *of* S1. Then what we learn about S2 in consequence of having detected these informative properties depends upon which inferences we draw from their presence.

Perhaps, then, Gibson's idea is that detecting the information that S1 contains about S2 is detecting the correlation between S1 and S2. But a moment's thought shows that this cannot be right either. To say (loosely) that S1 is correlated with S2 is to say that S1 and S2 belong to correlated *types* of states of affairs (see note 5). But, surely, you find out about correlations between types of states not by "detecting" the correlation but by processes of nondemonstrative (e.g., inductive) inference.

Something has clearly gone wrong, and it is not hard to see what it is. Having introduced the (purely relational) notion of states of affairs *containing information about* one another (i.e., being correlated) Gibson then slips over into talking of *the information in* a state of affairs. And, having once allowed himself to reify information in this way (to treat it as a thing, rather than a relation), it is a short step to thinking of detecting the information in the light on the model of, for example, detecting the frequency *of* the light; viz., as some sort of causal interaction between the information and the states of a perceptual mechanism (the information makes the perceptual mechanisms "resonate").

This is such an easy slide that it is essential to bear in mind that Gibson has no notion of information that warrants it. Information, in Gibson's sense, is not the sort of thing that can affect states of perceptual systems. What *can* function causally is *informative properties* of the medium, properties of the medium which are de facto informative because they are correlated with properties of the layout. So, for example, the frequency of the light can cause a state of a detector, and the frequency of the light can be de facto informative about the color of reflecting surfaces in virtue of a correlation that holds between frequency and color. But the fact that the frequency of the light is correlated with the color of reflecting surfaces cannot itself cause a state of a detector, and appeal to that fact exhausts Gibson's construal of the notion that the light contains information about the color of surfaces. So we are back in the old problem: how (by what mental processes) does the organism get from the detection of an informative property of the medium to the perception of a correlated property of the environment? How does the fact that certain properties of the medium are de facto informative manage to have any epistemic consequences? The function of the Establishment notion of perceptual inference is, of course, precisely to answer this question.

In short, "picking up the information in the light" must, given Gibson's account of information, come down to picking up features of the light that are correlated with features of the layout. Since the correlation is empirical (via the laws of ecological optics), it is perfectly possible that an organism should pick up a de facto informative property of the light but not *take it to be* informative, e.g., because the organism does not know about the correlation. In this case, picking up the information in the light will *not* lead to perceptual knowledge of the environment. Since this can happen (and does in innumerably many cases; see the discussion of the bird and the window in section 2.5), the theorist must face the question: what more than the pickup of de facto informative medium properties is required to mediate perceptual knowledge? The notion of inference may provide an answer; but, in any event, Gibson's notion of information does not. Information explains only what correlation explains, and the existence of a correlation between two states of affairs does not, in and of itself, explain how the detection of one of them could eventuate in perceptual knowledge of the other.

There is, we think, a deeper way of putting these points, and it is one that we will return to in the last section of our discussion. The fundamental difficulty for

Gibson is that "about" (as in "information *about* the layout in the light") is a semantic relation, and Gibson has no account *at all* of what it is to recognize a semantic relation. The reason this is so serious for Gibson is that it seems plausible that recognizing X to be about Y is a matter of mentally representing X in a certain way; e.g., as a premise in an inference from X to Y. And it is, of course, precisely the notion of mental representation that Gibson wants very much to do without. We have here a glimmer of Gibson's ultimate dilemma: the (correlational) notion of information that he allows himself simply will not serve for the identification of perception with information pickup. Whereas, the semantic notion of information that Gibson needs depends, so far as anyone knows, on precisely the mental representation construct that he deplores. The *point* of the inferential account of perception is to spell out what is involved in taking proximal (or ambient) stimulation as containing information about its distal causes. One cannot provide an alternative to that theory merely by assuming the notion of information as unexplicated, though that is, to all intents and purposes, just what Gibson does.

To summarize: Gibson has no notion of information over and above the notion of correlation. You can, no doubt, pick up properties of S1, and, no doubt, some of the properties of S1 that you can pick up may be correlated with properties of S2. But you cannot pick up the property of *being correlated with S2*, and it is hard to see how the mere existence of such a correlation could have epistemic consequences unless the correlation is mentally represented, e.g., as a premise in a perceptual inference. We can put it in a nutshell: sensible constraints on visual direct detection make properties of light its natural object. And then the question "how do you get from an epistemic relation to properties of the light (viz., pickup) to an epistemic relation to properties of the layout (viz., perception)?" seems to have only one conceivable answer: by inferential mediation, like the Establishment says.

The moral of all this is that when Gibson says that we perceive the layout "directly," one must not take him to be claiming that the perception of the layout is unmediated. Gibson, in fact, accepts that visual perception of the layout is mediated at least by the detection of properties of the light, and we have argued that he has suggested no alternative to the idea that such mediation also involves inference. Thus, if we want to find a disagreement between Gibson and the Establishment, we shall have to look to something other than the question whether the perception of distal visual layout involves inference from proximal visual stimulations; both sides agree that it does, albeit with unequal explicitness.

6   The Second Constraint on Pickup: Only Properties of "Effective Stimuli" Are Directly Detected

Since when Gibson says that perception is "direct" he is clearly not saying that it is unmediated, the question arises what alternative construal might be placed upon his claim. The following suggestion seems to be compatible with much of the text: Although perception of the layout is causally dependent upon pickup of properties of the medium, still the information about the layout that the medium makes available is so rich that the pickup of that information is, as it were, *tantamount* to the perception of the correlated layout properties. To all intents and purposes, this comes to the claim that a given configuration of the medium (e.g., of the ambient optical array) specifies a corresponding configuration of the layout uniquely.

There is a stronger and a weaker version of this claim. The stronger version is that (so long as we focus on the right properties of the medium) the information we find there is, under normal circumstances, *almost invariably* sufficient to specify the ecologically relevant properties of the layout. The weaker claim is that, although *some* of the perceptually available properties of the layout are uniquely specified by properties of the medium, it is left open that other such properties may not be. Gibson's exposition makes it clear that he intends the former of these claims, as indeed he must if there is to be a difference between his views and those of the Establishment.

The Establishment theory takes the connection between the distal layout and the states of the transducers to be something like this: certain properties of the medium are causal determinants of the output of the detectors. Some of these medium properties are, in turn, causally determined by properties of the distal layout. Since the relation of causal determination is transitive, the detector output is itself normally contingent upon particular features of the layout. If, as has usually been assumed, this relation between layout properties and detector outputs is more or less one-to-one (i.e., the mapping is reversible), then this view is entirely compatible with the weaker version of Gibson's claim. In both the Gibsonian account and the Establishment view, it is part of the explanation of the veridicality of perception that, in ecologically normal circumstances, many of the directly detectable properties of the light are specific to properties of the layout which cause them.

In short, the weak version of Gibson's claim is that there are *some* visual properties of the layout which are, to a first approximation, causally necessary and sufficient for properties of the light, which latter properties are themselves directly picked up. Our point has been that the Establishment theories say that too; in particular, the Establishment theories provide precisely that account in the case of the sensory properties of the layout, taking these to be, by stipulation, the properties of the layout which are causally responsible for the properties of the medium that transducers respond to.

Since the weak version of Gibson's claim does not distinguish his position from the Establishment's, let us consider the stronger version, which is that the light contains information that is specific to just about all the visual properties of the layout. By contrast, according to Establishment theories, the sensory properties are a very small subset of the visual properties, and it is *only* for the sensory properties that the medium-to-layout mapping is assumed to remotely approach uniqueness. Hence, the Establishment theory is *not* compatible with the strong version of Gibson's claim. Given this incompatibility, the next question is whether Gibson's claim is plausible on its strong construal. It turns out, however, that before we can raise this question, we have to face yet another trivialization problem.

Consider the claim that, for each visually perceptible property of the layout, there is a corresponding property of the light which is, in some non-vacuous sense, directly detectable and specific to the layout feature in question. For the moment, let us not worry about how the notion of a directly detectable property is to be constrained, and concentrate instead on the issue of specificity. Once again there is a way of trivializing Gibson's claim. The trivializing alternative arises if, among relevant properties of the medium, we allow properties of *arbitrary spatio-temporal cross sections of the light* (for example, the distribution of the light across the entire inhabited universe throughout some arbitrary segment of history, including the arrangement of the light reflected from all the pages of all the books in all the libraries, and all the dials on all the apparatus in all the scientific laboratories). If we take such an arbitrarily bounded sample of the light, then it may well be that its structure does uniquely specify every perceptible property of the corresponding layout. Indeed, it may be that the arrangement of all the light specifies a unique layout of all the objects, perceptual or otherwise. Whether this is true may be of considerable epistemological interest, since an epistemologist might well wonder whether there is enough data in the medium to determine a unique best theory of the world. The trouble is that, either way, the issue has no implications for the psychology of perception.

The important psychological question is whether the claim of specificity can be maintained for *appropriately bounded* samples of the ambient optic array, and the interest of the Establishment contention that perception is typically inferential depends in large part on the claim that the answer to this question is "no." The Establishment holds that there must be inference from medium to layout; but, as we have seen, that must be admitted by anyone who accepts the principle that only properties of the medium are detected directly. What is more contentious is the Establishment claim that layout properties are typically inferred on the basis of *relatively fragmentary* information about the structure of the medium; hence that the patterns of transducer outputs which serve as "premises" for perceptual inferences in general significantly *underdetermine* the percepts to which they give rise.[9] This is an issue on which Gibson and the Establishment certainly disagree. Our point has been that before it can be assessed, we need some independent criterion for what is to *count* as an appropriately bounded sample of the optic array.

We assume that the following is—or, anyhow, ought to be—untendentious: The goal of a theory of perception includes characterizing the sample of the ambient array which causes each percept. It is true that, in his most recent writings, Gibson sometimes seems to be saying that perception should not be viewed as caused by stimulation. Indeed, he appears to want to do away with the notion of the stimulus altogether. "I thought I had discovered that there were stimuli for perception in much the same way that there were known to be stimuli for sensations. This now seems to me to be a mistake. I failed to distinguish between stimulation proper and stimulus information" (p. 149). But, whatever this distinction may come to, it surely does not provide an argument against there being environmental causes of perception. And, as long as it is assumed that there are, giving a causal account of perceptual phenomena is surely one of the central aims that psychology ought to pursue. In particular, what we want is a specification of the sample of the ambient array which causes each distinct perceptual episode.

Just as the goal of specifying the environmental causes of percepts survives disagreements over whether what causes a percept is stimulation or stimulus information, so it also survives disagreements over how percepts ought to be described. Gibson says: "I should not have implied that a percept was an automatic response to a stimulus, as a sense impression is supposed to be. For even then I realized that perceiving is an act, not a response . . ." (Ibid). An adequate psychology might provide mappings from segments of the ambient array onto percepts, or onto some larger events, or patterns of behavior; in either case, perceptual episodes will be viewed as caused and the problem of specifying bounds on the causally efficacious sample of the ambient array will have to be faced.

In fact most of these worries are, in the invidious sense, academic. Gibson and the Establishment agree on what constitutes some clear cases of perceptual phenomena to be explained. When one performs an experiment by setting up certain displays and finds that subjects report seeing certain things, this is prima facie a relevant datum for perceptual theory. For example, Gibson (p. 190) makes much of an experiment by Kaplan involving progressive deletion or accretion of a random texture. He reports: "What observers saw was an edge, a cut edge, the edge of a sheet, and another surface behind it." This, then, is a perceptual phenomenon which everyone agrees requires causal explanation; and this agreement presupposes no general consensus about the ontological status of percepts.

On any account, then, percepts have causes, and among the causes of a percept will be some bounded spatio-temporal segments of the ambient optical array. Let us call such a segment the *effective stimulus* for the percept that it causes. Thus for every percept there is some effective stimulus which is its immediate environmental cause. Given this notion we can now ask the critical question: Is it true, in the general case, that each effective stimulus is uniquely correlated with the structure of a corresponding layout? We take it that this is the appropriate way to ask the question whether, in the general case, the structure of the medium specifies the structure of the layout uniquely.

When, however, we put the question this way, it seems obvious that the answer is "no." The mapping of layouts onto effective stimuli is certainly many-to-one, for it has been repeatedly shown in psychological laboratories that percepts can be caused by samples of the ambient medium which demonstrably underdetermine the corresponding layout. Nor is this phenomenon specific to vision. Consider, for example, the "phoneme restoration effect" (Warren, 1970) in psycholinguistics: Take a tape recording of an English word, and delete the part of the tape corresponding to one of the speech sounds. (For example, one can start with a recording of "determine" and produce a recording of "de#ermine.") Now record a cough-sound and splice it into the gap. The resulting tape is heard as containing the ungapped original word ("determine") with a cough-sound "in the background." The experiment thus demonstrates that an acoustic array which serves as an effective stimulus for the perception of a cough when heard in nonspeech contexts, can also serve as an effective stimulus for the percept /t/ when heard in the context "de#ermine," for the percept /k/ when heard in the context "es#ape," etc. The mapping from effective stimuli onto layouts is thus one-many in at least one case.[10]

Gibson is, of course, aware of such results, but he deprecates them on the grounds that providing a *richer* sample of the ambient array is often sufficient to change the organism's perception of the layout; as, for example, when one destroys the Ames' room illusion by allowing the viewer to move freely through the experimental environment or when, in the case of the phoneme restoration effect, one slows down the tape enough to hear what is "really" going on. (The latter case shows, by the way, that the "richer" stimulus—the one which leads to true perceptual beliefs—is by no means always the ecologically normal stimulus; there are illusions which occur in the normal situation, and in these cases it is the ecologically pathological stimulus which is required to produce the veridical percept). But Gibson's criticism of these results is irrelevant once one accepts the condition, enunciated above, that an adequate theory must account for the effects of *all* perceptually effective stimulations. True, we can alter the initial percept by adding to the input (supplying context); but it remains to be explained how the original "ecologically invalid" percept was caused. In effect, Gibson's criticism is telling only if one accepts the trivializing construal of his claim that the medium contains information sufficient to specify the layout, thereby avoiding the serious issue which is how much information the *effective stimulus* contains.

If, by contrast, we take the effective stimulus constraint seriously, the facts seem to be clear: percepts are often caused by effective stimulation which is not specific to a layout. In such cases, the properties of the medium that are picked up underdetermine the layout that is perceived. So we are in need of an answer to the question what processes *other than* the pickup of medium properties are implicated in the causation of percepts? The Establishment theory has an answer; viz., the occurrence of certain perceptual inferences. In particular, inferences *from* the detected properties of the fragmentary stimulus *to* the properties that a richer sample of the ambient array would reveal. Gibson has, thus far, provided no reason for rejecting that answer, nor has he shown how an alternative might be formulated.

To summarize: the claim that there is enough information in each sample of the light to specify a unique layout is empty without some constraint on what is to count as a sample. Gibson provides no such constraint, but it is fairly clear how one ought to do so: since the goal is a theory of the causation of percepts, the appropriate sample must be what we called the "effective stimulus." For, by stipulation, the effective stimulus just *is* an arrangement of the medium that is sufficient to cause a percept. But then the claim that, in the general case, effective stimuli uniquely specify layouts is patently false on empirical grounds. Note, finally, that the fact that the perception of the layout is generally veridical does *not* require that effective stimuli specify uniquely; indeed, the inferential account of perception is precisely an attempt to show how veridical perception could occur without unique specification. Since perception depends on ambient stimulation *together with inference*, the veridicality of perception requires only that the principles of inference should be truth preserving most of the time.

7   What Properties of the Effective Stimulus Are Directly Detected?

In view of the preceding discussion, one might well ask what remains of the ecological approach to visual perception. We will now see that Gibson can be construed as making a number of plausible objections to standard Establishment assumptions about which properties of the light are directly detected. Recall that we started by recognizing that the claim of immediate perception was vacuous unless constrained. We suggested that one such constraint is the requirement that generalizations which relate the inputs and outputs of detectors should be counterfactual supporting (i.e., that they should survive appropriate applications of the method of differences). A second constraint was that immediately detectable properties of the light should be properties of effective stimuli (i.e., of light samples which cause percepts). The present point is that within these constraints there is a real empirical issue as to what the correct inventory of detected properties is, and here Gibson departs in important ways from the assumptions that Establishment theorists have often made.

The version of Establishment theory against which Gibson typically pits his approach takes instantaneous point-intensities of the light impinging on a retinal surface as the only properties that are primitively detected in vision. Gibson's point is, at a minimum, that this decision cannot be defended on a priori grounds and that describing the directly detected stimulus as an instantaneous mosaic has profound and implausible implications for the rest of one's theory of perception. Both these points are well taken, and it is worth emphasizing that the pointillist view of the directly detected stimulus is not entailed by the constraints on transduction that we have proposed. There is nothing in these criteria to rule out there being directly detected properties of light distributed over much longer segments of space-time than has been widely assumed by Establishment theorists. Nor, as Gibson points out, do the physiological facts about the size of retinal receptive fields imply the pointillist view since, as we have repeatedly remarked, decisions as to what counts as a transducer—and hence decisions as to what properties are transduced—must ultimately be made on functional grounds.

The assumption of highly local detectors has often lead Establishment theorists to conclude that the perception of patterns over space and time *necessarily* involves construction and inference from information stored in memory. This conclusion is one of Gibson's favorite targets (see, for example, Gibson, 1966). He maintains that memory is not needed if we allow features of larger segments of space-time to be detected. And, strictly speaking, this is correct so long as the effective stimulus constraint is observed. There would, for example, be no need to posit the construction of such things as texture gradients and flows from snapshot memories if the organism could detect spatially and temporally extended light patterns. In the spatial case, such detection could proceed by the use of devices like spatial frequency filters and templates. Analogous methods are available in the temporal domain where tuned filters can be made to play the role of templates.

Similarly, as Gibson has frequently pointed out, it is incorrect to assume that the only way that one can perceive change is by detecting and comparing two instantaneous states, at least one of which is retained in memory. In the first place, there is nothing to prevent such mechanisms as speedometers, accelerometers or frequency meters from being primitive in the required sense. Yet all of these can be viewed as detecting change: A speedometer detects rate of change of distance, an accelerometer detects rate of change of velocity, and so on. In the second place, as the preceding examples suggest, whether one is detecting a given magnitude or a temporal derivative of some other magnitude is sometimes a matter of how one chooses to describe things. A transducer for acceleration (say in the vestibular system) can be viewed as detecting a magnitude (a force vector), or the rate of change of a magnitude (velocity), or even the second derivative of another magnitude (distance). The same applies to the visual modality, where the detection of the second derivative of a magnitude (number of photons incident on the receptor) can be viewed as the transduction of intensity change. In this case, there is no more need to posit memory to account for the detection of intensity *change* than there is to account for the detection of intensity *value*. Either could, in principle, be taken as primitive.

Even the absolute time over which a change can be primitively detected is an empirical question and cannot be settled in advance of the data. This is true for the same reason that rate and magnitude detection can be interchanged in certain situations. We saw above that when certain rates and magnitudes are nomologically related (e.g., force and acceleration), the question which one of them a mechanism detects may be without empirical import. The same principle holds over long time spans. Whenever an equivalence class of histories of some system is nomologically connected to the current state of that system, detecting the latter can be tantamount to detecting the former. Thus, the issue of how long a time period of changes can be primitively detected must be settled by actually studying the functional capacities of the organism in question. In particular, the spatial limits of the immediately detected visual properties may extend beyond the retinal field and their temporal limits may extend beyond the measured refractory period of the visual system as neuroanatomically defined. But if they do, of course, then the retina and the neuroanatomical structures involved do not constitute the whole transducer mechanism for these properties.

In short, the methodological constraints on transduction that we have discussed so far considerably underdetermine a census of the directly detected properties, and they are compatible with a view of these properties quite different from the pointillism that Gibson deplores. The pressing issue is thus to understand what sorts of empirical considerations are operative in deciding which properties of the light are transduced, and what the empirical consequences of such decisions are. In what follows, we briefly review three such considerations. For expository purposes, we will take some of our examples from phonetics rather than vision. The question of which (if any) phonetic properties are transduced is a classical problem in psycholinguistics, and one in which the theoretical consequences of the various options reveal themselves with particular clarity.

7.1 Productivity

There is a prima facie assumption that productive properties of the effective stimulus are not directly transduced. Roughly, a productive property is one which determines an infinite equivalence class of (actual and possible) discriminable stimuli, such that the organism is, at least in principle, capable of identifying arbitrary novel stimuli which belong to the class. We will call this set of stimuli the *associated set* for a productive property. The property of being a token of an English sentence is, in this sense, a productive property, and its associated set contains all and only the actual and possible token utterances of English sentences.

The reason that productive properties are prima facie not transduced is that, in many of the most interesting cases, membership in the associated set is inferred from a prior identification of the internal structure to the stimulus. For example, we presumably infer the sentencehood of a token from a prior analysis of its internal lexical and syntactic structure. Since inferential processes are ipso facto not transductive, cases in which productive properties are recognized via the assignment of internal structure are ipso facto not cases of direct detection.

There are, however, lots of examples where productive properties *are* transduced, and these raise theoretical issues of considerable importance. It is, for example, perfectly possible to build a detector which transduces—or, to borrow Gibson's term, "resonates to"—the frequency of ambient sound or light, so the fact that there are indefinitely many physical displays that the organism can recognize as tones or colors is no evidence against the direct detection of colorhood and tonehood. In general, where the associated set that a property determines can be specified in terms of the values of some physical parameter, it seems possible—in principle, if not in fact—that the mechanism for the recognition of that property might be a resonator which is "tuned" to the relevant parameter values.

These considerations suggest an argument which, though rarely explicit may well underlie the suspicion that the resonator model (and hence the direct detection theory) might after all provide a *general* account of perception. It may also help explain the emphasis on analogue models for perception that one finds in so many Gibsonian texts (see, for example, Prendle, Carello, and Turvey, 1980; Runeson, 1980). We digress to consider this argument.

Consider a productive property like token sentencehood which appears, at first blush, to be nontransducible.

1. It seems plausible that every token sentence, including a merely possible one, is identical with some actual or possible physical object. It presumably follows that, for every token sentence there is some or other *identifying physical description*; i.e., a description that is true of that token and no other.

2. We can therefore, in principle, specify a physical property P that is *counterpart* to the property of being an actual or possible sentence token. P is specified by forming the (presumably infinite) disjunction whose disjuncts are the identifying physical descriptions for each of the actual and possible sentence tokens.

3. P is a physical property; that is, it is specified solely in terms of physical parameters.

4. Therefore, it is possible (at least in principle) to build a resonator for P.

5. Therefore, it is possible (at least in principle) to build a resonator for token sentencehood.

6. If there could be a resonator for token sentencehood, then perhaps we detect that property by resonating to it. Similarly for any other productive property.

This argument is important because it seems to show that the mere fact that a class of stimuli is a class of physical objects implies the possibility-in-principle of a resonator for the property with which the class is associated. And it is a short step from that conclusion to the claim that the postulation of inferential processes in perceptual recognition is always *heuristic* in the sense that, if the associated class can be identified by an inferential system, it can also be identified by a resonator (albeit, in some cases, a very complicated one).

The usual objection to this line of argument is to challenge the inference from 3 to 4. Notice that P will be a transducible property only if there exists a nomologically possible device (a detector) whose states are causally dependent on the presence of P. But the nomological possibility of such a device is by no means implied just by the assumption that P is physically specifiable. Though we have every reason to suppose that there must be some physical property which is common to all and only the possible sentence tokens, we also have every reason to believe that it is a highly disjunctive and arbitrary property; one which may perfectly well fail even to be finitely specifiable. But if P is disjunctive and arbitrary, then presumably P is not projectible (there are no laws about P). And if P is not projectible, there is no reason to suppose that a device whose states are lawfully related to the presence of P—viz., a P-detector—is empirically possible.

We believe this rebuttal to be well taken. However, at first glance it may seem to be denying the following obvious fact. An English speaker is, presumably, a physical device; and English speakers are capable of distinguishing arbitrary token sentences from arbitrary token nonsentences. So it looks as though the very existence of English speakers constitutes a constructive proof of the possibility of physical systems that are selectively sensitive to P, and hence of the possibility of transducers for P. But if P is transducible and coextensive with token sentencehood in all possible worlds, then token sentencehood must be transducible after all.

This argument is attractive but fallacious, as is the argument from (1) through (6). In particular, you cannot infer the transducibility of P from the fact that English speakers are selectively sensitive to token sentencehood, and you cannot infer the transducibility of token sentencehood from the assumption that there is a resonator for P (as in the inference from [4] to [5]). Both inferences fail, and for the same reason: they both assume that the ability to detect membership in the associated set for a property implies the ability to detect the property. And this is wrong because it is perfectly possible for *distinct* properties to have the same associated set.

It is extremely tempting to assume that if two properties are coextensive for *both actual and possible* cases (as are, by assumption, P and token sentencehood) then the properties are identical, and the detection of one is the detection of the other. But this assumption is false. Distinct properties can be coextensive in all possible worlds, since properties that are coextensive in all possible worlds may nevertheless differ in their (higher order) properties.[11] This is by no means a quibble; it converts directly into differences in the empirical consequences of the hypothesis that English speakers respond selectively to token sentencehood, on the one hand, or to P on the other.

Consider the property of being a token sentence of Pig Latin (the property L_1). L_1 is very similar to English token sentencehood since you can pair any token English sentence with something which has L_1 by employing a trivial algorithm. But now consider the property P_1 which is the physical counterpart of L_1, in the same way that P is the physical counterpart of English token sentencehood. Suppose that $L_1 = P_1$ (i.e., that being a token sentence in Pig Latin is the same property as P_1). Then, since tokens of English and tokens of Pig Latin are similar in respect of their linguistic properties, and since we are assuming that their linguistic properties are *identical* to their physical properties (in particular, that being an English token *is* being P), it follows that tokens of English and tokens of Pig Latin must be similar in respect of their physical properties. But this consequence is false; a token of an English sentence may bear very little physical relation to a token of its Pig Latin translation.[12] Hence, token sentencehood cannot be the same property as P. To put the point quite generally, if two things are *similar* because one has A and the other A', but *dissimilar* because one has B and the other has B', it cannot be the case that A = B and A' = B'.

What we are saying is that even if token sentencehood and P are coextensive in all possible worlds, they nevertheless have different locations in the space of property similarities, and are thus *different properties*.[13] Hence the hypothesis that English speakers are responsive to token sentencehood leads to quite different predictions than the hypothesis that they are responsive to P. On the former hypothesis, it ought to be quite easy (having once learned to distinguish sentences from nonsentences) to then learn Pig Latin. Whereas, on the latter hypothesis it ought to be quite easy (having once learned to distinguish P from non-P) to learn to detect the property of being just like P except for some simple acoustical transformation—

like having the acoustic spectrum inverted or reversed. It is entirely clear which of these hypotheses is true of English speakers. Pig Latin is easy to learn, but very simple transformations of the physical signal can entirely destroy the intelligibility of speech. So when we respond selectively to tokens, it is sentencehood, and not P, that we are perceiving.

Since P and token sentencehood are not the same property, the assumption that P is transducible would not at all imply that it is possible to directly perceive sentencehood, and the fact that we can respond selectively to the associated set for sentencehood does not imply the nomological possibility of a transducer for P. It may be that the associated set for any perceptible property is a set of actual or possible physical objects. It does not follow that there could, even in principle, be a resonator for every perceptible property. Probably the right thing to say is that the only properties that can be transduced are the projectible ones: If a property is projectible, then by definition there are things whose states are lawfully connected to the presence of that property; i.e., things that detect that property. But it is by no means the case that all, or even most, of the properties that we can perceive are projectible.

As for P and token sentencehood, the right thing to say is probably that *neither* is transduced. We do not transduce P because P is not projectible, hence not the sort of physical property to which empirically possible detectors can be selectively tuned. And we do not transduce token sentencehood because the token sentencehood of a stimulus is inferred from the prior identification of its parts and their arrangement. The point to bear in mind is that *both* of these claims (and their conjunction) are compatible with the assumption that we are able to identify the members of the stimulus set that is associated with both token sentencehood and P.

7.2   Internal Structure and Generalization Gradients

As we saw in the preceding section, the reason that many productive properties cannot be viewed as transduced is that recognition of items belonging to their associated sets depends upon inference from assignments of internal structure: the items are recognized via a prior identification of the character and arrangement of their parts. In short, cases where perceptual recognition depends upon analysis of internal structure are cases where the direct perception model fails to apply.

The present question is how this criterion for nontransduction is to be applied; that is, how we can tell whether perceptual recognition is mediated by the assignment of internal structure. One answer is that, in such cases, the generalization gradient for the stimulus is often predictable from relations of similarity and identity defined over its parts.

As an illustration of what is at stake, consider the problem of deciding whether the perception of speech involves the direct detection of phones, or phonemes, or syllables or perhaps some higher level entities like words or sentences. The view that what is directly detected is one of the smaller units (e.g., phones) has as a consequence the prediction that segments which share a phone ought to be perceived as more similar than contrasted segments whose phonetic transcriptions do not overlap. By contrast, the view that larger units (such as syllables or words) are transduced would not lead directly to such predictions. Notice that this predictive asymmetry between the models holds even if the acoustic and phonetic structure of a speech segment are isomorphic, so that the phonetic similarity of segments guarantees their accoustic similarity. Suppose that a pair of segments have acoustically identical parts wherever they have phonetically identical parts. Even so, phonetic similarity warrants predictions of generalization only on the *further* assumption that the segments are identified via the prior identification of their parts—i.e., that the identification of the acoustic structure is nonholistic. On holistic assumptions (e.g., that recognition is accomplished by the application of a segment-length acoustic template), even the fact that a pair of segments exhibits partially identical acoustic substructures provides no grounds for predicting generalizations from one to the other.

Gibson appears to recognize the importance of the issue of internal structure in percepts, since he frequently refers to the perceptual objects in the environment as being "nested." However, he denies that the detection of such nested units is cascaded in the sense that the identification of the higher units is dependent upon the prior identification of the lower ones. He *must* deny this because the mechanisms in virtue of which the identification of the former is contingent upon the identification of the latter could only be inferential. Perhaps Gibson's view is that units at all relevant levels are simultaneously and independently detected. But, in and of itself, this assumption does little to explain the facts about generalization and similarity structure among percepts. What is required for that purpose is not merely that the information about lower level units be *recorded*, but also that the hierarchical and combinatorial relations among the various units should be among the properties of the stimulus which the organism registers in the course of perceptual identification. Thus, in order to account for the fact that /ba/ and /pa/ are perceived to be related in the same way as /bo/ and /po/, and that /ba/ and /ab/ are perceived to be related in the same way as /bo/ and /ob/, we need to assume the detection, not only of syllables and their constituent phones, but also of the relevant relations of order and inclusion.

Our point is not, of course, that making the appropriate predictions about generalization is *incompatible* with assuming the direct detection of higher-order units; only that their reconciliation often depends upon postulating ancillary mechanisms that the componential approach can do without. For example, one could assume holistic perception and account for generalization gradients by postulating a further process in which the internal structure of higher level units is retrieved by lookup (as in models of speech detection where syllabic identity is recovered first and phonetic structure is assigned by accessing a syllable dictionary). Such postulation is sometimes justifiable. For example, there is sometimes evidence that the higher units can be identified faster than their components, and such results provide prima facie (though by no means univocal) evidence for a "top down" order of processing. In any event, the need to account for the subject's perception of similarity and generalization structures among stimuli is real, and it provides a source of constraint on decisions about which of the properties of the stimulus should be viewed as directly detected.

7.3   Cognitive Penetrability

We have, in effect, been taking transducers to be devices whose output is lawfully dependent upon the character of their input. The output of a perceptual mechanism, by contrast, may show simultaneous effects of the character of its input and of the inferential operations that it performs. We now note an important consequence of this view of transduction: the character of a transducer's response is not, in general, sensitive to the beliefs and utilities of the organism. We refer to this as the "cognitive impenetrability" of transduction. (For general discussion, see Pylyshyn, 1980.)

It is notorious that the expectations and utilities of an organism selectively affect what it sees and hears. The subject biased to expect a picture of an old woman is not likely to see the ambiguous stimulus as a picture of a young girl; the hungry organism responds at low thresholds to food that the well fed organism misses altogether. The general consideration is that the range of "perceptual properties"— the range of properties that the perceptual system can respond to—is practically unbounded, and the mechanisms of perception can be selectively biased to very nearly any of them. This sounds surprising only if we forget that perception involves the integration of current inputs with background information; how the perceptual apparatus is cognitively tuned is largely a question of which such background information is being deployed. Whereas, since the output of a transducer is, by assumption, nomologically dependent upon the properties that it responds to, and since the number of properties that are lawfully connected with the output states of such devices is, in any event, very much smaller than the number of perceptible properties, the possibilities for the cognitive retuning of a transducer are correspondingly restricted relative to the possibilities for cognitive retuning in perception.[14]

The conclusion is that the right kind of cognitive penetrability is a counterindicant of transduction. The "right kind" of penetrability is exhibited when the property to which a mechanism responds proves to be arbitrarily sensitive to the content of the subject's goals, beliefs, and utilities.[15] We have qualified the claim in this way because we want to admit the possibility of such relatively undifferentiated effects of goals and beliefs on the behavior of transducer mechanisms as would be exhibited in cases of centripetal damping (as, for example, when the impedance of the ear or the aperture of the eye is altered as a mechanism of selective attention). Notice, however, that such examples typically concern modulation of the *amplitude* of a transducer's response rather than of the stimulus property to which its response is specific; and one would scarcely expect that such modulation would exhibit a *detailed* specificity to the content of the organism's cognitive states.

7.4 Cognitive Impenetrability and "Compiled Detectors"

It is important to notice that, though cognitive penetrability generally suggests nontransduction, the inverse does not hold. There are, in all probability, many cases of what might be called cognitive automatisms: computational processes which, though inferential, are nevertheless quite rigidly insensitive to modulation by beliefs and utilities. In fact, some of the most important work inspired by the Gibsonian tradition can be viewed as the identification of levels of mental representation which are computed by such processes.

We have seen that the general issue of specifying *which* properties of an effective stimulus are directly detected and which are constructed or inferred via processes that access the organism's tacit knowledge, is one of the fundamental problems of perception. Gibson is to be credited with promoting the view that many of the presuppositions of classical theories of perception were based upon untenable assumptions about how this question should be answered. Such assumptions, while not an inherent part of the Establishment view, dominated much of the early theorizing about vision which, for example, assumed that the input to a visual system should be described in terms of point-intensities on the retina at an instant of time. What such theorizing failed to appreciate, and what Gibson helped to dramatize, is that (a) there is no theoretically *neutral* description of a perceptual stimulus—the form that one's theory of perception takes is extremely sensitive to exactly what one assumes are the inputs to the perceptual system, and (b) what ought to be considered to be the input is an empirical question. Largely due to the efforts of Gibson and his coworkers there has been a revival of interest in viewing the input to the visual system as consisting of spatially and temporally distributed properties of the light array. For example, there has been much fruitful work on the perception of form and of motion which relies on the existence of reliable correlations between spatially extended optical texture gradients at the retina and such properties of the environment as the depth, slant and shape of surfaces (e.g., Stevens, 1979); between relative movements of elementary retinal features and the three dimensional shape of a moving rigid form (e.g., Ullman, 1979) or the movement of the observer (e.g., Prazdny, 1981); or between the retinal disparity of primitive features and the perception of depth (Marr and Poggio, 1976).

Although such correlations have long been known to be important for vision, the recent work has added an important new dimension to early speculative theories. Many of these investigations have located the precise features of the dynamic retinal pattern involved in the correlation, and have shown that there is a specifiable mathematical basis for its reliability. They have, in other words, succeeded in specifying *which* properties of the light constitute good indicators of perceived environmental properties, and *why* they do so. Thus, to take one example from the above list, Ullman has shown that if one assumes (a) that the organism can reliably determine which optical retinal features arise from the *same* point on a moving stimulus across time and (b) that the stimulus features maintain their relative three dimensional distances (i.e., that they are located on a rigid body), then given a sufficient sample of the dynamic retinal pattern, a computable one-to-one mapping onto the three dimensional form can be defined. Furthermore, the few assumptions made by this model have been verified empirically. It might thus be argued that the organism need not make complex, knowledge dependent inferences in order to determine the three dimensional shape of an object; it need not, in other words, go through any such process as that of using highly partial and sketchy cues to frame a hypothesis about the identity of the object, and then using its general world knowledge to infer the shape under observation. At least in this case, it appears that specific properties of the ambient array are able, as Gibson would put it, to specify the three dimensional shape uniquely.

Such results have helped kindle the current interest in Gibson's theory. Many investigators have even adopted some of Gibson's terminology, and describe these cases as illustrating the pickup of invariants. It is important, however, to see that such a terminological policy merely pays tribute to Gibson's attack on the pointil-list and static snapshot presuppositions of early Establishment theories. There is really nothing in the recent research that is at odds with the Establishment story (or, for that matter, with the Helmholtz story) about perceptual *inference*. In par-ticular, the fact that we can, in some cases, provide a precise account of a locus of a reliable correlation between light features and layout features—and, indeed, even show the conditions under which a perfect correlation is possible—does nothing to remove the need for postulating computational processes in accounting for the perceptual capacities of the organism.

Recall that we claimed that there are two aspects of the inferential model: the claim that properties of the layout are inferred from properties of the light, and the claim that the directly detected properties of the light generally underdetermine fea-tures of the layout. It is patent that nothing in the new research challenges the former claim; so long as the organism is detecting light patterns and not layout patterns, there is no way to avoid the conclusion that perceptual knowledge of the latter is inferred; this remains true no matter how perfect the correlation between light and layout may prove to be. What such results as Ullman's do is explain why such infer-ences are *sound* in specified circumstances.

More to the point, however, is the fact that such results *do not imply that the properties of the ambient optic array which correlate reliably with surface orienta-tions, shapes and motions of objects are the ones that are directly detected.* True, the findings suggest that the construction of certain levels of representation may be cognitively impenetrable by, for example, the subjects' prior beliefs about the stim-ulus that they are viewing. But, as we remarked above, while some notion of cog-nitive impenetrability provides a necessary condition for direct detection, it certainly does not provide a sufficient condition.

In particular, the research leaves open the possibility that the detection of such properties as, for example, the texture flow of the light when it is accelerating in a certain direction while systematically changing its textural density, is mediated by the detection of more primitive properties such as, perhaps, the relative magnitude of texture densities at various retinal locations, the relative rates of change of these densities in relation to their relative locations, the existence and locations of sharp discontinuities in these or other light features, and so on. The existence of such mediation in fact seems quite likely. As we argued earlier, we want to be able to account for the origins of percepts in terms of the properties of their effective stimuli, and this necessitates that we be able to detect subfeatures of the light like the ones just mentioned since they themselves can and do give rise to percepts. Since, moreover, the inference from the light to the layout depends upon details of the arrangement of such subfeatures in relation to one another and to global properties of the texture flow, it is, as we argued above, vastly implausible that the global feature detectors should be primitive. There are, after all, arbitrarily many ways in which such subfeatures can be arranged in the global array, and each of these arrangements has different implications for the organization of the layout and for the generalization gradients among percepts. It thus seems obvious that, barring the possibility of a primitive "resonator" that is selectively sensitive to these various proximal arrangements, the best assumption is that the output of the complex property detector must be *constructed* from primitively detected subfeatures.

What we have is, in effect, a conflict between the demands of the productivity and internal structure criteria, on the one hand, and the cognitive penetrability criterion, on the other. The discovery of cases where these criteria conflict may well be the most important contribution of the Gibsonian tradition to Establishment theory. Though the empirical research we have alluded to offers no support for direct perception of any kind, it does provide suggestive evidence for the existence of levels of complex detection which are autonomous, stimulus bound, cognitively impenetrable, and hence unmediated by a certain kind of deliberate deduction from generally available knowledge (e.g., the sort of deduction which enters into explicit question answering).

The notion of an autonomous computational "reflex," compiled from elementary constituents but impervious to general cognition, is one which finds widespread application. For example, there is good evidence that much of lexical identification, and even of syntactic analysis, may be of this type; and it may be that some of what goes under the name of "imagistic processing' belongs to this category. (See, however, Pylyshyn, 1980, for an argument that much imagistic processing is cognitively penetrable, hence not compiled). Similarly, Marr (1976) has argued for a level of complex representation in form recognition which he calls the "primal sketch" and which is assumed to be largely or entirely stimulus driven. The argument is that the computational processes eventuating in a primal sketch can be empirically demonstrated to be "reversible." Suppose that the primal sketch S arises from the ambient array A via the computational process C. It turns out that, if C is, in effect, applied backwards so as to generate an ambient array A' from S, A' will prove to be very nearly indistinguishable from A. This suggests that the mapping from stimulus arrays onto primary sketches must be very nearly one-to-one. If, however, a primal sketch is uniquely determined by an ambient pattern, then the processes which eventuate in its integration cannot be cognitively penetrable.

If the existence of processes of "compiled detection" is borne out by further research, that will indeed tell us something interesting about the modularity of perceptual systems. But it should be emphasized that such findings would have no particular bearing on the Gibsonian proposal of direct perception either of layout or of global features of the light. Transduction, as we have seen, is not to be inferred from cognitive impenetrability alone. Indeed, the only connection which a compiled detection theory of perception would have with the Gibsonian view is that they would share certain adversaries. They are both opposed to the old sense data theories, to the excesses of the "new look" in perception (cf. Bruner, 1957), and to those expectation-driven models, popular in certain quarters of artificial intelligence, which sometimes seem to deny that any significant amount of stimulus bound processing occurs after the activation of the rods and cones. But that is a fairly remote connection; the compiled detector story may be a revolution in the psychology of perception, but it is not a *Gibsonian* revolution.

Finally, it is worth bearing in mind that, while many perceptual processes may well be compiled, there is no reason to believe that all of them are. Object recognition, for example, is a perceptual process par excellence, and it appears to be cognitively penetrable through and through.

8 Conclusion: The Problem of Intentionality

Perception is interesting but cognition is more interesting still. It is, as we have seen, no small part of the importance of Gibson's revisionism that it is supposed to extend, not just to the theory of perception, but to cognitive processes at large. In this section, we argue that focusing on the problem of perception led Gibson seriously to underestimate the difficulty of constructing a cognitive psychology that dispenses with the mental representation construct. Our argument will be that (a) the prototypical perceptual relations (seeing, hearing, tasting, etc.) are extensional (and even where they are not, Gibson, in effect, treats them as though they were); (b) whereas, on the contrary, most other prototypical cognitive relations (believing, expecting, thinking about, seeing as, etc.) are intentional; and (c) the main work that the mental representation construct does in cognitive theory is to provide a basis for explaining the intentionality of cognitive relations. Our moral will be that one has not made a start on developing a representation-free cognitive psychology until one has (at least the outline of) a representation-free theory of intentionality; and that Gibson's concentration on perception led him to overlook this crucial point.

Compare *recognizing* with *recognizing as.* If you recognize the man on the white horse, and the man on the white horse is Tonto's best friend, then you recognize Tonto's best friend. Similarly with any other description true of the man on the white horse; if Tonto's best friend is The Lone Ranger, and you recognize Tonto's best friend, then you recognize The Lone Ranger. However, suppose that you recognize Tonto's best friend *as* the man on the white horse. Then, even though the man on the white horse is The Lone Ranger, it does *not* follow that you recognize the man on the white horse as The Lone Ranger. ("Who was that man on the white horse?" "That was *The Lone Ranger.*")

Roughly, *seeing* works like *recognizing,* and *seeing as* works like *recognizing as.* If you look up at the sky and see the Pole Star, then, in doing so, you see: a certain very large ball of hot flaming gasses; the star that the ancients used to steer by; a star that is not visible from South of the Equator; . . . etc. Whereas, if you look up at the sky and see the Pole Star *as* the Pole Star (i.e., you see the Pole Star and take it to be the Pole Star) it does not follow that you see the Pole Star as a large ball of hot flaming gasses, or as the star that the ancients used to steer by, or as a star that is not visible in the Southern Hemisphere. What you see when you see a thing depends on what the thing you see *is.* But what you see the thing *as* depends on what you know about what you are seeing. Contexts that work like *see* and *recognize* are called *extensional contexts.* Contexts that work like *see as* and *recognize as* are called *intentional contexts.*

We are not doing ordinary language analysis, so we do not care whether it is *precisely* true that the English verb "see" is uniformly extensional. The point is, rather, that a psychology which limits itself to considering only the extensional relations misses something that appears to be essential to explaining how our perceptual transactions with the world affect what we know and believe. Here is Smith at sea on a foggy evening, and as lost as ever he can be. Suddenly the skies clear, and Smith sees the Pole Star. What happens next? In particular, what are the consequences of what Smith perceives for what he comes to believe and do? Patently, that depends on what he sees the Pole Star *as*. If, for example, he sees the Pole Star as the star that is at the Celestial North Pole (plus or minus a degree or two), then Smith will know, to that extent, where he is; and we may confidently expect that he will utter "Saved!" and make for port. Whereas, if he sees the Pole Star but takes it to be a firefly, or takes it to be Alpha Centuri, or—knowing no astronomy at all—takes it to be just some star or other, then seeing the Pole Star may have no particular consequences for his behavior or his further cognitive states. Smith will be just as lost after he sees it as he was before.

If we want to make predictions from what someone perceives to what he does, or to the cognitive consequences of the perception, we must be able to distinguish between *merely* seeing the Pole Star and seeing the Pole Star *as* the Pole Star. In particular, since merely seeing the Pole Star and seeing it as the Pole Star have different psychological consequences, a cognitive theory must distinguish the state that the organism is in when it does the one from the state that it is when it does the other. And it must make the distinction *in the right way*. Whatever state the theory describes the organism as being in in consequence of having seen the Pole Star as such-and-such must be the right kind of state to explain the psychological consequences of seeing it that way. (If seeing the Pole Star as the Pole Star leads the astronomically sophisticated to jump with joy, then the state that the theory assigns to an organism which sees the Pole Star as the Pole Star must be such as to contribute appropriately to explaining the ensuing glee.) Our point is, then, that a theory of the intentional relations must be at the very heart of a cognitive psychology insofar as the psychologist seeks to derive predictive consequences from his claims about what the organism has perceived. To do cognitive psychology, you must know not just what the organism perceives, but how it takes what it perceives.

This is where the mental representation construct does its main theoretical work. In effect, it allows us to understand *seeing as* in terms of *seeing* and *mentally representing*. It thus comes to grips with the fact that the cognitive consequences of perception depend not just on *whether* the world is seen, but also on *how* it is seen. Just how the mental representation theory is supposed to work in this area is, of course, a matter of intense disagreement among Establishment theorists. But the general line is clear enough. To see the Pole Star as the Pole Star is (a) to see it; and (b) to take what one sees to satisfy some such representation as, for example, the open sentence "... is the Pole Star." It is perfectly possible for someone to see the Pole Star and *not* take it to satisfy a representation of that sort. For example, one might see it and believe only that it satisfies some such representation as "... is a firefly" or ". . . is some star or other." Since all these representational states are compatible with seeing the Pole Star, it is not surprising that seeing the Pole Star can have different consequences for different people or for the same person at different times. The cognitive (and hence the behavioral) consequences of what you see depend on how you represent what you see, assuming that the Establishment theory of the intentional relations is true.

Perhaps, however, it is *not* true. Our point is only that you need some theory or other to work in this area, and that the representational account is an open option. Conversely, if—like Gibson—you propose to do without the mental representation construct, you need a workable alternative to the representation account of the intentional relations. And this Gibson does not have.

We are now in a position to understand Gibson's basic strategy in some depth. To put the point as neutrally as we can, what *everybody* has to deal with, vis à vis the problem of intentionality, is the fact that stimuli enter into the causation of behavior under many different aspects. What one man responds to as the Morning Star, another responds to as the Evening Star, and their responses may, in consequence be quite different even though the Morning Star and the Evening Star are one and the same astronomical object.

The Establishment theory seeks to accommodate such facts by proliferating mental representations. The idea is that the very same object may be represented in many different ways, and someone who responds to Venus as the Morning Star differs from someone who responds to Venus as the Evening Star in respect of the ways that they represent the planet. Specifically, the locus of intentional distinctions, according to the Establishment theory, lies in the consideration that representations which differ in semantic content may nevertheless apply to the same object (Frege, 1949). The hope is, however, that theoretical appeals to the semantic content of mental representations will ultimately prove dispensable; in particular, that identities and differences among the semantic contents of mental representations will be reconstructable in terms of identities and differences among their functional (e.g., causal) roles. Such a functional account of the semantic properties of mental representations would then round out the Establishment theory of intentionality. (For discussion of this aspect of the relation between functionalism and representational theory of mind see Fodor, 1980, 1981; Loar, 1981; Field, 1978; and Pylshyn, 1980.)

What the Establishment does by proliferating *mental representations*, Gibson proposes to do by proliferating *properties*. Instead of saying that the same astronomical object is represented now as the Morning Star and now as the Evening Star, Gibson says, in effect, that the same object has the two distinct properties of being the Morning Star and being the Evening Star. Which way we respond to the object depends on which of these properties we happen to pick up.

It is not surprising that Gibson has this option. You can do with distinctions among properties a lot of what you can do with distinctions among the semantic contents of representations. This is because, according to at least one standard account, *property* and *meaning* are interdefinable notions: properties are distinct if they are expressed by nonsynonymous representations, and representations are synonymous if they express the same property.[16] Nothing much appears to be gained by chasing around this circle, which is why philosophers like Quine, who are vehemently suspicious about meaning, are equally vehemently suspicious about properties.

So, there is a sense—perhaps a rather uninteresting sense—in which Gibson can make do with distinct properties where Establishment theories postulate semantic distinctions among mental representations. But, of course, you have to pay the piper sometime. The price that Gibson pays is the failure of his theory of specification.

Property is an *intentional* notion in the sense that coextensive sets may correspond to distinct properties. (The Morning Star = the Evening Star, but *the property of being the Morning Star ≠ the property of being the Evening Star*. Or so, at least, we must assume if we are to explain differences in responses to Venus by appeal to differences in the properties picked up.) However, *specification* is an *extensional* notion. Specification comes down to correlation (see earlier), and if X is correlated with the Morning Star and the Morning Star = the Evening Star, then, of course, X is correlated with the Evening Star. Which is to say that, on Gibson's notion of specification, it must turn out that whatever specifies the Morning Star specifies the Evening Star too. Specification cannot, then, explain property pickup.

Everybody has to face the issue about intentionality somewhere. For Gibson, push comes to shove with the question: what is it for an event (a configuration of the light, etc.) to specify a *property*? To say that Gibson has no theory of intentionality is to say that he has no answer to that question. Or, to put it the other way around, the failure of Gibson's theory of specification is no minor flaw in his theory. It marks the precise point at which Gibson's treatment of intentionality proves to be bankrupt.

In a nutshell: the move from semantic distinctions among representations to ontological distinctions among properties, in and of itself, buys the psychologist nothing.

The problem of substance is to provide an independent account either of the meaning of a representation (Establishment style) or of the specification of a property (Gibson style). The former problem *may* be tractable since it may be that the meaning of a representation can be reconstructed by a reference to its functional role; that is the hope by which Establishment theories live. But Gibson gives no indication at all of how the latter problem is going to be solved. Where the Establishment line offers, anyhow, a pious hope, the Gibsonian line offers only a dead end.

We said that Gibson's basic strategy is to use the (intentional) notion of a property to do what Establishment theories do with the (intentional) notion of the semantic content of a representation. Exegesis is complicated, however, by the fact that Gibson's adherence to this program is only sporadic. To put the point very crudely, it seems clear that one's theory of intentionality will have to postulate two of *something* if it is to account for the two ways of seeing Venus. (In fact, of course, it will be necessary to postulate infinitely many of something since there are infinitely many ways of seeing Venus.) The Establishment proposal is that we postulate two different *mental representations of Venus*. Gibson's proposal is that we postulate two *properties* of Venus to which perceptual mechanisms can be selectively tuned. But there is a third option with which Gibson appears occasionally to flirt: namely, postulate *two Venuses*.

Consider, to vary the example once again, seeing the Pole Star as a distant ball of hot gasses. Seeing the Pole Star that way is a rather late achievement both ontogenetically and phylogenetically. It depends on knowing a lot about stars. Yet seeing the Pole Star *is* seeing a distant ball of hot gasses, so the question arises how you can see it and yet not see it that way. Since, however, Gibson has no account of intentionality, he is faced with the problem of developing a theory of perception which provides an account of *seeing* without raising that sort of issue about *seeing as*. Of the various possibilities, Gibson sometimes appears to want to take what strikes us as clearly the least advisable. He sometimes denies (or so a literal reading of the text suggests) that what you see when you look at the sky are stars.

The idea is, apparently, that there are two kinds of *things*: there are the little whitish things that you see when you look up, which count as bona fide ecological objects and hence as bona fide objects of perception; and there are also the large hot balls of gas that astronomers describe, which count as astronomical objects and hence as *not* bona fide objects of perception. This gets Gibson out of the need to explain how it could be that the very same object can be seen now as a little whitish thing and now as a (very distant) large ball of gasses. That is, it gets him out of the need for a theory of intentionality vis à vis what happens when you see a star. But for this Gibson pays an utterly unreasonable price; if we take him seriously, we will have to say that the astronomer is *wrong* when he claims to have discovered that the Pole Star, though it looks small and chilly and relatively close, is actually large and hot and very far away. He is wrong because, on Gibson's account, the (astronomical) object that is large and far away is not identical to the ecological object that looks small and close by. Gibson does not attempt to say what the relation between the astronomical object and the ecological object is, assuming that it is not identity. In this he is probably well advised.[17,18]

Perhaps, however, you are prepared to pay this price; in effect, to avoid the problem of seeing as by postulating many different things to see where a more plausible theory makes do with many different ways of seeing the *same* thing. Even so, the wriggle will not work. There is a subtle connection between Gibson's misleading talk of direct realism and his refusal to face the problem of intentionality. This point now needs to be addressed.

Remember that, though Gibson sometimes says that we see ecological properties of the layout "directly," it turns out that this sort of direct seeing is mediated by the pickup of information in the light. Gibson admits, in effect, that finding out about the layout depends on first finding out about the light. When we discussed this issue, we emphasized that Gibson's (tacit) concession raises the question of how—by what mental process—finding out about the light eventuates in finding out about the layout. We can now see that this whole issue is implicitly involved with problems of intentionality since *finding out* is itself an intentional relation.

If I find out that (see that, perceive that) the Pole Star is overhead, and the Pole Star is the star I ought to steer by, it does *not* follow that I find out that (see that, perceive that) the star I ought to steer by is overhead. More to the point, suppose that I find out that the light is in a certain configuration, and suppose that the light's being in that configuration is the same state of affairs as the light's being caused by a certain feature of the layout. It *does not follow* from these premises, that I have found out that the light is in a configuration caused by a certain feature of the layout. To get from finding out about the former to finding out about the latter, I have to get from representing the properties of the light in one way to representing them in another way; in effect, I have to make an inference. Missing the point about inference, missing the point about mental representations, and missing the point about intentionality are thus all aspects of missing the same point.

So, for example, Gibson writes that we correctly perceive the unchanging shape of rigidly moving objects ". . . not because we have formed associations between the optical elements, not even because the brain has organized the optical elements, but because the retinal mosaic is sensitive to transformations as such" (Gibson, 1957, p. 294; quoted in Ullman, 1980). But, to transformations of *what*? Not of the object per se, since that would be ruled out by the counterfactual support condition (see above). So, then, presumably, to transformations *of the light*. But the problem of perception is not how we get epistemically related to the transformations of the light; it is the problem of how we get perceptual knowledge of the shape of the object. Gibson must be thinking something like this: the visual system is sensitive to how the light is transformed; for the light to be transformed in a certain way is for it to be reflected from objects with a certain sort of structure; hence the visual system is sensitive to the structure of objects. But, as we have seen, the second premise is not true in the general case (vide the illusions) and, more to the present point, even if it were true the conclusion does not follow from the premises. To think it does is to fail to understand the intentionality of such key relations as "being sensitive to." Because he did not take the intentionality of these relations seriously, Gibson greatly underestimated the magnitude of the concession implicit in admitting that only the light is detected directly.

To summarize: Even if all you want is to construct a theory of perception, you cannot do much without encountering problems about intentionality, although it is true that many of the key perceptual relations are more or less extensional. When, however, you try to construct a theory about how perception relates to cognition at large (or, of course, of the nature of the non-perceptual cognitive processes) problems of intentionality come immediately to the fore.[19] According to the Establishment theory, this is no surprise: the mind is a mechanism for the manipulation of representations, and how what you see affects what you know is primarily a matter of how you represent what you know and see. This is what modern cognitive theory has inherited from the classical tradition in epistemology, and, as we remarked, it may be wrong. But there will be no successful anti-Establishment revolution in cognitive psychology until some alternative to this account is provided. What is finally and fundamentally wrong with the Gibsonian treatment is that it has not grasped that fact.

Notes

1. All references are to Gibson, 1979, except as otherwise noted.

2. The problem that we are raising against Gibson is, to all intents and purposes, identical to one that Chomsky (1959) raised against Skinner. Chomsky writes: "A typical example of *stimulus control* for Skinner would be the response ... to a painting ... *Dutch.* (Such

responses are said by Skinner to be 'under the control of extremely subtle properties of the physical object or event' (p. 108).) Suppose instead of saying *Dutch* we said *Clashes with the wallpaper, I thought you liked abstract work, Never saw it before* ..., or whatever else might come into our minds when looking at a picture ... Skinner could only say that each of these responses is under the control of some other stimulus property of the physical object. If we look at a red chair and say *red*, the response is under the control of the stimulus *redness*; if we say *chair*, it is under the control of (the property) *chairness*, and similarly for any other response. This device is as simple as it is empty ... properties are free for the asking ... (p. 52 in Block, 1980; Chomsky's page reference is to Skinner, 1957)." If one substitutes "the property picked up in perception" for "the stimulus property controlling behavior," it becomes apparent how similar in strategy are Skinner's antimentalism and Gibson's. There is, however, this difference: Skinner proposes to avoid vacuity by requiring that the "controlling stimulus" be physically specified, at least in principle. Chomsky's critique thus comes down to the (correct) observation that there is no reason to believe that anything physically specifiable *could* play the functional role vis à vis the causation of behavior that Skinner wants controlling stimuli to play; the point being that behavior is in fact the joint effect of impinging stimuli *together with the organism's mental states and processes*. Gibson has the corresponding problem of avoiding triviality by somehow constraining the objects of direct perception; but, as we shall see, he explicitly rejects the identification of the stimulus properties that get picked up with physical properties.

3. There is, nevertheless, a sense in which all perceptual processes, strictly so called, might be inferential. Perception is usually taken to affect what the organism knows, and it is conceivable that transducer-detected properties are epistemically inaccessible to the organism and subserve no purposes except those of perceptual integration. (Cf. Stich's [1978] discussion of "subdoxastic" states.) In that case, these non-inferential processes are nonperceptual, as it were, by definition. In deference to this consideration, we have generally avoided talking of transduced properties as directly *perceived*, preferring the less tendentious "directly picked up." Of course, this terminological issue does not jeopardize the observation in the text that processes of perceptual inference must begin from premises that are not themselves inferred. The present question is just whether the noninferential processes of pickup which make such premises available should themselves be referred to as perceptual. (See also the discussion in section 7.4.)

4. Some Gibsonians apparently want to read a sort of epistemological Realism as one of the morals of theories of direct perception (see, for example, Turvey, 1977), but that would seem quite unjustifiable. On the one hand, *every* theory will have to acknowledge the fact of at least *some* misperception, and if one is going to run skeptical arguments in epistemology, that is the premise one needs to get them started (e.g., "if you admit that perception is sometimes fallible, what reason is there to suppose that it isn't always wrong? ..." etc.). If you find such arguments persuasive, the idea that perception is direct *when it is veridical* will do nothing to soothe the skeptical itch, since that idea is compatible with the possibility that perception is *never* veridical. Correspondingly, an inference based theory of perception is perfectly compatible with a Realistic account of the information that perception delivers. All that is required for a perceptual inference to yield knowledge is that it should be sound. Gibson's views have philosophical implications, but not for epistemology.

5. Strictly, S1 and S2 are tokens of correlated types. We will not be explicit about the type token relation except where the intention is not clear from context.

6. Of course, knowing the physical/physiological structure of the organism can provide some constraints upon the assignment of transducers, since if there is *no* mechanism that is differentially sensitive to a given form of input energy, then that form of input *cannot* be a specifier for that organism. However, as we remarked earlier, this consideration does less than might be supposed since, in the general case, practically any form of ambient energy is likely to have *some effect* on the organism's neurological condition, and it is functional considerations which must decide which such effects are to count as transactions.

7. It is of prime importance that the employments of the method of differences should be *relevant* since, of course, there are *some* counterfactual conditions in which P will *not* produce S_i even if S *is* a transducer: e.g., the universe blows up, the organism dies, and so forth. The counterfactual supporting generalizations about transducers are thus like most counterfactual supporting generalizations in science in that they must be relativized to assumptions of "normal background conditions." Perhaps only the fundamental laws of microphysics are exempt from such relativization, these being assumed to hold, literally without exception, for all segments of space-time.

8. For our purposes, a world in which there were laws about grandmothers would be one in which some effect is a consequence of something being a grandmother, regardless of what other properties it may have. But, surely, this is not true in our world. Suppose, for example, that there are true empirical generalizations of the form $(\forall x) (\exists y)$ (x is a grandmother $\rightarrow$ Fy). Then it seems enormously plausible that such a generalization holds only because there is some property H *other than being a grandmother*, such that the generalization $(\forall x) (\exists y)$ (Hx $\rightarrow$ Fy) is true; and moreover that it is the latter generalization which supports counterfactuals in the critical cases. That is, if *a* were a grandmother but H*a* was false, then the former generalization would not hold for x = *a*.

9. For purposes of this discussion, we will usually speak of the epistemic states arising from perception as percepts. One could equally talk of perceptual beliefs, perceptual judgements, or any other epistemic state that an organism is in as a logical consequence of having perceived—as opposed to having guessed, deduced, remembered, or otherwise concluded—that P.

Talk of percepts, as opposed to beliefs about the world that do not arise directly from perception, implies a distinction between perceptual and cognitive processes (Dretske, 1978). Empirical grounds for drawing this distinction are discussed in, for example, Hochberg (1968). The present point is that all theories have to draw it somewhere, and the question about the richness of the ambient array arises specifically for the causation of perception, however it may be defined.

10. It might occur to a Gibsonian to avoid this conclusion by reanalyzing the effective stimuli. Whereas we assumed that the effective stimulus was *cough* (which, occurring in isolation is heard as a cough but occurring in speech-context is heard as a phone) a Gibsonian might want to argue that the isolated stimulus is actually # *silence-cough-silence*#. Since that stimulus is never presented in the speech condition, the appearance of a one-many stimulus-to-layout mapping is dissipated. This would be a typical Gibsonian tactic of appealing to context to avoid the problem of ambiguity.

The disadvantages of the tactic are, however, clearly revealed in this case. For, the stimulus #*noise-cough-noise*# *will*, in general, be heard as containing a cough; and this fact is rendered a mystery on the assumption that the right way to describe the effective stimulus for a cough perceived in isolation is as #silence-cough-silence#. Quite generally, what you gain vis à vis ambiguity by enlarging the effective stimulus, you lose vis à vis the perception of similarity. This is because the perception of similarity is so often mediated by the recognition of partial identity of the internal structures of the stimuli. See section 7.2.

11. This point is obvious, and widely admitted, independent of the present examples. Consider the properties of being an equilateral triangle and being an equiangular triangle, which, though distinct, are coextensive in all possible worlds.

For an argument which runs along lines similar to those in the text, see Sober (1980).

12. In general, linguistically natural transformations of sentences tend to be acoustically arbitrary, and vice versa. This is easy to understand on the assumption that P and token sentencehood are distinct properties. Roughly, a thing has the latter property in virtue of the identity and order of its segments, whereas a thing has the former property in virtue of the character of its acoustic analysis (e.g., in virtue of its formant structure). Not surprisingly, the linguistically natural transformations are (a subset of the ones that substitute for segments or rearrange them, and the acoustically natural transformations are (a subset of) the ones that operate on formant structure. It is these considerations that the argument in the text relies on.

13. Of course, difference in similarity relations is a sufficient, but not a necessary condition for the nonidentity of token sentencehood and P. The reader who does not accept the claims about similarity may nevertheless agree that the two properties are distinct since the former, but not the latter, determines a natural kind; there are presumably scientific generalizations about sentencehood—viz., in linguistics—but there are surely no such generalizations about P.

14. We stress that the relevant dependencies are those between stimulus properties and *output states* of the device. As we mentioned above, there is probably a large number of types of ambient energy to which the states of any physiological mechanism are responsive; however, most of these responses have no functional significance and hence do not count as outputs.

15. For these purposes, we have treated the cognitive impenetrability of transducers as simply a consequence of the fact that their inputs are nomologically sufficient for their outputs. There is, however, a deeper point. If, as we have argued, perception is an inferential process, then what goes on in perception is the construction of certain kinds of "arguments"—viz., from the premises that transducers make available to conclusions which express perceptual beliefs. We can then view cognitive penetration as a process which makes additional premises available to such arguments—e.g., premises which express background beliefs, goals, and utilities. But if that is right, if that is what cognitive penetration *is*, then it follows that there cannot, in principle, be cognitive penetration of noninferential processes like transduction.

16. It is, of course, possible that Gibson has some other (some nonsemantic) notion of property in mind. One cannot tell because the issue of property individuation is not one that Gibson discusses.

17. Gibson is rather less explicit about all this than we have perhaps made him seem, though there are passages which appear to admit no other interpretation of his views. For example: "The environment of animals and men is what they perceive. The environment is not the same as the physical world, if one means by that the world described by physics" (p. 15). What Gibson ought to have said is "The environment *as perceived* is not the world *as described by physics.*" The reason he did not say this is presumably that to do so would have been to make the category *ecological object* overtly intentional—an ecological object would then have been an object as represented in terms of ecological parameters. And Gibson could not do *that* because, as we have seen, he has no theory of intentionality.

18. Some of our best friends are prepared to quantify over intentional objects (e.g., for purposes of constructing model theoretic interpretations of modal expressions). But that is a far cry from taking intentional objects to be *objects of perception* as Gibson (and, by the way, Brentano before him) appears to be inclined to do. For one thing, if merely intentional (including non-actual) objects can be perceived, we will have to give up the enormously plausible principle that perception is mediated by causal transactions between perceiver and perceivee. Non-actual objects cannot, of course, be actual causes.

19. They crop up a lot earlier if you hold—as it is probably right to do—that every case of seeing a thing involves seeing the thing as something or other. True, you can see the Pole Star and not see it *as* the Pole Star. But, quite plausibly, you cannot see the Pole Star without seeing it as *either* the Pole Star or a little speck of light, or a firefly, or the star that Granny likes best . . . or *something*. If this is right then though *seeing* is an extensional relation, some of the logically necessary conditions on "x sees y" are intentional.

References

Block, N. (Ed.), (1980) *Readings in Philosophy of Psychology*. Cambridge, Mass., Harvard University Press.

Bruner, J. (1957) On Perceptual Readiness, *Psychol. Rev.,* 64, 123–152.

Chomsky, N. (1959) A Review of B. F. Skinner's *Verbal Behavior*, reprinted in Block, N. (Ed.) *Readings in Philosophy of Psychology, Vol. 1*. Cambridge, Mass., Harvard University Press.

Dretske, F. (1978) The Role of the Percept in Visual Cognition, in C. Wade Savage (Ed.) *Perception and Cognition, Issues in the Foundations of Psychology, Minnesota Studies in the Philosophy of Science, Vol. IX,* University of Minnesota Press, Minneapolis.

Field, H. (1978) Mental Representation. *Erkenntnis*, Vol. 13, pp. 9–61.

Fodor, J. (1980) *Representations*. Vermont, Bradford Books.

Fodor, J. (1981) The Mind-Body Problem, *Sci. Amer.,* 244, 114–123.

Frege, G. (1949) On Sense and Nominatum. Reprinted in H. Feigl and W. Sellars (Eds.) *Readings in Philosophical Analysis*, New York, Appleton Century Crofts.

Gibson, J. (1957) Optical Motions and Transformations as Stimuli for Visual Perception, *Psychol. Rev.,* 64, 288–295.

Gibson, J. (1966) *The Senses Considered as Perceptual Systems*. Boston, Houghton Mifflin.

Gibson, J. (1979) *The Ecological Approach to Visual Perception.* Boston, Houghton Mifflin.

Goodman, N. (1954) *Fact, Fiction and Forecast.* London, The Athlone Press.

Hess, E. (1975) The Role of Pupil Size in Communication. Reprinted in Atkinson and Atkinson (Eds.) *Mind and Behavior, Readings from Scientific American.* San Francisco, W. H. Freeman and Co., 1980.

Hochberg, J. (1968) In the Mind's Eye. In R. N. Haber (Ed.) *Contemporary Theory and Research in Visual Perception.* New York, Holt.

Loar, B. (1981) *Mind and Meaning.* Cambridge, Cambridge University Press.

Marr, D. (1976) Early Processing of Visual Information. *Philosoph. Trans. Royal Soc. London, 275,* 483–534.

Marr, D. and Poggio, T. (1976) Cooperative Computation of Stereo Disparity. *Science, 194,* 283–287.

Prazdny, K. (1981) Egomotion and Relative Depth Map from Optical Flow. *Bio. Cybernetics, 36,* 87–102.

Prendle, S., Carello, C. and Turvey, M. (1980) Animal-Environment Mutuality and Direct Perception. *The Behavioral and Brain Sciences,* in press.

Pylyshyn, Z. (1980) Computation and Cognition, Issues in the Foundations of Cognitive Science. *The Behavioral and Brain Sciences, 3*(1), 111–169.

Pylyshyn, Z. (1981) The Imagery Debate: Analog Media *versus* Tacit Knowledge. *Psycho. Rev., 88,* 16–45.

Reed, E. and Jones, R. (1978) Gibson's Theory of Perception: A Case of Hasty Epistemologizing? *Philosophy of Science, 45,* 519–530.

Runeson, S. (1980) There Is More to Psychological Meaningfulness than Computation and Representation. *The Behavioral and Brain Sciences,* in press.

Skinner, B. F. (1957) *Verbal Behavior,* New York, Appleton Century Crofts.

Stevens, Kent (1979) *Surface Perception from Local Analysis of Texture and Contour,* MIT Ph.D. Thesis.

Sober, E. (1980) Why Logically Equivalent Predicates May Pick Out Different Properties. Mimeog., University of Wisconsin.

Stich, S. (1978) Beliefs and Subdoxastic States. *Philosophy of Science, 45,* 499–518.

Turvey, M. (1977) Contrasting Orientations to the Theory of Visual Information Processing. *Psychol. Rev., 84,* 67–88.

Turvey, M. and Shaw, R. (1979) The Primacy of Perceiving: An Ecological Reformulation of Perception for Understanding Memory. In L. G. Nillson (Ed.) *Perspectives on Memory Research. Essays in Honor of Uppsala University's 500th Anniversary.* New Jersey, Erlbaum.

Ullman, S. (1979) *The Interpretation of Visual Motion,* Cambridge, Mass., MIT Press.

Ullman, S. (1980) Against Direct Perception. *The Behavioral and Brain Sciences, 3,* 373–415.

Uttal, W. (1967) Evoked Brain Potentials: Signs or Codes? *Perspectives in Biology and Medicine, 10,* 627–639.

Warren, R. (1970) Perceptual Restoration of Missing Speech Sounds. *Science, 167,* 392–393.

11

Selections from *Vision*

David Marr

General Introduction

What does it mean, to see? The plain man's answer (and Aristotle's, too) would be, to know what is where by looking. In other words, vision is the *process* of discovering from images what is present in the world, and where it is.

Vision is therefore, first and foremost, an information-processing task, but we cannot think of it just as a process. For if we are capable of knowing what is where in the world, our brains must somehow be capable of *representing* this information—in all its profusion of color and form, beauty, motion, and detail. The study of vision must therefore include not only the study of how to extract from images the various aspects of the world that are useful to us, but also an inquiry into the nature of the internal representations by which we capture this information and thus make it available as a basis for decisions about our thoughts and actions. This duality—the representation and the processing of information—lies at the heart of most information-processing tasks and will profoundly shape our investigation of the particular problems posed by vision.

The need to understand information-processing tasks and machines has arisen only quite recently. Until people began to dream of and then to build such machines, there was no very pressing need to think deeply about them. Once people did begin to speculate about such tasks and machines, however, it soon became clear that many aspects of the world around us could benefit from an information-processing point of view. Most of the phenomena that are central to us as human beings—the mysteries of life and evolution, of perception and feeling and thought—are primarily phenomena of information processing, and if we are ever to understand them fully, our thinking about them must include this perspective.

The next point—which has to be made rather quickly to those who inhabit a world in which the local utility's billing computer is still capable of sending a final demand for $0.00—is to emphasize that saying that a job is "only" an information-processing task or that an organism is "only" an information-processing machine is not a limiting or a pejorative description. Even more importantly, I shall in no way use such a description to try to limit the kind of explanations that are necessary. Quite the contrary, in fact. One of the fascinating features of information-processing machines is that in order to understand them completely, one has to be satisfied with one's explanations at many different levels.

For example, let us look at the range of perspectives that must be satisfied before one can be said, from a human and scientific point of view, to have understood visual perception. First, and I think foremost, there is the perspective of the plain man. He knows what it is like to see, and unless the bones of one's arguments and theories roughly correspond to what this person knows to be true at first hand, one will probably be wrong (a point made with force and elegance by Austin 1962). Second, there is the perspective of the brain scientists, the physiologists and anatomists who know a great deal about how the nervous system is built and how parts of it behave. The issues that concern them—how the cells are connected, why they respond as they do, the neuronal dogmas of Barlow (1972)—must be resolved and addressed in any full account of perception. And the same argument applies to the perspective of the experimental psychologists.

On the other hand, someone who has bought and played with a small home computer may make quite different demands. "If," he might say, "vision really is an information-processing task, then I should be able to make my computer do it, provided that it has sufficient power, memory, and some way of being connected to a home television camera." The explanation he wants is therefore a rather abstract one, telling him what to program and, if possible, a hint about the best algorithms for doing so. He doesn't what to know about rhodopsin, or the lateral geniculate nucleus, or inhibitory interneurons. He wants to know how to program vision.

The fundamental point is that in order to understand a device that performs an information-processing task, one needs many different kinds of explanations. Part I of this book is concerned with this point, and it plays a prominent role because one of the keystones of the book is the realization that we have had to be more careful about what constitutes an explanation than has been necessary in other recent scientific developments, like those in molecular biology. For the subject of vision, there *is* no single equation or view that explains everything. Each problem has to be addressed from several points of view—as a problem in representing information, as a computation capable of deriving that representation, and as a problem in the architecture of a computer capable of carrying out both things quickly and reliably.

If one keeps strongly in mind this necessarily rather broad aspect of the nature of explanation, one can avoid a number of pitfalls. One consequence of an emphasis on information processing might be, for example, to introduce a comparison between the human brain and a computer. In a sense, of course, the brain is a computer, but to say this without qualification is misleading, because the essence of the brain is not simply that it is a computer but that it is a computer which is in the habit of performing some rather particular computations. The term *computer* usually refers to a machine with a rather standard type of instruction set that usually runs serially but nowadays sometimes in parallel, under the control of programs that have been stored in a memory. In order to understand such a computer, one needs to understand what it is made of, how it is put together, what its instruction set is, how much memory it has and how it is accessed, and how the machine may be made to run. But this forms only a small part of understanding a computer that is performing an information-processing task.

This point bears reflection, because it is central to why most analogies between brains and computers are too superficial to be useful. Think, for example, of the international network of airline reservation computers, which performs the task of assigning flights for millions of passengers all over the world. To understand this system it is not enough to know how a modern computer works. One also has to understand a little about what aircraft are and what they do; about geography, time zones, fares, exchange rates, and connections; and something about politics, diets, and the various other aspects of human nature that happen to be relevant to this particular task.

Thus the critical point is that understanding computers is different from understanding computations. To understand a computer, one has to study that computer. To understand an information-processing task, one has to study that information-processing task. To understand fully a particular machine carrying out a particular information-processing task, one has to do both things. Neither alone will suffice.

From a philosophical point of view, the approach that I describe is an extension of what have sometimes been called representational theories of mind. On the whole, it rejects the more recent excursions into the philosophy of perception, with their arguments about sense-data, the molecules of perception, and the validity of what the senses tell us; instead, this approach looks back to an older view, according to which the senses are for the most part concerned with telling one what is there. Modern representational theories conceive of the mind as having access to systems of internal representations; mental states are characterized by asserting what the internal representations currently specify, and mental processes by how such internal representations are obtained and how they interact.

This scheme affords a comfortable framework for our study of visual perception, and I am content to let it form the point of departure for our inquiry. As we shall see, pursuing this approach will lead us away from traditional avenues into what is almost a new intellectual landscape. Some of the things we find will seem strange, and it will be hard to reconcile subjectively some of the ideas and theories that are forced on us with what actually goes on inside ourselves when we open our eyes and look at things. Even the basic notion of what constitutes an explanation will have to be developed and broadened a little, to ensure that we do not leave anything out and that every important perspective on the problem is satisfied or satisfiable.

The Philosophy and the Approach

1   Background

The problems of visual perception have attracted the curiosity of scientists for many centuries. Important early contributions were made by Newton (1704), who laid the foundations for modern work on color vision, and Helmholtz (1910), whose treatise on physiological optics generates interest even today. Early in this century, Wertheimer (1912, 1923) noticed the apparent motion not of individual dots but of wholes, or "fields," in images presented sequentially as in a movie. In much the same way we perceive the migration across the sky of a flock of geese: the flock somehow constitutes a single entity, and is not seen as individual birds. This observation started the Gestalt school of psychology, which was concerned with describing the qualities of wholes by using terms like *solidarity* and *distinctness*, and with trying to formulate the "laws" that governed the creation of these wholes. The attempt failed for various reasons, and the Gestalt school dissolved into the fog of subjectivism. With the death of the school, many of its early and genuine insights were unfortunately lost to the mainstream of experimental psychology.

Since then, students of the psychology of perception have made no serious attempts at an overall understanding of what perception is, concentrating instead on the analysis of properties and performance. The trichromatism of color vision was firmly established (see Brindley 1970), and the preoccupation with motion continued, with the most interesting developments perhaps being the experiments of Miles (1931) and of Wallach and O'Connell (1953), which established that under suitable conditions an unfamiliar three-dimensional shape can be correctly perceived from only its changing monocular projection.[1]

The development of the digital electronic computer made possible a similar discovery for binocular vision. In 1960 Bela Julesz devised computer-generated random-dot stereograms, which are image pairs constructed of dot patterns that appear random when viewed monocularly but fuse when viewed one through each eye to give a percept of shapes and surfaces with a clear three-dimensional structure. An example is shown in figure 11.1. Here the image for the left eye is a matrix of black and white squares generated at random by a computer program. The image for the right eye is made by copying the left image, shifting a square-shaped region at its center slightly to the left, and then providing a new random pattern to fill the gap that the shift creates. If each of the eyes sees only one matrix, as if the matrices were both in the same physical place, the result is the sensation of a square floating in space. Plainly, such percepts are caused solely by the stereo disparity between

Figure 11.1
A random-dot stereogram of the type used extensively by Bela Julesz. The left and right images are identical except for a central square region that is displaced slightly in one image. When fused binocularly, the images yield that impression of the central square floating in front of the background.

matching elements in the images presented to each eye; from such experiments, we know that the analysis of stereoscopic information, like the analysis of motion, can proceed independently in the absence of other information. Such findings are of critical importance because they help us to subdivide our study of perception into more specialized parts which can be treated separately. I shall refer to these as independent modules of perception.

The most recent contribution of psychophysics has been of a different kind but of equal importance. It arose from a combination of adaptation and threshold detection studies and originated from the demonstration by Campbell and Robson (1968) of the existence of independent, spatial-frequency-tuned channels—that is, channels sensitive to intensity variations in the image occurring at a particular scale or spatial interval—in the early stages of our perceptual apparatus. This paper led to an explosion of articles on various aspects of these channels, which culminated ten years later with quite satisfactory quantitative accounts of the characteristics of the first stages of visual perception (Wilson and Bergen 1979). I shall discuss this in detail later on.

Recently a rather different approach has attracted considerable attention. In 1971, Roger N. Shepard and Jacqueline Metzler made line drawings of simple objects that differed from one another either by a three-dimensional rotation or by a rotation plus a reflection (see figure 11.2). They asked how long it took to decide whether two depicted objects differed by a rotation and a reflection or merely a rotation. They found that the time taken depended on the three-dimensional angle of rotation necessary to bring the two objects into correspondence. Indeed, the time varied linearly with this angle. One is led thereby to the notion that a mental rotation of sorts is actually being performed—that a mental description of the first shape in a pair is being adjusted incrementally in orientation until it matches the second, such adjustment requiring greater time when greater angles are involved.

The significance of this approach lies not so much in its results, whose interpretation is controversial, as in the type of questions it raised. For until then, the notion of a representation was not one that visual psychologists took seriously. This type of experiment meant that the notion had to be considered. Although the early thoughts of visual psychologists were naive compared with those of the computer vision community, which had had to face the problem of representation from the beginning, it was not long before the thinking of psychologists became more sophisticated (see Shepard 1979).

But what of explanation? For a long time, the best hope seemed to lie along another line of investigation, that of electrophysiology. The development of ampli-

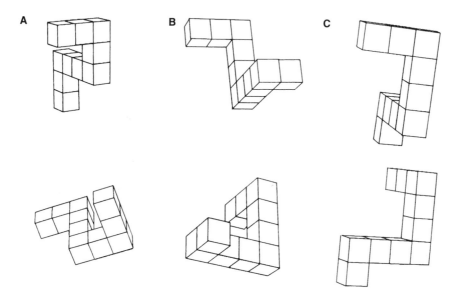

Figure 11.2
Some drawings similar to those used in Shepard and Metzler's experiments on mental rotation. The ones shown in (a) are identical, as a clockwise turning of this page by 80° will readily prove. Those in (b) are also identical, and again the relative angle between the two is 80°. Here, however, a rotation in depth will make the first coincide with the second. Finally, those in (c) are not at all identical, for no rotation will bring them into congruence. The time taken to decide whether a pair is the same was found to vary linearly with the angle through which one figure must be rotated to be brought into correspondence with the other. This suggested to the investigators that a stepwise mental rotation was in fact being performed by the subjects of their experiments.

fiers allowed Adrian (1928) and his colleagues to record the minute voltage changes that accompanied the transmission of nerve signals. Their investigations showed that the character of the sensation so produced depended on which fiber carried the message, not how the fiber was stimulated—as one might have expected from anatomical studies. This led to the view that the peripheral nerve fibers could be thought of as a simple mapping supplying the sensorium with a copy of the physical events at the body surface (Adrian 1947). The rest of the explanation, it was thought, could safely be left to the psychologists.

The next development was the technical improvement in amplification that made possible the recording of single neurons (Granit and Svaetichin 1939; Hartline 1938; Galambos and Davis 1943). This led to the notion of a cell's "receptive field" (Hartline 1940) and to the Harvard School's famous series of studies of the behavior of neurons at successively deeper levels of the visual pathway (Kuffler 1953; Hubel and Wiesel 1962, 1968). But perhaps the most exciting development was the new view that questions of psychological interest could be illuminated and perhaps even explained by neurophysiological experiments. The clearest early example of this was Barlow's (1953) study of ganglion cells in the frog retina, and I cannot put it better than he did:

If one explores the responsiveness of single ganglion cells in the frog's retina using handheld targets, one finds that one particular type of ganglion cell is most effectively driven by something like a black disc subtending a degree or so moved rapidly to and fro within the unit's receptive field. This causes a vigorous discharge which can be maintained without much decrement as long as the movement is continued. Now, if the stimulus which is optimal for this class of cells is presented to intact frogs, the behavioural response is often dramatic; they turn towards the target and make repeated feeding responses consisting of a jump and snap. The selectivity of the retinal neurons and the frog's reaction when they are selectively stimulated, suggest that they are "bug detectors" (Barlow 1953) performing a primitive but vitally important form of recognition.

The result makes one suddenly realize that a large part of the sensory machinery involved in a frog's feeding responses may actually reside in the retina rather than in mysterious "centres" that would be too difficult to understand by physiological methods. The essential lock-like property resides in each member of a whole class of neurons and allows the cell to discharge only to the appropriate key pattern of sensory stimulation. Lettvin et al. (1959) suggested that there were five different classes of cell in the frog, and Barlow, Hill and Levick (1964) found an even larger number of categories in the rabbit. [Barlow et al.] called these key patterns "trigger features," and Maturana et al. (1960) emphasized another important aspect of the behaviour of these ganglion cells; a cell continues to respond to the same trigger feature in spite of changes in light intensity over many decades. The properties of the retina are such that a ganglion cell can, figuratively speaking, reach out and determine that something specific is happening in front of the eye. Light is the agent by which it does this, but it is the detailed pattern of the light that carries the information, and the overall level of illumination prevailing at the time is almost totally disregarded. (p. 373)

Barlow (1972) then goes on to summarize these findings in the following way:

The cumulative effect of all the changes I have tried to outline above has been to make us realise that each *single neuron can perform a much more complex and subtle task than had previously been thought* (emphasis added). Neurons do not loosely and unreliably remap the luminous intensities of the visual image onto our sensorium, but instead they detect pattern elements, discriminate the depth of objects, ignore irrelevant causes of variation and are arranged in an intriguing hierarchy. Furthermore, there is evidence that they give prominence to what is informationally important, can respond with great reliability, and can have their pattern selectivity permanently modified by early visual experience. This amounts to a revolution in our outlook. It is now quite inappropriate to regard unit activity as a noisy indication of more basic and reliable processes involved in mental operations: instead, we must regard single neurons as the prime movers of these mechanisms. Thinking is brought about by neurons and we should not use phrases like "unit activity reflects, reveals, or monitors thought processes," because the activities of neurons, quite simply, are thought processes.

This revolution stemmed from physiological work and makes us realize that the activity of each single neuron may play a significant role in perception. (p. 380)

This aspect of his thinking led Barlow to formulate the first and most important of his five dogmas: "A description of that activity of a single nerve cell which is transmitted to and influences other nerve cells and of a nerve cell's response to such influences from other cells, is a complete enough description for functional under-standing of the nervous system. There is nothing else "looking at" or controlling this activity, which must therefore provide a basis for understanding how the brain controls behaviour" (Barlow 1972, p. 380).

I shall return later on to more carefully examine the validity of this point of view, but for now let us just enjoy it. The vigor and excitement of these ideas need no emphasis. At the time the eventual success of a reductionist approach seemed likely. Hubel and Wiesel's (1962, 1968) pioneering studies had shown the way; single-unit studies on stereopsis (Barlow, Blakemore, and Pettigrew 1967) and on color (DeValois, Abramov, and Mead 1967; Gouras 1968) seemed to confirm the close links between perception and single-cell recordings, and the intriguing results of Gross, Rocha-Miranda, and Bender (1972), who found "hand-detectors" in the inferotemporal cortex, seemed to show that the application of the reductionist approach would not be limited just to the early parts of the visual pathway.

It was, of course, recognized that physiologists had been lucky: If one probes around in a conventional electronic computer and records the behavior of single elements within it, one is unlikely to be able to discern what a given element is doing. But the brain, thanks to Barlow's first dogma, seemed to be built along more accommodating lines—people *were* able to determine the functions of single elements of the brain. There seemed no reason why the reductionist approach could not be taken all the way.

I was myself fully caught up in this excitement. Truth, I also believed, was basi-cally neural, and the central aim of all research was a thorough functional analysis of the structure of the central nervous system. My enthusiasm found expression in a theory of the cerebellar cortex (Marr 1969). According to this theory, the simple and regular cortical structure is interpreted as a simple but powerful memorizing device for learning motor skills; because of a simple combinatorial trick, each of the 15 million Purkinje cells in the cerebellum is capable of learning over 200 different patterns and discriminating them from unlearned patterns. Evidence is gradually accumulating that the cerebellum is involved in learning motor skills (Ito 1978), so that something like this theory may in fact be correct.

The way seemed clear. On the one hand we had new experimental techniques of proven power, and on the other, the beginnings of a theoretical approach that could back them up with a fine analysis of cortical structure. Psychophysics could tell us what needed explaining, and the recent advances in anatomy—the Fink-Heimer technique from Nauta's laboratory and the recent successful deployment by Szentagothai and others of the electron microscope—could provide the necessary information about the structure of the cerebral cortex.

But somewhere underneath, something was going wrong. The initial discoveries of the 1950s and 1960s were not being followed by equally dramatic discoveries in the 1970s. No neurophysiologists had recorded new and clear high-level correlates of perception. The leaders of the 1960s had turned away from what they had been doing—Hubel and Wiesel concentrated on anatomy, Barlow turned to psychophysics, and the mainstream of neurophysiology concentrated on development and plasticity (the concept that neural connections are not fixed) or on a more thorough analysis of the cells that had already been discovered (for example, Bishop, Coombs, and Henry 1971; Schiller, Finlay, and Volman 1976a, 1976b), or on cells in species like the owl (for example, Pettigrew and Konishi 1976). None of the new studies succeeded in elucidating the *function* of the visual cortex.

It is difficult to say precisely why this happened, because the reasoning was never made explicit and was probably largely unconscious. However, various factors are identifiable. In my own case, the cerebellar study had two effects. On the one hand, it suggested that one could eventually hope to understand cortical structure in functional terms, and this was exciting. But at the same time the study has disappointed me, because even if the theory was correct, it did not much enlighten one about the motor system—it did not, for example, tell one how to go about programming a mechanical arm. It suggested that if one wishes to program a mechanical arm so that it operates in a versatile way, then at some point a very large and rather simple type of memory will prove indispensable. But it did not say why, nor what that memory should contain.

The discoveries of the visual neurophysiologists left one in a similar situation. Suppose, for example, that one actually found the apocryphal grandmother cell.[2] Would that really tell us anything much at all? It would tell us that it existed— Gross's hand-detectors tell us almost that—but not *why* or even *how* such a thing may be constructed from the outputs of previously discovered cells. Do the single-unit recordings—the simple and complex cells—tell us much about how to detect edges or why one would want to, except in a rather general way through arguments based on economy and redundancy? If we really knew the answers, for example, we should be able to program them on a computer. But finding a hand-detector certainly did not allow us to program one.

As one reflected on these sorts of issues in the early 1970s, it gradually became clear that something important was missing that was not present in either of the disciplines of neurophysiology or psychophysics. The key observation is that neurophysiology and psychophysics have as their business to *describe* the behavior of cells or of subjects but not to *explain* such behavior. What are the visual areas of the cerebral cortex actually doing? What are the problems in doing it that need explaining, and at what level of description should such explanations be sought?

The best way of finding out the difficulties of doing something is to try to do it, so at this point I moved to the Artificial Intelligence Laboratory at MIT, where Marvin Minsky had collected a group of people and a powerful computer for the express purpose of addressing these questions.

The first great revelation was that the problems are difficult. Of course, these days this fact is a commonplace. But in the 1960s almost no one realized that machine vision was difficult. The field had to go through the same experience as the machine translation field did in its fiascoes of the 1950s before it was at last realized that here were some problems that had to be taken seriously. The reason for this misperception is that we humans are ourselves so good at vision. The notion of a feature detector was well established by Barlow and by Hubel and Wiesel, and the idea that extracting edges and lines from images might be at all difficult simply did not occur to those who had not tried to do it. It turned out to be an elusive problem: Edges that are of critical importance from a three-dimensional point of view often cannot be found at all by looking at the intensity changes in an image. Any kind of textured image gives a multitude of noisy edge segments; variations in reflectance and illumination cause no end of trouble; and even if an edge has a clear existence at one point, it is as likely as not to fade out quite soon, appearing only in patches along its length in the image. The common and almost despairing feeling of the early investigators like B. K. P. Horn and T. O. Binford was that practically anything could happen in an image and furthermore that practically everything did.

Three types of approach were taken to try to come to grips with these phenomena. The first was unashamedly empirical, associated most with Azriel Rosenfeld. His style was to take some new trick for edge detection, texture discrimination, or something similar, run it on images, and observe the result. Although several interesting ideas emerged in this way, including the simultaneous use of operators[3] of different sizes as an approach to increasing sensitivity and reducing noise (Rosenfeld and Thurston 1971), these studies were not as useful as they could have been because they were never accompanied by any serious assessment of how well the different algorithms performed. Few attempts were made to compare the merits of different operators (although Fram and Deutsch 1975, did try), and an approach like trying to prove mathematically which operator was optimal was not even attempted. Indeed, it could not be, because no one had yet formulated precisely what these operators should be trying to do. Nevertheless, considerable ingenuity was shown. The most clever was probably Hueckel's (1973) operator, which solved in an ingenious way the problem of finding the edge orientation that best fit a given intensity change in a small neighborhood of an image.

The second approach was to try for depth of analysis by restricting the scope to a world of single, illuminated, matte white toy blocks set against a black background. The blocks could occur in any shapes provided only that all faces were planar and all edges were straight. This restriction allowed more specialized techniques to be used, but it still did not make the problem easy. The Binford–Horn line finder (Horn 1973) was used to find edges, and both it and its sequel (described in Shirai 1973) made use of the special circumstances of the environment, such as the fact that all edges there were straight.

These techniques did work reasonably well, however, and they allowed a preliminary analysis of later problems to emerge—roughly, what does one do once a complete line drawing has been extracted from a scene? Studies of this had begun sometime before with Roberts (1965) and Guzman (1968), and they culminated in the works of Waltz (1975) and Mackworth (1973), which essentially solved the interpretation problem for line drawings derived from images of prismatic solids. Waltz's work had a particularly dramatic impact, because it was the first to show explicitly that an exhaustive analysis of all possible local physical arrangements of surfaces, edges, and shadows could lead to an effective and efficient algorithm for interpreting an actual image. Figure 11.3 and its legend convey the main ideas behind Waltz's theory.

The hope that lay behind this work was, of course, that once the toy world of white blocks had been understood, the solutions found there could be generalized, providing the basis for attacking the more complex problems posed by a richer visual environment. Unfortunately, this turned out not to be so. For the roots of the

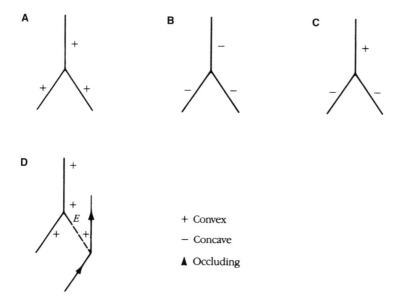

Figure 11.3
Some configurations of edges are physically realizable, and some are not. The trihedral junctions of three convex edges (a) or of three concave edges (b) are realizable, whereas the configuration (c) is impossible. Waltz catalogued all the possible junctions, including shadow edges, for up to four coincident edges. He then found that by using this catalog to implement consistency relations [requiring, for example, that an edge be of the same type all along its length like edge E in (d)], the solution to the labeling of a line drawing that included shadows was often uniquely determined.

approach that was eventually successful, we have to look at the third kind of development that was taking place then.

Two pieces of work were important here. Neither is probably of very great significance to human perception for what it actually accomplished—in the end, it is likely that neither will particularly reflect human visual processes—but they are both of importance because of the way in which they were formulated. The first was Land and McCann's (1971) work on the retinex theory of color vision, as developed by them and subsequently by Horn (1974). The starting point is the traditional one of regarding color as a perceptual approximation to reflectance. This allows the formulation of a clear computational question, namely, How can the effects of reflectance changes be separated from the vagaries of the prevailing illumination? Land and McCann suggested using the fact that changes in illumination are usually gradual, whereas changes in reflectance of a surface or of an object boundary are often quite sharp. Hence by filtering out slow changes, those changes due to the reflectance alone could be isolated. Horn devised a clever parallel algorithm for this, and I suggested how it might be implemented by neurons in the retina (Marr 1974).

I do not now believe that this is at all a correct analysis of color vision or of the retina, but it showed the possible style of a correct analysis. Gone are the ad hoc programs of computer vision; gone is the restriction to a special visual miniworld; gone is any explanation *in terms of* neurons—except as a way of implementing a method. And present is a clear understanding of what is to be computed, how it is to be done, the physical assumption on which the method is based, and some kind of analysis of algorithms that are capable of carrying it out.

The other piece of work was Horn's (1975) analysis of shape from shading, which was the first in what was to become a distinguished series of articles on the formation of images. By carefully analyzing the way in which the illumination, surface geometry, surface reflectance, and viewpoint conspired to create the measured intensity values in an image, Horn formulated a differential equation that related the image intensity values to the surface geometry. If the surface reflectance and illumination are known, one can solve for the surface geometry (see also Horn 1977). Thus from shading one can derive shape.

The message was plain. There must exist an additional level of understanding at which the character of the information-processing tasks carried out during perception are analyzed and understood in a way that is independent of the particular mechanisms and structures that implement them in our heads. This was what was missing—the analysis of the problem as an information-processing task. Such analysis does not usurp an understanding at the other levels—of neurons or of computer programs—but it is a necessary complement to them, since without it there can be no real understanding of the function of all those neurons.

This realization was arrived at independently and formulated together by Tomaso Poggio in Tübingen and myself (Marr and Poggio 1977; Marr 1977). It was not even quite new—Leon D. Harmon was saying something similar at about the same time, and others had paid lip service to a similar distinction. But the important point is that if the notion of different types of understanding is taken very seriously, it allows the study of the information-processing basis of perception to be made *rigorous*. It becomes possible, by separating explanations into different levels, to make explicit statements about what is being computed and why and to construct theories stating that what is being computed is optimal in some sense or is guaranteed to function correctly. The ad hoc element is removed, and heuristic computer programs are replaced by solid foundations on which a real subject can be built. This realization—the formulation of what was missing, together with a clear idea of how to supply it—formed the basic foundation for a new integrated approach, which it is the purpose of this book to describe

2   Understanding Complex Information-Processing Systems

Almost never can a complex system of any kind be understood as a simple extrapolation from the properties of its elementary components. Consider, for example, some gas in a bottle. A description of thermodynamic effects—temperature, pressure, density, and the relationships among these factors—is not formulated by using a large set of equations, one for each of the particles involved. Such effects are described at their own level, that of an enormous collection of particles; the effort is to show that in principle the microscopic and macroscopic descriptions are consistent with one another. If one hopes to achieve a full understanding of a system as complicated as a nervous system, a developing embryo, a set of metabolic pathways, a bottle of gas, or even a large computer program, then one must be prepared to contemplate different kinds of explanation at different levels of description that are linked, at least in principle, into a cohesive whole, even if linking the levels in complete detail is impractical. For the specific case of a system that solves an information-processing problem, there are in addition the twin strands of process and representation, and both these ideas need some discussion.

Representation and Description

A *representation* is a formal system for making explicit certain entities or types of information, together with a specification of how the system does this. And I shall call the result of using a representation to describe a given entity a *description* of the entity in that representation (Marr and Nishihara, 1978).

For example, the Arabic, Roman, and binary numeral systems are all formal systems for representing numbers. The Arabic representation consists of a string of symbols drawn from the set (0, 1, 2, 3, 4, 5, 6, 7, 8, 9), and the rule for constructing the description of a particular integer n is that one decomposes n into a sum of multiples of powers of 10 and unites these multiples into a string with the largest powers on the left and the smallest on the right. Thus, thirty-seven equals $3 \times 10^1 + 7 \times$

10^0, which becomes 37, the Arabic numeral system's description of the number. What this description makes explicit is the number's decomposition into powers of 10. The binary numeral system's description of the number thirty-seven is 100101, and this description makes explicit the number's decomposition into powers of 2. In the Roman numeral system, thirty-seven is represented as XXXVII.

This definition of a representation is quite general. For example, a representation for shape would be a formal scheme for describing some aspects of shape, together with rules that specify how the scheme is applied to any particular shape. A musical score provides a way of representing a symphony; the alphabet allows the construction of a written representation of words; and so forth. The phrase "formal scheme" is critical to the definition, but the reader should not be frightened by it. The reason is simply that we are dealing with information-processing machines, and the way such machines work is by using symbols to stand for things—to represent things, in our terminology. To say that something is a formal scheme means only that it is a set of symbols with rules for putting them together—no more and no less.

A representation, therefore, is not a foreign idea at all—we all use representations all the time. However, the notion that one can capture some aspect of reality by making a description of it using a symbol and that to do so can be useful seems to me a fascinating and powerful idea. But even the simple examples we have discussed introduce some rather general and important issues that arise whenever one chooses to use one particular representation. For example, if one chooses the Arabic numeral representation, it is easy to discover whether a number is a power of 10 but difficult to discover whether it is a power of 2. If one chooses the binary representation, the situation is reversed. Thus, there is a trade-off; any particular representation makes certain information explicit at the expense of information that is pushed into the background and may be quite hard to recover.

This issue is important, because how information is represented can greatly affect how easy it is to do different things with it. This is evident even from our numbers example: It is easy to add, to subtract, and even to multiply if the Arabic or binary representations are used, but it is not at all easy to do these things—especially multiplication—with Roman numerals. This is a key reason why the Roman culture failed to develop mathematics in the way the earlier Arabic cultures had.

An analogous problem faces computer engineers today. Electronic technology is much more suited to a binary number system than to the conventional base 10 system, yet humans supply their data and require the results in base 10. The design decision facing the engineer, therefore, is, Should one pay the cost of conversion into base 2, carry out the arithmetic in a binary representation, and then convert back into decimal numbers on output; or should one sacrifice efficiency of circuitry to carry out operations directly in a decimal representation? On the whole, business computers and pocket calculators take the second approach, and general purpose computers take the first. But even though one is not restricted to using just one representation system for a given type of information, the choice of which to use is important and cannot be taken lightly. It determines what information is made explicit and hence what is pushed further into the background, and it has a far-reaching effect on the ease and difficulty with which operations may subsequently be carried out on that information.

Process

The term *process* is very broad. For example, addition is a process, and so is taking a Fourier transform. But so is making a cup of tea, or going shopping. For the purposes of this chapter, I want to restrict our attention to the meanings associated with machines that are carrying out information-processing tasks. So let us examine in depth the notions behind one simple such device, a cash register at the checkout counter of a supermarket.

There are several levels at which one needs to understand such a device, and it is perhaps most useful to think in terms of three of them. The most abstract is the level of *what* the device does and *why*. What it does is arithmetic, so our first task is to master the theory of addition. Addition is a mapping, usually denoted by +, from pairs of numbers into single numbers; for example, + maps the pair $(3, 4)$ to 7, and I shall write this in the form $(3 + 4) \rightarrow 7$. Addition has a number of abstract properties, however. It is commutative: both $(3 + 4)$ and $(4 + 3)$ are equal to 7; and associative: the sum of $3 + (4 + 5)$ is the same as the sum of $(3 + 4) + 5$. Then there is the unique distinguished element, zero, the adding of which has no effect: $(4 + 0) \rightarrow 4$. Also, for every number there is a unique "inverse," written (-4) in the case of 4, which when added to the number gives zero: $[4 + (-4)] \rightarrow 0$.

Notice that these properties are part of the fundamental *theory* of addition. They are true no matter how the numbers are written—whether in binary, Arabic, or Roman representation—and no matter how the addition is executed. Thus part of this first level is something that might be characterized as *what* is being computed.

The other half of this level of explanation has to do with the question of *why* the cash register performs addition and not, for instance, multiplication when combining the prices of the purchased items to arrive at a final bill. The reason is that the rules we intuitively feel to be appropriate for combining the individual prices in fact define the mathematical operation of addition. These can be formulated as *constraints* in the following way:

1. If you buy nothing, it should cost you nothing; and buying nothing and something should cost the same as buying just the something. (The rules for zero.)

2. The order in which goods are presented to the cashier should not affect the total. (Commutativity.)

3. Arranging the goods into two piles and paying for each pile separately should not affect the total amount you pay. (Associativity; the basic operation for combining prices.)

4. If you buy an item and then return it for a refund, your total expenditure should be zero. (Inverses.)

It is a mathematical theorem that these conditions define the operation of addition, which is therefore the appropriate computation to use.

This whole argument is what I call the *computational theory* of the cash register. Its important features are (1) that it contains separate arguments about what is computed and why and (2) that the resulting operation is defined uniquely by the constraints it has to satisfy. In the theory of visual processes, the underlying task is to reliably derive properties of the world from images of it; the business of isolating constraints that are both powerful enough to allow a process to be defined and generally true of the world is a central theme of our inquiry.

In order that a process shall actually run, however, one has to realize it in some way and therefore choose a representation for the entities that the process manipulates. The second level of the analysis of a process, therefore, involves choosing two things: (1) a *representation* for the input and for the output of the process and (2) an *algorithm* by which the transformation may actually be accomplished. For addition, of course, the input and output representations can both be the same, because they both consist of numbers. However this is not true in general. In the case of a Fourier transform, for example, the input representation may be the time domain, and the output, the frequency domain. If the first of our levels specifies what and why, this second level specifies *how*. For addition, we might choose Arabic numerals for the representations, and for the algorithm we could follow the usual rules about adding the least significant digits first and "carrying" if the sum exceeds 9. Cash registers, whether mechanical or electronic, usually use this type of representation and algorithm.

There are three important points here. First, there is usually a wide choice of representation. Second, the choice of algorithm often depends rather critically on the particular representation that is employed. And third, even for a given fixed representation, there are often several possible algorithms for carrying out the same process. Which one is chosen will usually depend on any particularly desirable or undesirable characteristics that the algorithms may have; for example, one algorithm may be much more efficient than another, or another may be slightly less efficient but more robust (that is, less sensitive to slight inaccuracies in the data on which it must run). Or again, one algorithm may be parallel, and another, serial. The choice, then, may depend on the type of hardware or machinery in which the algorithm is to be embodied physically.

This brings us to the third level, that of the device in which the process is to be realized physically. The important point here is that, once again, the same algorithm may be implemented in quite different technologies. The child who methodically adds two numbers from right to left, carrying a digit when necessary, may be using the same algorithm that is implemented by the wires and transistors of the cash register in the neighborhood supermarket, but the physical realization of the algorithm is quite different in these two cases. Another example: Many people have written computer programs to play tic-tac-toe, and there is a more or less standard algorithm that cannot lose. This algorithm has in fact been implemented by W. D. Hillis and B. Silverman in a quite different technology, in a computer made out of Tinkertoys, a children's wooden building set. The whole monstrously ungainly engine, which actually works, currently resides in a museum at the University of Missouri in St. Louis.

Some styles of algorithm will suit some physical substrates better than others. For example, in conventional digital computers, the number of connections is comparable to the number of gates, while in a brain, the number of connections is much larger ($\times 10^4$) than the number of nerve cells. The underlying reason is that wires are rather cheap in biological architecture, because they can grow individually and in three dimensions. In conventional technology, wire laying is more or less restricted to two dimensions, which quite severely restricts the scope for using parallel techniques and algorithms; the same operations are often better carried out serially.

The Three Levels

We can summarize our discussion in something like the manner shown in figure 11.4, which illustrates the different levels at which an information-processing device must be understood before one can be said to have understood it completely. At

Computational theory	Representation and algorithm	Hardware implementation
What is the goal of the computation, why is it appropriate, and what is the logic of the strategy by which it can be carried out?	How can this computational theory be implemented? In particular, what is the representation for the input and output, and what is the algorithm for the transformation?	How can the representation and algorithm be realized physically?

Figure 11.4
The three levels at which any machine carrying out an information-processing task must be understood.

one extreme, the top level, is the abstract computational theory of the device, in which the performance of the device is characterized as a mapping from one kind of information to another, the abstract properties of this mapping are defined precisely, and its appropriateness and adequacy for the task at hand are demonstrated. In the center is the choice of representation for the input and output and the algorithm to be used to transform one into the other. And at the other extreme are the details of how the algorithm and representation are realized physically—the detailed computer architecture, so to speak. These three levels are coupled, but only loosely. The choice of an algorithm is influenced for example, by what it has to do and by the hardware in which it must run. But there is a wide choice available at each level, and the explication of each level involves issues that are rather independent of the other two.

Each of the three levels of description will have its place in the eventual understanding of perceptual information processing, and of course they are logically and causally related. But an important point to note is that since the three levels are only rather loosely related, some phenomena may be explained at only one or two of them. This means, for example, that a correct explanation of some psychophysical observation must be formulated at the appropriate level. In attempts to relate psychophysical problems to physiology, too often there is confusion about the level at which problems should be addressed. For instance, some are related mainly to the physical mechanisms of vision—such as afterimages (for example, the one you see after staring at a light bulb) or such as the fact that any color can be matched by a suitable mixture of the three primaries (a consequence principally of the fact that we humans have three types of cones). On the other hand, the ambiguity of the Necker cube (figure 11.5) seems to demand a different kind of explanation. To be sure, part of the explanation of its perceptual reversal must have to do with a

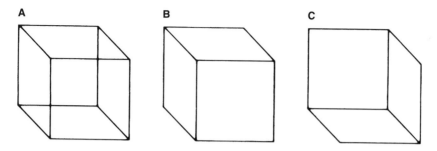

Figure 11.5
The so-called Necker illusion, named after L. A. Necker, the Swiss naturalist who developed it in 1832. The essence of the matter is that the two-dimensional representation (a) has collapsed the depth out of a cube and that a certain aspect of human vision is to recover this missing third dimension. The depth of the cube can indeed be perceived, but two interpretations are possible, (b) and (c). A person's perception characteristically flips from one to the other.

bistable neural network (that is, one with two distinct stable states) somewhere inside the brain, but few would feel satisfied by an account that failed to mention the existence of two different but perfectly plausible three-dimensional interpretations of this two-dimensional image.

For some phenomena, the type of explanation required is fairly obvious. Neuroanatomy, for example, is clearly tied principally to the third level, the physical realization of the computation. The same holds for synaptic mechanisms, action potentials, inhibitory interactions, and so forth. Neurophysiology, too, is related mostly to this level, but it can also help us to understand the type of representations being used, particularly if one accepts something along the lines of Barlow's views that I quoted earlier. But one has to exercise extreme caution in making inferences from neurophysiological findings about the algorithms and representations being used, particularly until one has a clear idea about what information needs to be represented and what processes need to be implemented.

Psychophysics, on the other hand, is related more directly to the level of algorithm and representation. Different algorithms tend to fail in radically different ways as they are pushed to the limits of their performance or are deprived of critical information. As we shall see, primarily psychophysical evidence proved to Poggio and myself that our first stereo-matching algorithm (Marr and Poggio, 1976) was not the one that is used by the brain, and the best evidence that our second algorithm (Marr and Poggio, 1979) *is* roughly the one that is used also comes from psychophysics. Of course, the underlying computational theory remained the same in both cases, only the algorithms were different.

Psychophysics can also help to determine the nature of a representation. The work of Roger Shepard (1975), Eleanor Rosch (1978), or Elizabeth Warrington (1975) provides some interesting hints in this direction. More specifically, Stevens (1979) argued from psychophysical experiments that surface orientation is represented by the coordinates of slant and tilt, rather than (for example) the more traditional (p,q) of gradient space. He also deduced from the uniformity of the size of errors made by subjects judging surface orientation over a wide range of orientations that the representational quantities used for slant and tilt are pure angles and not, for example, their cosines, sines, or tangents.

More generally, if the idea that different phenomena need to be explained at different levels is kept clearly in mind, it often helps in the assessment of the validity of the different kinds of objections that are raised from time to time. For example, one favorite is that the brain is quite different from a computer because one is parallel and the other serial. The answer to this, of course, is that the distinction between serial and parallel is a distinction at the level of algorithm; it is not fundamental at all—anything programmed in parallel can be rewritten serially (though not necessarily vice versa). The distinction, therefore, provides no grounds for arguing that the brain operates so differently from a computer that a computer could not be programmed to perform the same tasks.

Importance of Computational Theory

Although algorithms and mechanisms are empirically more accessible, it is the top level, the level of computational theory, which is critically important from an information-processing point of view. The reason for this is that the nature of the computations that underlie perception depends more upon the computational problems that have to be solved than upon the particular hardware in which their solutions are implemented. To phrase the matter another way, an algorithm is likely to be understood more readily by understanding the nature of the problem being solved than by examining the mechanism (and the hardware) in which it is embodied.

In a similar vein, trying to understand perception by studying only neurons is like trying to understand bird flight by studying only feathers: It just cannot be done. In order to understand bird flight, we have to understand aerodynamics; only then do the structure of feathers and the different shapes of birds' wings make sense.

More to the point, as we shall see, we cannot understand why retinal ganglion cells and lateral geniculate neurons have the receptive fields they do just by studying their anatomy and physiology. We can understand how these cells and neurons behave as they do by studying their wiring and interactions, but in order to understand *why* the receptive fields are as they are—why they are circularly symmetrical and why their excitatory and inhibitory regions have characteristic shapes and distributions— we have to know a little of the theory of differential operators, band-pass channels, and the mathematics of the uncertainty principle.

Perhaps it is not surprising that the very specialized empirical disciplines of the neurosciences failed to appreciate fully the absence of computational theory; but it is surprising that this level of approach did not play a more forceful role in the early development of artificial intelligence. For far too long, a heuristic program for carrying out some task was held to be a theory of that task, and the distinction between what a program did and how it did it was not taken seriously. As a result, (1) a style of explanation evolved that invoked the use of special mechanisms to solve particular problems, (2) particular data structures, such as the lists of attribute value pairs called property lists in the LISP programing language, were held to amount to theories of the representation of knowledge, and (3) there was frequently no way to determine whether a program would deal with a particular case other than by running the program.

Failure to recognize this theoretical distinction between *what* and *how* also greatly hampered communication between the fields of artificial intelligence and linguistics. Chomsky's (1965) theory of transformational grammar is a true computational theory in the sense defined earlier. It is concerned solely with specifying what the syntactic decomposition of an English sentence should be, and not at all with how that decomposition should be achieved. Chomsky himself was very clear about this—it is roughly his distinction between competence and performance, though his idea of performance did include other factors, like stopping in midutterance—but the fact that his theory was defined by transformations, which look like computations, seems to have confused many people. Winograd (1972), for example, felt able to criticize Chomsky's theory on the grounds that it cannot be inverted and so cannot be made to run on a computer; I had heard reflections of the same argument made by Chomsky's colleagues in linguistics as they turn their attention to how grammatical structure might actually be computed from a real English sentence.

The explanation is simply that finding algorithms by which Chomsky's theory may be implemented is a completely different endeavor from formulating the theory itself. In our terms, it is a study at a different level, and both tasks have to be done. This point was appreciated by Marcus (1980), who was concerned precisely with how Chomsky's theory can be realized and with the kinds of constraints on the power of the human grammatical processor that might give rise to the structural constraints in syntax that Chomsky found. It even appears that the emerging "trace" theory of grammar (Chomsky and Lasnik, 1977) may provide a way of synthesizing the two approaches—showing that, for example, some of the rather ad hoc restrictions that form part of the computational theory may be consequences of weaknesses in the computational power that is available for implementing syntactical decoding.

The Approach of J. J. Gibson

In perception, perhaps the nearest anyone came to the level of computational theory was Gibson (1966). However, although some aspects of his thinking were on the right lines, he did not understand properly what information processing was, which led him to seriously underestimate the complexity of the information-processing problems involved in vision and the consequent subtlety that is necessary in approaching them.

Gibson's important contribution was to take the debate away from the philosophical considerations of sense-data and the affective qualities of sensation and to note instead that the important thing about the senses is that they are channels for perception of the real world outside or, in the case of vision, of the visible surfaces. He therefore asked the critically important question, How does one obtain constant perceptions in everyday life on the basis of continually changing sensations? This is exactly the right question, showing that Gibson correctly regarded the problem of perception as that of recovering from sensory information "valid" properties of the external world. His problem was that he had a much oversimplified view of how this should be done. His approach led him to consider higher-order variables—stimulus energy, ratios, proportions, and so on—as "invariants" of the movement of an observer and of changes in stimulation intensity.

"These invariants," he wrote, "correspond to permanent properties of the environment. They constitute, therefore, information about the permanent environment." This led him to a view in which the function of the brain was to "detect invariants" despite changes in "sensations" of light, pressure, or loudness of sound. Thus, he says that the "function of the brain, when looped with its perceptual organs, is not to decode signals, nor to interpret messages, nor to accept images, nor to *organize* the sensory input or to *process* the data, in modern terminology. It is to seek and extract information about the environment from the flowing array of ambient energy," and he thought of the nervous system as in some way "resonating" to these invariants. He then embarked on a broad study of animals in their environments, looking for invariants to which they might resonate. This was the basic idea behind the notion of ecological optics (Gibson, 1966, 1979).

Although one can criticize certain shortcomings in the quality of Gibson's analysis, its major and, in my view, fatal shortcoming lies at a deeper level and results from a failure to realize two things. First, the detection of physical invariants, like image surfaces, is exactly and precisely an information-processing problem, in modern terminology. And second, he vastly underrated the sheer difficulty of such detection. In discussing the recovery of three-dimensional information from the movement of an observer, he says that "in motion, perspective information alone can be used" (Gibson, 1966, p. 202). And perhaps the key to Gibson is the following:

The detection of non-change when an object moves in the world is not as difficult as it might appear. It is only made to seem difficult when we assume that the perception of constant dimensions of the object must depend on the correcting of sensations of inconstant form and size. The information for the constant dimension of an object is normally carried by invariant relations in an optic array. Rigidity is *specified*. (emphasis added)

Yes, to be sure, but *how*? Detecting physical invariants is just as difficult as Gibson feared, but nevertheless we can do it. And the only way to understand how is to treat it as an information-processing problem.

The underlying point is that visual information processing is actually very complicated, and Gibson was not the only thinker who was misled by the apparent simplicity of the act of seeing. The whole tradition of philosophical inquiry into the nature of perception seems not to have taken seriously enough the complexity of the information processing involved. For example, Austin's (1962) *Sense and Sensibilia* entertainingly demolishes the argument, apparently favored by earlier philosophers, that since we are sometimes deluded by illusions (for example, a straight stick appears bent if it is partly submerged in water), we see sense-data rather than material things. The answer is simply that usually our perceptual processing does run correctly (it delivers a true description of what is there), but although evolution has seen to it that our processing allows for many changes (like inconstant illumination), the perturbation due to the refraction of light by water is not one of them. And incidentally, although the example of the bent stick has been discussed since Aristotle, I have seen no philosphical inquiry into the nature of the perceptions of, for instance, a heron, which is a bird that feeds by pecking up fish first seen from above the water surface. For such birds the visual correction might be present.

Anyway, my main point here is another one. Austin (1962) spends much time on the idea that perception tells one about real properties of the external world, and one thing he considers is "real shape," (p. 66), a notion which had cropped up earlier in his discussion of a coin that "looked elliptical" from some points of view. Even so,

> it had a real shape which remained unchanged. But coins in fact are rather special cases. For one thing their outlines are well defined and very highly stable, and for another they have a known and a nameable shape. But there are plenty of things of which this is not true. What is the real shape of a cloud? . . . or of a cat? Does its real shape change whenever it moves? If not, in what posture *is* its real shape on display? Furthermore, is its real shape such as to be fairly smooth outlines, or must it be finely enough serrated to take account of each hair? *It is pretty obvious that there is no answer to these questions—no rules according to which, no procedure by which, answers are to be determined.* (emphasis added) (p. 67)

But there *are* answers to these questions. There are ways of describing the shape of a cat to an arbitrary level of precision, and there are rules and procedures for arriving at such descriptions. That is exactly what vision is about, and precisely what makes it complicated.

3   A Representational Framework for Vision

Vision is a process that produces from images of the external world a description that is useful to the viewer and not cluttered with irrelevant information (Marr, 1976; Marr and Nishihara, 1978). We have already seen that a process may be thought of as a mapping from one representation to another, and in the case of human vision, the initial representation is in no doubt—it consists of arrays of image intensity values as detected by the photoreceptors in the retina.

It is quite proper to think of an image as a representation; the items that are made explicit are the image intensity values at each point in the array, which we can conveniently denote by $I(x,y)$ at coordinate (x,y). In order to simplify our discussion, we shall neglect for the moment the fact that there are several different types of receptor, and imagine instead that there is just one, so that the image is black-and-white. Each value of $I(x,y)$ thus specifies a particular level of gray; we shall refer to each detector as a picture element or *pixel* and to the whole array I as an image.

But what of the output of the process of vision? We have already agreed that it must consist of a useful description of the world, but that requirement is rather nebulous. Can we not do better? Well, it is perfectly true that, unlike the input, the result of vision is much harder to discern, let alone specify precisely, and an important aspect of this new approach is that it makes quite concrete proposals about what that end is. But before we begin that discussion, let us step back a little and spend a little time formulating the more general issues that are raised by these questions.

The Purpose of Vision

The usefulness of a representation depends upon how well suited it is to the purpose for which it is used. A pigeon uses vision to help it navigate, fly, and seek out food. Many types of jumping spider use vision to tell the difference between a potential meal and a potential mate. One type, for example, has a curious retina formed of two diagonal strips arranged in a V. If it detects a red V on the back of an object lying in front of it, the spider has found a mate. Otherwise, maybe a meal. The frog, as we have seen, detects bugs with its retina; and the rabbit retina is full of special gadgets, including what is apparently a hawk detector, since it responds well to the pattern made by a preying hawk hovering overhead. Human vision, on the other hand, seems to be very much more general, although it clearly contains a variety of special-purpose mechanisms that can, for example, direct the eye toward an unexpected movement in the visual field or cause one to blink or otherwise avoid something that approaches one's head too quickly.

Vision, in short, is used in such a bewildering variety of ways that the visual systems of different animals must differ significantly from one another. Can the type of formulation that I have been advocating, in terms of representations and processes, possibly prove adequate for them all? I think so. The general point here is that because vision is used by different animals for such a wide variety of purposes, it is inconceivable that all seeing animals use the same representations; each can confidently be expected to use one or more representations that are nicely tailored to the owner's purposes.

As an example, let us consider briefly a primitive but highly efficient visual system that has the added virtue of being well understood. Werner Reichardt's group in Tübingen has spent the last fourteen years patiently unraveling the visual flight-control system of the housefly, and in a famous collaboration, Reichardt and Tomaso Poggio have gone far toward solving the problem (Reichardt and Poggio,

1976, 1979; Poggio and Reichardt, 1976). Roughly speaking, the fly's visual apparatus controls its flight through a collection of about five independent, rigidly inflexible, very fast responding systems (the time from visual stimulus to change of torque is only 21 ms). For example, one of these systems is the landing system; if the visual field "explodes" fast enough (because a surface looms nearby), the fly automatically "lands" toward its center. If this center is above the fly, the fly automatically inverts to land upside down. When the feet touch, power to the wings is cut off. Conversely, to take off, the fly jumps; when the feet no longer touch the ground, power is restored to the wings, and the insect flies again.

In-flight control is achieved by independent systems controlling the fly's vertical velocity (through control of the lift generated by the wings) and horizontal direction (determined by the torque produced by the asymmetry of the horizontal thrust from the left and right wings). The visual input to the horizontal control system, for example, is completely described by the two terms

$$r(\psi)\dot{\psi} + D(\psi)$$

where r and D have the form illustrated in figure 11.6. This input describes how the fly tracks an object that is present at angle ψ in the visual field and has angular velocity $\dot{\psi}$. This system is triggered to track objects of a certain angular dimension

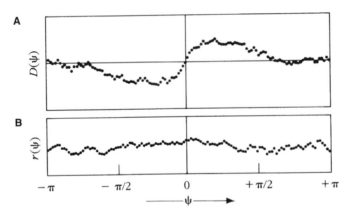

Figure 11.6
The horizontal component of the visual input R to the fly's flight system is described by the formula $R = D(\psi) - r(\psi)\dot{\psi}$, where ψ is the direction of the stimulus and $\dot{\psi}$ is its angular velocity in the fly's visual field. $D(\psi)$ is an odd function, shown in (a), which has the effect of keeping the target concerned in the fly's visual field; $r(\psi)$ is essentially constant as shown in (b).

in the visual field, and the motor strategy is such that if the visible object was another fly a few inches away, then it would be intercepted successfully. If the target was an elephant 100 yards away, interception would fail because the fly's built-in parameters are for another fly nearby, not an elephant far away.

Thus, fly vision delivers a representation in which at least these three things are specified: (1) whether the visual field is looming sufficiently fast that the fly should contemplate landing; (2) whether there is a small patch—it could be a black speck or, it turns out, a textured figure in front of a textured ground—having some kind of motion relative to its background; and if there is such a patch, (3) ψ and $\dot\psi$ for this patch are delivered to the motor system. And that is probably about 60% of fly vision. In particular, it is extremely unlikely that the fly has any explicit representation of the visual world around him—no true conception of a surface, for example, but just a few triggers and some specifically fly-centered parameters like ψ and $\dot\psi$.

It is clear that human vision is much more complex than this, although it may well incorporate subsystems not unlike the fly's to help with specific and rather low-level tasks like the control of pursuit eye movements. Nevertheless, as Poggio and Reichardt have shown, even these simple systems can be understood in the same sort of way, as information-processing tasks. And one of the fascinating aspects of their work is how they have managed not only to formulate the differential equations that accurately describe the visual control system of the fly but also to express these equations, using the Volterra series expansion, in a way that gives direct information about the minimum possible complexity of connections of the underlying neuronal networks.

Advanced Vision

Visual systems like the fly's serve adequately and with speed and precision the needs of their owners, but they are not very complicated; very little objective information about the world is obtained. The information is all very much subjective—the angular size of the stimulus as the fly sees it rather than the objective size of the object out there, the angle that the object has in the fly's visual field rather than its position relative to the fly or to some external reference, and the object's angular velocity, again in the fly's visual field, rather than any assessment of its true velocity relative to the fly or to some stationary reference point.

One reason for this simplicity must be that these facts provide the fly with sufficient information for it to survive. Of course, the information is not optimal and from time to time the fly will fritter away its energy chasing a falling leaf a medium distance away or an elephant a long way away as a direct consequence of the inadequacies of its perceptual system. But this apparently does not matter very much—the fly has sufficient excess energy for it to be able to absorb these extra costs. Another reason is certainly that translating these rather subjective measurements into more objective qualities involves much more computation. How, then, should one think about more advanced visual systems—human vision, for example. What are the issues? What kind of information is vision really delivering, and what are the representational issues involved?

My approach to these problems was very much influenced by the fascinating accounts of clinical neurology, such as Critchley (1953) and Warrington and Taylor (1973). Particularly important was a lecture that Elizabeth Warrington gave at MIT in October 1973, in which she described the capacities and limitations of patients who had suffered left or right parietal lesions. For me, the most important thing that she did was to draw a distinction between the two calsses of patient (see Warrington and Taylor, 1978). For those with lesions on the right side, recognition of a common object was possible *provided* that the patient's view of it was in some sense straightforward. She used the words *conventional* and *unconventional*—a water pail or a clarinet seen from the side gave "conventional" views but seen end-on gave "unconventional" views. If these patients recognized the object at all, they knew its name and its semantics—that is, its use and purpose, how big it was, how much it weighed, what it was made of, and so forth. If their view was unconventional—a pail seen from above, for example—not only would the patients fail to recognize it, but they would vehemently deny that it *could* be a view of a pail. Patients with left parietal lesions behaved completely differently. Often these patients had no language, so they were unable to name the viewed object or state its purpose and semantics. But they could convey that they correctly perceived its geometry—that is, its shape—even from the unconventional view.

Warrington's talk suggested two things. First, the representation of the shape of an object is stored in a different place and is therefore a quite different kind of thing from the representation of its use and purpose. And second, vision alone can deliver an internal description of the shape of a viewed object, even when the object was not recognized in the conventional sense of understanding its use and purpose.

This was an important moment for me for two reasons. The general trend in the computer vision community was to believe that recognition was so difficult that it required every possible kind of information. The results of this point of view duly appeared a few years later in programs like Freuder's (1974) and Tenenbaum and Barrow's (1976). In the latter program, knowledge about offices—for example, that desks have telephones on them and that telephones are black—was used to help "segment" out a black blob halfway up an image and "recognize" it as a telephone. Freuder's program used a similar approach to "segment" and "recognize" a hammer in a scene. Clearly, we do use such knowledge in real life; I once saw a brown blob quivering amongst the lettuce in my garden and correctly identified it as a rabbit, even though the visual information alone was inadequate. And yet here was this young woman calmly telling us not only that her patients could convey to her that they had grasped the shapes of things that she had shown them, even though they could not name the objects or say how they were used, but also that they could happily continue to do so even if she made the task extremely difficult visually by showing them peculiar views or by illuminating the objects in peculiar ways. It seemed clear that the intuitions of the computer vision people were completely wrong and that even in difficult circumstances shapes could be determined by vision alone.

The second important thing, I thought, was that Elizabeth Warrington had put her finger on what was somehow the quintessential fact of human vision—that it tells about shape and space and spatial arrangement. Here lay a way to formulate its purpose—building a description of the shapes and positions of things from images. Of course, that is by no means all that vision can do; it also tells about the illumination and about the reflectances of the surfacs that make the shapes—their brightnesses and colors and visual textures—and about their motion. But these things seemed secondary; they could be hung off a theory in which the main job of vision was to derive a representation of shape.

To the Desirable via the Possible
Finally, one has to come to terms with cold reality. Desirable as it may be to have vision deliver a completely invariant shape description from an image (whatever that may mean in detail), it is almost certainly impossible in only one step. We can only do what is possible and proceed from there toward what is desirable. Thus we arrived at the idea of a sequence of representations, starting with descriptions that could be obtained straight from an image but that are carefully designed to facilitate the subsequent recovery of gradually more objective, physical properties about an object's shape. The main stepping stone toward this goal is describing the geometry of the visible surfaces, since the information encoded in images, for example

Table 11.1
Representational Framework for Deriving Shape Information from Images

Name	Purpose	Primitives
Image(s)	Represents intensity.	Intensity value at each point in the image
Primal sketch	Makes explicit important information about the two-dimensional image, primarily the intensity changes there and their geometrical distribution and organization.	Zero-crossings Blobs Terminations and discontinuities Edge segments Virtual lines Groups Curvilinear organization Boundaries
$2\frac{1}{2}$-D sketch	Makes explicit the orientation and rough depth of the visible surfaces, and contours of discontinuities in these quantities in a viewer-centered coordinate frame.	Local surface orientation (the "needles" primitives) Distance from viewer Discontinuities in depth Discontinuities in surface orientation
3-D model representation	Describes shapes and their spatial organization in an object-centered coordinate frame, using a modular hierarchical representation that includes volumetric primitives (i.e., primitives that represent the volume of space that a shape occupies) as well as surface primitives.	3-D models arranged hierarchically, each one based on a spatial configuration of a few sticks or axes, to which volumetric or surface shape primitives are attached

by stereopsis, shading, texture, contours, or visual motion, is due to a shape's local surface properties. The objective of many early visual computations is to extract this information.

However, this description of the visible surfaces turns out to be unsuitable for recognition tasks. There are several reasons why, perhaps the most prominent being that like all early visual processes, it depends critically on the vantage point. The final step therefore consists of transforming the viewer-centered surface description into a representation of the three-dimensional shape and spatial arrangement of an object that does not depend upon the direction from which the object is being viewed. This final description is object centered rather than viewer centered.

The overall framework described here therefore divides the derivation of shape information from images into three representational stages (table 11.1): (1) the representation of properties of the two-dimensional image, such as intensity changes and local two-dimensional geometry; (2) the representation of properties of the visible surfaces in a viewer-centered coordinate system, such as surface orientation, distance from the viewer, and discontinuities in these quantities; surface reflectance; and some coarse description of the prevailing illumination; and (3) an object-centered representation of the three-dimensional structure and of the organization of the viewed shape, together with some description of its surface properties.

This framework is summarized in table 11.1.

Notes

1. The two-dimensional image seen by a single eye.

2. A cell that fires only when one's grandmother comes into view.

3. *Operator* refers to a local calculation to be applied at each location in the image, making use of the intensity there and in the immediate vicinity.

References

[*Editors' note:* Although Crichley 1953, Shepard 1979, and Wertheimer 1923 are cited in chapter 11, no references were provided in the original work.]

Adrian, E. D. 1928. *The Basis of Sensation.* London: Christophers. (Reprint ed. New York: Hafner, 1964.)

Adrian, E. D. 1947. *The Physical Background of Perception.* Oxford: Clarendon Press.

Austin, J. L. 1962. *Sense and Sensibilia.* Oxford: Clarendon Press.

Barlow, H. B. 1953. Summation and inhibition in the frog's retina. *J. Physiol. (Lond.) 119,* 69–88.

Barlow, H. B. 1972. Single units and sensation: a neuron doctrine for perceptual psychology? *Perception 1,* 371–394.

Barlow, H. B., C. Blakemore, and J. D. Pettigrew. 1967. The neural mechanism of binocular depth discrimination. *J. Physiol. (Lond.) 193,* 327–342.

Barlow, H. B., R. M. Hill, and W. R. Levick. 1964. Retinal ganglion cells responding selectively to direction and speed of image motion in the rabbit. *J. Physiol. (Lond.) 173,* 377–407.

Bishop, P. O., J. S. Coombs, and G. H. Henry. 1971. Responses to visual contours: Spatio-temporal aspects of excitation in the receptive fields of simple striate neurons. *J. Physiol. (Lond.) 219,* 625–657.

Brindley, G. S. 1970. *Physiology of the Retina and Visual Pathway.* Physiological Society Monograph no. 6. London: Edwin Arnold.

Campbell, F. W. C., and J. Robson. 1968. Application of Fourier analysis to the visibility of gratings. *J. Physiol. (Lond.) 197*, 551–566.

Chomsky, N. 1965. *Aspects of the Theory of Syntax*. Cambridge, MA: The MIT Press.

Chomsky, N., and H. Lasnik. 1977. Filters and control. *Linguistic Inquiry 8*, 425–504.

DeValois, R. L., I. Abramov, and W. R. Mead. 1967. Single cell analysis of wavelength discrimination at the lateral geniculate nucleus in the macaque. *J. Neurophysiol. 30*, 415–433.

Fram, J. R., and E. S. Deutsch. 1975. On the quantitative evaluation of edge detection schemes and their comparison with human performance. *IEEE Transactions on Computers C-24*, 616–628.

Freuder, E. C. 1974. A computer vision system for visual recognition using active knowledge. MIT A.I. Lab Tech. Rep. 345.

Galambos, R., and H. Davis. 1943. The response of single auditory-nerve fibres to acoustic stimulation. *J. Neurophysiol. 7*, 287–303.

Gibson, J. J. 1966. *The Senses Considered as Perceptual Systems*. Boston: Houghton Mifflin.

Gibson, J. J. 1979. *The Ecological Approach to Visual Perception*. Boston: Houghton Mifflin.

Gouras, P. 1968. Identification of cone mechanisms in monkey ganglion cells. *J. Physiol. (Lond.) 199*, 533–547.

Granit, R., and G. Svaetichin. 1939. Principles and technique of the electrophysiological analysis of colour reception with the aid of microelectrodes. *Upsala Lakraef Fath. 65*, 161–177.

Gross, C. G., C. E. Rocha-Miranda, and D. B. Bender. 1972. Visual properties of neurons in inferotemporal cortex of the macaque. *J. Neurophysiol. 35*, 96–111.

Guzman, A. 1968. Decomposition of a visual scene into three-dimensional bodies. In *AFIPS Conf. Proc. 33*, 291–304. Washington, DC: Thompson.

Hartline, H. K. 1938. The response of single optic nerve fibers of the vertebrate eye to illumination of the retina. *Am. J. Physiol. 121*, 400–415.

Hartline, H. K. 1940. The receptive fields of optic nerve fibers. *Am. J. Physiol. 130*, 690–699.

Helmholtz, H. L. F. von. 1910. *Treatise on Physiological Optics*. Translated by J. P. Southall, 1925. New York: Dover.

Horn, B. K. P. 1973. The Binford-Horn LINEFINDER. MIT A.I. Lab. Memo 285.

Horn, B. K. P. 1974. Determining lightness from an image. *Computer Graphics and Image Processing 3*, 277–299.

Horn, B. K. P. 1975. Obtaining shape from shading information. In *The Psychology of Computer Vision*, ed. P. H. Winston, 115–155. New York: McGraw-Hill.

Horn, B. K. P. 1977. Understanding image intensities. *Artificial Intelligence 8*, 201–231.

Hubel, D. H., and T. N. Wiesel. 1962. Receptive fields, binocular interaction and functional architecture in the cat's visual cortex. *J. Physiol. (Lond.) 166*, 106–154.

Hubel, D. H., and T. N. Wiesel. 1968. Receptive fields and functional architecture of monkey striate cortex. *J. Physiol. (Lond.) 195*, 215–243.

Hueckel, M. H. 1973. An operator which recognizes edges and lines. *J. Assoc. Comput. Mach. 20*, 634–647.

Ito, M. 1978. Recent advances in cerebellar physiology and pathology. In *Advances in Neurology*, ed. R. A. P. Kark, R. N. Rosenberg, and L. J. Shut 59–84. New York: Raven Press.

Julesz, B. 1960. Binocular depth perception of computer generated patterns. *Bell Syst. Tech. J. 39*, 1125–1162.

Kuffler, S. W. 1953. Discharge patterns and functional organization of mammalian retina. *J. Neurophysiol. 16*, 37–68.

Land, E. H., and J. J. McCann. 1971. Lightness and retinex theory. *J. Opt. Soc. Am. 61*, 1–11.

Lettvin, J. Y., R. R. Maturana, W. S. McCulloch, and W. H. Pitts. 1959. What the frog's eye tells the frog's brain. *Proc. Inst. Rad. Eng. 47*, 1940–1951.

Mackworth, A. K. 1973. Interpreting pictures of polyhedral scenes. *Art. Intel. 4*, 121–137.

Marcus, M. P. 1980. *A Theory of Syntactic Recognition for Natural Language*. Cambridge, MA: The MIT Press.

Marr, D. 1969. A theory of cerebellar cortex. *J. Physiol. (Lond.) 202*, 437–470.

Marr, D. 1974. The computation of lightness by the primate retina. *Vision Res. 14*, 1377–1388.

Marr, D. 1976. Early processing of visual information. *Phil Trans. R. Soc. Lond. B 275*, 483–524.

Marr, D. 1977. Artificial intelligence—a personal view. *Artificial Intelligence 9*, 37–48.

Marr, D., and H. K. Nishihara. 1978. Representation and recognition of the spatial organization of three-dimensional shapes. *Proc. R. Soc. Lond. B 200*, 269–294.

Marr, D., and T. Poggio. 1976. Cooperative computation of stereo disparity. *Science 194*, 283–287.

Marr, D., and T. Poggio. 1977. From understanding computation to understanding neural circuitry. *Neurosciences Res. Prog. Bull. 15*, 470–488.

Marr, D., and T. Poggio. 1979. A computational theory of human stereo vision. *Proc. R. Soc. Lond. B 204*, 301–328.

Maturana, H. R., J. Y. Lettvin, W. S. McCulloch, and W. H. Pitts. 1960. Anatomy and physiology of vision in the frog *(Rana pipiens). J. Gen. Physiol. 43* (suppl. No. 2, Mechanisms of Vision), 129–171.

Miles, W. R. 1931. Movement in interpretations of the silhouette of a revolving fan. *Am. J. Psychol. 43*, 392–404.

Newton, I. 1704. *Optics*. London.

Pettigrew, J. D., and M. Konishi. 1976. Neurons selective for orientation and binocular disparity in the visual wulst of the barn owl *(Tyto alba). Science 193*, 675–678.

Poggio, T., and W. Reichardt. 1976. Visual control of orientation behavior in the fly. Part II. Towards the underlying neural interactions. *Quart. Rev. Biophys. 9*, 377–438.

Reichardt, W., and T. Poggio. 1976. Visual control of orientation behavior in the fly. Part I. A quantitative analysis. *Quart. Rev. Biophys. 9*, 311–375.

Reichardt, W., and T. Poggio. 1979. Visual control of flight in flies. In *Recent Theoretical Developments in Neurobiology*, ed. W. E. Reichardt, V. B. Mountcastle, and T. Poggio.

Roberts, L. G. 1965. Machine perception of three-dimensional solids. In *Optical and electro optical information processing*, ed. J. T. Tippett et al., 159–197. Cambridge, MA: The MIT Press.

Rosch, E. 1978. Principles of categorization. In *Cognition and categorization*, ed. E. Rosch, and B. Lloyd, 27–48. Hillsdale, NJ: Lawrence Erlbaum Associates.

Rosenfeld, A., and M. Thurston. 1971. Edge and curve detection for visual scene analysis. *IEEE Trans. Comput. C-20*, 562–569.

Schiller, P. H., B. L. Finlay, and S. F. Volman. 1967a. Quantitative studies of single-cell properties in monkey striate cortex. I. Spatiotemporal organization of receptive fields. *J. Neurophysiol. 39*, 1288–1319.

Schiller, P. H., B. L. Finlay, and S. F. Volman. 1976b. Quantitative studies of single-cell properties in monkey striate cortex. II. Orientation specificity and ocular dominance. *J. Neurophysiol. 39*, 1320-1333.

Shepard, R. N. 1975. Form, formation and transformation of internal representations. In *Information Processing and Cognition: The Loyola Symposium*, ed. R. Solso, 87–122. Hillsdale, NJ: Lawrence Erlbaum Associates.

Shepard, R. N., and J. Metzler. 1971. Mental rotation of three-dimensional objects. *Science 171*, 701–703.

Shirai, Y. 1973. A context-sensitive line finder for recognition of polyhedra. *Artificial Intelligence 4*, 95–120.

Stevens, K. A. 1979. Surface perception from local analysis of texture and contour. Ph.D. diss. MIT. (Available as The information content of texture gradients. *Biol. Cybernetics 42* (1981), 95–105; also The visual interpretation of surface contours. *Artificial intelligence 17* (1981), 47–74.)

Tenenbaum, J. M., and H. G. Barrow. 1976. Experiments in interpretation-guided segmentation. Stanford Research Institute Tech. Note 123.

Wallach, H., and D. N. O'Connell. 1953. The kinetic depth effect. *J. Exp. Psychol. 45*, 205–217.

Waltz, D. 1975. Understanding line drawings of scenes with shadows. In *The Psychology of Computer Vision*, ed. P. H. Winston, 19–91. New York: McGraw-Hill.

Warrington, E. K. 1975. The selective impairment of semantic memory. *Quart. J. Exp. Psychol. 27*, 635–657.

Warrington, E. K., and A. M. Taylor. 1973. The contribution of the right parietal lobe to object recognition. *Cortex 9*, 152–164.

Warrington, E. K., and A. M. Taylor. 1978. Two categorical stages of object recognition. *Perception 7*, 695–705.

Wertheimer, M. 1912. Experimentalle Studien uber das Sehen von Bewegung. *Zeitschrift f. Psychol. 61*, 161–265.

Wilson, H. R., and J. R. Bergen. 1979. A four mechanism model for spatial vision. *Vision Res. 19*, 19–32.

Winograd, T. 1972. *Understanding Natural Language*. New York: Academic Press.

12

Sensation and the Content of Experience: A Distinction

Christopher Peacocke

Nothing is more fundamental to understanding the content of psychological states than sense experience. Time and again in this book we will need to appeal to it: in the accounts of observational concepts and of primitive demonstrative thought, and in the discussion of the Principle of Acquaintance. Elsewhere, in the account of the minimal conditions for the ascription of psychological states with content, we will need to make use of distinctions drawn from a particular theory of experience. If what I argue in this book is correct, we cannot fully understand these several areas if we remain unclear about experience.

But experience is not merely of instrumental interest. Having an experience is a psychological state in its own right, and one that raises many puzzles. How can senses as intrinsically different as sight and touch both serve as sources of knowledge about the spatial layout of our environment? Is the ancient tradition correct which holds that some concepts, those of secondary qualities, are more intimately related to experience than those of primary qualities? If so, must we acquiesce in the circular view that being red is to be explained in terms of looking red?[1]

The present chapter develops some claims and distinctions needed both for the discussion of those questions and for some later topics. As such, it has the character of a prelude. Nevertheless, it too has a venerable subject, one that would have been discussed by a classical British empiricist under the heading "Sensation and Perception." My claim in this chapter will be that concepts of sensation are indispensable to the description of the nature of any experience. This claim stands in opposition to the view that, while sensations may occur when a subject is asked to concentrate in a particular way on his own experience, or may occur as by-products of perception, they are not to be found in the mainstream of normal human experience, and certainly not in visual experience. But first we need to clarify the issues.

Historically, the distinction between putative perceptual experiences and sensations has been the distinction between those experiences which do in themselves represent the environment of the experiencer as being a certain way, and those experiences which have no such representational content. A visual perceptual experience enjoyed by someone sitting at a desk may represent various writing implements and items of furniture as having particular spatial relations to one another and to the experiencer, and as themselves having various qualities; a sensation of small, by contrast, may have no representational content of any sort, though of course the sensation will be of a distinctive kind. The representational content of a perceptual experience has to be given by a proposition, or set of propositions, which specifies the way the experience represents the world to be. To avoid any ambiguity, I will use the phrase "content of experience" only for the representational content of an experience, and never for a type of sensation: many past writers followed the opposite practice and used "object" or "meaning" for representational content. Corresponding to the historical distinction between sensation and perception, we can draw a distinction between sensational and representational properties of experience. Representational properties will be properties an experience has in virtue of features of its representational content; while sensational properties will be properties an experience has in virtue of some aspect—other than its representational content—of what it is like to have that experienct.[2]

The content of an experience is to be distinguished from the content of a judgement caused by the experience. A man may be familiar with a perfect *trompe l'œil* violin painted on a door, and be sure from his past experience that it is a *trompe l'œil*: nevertheless his experience may continue to represent a violin as hanging on the door in front of him. The possibility of such independence is one of the marks of the content of experience as opposed to the content of judgement. One of the earliest writers to state a distinction between sensation and perceptual experience, Thomas Reid, introduced it in terms which require that perceptual experience implies belief in the content of the experience.[3] In fact, we need a threefold distinction between sensation, perception, and judgement, to formulate the issues precisely.

This independence of the contents of judgement and experience does not mean that judgements cannot causally influence the content of experiences. In some cases they do. You may walk into your sitting-room and seem to hear rain falling outside. Then you notice that someone has left the stereo system on, and realize that the sound you hear is that of applause at the end of a concert. It happens to many people that after realizing this, the sound comes to be heard as applause: the content of experience is influenced by that of judgement. All the independence claim means is that this need not happen.

Among the many current uses of the term "information," there is one in particular from which the present notion of representational content should be distinguished. There is a sense in which a footprint contains the information that a person with a foot of such-and-such shape and size was at the location of the footprint earlier; and in which a fossil may contain the information that there was an organism of a certain kind at its location in the past. This is a clear and important use of "informational content," and it seems that it is, very roughly, to be explained along these lines (the details will not matter for us): x's being F at t has the informational content that there was something standing in R to x at some earlier time t' and which was then G, iff in normal circumstances an object's being F at some particular time is causally, and perhaps differentially, explained by there existing at some earlier time an object standing in R to it and which was then G.[4] An experience, or more strictly the occurrence to someone of an experience of a certain type at a certain time, will certainly have informational content in this sense. But informational content differs from representational content in at least four respects. First, the informational content of a visual experience will include the proposition that a bundle of light rays with such-and-such physical properties struck the retina; nothing like this will be in the representational content of the experience. Second, there are cases in which the representational content and the informational content of an experience are incompatible. This will be so for experiences of geometrical illusions. Such experiences are normally differentially explained by the presence of objects with properties incompatible with those they are represented by the experience as having. Third, though both informational content and representational content are specified by "that"-clauses, the contents are of different kinds. A specification of informational content is completely referentially transparent in genuine singular term position: this property it inherits from the corresponding transparency of "causally explains." In the representational content of an experience, on the other hand, objects are presented under perceptual modes of presentation. (This contrast applies not only to singular term position, but also to predicate position. We shall later wish to distinguish properties from modes of presentation of properties, and when that distinction is drawn, it will appear that only the properties themselves, and not properties under modes of presentation, enter causal explanations.) Finally, it is in the nature of representational content that it cannot be built up from concepts unless the subject of the experience himself has those concepts: the representational content is the way the experience presents the world as being, and it can hardly present the world as being that way if the subject is incapable of appreciating what that way is. Only those with the concept of a sphere can have an experience as of a sphere in front of them, and only those with spatial concepts can have experiences which represent things as distributed in depth in space.

By emphasizing these differences, I do not mean to exclude the possibility that possession of representational content can be analysed in terms of informational content (whether this is so is a complex and difficult matter). The present point is just that any such analysis would not consist in an identity. So when I argue that all experiences have nonrepresentational properties, this is *not* a claim to the effect that the intrinsic properties of experience are not determined by their informational content. It is rather a claim about the range of intrinsic properties themselves.

Those who say that sensation has almost no role to play in normal, mature human experience, or at least in normal human visual experience, commonly cite as their ground the fact that all visual experiences have some representational content. If this is indeed a fact, it shows that no human visual experience is a pure sensation. But it does not follow that such experiences do not have sensational properties. It is one thing to say that all mature visual experiences have representational content, another thing to say that no such experience has intrinsic properties (properties which help to specify what it is like to have the experience) explicable without reference to representational content. To assert that all experiences have sensational properties is not necessarily to return to the views of Wundt and his followers.[5] My aim is just to argue that every experience has some sensational properties, and I will concentrate on visual experience as the most challenging case. We can label those who dispute this view, and hold that all intrinsic properties of mature human visual experiences are possessed in virtue of their representational content, "extreme perceptual theorists."

Again, we need to sharpen the dispute. One way to do so is to introduce for consideration what I will call the *Adequacy Thesis* (AT). The AT states that a complete intrinsic characterization of an experience can be given by embedding within an operator like "it visually appears to the subject that . . ." some complex condition concerning physical objects. One component of the condition might be that there is a black telephone in front of oneself and a bookshelf a certain distance and direction to one's left, above and behind which is a window. Such contents can equally be the contents of perceptual or hallucinatory experiences.[6] The content need not be restricted to the qualitative properties of objects, their spatial relations to one another and to the location of the experiencer. It can also concern the relations of the objects and the experiencer to some environmental dimension: the experience of being in a tilted room is different from that of being in the same room when it is upright and the experiencer's body is tilted. Or again, a visual experience as of everything around one swinging to one's left can be distinguished from the visual experience as of oneself revolving rightwards on one's vertical axis. The specification of content may also need in some way to make reference to individuals whom the subject of the experience can recognize: a visual experience can represent Nixon as giving a speech in front of one. The representational content of a visual experience seems always to contain the indexical notions "now" and "I", and almost always "here" and "there". It should be emphasized that the propositional contents available to the defender of the AT are not all restricted to those features of experience which do not result from unconscious cognitive processing. If there are indeed unconscious mechanisms analogous, say, to inference in the production of experience, then certainly many features of the representational content of an experience will result from the operation of these mechanisms. The important point about representational content, as the notion is used here, is not its freedom from processing but its simultaneous possession of two features. The first is that the representational content concerns the world external to the experiencer, and as such is assessable as true or false. The second feature is that this content is something intrinsic to the experience itself—any experience which does not represent to the subject the world as being the way that this content specifies is phenomenologically different, an experience of a different type. It is quite consistent with these two features that the presence of experiences with a given representational content has been caused by past experience and learning. What one must not do is to suppose that such explanations show that representational content is a matter of judgement caused by some purer experience: even when an experience has a rich representational content, the judgement of the subject may still endorse or reject this content.

The extreme perceptual theorist is committed to the AT. For if the AT is false, there are intrinsic features of visual experience which are not captured by representational content. My initial strategy in opposition to the extreme perceptual theorist will be to argue against the AT by counterexamples. There is no obvious defender of the AT whose views one can take as a stalking horse, no doubt partly because the sensational/representational distinction seems not to have been sufficiently sharply formulated. There are, though, strong hints of the thesis in Hintikka.

He writes "The appropriate way of speaking of our spontaneous perceptions is to use the same vocabulary and the same syntax as we apply to the objects of perception . . . *all* there is (in principle) to perception (at this level of analysis) is a specification of the information in question" (Hintikka's emphasis). He is not here using "information" in the sense of informational content, for he writes of the information that our perceptual systems give *us*.[7]

There are at least three types of example which are *prima facie* evidence against the AT. I will give all three before discussing ways in which the extreme perceptual theorist might try to account for each type; for any satisfactory account must accommodate all three types. The point in giving these examples is not to cite newly discovered phenomena—on the contrary, all the phenomena are familiar. The point is rather to consider their bearing on the correct conception of the representational and sensational properties of experience. Any novelty lies in claims about this bearing.

Since I shall be arguing by counterexample, the extreme perceptualist's reasons for his view will not initially affect the argument. But his views do not come from nowhere, and if the counter-examples are sound, the extreme perceptualist's reasons for his views must be insufficient: in so far as there are true beliefs amongst his reasons, those beliefs cannot carry him all the way to his extreme perceptualism. The extreme perceptualist's main motivation is likely to be the thought that if the AT is false, then there are intrinsic features of an experience which are unknowable by anyone not actually having that experience. This thought may be backed by the following superficially plausible argument. We can tell what kind of experience someone has if we know his desires and intentions, and find that he is disposed to act in such-and-such ways when he takes his experience at face value. If, for instance, he wants to travel to a certain place, and takes the shortest available route even though this is not on a straight line, we can come to have reason to believe that he perceives an obstacle on the most direct route: this hypothesis could be inductively confirmed. But it seems that techniques of this sort could only ever reveal representational properties of the subject's experience: for the technique consists in checking that he acts in ways appropriate to the world being as his experience represents it. If this is the only way in which we could come to know the intrinsic properties of another's experiences, the nonrepresentational properties of another's experiences would be unknowable. If the counterexamples below are correct, there must be a gap in this argument. Though the massive general topic of our understanding of consciousness in others is beyond the scope of this book, I will try to indicate at suitable points how we might know of the sensational properties of others' experiences.

There is one last preliminary. Our perceptual experience is always of a more determinate character than our observational concepts which we might use in characterizing it. A normal person does not, and possibly could not, have observational concepts of every possible shade of colour, where shades are individuated by Goodman's identity condition for qualia.[8] Even concepts like "yellow ochre" and "burnt sienna" will not distinguish every such shade; and in any case not everyone has such concepts. Thus if the extreme perceptualist is not to be mistaken for trivial reasons, the most that he can maintain is this: the intrinsic properties of a visual experience are exhausted by a specification of its representational content together with some more specific determination of the properties mentioned in that content. I will not trade on this qualification.

Here then are the examples:

(1) Suppose you are standing on a road which stretches from you in a straight line to the horizon. There are two trees at the roadside, one a hundred yards from you, the other two hundred. Your experience represents these objets as being of the same physical height and other dimensions; that is, taking your experience at face value you would judge that the trees are roughly the same physical size, just as in the *trompe l'œil* example, without countervailing beliefs you would judge that there is a violin on the door; and in this case we can suppose that the experience is a perception of the scene around you. Yet there is also some sense in which the nearer tree occupies more of your visual field than the more distant tree. This is as much a feature of your experience itself as is its representing the trees as being the same height. The experience can possess this feature without your having any concept of the feature or of the visual field: you simply enjoy an experience which has the feature. It is a feature which makes Rock say that the greater size of the retinal image of the nearer tree is not without some reflection in consciousness, and may be what earlier writers such as Ward meant when they wrote of differences in extensity.[9] It presents an initial challenge to the Adequacy Thesis, since no veridical experience can represent one tree as larger than another and also as the same size as the other. The challenge to the extreme perceptual theorist is to account for these facts about size in the visual field without abandoning the AT. We can label this problem "the problem of the additional characterization."

The problem of the additional characterization does not arise only for size in the visual field, or for properties such as speed of movement in the visual field which are defined in terms of it. It can arise for colours and sounds. Imagine you are in a room looking at a corner formed by two of its walls. The walls are covered with paper of a uniform hue, brightness and saturation. But one wall is more brightly illuminated than the other. In these circumstances, your experience can represent both walls as being the same colour: it does not look to you as if one of the walls is painted with brighter paint than the other. Yet it is equally an aspect of your visual experience itself that the region of the visual field in which one wall is presented is brighter than that in which the other is presented. An example of the same type of phenomenon involving hearing might be this. You see two cars at different distances from yourself, both with their engines running. Your experience can represent the engines as running equally loudly (if you are searching for a quiet car, your experience gives you no reason to prefer one over the other); but again it seems undeniable that in some sense the nearer car sounds louder.

(2) All these illustrations of the problem of the additional characterization were in some way related to the duality of representational properties and properties of the two-dimensional visual field, but they were not cases in which the additional characterization apparently omitted by representational properties was something which could vary even though representational content is held constant. Yet there are also examples of this, examples in which a pair of experiences in the same sense-modality have the same representational content, but differ in some other intrinsic respect. Suppose you look at an array of pieces of furniture with one eye closed. Some of the pieces of furniture may be represented by your experience as being in front of others. Imagine now that you look at the same scene with both eyes. The experience is different. It may be tempting to try to express this difference by saying that some chairs now appear to be in front of others, but this cannot suffice: for the monocular experience also represented certain objects as being in front of others. Taking your monocular experience at face value, you would judge that some pieces of furniture are in front of others: objects do not suddenly seem to be at no distance from you when you close one eye. The experiential difference between monocular and binocular vision is independent of the double images of unfocussed objects produced by binocular vision. The extra way depth is indicated in binocular vision is present when you look into a child's stereoscope, and there need not be any double images when you do.[10] (There are not many examples of this phenomenon with the other senses, but one such might be this. A stereophonic recording of a wave breaking sounds quite different from a monaural recording, even if one cannot locate aurally the various directions of the components of the whole sound.)

The situation in the visual example is more complex than it may at first seem. The complexity can be brought out by reflecting that there are pairs of experiences which differ in the way in which the experiences of monocular and binocular vision of an ordinary scene differ, and in which only the binocular experience contains any dimension of depth. Consider two arrays of dots, one a random array and the other random except in some region in which the dots are arranged as they are in the corresponding region of the first array, but slightly displaced to take account of binocular disparity. These are the Julesz random-dot patterns.[11] When viewed with two eyes, some dots are seen as being in front of others: when the arrays are seen with only one eye, there is no impression of depth. There are two different attitudes one could take to this example. One, incompatible with what we have so far said, would be that the example shows that though there is indeed an additional way in which depth is represented in binocular as opposed to monocular vision, the extra feature is purely representational; and it is this additional purely representational feature which is present in binocular vision of the random-dot patterns. The second attitude is that even in the random-dot case, the difference between monocular and binocular vision is both sensational and representational. This is the attitude for which I shall argue.

On the second attitude, there is a sensational property which in normal human experience is indeed associated with the representation of depth. If it is granted that visual field properties are sensational, we already have other examples of such association, since in normal humans perceiving an ordinary scene, the visual field properties are associated with a representational content. The difference between the two attitudes lies in the fact that according to the first, it ought to be impossible to conceive of cases in which the alleged sensational property is present, but in which a representation of certain objects as being behind others in the environment is absent. According to the second attitude, this ought to be conceivable.

But it does seem to be conceivable. It could be that there is a being for whom visual experience is in certain respects like the experience enjoyed by a congenitally blind user of a tactile–vision substitution system (TVSS).[12] A TVSS consists of a television camera, the output of which is connected to a two-dimensional array of vibrating rods on the user's back. After using the TVSS for a short time, the congenitally blind subject has intrinsically spatial sensations resulting from the vibrations, sensations which are not those of pressure or vibration on his back, and which are reported to be quite unlike those of touch. These sensations are arranged in a two-dimensional space, and they do not seem to the experiencer to be of objects in the space around him. That is, the space of the sensations is not experienced as bearing any spatial relations to the physical space in which the experiencer is located.[13] The subjects report that the sensations are not as of anything "out there." Now it seems that we can also conceive, at least as a logical possibility, of such sensations (perhaps resulting from the output of two cameras) existing in a three-dimensional space, which is nevertheless still not experienced as the space around the perceiver. Finally, it seems that we can conceive of someone's visual experience being like that of the subject in his hypothetical three-dimensional case: someone with tactile experience of the world around him and suddenly given stereoscopic vision of unfamiliar objects (such as small blobs randomly distributed in three-dimensional space) could conceivably be so. Here then a sensational third dimension would be present; but there would be no representation of depth in the sense that the experience itself represents some things as being further away than others in the forward direction in the physical space in which the experiencer is located. There is, then, a dangerous ambiguity in the term "depth." It is indeed true that whenever the extra feature which distinguishes binocular from monocular vision is present, there will be an impression of depth; but since on the sense in which this must be so, depth is a sensational property, the point cannot be used to argue that the difference between monocular and binocular vision is purely representaional.[14]

(3) The third type of problem is illustrated by the switching of aspects under which some object or array of objects is seen. Consider an example in which a wire framework in the shape of a cube is viewed with one eye and is seen first with one of its faces in front, the face parallel to this face being seen as behind it, and is then suddenly seen, without any change in the cube or alteration of its position, with that former face now behind the other. The successive experiences have different representational contents. The first experience represents a face ABCD as nearer oneself than the face EFGH, the later experience represents the presence of a state of affairs incompatible with its being nearer. Yet there seems to be some additional level of classification at which the successive experiences fall under the same type; indeed that something like this is so seems to be a feature of the experience of a switch in aspect—as Wittgenstein writes, "I *see* that it has not changed."[15] We have here another example of apparently nonrepresentational similarities between experiences.

The challenge to the extreme perceptual theorist is to explain how there can be nonrepresentational similarities between experiences without giving up the AT. He might propose simply to introduce a new classification of visual experience by means of a content which still conforms to the spirit of the AT, but which relates to some time just before the occurrence of the experience: the content would presumably be that the scene around oneself has not altered. But this view ignores the fact that, in normal circumstances, with memory errors aside, the presence of the impression that the scene has or has not altered surely depends on the character of the successive experiences. If we just added this new type of experience to our characterizations, we would still have to say on what properties of successive experiences its presence or absence depends. This suggestion also fails to cope with an aspect switch accompanied by loss of memory of the earlier experience: for here there need be no impression that the scene has not altered. Finally, the suggestion does not capture the nonrepresentational similarity between the experiences of two different subjects looking at the cube, one seeing a certain face in front, the other seeing it as behind. It is not only between successive experiences of a single person that there are nonrepresentational similarities. We do then have a third type of problem for the extreme perceptual theorist.

Why have I chosen to use the example of monocular vision of a three-dimensional wire frame to make these points, rather than the traditional duck–rabbit figure? The reason lies in this: when a subject undergoes an aspect switch while looking at that figure, there is nothing which is seen first as a duck, and then as a rabbit—rather, something is seen first as a representation of a duck, and then is seen as a representation of a rabbit. But then what is so seen, an arrangement of lines on paper, remains constant in the representational content of the successive experiences. So the example does not serve the purpose of showing that there can be nonrepresentational similarities between experiences, since someone who denies that could simply say that in this example the component of representational content concerning the arrangement of the lines on paper remains constant, and accounts for the similarity. In the example of the wire cube, this reply is not available: for after the aspect switch, the wires do not all seem to be in the same relative positions as before.[16]

A natural reaction of the extreme perceptual theorist to examples of these three types is to claim that all the statements whose truth seems to conflict with the Adequacy Thesis can be translated into statements which do not attribute to experiences any features going beyond those countenanced by the AT.[17] Let us consider this translational response as applied to size in the visual field and the two trees on the road. It might be suggested that the statement "The nearer tree takes up more of the visual field" could be approximately translated by the counterfactual "For any plane perpendicular to the subject's line of sight and lying between him and the two trees, a larger area of that place would have to be made opaque precisely to obscure the nearer tree than would have to be made opaque precisely to obscure the more distant tree." It is not clear how the translational response could be implemented in the second kind of example, but does it succeed even for the first kind?

Of what is this translational suggestion offered as an explanation? A first possibility is that it might be offered as an explanation of why we use the same spatial vocabulary as applies to extended objects in space in connection with the visual field. As an explanation of this it is satisfying, and can be extended to such relations as *above* and *next to* in the visual field. But the defender of the AT needs more than this. If this account of the content of experience is to be adequate, he needs this suggestion to supply an account of what it means to say that one object is larger than another in the subject's visual field. This is the second possibility. As a meaning-giving account, the suggestion seems quite inadequate. When we reflect on the possibility that light rays might bend locally, or that the experience might have astigmatism, it seems clear that the counterfactual which is alleged to translate the statement "The nearer tree takes up more of the visual field than the further tree" is in general neither necessary nor sufficient for the truth of that statement. There is also an objection of principle to a counterfactual analysis of an intrinsic property of experience. Whether one object is larger than another in the subject's visual field is a property of his experience in the actual world, be counterfactual circumstances as they may. An account of size in the visual field should make it dependent only upon the actual properties of the experience itself.

The distinction between the acceptable and the unacceptable components of the translational view can be explained in terms of a partial parallel with Kripke's distinction between fixing the referent of an expression and giving its meaning.[18] Kripke noted that though one may fix the reference of a proper name "Bright" by stipulating that it is to refer to the man who invented the wheel, nevertheless the sentence "It might have been that Bright never invented the wheel" is true. Now to understand this last sentence, we have to have some grasp of the possibility of a person who actually meets a condition failing to meet it. Similarly, experiences of such a type that the nearer tree is larger in the visual field than the further do actually meet the condition that more of the previously mentioned plane must be obscured precisely to block perception of the nearer tree. This condition fixes the type of the experience, but this type might have failed to meet that condition, just as it might have been that Bright was less inventive. What the translational defender of the extreme perceptual view fails to supply is any account of sameness of experience which allows for the possibility that the type of experience which in fact meets his translational condition fails to do so.

A different strategy in defence of the Adequacy Thesis would be to expand the range of representational contents. It would be conceded that the three types of example make trouble for the AT if we confine ourselves to representational contents of the sorts already considered; but there would be no difficulty, it may be said, if for instance we included in representational content the angle subtended by an object. Such is the view of Rock, who regards perceived visual angle and perceived objective size as simply different aspects of perception. He follows the practice of calling experiences of the former type 'proximal mode experiences' and writes, "Proximal mode experiences are best thought of as perceptions rather than sensations."[19] Despite his important contributions on the issues of this section, Rock's views here are open to criticism. As we emphasized, it is a conceptual truth that no one can have an experience with a given representational content unless he possesses the concepts from which that content is built up: an experience cannot represent the world to the subject of experience as being a certain way if he is not capable of grasping what that way is. This conceptual point entails that adding contents concerning the visual angle to representational content to save the AT is illegitimate: for an unsophisticated perceiver who does not have the concept of subtended angle it is nevertheless true that one object takes up more of his visual field than another, just as it does for a more sophisticated theorist.[20] This criticism would equally apply to a view once endorsed by Boring, who, after asking what "observation would demonstrate" that a subject is perceiving the size of his own retinal image, continued: "For a man to perceive the size of his own retinal images his perception of size must remain invariant under all transformations that leave the size of the retinal images invariant."[21] If this is a sufficient condition, it is one that can be met by a man who has never heard of a retina. It would also involve a fundamental overdeterminacy of the representational content of experience, since transformations that leave the size of the retinal image invariant will equally leave suitable cross-sections of the light rays in a given plane within the eye unaltered in area, and by Boring's lights this could equally be taken as the content of the perception. These problems result from trying to construe a sensational property, size in the visual field, as a representational property.

It will help at this point if we introduce a simple piece of notation. If a particular experience *e* has the familiar sensational property which in normal circumstances is produced by a white object (such as a tilted plate) which would be precisely obscured by an opaque elliptical region (r, say) of the imagined interposed plane, let us express this fact in the notation "elliptical' (r, e) and white' (r, e)." These primed predicates "elliptical'" and "white'" should not be confused with their unprimed homonyms. In using the notation, we are not thereby saying that experiences have colour properties or spatial properties. With this apparatus we can express what would more traditionally have been expressed by saying "There is a yellow elliptical region of the visual field next to a white square region." Thus, using logical notation:

$$\exists\, r\, \exists\, s\ (\text{elliptical}'\ (r, e)\ \&\ \text{yellow}'\ (r, e)\ \&\ \text{square}'\ (s, e)\ \&\ \text{white}'\ (s, e)\ \&\ \text{next}'\ (r, s)).[22]$$

We said earlier that the means by which these expressions containing primes have been introduced serves only to fix which properties they pick out. The point of invoking Kripke's distinction between fixing the referent and giving the meaning was to emphasize a modal point: that we can conceive of circumstances in which, for example, a tilted plate does not produce an elliptical region of the visual field. But the phrase "it fixes the referent rather than gives the meaning" is potentially misleading: it may suggest that there is more to understanding "red'" than knowing that it is the sensational property of the visual field in which a red thing is presented in normal circumstances. But there is not more than this. Anyone who knows what it is like to have an experience as of something red and has the concept of the visual field knows what it is like to have an experience which is red' (relative to some region). In this respect the means by which we have fixed which property "red'" refers to does indeed play a special role in understanding that primed predicate. It would be equally true to say that the property of being red' is that property of the visual field normally produced by the presence of an object with such-and-such physical reflectance properties. This description would not convey understanding of "red'," except in the presence of additional knowledge of which sensational property it is that meets the physically specified condition.

The sensational properties of an experience, like its representational properties, have reliable and publicly identifiable causes. We argued that the property of being presented in a large region of the visual field cannot be identified with the property of being represented as subtending a large visual angle: but nevertheless the fact that an object does subtend a large visual angle does causally explain its presentation in a large region of the visual field. This explanatory fact is one which concerns the physical spatial relations of the perceiver to the physical objects in his environment.

Nor is it true that the sensational properties of an experience cannot explain a subject's behaviour. We can conceive of someone who does indeed want to obscure precisely certain objects by attaching opaque surfaces to a glass plane which is perpendicular to his line of sight. At first, he may have to learn from experience with several particular objects what shape of surface to place on the plane. But it seems clear that we can also imagine that his learning successfully transfers to shapes quite different from those cases in which he learned which shape to choose, and that he comes to need no more than his ordinary visual experience in order to make a selection of the shape. At this stage, the sensational properties of his experience would have to be cited in the explanation of why he chooses one shape rather than another to obscure precisely some particular kind of object seen for the first time behind the glass. It is not clear that the sensational properties of experience are in principle any more problematic epistemologically than are the representational properties (which are, certainly, problematic enough).

These points about sensational properties have been tailored to the first type of example offered against the Adequacy Thesis. But they apply equally to the second: they apply pari passu if we introduce a primed relation "behind'" and fix its reference in terms of the physical conditions which normally produce the sensational property it stands for—the conditions for binocular vision of objects at different depths. I suggest that in the third kind of case, nonrepresentational similarity of experiences consists in sameness or similarity of sensational properties. In all the standard cases of switches of aspect, the successive experiences have the same primed sensational properties, those fixed in terms of the imagined interposed plane. Such identity of sensational properties is also not confined to successive experiences of one individual. This explanation of the third type of case also generalizes to an example with which it is hard to reconcile the AT. A person can have the experience of waking up in an unfamiliar position or place, and his experience initially has a minimal representational content. The content may be just that there are surfaces at various angles to him, without even a rough specification of distances. Suddenly, everything falls into place, and he has an experience with a rich representational content: he sees that nothing has altered in the scene in the sense in which one sees this when experiencing an aspect switch with the wire cube. Again, the primed sensational properties of the successive experiences are identical.

If this treatment of the examples is correct, then neither one of representational content and sensational properties determines the other. The cases of change of aspect show that sensational properties do not determine representational content, while the case of binocular vision of depth shows that representational content in a given sense-modality does not determine sensational properties. Concepts of both types are needed for a full description.[23]

Sensational properties are ubiquitous features of visual experiences: indeed it seems impossible to conceive of an experience devoid of all sensational properties. This is one reason why the visual properties which have been argued here to be sensational should be distinguished from the early Gibsonian conception of the visual field. Concepts of the Gibsonian visual field apply not to ordinary visual experience, but only to a special kind of experience we can have when we adopt the attitude a painter adopts to his experience. "By adopting the appropriate attitude, one can have either kind of visual experience . . . The visual field is a product of the chronic habit of civilized men of seeing the world as a picture . . . The visual field is a picture-like phenomenal experience at a presumptive phenomenal distance from the eyes, consisting of perspective size-impressions."[24] Gibsonian visual field experiences can occur only to those who have the concept of a planar representation of the environment. It would perhaps be open to a Gibsonian to hold that the pictorial attitude and the special experiences it produces merely emphasize features already present in ordinary visual experience. This is indeed the position I have been defending, but on such a defence the account of the nature of these features cannot make essential reference to pictorial representation.

Where do the phenomena to which the Gestalt psychologists referred with the label "grouping" fall within this classification? One such phenomenon is given by the fact that we see the array

as three columns of dots rather than as four rows. Two points make it plausible to classify grouping phenomena as generally sensational properties of experience. One is that it is manifested simply in the exercise of experientially-based discriminative capacities. Someone who perceives the array grouped into three columns will find this array subjectively more similar to than to

---

Instances of a three-place relation of comparative subjective similarity can be manifested in experientially-based discriminative reactions. Quine emphasized this point in *The Roots of Reference*,[25] and in this he was in agreement with the experimental techniques of the Gestalt psychologists themselves.[26] A second reason for saying that grouping properties are sensational rather than representational is that they are found in experiences which have no representational properties. In listening to the rhythms produced by a solo drum player, each sound is grouped with some but not with other sounds.[27] It is true that in our initial example, the very description of the case "seen as three columns rather than four rows" seems to suggest that we are concerned with a representational, not a sensational, property: the concept of a column enters the content. But this is because experiences with a particular sensational property also have, in normal mature humans, a certain representational property. Many of the examples given by Gestalt psychologists are ones in which there are distinctive grouping properties, groupings in particular curves and shapes, and in which the subject of the experience has no concept in advance with which to pick out the curve or shape in question.[28]

Grouping phenomena do however raise two closely related problems for what I have so far said about the category of sensational properties. In some cases we can perceive one and the same array as differently grouped in successive experiences. This array

○　○　○　○
●　●　●　●
○　○　○　○
●　●　●　●
○　○　○　○
●　●　●　●

[after Rock, *Introduction to Perception*]

can be seen as either rows or columns. The first problem now is this: we earlier said that in switches of aspect the sensational properties of the successive experiences remained constant. But now, in the case of switches of grouping, we are distinguishing switches *within* the class of sensational properties of experience according to the account so far given. No doubt aspect—and grouping—switches are to be distinguished, but the impression after a switch of either type that nothing has altered seems to have a similar basis; yet the account seems to leave no room for saying that it does. That is the first problem. The second problem, now that grouping is included as a sensational property, is how the particular sensational properties an experience may possess are to be explained. For the primed properties of the successive experiences, for someone who views our most recent array and undergoes a switch of grouping, may be identical; and yet their sensational properties are different.

A full treatment of these problems would give a detailed theory of the types of sensational properties and the relations between them. Here I will just note a distinction which can be applied to the problem. The facts about grouping show that many different types of experience may be produced in normal circumstances by a given pattern of light on the imagined frontal glass plane. We can capture the non-representational differences between these types by using again the fact that if an experience has a particular grouping, it will be subjectively more similar to a second experience with different primed properties than it is to a third. There are at least two levels of classification of visual experience in sensational terms: a basic level, at which terms for the properties have their references fixed by means of the imagined frontal glass plane; and a second level, determined by different possible patterns of comparative subjective similarity between experiences falling under these basic types. The difference between the case in which a given array is seen to be grouped in columns and the case in which it is seen to be grouped in rows is captured at this second level. The difference remains a difference within the class of sensational properties.

Notes

1. For a clear statement of this last problem, see B. Williams, *Descartes: The Project of Pure Enquiry* (London: Penguin, 1978), at pp. 243–4.

2. Brian O'Shaughnessy in *The Will: A Dual Aspect Theory* (Cambridge: CUP, 1980) says that experiences with content are the causal consequences of sensations (vol. 1, pp. 172–3; vol. 2, pp. 68–74 and 139–42). I have set up the issues in such a way that sensational properties, if they exist, are properties of the very same thing, the experience, which has representational properties. That some properties of the experience are causally responsible for others would be an empirical psychological hypothesis, and one which involves simultane-

ous causation. O'Shaughnessy also writes, as I do not, of seeing sensations. Despite these differences and others noted later, much of what O'Shaughnessy says about sensation is congenial and complementary to the main theses of this chapter, in particular his emphasis on the inseparability of sensation from experience and on the nonconceptual character of sensation.

3. Essay II (ch. XVI) of *Essays on the Intellectual Powers of Man* (Edinburgh: Thin, 1895), p. 312: "sensation, taken by itself, implies neither the conception nor the belief of any external object . . . Perception implies an immediate conviction and belief of something external—something different both from the mind that perceives, and from the act of perception."

4. For differential explanation, see Ch. 2 of my *Holistic Explanation* (Oxford: OUP, 1979).

5. W. Wundt, *Outlines of Psychology* (Leipzig: Engelmann, 1907).

6. If we are to be strict, the attribution of a common existential content to perceptual and hallucinatory experience is too crude. There is a sense in which, as one incompetently says, a hallucination presents a *particular* nonexistent object, and so has more than a general existential content. (This can be important in explaining such sentences as "He hallucinated a cup; he believed it to be medieval, and tried to pick it up; later he came to think it a fake.") To capture this the common content of perception and hallucination could be given by specifying perceptual *types* of modes of presentation of objects, types which do not in every context determine an object.

7. "Information, Causality and the Logic of Perception", in *The Intentions of Intentionality and Other New Models for Modality* (Dordrecht: Reidel, 1957), pp. 60–2.

8. *The Structure of Appearance* (Indianapolis: Bobbs-Merrill, 1966), p. 290.

9. I. Rock, "In Defense of Unconscious Inference," in *Stability and Constancy in Visual Perception* (New York: Wiley, 1977), ed. W. Epstein; J. Ward *Psychological Principles* (Cambridge: CUP, 1920).

10. In *The Perception of the Visual World* (Boston: Houghton Mifflin, 1950); J. J. Gibson says of the impression of distance in depth in binocular vision that "You can reduce the distance somewhat by closing one eye" (p. 42). Even if this is in fact true in all cases, it cannot be definitional of the distinctive impression produced by depth in binocular vision: one can imagine that closing one eye eliminates this impression even though as a result nothing looks closer than it did before.

11. B. Julesz, "Texture and visual perception," *Scientific American*, February 1965.

12. P. Bach-y-Rita et al, "Vision Substitution by Tactile Image Projection," *Nature* 221 (1969), 963–4; G. Guarniero, "Experience of tactile vision," *Perception* 3 (1974), 101–4.

13. Cp. Guarniero, p. 104: "By this time objects had come to have a top and a bottom; a right side and a left; but no depth—they existed in an ordered two-dimensional space, the precise location of which has not yet been determined."

14. My position here is incompatible with that of O'Shaughnessy, *The Will*, vol. 1, pp. 171–3, where he argues that (in my terminology) depth is never a sensational property. He offers three reasons, the first two of which aim to show that "concepts play a causal role in the genesis of visual depth experience." The first reason is that "*any* visual depth experience depends upon one's seeing one's visual depth sensations *as* contributing the colour of

physical items situated at some distance from one." This begs the question by presuming that the third dimension in the space of the sensations must represent to the experiencer depth in the physical space around him. The text above gives an imagined counterexample to this claim of necessary coincidence. The second reason given is that "two visual fields of sensations could be internally indistinguishable and yet thanks to the diverse concepts and beliefs of their owners cause different *veridical* visual depth impressions." But when there are stereoscopic depth impressions resulting from binocular vision, the three-dimensional visual field properties are not compatible with different depth impressions, at least in respect of the distribution in three dimensions of the surface actually seen. O'Shaughnessy's third reason is that his view is corroborated by the optical facts: but he considers only the bundle of light rays reaching a single eye. In the nature of the case, monocular vision is insufficient for stereopsis; and the optical facts when we consider binocular vision not only make depth as a sensational property intelligible, but also explain why the property should peter out at greater distances.

15. *Philosophical Investigations* (Oxford: Blackwell, 1958), p. 193; cp. also *Remarks on the Philosophy of Psychology* (Oxford: Blackwell, 1980), vol. 1, section 33.

16. The possibility of the notion of representation itself entering the content of an experience would allow one to give this explanation of the difference between seeing one area as figure and another as ground: the whole is seen as a representation in which the former area is represented as being in front of the latter.

17. In effect, some philosophers reacted this way to Gibson's use in his earlier writings of the concept of the visual field; D. W. Hamlyn for instance wrote ". . . the properties which Gibson ascribes to the visual field are all logically derivative from those ascribable to the visual world." See "The Visual Field and Perception." *Proceedings of the Aristotelian Society*, supplementary volume 31 (1957) at p. 121. (I should add that Hamlyn later changed his mind on this question.)

18. *Naming and Necessity* (Oxford: Blackwell, 1980).

19. "In Defense of Unconscious Inference," p. 349, and also in his *Introduction to Perception* (New York: Macmillan, 1975), pp. 39, 47, 56.

20. Even if the perceiver does have the concept of the subtended angle and it enters the representational content of his experience, it is not clear that the suggestion works. For it would rule out *a priori* the following possibility. There is someone who suffers from unsystematic distortion in a particular region of his visual field. He knows this, and after a time objects presented in that region of his visual field are no longer presented as being as determinate in size in the way those presented elsewhere are so represented. If this is possible, then an object may be presented outside the distorting region, and be presented as subtending a certain angle, and it may occupy the same size of region of the visual field as an object in the distorting region which is not presented as subtending any particular angle.

21. "Visual Perception and Invariance," *Psychological Review* 59 (1952), 141–8, at p. 145.

22. The visual field sensational properties caused by an object can of course be influenced by the properties of the other objects perceived: geometrical illusions again illustrate the point. A more complex means of introducing the primed properties would take account of this relativity.

23. A listener hearing an earlier version of this chapter drew my attention to David Lewis's unduly neglected "Percepts and Color Mosaics in Visual Experience," *Philosophical Review* 75 (1966), 375–68. Lewis's notion of experiences which are modification-equivalent and his claims concerning it are clearly close to what I would call the relation of having the same sensational properties and the claim that sensational properties are distinct from representational properties. But readers wishing to compare his views with those of this chapter should note that Lewis's percept and my representational content are not to be identified. He writes of percepts which are pure percepts of colour mosaic and nothing else (p. 363): such experiences do not in my sense have representational content. Like the early experiences of the TVSS user, they do not represent the world in the environment of the subject as being a particular way. Correspondingly they are not directly assessable as veridical or otherwise. (Less direct relations of correspondence could though be defined.)

24. J. J. Gibson, "The Visual Field and the Visual World," *Psychological Review* 59 (1952), 149–51.

25. La Salle, Illinois: Open Court, 1974.

26. W. Köhler, *Gestalt Psychology* (New York: Liveright, 1947), Ch. 5.

27. Compare also hearing a chord as an augmented fourth rather than as a diminished fifth. Someone can have this experience without having the concept of an augmented fourth. His hearing it that way is necessarily linked to the resolutions of that chord which sound right to him. If it is true that different groupings are sensational properties, any proposal to include both grouping phenomena and switches in the aspect under which an object is perceived under the common label of "organization in experience", needs some positive justification. Note also that the fact that there seems to be a conceptual distinction between grouping and seeing something as an instance of a particular concept may underlie Wittgenstein's otherwise somewhat obscure remark in his discussion of seeing-as—that one has to distinguish "purely optical" aspects from those "*mainly* determined by thoughts and associations": see *Remarks on the Philosophy of Psychology* vol. 1, sections 970, 1017.

28. For sample illustrations, see Köhler, op. cit., and Rock, *Introduction to Perception.*

13

Linking Propositions

Davida Y. Teller

Introduction

Visual science is an eclectic discipline. Visual scientists are interested in what people see, as measured by psychophysical experiments and described by phenomenal reports. They are also interested in the physiology of the visual system, and in all elements of the substrate upon which human visual capacities are based. And finally, they are interested in the relationships between visual capacities and the neural substrates of vision; that is, in some sense, in explaining how we see on the basis of the properties of the machinery that makes seeing possible. This last is a very difficult problem, in part because of the inherent complexity of the first two topics, and in part because of the logical and philosophical difficulties involved in explanatory efforts which span between such different scientific disciplines (cf. Uttal 1981).

The fact that physical/physiological statements and psychophysical/phenomenal statements are from such different sciences has often led to the presumption that some special kinds of logical links will be needed to bring them into a single domain. These special linking statements have been variously called *psychophysical axioms* (Müller 1896), *psychophysical linking hypotheses* (Brindley 1960, 1970) and *linking propositions* (Teller 1981; Teller and Pugh 1983). Statements that the shape of the dark-adapted spectral sensitivity curve is due largely to the absorption spectrum of rhodopsin, that the low-frequency falloff of the spatial contrast sensitivity function is caused by center-surround antagonism in receptive fields, that the mutual exclusivity of certain hues implies the existence of opponent neural coding, or that cortical simple cells are involved in form perception, may be cited as examples of linking propositions. Insofar as visual scientists are interested in explaining psychophysical data on the basis of the properties of the neural substrate, we must be said to be interested precisely in the formulation, testing, accepting and falsifying of linking propositions. Yet explicit, systematic discussions of linking propositions remain scarce in the vision literature.

The purpose of the present paper is five-fold. First, the concept of a linking proposition will be discussed and expanded briefly in the historical context and a general definition of the concept will be proposed. Second, a preliminary systematization of general linking propositions will be presented, including five families of propositions which are in common usage in visual science. Third, some specific linking propositions concerning the relation between single neurons and perception will be articulated, and used to develop a set of evaluative criteria for judging linking propositions involving single neurons. Fourth, linking propositions concerning the canonical forms that visual information must be assumed to take will be examined. And finally, a brief analysis will be attempted of the extent to which linking propositions are subject to empirical test.

Linking Propositions: Evolution of the Concept

The early psychophysicists, without the tools of modern electrophysiology, studied psychophysics in part as a way of discovering the properties of the brain. They developed the concept that phenomenal states and physiological states must be, in some way, lawfully related and worked out a list of relationships that could be assumed by consensus to hold between mental events and material events. These culminated in the *psychophysical axioms* articulated by G. E. Müller in 1896. Boring (1942, p. 89) quotes the first three axioms as follows:

1. The ground of every state of consciousness is a material process, a psychophysical process so-called, to whose occurrence the presence of the conscious state is joined.

2. To an equality, similarity, or difference in the constitution of sensations . . . there corresponds an equality, similarity, or difference in the constitution of the psychophysical process, and conversely. Moreover, to a greater or lesser similarity of sensations, there also corresponds respectively a greater or lesser similarity of the psychophysical process, and conversely.

3. If the changes through which a sensation passes have the same direction, or if the differences which exist between series of given sensations are of like direction, then the changes through which the psychophysical process passes, or the differences of the given psychophysical processes, have like direction. Moreover, if a sen-

sation is variable in n directions, then the psychophysical process lying at the basis of it must also be variable in n directions, and conversely. . . .

Two characteristics of these linking propositions deserve special mention. First, they were assigned the logical status of axioms, i.e. they had to be accepted as fundamental, necessary and unprovable. And second, there were several of them, including such concepts as identity, similarity, difference, directionality and dimensionality, with the result that many different sensory and perceptual characteristics could be used to infer properties of the unobservable "material process."

Over the ensuing years, technological progress has allowed more direct knowledge of the optical, photochemical, anatomical and physiological characteristics of the visual system. Reliance on inferences from psychophysical experiments as a direct source of knowledge about physiological processes has diminished in consequence. In this new context, the question of the relation between psychophysical and physiological data was brought again to the attention of visual scientists by Brindley (1960).

Brindley was writing as a visual physiologist, and his primary interest was in the formulation and testing of physiological hypotheses. He noted that in visual science, in addition to purely physiological data, one has available data from what he calls "sensory experiments; that is, experiments in which an essential part of the results is a subject's report of his own sensations" (p. 144). Brindley's question was what is the place and value of sensory reports in the testing of physiological hypotheses? He formulated the argument that phenomenal terms and physiological terms are from different realms of discourse and that, if terms from the two different realms were to be used together in a single sentence, explicit bridging statements would be needed. He called such statements *psychophysical linking hypotheses*.

Brindley was able to discover only one general linking hypothesis which met his criteria for adequate rigor. This linking hypothesis, which he suggested may be a truism, was stated as follows (1960, p. 144):

. . . whenever two stimuli cause physically indistinguishable signals to be sent from the sense organs to the brain, the sensations produced by those stimuli, as reported by the subject in words, symbols or actions, must also be indistinguishable.

Other general linking propositions, use of which would allow physiological inferences to be drawn from experiments (p. 145) "in which the subject must describe the quality or intensity of his sensations, or abstract from two different sensations some aspect in which they are alike . . . ," were deemed to be generally lacking in rigor, and were omitted from specific discussion. Thus, through the adoption of extremely strict criteria of admissibility, most of Müller's axioms were discarded, and only a single general proposition, concerning the indistinguishability of physiological or perceptual states, survived.[1]

In addition to the single acceptable general linking hypothesis, Brindley identified several very specific ones that seemed to him well established. These dealt mostly with the anatomical causes of various entoptic phenomena; for example, he argued that the hypothesis that the perceptual "retinal tree" is caused by the shadow cast by the retinal blood vessels on the receptors was extremely well established. He argued that the truth of such special linking statements could be established by "correlating very many features of a sensory phenomenon with corresponding features of an objectively determined one" (p. 149); in other words, that special linking propositions were at least in principle subject to empirical test.

Over the past 20 years, an enormous amount of information has accumulated concerning the response properties of single neurons at many levels of the visual system. Visual physiologists have learned a great deal about how and where information of various kinds is lost, how it is carried at each level of the visual system and how and where it is transformed from one format to another. In this context it is sometimes feasible, and always tempting, to try to attribute psychophysical and perceptual phenomena to the properties or activities of individual neurons or sets of neurons at particular levels of the visual system, and explanatory efforts of this kind are now a major thrust of visual science.

A reformulation of the concept of a linking proposition, which encompasses earlier points of view and emphasizes use of the modern detailed knowledge of the activities of neurons at many levels of the visual system, has been put forward recently by Teller and Pugh (1983). For the sake of discussion, Teller and Pugh describe the process of vision as a sequence of deterministic maps, with information being mapped from the visual world to the retinal image, to the quantum catch states of all receptors, to the set of all receptor outputs, and so on through the visual system. In their formulation, the mapping from any earlier to any later stage may be thought of as a composite map.

Eventually the states of some large or small subset of these neurons must be mapped to subjective visual perception. Partly as a means of dealing with this final mapping, Teller and Pugh introduce the term *bridge locus*, as follows (p. 581, phrase in parentheses added):

Most visual scientists probably believe that there exists a set of neurons with visual system input, whose activities form the immediate substrate of visual perception. We single out this one particular neural stage, with a name: the *bridge locus*. The occurrence of a particular activity pattern in these bridge locus neurons is necessary for the occurrence of a particular perceptual state; neural activity elsewhere in the visual system is not necessary. The physical location of these neurons in the brain is of course unknown. However, we feel that most visual scientists would agree that they are certainly not in the retina (i.e. that they consist of a central rather than a peripheral subset of visual system neurons). For if one could set up conditions for properly stimulating them in the absence of the retina, the correlated perceptual state presumably would occur.

In this context, a linking proposition may be defined as *a claim that a particular mapping occurs, or a particular mapping principle applies, between perceptual and physiological states* (cf. Teller and Pugh 1983, p. 581). Such a claim can be general, as were Müller's axioms and Brindley's general linking hypothesis, or it can be specific to a particular perceptual phenomenon or a particular set of optical, photochemical or neural elements. The location of the neural elements can be unspecified, and a claim made only that, since a particular perceptual state occurs, neurons having particular properties must exist somewhere within the visual system; or that visual information must somewhere be encoded in a particular form when a particular perceptual state occurs. Alternately, the linking proposition can involve specified neural elements at any location, peripheral or central, at or prior to the bridge locus. The more peripheral the neurons, the more complex is the implied composite map; and, most importantly, in all cases the implied composite map includes the mapping from the bridge locus neurons to perceptual states.

In addition to these reformulations, it is philosophically appropriate in the mid-1980s to adopt an analytical rather than a proscriptive attitude toward linking propositions (cf. Suppe 1977, esp. pp. 650–730). Rather than prejudging the logical status of linking propositions, or condemning them for lack of rigor, one can simply state that there is a consensus among many visual scientists that physiological and perceptual facts together make up a viable scientific domain (Shapere 1977; Suppe 1977, pp. 686ff), and that linking propositions form some of the necessary elements of that domain. The question then becomes, what kinds of linking propositions do visual scientists use, what are their logical interrelationships and truth-values, and what roles do they play in the structure of modern visual science?

In the next three sections, three kinds of linking propositions will be examined: general linking propositions; linking propositions involving single cells; and linking propositions concerning the canonical forms that visual information must take before it can form the substrate of visual perception.

General Linking Propositions: A Preliminary Systematization

In the present section, a preliminary systematization of general linking propositions will be presented. Two main points will be made. The first is that general linking propositions come in logically organized groups or families. The second is that there are at least four such families, which can be called Identity, Similarity, Mutual Exclusivity and Simplicity, along with a less well organized proposition that can be called Analogy. As should be obvious, the point of the exercise is not to claim that the various propositions are true by logical necessity, or even that they are necessarily workable or even sensible; but rather to articulate them in order to make such evaluative judgments possible.

The logical structure of the first four families is shown in figure 13.1. By definition, a linking proposition is a statement that contains both physiological (ϕ) and psychological (ψ) terms. On the first line of figure 13.1 is portrayed a linking statement that ϕ implies ψ; i.e. that some characteristic of the state of the physiological substrate implies some characteristic of the perceptual phenomenon. On the second line is the Contrapositive (the negative of the converse) of the first line: $\bar{\psi}$ implies $\bar{\phi}$ ("not ψ" implies "not ϕ"). These two statements are logically equivalent because any statement implies the negative of its converse: If A implies B, $\bar{B}$ implies $\bar{A}$. On the third line is stated the Converse of the first line: ψ implies ϕ; i.e., that some characteristic of the psychophysical data implies some characteristic of the substrate. The truth of the Converse, of course, is not implied by the truth of the original statement. This point was explicitly made and appreciated by the early psychophysicists, as is shown by Müller's inclusion of the separate phrase "and con-

1. Initial proposition	$\phi \rightarrow \psi$
*2. Contrapositive	$\bar{\psi} \rightarrow \bar{\phi}$
*3. Converse	$\psi \rightarrow \phi$
4. Converse Contrapositive (CC)	$\bar{\phi} \rightarrow \bar{\psi}$

Figure 13.1
The logical structure of the first four families of linking propositions. Line 1 states a proposition that a particular characteristic of the physiological state (ϕ) implies a particular characteristic of the perceptual state (ψ). Line 2 is the Contrapositive of line 1 and is implied by line 1. Line 3 is the Converse of line 1 and states a proposition that a particular characteristic of the perceptual state implies a particular characteristic of the physiological state. Line 4 is the Contrapositive of the Converse and is implied by line 3.

versely" in the axioms quoted above. And on the fourth line is the Converse Contrapositive: $\bar{\phi}$ implies $\bar{\psi}$. The third and fourth lines, like the first and second, are logically equivalent to one another.

There is another interesting interrelationship among subsets of these propositions. Propositions 1 and 4 have to do with drawing conclusions about psychophysical phenomena from physiological data, while propositions 2 and 3, which are starred in figure 13.1, have to do with drawing physiological conclusions from psychophysical data. The latter direction of inference—from psychophysical data to physiological conclusions—has played the larger role in the history of visual science, largely because we have had access to psychophysical data for a much longer time than we have had access to any very detailed information about the physiological substrate. With the increasing availability of physiological data, the two directions of inference may well come to play more equal roles. Nonetheless, most of the examples that will be discussed below are examples of using propositions 2 and 3, the Contrapositive and the Converse, to argue from psychophysical data to physiological conclusions.

And finally, in deciding to do a psychophysical experiment, one commits oneself to the use of either the Contrapositive or the Converse, or both together. But one cannot choose which linking proposition one will use ahead of time, because that depends on the results of the experiment: on whether the outcome shows ψ or $\bar{\psi}$ to be true.

The first family of linking propositions, the Identity family, is shown in figure 13.2. The initial Identity proposition, line 1, is that identical ϕ imply identical ψ; i.e. that identical states of the nervous system must lead to identical sensations. The Contrapositive, line 2, is that if two sensations are discriminable the underlying physiological states must also differ.

A specific form of the Identity proposition, stated in the context of the physical stimuli used to produce the sensations in the psychophysical experiment, is

1. Identity	Identical	ϕ	$\rightarrow$	Identical	ψ
*2. Contrapositive Identity	Non-Identical	ψ	$\rightarrow$	Non-Identical	ϕ
*3. Converse Identity	Identical	ψ	$\rightarrow$	Identical	ϕ
4. CC Identity	Non-Identical	ϕ	$\rightarrow$	Non-Identical	ψ

Figure 13.2
The Identity family.

familiar as the one Brindley felt was both acceptably general and acceptably certain, viz., "If two stimuli cause physically indistinguishable signals to be sent from the sense organs to the brain, the sensations . . . will also be indistinguishable." The use of the Contrapositive was also made explicit by Brindley in his example of hypothesis testing. He argued that the non-identity of two sensations implies the non-identity of physiological states, and thus that the psychophysical finding of discrimination between two stimuli allows the rejection of any physiological hypothesis which predicts that the two stimuli cause physically indistinguishable signals to be sent from the sense organs to the brain.

The logical status of the Identity and Contrapositive Identity propositions is very strong. They are probably the most universally accepted of any of the general linking propositions to be discussed here. In Brindley's formulation—phrased in terms of the discriminability of stimuli—they are restatements of the more general scientific axiom that information that is lost at one level of an information processing system cannot be recreated by later levels. In the present formulation—phrased in terms of the non-identity of sensations—they amount to the statement that the mapping between brain states and phenomenal states is 1:1 or many:1, but not 1:many (Feigl 1958). Most visual scientists would doubtless accept this statement also as axiomatic (but cf. Eccles 1977).

At the same time, H. B. Barlow (personal communication) and others have argued convincingly that, in the original form, these propositions run the risk of being useless. That is, because of noise in both the stimulus and the neural system, even the same stimulus will generate a variable response from one trial to the next. For this reason, a proposition that requires the existence of two identical physiological states, generated by the same *or* different stimuli, even if logically unassailable, may refer to an empty set.

To alleviate this problem, one must speak of statistical rather than absolute identity or non-identity, of stimuli, sensations and neural states, over a series of trials. The reformulated identity proposition would be that statistically identical neural signals imply statistically indiscriminable sensations; and the reformulated Contrapositive Identity proposition would be that statistically discriminable sensations imply statistically discriminable physiological states. In this form the Identity proposition and its Contrapositive appear to be both logically strong and applicable to real psychophysical cases. The statistical discriminability of stimuli implies the statistical discriminability of the corresponding sensations, and hence the statistical discriminability of the corresponding physiological states.

The third line of figure 13.2 states the Converse Identity proposition (cf. Brindley 1957; Boynton and Onley 1962). It is that identical ψ imply identical φ; or, that statistically indiscriminable sensations imply statistically identical states of the visual system. The fourth line is the Contrapositive Converse Identity proposition: that statistically discriminable states of the nervous system imply statistically discriminable sensations.

The Converse and Converse Contrapositive identity propositions are clearly not analytically nor universally true, for several reasons. In the first place, there are many instances in which two different stimuli are believed to lead to different quantum catches, for example, and yet are psychophysically indiscriminable, precisely because the two neural signals are rendered indiscriminable at some subsequent stage of neural processing. Such cases of information loss within the visual system are among the most interesting and intensively researched phenomena in visual science. The elevations of threshold in the early stages of dark adaptation provide the classic example, and many other cases could be cited (cf. Ratliff and Sirovich 1978).

This problem serves to illustrate the usefulness of the concept of a bridge locus and the bridge locus neurons, the central neurons that form the most immediate substrate of conscious perceptual events. In many cases, the bridge locus neurons will be the neurons whose states one will have the most direct means of inferring by using contrapositive or converse linking propositions in combination with psychophysical data. Inferences about the states of neurons at earlier levels of the serial processing system will necessarily be less direct, and the Converse Identity proposition needs to be reformulated to take the possibility of information loss in the earlier stages of visual processing into account.

To allow for the option of neural information loss, one may propose that the meaning of the Converse and Converse Contrapositive Identity linking propositions be stipulated as follows: if two different stimuli (or their resulting sensations) are statistically indiscriminable, the corresponding neural signals must be rendered statistically indiscriminable somewhere within the sensory system, at or prior to the bridge locus.[2]

Even so, the Converse and Converse Contrapositive Identity propositions are clearly not logical necessities. Few visual scientists would argue that indiscriminable sensations necessarily imply identical physiological states, even at the bridge locus, because to claim this is to claim that one is capable of sensing every different state of the bridge locus neurons; i.e. that the mapping at the bridge locus is 1:1. Visual scientists probably tend to believe that the mapping of physiological states to perceptual states is many : 1, with there being more different states of the bridge locus neurons than there are sensations. This point is probably not addressable empirically; its logical consequences are explored further by Teller and Pugh (1983).

Despite this remaining logical difficulty, the Converse Identity proposition has often been used in the history of visual science and inference structures which have included it have often led to correct conclusions. It has provided us with some of our most striking successes, and is very much in use today. For example, the existence of metamers—stimuli of different wavelength composition which produce identical sensations—inspired the insight that color vision might be subserved by only a few kinds of receptors, each one of which loses wavelength information.

No instances in which the careful use of the reformulated Converse Identity proposition has led to false conclusions have yet come to the writer's attention. It is therefore proposed that Converse Identity be accepted as generally useful until at least one counterexample is found.

What kinds of psychophysical data are used in conjunction with Identity propositions? Clearly the relevant experiments are those which Brindley (1960, 1970) called Class A—experiments in which the subject is asked to judge the identity or non-identity of the sensations resulting from two different stimuli. Brindley put matching experiments and threshold experiments in this category, the latter presumably because in a threshold experiment the subject must judge whether or not the presence and the absence of the test stimulus lead to identical sensations (but cf. Boynton and Onley 1962). In classical psychophysical terminology, Brindley's matching experiments can be identified with *discrimination* (since if two stimuli are indiscriminable they can be said to match) and Brindley's threshold category can be identified with *detection*.

When one tries, then, to draw physiological conclusions from the data of detection or discrimination experiments, Identity propositions will always be involved. Which Identity proposition will be involved depends upon the outcome of the experiment. From failures to detect or discriminate, one can risk inferring the identity of physiological states. These inferences will employ the Converse Identity proposition. They would seem to be relatively safe if confined to the bridge locus, and more risky if used to infer the states of more peripheral sites. From correct detections or discriminations, one can infer the non-identity of physiological states. These inferences will employ the Contrapositive Identity proposition, and would seem to be remarkably safe.

1. Similarity	Similar	ϕ	$\rightarrow$	Similar	ψ
*2. Contrapositive Similarity	Dissimilar	ψ	$\rightarrow$	Dissimilar	ϕ
*3. Converse Similarity	Similar	ψ	$\rightarrow$	Similar	ϕ
4. CC Similarity	Dissimilar	ϕ	$\rightarrow$	Dissimilar	ψ

Figure 13.3
The Similarity family.

The next family of linking propositions—Similarity—is shown in figure 13.3. Line 1 states the basic Similarity proposition, that similar states of the sensory system will lead to similar sensations. Phrased in terms of stimuli, and following Brindley's formulation of Identity, a more specific form would be, if two stimuli cause similar signals to be sent from the sense organs to the brain, the sensations produced by these stimuli will also be similar. Line 3 states the Converse, that similar sensations imply similar states of the nervous system.

Neither of these propositions is a logical necessity, nor universally true, and these propositions are subject to modified versions of all of the limitations of the Identity propositions discussed above. In particular, Similarity propositions would seem to be a better bet when used to relate central, rather than peripheral, physiological states to phenomenal states, because stimuli which appear similar can sometimes be very different physically, and hence often very different at the earliest stages of neural coding.

As is the case with the Identity family, it is Converse Similarity that has historically received the greatest usage in visual science. In fact, Converse Similarity is in common use, and is perhaps even indispensable to visual science. For example, we use the Converse Similarity proposition in discussions of the perceptual orderliness of the variation of hue with wavelength across the spectrum. It is in use when we assume that, since long wavelength and short wavelength light produce similar (reddish) sensations, these two wavelength bands must have similar neural codes; or when we assume that a blue sensation created by simultaneous contrast creates a neural state similar to that created by a 470 nm light. Even more strikingly, it is involved in discussions of the Benham top phenomenon, when we propose any explanation that assumes that the neural signals produced by the Benham top stimuli must be similar to the signals produced by the chromatic stimuli they resemble. These assumptions are not logical necessities; yet, if one did not make these assumptions, it is not clear how one would go about searching for an explanation for the Benham top phenomenon, or recognize an explanation when one had found it.

There is also a second form of Similarity proposition, perhaps closely related to the *n*-dimensionality discussed by Müller and others. For example, in heterochromatic brightness matching—the matching of brightness across differences in hue—or studies of the Bezold–Brücke hue shift—matching of hue across differences in brightness—the subject judges two non-identical sensations to be matched on one perceptual dimension but not on another. The matching of hue across variations of size and eccentricity provides another example. Converse Similarity propositions are involved when we model these data by assuming that lights that match in hue will have important elements of neural coding in common, as will lights that match in brightness.

One also suspects that the Similarity family has a lot of cousins, concerned with the degree of similarity between two sensations. For example, there is probably a Continuity family, containing assertions to the effect that continuous (or discontinuous) changes in neural activity imply continuous (or discontinuous) changes in sensations and vice versa; a Montonicity family, with propositions to the effect that monotonic variation in neural activity implies a monotonic variation in sensation and vice versa; and perhaps also quantitative versions of these, for example, that a doubling of judged brightness implies the doubling of a value in a neural code and vice versa.

Experiments relevant to Similarity propositions will be a subset of the kind which Brindley called Class B; i.e., experiments in which the subject is asked to abstract from two distinguishable sensations ways in which they are alike. For the first kind of Similarity, judgments would concern subjective order. For the second kind, judgments would concern identity or similarity on one subjective dimension at a time. For the cousins of Similarity, the psychophysical data would be provided by other kinds of Class B experiments, such as the ordering or scaling of brightness or the matching or naming of hue.

The next two families of linking propositions—Mutual Exclusivity and Simplicity—both have their primary exemplars in opponent process theories of color vision. The origins of psychophysical opponent process theories rest heavily upon two subjective characteristics of colors: that some colors—red, yellow, green and blue—seem more *unique* or *simpler* than others; and that these four colors divide themselves into two pairs, red–green and yellow–blue, the members of a pair being *mutually exclusive* in the sense that the two hues cannot be perceived in the same place at the same time. Opponent process theories typically assume that the mutual exclusivity is caused by color coding channels that take on either of two mutually

1. Mutual Exclusivity	Mutually Exclusive	ϕ	$\rightarrow$	Mutually Exclusive	ψ
*2. Contrapositive Mutual Exclusivity	Mutually Compatible	ψ	$\rightarrow$	Mutually Compatible	ϕ
*3. Converse Mutual Exclusivity	Mutually Exclusive	ψ	$\rightarrow$	Mutually Exclusive	ϕ
4. CC Mutual Exclusivity	Mutually Compatible	ϕ	$\rightarrow$	Mutually Compatible	ψ

Figure 13.4
The Mutual Exclusivity family.

exclusive states; and that the unique hues occur at wavelengths for which one of two such channels is at its null point.

The third family of linking propositions, then, can be called Mutual Exclusivity, and is shown in figure 13.4. The basic Mutual Exclusivity proposition is: Whenever two stimuli cause mutually exclusive neural signals, the sensations produced by these stimuli must also be mutually exclusive; or, mutually exclusive neural states will correspond to sensations which never occur together. The Contrapositive, which is easier to think about, is: if two sensations can occur together, their corresponding neural signals must also be compatible. The Converse Mutual Exclusivity proposition is: mutually exclusive sensations imply mutually exclusive states of the nervous system.

Psychophysical experiments relevant to the Mutual Exclusivity propositions would be those in which a subject is asked to judge the mutual compatibility or exclusivity of sensations. The judgment of mutual exclusivity of redness and greenness, and of yellowness and blueness, provides the major historical example. Reversible figures may be taken to provide a second example. Many subjects would judge that the two perceptual configurations of the Necker cube, for example, cannot happen at the same time. This observation has often been taken to imply that the Necker cube leads to the setting up of one of two alternative and mutually exclusive physiological states, or to a "bistable state" (cf. Marr 1982, pp. 25–26). The author has thought for a while about whether seeing a cross excludes seeing the vertical and horizontal lines that make it up, but is unable to decide this issue on the basis of her own introspections. If the two sensations are mutually exclusive, then Mutual Exclusivity propositions might have some relevance to the question of whether cortical cells that respond to lines can form the physiological basis of the perception of complex patterns.

The logical status of the various Mutual Exclusivity propositions is difficult to assess. One of the problems is that, unlike the cases of Identity and Similarity, inferences from Mutual Exclusivity propositions do not seem to be safer when applied at the bridge locus than at more peripheral sites. That is, if the physiological states created by two stimuli are mutually exclusive at *any single* neural stage, the two sensations should never occur together, but as noted by Teller and Pugh (1983, p. 586, parentheses added): ". . . logic does not require that an opponent code be maintained all the way through the system to the bridge locus. At later stages the codes for . . . redness and greenness need not be mutually exclusive: they simply (would) never occur together in normal visual experience, because of the mutual exclusivity of their causal precursors at a critical locus early in the visual system." A recent report of a set of highly unnatural conditions under which the perception of a reddish–greenish hue is reported by some subjects (Crane and Piantanida 1983) lends further force to this argument.

Given these problems, the Mutual Exclusivity proposition is in need of a more circumscribed formulation, perhaps as follows: if two neural states are mutually exclusive at any single stage of neural processing, the corresponding sensations will ordinarily never occur together. However, if the coding is not mutually exclusive at the bridge locus, and if a way can be found to activate both neural codes together at the bridge locus, then the two sensations can be made to occur together. Similarly, the Contrapositive would be, if two sensations are ordinarily mutually compatible, their neural codes are compatible at all stages of neural coding.

The Converse Mutual Exclusivity proposition might be similarly elaborated, more or less as follows: if two sensations do not ordinarily occur together, there exists a stage of neural processing, at or before the bridge locus, at which the neural codes for the two sensations are mutually exclusive. In this context, if stimulus conditions are found under which the two sensations do occur together, it would follow that the stage at which the two codes are mutually exclusive must be prior to the bridge locus, and that at the bridge locus the two codes are compatible. However, even in these modified forms, the truth values of mutual exclusivity propositions remain difficult to assess.

Another problem with the property of Mutual Exclusivity is that it appears to have strong and weak forms. In the strong form, as used in opponent process theory, mutually exclusive signals are those which depart in opposite directions from a null state. But in the weak form, any two different output states for a neuron would seem to be mutually exclusive, in that they cannot both occur at the same time.

1. Simplicity	Simple	φ	→	Simple	ψ
*2. Contrapositive Simplicity	Non-Simple	ψ	→	Non-Simple	φ
*3. Converse Simplicity	Simple	ψ	→	Simple	φ
4. CC Simplicity	Non-Simple	φ	→	Non-Simple	ψ

Figure 13.5
The Simplicity family.

Psychophysically, redness and greenness are strongly mutually exclusive, but yellowish–green and greenish–yellow would also seem to be mutually exclusive in some weaker sense. In sum, the concept of mutual exclusivity is a complex and slippery one, and it would doubtless profit from formal analysis at definitional and conceptual, as well as phenomenal and physiological, levels.

The fourth family of linking propositions, that of Simplicity (figure 13.5), also has its main historical illustration in opponent process theory. The basic hypothesis is: whenever a stimulus causes the occurrence of a particularly simple signal, the sensation produced by that stimulus will be particularly simple; or, simple states of the nervous system will produce simple sensations. The Converse is that sensations that are particularly simple imply the presence of particular elements of simplicity in the neural code.

Like Converse Mutual Exclusivity, Converse Simplicity plays a role in opponent process theory: the particularly simple sensation is a unique hue, and the particularly simple signal is a signal in which one of the two chromatic channels remains at its null point.

Simplicity propositions seem to be particularly intuitively appealing, but at the same time particularly weak, because the notion of what is simple may vary from context to context and from person to person. Visual scientists may not have the same implicit consensus on what is simple that we may have on identity, mutual exclusivity or similarity. For example, whether one thinks that the assumption that a neural network performs a crude Fourier analysis is a simplicity or not depends on how one feels about Fourier analysis. In addition to a possible lack of consensus at any one time in history, the notion of simplicity also seems to change from one decade to the next, and it will have to be redefined as the science goes along. The Simplicity propositions, however, will probably maintain an implicit and powerful role in our thinking processes, while our concrete notions of simplicity change around them.

φ "Looks Like" ψ   →   φ   Explains   ψ

Figure 13.6
The Analogy proposition.

The Simplicity family may well form the basis of much of the intuitive appeal that visual scientists of the present era have found in single cell models of visual phenomena. Line detectors have been appealing as candidates for the mapping of line stimuli into the perception of lines, because intuitively lines are among the simple elements from which a spatial pattern could be made up; and the firing of one particular cell out of a population of cells, for a line at each orientation at each position, has a ring of simplicity about it. The Neuron Doctrine so beautifully explicated by Barlow (1972) illustrates the implicit involvement of Simplicity assumptions, as when he says that "the activity of each single cell is . . . thought to be related quite simply to our subjective experience . . ." (p. 371) or in his Fourth Dogma that ". . . the active high-level neurons directly and simply cause the elements of our perception" (p. 381).

The last general linking proposition to be discussed here can be called Analogy. The Analogy proposition departs from the logical structure of the previous four families. The proposition is shown in figure 13.6; it is: if φ "looks like" ψ, then φ explains ψ (see Teller 1980 for an earlier discussion of the concept of "looking like"). This means, roughly, that if psychophysical and physiological data can be manipulated in such a way that they can be plotted on meaningfully similar axes, such that the two graphs have similar shapes, then that physiological phenomenon is a major causal factor in producing that psychophysical phenomenon. This kind of linking proposition appears in many forms, and is extremely commonly used, either explicitly or implicitly. The explanation of the shape of the scotopic spectral sensitivity curve by the absorption spectrum of rhodopsin (in combination with absorption in the optic media) is an example of a strong use of analogy, bolstered by many other elements of fact and logic. The explanation of Mach bands by the spatial pattern of activity in ganglion cells, discussed in detail below, is a good example of weak and implicit use of Analogy. The analogy between opponent cells and opponent colors has been explored recently by Hood and Finkelstein (1983). The explicit use of analogy in relating the states of central neurons to perceptual phenomena is best exemplified in the work of De Valois and his colleagues (e.g., De Valois 1965).

The Analogy proposition is the first of the general propositions to contain both a psychophysical and a physiological referent on both sides of the arrow. This fact adds some conceptual complexity to the evaluation of Analogy propositions, because to use all the earlier families one had only to make judgments about the properties—identity, similarity, etc.—of physiological states with respect to each other and perceptual states with respect to each other. Here, one must judge the quality of the analogy between psychophysical and physiological data sets.

The degree of acceptability of Analogy propositions varies widely, and many potentially rigorous linking propositions probably enter the discipline by this route (cf. Suppe 1977, p. 687). Ideally, the initial analogy will be followed up by exploring its implications, and subjecting it to the usual kinds of tests that lead to the acceptance or rejection of other scientific propositions. On the other hand the fact that two curves look alike ought not to be taken as, in itself, an explanation of the psychophysical by the physiological phenomenon. It is the author's contention that the explication of criteria of acceptability and testability of Analogy propositions is an area in which additional analytical work is badly needed.

In summary, these five families—Identity, Similarity, Mutual Exclusivity, Simplicity and Analogy—are offered as the first step toward a modern systematization of general linking propositions. They are surely not an exhaustive list, and additional classes of general linking propositions will doubtless be added. A cataloging of the ways in which each proposition is used—as axiom, assumption, hypothesis, conclusion or speculation—needs to be undertaken, along with an examination of the mutual compatibility of the linking propositions that are in most common use. More examples of successful and unsuccessful uses of each proposition, both historical and modern, need to be developed. In particular, the scheme is in need of good counterexamples; i.e., instances in which one or another of the propositions has been found to be limited, misleading or useless in relating specific psychophysical to specific physiological phenomena. Some such specific counterexamples are explored in the next section.

Specific Linking Propositions Involving Single Cells

Many of the linking propositions involved in visual theory in the last decade or two have had as their ϕ terms the activities of single neurons or regular populations of single neurons. To each visual scientist, some such linking propositions seem credible, while others seem foolish; but the criteria by which such evaluations are made have seldom been stated explicitly. Two cases of popular but faulty "textbook explanations" (Hood and Finkelstein 1983) of perceptual phenomena will be analyzed here. The first case is the usual textbook explanation of Mach bands, and the second is the use of the concepts of *trigger features or detectors* as explanations of part of the neural processing that enters into form perception. The purpose of the exercise is to try, by analyzing these examples, to begin to develop a set of criteria for the evaluation of single unit linking propositions.

Mach bands are the illusory bright and dark bands seen at the intensity transition regions of a ramp pattern of intensity. The common explanation for Mach bands is that, if one could trace out the firing rates of cells—say, a subclass of retinal ganglion cells—in the presence of a ramp pattern, one would find maxima and minima in firing rates in the regions where subjects report Mach bands. In fact, many people have tried this experiment in cat ganglion cells, and some of them have indeed found minima and maxima of activity in about the right places (cf. Robson 1980). Under the right conditions, the physiological data "look like" the psychophysical data. The analogy is very appealing, but the question is, to what extent, or in what sense, do these results provide an explanation of why we see Mach bands?

Obviously there is an implicit linking proposition involved in this argument—that *the set of firing rates across a row of ganglion cells maps to the set of perceived brightnesses across the visual field*. At least three reservations about this proposition should be expressed: its intended range of applicability, its assumption of homogeneity, and its peripherality. They are illustrative of problems one can readily find implicit in many single cell models of visual phenomena.

First, what is the intended range of applicability of this linking proposition? Over how many of the phenomena of brightness perception would this correlation be expected to hold? If one were serious about this explanation, one would have to show a correspondence of details between the psychophysical and physiological phenomena (cf. Brindley 1960, p. 149). For example, one would have to show that the maxima and minima are largest when the Mach bands are most prominent and absent when Mach bands are not reported, and that the correlation holds for a broader range of brightness phenomena, including the brightness of isolated spots of light, the perception of brightness across sinusoidal gratings, the growth of subjective contrast with stimulus contrast, and so on. In the absence of exploration of its range of applicability, such a linking assumption seems to be too ad hoc to have much explanatory power.

The second reservation concerns the implicit assumption, rarely tested empirically, that there exists a class of retinal ganglion cells with adequate homogeneity to support the linking proposition. Since it is impractical to record from each of several ganglion cells at once, physiological Mach band experiments are carried out by recording from a single cell, and placing the physical ramp pattern at a series of positions with respect to the cell being recorded. It is then assumed that many such cells exist, and that, if one could present the ramp pattern in a single location and record from each cell in the row in turn, one would see a pattern with maxima and minima at the ends of the ramp. But for this explanation to work, one must believe that the cells are homogeneous enough that the relatively small variations across the Mach band pattern will constitute a meaningful perturbation against the variation of firing characteristics from one cell to the next. This is to some degree an empirical question, but it is not often treated in the physiological literature.

The third reservation about this linking proposition is its peripherality: it states a causal or explanatory relationship between the activity of single cells at a peripheral level of the nervous system and a perceptual or behavioral phenomenon, without any accompanying proposal as to how this pattern maintains itself through the system. The proposition includes an implicit appeal to the "nothing mucks it up" proviso (Teller 1980). But one could well argue that serious hypotheses proposing explanatory relationships between the activities of peripheral neural units and perceptual or psychophysical data should be accompanied by an explicit treatment of the problem of how the rest of the system manages not to muck up the relationship or, put more elegantly, of the constraints that the hypothesis puts on models of the composite map from the peripheral neural level to the bridge locus, and between the bridge locus and phenomenal states.

In the absence of any explicit treatment of these problems, the Mach band proposition would seem to amount to nothing more than a remote homunculus theory: the Mach band stimulus sets up the pattern of activity in the ganglion cells that "looks like" Mach bands, and the homunculus peers down at the ganglion cells through a magical Maxwellian telescope and sees Mach bands.

Many visual scientists acknowledge these problems, but argue that this explanation of Mach bands nonetheless provides an important heuristic for thinking about how Mach bands might come about. But one can argue the opposite: that it is all too common in visual science to find some superficial analogy between the activity of single cells and the results of perceptual or psychophysical experiments, and conclude that the former has something to do with, or even causes or explains, the latter. The crux of the argument concerns precisely the difference between a superficial analogy and an acceptable and well-founded explanation. Problems of range, homogeneity and peripherality would all seem to require further treatment before the value of the analogy can be assessed.

The second specific example to be discussed is the concept of trigger features or detectors, or more broadly, the role of individual cortical neurons in pattern perception. Many neurons in visual cortex seem to be "tuned" to respond with a rapid firing rate to light or dark bars at specific retinal orientations. Bars at non-optimal orientations lead to a lower firing rate, or no change from spontaneous activity levels. Since the discovery of these kinds of cortical cells (Hubel and Wiesel 1959, 1968) it has been commonplace in textbook visual theory to presume that these so-called "line detectors" play a fundamental (if not always clearly specified) role in the perception of oriented contours. Visual scientists have also been known to speculate that cells with even more specific trigger features will be found at higher levels of the visual system, and that activity in these cells will underlie the perception of the specific patterns or objects that make them fire fastest.

The linking proposition involved in such arguments is that *a neuron's role in the neural code is to signal the presence of the stimulus which makes that neuron respond most vigorously.* And, as was the case with the linking proposition used in the Mach band explanation, several reservations again must be expressed. In addition to range and peripherality problems like those discussed above, this linking proposition would seem to be lacking in face validity with respect to reasonable principles of neural coding.

To discuss these problems, it is useful to start with a digression, to introduce the concept of an *Equivalence Class* (cf. Carnap 1966, Chap. 5; Ratliff and Sirovich 1978) as it applies to the activities of single neurons. An equivalence class is a set of objects or stimuli which may differ from each other in many ways, but which are rendered identical by a particular measurement operation or classification scheme. All objects that have the same weight are an equivalence class with respect to weight, and all stimuli that lead to the same output from a neuron are an equivalence class for that neuron. Each neuron, as a univariant information channel, collapses a large set of stimuli into a smaller set of neural outputs, and necessarily confounds all members of each equivalence class.

This concept is very familiar in the consideration of photoreceptors. Under steady-state conditions, an individual rod or cone is nothing more than a quantum counter. Many different patches of light of many different wavelengths and wavelength mixtures will lead to statistically equal quantum catches, and thus will yield statistically identical outputs from that receptor. These patches of light are an equivalence class for that cell. Similarly, if one doubles the intensity of each of those patches of light, each patch will each now lead to twice the average quantum catch, putting the receptor in an average state different from that of the first equivalence class; these new patches of light will be a second equivalence class.

Now, a receptor has a broad action spectrum. The probability of absorption of a quantum varies with wavelength, and given a set of stimuli of equal irradiances, there will be one stimulus that leads to the maximum output from the receptor. But there is no sense in which one would want to say that a receptor with maximum sensitivity at 570 nm is specialized to signal 570 nm light. It is not called a 570-nm detector, nor is its trigger feature said to be a light of 570 nm. The emphasis in color theory is rather on the fact that equivalence classes exist for this cell; that the cell confounds wavelength and intensity information; and that, if wavelength information is to pass through a set of receptors, it must do so encoded in the relative activity levels of different receptor types.

Single simple cells in area 17 are often described as being triggered by, or detecting, the presence of bars of light at particular orientations. The reason that they are characterized in this way is that, of the stimulus set that has been tried, an oriented bar of light seems to make the cell fire fastest. But to say that the cell has a special role in encoding the stimulus which makes it fire fastest is to commit the same fallacy as to say that a cone with maximum sensitivity at 570 nm is a 570-nm detector. It would seem to make more sense to assume that each perceptual element is coded by a pattern of firing among many neurons, and that each different firing rate of each cortical cell is important to the neural code. To understand the part particular classes of cells are playing in the overall neural code, it will be necessary to use a large universe of stimuli, and to explore the equivalence classes for each different level of activity, for each different kind of cell (cf. Boynton 1979; Daugman 1980; Hood and Finkelstein 1983).

In a recent detailed analysis of this kind, Peter Lennie and Anthony Movshon (personal communication) have undertaken experiments to establish whether or not cortical cells are univariant; i.e., whether the response to a stimulus having one spatial configuration is distinguishable from the response to a second stimulus having a different spatial configuration suitably adjusted in contrast. Neurons in area 17 of the cat were stimulated by moving gratings of a range of spatial frequencies and orientations that spanned the optimum for each cell. For each combination of orientation and spatial frequency, gratings were presented at a series of different contrasts, and the times of occurrence of impulses were recorded precisely. By any of several different analyses of the discharge, there existed sets of stimuli, differing in spatial frequency, orientation and contrast, that gave rise to identical responses. Hence, exact equivalence classes could be identified for cortical cells. Doubtless, had the range of stimulus parameters been expanded to include wavelength, field size, etc., larger equivalence classes would have been found. With such information available, one might begin to think more clearly about the roles of cortical cells, and the ways in which univariant cells with different equivalence classes work together to preserve information, just as the three receptor types do in color vision.[3]

To what extent can the existence of equivalence classes be reconciled with the concept of trigger features or detectors? To use the concept of a trigger feature appears to be to claim implicitly three things: that for any given cortical cell most of the stimuli in the universe are in the null class, i.e. they do not influence the firing of the cell; that the set of stimuli that makes any appreciable response in the cell is small and homogeneous; and that the later elements which receive inputs from the cell ignore variations in the firing rate of the cell and treat the cell as binary—either firing or not firing. These assumptions would seem to be important and empirically testable. But in the virtual absence of data it is hard to set aside the convictions that all of the possible firing rates of cortical cells play a role in the neural code; and that the use of broader universes of stimuli in physiological experiments would reveal the size and heterogeneity of the equivalence classes of neurons. Such findings would re-insert a justified complexity into our thinking about the functions of cortical neurons. If these arguments are valid, they seriously challenge the validity of the notion of detectors and the ultimate value of physiological experiments employing narrowly limited stimulus sets.

In regard to intended range, it is sufficient to point out that the linking proposition involved in the notion of a detector—that the presence of the stimulus that makes a cell fire fastest is coded by the activity of that cell—is not universally invoked. It is not applied to receptors, nor to ganglion cells; and, in fact, it contradicts the Mach band brightness assumption, which includes the idea that the graded firing rates of the neurons across the Mach band pattern encode the graded range of perceived brightnesses. It is also contradictory to one of the fundamental assumptions of opponent process theories of color vision; namely, that the null signal from one opponent channel is a fundamental element of the neural code for the unique hues represented by departures from the null state in the other opponent channel. In short, if the "fastest firing rate" linking proposition is to be saved, its intended range of applicability must be specified and justified on other than an ad hoc basis.

In regard to peripherality, it is interesting to note that our views on whether cortical cells are "central" or "peripheral" have changed drastically in the last 20 years. Twenty years ago, the properties of visual cortical cells were still shrouded in mystery. It was easy to think of these cells as being very "central," and perhaps even forming the immediate neural substrate of perceptual events. Today Area 17 is often regarded as being a relatively peripheral stage of neural processing (cf. Marr 1982). In that case, if the properties of Area 17 cells are to be used to explain the elements of our perceptions, a "nothing mucks it up" theory is needed to bridge the gap between the Area 17 cell and the still more central sites which are now implicitly assumed to form the immediate neural substrates of conscious perceptions. This objection would not, of course, count against the use of the "fastest firing rate" linking proposition at the most central levels (i.e., the bridge locus), but the objections of range and face validity would still apply.

In sum, this section has been an attempt to use two common textbook explanations to explicate two common but mutually inconsistent linking propositions, and to begin to generate a set of criteria—range of applicability, homogeneity, peripherality, face validity and mutual consistency—by which one might attempt to evaluate a wider set of linking propositions. The suggestion is also made that the empirical analysis of equivalence classes for central neurons would be a worthwhile undertaking.

Canonical Forms

We come finally to the question of canonical forms. The question is, does one wish to argue that there is a necessary form that the information coded in the visual neurons must eventually take, in order for particular perceptual states to occur? Claims of canonical form involve linking propositions, insofar as they claim that the existence of a particular brain state is a necessary condition for the occurrence of a particular perceptual state.

One area in which the question of canonical form manifests itself may be called the convergence dilemma, or the problem of pattern codes (cf. Barlow 1972; Hood and Finkelstein 1983). The question is, if two or more neurons are to act jointly to determine a perceptual state, must their outputs necessarily converge upon a successor neuron whose state uniquely determines the perceptual state? Must the physiological basis for each separate perceptual state be the activity of a different single neuron, or may it be the *pattern* of activity in a set of non-interacting neurons? In brief, if one chooses the first horn of the dilemma and allows the possibility of a pattern code, one must deal with the problem of how two or more cells can have a joint causal role without interacting. The best approach is probably through the concept of emergent properties (e.g., Hofstadter 1980). But if one chooses instead the second horn, and argues that convergence is necessary, one must be ready to argue that there are enough eligible neurons to go around. The author knows of no comfortable place to hide from this dilemma.

An example from color vision theory may clarify the problem. As an opponent process theorist, one might argue that the joint states of three bridge locus neurons— a Redness/Greenness neuron, a Yellowness/Blueness neuron and a Blackness/Whiteness neuron—determine perceived hue, brightness and saturation in a region of the visual world; and further, that the outputs of three such neurons need not converge upon any other single neuron in order to act jointly to determine the perceptual state. Alternately, one might believe that there must exist a (later) stage of the visual system at which a different neuron would be active for the perception of each different combination of hue, brightness, and saturation, and that until this stage is found the neural correlates of perceived hue will not be properly understood.

A second example may be taken from the "second quantitative law of perception" formulated recently by Barlow (1983): "... the essential work done in perception is to construct a representation using symbols of high relative entropy from sensory messages in which the symbols have low relative entropy because of numerous forms of redundancy." It is not however, clear that this proposition is a canonical claim, because it is also said to be subject to empirical verification or falsification.

A third example may be taken from the work on Marr (1982). Marr argues (p. 36) that the fundamental purpose of vision is that it "... tells about shape and space and spatial arrangement ..." and therefore that (p. 326, parentheses added) "... it is clear in principle that the brain must construct (explicit) three-dimensional representations of object, and the space they occupy. ... In order to recognize an object by its shape ... some kind of three-dimensional representation must be built from the image and matched in some way to a stored three-dimensional representation with which other knowledge is already associated." Although the physiological interpretation of the concept of explicit representation is purposely left unspecified (pp. 336–343), this is clearly an abstract argument that there is a canonical form that visual information must take and Marr's theory of pattern vision consists of ingeneous speculations about how the information could take that form. To a large degree the value of Marr's formulations to visual science will rest on the question of whether his argument for the explicit representation of form is true, whether it can be given a physiologically useful interpretation, and whether it can be rendered as a specific psychophysiological linking proposition.

As a final exercise, it is of interest to consider the following four questions, all of which involve assumptions about canonical forms. First, why do we see the world right side up when the retinal image is upside down? Second, why do we see the world as non-distorted when the map on the visual cortex is distorted? Third, why do we see a continuous visual scene, with no division at the midline, when left and right visual fields project to separate hemispheres? And fourth (Barlow 1983), where in the brain are the cues of binocular parallex, motion parallax and texture gradients brought together to add the third dimension to our perceptual world? In modern visual science, the first two questions are usually considered to be pseudo-questions, not in need of answers. The third and fourth are usually considered to be real questions, and the postulated physiological communication pathways and convergence loci are taken as logical necessities. The point is that each of the four questions involves a linking proposition. Our implicit acceptance or rejection of particular linking propositions forms the basis for very fundamental decisions about which questions require answers, and what properties are to be studied in anatomical and physiological experiments.

Testability of Linking Propositions

We now return to the question of the empirical testability of linking propositions. A full treatment of this question remains to be undertaken, but a few brief comments can be made. It has been argued above that there are many kinds of linking propositions, and that different linking propositions take on different roles—as fundamental axioms, broad but non-universal generalizations, tentative assumptions, hypotheses or speculations—in the nomological network of visual science. If this is so, the testability or falsifiability of linking propositions will also vary widely, depending upon the role the specific proposition is playing in a given experimental or theoretical context.

At one extreme lie some general linking propositions dealing with information loss—Identity and Contrapositive Identity—which stand as axiomatic in visual science and its parent disciplines. These would not be subject to empirical falsification without major upheavals in a broad range of scientific disciplines. At the other extreme lie linking propositions to the effect that a specific mapping occurs between the states of particular, well-characterized visual neurons and particular perceptual states; i.e. propositions of the form: human beings perceive X whenever the set of neurons Y is in the set of states Z. Leaving aside the standard problems of anesthesia and cross-species generalizations, such a proposition seems eminently testable. To test it one would make the most inclusive possible collection of objects and stimulus configurations that produce the perception X, along with an equally varied collection that do not; and see whether or not presentation of each of them produces the predicted neural states. There does not appear to be any particular logical difficulty associated with such an approach, as long as the perceptual facts are available, the cell types can be identified unambiguously, and the linking proposition is stated with sufficient clarity and precision.

If such an experiment were carried out, and the proposed correspondence were shown to hold, one might well produce an empirically validated Analogy, with an established, broad range of applicability. The quality and explanatory value of the analogy would remain to be judged, and I have argued above that the criteria for judging the value of such analogies are greatly in need of explication and clarification.

Conclusion

Twenty years ago, Brindley pointed out that in using linking hypotheses, visual scientists often introduce unacknowledged, non-rigorous steps into their arguments. Brindley's remarks correctly sensitized us to the lack of rigor with which linking propositions have undoubtedly often been used, but led to few detailed, explicit discussions of linking propositions. It would seem useful to encourage such discussions, and to encourage visual scientists to make linking propositions explicit, so that linking propositions can be subjected to the requirements of consistency and the risks of falsification appropriate to the evaluation of all scientific propositions.

Perhaps we should include more often in our publications a paragraph or two making our linking propositions explicit. It will be important to define the ranges of intended applicability of individual linking propositions, the kinds of support they receive from prior experiments, their consistency with other broadly accepted linking propositions, the constraints they place on the composite map, the ancillary assumptions involved and the overall fit of the linking propositions into the current theoretical network of visual science. Within a few years, enough such descriptions should become available that it would be possible to refer to and build upon earlier explications, rather than starting from scratch each time. Similarly, perhaps reviewers could be encouraged to use the explicitness and potential values of linking propositions as one of the criteria of excellence for papers in which arguments containing linking propositions are explicitly or implicitly made.

Acknowledgements

Preparation of this paper was supported by grant BNS 81-11927 from the National Science Foundation and a Sabbatical Award from the James McKeen Cattell Fund. I thank Denise Varner and Angela Brown for comments on several drafts of the manuscript, Peter Lennie for timely encouragement and advice, Marjorie Zachow for secretarial assistance and many colleagues for valuable discussions.

Notes

Portions of this work were originally presented at the symposium, "Relating psychophysics to physiology: Current problems and approaches," 12th Symposium of the Center for Visual Sciences, Rochester, New York, 18–20 June 1981.

1. Brindley's view subsequently became somewhat more liberal. In the 1970 edition of his book, the chapter on linking hypotheses is still much the same, but in the chapter on color vision Brindley included for the first time a discussion of Hering's contributions to color vision theory. In the context of this discussion he remarked (p. 208, parentheses added) that "(Hering's) argument from the appearance of colours . . . though non-rigorous is not necessarily bad; it is hard to judge because it comes from a kind of thinking that is outside the main tradition of natural science. . . . (If) Hering's argument is vindicated . . . it will help us decide whether in future to pay attention to arguments from Class B (i.e., subjective) sensory phenomena, or to disregard them."

2. Walter Makous (personal communication) and others have argued that if two stimuli lead to behaviorally indistinguishable responses, the neural signals underlying these responses *must* be indistinguishable some where, even if only at the level of the motor neurons. Under this interpretation, the Converse Identity proposition, like the Identity proposition, is true and tautological. However, this is not the interpretation in common use. When visual scientists employ the Converse Identity proposition, I believe they specifically mean to assume that two signals are rendered identical within the *sensory* visual system. Where the sensory visual system leaves off and the central or motor systems begin is, of course, very much an unsolved problem in its own right.

3. These arguments would seem to be inconsistent with Barlow's (1972) fifth dogma; i.e., that: "The frequency of neural impulses codes subjective certainty; a high impulse frequency in a given neuron corresponds to a high degree of confidence that the cause of the percept is present in the external world" (p. 381).

References

Barlow H. B. (1972) Single units and sensation: a neuron doctrine for perceptual psychology? *Perception* 1, 371–394.

Barlow H. B. (1983) Perception: What quantitative laws govern the acquisition of knowledge from the senses. In *Functions of the Brain*, Wolfson College Lectures (Edited by Coen C.). Oxford University Press, Oxford.

Boring E. G. (1942) *Sensation and Perception in the History of Experimental Psychology.* Appleton–Century–Crofts, New York.

Boynton R. M. (1979) *Human Color Vision.* Holt, Rinehart & Winston, New York.

Boynton R. M. and Onley J. (1962) A critique of the special status assigned by Brindley to "Psychophysical Linking Hypotheses" of Class A. *Vision Res.* 2, 383–390.

Brindley G. (1957) Two theorems in colour vision. *Q. Jl exp. Psychol.* 9, 101–104.

————(1960) *Physiology of the Retina and Visual Pathways*, 1st Edition. Edward Arnold, London.

————(1970) *Physiology of the Retina and Visual Pathways*, 2nd Edition. Williams & Wilkins, Baltimore.

Carnap R. (1966) *An Introduction to the Philosophy of Science* (Edited by Gardner M.). Basic Books, New York.

Crane H. and Piantanida T. (1983) On seeing reddish-green and yellowish-blue. *Science* 221, 1078–1080.

Daugman J. G. (1980) Two-dimensional spectral analysis of cortical receptive field profiles. *Vision Res.* 20, 847–856.

De Valois R. L. (1965) Analysis and coding of color vision in the primate visual system. In *Cold Spring Harbor Symposia on Quantitative Biology, Vol. XXX. Sensory Receptors.* Cold Spring Harbor Laboratory of Quantitative Biology, Cold Spring Harbor, NY.

Eccles J. C. (1977) In *The Self and its Brain* (Edited by Popper K. R. and Eccles J. C.), Part II. Springer, Berlin.

Feigl H. (1958) The "mental" and the "physical." In *Minnesota Studies in the Philosophy of Science, Vol. II. Concepts, Theories, and the Mind–Body Problem.* University of Minnesota Press.

Hofstadter D. R. (1980) *Gödel, Escher, Bach: an Eternal Golden Braid.* Random House, New York.

Hood D. C. and Finkelstein M. A. (1983) A case for the revision of textbook models of color vision: the detection and appearance of small brief lights. In *Colour Vision: Physiology and Psychophysics* (Edited by Mollon J. D. and Sharpe L. T.). Academic Press, London.

Hubel D. H. and Wiesel T. N. (1959) Receptive fields of single neurons in the cat's striate cortex. *J. Physiol.* 148, 574–591.

Hubel D. H. and Wiesel T. N. (1968) Receptive fields and functional architecture of monkey striate cortex. *J. Physiol.* 195, 215–243.

Marr D. (1982) *Vision.* W. H. Freeman, San Francisco, CA.

Ratliff F. and Sirovich L. (1978) Equivalence classes of visual stimuli. *Vision Res.* 18, 845–851.

Robson J. (1980) The physiological basis of spatial vision. In *Visual Coding and Adaptability* (Edited by Harris C. H.). Erlbaum Associates, Hillsdale, NJ.

Shapere D. (1977) Scientific theories and their domains. In *The Structure of Scientific Theories* (Edited by Suppe F.) 2nd Edition. University of Illinois Press, Urbana.

Suppe F. (1977) *The Structure of Scientific Theories*, 2nd Edition. University of Illinois Press, Urbana.

Teller D. Y. (1980) Locus questions in visual science, In *Visual Coding and Adaptability* (Edited by Harris C.). Erlbaum Associates, Hillsdale, NJ.

Teller D. Y. and Pugh E. N. Jr (1983) Linking propositions in color vision. In *Colour Vision: Physiology and Psychophysics* (Edited by Mollon J. D. and Sharpe L. T.). Academic Press, London.

Uttal W. R. (1981) *A Taxonomy of Visual Processes.* Erlbaum Associates, Hillsdale, NJ.

14

Molyneux's Question

Gareth Evans

I

William Molyneux posed the following question in a letter to Locke:

Suppose a man born blind, and now adult, and taught by his touch to distinguish between a cube and a sphere of the same metal, and nighly of the same bigness, so as to tell, when he felt one and the other, which is the cube, which the sphere. Suppose then the cube and sphere placed on a table, and the blind man to be made to see; *quaere*, Whether by his sight, before he touched them, he could now distinguish and tell which is the globe, and which the cube?[1]

This question aroused tremendous interest among philosophers and psychologists on both sides of the Channel, so much so that Cassirer was able to claim that it formed the central question of eighteenth-century epistemology and psychology.[2] In fact, Molyneux's Question raises many different issues, not all of which are of as great interest now as they were in earlier times. Nevertheless, there seems to me to be one issue at the heart of the controversy which is very important and upon which it is still possible to make some progress. In this introductory section, I shall try to identify this issue as sharply as I can. The issue I want to discuss arises only on the assumption that the blind possess genuine spatial concepts, and so I shall begin by saying a word about that background assumption. Having stated the question as precisely as is possible, I shall distinguish it from other issues which have become entangled with it. In the second section, I shall try to make clear what is involved in the presumed ability of the blind to perceive spatially, and in the final section, I consider how the spatiality of vision is to be thought of in relation to that ability.

Even before proceeding with this programme, I want to make two points about the terms in which the question is posed. First, I shall make a simplification of the situation originally suggested by Diderot.[3] Molyneux asked whether or not the blind man would be able to apply three-dimensional spatial concepts, such as *sphere* and *cube*, upon the basis of his newly acquired vision; he also seems to have been interested in whether the blind man would see things as at various distances from him.[4] There is nothing wrong with these questions, but they are in a sense less interesting than whether he would be able to extend two-dimensional concepts, like *square* and *circle*, since there is less antecedent expectation that the newly sighted man would be able to appreciate the depth cues available in visual perception. Although most disputants in the controversy retained the terms in which Molyneux originally posed it, it transpires that their fundamental disagreement is about whether the blind man would be able to extend his two-dimensional concepts.[5]

Secondly, I must stress that Molyneux's Question is about whether a born-blind man *who can see* a circle and a square would extend his concepts to them. It is not a question about how soon after the operation, and via what process, a newly sighted man would be able to see. Molyneux's Question requires only that the newly sighted man would be able to have visual experiences of circles and squares without his, or his brain's, having had a chance to establish correlations between the old and the new information.

Several thinkers have returned a negative answer to Molyneux's Question not because they held a view about the difference between the spatial concepts of the blind and those connected with visual experience, but because they held that the blind do not have any genuinely spatial concepts at all. The first explicit statement of this view that I have been able to find occurs in Platner's *Philosophische Aphorismen* (1793), though antecedents can certainly be found in Berkeley's *New Theory of Vision*. Platner wrote:

In reality, it is time that serves, for the man born blind, as space. Remoteness and proximity only mean to him the time, more or less long, and the number, more or less, of intermediaries which he needs in passing from one tactual impression to another.[6]

Echoing this, Lotze wrote:

the space of a blind man may not be so much what we mean by space, as an artificial system of conceptions of movement, time and effort.[7]

The line of thought behind this position can be seen in the following passage from von Senden, the most recent, and most dogmatic, of its proponents:

Nothing is given to the blind man simultaneously, either by touch or the other senses; everything is resolved into successions . . . Only the variety furnished by a temporally ordered series of experiences can furnish him with knowledge. . . .

Since nothing is given simultaneously to his senses as spatial, it must be mentally strung together in time. . . . A spatial line must be replaced by a temporal sequence.[8]

On this view, the perceptions of the blind cannot represent several objects existing simultaneously; they amount to no more than the *succession* of tactual experiences, perhaps linked by, or embroidered with, kinaesthetic and muscular experiences. When a blind man traces the outline of a square—e.g. by tracing the edge of one face of a cube, or a wire figure—he receives just such a sequence of impressions, and his concept of *square*, though it is abstract, and can be applied, for example, to the arrangement of houses in the village, remains the concept of a certain kind of *succession*, like the concept of a *fugue* or a *tune*.

It is not surprising that those who hold this view about the spatial concepts of the blind will say "Not" to Molyneux's Question; as Bain put it:

But how a vision to the eye can reveal beforehand what would be the experience of the hand or the other moving members I am unable to understand.[9]

The implication here is perhaps not watertight, but I shall not elaborate since the claim about the spatial concepts of the blind surely cannot be sustained. It is true, and I think important, that spatial concepts are concepts that involve the thought of distinct objects or elements existing simultaneously. Nor do I wish to quarrel with the view that someone who has spatial *concepts* must also have the ability to form, or enjoy, *perceptual* representations of distinct but simultaneously existing objects. Of course, not all spatial concepts need relate immediately to perceptual experience. Once some spatial concepts are possessed, a great many other spatial concepts, like that of a *fifteen-sided plane figure*, can be understood by means of their relation to those basic concepts. Even what we like to think of as very elementary spatial concepts—such as *triangle* and *square*—can only fully be grasped via their connection with simpler concepts, such as *between, longer, straight, angle*, etc. But ultimately, possession of some concepts will require a capacity to use the concept in response to the appropriate perceptual experience, and if they, and all concepts explicable in terms of them, are to have the essential character of applying to arrangements of distinct but simultaneously existing objects, then the perceptions to which they relate must involve the presentation or representation of distinct objects. It follows that it is not sufficient for the possession of genuine spatial concepts that one can correctly use spatial terms of a public language, for it is possible that this could be done without the appropriate perceptual representations; in much the way that someone might be able to apply colour terms correctly by analysis of wavelength of light, or as someone might be able to apply "to the right" and "to the left" to sounds simply upon the basis of the difference in the time the sound waves meet the two ears, and with no spatial meaning at all.[10]

My disagreement with this tradition comes at the point where it is claimed that the blind cannot form or enjoy perceptual representations of space—of distinct objects existing simultaneously and related spatially. I do not wish to object, as one might object, on the ground that the blind can perceive distinct things simultaneously, by touching them with both hands, for example, or by feeling the parts of something small enough to be placed within the hand. For, although this is true, to locate this as the point of objection is to concede far too much to the theory of perception on which the position is based. I would still want to object to the conclusion even if the blind had only a single hand in a world in which all the objects were too large to be grasped in it.

It is unacceptable to argue from the successiveness of *sensation* to the successiveness of *perception*. One can surely make sense of the idea of a perceiving organism which uses a sequence of impressions or stimulations to build up a perceptual representation of a spatial world, in which the information contained in the sequence of stimulations is integrated into, or interpreted in terms of, a unitary representation of the perceiver's surroundings. As Gibson has been at pains to point out, the supposedly unproblematic spatial perception provided by vision depends to a very considerable extent upon precisely such a process.[11] Now, I do not pretend that this concept is clear; indeed, it is one of the main tasks of this paper to get it clear. For the time being I shall appeal to an intuitive understanding of the idea. The point is made at this intuitive level by Pierre Villey, a blind Montaigne scholar who was obviously riled by the suggestion that the blind did not have genuine spatial concepts (and by the implication of intellectual inferiority that often went with it), and he wrote a book, from which the following quotation is taken, in order to refute it. Villey concedes that his tactual perception of the chair is successive, but writes:

... if, an hour after feeling it, I search in my consciousness for the memory of the vanished chair ... I do not reconstruct it by means of fragmentary and successive images. It appears immediately and as a whole in its essential parts ... There is no procession, even rapid, of representations ... I couldn't tell in what order the parts were perceived by me.[12]

Of course, the attribution to a subject of a perceptual representation of space is to be justified upon the basis of behavioural and reasoning skills which it explains, but this anecdotal evidence is not worthless. If von Senden and his predecessors are right, Villey's memory of a chair would have to be ordered in time; yet his incapacity to remember the order in which he perceived the chair, or to acknowledge a succession in what is remembered, directly contradicts this.

There is, indeed, the possibility of a deeper argument on this point. Kant argued with tremendous force that it was not possible to have a conception of an objective world—a world whose states and constituents are independent of one's perception of them—without conceiving of that world as spatial, with oneself as located within it and tracing a continuous path through it. The argument connects objectivity with space—but space as conceived in "genuine" spatial concepts, i.e. concepts which connect up with simultaneous perceptual representations of the world. (I shall occasionally call these "simultaneous representations" and the concepts based upon them "simultaneous concepts.") If the concepts of the blind were really no more than concepts of certain kinds of succession in experience, then they could not be regarded as having a concept of an independently existing world at all. The blind would have to think as the phenomenalists would have us all think, in terms of actual and possible sense experiences.

In what follows, I shall assume that the blind do have simultaneous perceptual representations of space, and hence that they have genuine, simultaneous spatial concepts. Although there are many experiments which show that the blind are inferior to the sighted in spatial ability and reasoning,[13] there are equally many which show the blind to be capable of behaviour which seems to show that they are able to form simultaneous representations of the world—whether in perception, or imagery.[14] The issue I want to discuss, and which I believe was the issue on which Locke, Berkeley, Leibniz, Condillac, and others were taking up positions, is that of the relation between the perceptual representations of space attributable to the blind, and the perceptual representation of space available in visual perception. For this reason, I shall not consider the school of thought, represented most notably by J. S. Mill and Henri Poincaré, who held, partly with a view to avoiding the consequence that the spatial concepts of the blind and the sighted are different, that *our* spatial concepts have precisely the character assigned by von Senden and his predecessors to the concepts of the blind. Poincaré wrote:

To localize an object simply means to represent to oneself the movements that would be necessary to reach it. It is not a question of representing the movements themselves in space, but solely of representing to oneself the muscular sensations which accompany these movements and which do not presuppose the existence of space.[15]

These philosophers take account of a point which is of the greatest importance in the theory of space perception, but distort it. This fundamental point is that no explanation can be given of what it is to have a perceptual representation of space—

to be given perceptually the information that objects of such-and-such a character are arranged in such-and-such a way in one's vicinity—except in terms of the behavioural propensities and dispositions to which such information gives rise. The distortion comes in at the point where an attempt is made to *reduce* spatial propositions to propositions about time, kinaesthetic and tactual sensation—at the point, that is, where Poincaré suggests not only that the information embodied in these perceptual representations cannot be explained without reference to bodily movements, but also that the concepts of the relevant bodily movements *can* be explained without reference to space. I shall return to this point below.

I have not placed Berkeley of the *New Theory of Vision* in the Mill–Poincaré tradition, despite the fact that there is much that he says with which they would agree. When Berkeley is thinking about "outness"—distance away from the observer—he belongs squarely with Mill and Poincaré. In the *Principles*, he summarized the position he thought he had established in the *New Theory of Vision*:

. . . in strict truth the ideas of sight, . . . do not suggest or mark out to us things actually existing at a distance, but only admonish us that ideas of touch will be imprinted in our minds at such and such distances of time, and in consequence of such and such actions.[16]

But I do not think that Berkeley held that the *two*-dimensional concepts which we are able to form on the basis of touch—like the concept he called *tangible square*—were concepts of succession, and so I do not think that his reason for giving a negative answer to Molyneux's Question is the same as von Senden's. Berkeley is quite explicit:

Sounds, for example, perceived at the same instant, are apt to coalesce, if I may so say, into one sound: but we can perceive at the same time great variety of visible objects, very separate and distinct from each other. Now *tangible extension being made up of several distinct coexistent parts*, we may hence gather another reason that may dispose us to imagine a likeness or an analogy between the immediate objects of sight and touch.[17]

In view of this, it is certain that in answering Molyneux's Question negatively, Berkeley was taking up a position upon the most fundamental issue posed by that question—an issue which only arises on the assumption that the blind do have simultaneous spatial concepts. It is to that issue that I now turn.

To bring it out, let us consider first the position of a philosopher, whom I shall call "V," who insists that, on the conditions given, the newly sighted man must be able to apply his concepts to the visually presented array—must, to use a convenient term, "generalize." (Curiously enough, there is no historical figure who has taken exactly this position; as I will explain, even Leibniz's "Yes" to Molyneux's

Question indicates a position weaker than V's.) For V, the case presented by Molyneux's Question is no different from that involved in the following speculation: whether a man born deaf, and taught to apply the terms "continuous" and "pulsating" to stimulations made on his skin, would, on gaining his hearing and being presented with two tones, one continuous and the other pulsating, be able to apply the terms correctly. Few of us have a doubt about the outcome of this experiment, but, more important, if the born-deaf man failed to apply the terms in this new case, we should feel obliged to interpret this as casting doubt upon his understanding of the terms which we thought we had introduced to him, just as if he had, incomprehensibly, been unable to apply the terms to stimulations made on a hitherto unused part of his skin. We should say that he had not fully mastered the concept of *pulsation* simply because he had been presented with a case to which the concept manifestly applied, and had failed to apply it. No obligation attaches to one who holds this position to provide an alternative interpretation of the subject's previous utterances; it is not, indeed, part of his position that they are intelligible. What he does claim is that there is a unitary conceptual capacity which most people have with the word "pulsating" which this born-deaf man must be acknowledged to lack.[18]

In the same way, V holds, there is a unitary conceptual ability associated in the case of most adults with the word "square"—mastery of a single concept. Now, the fact of the matter is that this concept *applies* in the case of a visually presented square, or in the case of four points of light arranged in a square. If a man does not perceive the shape, or the points of light, then his inability to apply the term "square" in no way casts doubt upon his understanding of it. But if we build into the description of the case that the newly-sighted man does see the square, or the four dots—does, if you like, have a visual experience of the same character as leads the normally sighted to apply the term—then he is presented with something which falls under the concept, and an incapacity to apply the term in this new case must show that he does not possess the (unitary) concept of a square.

V finds it impossible to conceive of a coherent concept which applies to items simultaneously existing, which is therefore exercised most directly in connection with perceptual representations of several distinct objects existing simultaneously, and yet which stops short of applying in the case where the items are visually perceived. V simply cannot find room for *two* genuine, i.e. simultaneous, concepts of a square, or for *two* genuine concepts of *between*, *straight line*, etc., each set of concepts generating its own geometry.

If V is sophisticated, he will make no appeal to the notion of *similarity*. His position is not that the tactual perceptual representation of a square *resembles* the visual perceptual representation of a square. His point is that if both are simultaneous representations, the only concept which he can understand applies (or seems to apply) in both cases.[19]

The opposing position is essentially that advanced by Berkeley in the *New Theory of Vision*, though I shall call its proponent "B" so as to allow him to deviate a little from the historical Berkeley. B denies that there is a single concept *square*, which may or may not be possessed by the blind man, and whose possession is tested by whether he generalizes when he regains his sight. The sighted adult's use of the word "square" rests upon two separable and conceptually unconnected abilities.[20] Both of the concepts apply to arrangements of simultaneously existing objects, but nevertheless they are distinct.

No one can say that B's position is, on the face of it, a wildly attractive one; to see why it has attracted so many adherents, we must look at the reason B can advance for opposing V's simple idea of the single conceptual capacity. Many reasons have been advanced, but the one I want to focus upon as being particularly important arises from the way B regards visual experience. B supposes that a subject could enjoy visual experience without regarding it as *of* a world distinct from himself at all. In this condition, the subject would not conceive of the items of which he was aware as *outside* himself, or as located at any distance from himself, but even so, B thinks, his visual experience would acquaint the subject with a two-dimensional mosaic of colours. Now, B supposes that it would be possible for the subject to abstract from this experience colour concepts, such as "red," "blue," etc., and B supposes that the subject might respond in a similar way to shape-resemblances in the colour mosaics, and thereby form (two-dimensional) shape concepts. Such are the concepts which B terms *visible square, visible circle*—abstracted from an experience which has no reference to an external reality at all. These concepts, B thinks, are the concepts which V is prepared to ascribe to the blind man. But this is what B cannot understand. How is it possible for a man who cannot form the least idea of visual experience to acquire a concept capable of being abstracted so directly from it—related to it in the same way in which colour concepts are related to it?

These reflections certainly do not constitute a decisive argument against V's position, but they do focus attention upon an unease which will not be removed until visual experience and its spatiality are fundamentally rethought.

I have located the main reason for B's position here, rather than in *anti-abstractionism* where it is sometimes located, for two reasons. First, Berkeley's only sound point concerns a spurious explanation (in terms of images) of our generalizing capacities; it cannot be used to place a limit upon the range of those capacities themselves. If Berkeley were to claim that the supposed concept of a square which V attributes to the blind man cannot exist, because, being free of sensory elements from either modality, it could not consist in any image, V should reply by citing Berkeley's own observation that the concept of a visible triangle cannot consist in an image either. Secondly, the anti-abstractionism considerations, even if they were valid, are considerations of the wrong kind to sustain B's position. They rule out V's concepts simply because they are a-modal (i.e. supra-sensible or neutral with respect to sense modality), and this would mean that B's objection to giving an affirmative answer to Molyneux's Question is no stronger than an objection to giving a similar answer about the man born deaf who has to generalize the concept *pulsating*. I want to give B a position which would enable him to discriminate between the two cases.[21]

If I have identified in the dispute between B and V the central issue raised by Molyneux's Question, then we can see that this issue was missed by two contemporary discussions of the question.

In a recent book on Molyneux's Question, the psychologist M. J. Morgan writes as though the main issue was one of *innateness*. He writes, for example:

Locke replied "Not" to Molyneux's Question to avoid postulating a common representational scheme for the different senses, because such a schema implies an innate supra-sensible structure to the mind.[22]

The reasoning comes out in the following passage:

The real question was whether he could name what he saw. And the answer to this was "Not" because to name the visual impression he would have to compare it to some other idea, an idea common between touch and vision. Plainly, such an idea could not be a simple "sensory impression"; it would have to be something transcending individual impressions, and to which these individual impressions could be referred. The *Essay* was written against such innate ideas . . .[23]

It seems to me that the issue of innateness cuts right across the dispute between B and V. In the first place, I see no particular reason why the concept which V attributes to the blind man has to be innate. Whether it can be accounted for by empiricist learning mechanisms depends upon what we conceive those mechanisms to be. I suppose that, according to the most radical empiricist position, an organism has an innate similarity-space defined over *sensations*, and concepts simply result from a partitioning of that space.[24] It is perfectly true, on that position, that no account can be given of the spatial concepts which V attributes to the blind man. This is not because the required concept is supra-sensible (i.e. a-modal). There is nothing on the radical empiricist view that precludes sensations produced by the stimulation of different sense modalities being sufficiently close together in the innate similarity space for responses conditioned to the one to generalize to the other. There is nothing particularly upsetting to an empiricist theory of concept formation in the suggestion that human subjects who are trained with the use of "harmonious" in the case of sounds might generalize its use (without further training) to the case of certain combinations of colours. Rather, the difficulty arises in the case of shape concepts because on the simple model there is no way for the gap between succession and simultaneity to be bridged. However, such a radical empiricism is not an attractive position, nor is it clear that B could appeal to it, since he too acknowledges that the concept *tangible square* is a simultaneous concept.

A much more reasonable position would be to suppose that spatial concepts can be learned through the subject's capacity to *perceive* spatially. A perceptual spatial representation, although it embodies spatial information, is not a *conceptual* representation, and there is room for the explanation of our acquisition of *concepts* like *square*, with their characteristic generality, in terms of our exposure, in perception, to a range of squares.[25] It is not clear why the concept which V attributes to the blind man, and which is open to generalization, could not have been acquired in this way. Of course, it is B's thesis that no concept acquired in this way can be directly applied on the basis of vision, but that, V holds, is because B fails to take into account what is involved in tactual-kinaesthetic spatial perception, and has a false view about the nature of visual experience. Their dispute is about these things, not about innate ideas.[26]

In the second place, far from innateness being an essential ingredient of V's position, it is an element of a perfectly possible variant of B's position. B holds that there is no *conceptual* connection between *tangible square* and *visible square*, but this leaves it open how the move from the visible to the tangible is made. Berkeley held that we *learn* the connection by experience, but an alternative hypothesis is that the connection is pre-programmed into the brain. (I assume that it is a coherent hypothesis with respect to anything which is learned that it should have been innate.) It follows from this observation that Molyneux's Question is not in fact a crucial experiment in the dispute between B and V, for although a negative answer would refute V, a positive answer would be consistent both with V's position, and with this nativist version of B's position.

In a second recent work on Molyneux's Question, Judith Jarvis Thompson takes the central issue to be whether a world is conceivable in which tactual circles give rise to the visual impression of a square, and tactual squares give rise to the visual impression of a circle. She writes:

I am inclined to think that what was in Molyneux's mind, because of which he drew that conclusion [that the blind man would not generalize] from those premises [the blind man has not yet attained the experience that what affects his touch so or so, must affect his sight so and so], was this: that what affects one's touch so or so *could* have affected one's sight such and such instead of so and so. . . .[27]

Borrowing an idea from Grice,[28] she attempts to show that no such world is conceivable. For example, when three tactual circles are brought together, empty space can be felt between them, but there is nothing corresponding to this in the case of three visual squares. I shall not go into detail here, because this line of thought seems to me to be beside the point. For what position would this reflection support on the debate between B and V? If Mrs Thompson's reasoning is cogent, and if the blind man can be expected to rehearse it, it follows that he can *work out* which visual shape corresponds to which tactual shape, *on the assumption that he knows that some such correspondence exists*. But, according to V, no such assumption is necessary. V holds that, on seeing the square or the four points arranged in a square, the blind man is confronted with an instance of his antecedently existing concept, and hence should be disposed to apply it without any additional information or instruction at all. There is no question of his having to *work out* how to apply it. We don't suppose that the man who regained his hearing would need to be told that one of the sounds he was to hear was going to be continuous and the other pulsating in order to be able to apply his concept in the new case, and this is the position V takes on Molyneux's Question.

Although she does not mention any of this work, Mrs. Thompson's paper is the last in a long line, beginning with Leibniz, of answers to Molyneux's Question. Leibniz held that the blind man would be able to work out which was which, on the ground:

that in the globe there are no points distinguishable on the side of the globe itself, all being level there without angles, whereas in the cube there are eight points distinguished from all the others.[29]

Hence, Leibniz thought that if one was to set up a correspondence between the visual and the tactual, one could not map the visual circle on to the tactual square in such a way as to generate analogues in the visual world to each structural property and relation perceivable in the tactual world. Mrs. Thompson and Leibniz focus on different examples of properties that would not be representable in the visual domain in the unnatural correspondence, but their arguments have the same structure. However, Leibniz realized the limitations of this argument, in a way which Mrs. Thompson apparently does not. Leibniz wrote:

Perhaps Molyneux and the author of the *Essay* are not so far from my opinion as at first appears. . . . If you will weigh my answer, ["Yes" to Molyneux's Question] you will find that I have put a condition upon it which can be considered as included in the question: it is, that the only thing in question is that of distinguishing, and the blind man knows that the two figured bodies which he must distinguish are there, and thus that each of the appearances which he sees is that of the cube or that of the globe.[30]

In other words, Leibniz was refusing to support V's position, since by implication, he suggests that in the absence of instruction, the newly sighted man might enjoy visual experiences of squares and circles without being put in mind of the shapes discernible by touch at all. Hence, Leibniz's qualified affirmative answer shows him to be an adherent of a version of B's position. After all, Berkeley himself was prepared to allow that "the visible square is fitter than the visible circle to represent the tangible square"[31] on the ground that the visible square had, as the visible circle did not, several distinguishable parts, and it would not matter to the fundamental disagreement that he has with V that the visible square is *uniquely* fitted to represent the tangible square. It remains the case that the one *represents* the other, rather than being both instances of a common concept. It remains the case, that is, that there is an intelligible and separable conceptual capacity whose range is restricted to the set of tactually perceived squares.

As we have seen, the result of Molyneux's experiment bears somewhat indirectly upon what I have identified as the main issue raised by his question. (See figure 14.1.) It is true that a negative result to the experiment does undermine V's position, and it might be thought that enough negative answers had been collected to make further speculation unnecessary. However, almost all of the experiments which are cited as providing a negative result to Molyneux's Question do no such thing, for while it is true that subjects cannot name the circle and the square, this is because they do not have any visual figure perception at all but are restricted to a confusing succession of experiences of light and colour. Even Berkeley missed this point, and cites Chiselden's case in defence of his position; quite unsuitably for even as Berkeley reported it, the subject in that case "knew not the shape of anything, nor any one thing from another, however different in shape or magnitude."[32] Von Senden cites only one or two cases in which it is claimed that the subject could dis-

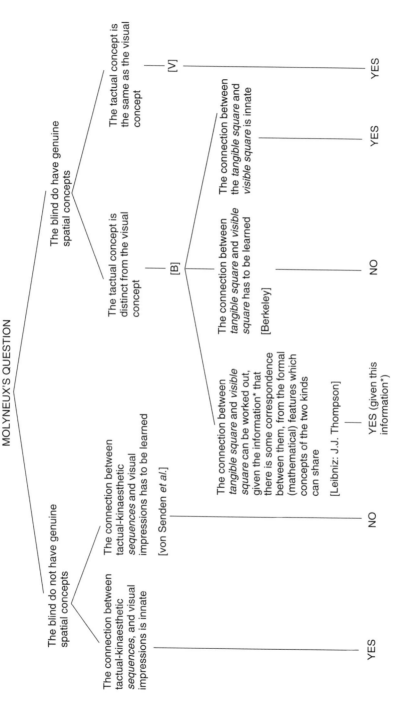

Figure 14.1

tinguish the circle from the square, yet could not name them correctly, but even these results are not guaranteed to be relevant to the central issue, since a capacity to make gross "same/different" judgements is far from establishing visual perception of the figure. A more recent case studied by Gregory seems to confirm a positive answer to Molyneux's Question, but unfortunately the experiments were only carried out a considerable time after the operation.[33] I have been able to track down only two reports of relevant experiments since then, and neither bears unequivocally upon the issue.[34] In view of the delicacy of the experimental conditions, it might be thought to be worth while to make a more theoretical examination of the issue by considering what background theories of perception might sustain the respective positions of B and V, and whether any arguments might be offered for or against them.

II

The next section of our path lies across a minefield. We cannot get closer to the dispute between B and V without getting at least a little clearer about what is involved in a blind subject's (forming a) simultaneous perceptual representation of his vicinity, and to do this, we must work within the framework of some theory of perception and perceptual experience. Fortunately our task is not the elaboration and defence of such a theory, and there will be little in the very general account that I shall put forward with which either party to the dispute is committed to disagree, so that once the minefield is crossed, we can continue our journey on safer terrain.

I want to begin by considering the spatial element in auditory perception. What is involved in a subject's hearing a sound as coming from such-and-such a position in space? I assume that the apparent direction of a sound is a *phenomenal* property of the perception of the sound; just as we hear sounds as high or low, discordant or harmonious, we hear them as coming from this or that direction. I have already mentioned one very important, negative, point: it is not sufficient for an organism to perceive the direction of a sound that it be capable of discriminating, i.e. responding differentially to, sounds which have different directions. "[A]n organism could perfectly well discriminate between values on all the proximal variables that specify position in the third dimension, and yet have no awareness of position in the third dimension *per se*."[35] When we envisage such an organism, we envisage one that can be conditioned to respond differentially to those different values of the proximal stimulus which code the direction of sound, e.g. by pressing a button, yet in whom the difference in stimulus is not connected to any difference in spatial *behaviour*. "Awareness of position in the third dimension" at least involves such a connection. George Pitcher makes this point effectively in his recent book. He considers the suggestion that "position in the auditory field" is a phenomenal property without any intrinsic connection with behaviour, and writes:

> ... suppose the idea is legitimate; suppose, that is, that the direction from which a (phenomenal) sound comes is a purely auditory matter, that it is just another aspect of the perceiver's auditory sense-datum. If so, then it ought to be logically possible for someone to hear the direction from which a certain single sound (a bird-call, for example) is coming, and yet for him not to know in what direction he must point (or walk) if he is to point (or walk) in the direction from which the sound is coming, not to know in what direction he must look if he is to look in that direction, ... and so on for all related abilities.[36]

We do not hear a sound as coming from a certain direction, and then have to *think* or *calculate* which way to turn our heads to look for the source of the sound etc. If this were so, then it should be possible for two people to hear the sound as coming from the same place ("having the same position in the auditory field") and yet be disposed to do quite different things in reacting to the sound. Since this does not appear to make sense, we must say that having the perceptual information at least partly consists in being disposed to do various things (always given, of course, other beliefs and desires which make that reaction to the sound source a sensible thing to do).

The same point also comes out very clearly if we reflect upon how we might specify the spatial information which we imagine the perception to embody. The subject hears the sound as coming from such-and-such a position, but how is that position to be specified? We envisage specifications like this: he hears the sound *up*, or *down*, *to the right* or *to the left*, *in front* or *behind*, or *over there*. It is clear that these terms are *egocentric* terms; they involve the specification of the position of the sound in relation to the observer's own body. But these egocentric terms derive their meaning from their (complicated) connections with the actions of the subject. Some people—including, apparently, Freud—are only able to understand the word "right" via the rule linking it to the hand they write with, and I suppose a similar defect might force someone to rely upon the connection between "down" and the earth's surface, though such a person should not travel into space. But when these terms are understood in this way, they are not suitable for specifying the content of the information embodied in directional perception. No one hears a sound *as coming from the same side as the hand he writes with* in the sense, that, having heard it thus, he has to say to himself "Now I write with this hand" (wiggling his right hand) "so that sound must be coming from over there" (pointing with his right hand). Rather, he can immediately say to himself "It's coming from over there" (pointing with what is in fact his right hand), and may then reflect as an afterthought "and that's the hand I write with." Thus Charles Taylor writes:

Our perceptual field has an orientational structure, a foreground and a background, an up and down. . . . Now this orientational structure marks our field as essentially that of an embodied agent. It is not just that the field's perspective centres on where I am bodily—this by itself doesn't show that I am essentially agent. But take the up–down directionality of the field. What is it based on? Up and down are not simply related to my body; up is not just where my head is and down where my feet are. For I can be lying down, or bending over, or upside down; and in all these cases 'up' in my field is not the direction of my head. Nor are up and down defined by certain paradigm objects in the field, such as earth or sky: the earth can slope for instance . . . Rather, up and down are related to how one would move and act in the field.[37]

Auditory input, or rather, the complex property of auditory input which codes the direction of sound, acquires a spatial *content* for an organism by being linked with behavioural output in an advantageous way. But, at least in the case of adult human beings, the connection is very complex, for the behaviour which is appropriate to a sound at such and such a position is, when described in muscular terms, indefinitely various. This is not merely because the behaviour may involve the movement of different parts of the body; one can run, walk, crawl, or, as in the case of rats in a famous experiment, swim, to a target position. Even if we focus upon a particular kind of behaviour, such as reaching out with the hand for a rattle heard in the dark, there is a similar kind of complexity, since an indefinite range of reaching responses (identified in muscular terms) will be appropriate, depending upon the starting position of the limb, and the route it follows—which need not, and often cannot, be the most direct. It may well be that the input-output connections can only be finitely stated if the output is described in explicitly spatial terms—for example, "extending the arm," "walking forward two feet," etc.—and if this is so, there would certainly not be the reduction, claimed by Poincaré, of this egocentric spatial vocabulary to a muscular vocabulary. Such a reduction is not needed for the point being urged here, which is that the spatial information embodied in auditory perception is only specifiable in a vocabulary whose terms derive their meaning from being linked with bodily actions. Even given an irreducibility, it would remain the case that possession of such information is directly manifestable in uncalculated behaviour; there would just be indefinitely many ways in which the manifestation can be made.[38]

I have used the term "egocentric" in what is close to its literal meaning, and without intending to link my views with any others expressed with the use of the term. I shall occasionally allow myself the shorthand way of speaking in terms of information "specifying a position in behavioural space," but in doing so I shall not be talking about information about a special kind of space, but about a special kind of information about space—information of the type one would possess if one had mastered an egocentric spatial vocabulary, and had received and understood information expressed in it. It is perfectly consistent with the *sense* that I have assigned to this vocabulary that its terms should *refer* to points in a public three-dimensional space.[39]

Although we have told part of the story of what is involved in a subject's having an auditory perception embodying spatial information, we have not told the whole of it. The dispute between B and V concerns the conceptual response of a thinking subject to his perceptual experience, and so the perceptual representations which the debate forces us to consider are states of conscious subjects. When we were thinking of the (simultaneous) perceptual representation which a blind man might form of his immediate environment, we were thinking, however inchoately, of something the possession of which would constitute a perceptual *experience*, i.e. a state of consciousness. But, however addicted we may be to thinking of the links between auditory input and behavioural output in information-processing terms—in terms of computing the solution to simultaneous equations[40]—it seems abundantly clear that evolution could throw up an organism in which such advantageous links were established long before it had provided us with a conscious subject of experience. If this point is not immediately obvious, it can be brought out by reflection on the following possibility. A conscious adult may display fairly normal responses to stimuli (including directional responses to spatially varying stimuli) and yet might have no conscious experience, might sincerely deny that he perceives anything at all. A dramatic illustration is provided by the case of a brain-damaged patient studied by Weiskrantz, who was able to point to a source of light despite claiming that he could not see anything at all.[41]

Reflecting upon this kind of case, philosophers and psychologists have thought that what is required for the application of our intuitive concept of conscious experience is that the subject be able to ascribe the experience to himself: to say or think

"I am having such and such an experience." It is understandable, if one looks at matters in this way, that one should find the concept of little interest; surely, one might think, the experience can antedate thoughts about it. But, though it is true that our intuitive concept requires a subject of experience to have *thoughts*, it is not thoughts about the experience that matter, but thoughts about the world. In other words, we arrive at conscious perceptual experience only when sensory input is not only connected to behavioural dispositions in the way outlined—perhaps in some phylogenetically more ancient part of the brain—but also serves as the input to a thinking, concept-applying, and reasoning system, so that the subject's thoughts, plans and deliberations are also systematically dependent upon the informational properties of the input. (Psychologists sometimes refer to the link I have in mind as "perceptual-verbal encoding.") When there is such a link, we can say that he, the person, rather than just some part of his brain, receives and possesses the information. Of course, these thoughts are not epiphenomena; what a conscious subject does critically depends upon his thoughts, and so there must be links between the system I mention and behaviour. After all, it is only these links that enable us to ascribe any (conceptual) content to those thoughts. Further the intelligibility of the system I have described depends upon there being a *harmony* between the thoughts and the behaviour to which a given sensory state gives rise, but this will seem adventitious only to those who forget that concepts exercised in thought are learned by an organism in whom the links between sensory input and behaviour have already been established. Now, I do not mean to suggest that only those information-bearing aspects of the sensory input for which the subject has concepts can figure in a report of his experience. It is not necessary, for example, that the subject possess the egocentric *concepts* "to the right" etc., for him to have the experience of a sound as being from the right. All I am requiring for conscious experience is that the subject have *some* concepts, some thoughts, and that the content of those thoughts should systematically depend upon the informational properties of the input.

So, to return to our original question, we can say that a subject perceives the directionality of sound if *he* is in an informational state whose content is reportable (not necessarily by him) in egocentric spatial terms. And we must understand *the subject's* possession of the information in terms not only of his unreflective behaviour's systematic dependence upon the sensory input, but also, necessarily, of his thought's systematic dependence on that input too. We have not yet built in, or required, that the subject should be able to hear sounds from different positions simultaneously, but even in the absence of that requirement, we have, in this informational state, a "simultaneous" spatial representation. For the subject hears a sound from one among indefinitely many simultaneously existing positions which define behavioural space. However, it is easy to understand what is involved in the subject's having a simultaneous representation in the stronger sense, of simultaneously hearing two sounds coming from different positions in space. He would then be in a complex informational state the content of which entails the egocentric location of two distinct sounds.

Let us bring these reflections to bear upon the "simultaneous" perceptual representations of space, which earlier we argued the blind man could possess. The spatial information available to him upon the basis of tactual-kinaesthetic perception is much *richer* than that available by hearing, and quite different perceptible phenomena, of course, are specified as located at different positions. However, there is a fundamental point of similarity; when we think of the spatial content of tactual-kinaesthetic perception, we also think of it as specifiable in egocentric terms. Indeed, when he uses his hand, the blind man gains information whose content is partly determined by the disposition he has thereby exercised—for example, that *if* he moves his hand forward such-and-such a distance and to the right he will encounter the top part of a chair. And when we think of a blind man synthesizing the information he receives by a sequence of haptic perceptions of a chair into a unitary representation, we can think of him ending the process by being in a complex informational state which embodies information concerning the egocentric location of each of the parts of the chair; the top *over there, to the right* (here, he is inclined to point or reach out), the back running from *there* to *here*, and so on. Each bit of the information is directly manifestable in his behaviour, and is equally and immediately influential upon his thoughts. One, but not the only, manifestation of this latter state of affairs is the subject's judging that there is a chair-shaped object in front of him.

We started off by thinking about what is involved in perceptions which specify the egocentric position of a stimulus, and we find that we have captured perceptions which convey, at least in a rudimentary way, *shape* or *figure*—i.e. perceptions upon the basis of which shape concepts could be applied. To make the transition, it is necessary to move from auditory spatial perception, which specifies the direction but not the distance of a sound, to a mode of perception which also conveys information about the distance of perceptible phenomena from the subject, so that he can think of a series of points as lying on a plane, and as all being equidistant from him. But no new theoretical departure is made; the content of this information is still specifiable egocentrically—we are still dealing with behavioural space.

It is a consequence of the fact that the spatial content of auditory and tactual-kinaesthetic perceptions must be specified in the same, egocentric, terms, that perceptions from both systems will be used to build up a unitary picture of the world, and hence that spatial concepts applicable upon the basis of one mode of perception must generalize to the other. There is only one behavioural space.[42]

III

There is nothing in the description that I have offered of the spatiality of tactual-kinaesthetic perception with which either party need disagree. Berkeley himself emphasized the egocentricity of the spatial information provided by the tactual-kinaesthetic mode of perception. For example, in the *New Theory of Vision* he writes:

... by touch he [the blind man] could not perceive any motion but what was up or down, to the right or left, nearer or farther from him; besides these and their several varieties or complications, it is impossible he should have any idea of motion.[43]

And it becomes clear that one of Berkeley's main arguments for his negative answer to Molyneux's Question is precisely that the spatiality of vision has nothing to do with the egocentrically specifiable spatial information. In the same section, he continues:

He [the blind man] would not therefore think anything to be motion, or give the name motion to any idea which he could not range under some or other of those particular kinds thereof. But ... it is plain that by the mere act of vision he could not know motion upwards or downwards, to the right or left, or in any other possible direction.

An angel, or unembodied spirit, who had no sense of touch, and who could not act, would have no notions of *up, down, left, right, forwards,* and *backwards,* but, says Berkeley, it could see perfectly well: "i.e. having a clear perception of the proper and immediate objects of sight."[44]

We come here to a theoretical disagreement about the nature of visual perception which might be seen to underlie the dispute between B and V. For, suppose one took a view of the nature of visual perception radically different from the one expressed by Berkeley, by holding that the spatiality of vision is not a primitive datum, but something to be explained in the way we have explained the spatiality of auditory and tactual-kinaesthetic perception. To hold this is to hold that any visual experience of distinct but spatially related phenomena must consist in the subject's possession of spatial information specifiable in egocentric terms. This would then provide a common basis for the application of at least certain fundamental spatial concepts. To explore this possibility further, I want to concentrate upon a streamlined version of Molyneux's Question.

It has been known for many years that direct electrical stimulation of the visual cortex in human subjects produces the experience of a flash of light, or a "phosphene."[45] It is also known that phosphenes can be produced in this way in subjects who have been blind for many years,[46] though, to the best of my knowledge, no attempt has ever been made to produce phosphenes by direct cortical stimulation of the congenitally blind.[47] The repeated stimulation of a given site of the visual cortex with a given intensity reliably produces a phosphene located at the same position in the visual field, and the simultaneous stimulation of two or more distinct sites produces the experience of simple patterns. However, as with the after-images, the phosphenes are experienced as moving when the eye moves. There has been a certain amount of research devoted to the possibility of exploiting this fact to provide a visual prosthesis for the blind.[48] G. S. Brindley, the pioneer of this work, has made long-term cortical implants in two patients, and used them to produce recognizable patterns corresponding to letters of the alphabet, including a fairly good question mark.[49]

The simplified version of Molyneux's Question that I want to consider is this. Suppose it is possible to produce in a congenitally blind man, by the use of a Brindley implant, a pattern of phosphenes exemplifying a shape which previously he had been able to name when he tactually perceived it (for example, a square, or the letter "A"), would he then be able to name the shape correctly? This version of Molyneux's Question avoids certain difficulties in the original question which arise from the complexity of the information which a newly sighted man would receive upon opening his eyes, from the confusion introduced by the movement of his eyes and head, and from the need to separate figure and ground. But the essence of the question is preserved. And I am suggesting that one way in which V could defend his expectation that the blind man will be able to generalize is by arguing as follows. To have the visual experience of four points of light arranged in a square amounts to no more than being in a complex informational state which embodies information about the egocentric location of those lights; for example, one is perceived up and off to the left, another below it, a third up and off to the right, and so on. Now, we are assuming that the subject has been able to form simultaneous perceptual representations of the locations of tactually perceived objects, and this means that he has been in a complex informational state of just this kind before, perhaps when he felt the four corners of a wire square to be occupying these, or similarly related, positions in behavioural space. Of course, the perceptible phenomena apparently located at the various positions in behavioural space in the two cases are different, but the spatial ingredient of the information would be specifiable in the same vocabulary, so that if receipt of such information was sufficient to prompt application of the concept *square* in the tactual case, it is not clear why it should not do so in the visual case.

There is a complication. Although phosphenes are assigned positions "in the visual field," the position does not involve the specification of distance from the observer; in this very pared-down case, visual localization is like auditory localization:

Sperling: Could the woman equate those phosphenes with any prior visual experience?

Brindley: Yes, certainly. She said that they were like stars in the sky. This raises the question of whether they appear to be distant or close to her, but when I tried to probe her on that, and when other people questioned her on that, she was not very consistent. I do not think that she has a definite impression that they are a long way away, or that they are close.[50]

If the blind man was to apply the two-dimensional concept *square*, he would have to think of the points of light as equally far away. Although this is a natural assumption for sighted people when looking at the night sky, since none of the normal distance cues, like occlusion, is present, we cannot say that this would be a natural assumption for the blind man, who has never responded to those cues. So, strictly speaking, a defence of V's position based upon the view of the spatiality of vision being outlined, carries with it the need to enter a slight qualification to his affirmative answer to Molyneux's Question. However, I do not think that it significantly diminishes the interest of his conclusion.

V's position is therefore essentially that advanced by the great Scottish philosopher, Thomas Reid:

To set this matter in another light, let us distinguish betwixt the *position* of objects with regard to the eye, and their *distance* from it. Objects that lie in the same right line drawn from the centre of the eye, have the same position, however different their distances from the eye may be: but objects which lie in different right lines drawn from the eye's centre, have a different position; and this difference of position is greater or less, in proportion to the angle made at the eye by the right lines mentioned. Having thus defined what we mean by the position of objects with regard to the eye, it is evident, that as the real figure of a body consists in the situation of its several parts with regard to one another, so its visible figure consists in the position of its several parts with regard to the eye; and as he that hath a distinct conception of the situation of the parts of the body with regard to one another, must have a distinct conception of its real figure; so he that conceives distinctly the position of its several parts with regard to the eye, must have a distinct conception of its visible figure.[51]

Visual localization is complicated in the normal case by the fact that the eyes can move, so that, even given a single orientation of the head, there is no simple correspondence between points on the two retinas and points in behavioural space. It is not necessary, however, for V to argue that the mechanism whereby account is taken of eye position in computing position in behavioural space must be present at the inception of visual experience. His position is that apparent location in behavioural space is an essential feature of any visual experience which permits the application of two-dimensional spatial concepts, not that the apparent location is accurate, or likely to be accurate, were the visual cortex to be connected to the retina in the standard way.

Nor is it necessary for V to argue that the capacity to apply visual shape concepts rests upon no more than the capacity for visual localization. It obviously does not. I have already mentioned the separation of figure and ground, which is closely tied to the capacity to perceive an object as the same as it moves about in the visual field. Furthermore, sighted people clearly have a capacity to respond to the purely visual similarities of things, as when they recognize a friend by his face, or detect a family resemblance in the faces of father and son, and the application of many visual shape concepts depends upon this capacity. V's position is that if a visual system is capable of providing the experience of distinct but spatially related phenomena then it is *at least* a system which provides the subject with information about the position such phenomena occupy in behavioural space, and that this fact provides a basis for the application of certain very fundamental spatial concepts which is common to vision and touch. What matters to V is that the application of concepts like *straight*, *square*, *between*, etc., should be independent of the capacity to respond to the characteristic look that things have, and not that the application of all shape concepts should be independent of that capacity.

There is certainly nothing in the literature on direct cortical stimulation that contradicts V's contention. What experimenters mean by "point in the visual field" is "apparent point in behavioural space"; when they map cells on to points in the visual field, the subject is asked to point to the apparent source of the light. This, however, may not impress B, since all those studied are late-blind; but it is extremely difficult to see how the spatiality of the experience could be established experimentally in the absence of any links with behavioural space. There *is* a certain amount of evidence that visual localization, and visual shape perception are subserved by different parts of the brain in certain mammals, and that with suitable lesions, they can be separated. Schneider claims that "undercutting the superior colliculus [in a hamster] abolishes the ability to orient toward an object, but not the ability to identify it according to tests of pattern discrimination learning."[52] However, I do not think that this undermines V's position, which concerns the nature of conscious visual experience. It is not difficult to envisage feature detectors of the Hubel and Wiesel type, capable of responding selectively to certain pattern and shape features of the retinal stimulus, operating in the absence of any of the links between stimulus and behaviour which we earlier saw were necessary if the stimulus is to embody localization information. These feature detectors could then be exploited in discriminatory behaviour. But such a system could not provide the basis for the visual experience of shape. When we have the experience of seeing a square, we do not unaccountably find ourselves inclined to judge that there is a square somewhere in the vicinity; we possess information about each of the parts of the square and their relations to one another. The experience of seeing a square, we might say, is a *complex* psychological state. And this, V argues, is because it involves the possession of information about the location of each of the parts of the square in behavioural space. To this claim, Schneider's findings are plainly irrelevant.[53]

So far, I have considered the position on the spatiality of vision which might sustain V's answer to Molyneux's Question to be an empirical theory about the visual system in humans. I want to end by canvassing the possibility that the position can be defended on *conceptual* grounds—the possibility that there are grounds for holding that it does not *make sense* to talk of a subject's perceiving spatially distinct points of light in an extended visual field, unless this can be explained in terms of the subject's receiving information about the location of phenomena in behavioural space. Now, I think sighted people *do* have an incapacity to conceive (i.e. imagine) a visual experience of an array of lights which are not at the same time referred to points in behavioural space, but I do not think that we can rest any weight on this incapacity, which B will argue shows nothing more than our extreme familiarity with the association of points in visual and behavioural space. However, there are weightier considerations.

The first argument is very familiar, and I shall only mention it briefly. B's notion of a visual field generates what we may call *necessarily private facts*. B presumably thinks of the subject's visual field as having an orientation—four distinguishable sides—so that the experience of A is distinguishable from the experience of ∀. (Were this not so, it would not make sense to speak of the motion of something across, or the rotation of something in, the visual field.) The visual field, then, has four sides, *a*, *b*, *c*, *d*, which can be identified from occasion to occasion, and what makes the experience of **A** different from that of ∀ is that in the first case the apex of the **A** is closest to the *a*-side, and in the second it is closest to the *c*-side. Now, on B's theory, the sides of the visual field cannot be distinguished by reference to anything outside the field, and consequently, in identifying them from occasion to occasion, the subject is engaged in the application of a necessarily private concept, something which I believe Wittgenstein has shown to be highly problematic. For there does not appear to be a distinction between the correct and the incorrect application of the names "a," "b," "c," and "d." As I said, this argument is very familiar, and since the present application of the argument introduces nothing new, I shall not say anything further about it.

One who uses this argument of Wittgenstein's plays along with B's notion of the visual field, only to discredit it, so to speak, from the inside. The second argument I want to mention questions the legitimacy of B's describing the visual experience in spatial terms at all. We may start by taking note of the fact that many of the spatial descriptions of visual experience which we are inclined to give are obviously metaphorical. For example, I myself have been speaking of cortical stimulation "producing a pattern of phosphenes arranged in a square," and the literature is replete with such metaphorical talk. It is clear that such descriptions cannot be taken literally; there are not literally four points of light, or indeed four things of any kind, arranged in a square. To think that when a subject seems to see four points of light arranged in a square, there really are four (mental) items *actually* arranged in a square is to commit the sense-datum fallacy. It might be better to call it "the homunculus fallacy," to which it inescapably gives rise. One commits the homunculus fallacy when one attempts to explain what is involved in a subject's being related to objects in the external world by appealing to the existence of an inner situation which recapitulates the essential features of the original situation to be explained— by introducing a relation between the subject and inner objects of essentially the same kind as the relation existing between the subject and outer objects. Thus, we start by wondering what is involved in a subject's gaining knowledge of the spatial relations of outer objects, and we appeal, quite correctly, to an inner, psychological, state—a perceptual experience "of items disposed in the visual field." We cannot then go on to take the "visual field" description literally, by supposing that there are certain items which *in fact* stand in spatial relations. For the question arises again: how are we to understand the subject's capacity to gain knowledge of these relations?[54]

We must therefore always be prepared to replace our metaphorical descriptions of experience in terms of mental items—colour patches, phosphenes, and the like—

with conceptually more innocent descriptions. V's way of thinking about the spatiality of visual experience enables him to do this; "the subject experiences four phosphenes arranged in a square" describes a subject as being in a complex informational state embodying the (non-conceptual) information (or misinformation) that there are four lights located at various positions in his immediate vicinity. Notice: the subject *has* this information, he does not confront it on an inner screen.

How can B cash the metaphor of the four lights in the visual field? He can certainly do nothing along V's lines. It is essential to V's way of avoiding the inner screen that he thinks of a visual experience as an informational, or representational, state—a state which can be assessed as true or false, and hence which refers to something outside itself. The spatiality of the experience is explained in terms of its embodying information about the spatial relations of things. But on B's view, points in the blind man's visual field bear no relation to points in physical space, and this precludes him from conceiving of visual experience as representational. If the existence and spatial relations of objects in the subject's immediate vicinity are not represented, it is difficult to believe that the existence and spatial relations of any other group of objects can be.

B wishes to hold that cortical stimulation of a congenitally blind man may cause him to have an experience which can be described in spatial terms, even though he does not perceive points of light as having positions in behavioural space. When we were content with metaphorical descriptions, there did not seem to be any difficulty—the simulation produced four phosphenes arranged in a square. But once we attempt to dispense with the metaphor, it is not clear that the description of the experience in spatial terms can be defended. If "arranged in a square" cannot come in literally, as a description of the position of phosphenes, and if it cannot come in indirectly, as a description of the apparent position of lights in space, it is not clear that it can come in at all. It certainly cannot come in by virtue of the fact that it is the description that the subject himself is inclined to offer—at least not if B is to continue to give a negative answer to Molyneux's Question.

Much more needs to be said about both of the arguments against B's position which I have mentioned. For example, a full treatment of the subject would involve an extended discussion of the results of the inverting prism experiments.[55] I shall be content if I have shown how Molyneux's Question is linked to these other fundamental issues in the philosophy of mind and perception, and if I have shown that V is not entirely without resources to defend himself.

Notes

[Written during the Winter of 1978, the paper was read at several universities in the first half of 1979. It must be emphasized that in its present form it is a first draft: Evans intended to make substantial revisions, and to incorporate new material. Had he had the opportunity of writing a final version, and preparing it for publication, he would have made acknowledgements where due. Ed. (John McDowell)]

1. Quoted in Locke's *Essay Concerning Human Understanding* II, ix, 8.

2. E. Cassirer, *The Philosophy of the Enlightenment* (Boston, Mass.: Beacon Press, 1951), p. 108.

3. Diderot, *Lettre sur les Aveugles*, translated in M. J. Morgan's *Molyneux's Question* (Cambridge: Cambridge University Press, 1977), p. 108.

4. See the original letter Molyneux sent to Locke in 1688, four years before the one Locke cites in the *Essay* (in the Bodleian Library (MS Locke c. 16, fol. 92)). I owe this reference to W. von Leyden, *Seventeenth Century Metaphysics* (London: Duckworth, 1968), p. 277. See also the letter no. 1064 in *The Correspondence of Locke*, vol. 3, ed. E. de Beer (Oxford: Clarendon Press, 1978).

5. John Mackie claims, in his *Problems from Locke* (Oxford: Clarendon Press, 1976), p. 30, that Locke's negative answer was only to Molyneux's original question, and that he would have answered "Yes" to Diderot's later version. I do not think that this interpretation of Locke can be sustained. See especially the passage immediately following the discussion of Molyneux's Question: ". . . sight . . . conveying to our minds the ideas of light and colours which are peculiar only to that sense; and also the far different ideas of space, figure and motion, the several varieties whereof change the appearance of *its proper object*, viz., light and colours; we bring ourselves *by use* to judge of the one by the other," (*Essay* II, ix, 9— my italics.) This seems to express the straight Berkeleyan position on visual perception of space, and would obviously require a negative answer to Diderot's version of Molyneux's Question also.

6. Quoted in J. S. Mill, *An Examination of William Hamilton's Philosophy* (London: Longmans, 1872), pp. 283–4.

7. H. Lotze, *Metaphysic* II (Oxford: Clarendon Press, 1887), pp. 272–3.

8. M. von Senden, *Space and Sight*, trans. P. Heath (London: Methuen, 1960), pp. 285–6.

9. A. Bain, *The Senses and the Intellect*, 2nd ed., p. 376.

10. This last example comes from T. G. R. Bower's book *Development in Infancy* (San Francisco, Calif.: Freeman, 1974), p. 29. I quite agree with Bower that it is not enough to establish mastery of spatial concepts to show that babies are capable of being conditioned to respond differentially to stimuli whose differences *we* describe in spatial terms.

11. J. J. Gibson, *The Senses Considered as Perceptual Systems* (London: Allen & Unwin, 1968), chap. 13.

12. Pierre Villey, *The World of the Blind* (London: Simpkin, Marshall, Hamilton, Kent & Co., 1922), pp. 183–4.

13. See, e.g., S. Millar, "Spatial Memory by Blind and Sighted Children," *British Journal of Psychology* (1975); "Spatial Representations by Blind and Sighted Children," *Journal of Experimental and Child Psychology* (1976), and L. C. Hartlage, "Development of Spatial Concepts in Visually Deprived Children," *Perceptual and Motor Skills* 42 (1976), pp. 255–8.

14. B. Jones, "The Spatial Perception of the Blind", *British Journal of Psychology* (1975); M. Robin and P. Pecheux, "Problèmes Posés par la réproduction des modèles spatiaux chez les enfants aveugles," *Perception* (1976); J. Juurmaa, "Transposition in Mental Spatial Manipulation" (American Foundation for the Blind Research Bulletin no. 26, June 1973), pp. 87–134. For some further general reflections on the spatial concepts of the blind, see G. Revesz, *The Human Hand* (London: Routledge & Kegan Paul, 1958) and *The Psychology and Art of the Blind* (London: Longmans, 1950); K. Lashley, "Psychological Problems in the Development of Instrumental Aids for the Blind," in P. A. Zahl (ed.) *Blindness* (New York: Haffner, 1962); G. Warnock, "Significance for Philosophy," Appendix to von Senden, op. cit.; and D. Rosencranz and R. Suslick, "Cognitive Models for Spatial Representations in Congenitally Blind, Adventitiously Blind and Sighted Subjects," in *New Outlook for the Blind* 70 (1976), pp. 188–94.

15. H. Poincaré, *The Value of Science* (New York: Dover, 1958), p. 47. See also J. S. Mill, *An Examination of William Hamilton's Philosophy*, 13.

16. *Principles of Human Knowledge*, ed. M. R. Ayers (London: Dent, 1975), sect. 44, p. 89.

17. *New Theory of Vision*, ed. Ayers, sect. 145, p. 51 (my italics).

18. [Evans subsequently noted that there is a disanalogy between this case and Molyneux's, for in the former the concepts *continuous* and *pulsating* apply literally to the experience itself, rather than figuring in the specification of its representational content. Ed. (John McDowell)].

19. The qualification "seems to apply" is designed to take account of the possibility that either representation might be illusory. [Evans was dissatisfied with this paragraph and probably would have rewritten it. ed. (John McDowell)]

20. The qualification "conceptually unconnected" is required so as to preclude a trivialization of B's position; *tangible square* and *visible square* must not be analysable as *square and tangible*, and as *square and visible* respectively.

21. Berkeley himself was clear on this. See the *New Theory of Vision*, sect. 127: "It having been shown that there are no abstract ideas of figure . . . the question now remaining is, whether the particular extensions, figures, and motions perceived by sight be of the same kind with the particular extensions, figures, and motions perceived by touch?"

22. Op. cit., p. 14.

23. Ibid., p. 7. In fairness to Morgan, it should be pointed out that he ends the book with the view that the nativist/empiricist distinction is not a very useful one in terms of which to think of approaches to Molyneux's Question.

24. For the notion of "innate similarity-space" see, e.g., W. V. O. Quine, *Roots of Reference* (La Salle, Ill.: Open Court, 1973), sect. 5. "Some implicit standard . . . for ordering our episodes as more or less similar must therefore antedate all learning, and be innate." See also Quine's "Linguistics and Philosophy," in S. Hook, *Language and Philosophy* (New York: New York University Press, 1969), pp. 95–8.

25. For further explanation of the distinction between conceptual and perceptual representations, see the Appendix to this paper. [This Appendix must be one that Evans planned to write, for as far as I know it does not exist. See instead *The Varieties of Reference* (Oxford: Clarendon Press, 1982), chap. 5, pp. 122–9. Ed. (John McDowell)].

26. Nor is the innateness of the blind man's capacity to perceive spatially the ground of the dispute between them. On my construal of the debate, both B and V attribute to the blind man this capacity, hence arguments, or evidence, for the innateness of this capacity affects both of them equally.

27. "Molyneux's Question," *Journal of Philosophy* 71 (1974), p. 637.

28. H. P. Grice, "Some Remarks about the Senses," in R. J. Butler (ed.), *Analytical Philosophy* (Oxford: Blackwell, 1962).

29. *New Essays on the Human Understanding*, IX, 8.

30. Ibid.

31. Berkeley, *New Theory of Vision*, sect. 142.

32. *The Theory of Vision Vindicated and Explained*, sect. 71.

33. R. L. Gregory and J. Wallace, "Recovery from Early Blindness—a case study," in R. L. Gregory, *Concepts and Mechanisms of Perception* (London: Duckworth, 1974), pp. 65–129.

34. A. Valvo, *Sight Restoration after Long Term Blindness* (New York: American Foundation for the Blind, 1971); H. Umezu, S. Torii, and Y. Uemura, "Postoperative Formation of Visual Perception in the Early Blind," *Psychologia* 18 (1975), pp. 171–86.

35. T. G. R. Bower, "Infant Perception of the Third Dimension and Object Concept Development," in L. Cohen and P. Salapatek (eds.), *Infant Perception* (New York: Academic Press, 1975), p. 34. Bower credits the point to Irving Rock.

36. G. Pitcher, *A Theory of Perception* (Princeton, N.J.: Princeton University Press, 1971), p. 189.

37. C. Taylor, "The Validity of Transcendental Arguments," *Proceedings of the Aristotelian Society* (1979), p. 154.

38. Egocentric spatial terms, and spatial descriptions of bodily movement would then form a structure familiar to philosophers under the title "holistic." For a study of concepts interrelated in this way, see C. A. B. Peacocke, *Holistic Explanation* (Oxford: Clarendon Press, 1979).

39. Since coining the term "behavioural space," I have found it used in roughly the same sense by C. B. Trevarthen; see "Two Mechanisms of Perception in Primates," in *Psychologische Forschung* 31 (1968), p. 302: "Animals act as though they were continuously cognizant of a space for behaviour around the body. . . . In this world acts are made from the body as centre and origin. Therefore the spatial frame for activity has a symmetry imposed upon it; it is bisymmetric with the midplane of the body and polarized in the antero-posterior direction of the body axis. I shall call this body-centred space *behavioural space*."

40. For the mechanism of auditory localization, see, e.g., P. H. Lindsay and D. A. Norman, *Human Information Processing* (New York: Academic Press, 1977), pp. 178–88. For the writings of an addict, see J. Fodor, *The Language of Thought* (Brighton, Sussex: Harvester

Press, 1976), pp. 42–53. One of the disadvantages of the addiction is that it tends to blur the distinction I am trying to explain.

41. L. Weiskrantz, E. K. Warrington, M. D. Saunders and J. Marshall, "Visual Capacity in the Hemianopic Field following a Restricted Occipital Ablation," *Brain* 97 (1974), pp. 709–28. "But always he was at a loss for words to describe any conscious perception, and repeatedly stressed that he saw nothing at all in the sense of 'seeing,' and that he was merely guessing" (p. 721).

42. See S. J. Freedman and J. H. Rekosh, "The Functional Integrity of Spatial Behaviour," in S. J. Freedman (ed.), *The Neuropsychology of Spatially Oriented Behaviour* (Homewood. Ill.: Dorsey, 1968).

43. *New Theory of Vision*, sect. 137.

44. Ibid., sect. 95.

45. For a review, see G. S. Brindley "Sensory Effects of Electrical Stimulation of the Visual and Paravisual Cortex," in R. Jung (ed.), *Visual Centres of the Brain*, Handbook of Sensory Physiology 7, 3, *b* (Berlin: Springer-Verlag, 1973), chap. 26.

46. W. H. Dobelle, M. G. Mladejovesky, and J. P. Girvan, 'Artificial Vision for the Blind', *Science* 183 (1974), pp. 440–4.

47. The closest we come to a study of phosphenes in the congenitally blind is in the report of W. Schodtman ("Ein Beitrag zur lehre von der Optischen Lokalisati bei Blindgebronen," *Archiv für Ophthalmologie* 54 (1902), pp. 256–67) who claimed that 'pressure phosphenes' could be produced in such subjects by pressure on their eyes, and that these phosphenes were located in behavioural space; located "up" if the pressure was on the lower part of the eyeball, and "down" if on the upper. However, there is a certain amount of doubt about whether this claim can be believed. I owe the reference to I. Rock.

48. For a recent review, see W. H. Dobelle, "Current State of Research on Providing Sight to the Blind by Electrical Stimulation of the Brain," *Journal of Impairment and Blindness* 71 (1977), pp. 290–7. See also T. D. Sperling (ed.), *Visual Prosthesis* (New York: Academic Press, 1971).

49. G. S. Brindley and W. S. Lewin, "The Sensations Produced by Electrical Stimulation of the Visual Cortex," *Journal of Physiology* 196 (1968), pp. 479–93.

50. Telephone conversation with G. S. Brindley, in *Visual Prosthesis*, op. cit., p. 48.

51. Thomas Reid, *An Inquiry into the Human Mind*, ed. T. Duggan (Chicago, Ill.: University of Chicago Press, 1970), p. 113. I presume Reid must mean to be referring to "the Cyclopean eye."

52. G. S. Schneider, "Two Visual Systems," in *Science* 163 (1969), p. 901. A similar but by no means identical distinction between "ambient" and "focal" perception has been suggested by C. Trevarthen, in the paper cited earlier.

53. The considerations of this paragraph strongly suggest that a great deal of the work on computer vision—computer simulation of visual perception—is based upon a mistake. The problem is conceived to be that of simulating the human subject's capacity to describe his environment, and so, fundamentally a problem of devising a sufficiently complicated pattern-recognizing program. Whatever it is that one may reach by this route, it does not remotely

resemble the psychology of a conscious human subject, since there is nothing which corresponds to the human's non-conceptual representation of his environment—i.e. nothing which corresponds to visual experience. If the argument of this paper is along anything like the right lines, that defect will not be rectified until attention shifts to the study of programs for computers which control behaviour in a spatial world.

54. The link between the sense-datum fallacy and the homunculus fallacy is brought out well in Ryle's *Concept of Mind* (Harmondsworth: Penguin, 1963), pp. 200–11.

55. For such a discussion, see I. Rock, *The Nature of Perceptual Adaptation* (New York: Basic Books, 1966).

15

Ways of Coloring: Comparative Color Vision as a Case Study for Cognitive Science

Evan Thompson, Adrian Palacios, and Francisco J. Varela

The study of color vision provides a microcosm of research in cognitive science: Each of the disciplines that compose cognitive science has made significant contributions to our understanding of color. Neuroscientists have had some success in uncovering the anatomical and physiological correlates of color vision in the visual system, primarily in primates (DeValois and DeValois 1975; Livingstone and Hubel 1984; Zeki 1983); cellular biologists have characterized the retinal basis of sensitivity (Brown and Wald 1964; Dartnall et al. 1983; Svaetichin and MacNichol 1958); molecular biologists have isolated and sequenced the genes for the three different types of color-sensitive photopigments in the human eye (Nathans et al. 1986); psychophysicists have contributed quantitative models for human visual performance (Hurvich 1985; Hurvich and Jameson 1957; Jameson 1985); cognitive psychologists have provided models of the structure of human color categories (Heider 1972; Rosch 1973); linguists have shown that human languages contain a limited number of "basic" color terms (Berlin and Kay 1969) and have provided models to derive these semantic universals from properties of the visual system (Kay and McDaniel 1978); researchers in computational vision and artificial intelligence have devised computational models and algorithms for color constancy (Gershon 1987; Hurlbert 1986; Land 1983; Maloney 1985; Maloney and Wandell 1986); and finally, philosophers have discussed the ontological status of color and its implications for theories of mind and perception (Hardin 1988; Hilbert 1987; Thompson 1989).

This target article is intended as a contribution to this ongoing interdisciplinary effort. We propose to offer here a new empirical and philosophical perspective on color vision, one based on recent experimental research in *comparative* color vision—studies of color vision in various animal species. We do not intend to provide a detailed scientific review of current research on this topic (see Goldsmith

1990; Jacobs 1981; and Nuboer 1986). Rather, we wish to draw on this material, especially recent research on fishes, birds, and insects, to cast new light on some fundamental questions in visual perception, cognitive science, and the philosophy of mind.

Our presentation has three stages. In the first, we provide an overview of various types of explanation for color vision in contemporary visual science, showing how particular types of explanation have been used to motivate various views about what color *is*, that is, about the ontology of color. As we shall see, those who favor objectivism about color, the view that colors are perceiver-independent physical properties (Hilbert 1987; Matthen 1988), rely on computational vision, whereas those who favor subjectivism, the view that colors are internal sensory qualities (Hardin 1988), rely on psychophysics and neurophysiology. In the second stage, we propose a broader comparative and evolutionary perspective on color vision. We present what we call "the comparative argument," which purports to show that an adequate account of color must be *experientialist* (unlike objectivism) and *ecological* (unlike subjectivism). In the third stage, we explore the implications of the comparative argument for vision research. We argue that the typical emphasis in computational vision on optimally "recovering" prespecified features of the environment (i.e., distal properties whose specification is thought to be independent of the sensory-motor capacities of the animal) is unsatisfactory. Instead, visual perception is better conceived as the visual guidance of activity in an environment that is constituted largely by that very activity. Here we present what we call an "enactive" approach to perception (proposed originally by Varela 1979; 1984; 1989; 1991a; and developed subsequently by Varela et al. 1991). We then suggest some directions for further research that follow from our discussion.

1   Explanation in Visual Science and the Ontology of Color

1.1   Levels of Explanation: A Brief Overview

A central concern in contemporary visual science (indeed throughout all cognitive science) is the relation among various levels of generalization and explanation. Following Churchland and Sejnowski (1988), we can distinguish several notions of "level" at work in cognitive science: levels of analysis, of organization, and of operation ("processing"). Because these notions will prove to be of use in our discussion of color vision, we review them briefly here.

In vision research, the notion of levels of analysis is most familiar from the work of Marr and Poggio (1977). In their framework, vision requires analysis and explanation at three different levels: (i) the level of computational theory; (ii) the level of algorithm; and (iii) the level of physical implementation. The computational level is an abstract analysis of the problem or task, which for early vision, according to Marr and Poggio, is the recovery of three-dimensional scenes from ambiguous two-dimensional projections, otherwise known as "inverse optics" (Marr 1982; Poggio et al. 1985). For color vision, the inverse optics problem is to recover the invariant surface spectral reflectances of objects in a scene. The algorithmic level is concerned with the specific formal procedures required to perform a given computational task. Finally, the level of physical implementation is concerned with how the algorithms are physically realized in biological or artificial systems.

It is well known that Marr (1982) claimed that these three levels of analysis were largely independent. In the study of biological vision, Marr also supposed that the algorithmic level corresponds to psychophysics and to parts of neurophysiology, whereas the implementational level corresponds to most of neurophysiology and neuroanatomy (1982, p. 26). This conception of explanation in visual science, especially as applied to the study of natural vision, has generated considerable discussion and debate. Among other things, many dispute Marr's (1982) claim that the three levels of analysis are largely independent. Some favor a more "bottom up" approach to the explanation of visual processes, and some criticize Marr's assumption of optimality at the computational level, that is, that "what is being computed is optimal in some sense or is guaranteed to function correctly" (1982, p. 19) [see also Schoemaker, "The Quest for Optimality: A Positive Heuristic of Science?" *BBS* 14(2) 1991; and Anderson, "Is Human Cognition Adaptive?" *BBS* 14(3) 1991.] We do not intend to review all of these controversies here.[1] We mention them, rather, as pointers toward some of the issues that will arise shortly when we discuss models of color vision, and when we present our alternative "enactive" approach to visual perception in section 3.

In contrast to the notion of levels of analysis, the notion of levels of organization is relatively straightforward. In the nervous system, we find highly organized structures at many different scales from molecules to synapses, neurons, neuronal ensembles, neural networks, maps, systems, and so on. Each level has properties specific to it, which in turn require different techniques for their investigation. Such organizational complexity is certainly evident in color vision, ranging from the chemical properties of receptor photopigments to the network properties of retinal and cortical cells.

Finally, in addition to these levels of organization, we find many levels of operation in the nervous system. How these levels are to be assigned, however, is considerably less clear than it is for levels of organization. The typical procedure is to order the levels hierarchically from peripheral (lower) to central (higher) areas (measured in terms of synaptic distance from sensory stimulation), thereby suggesting that "processing" in the nervous system proceeds sequentially. We wish, however, to dissociate the notion of levels of operation from the idea that processing among the levels is sequential. If (as we and many others believe) "higher" levels can significantly affect the processing in "lower" levels, then the notion of sequential processing will be of limited application, or at least will have to be modified considerably. To cite just one example that is relevant for our discussion here: Although the visual system is typically described as carrying out sequential processing from retina to lateral geniculate nucleus (LGN) to visual cortex, it is also well known that there are massive back-projections from all areas of the cortex to the thalamic nuclei (Steriade and Deschenes 1985). In the case of the visual system, there are actually more fibers going down from the visual cortex to the LGN than go in the reverse direction (Robson 1983). This organization suggests that neuronal activity in central levels may considerably modulate the activity at peripheral levels, an idea that is also supported by some recent experiments (e.g., Varela and Singer 1987). We set this issue aside here. However the relations among levels of operation must ultimately be conceptualized, it is obvious that there are various levels to be distinguished. For example, in primate color vision, we need to understand at the very least the two-way interactions between operations in the retina, thalamus, striate (VI) and peristriate (V4) visual cortex.

With these three notions of "level" in hand we can now turn specifically to color vision. In the remainder of section 1 we give a brief overview of the types of explanation offered for color vision, showing how they have been used to motivate contrasting philosophical positions on the ontology of color.

1.2   Color Space: Psychophysics and Neurophysiology

In general, psychophysics and neurophysiology have taken as their point of departure what is known as "color space." This is the closed space formed by the three semi-independent dimensions of color known as hue, chroma or saturation, and value or brightness (figure 15.1).[2] Hue obviously refers to the redness, greenness, yellowness, or blueness of a given color. Saturation refers to the proportion of hue in a given color relative to the achromatic (white-black) dimension: Saturated colors have a comparatively greater degree of hue, whereas desaturated colors are comparatively closer to gray. Brightness refers to the achromatic or white-black dimen-

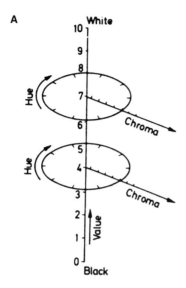

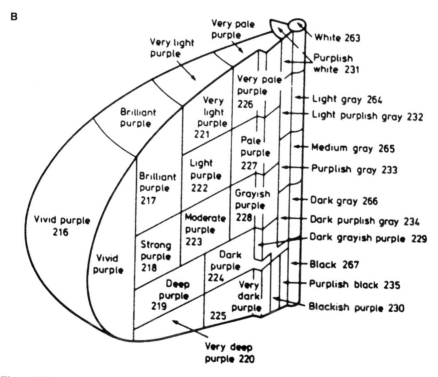

Figure 15.1

The phenomenal structure of human color space. (a) The three-dimensional space of hue, saturation or chroma, and brightness. We use here the standard Munsell color space. (b) A slice in color space for the purple sector (Munsell values 3P–9P), using the ISCC-NBS color names (or equivalent centroid numbers).

sion. In this space, colors can be seen to exhibit certain relations among themselves, such as the hue-opponency of red and green, and yellow and blue. These kind of relations compose what we call the *phenomenal structure of color space*, or simply the *phenomenal structure of color*.

How are we to explain the generation of this phenomenal structure? Why does (our) color space have this phenomenal structure and not some other? It is primarily this question that has motivated the psychophysical and neurophysiological study of color vision. Rather than review this enormous field, we present merely a few points that are relevant for our purposes in this paper.[3] The basic idea is to provide a mapping from the phenomenal color space of Figure 1 into a new color space whose coordinates correspond to psychophysical and/or neurophysiological processes relevant for color vision. We call the axes of these new color spaces "color channels." Strictly speaking, channels are specified psychophysically and so are not isomorphic with unique neuronal pathways (Boynton 1988, p. 77), but we intend to use the term "channel" both in this psychophysical sense and somewhat more loosely to refer to underlying neurophysiological processes (such as color opponent receptive field properties) that can be studied at various levels of analysis, organization, and operation.

We should note that the following maps of color space are idealized. We do not intend to suggest that they provide full-fledged "linking propositions" needed to identify chromatic perceptual states and states of the visual substrate (see Teller 1984; 1990; Teller and Pugh 1983). Visual science is still far from being able to provide the full story of how the activity in multiple neuronal areas becomes integrated to form our experience of color. Our intention, however, is simply to provide some illustrations of the kinds of covariance that have been established between aspects of the phenomenal and the biological.

We begin with the three kinds of retinal cones, short-wave ($S^1 = S$), medium-wave ($S^2 = M$), and long-wave ($S^3 = L$), which respond with a differential sensitivity to wavelength according to the photopigment they carry in their outer segments (figure 15.2a, bottom). At this level, we can construct a rudimentary map of color space whose coordinates correspond to the relative activity of the cones, which are present (in various proportions) at each point of the visual field. This map corresponds to a vector $\vec{s}_r = \langle S^1, S^2, S^3 \rangle((\vec{r})$, where $\vec{r}$ is the surface coordinate. A convenient representation is a (Maxwell) triangle (figure 15.2b) instead of a 3-D graph to depict the spectral loci of monochromatic lights: The three kinds of cone receptor appropriately adjusted in activation are required to match a test-light of any spectral composition and intensity. This property corresponds to the *trichromacy* of normal human color vision.

We refer to this mapping of color space as "rudimentary" because it takes into account only the relative absorptions of the cone photopigments. Postreceptor cells, however, both combine and compare (substract) cone signals, thereby giving rise to three new types of color channels: two opponent chromatic channels (R-G, Y-B) and one nonopponent achromatic channel (Wh-Bk), which can be found in primates at the retinal and thalamic levels (figure 15.2c). These new channels result, then, from linear combinations of the receptor activations, which can be written vectorially as $\vec{c}_r = \mathrm{M} \cdot \vec{s}_r$, $\vec{c}_r = \langle C^1, C^2, C^3 \rangle (\vec{r})$, with C^1 = Wh-Bk, C^2 = R-G, C^3 = Y-B. The matrix M for constructing the channels is at the core of various color vision theories (Wyszecki and Stiles 1982); we return to provide an algorithm for its determination below in section 2. These three color channels proper can be used to provide a set of axes for color space (figure 15.2c). This diagram thus displays the trivariance of human color vision mapped onto the three dimensions of color space at the physiological level.

This mapping, too, has limitations, for it relies on an analogy between the existence of opponent colors and the existence of chromatically opponent cells, which though obviously promising nonetheless neglects many details of the fit between properties of color perception and the properties of these peripheral cells (Hood and Finklestein 1983; Teller 1990). It also does not take into account the multilevel neuronal interactions in the visual pathway that somehow constitute our entire experience of color (Livingstone and Hubel 1984; Zeki 1983).

To obtain axes more appropriate for this level we need to use psychophysical global response functions. The functions chosen will depend on which aspect of color experience we are interested in quantifying more precisely, for example, chromatic sensitivity, discrimination. or color mixing (see Wyszecki and Stiles 1982). For our purposes here, one useful standard set comprises the empirically determined CIE (Commission Internationale de l'Eclairage) color-matching functions $\langle x, y, z \rangle (\lambda)$, which specify the well-known human chromaticity diagram (figure 15.2d). To project our three-dimensional color space into this two-dimensional plane we equalize for brightness. At the center is the achromatic neutral (white/gray) point: movements away from the point indicate an increase in saturation, with the maximally saturated hues along the periphery. In this chromaticity diagram, we find complementary colors at the opposite ends of the space, the pure spectral locus at the outermost boundary, and the purple range as "nonspectral" loci. Thus *any* color

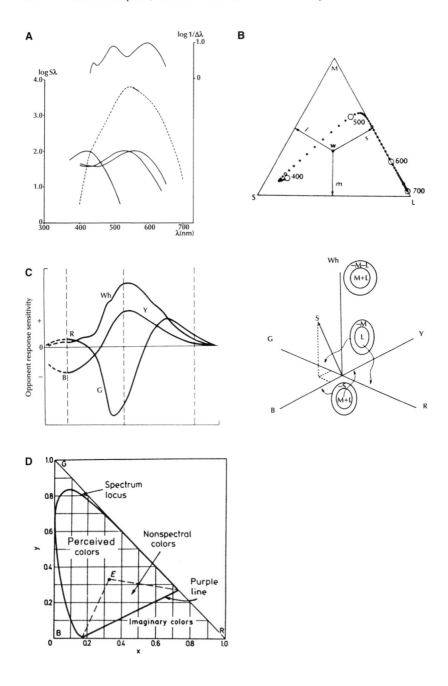

we perceive can be matched in this space by an appropriate value of the underlying channels (global response functions). It should be made clear that although strictly speaking the CIE diagram is a *stimulus* space, the stimuli are useful in characterizing color experience by mapping its extent, and so the CIE diagram can be read as a mapping of one aspect of color experience. (This point will also apply to the relation between the stimulus spaces and color perception in other animals as discussed below).

These color-matching functions were derived mostly for purely psychophysical and industrial purposes and so are not particularly useful as a guide to underlying neuronal processes. Nevertheless, they do provide a more precise and quantitative way of mapping some aspects of the phenomenal structure of color space. It should be noted that alternative color channels motivated by computational algorithms (Land 1983) and perceptual and neurobiological data (Zeki 1980; 1983; 1985) have been proposed by taking into account the global integration properties of visual mechanisms, because a local description (i.e., independent of the rest of the visual field) violates perceptual evidence and neurophysiological data. For example, Land (1983) proposes three lightness "indicators," which result from discarding the illuminant from the receptor activity after long-range integration of local values.

◀ Figure 15.2
Biological mappings of human color space at various levels. (a) The spectral absorption of human cone pigments and the overall photopic sensitivity curve for humans (in discontinuous lines). In the upper part a plot of the wavelength discrimination curve (reciprocal of the just noticeable difference in wavelength necessary for wavelength discrimination). Modified from Nuboer (1986). (b) For any light, the relative Long/Medium/Short wave length absorptions (L, M, S) can be plotted as relative activity on a Maxwell triangle with orthogonal axes l, m, s of unit length. The loci of pure spectral colors are shown calculated by normalizing the pigment spectra for equal areas and computing the quantum catch. Equal absorption for all three areas is labeled as w. From Goldsmith (1990). (c) On the left, opponent neural system obtained by the weighted excitatory and inhibitory responses between retinal elements. On the right, a diagram showing how each of these channels can be used to provide a set of axes for color space. The Wh-Bk (White-Black) channel receives excitatory input mostly from L and M cones, whereas the two antagonistic channels receive both excitatory and inhibitory inputs: $+L - M$ for the R-G (Red-Green) channel, and $(M + L) - S$ for the Y-B (Yellow-Blue) channel. From Hurvich (1981) and Ingling and Tsou (1977). (d) Chromacity diagram computed from the three CIE (Commission Internationale de l'Eclairage) 1931 color matching functions. As in (b) the relative activities have been normalized so that two values suffice to locate all points in this modified triangle.

We have now provided enough illustrations of the various neurophysiological and psychophysical mappings of color space for this target article. Henceforth, we will use the term "color space" to refer to this kind of composite representation in which the phenomenal structure of color and the structure of the visual system covary. For our purposes here, then, color space refers to the following multilevel description:

(i) receptor space: the raw array of local activity under given illumination conditions in a scene;

(ii) "lightness" indicator space: the globally integrated activity at various levels after discarding the illuminant from the receptor space via lateral interactions;

(iii) physiological channels space: the local activity of subtraction and addition of integrated values to conform to antagonistic mechanisms obtained from indicator values;

(iv) psychophysical channel space: the perceptual, high-level integration into separable mechanisms, obtained on the basis of the underlying physiological activity relevant to color channels;

(v) phenomenal space: the color appearance space of hue, saturation, and brightness.

The main task of the psychophysical and neurophysiological study of color vision is to uncover the appropriate biological processes underlying all these levels and to formulate, test, and establish the "linking propositions" needed to relate the various levels (Teller 1984; 1990; Teller and Pugh 1983). As a matter of general principle, however, it is clear that the phenomenal structure of color covaries with the structure (and, as we shall see later, the ecological interactions) of the perceiver. If we wish to explore this fact, we should determine whether and how changes in the structure (and ecological interactions) of the perceiver can be correlated with changes in the phenomenal structure that color exemplifies. This is the main task of this target article.

1.3 Computational Color Vision

A full explanation of color vision requires that we also understand how color appearances remain relatively stable or constant in natural light environments—a phenomenon known as *color constancy*. Computational color vision is particularly concerned with this phenomenon. Because the retinal activity from a given point hopelessly confounds the illumination with the reflectance properties of surfaces, the core problem is to disentangle these variables and assign colors that correlate with surface properties.

In what follows, the ideas we present naturally take a mathematical form, which cannot be simplified without losing some important features. The nonmathematical reader can skip the formulae, however, without losing the basic points we need for our argument here. (Our presentation throughout this section is indebted to the more detailed treatment in Hurlbert 1989, ch. 3).

Most computational models simplify the overall situation by considering only the surface reflectance (or albedo), which depends on object properties, not on viewing geometry, as in [1]:

$$I(\lambda, \vec{r}) = \rho(\lambda, \vec{r}) E(\lambda, \vec{r}) \tag{1}$$

where I is the irradiance, λ is wavelength, E is the surface illumination, and ρ is the reflectance, and $\vec{r}$, as before, is the surface coordinate. The irradiance affects an array of sensors which have a specific nonlinear response function $R^i(\lambda)$, $i = 1, \ldots, n_{recep}$, comprising a number of different cone classes (e.g., for primates $n_{recep} = 3$). Under these conditions the raw receptor response corresponding to a point $\vec{r}$ from a surface is the integral:

$$S^i(\vec{r}) = \int_{visible\ window} d\lambda\ R^i(\lambda) \rho(\lambda, \vec{r}) E(\lambda, \vec{r}) \tag{2}$$

We have written "visible window" simply to indicate the extent of the wavelength sensitivity depending on the species being considered. For primates, this "visible" range is approximately 400–700 nm: for insects it shifts down to approximately 310–590 nm; in birds it broadens to approximately 350–720 nm.

As we mentioned above, the computational approach to color constancy is a prime example of inverse optics—the recovery of what are taken to be objective attributes of three-dimensional scenes from ambiguous two-dimensional projections. In the case of color vision, the problem is to discard the source illuminant E and retain the invariant spectral reflectances ρ of object surfaces given only the retinal activity S. This problem—like inverse optics problems generally—is underscored or ill-posed. (Poggio et al. 1985). To solve an ill-posed problem one must restrict the class of admissible solutions by introducing constraints; these constraints are said to "regularize" the problem. In the case of color vision, a combination of empirical evidence and task-level analysis has shown that these constraints are basically of three kinds: (i) low-dimensional models of lights and reflectance; (ii) global computations; and (iii) spatial segmentation.

1.3.1 Low Dimensionality. Naturally occurring illuminants and object reflectances can be described as lying within a low-dimensional space: A few basis functions, when added together in the correct proportions, suffice to span the entire diversity of actual lights and reflectances. Formally expressed this becomes:

$$E(\lambda, \vec{r}) = \sum_{j=1}^{n_{illum}} \varepsilon_j(\vec{r}) E_j(\lambda)$$

$$\rho(\lambda, \vec{r}) = \sum_{k=1}^{n_{reflec}} \zeta_k(\vec{r}) \rho_x(\lambda) \tag{3}$$

where E_j and ρ_k are basis functions, and ε_j and ζ_k are spatially varying coefficients. On the basis of empirical evidence from measurements of typical ambient conditions and object reflectances, n_{illum} and n_{reflec} are usually taken to be 3 or at most 6 (Maloney 1985). It is typically further assumed that illumination is quite uniform over space,

$$E(\lambda, \vec{r}) = E(\lambda), \varepsilon_j(\vec{r}) = \varepsilon_j \tag{4}$$

and that reflectance is invariant under changes in viewing geometry (i.e., a Lambertian reflection model). Thus, computational color vision is fundamentally constrained by the low dimensionally of *both* the stimuli and the receptor types, because these are known to come in small numbers.

Under these conditions the irradiance equation (2) takes the general form:

$$S^i(\vec{r}) = T^{ik}(\varepsilon)\zeta_k(\vec{r}) \tag{5}$$

where

$$T^{ik}(\varepsilon) = \sum_j \varepsilon_j \tau_{jik}, = \int d\lambda \, R^i(\lambda)\rho_k(\lambda)E_j(\lambda) \tag{6}$$

The matrix, $T^{ik}(\varepsilon)$ (which Maloney calls the "light transformation matrix"), depends on the illuminance and reflectance basis functions, the sensory sensitivities, which are fixed, and the illuminant, which is variable. Clearly, since this matrix and the $\zeta_k(\vec{r})$ are, in general, not entirely known, the equations are underdetermined, and to find solutions further constraints need to be introduced. These take various forms. For example, Buchsbaum (1980) requires that a weighted average of all reflectances in a given scene be known. In contrast, Maloney and Wandell (1986), and Yuille (1984), assume that there is at least one more sensor type than there are reflectance components. This assumption obviates the need for the previous ones, and exploits instead the various sensors at each location. For instance, using only photoreceptors, these algorithms would recover constant colors for materials that can be described using no more than two basis functions. Finally, D'Zmura and Lennie (1986) introduce eye movements and light adaptations to recover illuminants.

1.3.2 Global Computations. The foregoing discussion focused on the quality of the light signals and the number of receptors, but it did not take into account the way the local activity of a photoreceptor, $S^i(\vec{r})$, is not the most significant variable. More relevant to account for color constancy and chromatic induction is the interaction of receptor activity over distant places in the visual scene, which transforms luminance (a quantity which expresses a local level of activity) into "lightness," $L^i(\vec{r})$, a level of activity closer to reflectance (and one that is relative to other levels of activity in the scene). These global interactions can all be understood as a manifestation of the lateral interactions and reentrant circuits typical of both the retina and parts of the visual system, which lead to internally specified values rather than raw sensory values.

There are a number of equivalent "lightness" algorithms (Hurlbert 1986). In general, though, lightness algorithms proceed by (i) taking a differential of values of the intensity over different locations of space: (ii) applying a threshold operation that eliminates small values because of smooth changes in the illumination and retains large values resulting from abrupt changes in reflectance at the borders between patches; and (iii) integrating the result of this operation back into reflectance values for each position in space. For example, one of the first algorithms, proposed by Horn (1974), obtains lightness by simulating a diffusion of the activity of one receptor over the entire layer. Mathematically, this is expressed as a solution to the Poisson equation on the receptor activity:

$$\nabla^2 L^i(\vec{r}) = \theta[\nabla^2 S^i(\vec{r})] \tag{7}$$

where $\theta[.]$ is a thresholding operation performed on the Laplacian operator ∇^2, which embodies the neural lateral interactions. When the sensor array is finite, and surrounded by a constant boundary condition, [7] can be solved explicitly. More recently, global computations have been approached by noticing that each sensory receptive field has an excitatory center and an inhibitory periphery that can be seen as a filter for the light signal. It is also known that these receptive fields have various sizes and degrees of steepness. Thus, a family of recent algorithms assumes that the sensor array is convolved through a center-periphery profile at each point of the visual scene (Land 1986) and at various scales (Hurlbert 1986). In this case:

$$L^i(\vec{r}) = \int_{\text{Scale range}} d\mu \int_{\text{Region}} d\vec{q} \Theta[\nabla^2 G(\vec{r}-\vec{q};\mu)S^i(\vec{q})] \qquad (8)$$

where G is a Gaussian function, with a continuum of parameters μ. The Laplacian of G is roughly equivalent to a difference of Gaussians (DOG function), similar to receptive fields. Expression (8) degrades when approximated in the discrete case, but sums over ten scales of μ yield reasonable lightness values for so-called "Mondrian" scenes (displays consisting of about 100 different colored papers arranged arbitrarily that resemble the paintings of Piet Mondrian).

1.3.3 Spatial Segmentation. Even with low-dimensional constraints and network global computations, reflectances are still underdetermined. One missing key element is the way a scene is segmented into the relevant patches on which the calculation of reflectance will be performed. Some extra assumptions about surfaces (abruptness of change, distributed averages, etc.) must therefore be brought to bear. These assumptions in part miss the purpose of color vision, which is presumably important in object discrimination and identification (D'Zmura and Lennie 1986), a point to which we return in later sections. The overall effect of segmentation is to make reflectance values correspond not to local scene coordinates r, but to regions σ, yielding lightness values over *regions*, L^i_σ, $\sigma \varepsilon \Sigma$. One of the better known segmentation algorithms is the one from Rubin and Richards (1982; 1988), which seeks to determine where material changes occur in a scene using only spectral intensity responses in separate points on the retina. For example, we can state this idea by considering two different receptors, which will have a spectral crosspoint on opposite sides of an edge when:

$$[S^i(\vec{r}_1) - S^i(\vec{r}_2)][S^j(\vec{r}_1) - S^j(\vec{r}_2)] < 0 \qquad (9)$$

If the product is negative, one channel increases while the other decreases. Such a crosspoint will be produced only by material changes, under such simplifying assumptions as uniform illumination. In addition, one can consider the signs of the slopes of each response function (opposite slope sign condition). There are conditions in which these algorithms will not segment a scene into material discontinuities but will give false positives because of shadows, occlusions, or illuminant variations.

Another model for segmentation is provided by D'Zmura and Lennie (1986). In this model, mechanisms of light adaptation ("a multiplicative change in sensitivity in the independent cone mechanisms followed by an adaptive linear transformation of scaled cone signals at color-opponent sites" [p. 1670]), combined with eye movements that expose the eyes to the average light reflected from the field of view, are used to evaluate and discount the illuminant, thereby recovering reflectance designators. This scheme does not rely on a prior segmentation of the scene. Instead, the designators are transformed to yield estimates of hue, which is, compared to saturation and lightness, relatively independent of object shape and viewing geometry. These hue estimates can then be used in the task of segmentation.

These three elements—low-dimensional constraints, global integration, and scene segmentation—must come together for artificial systems to regularize the ill-posed problem of recovering reflectance. Since the assumptions introduced are about the natural world, they can be expected to fail when they are not satisfied in the world. For example, with a few exceptions (e.g., D'Zmura and Lennie 1986) most current computational algorithms do not perform well in the presence of significant specular components; the algorithms require a virtually uniform illumination, and the collection of surface reflectances must average to the same "gray" in every scene.

Our purpose is not to provide a comprehensive discussion of computational color vision. Enough has been said to indicate that there are at present different approaches to color vision, which focus on different respective kinds of color phenomena: On the one hand, we have computational theories of color constancy, on the other hand, psychophysical and neurophysiological investigations of a range of such chromatic phenomena as constancy, contrast, color matching, color blindness, and so on. At the present stage of research, the question of how these approaches to color vision might be related does not admit of a clear and nonpartisan answer. Only a handful of studies explore possible links among the various levels of analysis and kinds of phenomena—for example, Zeki's (1980; 1983; 1985) neurophysiological studies of the cortical mechanisms underlying color constancy, or Buchsbaum and Gottschalk's (1983) formal analysis of opponent color mechanisms. This question does raise a number of conceptual and empirical issues, however, which in turn have considerable implications for the ontology of color.

1.4   Current Ontologies

To discern these issues consider that human color vision exhibits only *approximate* color constancy. Many factors can affect constancy; among the best documented are the effects of sensitivity to the spectral quality of the illumination (Helson 1938; Helson and Jeffers 1940; Judd 1940). As Jameson and Hurvich (1989, p. 7) note in a recent review: "Departures from perfect color constancy with changes in the spectral quality of illumination . . . imply that perceived contrast between objects of different surface reflectance varies with the level and kind of illumination in which they are seen and to which the visual system is adapted."

From the standpoint of the computational level of analysis, the approximate constancy of human color vision is not surprising. For example, in Maloney and Wandell's (1986) model, surface reflectance can be completely recovered only if there are more sensor types than degrees of freedom in reflectance. Since naturally occurring reflectances require 3 to 6 degrees of freedom for their full specification (Maloney 1985) and human color vision is trichromatic (3 receptor types), Maloney and Wandell's model predicts that there are chromatic differences among naturally occurring surface reflectances that cannot be detected by a trichromatic system (assuming, of course, that no other kind of disambiguation is available).

So far, then, we have an overall agreement between psychophysics and computational vision. The problems arise when we ask how the approximate constancy of natural color vision is to be *explained*. It is in the kind of answer given to this question that we find the motivation for current views on the ontology of color.

Starting from the computational level of analysis as outlined above, we assume that the function of color vision is the achievement of color constancy, defined as the recovery of the invariant surface spectral reflectances in a scene. We then are led to explain approximate color constancy as a departure from ideal or perfect color constancy, the implication being that such a departure constitutes a visual shortcoming or error (cf. Maloney and Wandell 1986, p. 32). Obviously, once such a conceptual framework is in place, it is natural to suppose that color is simply the property of surface spectral reflectance. Thus, consider the following passage from Maloney (1985):

The analyses of Chapter 2 [those presenting finite-dimensional linear models of lights and reflectances] used data appropriate to human environments and suggested that what we call color corresponds to an objective property of physical surfaces. Depending on the lights and surfaces present in a scene, we succeed or fail in estimating these properties. Failures of color constancy, from this viewpoint, can be considered as visual illusions. We misestimate true color as we might misestimate true height in an Ames room (p. 119).[4]

We might wonder, however, whether this "top-down" computational approach, although consistent with the approximate constancy of natural color vision, should be accorded the status of an explanation. If we wish to design a visual system that exhibits complete constancy, and the system exhibits only approximate constancy, then we are justified in saying that the system does not perform optimally, that it fails to achieve the task *for which it was designed*. But because natural color vision presumably resulted from evolutionary tinkering involving "trade-offs" rather than optimal design, why should the approximate constancy of natural color vision be explained by appealing to such a strong, engineering notion of optimality? Furthermore, even if natural color vision is in some sense optimal (relative to a given species and its niche), it might exhibit approximate constancy for biological and ecological reasons that preclude designating this kind of constancy as involving visual error. For example, most computational approaches seem to assume that color vision is concerned primarily with the reflecting properties of surfaces. As a result, illumination conditions are treated merely as something to be "discounted" in the task of recovering reflectance. Natural color vision appears to be concerned with illumination conditions in their own right, however, for these provide indications about weather conditions, time of day, and so forth (Jameson and Hurvich 1989). To emphasize color constancy at the expense of sensitivity to the illumination in its own right would therefore seriously prejudge the behaviors that natural color vision serves.

Consider, then, what happens if we proceed in a more "bottom-up" direction by taking the performance of natural color vision and its biological embodiment as our reference point. Here our point of departure is color space and its dimensions. That color constancy is only approximate provides an example of how these dimensions (hue-saturation-brightness) can shift depending on the state of the perceiver and the conditions of viewing. We therefore give more attention to the local, context-dependent features of perception than to the high-level, physically invariant properties of the environment. Furthermore, because our point of departure is color understood phenomenally, we are less likely to play favorites among the different ways colors can be encountered. For example, afterimage colors as well as surface colors require explanation. These both count as genuine color phenomena because they exhibit the three dimensions of hue, saturation, and brightness. It therefore becomes natural to identify color with this phenomenal structure. And because this structure does not reduce to properties of either light waves or surface reflectance (more on this later), we will probably be led to embrace subjectivism. Thus, consider the following passage from the conclusion of Zeki's (1983) pioneering study of cortical cell responses to both surface colors and after-image colors:

The results described here . . . suggest that *the nervous system, rather than analyze colors, takes what information there is in the external environment, namely, the reflectance of different surfaces for different wavelengths of light, and transforms that information to construct colors,* using its own algorithms to do so. In other words, it constructs something which is a property of the brain, not the world outside. (Emphasis in original, p. 764)

If we compare the above passage from Maloney (1985) with this remark of Zeki's, we can see that despite the considerable advances made in the study of color vision in recent years, disagreement remains among vision researchers on the ontology of color. Ontology is more the specialty of philosophers, but they do not agree either. In fact, the two positions just outlined, with their respective links to computational vision and to neurophysiology, correspond precisely to the most recent discussions by philosophers: Hilbert (1987) and Matthen (1988) defend objectivism largely on the basis of computational color vision (Maloney and Wandell's model and Land's retinex theory); Hardin (1988) defends subjectivism largely on the basis of neurophysiology and psychophysics (opponent-process theories).

Two basic claims constitute Hilbert's version of objectivism. First, the centerpiece of his position is the typical objectivist claim that we must distinguish between color as an objective property of the world and color as we perceive it. For Hilbert, each objective color is identical with a distinct spectral reflectance. Objects that have identical surface spectral reflectances have the same color; objects that have different surface spectral reflectances have different colors. Second, Hilbert claims that since our color perception and color terms are indeterminate with respect to surface reflectance, they give us only "anthropocentrically defined colors and not colors themselves" (p. 27). For Hilbert, "red," "green," "yellow," and "blue" do not name determinate spectral reflectances; rather, they name indeterminate kinds of spectral reflectance whose specifications are arbitrary from a purely physical standpoint, but nonetheless of interest in relation to the structure of the human visual system. Hilbert accordingly calls his position "anthropocentric realism."

Matthen (1988) defends a similar view by first developing a theory of perceptual content. In his view, perceptual states have content because they have the function to detect things of a certain type. Matthen then argues on the basis of Land's retinex theory (Land 1977; 1983) that the function of color vision is to detect surface reflectance. Because Matthen identifies the contents of types of chromatic perceptual states with the distal property they supposedly have the function to detect, he is naturally led to claim that color simply is that distal property, namely, surface reflectance.

Hardin (1988), on the other hand, develops an extensive argument against objectivism, which consists of two basic points: First, surface spectral reflectance is only one of the many kinds of stimuli that can give rise to color experience; second, the properties of color—for example, the uniqueness and binariness of hue and hue-opponency—cannot be found in properties of the (distal or proximal) physical stimuli for color vision. The second is the more important point, for it consists in the claim that there is no mapping from physical stimuli to phenomenal color space that is sufficient to ground objectivism. As we saw above, however, there are mappings from color space to the visual system at various levels of organization and operation. Hardin relies precisely on these kinds of mappings, especially opponent-process theories, to support his subjectivist view that there are no "extradermal" colored objects; there are only chromatic perceptual states. In his words: "Colored objects are illusions, but not unfounded illusions. We are normally in chromatic perceptual states, and these are neural states . . . We are to be eliminativists with respect to color as a property of objects, but reductivists with respect to color experiences" (pp. 111–12).

We refer to these two positions as "computational objectivism" and "neurophysiological subjectivism," respectively, thus highlighting the link between current color ontologies and explanation in visual science. The debate between these two positions has so far proceeded with computational objectivists downplaying the phenomenal structure of color and neurophysiological subjectivists responding by emphasizing the context-dependent, approximate constancy of human surface color perception.

Our intention in the remainder of this chapter is to move beyond this debate by offering a broader empirical and philosophical perspective grounded in comparative color vision. Before we proceed, let us lay our cards on the table. With respect to the debate as outlined so far, we are fundamentally in agreement with Hardin's claim that "every attempt . . . to type-identify chromatic sensory states in terms of their stimuli is fundamentally misguided" (1989, p. 3). Nonetheless, we believe that Hardin's neurophysiological subjectivism is far too restrictive, for there are dimensions of color vision that do not yield to analysis purely in terms of the neurophysiological structure of the perceiver. These dimensions are, we argue, ecological. Hardin (1990) has recently begun to emphasize some of these dimensions, but we believe he has not gone far enough. On the other hand, although computational objectivism does emphasize the environmental context of color vision, it usually does so in a profoundly unbiological and unecological way by making animal-independent, distal properties the ultimate point of reference.

2   The Comparative Argument

2.1   Overview

Two pervasive phenomena of natural color vision form the basis for the comparative argument:

1. Animals whose neural apparatuses have little in common beyond the peripheral photoreceptor level (e.g., insects, fishes, birds, and primates), and that inhabit considerably diverse environmental contexts, nonetheless possess color vision.

2. Despite this commonality, color vision varies across species and animal groups. Among the most salient variations are the *type* (dimensionality) and *amount* (sensitivity) of color vision and its neural substrates. These variations imply different phenomenal color spaces, some of which are incommensurable.

These two phenomena constrain any attempt to explain color vision and the ontology of color. Our claim is that they constrain such a theory to be *experientialist* and *ecological*: Color can be understood only in relation to the visual perception of a given individual or species (contrary to objectivism); but such visual experience can be understood only in the context of its ecological embodiment (contrary to subjectivism).

Consider (1) first. Why do so many species of invertebrates, nonmammalian vertebrates, and mammals possess color vision? To answer we must appeal not only to comparative physiology, but also to the evolutionary histories of seeing animals (probably at several levels of selection), to common features among the diverse environmental contexts of color vision, and to changes in the environment that are a function of animal-environment coevolution (we mention examples later).

These ecological dimensions of color vision have generally been taken to support computational objectivism. Among computational visual scientists, the argument (which usually goes unstated) is that because color vision is biologically pervasive, the evolution of color vision must consist in various species devising their own unique "solutions" to the information-processing problem of recovering surface reflectance in their respective environments. Among philosophers, this argument takes the form we reviewed above: The contents of perceptual states are to be type-identified by the (distal) properties they have the function to detect; the function of color vision is to detect surface reflectance; therefore color can be identified with surface reflectance (Matthen 1988).

In this section, we argue at some length against this view on the basis of (2) above, which develops into three related points:

(i) The properties of color, especially of different and sometimes incommensurable color spaces, cannot be modelled on the basis of properties of physical stimuli like surface reflectance. Hence color cannot be identified with surface spectral reflectance.

(ii) Given considerable variation in the dimensionality and sensitivity of color vision, and given a role for color vision in determining the boundaries of surfaces, the segmentation of the visual scene and therefore of what counts as a distinct surface to be perceived may in fact be relative to the structure of the perceiving animal. Thus surfaces may themselves be relational like color, providing no animal-independent anchor for objective color as surface spectral reflectance.

(iii) Natural color vision is concerned not just with detecting surfaces but also with a variety of other tasks in various terrestrial, aquatic, and aerial contexts. Among these are the discrimination of illumination conditions and the generation of a set of perceptual categories that have "cognitive significance" for animals in a variety of interactions. For these reasons, it is a mistake to suppose that the one and only (or even primary) function of color vision is the recovery of surface spectral reflectance.

Because each of these points rests on the idea of differences in color space, we begin by discussing the evidence for the existence of different kinds of color space among perceiving animals.

2.2   The Color Space of Other Animals

It is tempting to assume that our visual abilities provide the norm for understanding color vision. This assumption might be justifiable if humans—or our primate relatives—were unique in possessing color vision. In reality, however, color vision is widespread throughout the animal world. Indeed, it seems that virtually every animal class has some species with trichromatic vision (Jacobs 1981, p. 153). But it would also be a mistake to take trichromacy as the norm. Many animals are *dichromats* (e.g., squirrels, rabbits, tree shrews, some fishes, possibly cats and dogs, some New World monkeys); others appear to be *tetrachromats* (e.g., goldfish, the Japanese dace, turtles), perhaps even *pentachromats* (pigeons, ducks).

Before discussing the evidence for higher dimensional color spaces, it is important to consider how color vision also varies considerably in its amount or sensitivity as determined by the spectral sensitivity, wavelength discrimination, and colorimetric purity functions. By measuring these functions for various animals, one can compare their overall sensitivities to spectral stimuli, their abilities to discriminate on the basis of wavelength, and whether spectral stimuli appear more or less saturated.

Each of these functions will differ for color vision of different dimensionality. The wavelength discrimination curve is of particular interest here, for it can also be taken as an indication of the type of color vision system: A maximum or minimum is expected where there is a crossover between two primary responses. For example, our three primaries are revealed in our wavelength discrimination curve, which has two maxima (figure 15.2a, top). These maxima correspond to the two regions in the spectrum where our hue discrimination is finest (580 nm and 470 nm). The curve for the goldfish, however, shows three regions of best hue discrimination at 610 nm, 500 nm, and 400 nm (Neumeyer 1985; 1986). This finding suggests that the goldfish has four active primaries and so is potentially a tetrachromat (Crawford et al. 1990; Neumeyer 1988). In contrast, the wavelength discrimination curve for the pigeon shows four regions of best hue discrimination at 390 nm, 450 nm, 540 nm, and 600 nm (Emmerton and Delius 1980), suggesting that the pigeon has five active primary mechanisms, and so is potentially a pentachromat. Three of the minima not including the one at 390 nm in the UV region are shown in figure 15.4c (Palacios et al. 1990a).

The three functions also differ among animals that have color vision of the same dimensionality, among "normal" and "anomalous" individuals, and even among "normal" individuals. To cite examples of each kind of variation: (i) Humans and forager honey bees are both trichromats, but bee color vision is shifted toward the ultraviolet, with the points of best hue discrimination at about 400 nm and 490 nm (Menzel 1979; 1989), as can be seen in figure 15.3, which also shows the receptor-level and the opponent channel color space for these insects. (ii) For normal human trichromats, spectral sensitivity peaks at about 555 nm; the spectral sensitivity of deuteranomalous trichromats, however, is shifted toward longer wavelengths, whereas that of protanomalous trichromats is shifted toward shorter wavelengths. (iii) Finally, each of the three functions can differ slightly among "normal" individuals: For example, men and women appear to differ in their color mixtures (Neitz and Jacobs 1986).

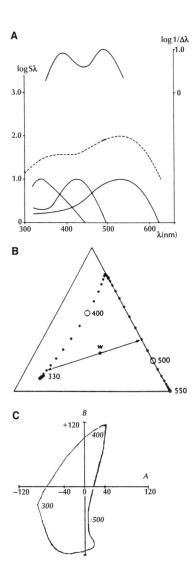

Figure 15.3
The honey bee: an alternative trichromatic color space. (a) Spectral sensitivities of the three pigments present in the forager honey bee's retina (*Apis mellifera*), with the overall sensitivity curve (discontinuous line) and the two-peaked wave-length discrimination function. Modified from Nuboer (1986). (b) Maxwell triangle for photoreceptor activities, indicating the spectral loci. Compare with figure 15.2b. From Goldsmith (1990). (c) Chromaticity diagram for constant brightness, calculated on the basis of two antagonistic channels postulated for the bee from phsiological findings: A = +UV − B − G; B = UV − B + G. From Menzel (1989).

Now that we have introduced the idea of variations in the dimensionality and sensitivity of color vision, we can turn to what these variations tell us about color space. We focus first on color vision in birds, for as J. K. Bowmaker remarked some years ago: "The true culmination of the evolution of color vision in vertebrates is probably to be found in the highly evolved diurnal animals, perhaps best represented by diurnal birds, and it is within these species that we should look for color vision significantly more complex than our own and utilizing more of the available spectrum" (1980b, p. 196).

As we mentioned above, evidence that is now being accumulated indicates that such diurnal birds as the pigeon and the duck are at least tetrachromats, perhaps even pentachromats (Jane and Bowmaker 1988; Burkhardt 1989; Chen et al. 1984; Goldsmith 1990; Palacios 1991; Palacios and Varela 1992; Palacios et al. 1990b; Varela et al. 1991). This evidence is derived from a variety of experiments with species ranging over various families within each order. The evidence also pertains to several levels, from the photoreceptor and retinal constitution, to the neurophysiological, and psychophysical or behavioral levels.

To begin at the retinal level, *five* different types of cone-oil droplet combinations have been described in the retinas of various birds such as pigeons, ducks, and penguins; passerines have at least four such combinations (Bowmaker 1977; Chen and Goldsmith 1986; Chen et al. 1984; Jane and Bowmaker 1988). As can be seen from figure 15.4a, the "visible" spectral range available to diurnal birds includes that available to humans, but it also extends considerably further into the short-wave region. Indeed, it is now generally agreed that many birds have color vision in the near-ultraviolet region. For example, Wright (1972) found that the removal of an ultraviolet component changes the color of certain stimuli for the pigeon; and Goldsmith (1980) found that hummingbirds can distinguish near-ultraviolet light (370 nm) from darkness, and from white light lacking wavelengths below 400 nm. Humans cannot perform either of these tasks.[5]

The cones in the avian retina, unlike those in mammals and insects, also possess oil droplet inclusions, which appear to act as cut-off filters, thereby increasing in number the combination of receptor sensitivities (Bowmaker 1980b). Oil droplets are also found in the retinas of some fishes, amphibians, and reptiles. In the pigeon retina, for example, there are up to four types of colored oil droplets in combination with three types of cone photopigment for the long-wave region alone (figure 15.4b) (Bowmaker 1977). Furthermore, this information about retinal organization is regional, because in birds like the pigeon there are two foveal regions that mediate

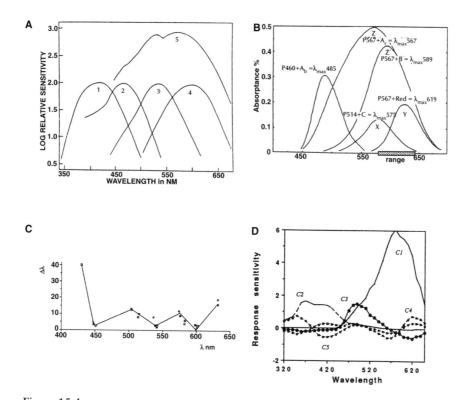

Figure 15.4
The color hyperspace of diurnal birds. (a) Relative spectral sensitivities of the five major cone classes of the mallard duck (*Anas platyrhynchos L.*) calculated by taking into account both oil droplet and ocular media absorption. The fifth curve has been shifted up one log unit arbitrarily for clarity. From Jane and Bowmaker (1988). (b) The cone photopigments (maxima at 460 nm, 514 nm and 567 nm) and oil droplet (50% cutoff transmission at 476 nm, 476 nm, 554 nm, 610 nm, and 570 nm, respectively) combinations actually present in the pigeon's retinal "red" field. The sector designated "range," the long-wave window 580–640 nm, is compatible with trichromacy according to color-mixture data. From Palacios, Martinoya, Block and Varela (1990), based on data from Bowmaker (1977). (c) A behavioral determination of the wavelength discrimination function for the pigeon (*Columbia livia*) not including the UV region, showing three conspicuous minima. Data from Palacios, Bonnardel and Varela (1990a). (d) Proposed chromatic opponent channels for the pigeon, based on weighted subtractions and additions that maximally decorrelate primary responses (see text). The primary responses considered were maxima at 360 nm, 415 nm, 520 nm and 620 nm. These channels can adequately predict the known photopic sensitivity, wavelength discrimination curve, and color mixture in pigeons. From Palacios (1991).

different behavioral roles (Bloch and Martinoya 1983; Maldonado et al. 1988); evidence indicates that sensitivity and discrimination are different in these two visual regions (Nuboer and Wortel 1987; Remy and Emmerton 1989). These regional differences increase even more the complexity of pigeon color vision, for the color perceived depends on the visual field being attended.

Turning now to psychophysics, wavelength discrimination curves, as we have already mentioned, show four distinct minima (Emmerton and Delius 1980; Palacios et al. 1990a). Color-mixture experiments for the pigeon provide direct evidence for tetrachromacy (Palacios and Varela 1991; Palacios et al. 1990b). A definitive proof of pentachromacy would require five-way color-mixture experiments, which have yet to be performed.

There is unfortunately little evidence at present about the neural basis for avian chromatic channels in general (see Maturana and Varela 1982; Varela et al. 1983). It is nevertheless possible to form an educated guess about the possible shape of the pigeon's color channels, comparable to those shown in figures 15.2c and 15.3c for humans and bees, respectively. The basic idea, introduced by Buchsbaum and Gottschalk (1983), is to obtain the weighted combination of mutual excitation and inhibition that maximally *decorrelates* the primary photoreceptor responses (see appendix A). In their original calculations, Buchsbaum and Gottschalk (1983) used the Vos-Walraven primary responses for humans, which are psychophysically derived. The resulting channels correspond remarkably well with the Wh-Bk (White-Black), R-G (Red-Green), and Y-B (Yellow-Blue) channels known to the psychophysicist, and to color-opponent profiles at the retinal or geniculate level known to the neurophysiologist.

We have applied this same procedure to other species, as explained in Appendix A. Unlike the human data, the animal data are incomplete; at present, the best one has to work with are raw microspectrophotometric data. The proposed channels can be validated by their capacity to *predict* known behavioral evidence, such as sensitivity, discrimination, and color mixture. In figure 15.4d we show the result of the decorrelation of the primary responses of the pigeon, thereby giving a set of putative channels. These channels adequately predict the known data on sensitivity, wavelength discrimination, and color mixture (Palacios 1991). We typically find that we need *five* channels to account for the available data: one achromatic luminance channel (C1) and four color-opponent channels (C2, C3, C4, C5) with different zero crossings (figure 15.4d).[6]

It is important to realize that such an increase in chromatic dimensionality does not mean that pigeons exhibit greater sensitivity to the monochromatic hues that we see. For example, we should not suppose that since the hue discrimination of the pigeon is best around 600 nm, and since we see a 600 nm stimulus as orange, pigeons are better at discriminating spectral hues of orange than we are. Indeed, we have reason to believe that such a mapping of our hue terms onto the pigeon would be an error: In an experiment designed to determine whether and how pigeons group spectral stimuli into hue categories, Wright and Cummings (1971) found that pigeons treat wavelengths to either side of 540 nm as falling into different hue categories, whereas humans do not. As Jacobs (1981, p. 118) notes in his discussion of this experiment: "Among other things, this result strongly emphasizes how misleading it may be to use human hue designations to describe color vision in non-human species."

This point can be made even more forcefully, however, when it is a difference in the *dimensionality* of color vision that we are considering. An increase in the dimensionality of color vision indicates a fundamentally different kind of color space. We are familiar with trichromatic color spaces such as our own, which require three independent axes for their specification, given either as receptor activation or as color channels (figure 15.2). A tetrachromatic color space obviously requires four dimensions for its specification. It is thus an example of what can be called a *color hyperspace*.

The difference between a tetrachromatic and a trichromatic color space is therefore not like the difference between two trichromatic color spaces: The former two color spaces are *incommensurable* in a precise mathematical sense, for there is no way to map the kinds of distinctions available in four dimensions into the kinds of distinctions available in three dimensions without remainder. One might object that such incommensurability does not prevent one from "projecting" the higher-dimensional space onto the lower; hence the difference in dimensionality simply means that the higher space contains more perceptual content than the lower. Such an interpretation, however, begs the fundamental question of how one is to choose to "project" the higher space onto the lower. Because the spaces are not isomorphic, there is no unique projection relation. Furthermore, to pass from one space to another, one needs to specify the appropriate axes (color channels), which differ according to the animal (even for animals that have color vision of the same dimensionality).

To mark this kind of difference in color space, consider the color space of the forager honey bee, which we presented in figure 15.3 above. If bees are able to enjoy the experience of hue, the hues they perceive are likely to be different from ours, because they match wavelengths to which we are also sensitive with lights drawn from the near-ultraviolet region of the spectrum, which we cannot see. In spite of this difference, there is a sense in which bee color space and human color space can be said to be commensurable, for the dimensionalities of the spaces are the same, and so a precise correspondence can be provided between these two perceptual spaces. In the case of tetrachromats or pentachromats such a correspondence is not possible.

This incommensurability can be more easily envisioned with the help of the evidence for tetrachromacy in teleost fishes, especially the goldfish (Neumeyer 1988). In figure 15.5a, we present the pigment triangle for the goldfish, which should be compared with the previously presented triangles for humans (figure 15.2b) and the bee (figure 15.3b). Here the familiar Maxwell triangle has been doubled to accommodate the additional coordinate needed to map spectral loci. This representation was first proposed by Neumeyer (1988) for goldfish and independently by Burkhardt (1989) for the color vision of birds. We also reproduce here Goldsmith's (1990) suggestive rendering of the same idea as a pigment *tetrahedron* for an "imaginary" turtle with a retina whose photoreceptors have no oil droplets (figure 15.5b).

To generate these kinds of color hyperspaces at the physiological and psychophysical levels, we need at least four channels. For teleost fish, these channels can be obtained in a manner similar to those for the pigeon—by maximally decorrelating the primary responses as known from microspectrophotometric and physiological data (Harosi and Hashimoto 1983; Neumeyer 1988). In this case, the transformation matrix from primary responses to channels is explicitly given in appendix A. Here again the putative channels can correctly predict the known behavioral evidence for sensitivity, wavelength discrimination, and color mixture for the goldfish (Palacios 1991). It is interesting to note that Neumeyer and Arnold (1989) have recently shown that the goldfish switches from trichromatic to tetrachromatic modes depending on light conditions—an indication that the ecological embeddedness of the animal is quite pertinent even at this level of description.

This complex of issues can also be approached from a frequency analysis of color signals and responses that could provide a way to ascertain the dimensionality of color space directly. The basic idea was first proposed by Barlow (1982; see also

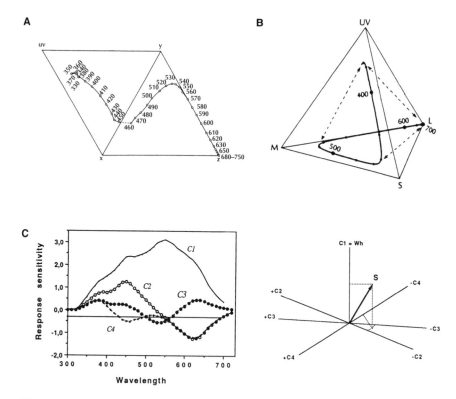

Figure 15.5
Tetrachromatic color hyperspaces. (a) Pigment color space for the goldfish, requiring four relative values to span the entire space. In contrast to figures 15.2 and 15.3, the representation demands an extra dimension, which is obtained by doubling the color triangle. The spectral loci thus obtained from pigment absorption data no longer fall on the boundaries of the space, but inside them. From Neumeyer (1988). (b) Pigment tetrahedron for an "imaginary" turtle with no oil droplets in its cones, with visual pigment maxima at 370 nm, 450 nm, 520 nm, and 620 nm. In this format it is easy to see that the animal is likely to have three nonspectral stimulus regions (see figure 15.2), which would fall along the dashed lines. From Goldsmith (1990). (c) Proposed chromatic opponent channels for the goldfish, by maximal decorrelation of the pigment data form Harosi and Hashimoto (1983). An achromatic channel and three opponent channels are found. These four channels adequately predict sensitivity, wavelength discrimination, and color-mixture data, as well as physiological data from the fish retina. From Palacios (1991). To the right, the putative channels are used as axes of a color hyperspace of four dimensions (labeled here simply as +C1 – C1, +C2 – C2, etc.), plus the achromatic or brightness axis (C1 = Wh). Compare with figures 15.2c and 15.3c for the trichromatic spaces of humans and the bee respectively.

Bowmaker 1983), but since it is rather novel, we have relegated our treatment to an appendix (see appendix B).

In this section, we have presented an array of evidence for the existence of different kinds of color space among perceiving animals. The evidence includes the diversity of kinds of photopigments and sensitivity functions, wavelength discrimination and categorical perception, color mixture, physiological processes, and ethology. Although each form of evidence taken in isolation might be unconvincing, taken as a whole it makes a strong case for the existence of significant variations in the dimensionalities of color space among perceiving animals. We must now wonder what these differences might mean in experiential or phenomenal terms. What do these comparative variations in color space imply for our understanding of color experience?

2.3 Novel Hues and Diversity in Color Experience

Since some readers may be sceptical about attributing color experience to creatures other than ourselves (or our primate relatives), let us first attempt to distinguish more precisely between color vision and color experience. Although it is difficult to draw a principled distinction between mere wavelength-specific behavior and color vision (Menzel 1979), color vision is sometimes defined as the ability to discriminate wavelengths independent of their relative intensities. This ability would not seem to entail the enjoyment of color experience, however, for it seems possible to imagine the former without the latter. Unfortunately, it is also not clear how to draw a principled distinction between color vision as wavelength discrimination and the full-fledged perceptual experience of color.

A more satisfactory approach to this problem is to hold that color perception involves at least three important phenomena: additive color mixture (hue, saturation, and brightness matches for spectral stimuli), color contrast (simultaneous and successive) and color constancy. In particular, it seems reasonable to suppose that color contrast and color constancy are necessary for color experiences.[7] It is therefore interesting to note that these chromatic phenomena have now been demonstrated for a variety of species. Color constancy and color induction have been found in bees (Neumeyer 1980; 1981), goldfish (Ingle 1985), and pigeons (Varela et al. 1991). In the case of pigeons, we have also seen that these animals group adjacent wavelengths into categories, which though different from the groupings humans perform, nonetheless seem to be categories of hue (Wright and Cummings 1971).

Given these psychophysical results, then, it does not seem unreasonable to suppose that these animals, especially birds and fishes, experience color.

Let us now consider color vision of higher dimensionality than our own. When they hear of the evidence for tetrachromacy or pentachromacy many people respond by asking: "Well, what are the extra colors that these perceivers see?" This question is understandable, but somewhat naive, for, as pointed out above, we should not suppose that tetrachromats or pentachromats are simply better at seeing the colors that we see. On the contrary, to see in four or five dimensions, as it were, is not to discriminate more finely in three dimensions. In other words, tetrachromats and pentachromats should not be conceived as perceivers who simply make finer hue-saturation-brightness discriminations among, say, blue and green or red and yellow (like perceivers who simply see finer shades of our colors). Such an ability would not amount to an increase in the *dimensionality* of color space; it would consist only in a relative increase in hue-saturation-brightness sensitivity within the dimensions of our trichromatic color space. If we wish to understand what tetrachromacy and pentachromacy imply for color experience, we must instead ask what the possession of additional dimensions to make chromatic distinctions could mean in experiential or phenomenal terms.

At this point, we can offer only imaginative speculation, for we still lack knowledge of the post-retinal neuronal processes involved in tetrachromatic and pentachromatic perception and we obviously do not know what such perception is *like* from the point of view of the goldfish or the pigeon.[8] By returning to consider our color space, however, and by asking how this space would be transformed by the addition of a new dimension, we can perhaps achieve an indirect appreciation of what a tetrachromatic color hyperspace might be like. Recall, then, that because our visual system has two chromatically opponent channels, we are able to experience four unique hues (red, green, yellow, and blue) and their binary combinations (orange, purple, etc.). A tetravariant visual system, however, like that suggested for the goldfish (figure 15.5), would contain three chromatically opponent channels. We are therefore entitled to speculate that these three channels (call them r-g, y-b, and p-q) would enable a tetrachromat to experience six basic hue components (r, g, y, b, p, q), binary combinations of these hues (e.g., r + y, y + p, etc.), and *ternary* combinations as well (e.g., r + y + p, g + y + p). Thus the color hyperspace of a tetrachromat might reflect a phenomenal structure composed not only of two new basic hue components, which would combine to form novel binaries, but also an entirely *new kind of hue* not found in the phenomenal structure of our color space, namely, ternary hues.[9] These ternary hues would correspond to the additional kind of chromatic distinction available to a tetrachromat, but not to a trichromat.

This point about novel colors can be made more accessible with the help of the diagrams presented in figures 15.2, 15.4, and 15.5. To represent tetrachromatic stimulus mixtures we found that we had to add an additional axis to the plane so that it became a volume (figure 15.5). Therefore, as Burkhardt (1989) notes: "While in man s chromaticity diagram there is only one intermediate color which does not occur in the daylight spectrum, namely, purple, in tetrachromatic vision there would be three intermediate colors which are not present in the daylight spectrum, namely, mixtures of red and blue (purple), of green and UV, and of red and UV . . ." (pp. 794–95). Similar kinds of novel, nonspectral stimulus mixtures are indicated by the dashed lines in Goldsmith's (1990) pigment tetrahedron for an imaginary turtle (figure 15.5b). If such novel, nonspectral stimulus mixtures can be shown to be treated as colors by the animal through its behavior, then the existence of color hyperspace as a domain of behaviorally significant distinctions would be strongly reinforced.

2.4   Computational Objectivism Revisited

We now pursue the implications of our comparative discussion, beginning with the view that we call "computational objectivism." Our first task is to determine whether some sufficient subset of the properties of color can be identified with such physical properties as surface spectral reflectance. If these properties of color cannot be so identified then we have reason to reject the objectivist's claim that color is simply surface spectral reflectance.

The obvious place to begin is color space. For something to be a color it must have a location in some color space; that is, it must be specifiable in terms of hue, saturation, and brightness. By taking these three properties as our reference point, we can construct an argument against the identification of color with surface spectral reflectance, which we will call the "argument from external irreducibility." (The main features of this argument were originally proposed by Hardin [1984; 1988, pp. 66–67].)

The Argument from External Irreducibility

1. For something to be a (chromatic) color it must be a hue.

2. For something to be a hue it must be either unique or binary (or ternary).

3. Therefore, if hues are to be reductively identified with physical properties, these physical properties must admit of corresponding unique, binary (or ternary) divisions.

4. Organism-independent, external properties such as light-waves and spectral reflectances do not admit of such divisions.

5. Therefore, color cannot be reductively identified with such organism-independent, external properties.

Although this argument has conceptual components, we do not intend it to be primarily conceptual. We are interested not in conceptual analysis, (i.e., in making claims about the essential features of the concept of color), but in determining what color is, given the concept of color as it figures in visual science, especially in psychophysical explanation. Thus (1) and (2) should be read as consequences that follow from how color is conceptually and empirically specified in visual science.

The main empirical claim in the argument is obviously (4). To put the point another way: Given only light wavelengths or the spectral reflectance profiles for surfaces, we cannot model or state generalizations about hue. Light waves or surface spectral reflectances do not stand in relations to each other that can be described as unique or binary, or for that matter opponent or nonopponent, balanced or unbalanced, saturated or desaturated, and so forth. There is simply no mapping from such physical properties to the properties of color that is sufficient to establish the objectivist identification.[10]

This argument obviously depends on considerations about what properties a mapping must have to be sufficient to establish objectivism. We are supposing that such a mapping must enable us to state generalizations about features of color such as the unique/binary structure of hue and the opponent relations. The objectivist might deny this point. Such a denial would be tantamount to claiming, contrary to (1)–(3) above, that we should replace our current understanding of color in visual science with a new concept of physical color as surface spectral reflectance. It is tempting to dismiss this conceptual replacement idea out of hand: It is one thing to argue for a distinction between physical color and perceived color, but it is quite another to uphold the distinction by divesting hue, and thereby color, of those properties used in its conceptual and empirical specification in visual science. If the properties of hue, such as being unique or binary, and the opponent relations, could be successfully identified with some set of physical properties such as surface spectral reflectances, then statements about these physical properties would provide us with an alternative theoretical access to the properties of color that figure in psychophysical explanation. We would then have reason for accepting a new notion of physical color. But because we have no physical model for these properties of color, what is to motivate such a notion?

The argument from external irreducibility could be and indeed has been advanced without taking into consideration comparative color spaces (Hardin 1984; 1988). We present the argument here because it becomes even stronger when we place it in the context of comparative color vision. Consider hue as it varies across dichromatic, trichromatic, and tetrachromatic (to say nothing of pentachromatic) color spaces. As we know from studies of human color blindness (see Hurvich 1981 for an overview), a dichromat has only one opponent-hue pair (yellow-blue or more rarely red-green). Therefore, unlike a trichromatic color space, a purely dichromatic color space contains no binary hues. Similarly, a tetrachromatic color hyperspace would contain ternary hues not found in a trichromatic color space. There are thus different *kinds* of hue to be found in each of these color spaces. The unique, binary, and ternary structures that compose these different kinds of hue do not map onto properties of surface spectral reflectance. Neither the unity among the phenomena (color *qua* hue-saturation-brightness relations) nor the relevant diversity (different dimensionalities and hence kinds of hue) is to be found at the purely physical level of spectral reflectance.

At this point, the objectivist will no doubt appeal to the idea that the contents of (types) of perceptual states should be identified according to the distal properties they have the function to detect, that the function of color vision is to detect surface spectral reflectance, and that this functionalist type-identification is sufficient to establish the claim that color is surface spectral reflectance (Matthen 1988).

Even if the function of color vision is to detect surface reflectance, it does not follow that color is surface reflectance. In fact, computational objectivists often simply beg the question about the status of color by building objectivism into their representationist theories of perception. But there is an even more fundamental problem we wish to stress: The claim that the function of color vision is to detect surface reflectance is at best considerably misleading and at worst seriously flawed. It is misleading because a comparative ecological examination of color vision reveals that color vision has many other biological functions besides those involved in the detection of surfaces. Most notably, color vision is concerned with illumination conditions in their own right and with the perceptual significance of color in guiding behavioral interactions (we provide examples shortly). It is flawed because it is not at all clear that surfaces are themselves perceiver-independent in the way the objectivist supposes. Let us begin with this point, because it is the more controversial.[11]

In the top-down functional decomposition characteristic of the computational level of analysis (such as inverse optics), vision is decomposed into various more-or-less modular tasks. In the case of color vision, the task is to recover information about surface spectral reflectance given a collection of objects. This statement of the "problem" of color vision assumes that the visual scene has already been segmented into areas that correspond to distinct objects and their surfaces. But this assumption begs the question of the purposes that color vision may serve. As D'Zmura and Lennie (1986, p. 1666) note: "To find the loci of responses that correspond to different objects, one must already have segmented the scene to establish which lights come from which objects. This begs the question of the purpose of color vision, which we believe plays an important role in the discrimination among objects and in their identification."

Consider the regularization constraints that we discussed above. Among these is the fact that naturally occurring illuminants and reflectances can be adequately modelled in a low-dimensional space. What, we might ask, constitutes a "naturally occurring reflectance"? If we examine these models, we see that so-called natural reflectances correspond to the surface reflectances of typical objects from our human environment (e.g., bricks, grass, buildings, etc.). Given a class of such objects, one measures their surface spectral reflectances and then determines which finite set of basis reflectance functions best models the variance in the class. The visual system, however, is never simply presented with such prespecified objects. On the contrary, the determination of what and where an object is, as well as its surface texture and orientation (hence the overall context in which color is perceived), is a complex process that the visual system must achieve.

In fact, we have already seen that color vision contributes to this process of spatial segmentation. For example, we reviewed Rubin and Richards's (1982; 1988) idea that an early goal of biological color vision is to determine where material changes occur in a scene using spectral crosspoints and opposite slope signs. Another example comes from D'Zmura and Lennie (1986), who propose an algorithm for color constancy in which the geometric stability of hue contributes to segmenting a scene whereas variations in lightness and saturation contribute to establishing an object's shape and position. Finally, at the neurophysiological level, it is generally held that distinct retinal-geniculate-cortical pathways are involved in color, form, and movement perception (De Yoe and Van Essen 1988; Lennie 1984; Livingstone and Hubel 1988), but there is disagreement over the properties of these pathways and their relations (Lennie et al. 1990; Logothetis et al. 1990; Mollon 1990; Schiller et al. 1990). Nonetheless, it seems safe to say that not only the achromatic process involving the lightness dimension of surface color, but also the chromatically opponent processes play a role in spatial segmentation (e.g., color contrasts can be used to determine borders), to say nothing of how the specification of color and shape may be combined in, say, V4 (Heywood and Cowey 1987).

This interdependency between color vision and spatial segmentation is downplayed by computational objectivism. This view simply assumes that the surfaces of objects provide a perceiver-independent peg on which to hang objective color as spectral reflectance. The objectivist presumably thinks that the assumption needs no defence, since surface spectral reflectances can be specified in physical terms. But although the *reflectance* at any point in the scene can be specified in physical terms, what counts as a *surface* may in fact involve tacit reference to a type of perceiver. This point has not been evident for several reasons which we need to explore.

First, it is usually simply assumed that surfaces are properties of the world found at a purely physical level of description. At the level of description found in perceptual theory, however, surfaces also figure as properties of the *perceptual object*, that is, the object as construed in relation to the sensory-motor capacities of perceiving animals. Here surfaces are treated in relation to the bodyscaling of the animal, and, in the case of vision, to properties like visual shape, texture, orientation, lightness, and color. How surfaces at this perceptual level are to be linked to the purely physical level is precisely the issue. Simply to assume that this link can be made without implicating the sensory-motor capacities of the animal is to beg the question. For example, the visual system responds to singularities at many scales that characterize apparent contours in edges, yet these scales are integrated into a unified behavioral designation. This integration, however, is not implicit in the singularities themselves: it depends on how the neuronal processes treat them (DeValois and DeValois 1988).[12]

Second, such issues often remain hidden because many theories of perception focus on tasks (e.g., recovering reflectance) in an already well-specified or easily segmented context (e.g., Mondrian displays). Uncritical attention to visual tasks in such artificially simplified contexts makes one forget the complexities involved in spatial segmentation itself.

Third, virtually all theories of perception focus on our familiar human environment rather than the considerably different environments of, say, birds, fishes, or insects. For example, the prespecified objects in low-dimensional models of reflectance are typically middle-sized, frontally viewed, "human" objects, such as bricks, grass, buildings, Munsell color chips, Mondrian displays, and so forth. They are not, for example, silhouettes against the background sky, as seen frontally and laterally by birds, ultraviolet reflectance patterns of flowers, as seen by birds and bees, aquatic objects that contrast with the volume colors of the downwelling or background space light as viewed by fishes, and so on. Because of this attention to prespecified human objects, the issue of how the world comes to be segmented into a given collection of surfaces by different perceiving animals is hardly ever empirically raised, or explored philosophically (but see Stroll 1986).

Finally, if, as Gouras and Zrenner (1981, p. 172) claim, "it is impossible to separate the object sensed from its color because it is the color contrast itself that forms the object," then what counts as the perceptual object may vary considerably depending on the type of color vision system involved.[13] Gouras and Zrenner are referring here to the perceptual object. Nonetheless, the interdependency between color and surface perception is enough to show that at the level of description revelant to perception, it is not at all evident, as computational objectivism assumes, that the specification of surfaces is not relative to the perceiver. In other words, the kinds of surfaces that populate the world as visually perceived by a given animal may depend for their specification on the processes by which that animal segments its visual scene.

Let us summarize this line of argument, which we call the "argument from perceiver-relativity":

The Argument from Perceiver-Relativity

1. Color vision contributes to the task of segmenting the visual scene into regions of distinct surfaces and/or objects.

2. Color vision varies considerably throughout the animal world.

3. We may accordingly expect spatial segmentation to vary as well.

4. What counts as the surface of an object (for perception theory) therefore has to be specified in relation to the perceiving animal.

We take this argument to be conditional, based on a reasoned hypothesis or conjecture that requires further empirical investigation in a comparative neurophysiological and ecological context. Nonetheless, we believe its plausibility undermines much of the computational objectivist's assumption that surfaces provide a perceiver-independent anchor for color.

The comparative ecology of color vision reveals several other points where computational objectivism is inadequate. The computational objectivist typically assumes that the sole or genuine function of color vision is object detection. Matthen (1988), for example, argues that the "biological function" of color vision is object detection via the recovery of surface reflectance. He claims that nonsurface modes of color appearance, such as the blue of the sky, should be explained as the result of "normal misperception," that is, as cases of visual representation that are nonveridical, but do not result from the malfunction or maladaptation of the visual system. Thus Matthen tries to ground the philosophical claim that only surfaces are genuinely colored by relying on a notion of "biological function." The irony of this proposal is that Matthen's claim about the *biological* function of color vision is advanced on the basis of a rather controversial *computational* model (Land's retinex theory) and is undermined by the actual biological and ecological operation of color vision. Color vision is not limited to the perception of surfaces; it includes the perception of the ambient lighting conditions in their own right (not merely as "information to be discounted"), for these are relevant to a variety of environmental conditions, such as weather and time of day (Jameson and Hurvich 1989). Nonsurface modes of color vision also serve to heighten contrast between aerial or aquatic backgrounds (volume colors) and foreground objects (surface colors) (Levine and MacNichol 1982; Lythgoe 1979).

Although we still lack extensive knowledge of the ecological function of color vision in various animal species, the evidence we do have is sufficient to demonstrate that speculations about color vision should not be dictated by top-down computational models that rely on a considerably simplified human perceptual context. Instead, as the following examples will illustrate, color vision must be understood within the context of the quite different behavioral repertoires available to perceiving animals.

Consider first the link in chromatic ecology between visual pigments and animal niches. Studies of aquatic visual ecologies have shown that the retinas of deep sea fishes have been reduced to one rhodopsin pigment, with a sensitivity maxima around 470–490 nm (Levine and MacNichol 1979; Loew and Lythgoe 1978; Partridge et al. 1989). According to one interpretation, this range would permit the maximum of contrast sensitivity for movement (Crescitelli et al. 1985; Muntz 1975). In contrast, for species that have a bioluminescent organ, a different pigment of the porphyropsin family, whose sensitivity maximum (513–539 nm) coincides with the main luminous emission of the organ, has been described (Bowmaker et al. 1988; Partridge et al. 1989). As one moves upward toward more illuminated depths, all species have a larger diversity of photopigments and retinal arrangements, from which one may conclude that different visual objects are pertinent for each species (Lythgoe 1979). This ecological link between photopigments and environments becomes even more striking in migratory fishes, which go from river to sea: Here the relative amounts of rhodopsin and porphyropsin change according to the time of day and season (Beatty 1969; 1984; Bridges 1972; Muntz and McFarland 1977; Muntz and Mouat 1984; Whitmore and Bowmaker 1989). Such polymorphism is also present among other nonmigratory species (Archer and Lythgoe 1990; Archer et al. 1987; Whitmore and Bowmaker 1989). Neumeyer and Arnold (1989) have also recently shown, as we mentioned above, that the goldfish is tetrachromatic for an ambient illumination of 25 lux, but trichromatic for a lower illumination around 1.5 lux. They suggest that this capacity for a dimensional shift is likely to have an ecological interpretation. This evidence for aquatic ecologies is admittedly fragmentary, yet it serves to indicate the need to link chromatic performance to the ecological setting of the animal (Muntz 1975; Wheeler 1982).

Among birds, the retinal oil droplets vary considerably even for species with similar global living conditions (Budnik et al. 1984; Jane and Bowmaker 1988; Martin 1977; Martin and Lett 1985). For example, the common tern, a predator bird, has a significant amount of red and yellow droplets in the dorsal retina, while the barn swallow, which catches insects, has a large quantity of translucent droplets (Goldsmith et al. 1984). In fact, Partridge et al. (1989) has shown by means of cluster analysis that the ecological niche (herbivore, fishing, etc.) is more important in predicting the kinds and distribution of oil droplets than strict phylogenic kinship. The presence of ultraviolet pigments in birds also provides an example. These pigments can be linked to bird-fruit coevolution, including the dissemination of kernels (Snow 1971; Burkhardt 1982), and to ethological factors involving animal recognition, for bird plumages have been shown to have high frequency content, and so might require higher-dimensional color spaces for their recognition (Brush 1990; Burkhardt 1989; Durrer 1986; Hudon and Brush 1989; Weedon 1963).

Ultraviolet sensitivity in birds may also be used in aerial navigation. As we have seen, pigeons have excellent short-wave and near-ultraviolet discrimination. It is possible that, in Nuboer's (1986, pp. 370–71) words, "the excellent spectral discrimination within this range . . . represents an adaptation to the coloration of an unclouded sky. This property enables the pigeon to evaluate short-wave gradients in the sky, ranging from white at the sun's locus to highly saturated (ultra) violet at angles of 90° to the axis between observer and sun." Furthermore, since pigeon navigation is based on orientation with respect to the sun's azimuth, "the perception of colour gradients in the sky may control navigation indirectly when the sun is hidden by clouds."

A different, but perhaps even more important feature of the ecological function of color vision is to yield a set of perceptual categories that have "cognitive significance" for perceiving animals in a variety of behavioral interactions (Jacobs 1981, pp. 170–71). A color category can guide behavior in various ways depending on the things which exemplify it: In the case of fruits, it guides feeding; in the case of animal coloration, it may guide various social interactions, such as mating. Pigeons have been shown to group spectral stimuli into hue categories, and the brightly colored feathers of birds must have cognitive significance for behavior, especially behavior involving sexual recognition. Finally, although object discrimination is obviously important for these kinds of behavior, the cognitive significance of color may have an affective dimension (perhaps related to the overall hormonal/motivational level of the animal) that cannot be explained simply as a function of object discrimination (Varela et al. 1983).

Much research remains to be done on the relations among color vision, perceptual color categories, and animal behavior (Burtt 1979; Hailman 1977). Although color as a perceptual category with cognitive significance obviously plays a great role in human life, there is still little evidence about this dimension of color perception in nonhuman animals, especially nonprimates. In the case of birds, however, it seems safe to conclude that this kind of color experience does exist, as we have been arguing here. In any case, the evidence that we have presented in the previous paragraphs serves to demonstrate our point that the functions of color vision should be understood in the context of the actual behavioral repertoires and visual ecologies of perceiving animals.

2.5   Neurophysiological Subjectivism Revisited

To emphasize the active role that color vision plays in tasks such as spatial segmentation and in guiding the interactions of perceiving animals implies an approach to color perception that is also different from neurophysiological subjectivism. To demonstrate this point, we need to consider Hardin's (1988; 1990) defense of neurophysiological subjectivism.

Hardin's strategy is to offer what we can call an "argument from internal reducibility" whose main claim is that the properties of hue (e.g., uniqueness, binariness) can be reductively identified with psychophysical and eventually neural properties of the visual system. This argument, coupled with the "argument from external irreducibility," leads Hardin to the position that there are no "extradermal" colored objects: there are only chromatic neural states. Hardin's defense of this idea is worth quoting:

> We have no good reasons for thinking that such a replacement of the one [phenomenal] description by the other [neural] description would leave anything out, with a consequent loss of information. On the contrary, we have reason to expect that a proper neural description would be richer, more complete, and, in principle, more penetrable by the intellect. Problems that are intractable at the extradermal physical level or at the phenomenal level promise to yield analysis in neurological terms. (1988, p. 111)

Two points appear to be contained in this remark, one ontological, the other methodological. The ontological claim is that color, or rather chromatic experience, is a type of neural state or process. The methodological claim is that color phenomena can be analyzed in neurological terms. These two claims obviously support each other: If colors are really neural states, then we have reason to pursue a neurological analysis of color phenomena: on the other hand, if we can give a neurological analysis of color phenomena (and we cannot give a comparable physical analysis), then we have reason to believe colors are neural states. We make this distinction not to be pedantic, but because it is primarily the methodological issue that we wish to address here, not the ontological one. In other words, we do not intend to evaluate Hardin's position by embarking upon a discussion of the mind-body problem for visual experience. It is, rather, the scope and limits of a purely neurological approach to color phenomena that interests us.

Our aim in this final section of the comparative argument will be to show that there are indeed phenomena that, intractable as they are at the extradermal and organism-independent physical level as well as the phenomenal level, nonetheless fail to yield to analysis in purely neurological terms. These phenomena are ecological in the broadest sense; that is, they encompass not only the extradermal world as an animal environment, but also perceiving animals as both assemblies of sensory-motor networks and as organismic unities that *shape the extradermal world into an environment in their interactions.*

Consider first the polymorphism in the color vision of the squirrel monkey and the spider monkey (Jacobs 1986). In these species, all males are dichromats, whereas three-quarters of the females are trichromats. Several explanations have been proposed for this polymorphism (Mollon et al. 1984; Nuboer 1986). According to one, it has resulted from adaptation to the spatial heterogeneity of the environment: It is possible that different phenotypes inhabit regions of the jungle that differ in the spectral composition of their ambient light. A second proposal appeals to the hypothesis of group selection: It might be advantageous for the animal community to have members with several forms of color vision. A third proposal appeals to frequency dependent selection: There may be an ecological balance between the availability of certain fruits and the number of phenotypes that can detect them. Finally, another hypothesis holds that the colors of local fruits coevolved with the differences in color vision (Snodderly 1979).

Our second example comes from the color vision of bees. We have seen that bees have trichromatic vision that is shifted towards the ultraviolet. It has been argued that this distinctive form of trichromacy coevolved with the colors of flowers, which often have contrasting patterns in ultraviolet light (Earth 1985; Lythgoe 1979; Menzel 1989; Nuboer 1986). On the one hand, flowers attract pollinators by their food content, and so must be conspicuous and yet different from flowers of other species. On the other hand, bees gather food from flowers, and so need to recognize flowers from a distance. This mutual advantage seems to have determined a coevolution of plant features and sensory-neural capacities in the bee.

Finally, consider that the colored "objects" that animals discriminate are often (perhaps typically) other animals. Therefore, within an ecological framework our inquiry should be concerned just as much with animal coloration—indeed with the coloration of living things in general—as with animal color vision (see Burkhardt 1989; Burtt 1979; Hailman 1977; Lythgoe 1979). Coloration obviously affects an animal's visibility, both to conspecifics and to members of other species in its environment. It is therefore not surprising to find coloration involved in camouflage and in many kinds of visual recognition (e.g., species recognition, sexual recognition, individual recognition, recognition of motivational state, etc.; Baylis 1979; Rowland 1979). Indeed, the ecological entanglement of color vision and animal coloration is truly astounding. Consider, for example, the variations in color vision and coloration among fishes in a tropical coral reef, perhaps one of the richest of color environments.

These kinds of phenomena indicate that a purely neural explanation for color vision is incomplete. To explain the polymorphism in spider and squirrel monkey color vision, and hence the differences in the perceptual experiences of these animals, we must appeal not simply to the neurophysiological constitution of these animals, but also to the evolutionary histories of their environmental interactions, perhaps at several levels of selection.[14] Similarly, to understand why bee color vision is shifted toward the ultraviolet, and hence why the color space of the bee might comprise novel hues, we must appeal to animal-environment coevolution. Finally, to understand the relations among color vision, animal coloration, visual recognition, and animal communication, we must appeal to a broad range of physiological, ecological, and evolutionary considerations, ranging from the physiological functions of pigmentation, to coordinated inter- and intraspecific animal interactions, to the coevolution of the various behavioral partners (Burtt 1979).

We expect that Hardin would not deny any of these points. Indeed, Hardin has recently drawn on evolutionary—or more broadly, ecological—considerations to defend his view that although chromatic categories (red, green, yellow, and blue) have no counterparts in the extradermal world, such categories confer evolutionary advantages on perceiving organisms (Hardin 1990). Hardin argues that color vision does not represent the world as it really is, but rather "encodes information" about light, reflectance, and so forth, in a subjectively generated form that is salient, vivid, and of great practical value for the perceiver. The salience and vividness are to be explained neurophysiologically, whereas the practical value is to be explained ecologically.

We believe, however, that Hardin has not yet appreciated the moral that evolutionary and ecological considerations have for his neurophysiological subjectivism. Color vision does not merely provide practical knowledge of the environment; it also participates in the *codetermination* of perceiving animals and their environments. By codetermination we mean both (1) that animals select properties in the physical world relevant to their structure (body-scaling, sensory-motor capacities, etc.), shaping these properties into environments that have behavioral significance; and (2) that environments select sensory-motor capacities in the animal and thereby constrain animal activity (Levins and Lewontin 1983; 1985). Consider once again the coevolution of plant features and sensory-neural capacities in the bee (and other invertebrates). This coevolution implies not only that bee color vision is sensitive to ultraviolet because it is advantageous for bees to detect flowers that have ultraviolet reflectances, but also that flowers have ultraviolet reflectances because it is advantageous for them to be seen by bees. Thus, the evolution of bee color vision did not simply provide the bee with a practical knowledge of its environment; it also contributed to the very determination of that environment. As Barth (1985) says in his wonderful study of insects and flowers: "The colorful field of flowers is an insect environment that reflects the insects themselves (p. vii) . . . the plants and their pollinators are environment and reflection of one another" (p. 266). Such sensory-neural and environment coevolution provides, then, a particularly dramatic example of how the visual environment is not only relative to the animal, but also partly determined by the visually guided activity of the animal itself.

Such animal-environment codetermination is not limited to invertebrates. As Humphrey (1984) has observed, most of the world's colors are organic colors carried by the pigments of plants and animals—for example, the colors of flowers and fruits, of plumages, of tropical fishes, and so on. Such organic colors have been selected because of their biological significance to those who can see them. It is interesting to note that some pigments, for example, carotenoids, play a key role both on the side of the discriminated object (plants, fruits, feathers), and on the side of the primary processes in the retina (visual pigments, oil droplets). Thus the presence of carotenoids is emblematic of the evolutionary codetermination of perceiving animals and their environments (Rothschild 1975).

Hardin's subjectivism neglects this role that visual perception plays in animal-environment codetermination. The neglect derives, we believe, from Hardin's implicit acceptance of the subjectivist-objectivist framework for evaluating perception derived from Galileo, Newton, and Locke. Thus although Hardin has emphasized the role that color vision plays in generating chromatic categories that have intersubjective, cognitive significance for perceiving animals in their interactions, he nonetheless wishes to drive a principled wedge between, on the one hand, color construed as a subjective encoding of information about the world, and on the other hand, surface reflectances construed as objective properties of the world. He claims, for example, that colors are subjective because he supposes that if there were no perceiving animals in the world, there would be no colors; since objects and their surfaces would remain, however, these are objective (Hardin 1990). (This same argument was in fact given by Galileo in 1623: ". . . Colors and so on are no more than mere names so far as the object in which we place them is concerned, and . . . they reside only in the consciousness. Hence if the living creatures were removed, all these qualities would be wiped away and annihilated" [Drake 1957, p. 274].)

This line of argument not only overlooks but actually does violence to virtually every aspect of the ecologically entangled relations of perceiving animals and their environments. First, it overlooks the fact just mentioned that most of the world's colors are organic colors. The evolution of color vision is inextricably linked to the evolution of organic coloration—so much so that "in a world without animals that possessed colour vision there would be very little colour" (Humphrey 1984, p. 146).

It is therefore irrelevant—perhaps even somewhat perverse—to appeal to *meta-physical* intuitions about what the world would be like "if the living creatures were removed" when one's concern is to provide a *naturalistic* explanation of perceiving animals and their environments.

Second, Hardin's argument overlooks the role that color vision plays in spatial segmentation and hence the relational nature of the surfaces of perceptual objects, which we reviewed above. Elsewhere Hardin (1988, pp. 111–12) has himself drawn attention to a similar point: "Because perceptions of color differences and perceptions of boundaries are closely intertwined neural processes, we see colors and shapes together. Roughly speaking, as color goes, so goes visual shape." For Hardin, however, there is an important difference between color and shape; thus he continues: "Consequently, there are no visual shapes in the ultimate sense, just as there are no colors. But visual shapes have their structural analogues in the physical world, namely, shapes *simpliciter*, and colors do not."[15] We find this point unclear, for Hardin does not tell us exactly what he means by "structurally analogous" and "shapes simpliciter." We obviously agree with Hardin that colors do not have structural analogues in the physical world *in the way that objectivists have supposed*— that is, analogues that do not depend in any way upon the existence of perceivers. This point, however, does not prevent our specifying *context-dependent and interest-relative* structural analogues of color, as the science of colorimetry and its associated color technologies clearly indicate (see Hurvich 1981, Chapters 20–21). This point might strike some as unfair, since Hardin's claim might be that there are no context-independent and non-interest-relative structural analogues for color, whereas there are for visual shape. But if this is Hardin's point, then we are not at all convinced it is true. Unlike Newton and Locke, we no longer take shape to be among the fundamental, microscopic properties of matter (cf. Priest 1989). And, as a macroscopic property, what gets picked out as a given shape may depend on the interests and capacities of those performing the specification. In this sense, surfaces as specified in terms of shapes and boundaries might be more properly thought to belong not to the physical world per se (the world at a purely physical level of description), but rather to what Gibson (1979) calls the "ecological environment," that is, the world as construed in relation to certain animal capacities (cf. Stroll 1986).

The moral of these considerations, we believe, is that the empirical study of color vision—indeed, of perception in general—should not be saddled with some a priori subjective/objective distinction. There is nothing wrong with drawing a distinction between subjective and objective, or internal and external, relative to the framework of a given neurophysiological, psychophysical, or behavioral experiment. The problems arise, rather, when we attempt to force perception theory as a whole into some absolute, subjective/objective straitjacket derived from the empiricist tradition. Hardin (1988) has already impressively demolished many of the dogmas about color in this tradition. He has rightly built his case from biological evidence, but this evidence demands a more sophisticated interactionist approach to color vision than neurophysiological subjectivism delivers. We now turn to the more constructive task of outlining such an approach.

3   Toward an Enactive View of Color Vision

Although the shortcomings of computational objectivism and neurophysiological subjectivism are different, they are related. Computational objectivism conceives of color vision as the "recovery" of animal-independent, distal properties; neurophysiological subjectivism conceives of color vision as the "projection" of subjectively generated qualities onto a distal world of objects and their surfaces. In either case, the role that vision plays in the codetermination of animal and environment is neglected.

Consider the question: "Which came first, the world or the image?" The answer of inverse optics is given ambiguously by the names of the tasks investigated—to recover shape from shading, surface reflectance from varying illuminants, and so on. We call this stance the "chicken position":

Chicken position: The distal world can be specified independently of the animal; it casts images on the perceptual system whose task is to recover the world appropriately from them.

This position is so ingrained that we tend to think the only alternative is the "egg position":

Egg position: The perceptual system projects its own world and the apparent reality of this world is merely a reflection of internal laws of the system.

Our discussion of color vision, however, indicates that neither position is satisfactory. We have seen that colors are not already labelled properties in the world which the perceiving animal must simply recover (objectivism). On the other hand, we have seen that they are not internally generated qualities that the animal simply projects onto the world (subjectivism). Rather, colors are properties of the world that result from animal-environment codetermination. Our case study of color vision suggests that the world and the perceiving animal determine each other, like chicken and egg.

To situate our discussion of vision within the context of animal-environment codetermination, it is worth repeating the summary provided by Levins and Lewontin (1983; 1985) of how organisms "construct" their environments: (1) Organisms determine in and through their interactions what in the physical environment constitutes their relative environments; (2) organisms alter the world external to them as they interact with it; (3) organisms transduce the physical signals that reach them, and so the significance of these signals depends on the structure of the organism; (4) organisms transform the statistical pattern of environmental variation in the world external to them; and (5) the organism-environment relationship defines the "traits" selected for in evolution (cf. Oyama 1985). These five kinds of phenomena involve circular and reciprocal (though not symmetrical) processes of interaction in which the structure of the environment constrains the activity of the organism, but the activity of the organism shapes the environment, and so contributes to the constitution of the environmental constraints (cf. Odling-Smee 1988). It is on the basis of these interactive processes that Levins and Lewontin claim that "the environment and the organism actively co-determine each other" (1985, p. 89).

The implications of this codetermination of animals and their environments have been mostly neglected in perceptual theory, not only by the computational research program of inverse optics, but even by proponents of the so-called "ecological" approach to visual perception (Gibson 1979; Turvey et al. 1981). We will comment on the ecological approach presently; at the moment, we wish to delve further into the reasons for the neglect of animal-environment codetermination in the research program of inverse optics (Marr 1982; Poggio et al. 1985).

Simplifying for the purposes of brevity, inverse optics claims that the animal visually perceives by instantiating various functions that map from two-dimensional images on the receptor array (input) to perceptions of the three-dimensional world (output) via intermediate representations (and given various independent physical constraints). So stated, this account of perception has at least three important consequences that run counter to the idea that visual perception participates in animal-environment codetermination.

First, animal and environment are treated as fundamentally separate systems: The distal environment (objects, surfaces, etc.) is specified in advance; it provides a source of input that is independent of the animal. The perceiving animal, on the other hand, is treated as an input-output system whose function is to solve the ill-posed problem of recovering this prespecified environment. Second, perceptual and motor mechanisms are treated as fundamentally distinct subsystems of the animal. Since the "outputs" of perceptual systems are considered to be perceptual beliefs about the distal scene, perceptual systems form a mechanism for the fixation of belief. On the basis of its perceptual beliefs, the animal may adjust its activity, but the adjustment of activity per se is not treated as part of the perceptual process. Third, perception does not in any way shape the environment; it merely recovers the environment. It might be admitted that animal activity can perturb, select, or construct the environment, but since perception is considered to be fundamentally distinct from action, perception per se does not participate in animal-environment codetermination.

This account of perception is based in a well-established empirical research program and so should not be dismissed either on conceptual grounds or simply by adducing counterexamples. It can be challenged, however, by offering an alternative theoretical and empirical framework as a rival research program. At this point in our target article we obviously do not intend to embark on a detailed defense of such an alternative research program.[16] Our intention here is simply to outline briefly a framework for understanding visual perception in which we take seriously the role of vision in the codetermination of animal and environment.

The first step for perceptual theory is to refuse to separate perception from action, or, more generally, from perceptually guided activity. This refusal is in fact common to a number of different research programs, such as the "ecological approach" of Gibson (1979) and his followers (Turvey et al. 1981), the biological approach to cognition of Maturana and Varela (1980; 1987), Freeman's view of brain processes (Freeman 1975; Freeman and Skarda 1985; Skarda and Freeman 1987), and the recent work in AI and robotics of Brooks (1986; 1987; 1989). All of these research programs take as central the fact that perception and action have evolved together—that perception is always *perceptually guided activity*. But whereas the first research program (Gibson's) chooses to focus on properties of the animal environment and optical properties of the ambient light, the others focus on the sensory-motor structure of the animal, either as neuronal networks that link sensory and motor surfaces or as "layers" of "activity producing systems" in artificial robotic "creatures."

We must encompass both the extradermal world conceived as the animal's environment and the sensory-motor structure of the animal in any adequate theory of perception. We believe that the original Gibsonian program exaggerated the role of invariances in the receptor array activity and their hypothesized specification of the environment. That program neglected not only the complex neural processes that are required to guide activity, but also how those processes contribute to shaping different environments depending on the animal. The original Gibsonian program remains unsatisfactory precisely because it does not take this further step, namely that of shifting the reference point for understanding perception from the environment to the structure of the perceiving animal, understood as the kinds of self-organizing neuronal networks that couple sensory and motor surfaces, which determine both how the animal can be modulated by environmental events and how sensory-motor activity participates in animal-environment codetermination. [See also Ullman: "Against Direct Perception" *BBS* 3(3) 1980.] Elsewhere one of us has argued that a consistent application of this shift in perspective is tantamount to treating the animal as an autonomous self-organizing system rather than as a heteronomous input–output system (Varela 1979; 1984; 1989; see also Freeman and Skarda 1985; Skarda and Freeman 1987). We do not intend to repeat these arguments here; we mention the point because it is primarily this second step—emphasizing the autonomous organization of the animal—that marks the difference between our emphasis on perceptually guided activity and Gibson's. In contrast, many Gibsonians continue to treat perception in largely optical terms, and so attempt to build up the theory of perception almost entirely from the side of the environment. We believe this tendency is largely the result of Gibson's belief that the only alternative to the mistaken sense-data view of perception is direct realism (see Gibson 1967; Turvey 1977). Our approach, however, like that of some more recent Gibsonians (e.g., Kelso and Kay 1987), takes from Gibson the deep insight that perception must be understood within the ecological context of guided activity, but we develop this insight in two important ways: (1) by focusing on the self-organizing properties of neural networks as the proper substrate of animal activity; and (2) by treating the environment not simply as the ecological setting for animal activity, but also as something determined by that very activity. To label this concern with perceptually guided activity thus understood, we will use the term *enactive* as proposed by Varela (1989; 1991a), and as subsequently developed by Varela et al. (1991).

The point of departure for an enactive approach to vision, then, is not the problem of recovering a prespecified distal world. Rather, it is to specify the sensory-motor patterns that underlie the visual guidance of animal activity in its local situation. Our examination of differences in color vision led us to hypothesize that animals with different sensory-motor capacities would segment the world in different ways. As a corollary, we claim that the prespecified world we find in, say, low-dimensional models of surface reflectance is actually the world as described in relation to the sensory-motor capacities of the higher primates. It is perhaps a legitimate simplification to specify or label the world in advance when studying our own visual capacities (or those of animals very much like us). It is not legitimate, however, when studying perception in animals that differ considerably from us.

To make this point clearer, consider again the visual system of birds, which provides such a stark contrast to the visual systems of the more familiar mammals. As we mentioned above, the avian retina has two regions of high neuronal density (foveas), which give rise to distinct frontal and lateral visual fields that in turn correspond roughly to further anatomical projections in the brain—the parallel thalamo-fugal and tecto-fugal pathways. Experiments reveal interesting differences between these two visual fields: Frontal fixation is used for static and slow stimuli, and lateral fixation for fast-moving stimuli (Maldonado et al. 1988). There are also differences in accommodation, depth of focus (Bloch and Martinoya 1983), spectral sensitivity (Nuboer and Wortel 1987; Remy and Emmerton 1989), and probably chromatic vision (Varela et al. 1983). Thus, visual discrimination for birds is not a cyclopean image reconstruction but a contextualized specification according to avian sensory-motor activity—a visual world-to-the-front and a visual world-to-the-side are enacted by the animal. It is the visuomotor behavior that actually reveals what constitutes a relevant world for the animal, not a reconstruction of the world as it appears visually to us.

This emphasis on sensory-motor patterns of activity is not, of course, incompatible with abstract task-analyses for vision per se. Our objection, rather, is to the biologically implausible idea of a prespecified or already labelled world that the perceiving animal must recover appropriately. Although this assumption is built into Marr's conception of the computational level of analysis and of vision as inverse optics, it need not be accepted by those who wish to provide abstract task-analyses for vision and to build artificial visual systems. Indeed, there are models that considerably relax this assumption, such as Grossberg's (1984; Carpenter and Grossberg 1987) adaptive resonant neuronal networks and Edelman's selective recognition automata (Reeke and Edelman 1988). Similarly, in Brooks's (1986; 1987; 1989) recent works in robotics, the ongoing updating of sensory-motor activity is the key for successful design, rather than the representation of prespecified features of the world. By construing visual perception not as recovery or representation, but as guided activity, these models implicitly embody the shift in perspective that we are calling "enaction."

This enactive orientation also implies an understanding of the relationship between the physical and the perceptual different from the usual one in the computational level of analysis. Inverse optics typically assumes that the task of perception is simply to recover properties of the physical world. The enactive approach suggests that perception is not about the physical world in this way. The world that a given animal perceives cannot be given a purely physical-level specification, for what an animal perceives depends on three kinds of factors: (1) physical-level constraints; (2) sensory-motor activity as constituted by neuronal processes and developmental constraints: and (3) evolutionary history. For example, such physical-level constraints as spectral reflectances and light signals are certainly ingredients of what the animal sees. They are not sufficient to determine the *perceptual object*, however, for, as we have seen, color spaces of different dimensionalities can be constructed on the basis of the same physical signals. To account for these differences and hence for the differences in color among the relevant perceptual objects, we must in addition appeal to sensory-motor activity and evolutionary history. Each of these three factors is necessary to determine the perceptual object; in the absence of any one of them, therefore, the perceptual object cannot be properly explained.

This claim about the status of the perceptual object also serves to mark the difference between enaction and subjectivism. Hardin's subjectivism implies that the perceptual object is simply "in the head," and so can be reconstructed in entirely neural terms. As he says: "The tactic that suggests itself is to show how phenomena of the visual field are represented in the visual cortex and then to show how descriptions of the visual field may be replaced by descriptions of neural processes" (Hardin 1988, p. 111). Our critique of neurophysiological subjectivism in the previous section implies that the perceptual object, though experiential, is also ineliminably ecological, and so, contrary to Hardin, is not simply "in the head."

The enactive view of perceptual content is also different from both the "externalist" view that perceptual content is provided by distal physical properties and the "internalist" view that perceptual content is provided by subjective qualities (qualia). According to the enactive view, the contents of perceptual states are to be type-identified by way of the ecological properties perceived, and these ecological properties are to be type-identified by way of the states that perceive them. One should not be put off by this circularity, for it is informative. To specify perceptual content for a given animal we must investigate the relevant environmental properties, and to determine the relevant environmental properties we must investigate the sensory-motor patterns of activity that constitute the animal's perceptual states. This circularity is also empirically well-founded: Recall the discussion of how color vision and the ecological properties detected by color vision (e.g., plant and animal coloration) have in the course of evolution been selected for each other. The enactive view of perceptual content thus follows from animal-environment code-termination.

Now that we have provided an idea of the kind of conceptual space in which an enactive approach to vision could grow, let us return specifically to color vision. According to enactivism, color is neither a perceiver-independent property, as in objectivism nor is it merely a projection or property of the brain, as in subjectivism. Rather, it is a property of the enacted perceptual environments experienced by animals in their visually guided interactions. Unlike computational objectivism and neurophysiological subjectivism, this does not lead to an eliminativist position regarding color: color is not divested of its phenomenal or experiential structure in favor of spectral reflectance; nor is it divested of its extradermal locus in favor of neural states. Instead, color is a property of the extradermal world understood as an animal's environment, a world that is enacted by animal-environment codetermination. Thus we arrive at the view announced at the beginning of this paper, according to which color is both ecological and experiential.

Our view might in some respects recall Locke's (1690/1975) concept of color as a relational property, but there are significant differences. Locke held that color is relational because it is a "secondary quality," a disposition of objects to cause color sensations in a perceiver. According to the Lockean view, then, color is not merely *relational*, but also *dispositional* and *subjective* (see Bennett 1971). Ecological experientialism, however, does not imply that color is dispositional and subjective. We have not tried to explicate the relational nature of color by attempting to link dispositional properties of an organism-independent physical world, and private sensations, qualia, or sense-data. This is not feasible, we feel, despite repeated empiricist attempts (Westphal 1987; Thompson 1989). Nor does ecological experientialism rest on the distinction between primary and secondary qualities. On the contrary, our argument that not only color but also other high-level, spatial properties of the scene (object surfaces as determined by shapes and boundaries) are relational runs directly counter to the Lockean and Newtonian attempt to draw a principled distinction between color as a secondary quality, and size, shape, and so forth, as primary qualities. Rather, we have emphasized the relational nature of the perceptual environment as a whole resulting from the enactive dimensions of visually guided activity.

Our intention in this target article has been to offer a broad, comparative framework for the ongoing, interdisciplinary effort to understand color vision and visual perception in cognitive science. This framework suggests specific directions for further research.

(i) The first concern of our comparative approach is to determine more precisely the kinds of color space there are in the animal world. For tetrachromacy, we need further evidence of four-way color mixture; to establish pentachromacy, we need evidence of five-way color mixture. Frequency modulation in the study of color vision (as described in appendix B) might be useful in this area.

(ii) A related question concerns how the relevant color vision mechanisms and the dimensionalities of color space are related to perceptual phenomena such as constancy and segmentation of the visual scene. Of particular interest here is how color and other visual phenomena such as visual shape, texture, and space, interact to constitute different perceptual objects for various perceiving animals.

(iii) A third research objective is to determine (at least to a degree comparable to what is known of primates) the neuronal mechanisms underlying the variety of color spaces of different animal groups, especially fishes and birds. This is the key to understanding how color vision figures in the larger context of animal life and behavior.

(iv) Finally, the ecological aspects of the perceptual environment need to be investigated, for example, local illuminance and reflectance conditions, animal coloration, and animal communication. The task here is to develop further the means to describe the perceptual environment from a given animal's point of view, rather than imposing anthropocentric assumptions about such environments.

These questions have hardly begun to be addressed in detail in visual science, but we can expect their investigation to reveal even further the splendor of color as a naturalized aesthetic, or, in the words of Cézanne, "the place where our brain and the universe meet" (Merleau-Ponty 1964, p. 67).

Appendix A

Decorrelation Procedure for Calculating Chromatic Channels
(Buchsbaum and Gottschalk 1983; Palacios, 1992)
Consider responses r_i to an arbitrary illuminant belonging to a set $\{I(\lambda)\}$,

$$r_1 = \int d\lambda \, w_i R^i(\lambda) I(\lambda)$$

where the w_i are weighting factors for each primary response (as explained below). Next construct a covariance matrix Γ between the receptor response as follows:

$$
\Gamma =
\begin{array}{ccccc}
\gamma_{11} & \cdot & \cdot & \cdot & \gamma_{1n_{recep}} \\
\cdot & & \cdot & & \cdot \\
\cdot & & & \cdot & \cdot \\
\cdot & & & \cdot & \cdot \\
\gamma_{n_{recep}1} & \cdot & \cdot & \cdot & \gamma_{n_{recep}n_{recep}}
\end{array}
$$

with

$$\gamma_{ij} = Ex\{r_i r_j\} - Ex\{r_i\} \cdot Ex\{r_j\} \tag{11}$$

where Ex is the expectation operator. To achieve optimal decorrelation the obvious step is to obtain the eigenvalues φ_i and eigenvectors for Γ, and the new matrix A constituted of the eigenvectors and their transpose A^T so that:

$$
A^T \circ \Gamma \circ A =
\begin{bmatrix}
\varphi_1 & 0 & 0 \\
0 & \cdot & 0 \\
0 & 0 & \varphi_{n_{recep}}
\end{bmatrix}
$$

The eigenvector transformation is now well defined by:

$$\vec{c}_r = A^T \cdot \vec{s}_r \tag{12}$$

and the postulated chromatic channels ($C^1, \ldots, C^n_{recep}$) thus calculated can be compared with the available experimental evidence. As Buchsbaum and Gottschalk (1983) emphasize, the covariance matrix depends not only on the shape of the primary responses, but also on the ensemble properties of the illuminants $\{I(\lambda)\}$. In fact, to arrive at an explicit expression for the correlations, we need to make some assumptions about the expectations $Ex\{I(\lambda)\}$ of the ensemble. A correlation $R(\lambda,\mu)$ and a covariance $K(\lambda,\mu)$ function can be defined as follows:

$$
\begin{aligned}
R(\lambda,\mu) &= Ex\{I(\lambda)/(\mu)\} \\
K(\lambda,\mu) &= R(\lambda,\mu) - Ex\{(I-(\lambda)\}\,Ex\{I(\mu)\}.
\end{aligned}
\tag{13}
$$

If the choice is $K(\lambda,\mu) = \delta(\lambda - \mu)$ where δ is the Dirac delta function, this amounts to using monochromatic illuminants. Inserting (13) into (11) finally yields an explicit form for the entries in the covariance matrix (11):

$$\gamma_{ij} = \int d\lambda\, R^i(\lambda)R^j(\lambda) \tag{14}$$

Thus the relative contributions from each class of retinal receptors need to be filled in by weighting factors previously mentioned. These are the only unknowns in our calculations; we have adjusted them so that the resulting channels have a good fit with experiments. These values should not be seen as ad hoc, however, but as proportions that should covary with neural characteristics.

For example, in the case of the goldfish this procedure yields:

$$
\begin{matrix}
C^1 \\
C^2 \\
C^3 \\
C^4
\end{matrix}
\;=\;
\begin{matrix}
0.11 & 0.37 & 0.72 & 0.58 \\
0.83 & -0.5 & 0.23 & -0.12 \\
0.26 & 0.68 & 0.15 & -0.67 \\
-0.48 & -0.4 & 0.64 & -0.44
\end{matrix}
\;
\begin{matrix}
R^1 \\
R^2 \\
R^3 \\
R^4
\end{matrix}
$$

For the putative color channels of the pigeon, see figure 15.4d.

Appendix B

**Frequency Analysis of Color Vision
(Barlow 1982; Bonnardel and Varela 1989)**

The basic strategy is to consider an illuminant (or a response capacity of the visual system) in the *frequency* domain, that is, to examine the spectral power distribution of the signal (or the response mechanism) in terms of cycles over "visible" window. For example, we can consider the frequency response of the three chromatic channels required for human vision. The channels proposed by Hurvich and Jameson, when studied under Fourier analysis, predict that beyond 2–3 cycles/300 nm there should be little response, with a peak of sensitivity for signals around 1.7 cycles/300 nm. These predictions correspond well with the first measurements of such a *modulation sensitivity function* (MSF) obtained with a specially built apparatus that can produce sinusoidally modulated illuminants with controlled contrast, frequency, and phase (Bonnardel and Varela 1989). The conclusion is that the signals for color vision are *band-limited*, that is, bounded in both the variable ("visible" window) and the frequency (cycles per "visible" window) domain. Now a nontrivial relationship exists between a collection of such band-limited signals and the number of significant independent samples required to reconstruct with sufficient accuracy any function in the collection (Buchsbaum and Gottschalk 1983; Dym and McKean 1975). Specifically, it can be shown that:

$$n_{sample} = \Phi[BT] + 1 \tag{15}$$

where $\Phi[x]$ stands for the highest integer smaller than x; and n_{sample} is the number of independent channels required to sample the space of signals limited by B (in the frequency domain) and by T (in the wavelength domain).[17] For example, if we take $n_{sample} = 3$, and $T = 300\,nm$, as in the human trichromatic system, a band-limitation $B = 1.5$ cycle/300 nm is predicted. This limitation is within the range of the measured band-limitation of human natural scenes, which contain about 98% of all reflectances within the 1.5 cyc/300 nm limit (Maloney 1985) but falls a little short of the observed MTF in humans which peaks at this value. In contrast, if $n_{sample} = 4$ and $T = 330\,nm$, as is the case in birds, one would predict a band-limit of $B = 0.001$ cyc/nm. This result is due in part to the avian sensitivity window being large into 370 nm, and on the other hand, to the pigment sensitivities being narrower: the combination of these two allows for less demodulation of the MSF at higher frequencies and corresponds to the higher frequency content directly visible in the putative channels discussed before.

Briefly stated, then different chromatic dimensions will satisfy the sampling theorem with different combinations of the three quantities involved (n_{sample}, B and T), thus permitting quantitative comparisons of diverse color vision mechanisms. In particular, the measurements of MSF might represent a way to ascertain directly the dimensionality of a color space. On the basis of such a determination of color space, one could then undertake a comparison of the frequency-limitations of color vision mechanisms with the frequency-limitations of the reflectances of the relevant objects in the animal's environment. As we mentioned above, data have been collected concerning the frequency-limitations of human natural scenes (Maloney 1985); in the case of birds, some data have been collected about the reflectance properties of objects such as feathers, which, not surprisingly, have higher frequency contents than those of human natural objects (Burkhardt 1989). Obviously, work in this area is just beginning.

Acknowledgments

We have discussed the material presented in this paper with a number of people. In particular we wish to thank: Mark Ansprach, Ronald deSousa, Daniel Dennett, Lynd Forguson, Timothy Goldsmith, C. L. Hardin, David R. Hilbert, André Kukla, Jim McGilvray, Christa Neumeyer, William Seager, and Mark Thornton.

During the preparation of this paper ET was supported by a Social Sciences and Humanities Research Council of Canada Postdoctoral Fellowship (#456-89-0236). AP was supported by the Simone et Cino del Duca, and the Philippe Foundations. The financial support to FV from Fondation de France (Chaire Scientifique), CNRS,

Ministère de la Recherche et la Technologie, and the Prince Trust Fund is gratefully acknowledged.

Notes

1. For further discussion, see Churchland and Sejnowski (1988), Sejnowski et al. (1988), and Boden (1988). Marr's optimality assumption has been criticized by Kitcher (1988); for some related points see Ramachandran (1985).

2. In visual science there is confusion and some disagreement over the use of the terms "brightness" and "lightness." According to Wyszecki and Stiles (1982, pp. 493–500), *brightness* is the "attribute of a visual sensation according to which a given visual stimulus appears to be more or less intense" (p. 493), whereas *lightness* is the "attribute of a visual sensation according to which the area in which the visual stimulus is presented appears to emit more or less light in proportion to that emitted by a similarly illuminated area perceived as a 'white' stimulus" (p. 494). Strictly speaking, then, "brightness" refers to a dim-to-dazzling scale, whereas "lightness" refers to the gray scale of black and white. Nevertheless, many visual scientists, a large number of whom we cite in this paper, use "brightness" to refer to the white-black dimension. Furthermore, "lightness" has also been used in a related, but somewhat different sense by Land (1977; 1983), and by other researchers in computational color vision (Hurlbert 1986), to mean the psychophysical correlate of average relative reflectance (Land 1983) or scaled integrated reflectance (McCann et al. 1976). To avoid confusion, then, we use "brightness" for the achromatic dimension.

3. The material on which we are drawing here can be found in Boynton (1979), Hurvich (1981), Wyszecki and Stiles (1982), Mollon and Sharpe (1983), and Ottoson and Zeki (1985).

4. Our point in citing this passage is not that computational color vision commits one to objectivism about color—Land (1978; 1983), for example, holds distinctly nonobjectivist views. It is, rather, that the computational conception of color vision as concerned almost exclusively with the task of recovering surface reflectance suggests a form of objectivism.

5. For additional studies of near-ultraviolet sensitivity in bird vision, see Wright (1979), Delius and Emmerton (1979), Emmerton and Delius (1980), Emmerton (1983), Burkhardt (1982; 1989), and Burkhardt and Maier (1989). Cones with peak sensitivity in the near-ultraviolet have also been found in fishes: Harosi and Hashimoto (1983); Neumeyer (1985); Bowmaker and Kunz (1987).

6. Notice that channel C2 in figure 15.4d has the *appearance* of an achromatic channel because of very small negative contributions from the long-wave primaries. This issue, as well as the general problem of the relative merits of a tetrachromatic or pentachromatic model for explaining the empirical data on pigeon color vision, require more elaborate discussion than we can provide here (see Palacios 1991).

7. This point is made clearly by Gouras (1985, p. 386), though it is a familiar theme in the history of color science. See Wasserman (1979) for a historical survey.

8. Some philosophers would no doubt go even further and argue that we cannot know what tetrachromatic or pentachromatic perception is like because the revelant facts (tetrachromatic

or pentachromatic experience) are accessible only from the point of view of tetrachromatic and pentachromatic perceivers (cf. Nagel 1974/1980). Although this claim is certainly relevant to our discussion, space constraints do not allow us to consider the various arguments here. We will therefore reserve discussion of this matter for another occasion (see Akins 1990; P. M. Churchland 1985; and Jackson 1982).

9. Hardin (1988, p. 146) notes this possibility of ternary hues by imagining a hypothetical tetrachromatic "visual super-woman," but does not extend his discussion to actual tetrachromacy among vertebrates such as birds and fishes.

10. Several objectivists (P. M. Churchland 1985; 1986; Hilbert 1987, pp. 111–18; Matthen 1988) have argued that such a mapping can be found in Edwin Land's (1977; 1983) retinex color space in which colors correspond to points in a three-dimensional space whose axes correspond to values of lightness calculated independently in each of three long-, middle-, and short-wave bands based on the sensitivities of the human (cone) photoreceptors. These arguments overlook two features of Land's model: (i) The axes of Land's color space are usually given as axes of lightness, not (average relative) reflectance. This is important because lightness is a sensation that can be measured only by a visual system, and problems arise for the straightforward identification of lightness with reflectance just as they do for color. (ii) Since the retinex color space attempts to specify colors purely in terms of lightness values it does not model the opponent relations and unique/binary structure of hue. In fact, we cannot at present be said to understand how (chromatic) color could be generated purely from (achromatic) lightness comparisons.

11. It should also be noted that computational objectivist arguments such as Matthen's (1988) rely on a very strong notion of adaptive biological functions. We believe there are serious problems with this notion, but we will not pursue this point here. See Varela (1984); Maturana and Varela (1980).

12. We intend to investigate this issue in greater detail in another essay.

13. This claim is similar to one made by Berkeley (1710, Part I, para. 10). See also Wilson (1987).

14. A similar claim could be made for polymorphism in the evolution of human color vision, for example, red-green color blindness in human males.

15. This line of argument corresponds closely to one of Locke's (1690/1975) formulations of the primary/secondary quality distinction. Locke held that in the case of shape, our ideas (visual shapes) resemble (are structurally analogous to) their physical causes (shapes simpliciter), whereas in the case of color, they do not. Our criticism of this view as espoused by Hardin is similar to Berkeley's rejection of the view as espoused by Locke (see note 13).

16. For extensive elaboration of a research program for neuroscience in which the perceiving animal is treated not as an input-output system specified in terms of external mechanisms of control, but rather as an autonomous self-organizing system, see Maturana and Varela (1980; 1987), and Varela (1979; 1984; 1989; 1991a; 1991b), and Varela et al. (1991).

17. This so-called sampling theorem requires, however, that the ensemble of band-limited functions have stringent averages (Brill and Benzschawel 1985).

References

Akins, K. (1990) Science and our inner lives: Birds of prey, bats, and the common (featherless) bi-ped. In *Interpretation and explanation in the study of animal behavior*, ed. M. Bekoff and D. Jamieson. Westview.

Archer, S. N., and Lythgoe, J. N. (1990) The visual pigment basis for cone polymorphism in the guppy (*Poecilia reticulata*). *Vision Research* 30: 225–233.

Archer, S. N., Endler, J. A., Lythgoe, J. N., and Partridge, J. C. (1987) Visual pigment polymorphism in the guppy (*Poecilia reticulata*). *Vision Research* 27: 1243–1252.

Barlow, H. B. (1982) What causes trichromacy? A theoretical analysis using comb-filtered spectra. *Vision Research* 22: 635–643.

Barth, F. G. (1985) *Insects and flowers: The biology of a partnership*. Translated from the German by M. A. Biederman-Thorson. Princeton University Press.

Baylis, J. R. (1979) Optical signals and interspecific communication. In *The behavioral significance of color*, ed. E. H. Burtt. Garland STPM Press.

Beatty, D. D. (1969) Visual pigments of the burdot (*Lota lota*) and seasonal changes in their relative proportions. *Vision Research* 9: 1173–1183.

Beatty, D. D. (1984) Visual pigments and the labile scotopic visual system of fish. *Vision Research* 24: 1563–1573.

Bennett, J. (1971) *Locke, Berkeley, Hume: Central themes*. Oxford University Press (Oxford).

Berkeley, G. (1710/1965) The principles of human knowledge. In *Berkeley's philosophical writings*, ed. D. M. Armstrong. Macmillan.

Berlin, B., and Kay, P. (1969) *Basic color terms: Their universality and evolution*. University of California Press.

Bloch, S., and Martinoya, C. (1983) Specialization of visual functions for the different retinal areas in the pigeon. In *Advances in behavioral neuroethology*, ed. P. Ewert, R. Capranica and D. Ingle. Plenum Press.

Boden, M. (1988) *Computer models of mind*. Cambridge University Press.

Bonnardel, V., and Varela, F. J. (1989) Response of the human color vision system to sinusoidal power distributions. *Neuroscience Abstracts* 15(1): 625.

Bowmaker, J. K. (1977) The visual pigments, oil droplets and spectral sensitivity of the pigeon. Vision Research 17: 1129–1138.

Bowmaker, J. K. (1980a) Birds see ultraviolet light. *Nature* 284: 306.

Bowmaker, J. K. (1980b) Colour vision in birds and the role of oil droplets. *Trends in Neurosciences* 3: 196–199.

Bowmaker, J. K. (1983) Trichromatic colour vision: Why only three receptor types? *Trends in Neurosciences* 6: 41–43.

Bowmaker, J. K., and Kunz, Y. W. (1987) Ultraviolet receptors, tetrachromatic colour vision and retinal mosaics in the brown trout (*Salmo trutta*): Age-dependent changes. *Vision Research* 27: 2101–2108.

Bowmaker, J. K., Dartnall, H. J., and Herring, P. J. (1988) Longwave-sensitive visual pigments in some deep-sea fishes: Segregation of "paired" rhodopsine and porphyropsins. *Journal of Comparative Psychology A* 163: 685–698.

Boynton, R. M. (1979) *Human color vision*. Holt, Rinehart, and Winston.

Boynton, R. M. (1988) Color vision. *Annual Review of Psychology* 39: 69–100.

Bridges, C. D. (1972) The rhodopsin-porphyropsin visual system. In *Handbook of sensory physiology, VII/1*, ed. H. J. Dantall. Springer-Verlag.

Brill, M., and Benzschawel, T. (1985) Remarks on signal-processing explanations of the trichromacy of vision. *Journal of the Optical Society of America A* 2: 1794–1796.

Brooks, R. (1986) Achieving artificial intelligence through building robots. *AI Memo 889*. MIT Artifical Intelligence Laboratory.

Brooks, R. (1987) Autonomous mobile robots. In *AI in the 1980s and beyond*, ed. W. E. L. Grimson and R. S. Patil. The MIT Press.

Brooks, R. (1989) A robot that walks: Emergent behaviors from a carefully evolved network. *AI Memo 1091*, MIT Artificial Intelligence Laboratory.

Brown, P. K., and Wald, G. (1964) Visual pigments in single rods and cones of the human retina. *Science* 144: 45–52.

Brush, A. H. (1990) Metabolism of carotenoid pigments in birds. *FASEB* 4: 2969–2977.

Buchsbaum, G. (1980) A spatial processor model for object colour perception. *Journal of the Franklin Institute* 310: 1–26.

Buchsbaum, G., and Gottschalk, A. (1983) Trichromacy, opponent colours coding, and optimum colour information transmission in the retina. *Proceedings of the Royal Society of London B* 220: 89–113.

Budnik, V., Mpodozis, J., Varela, F. J., and Maturana, H. R. (1984) Regional specialization of the quail retina: Ganglion cell density and oil droplet distribution. *Neurosciences Letters* 51: 145–150.

Burkhardt, D. (1982) Birds, berries and UV: A note on some consequences of UV vision in birds. *Naturwissenschaften* 69: 153–157.

Burkhardt, D. (1989) UV vision: A bird's eye view of feathers. *Journal of Comparative Physiology A* 164: 787–796.

Burkhardt, D., and Maier, E. (1989) The spectral sensitivity of a passerine bird is highest in the UV. *Naturwissenschaften* 76: 82–83.

Burtt, E. H. Jr., ed. (1979) *The behavioral significance of color*. Garland STPM Press.

Carpenter, G., and Grossberg, S. (1987) A massively parallel architecture for a self-organizing neural pattern recognition machine. *Computer Vision, Graphics, and Image Processing* 37: 54–115.

Chen, D. M., and Goldsmith, T. H. (1986) Four spectral classes of cones in the retinas of birds. *Journal of Comparative Physiology A* 159: 473–479.

Chen, D. M., Collins, J. S., and Goldsmith, T. H. (1984) The ultraviolet receptor of bird retinas. *Science* 225: 337–340.

Churchland, P. M. (1985) Reduction, qualia, and the direct introspection of brain states. *Journal of Philosophy* 82: 8–28.

Churchland, P. M. (1986) Some reductive strategies in cognitive neurobiology. *Mind* 95: 279–309.

Churchland, P. S., and Sejnowski, T. J. (1988) Perspectives on cognitive neuroscience. *Science* 242: 741–745.

Crawford, M. L. J., Anderson, R. A., Blake, R., Jacobs, G. H., and Neumeyer, C. (1990) Interspecies comparisons in the understanding of human visual perception. In *Visual perception. The neurophysiological foundations*, ed. L. Spillman and J. S. Werner. Academic Press.

Crescitelli, F., McFall-Ngai, M., and Horwitz, J. (1985) The visual pigment sensitivity hypothesis: Further evidence from fishes of varying habitats. *Journal of Comparative Physiology A* 157: 323–333.

Dartnall, H. J. A., Bowmaker, J. K., and Mollon, J. D. (1983) Human visual pigments: Microspectrophotometric results from the eyes of seven persons. *Proceedings of the Royal Society of London B* 220: 115–130.

Delius, J. D., and Emmerton, J. (1979) Visual performance of pigeons. In *Neural mechanisms of behavior in the pigeon*, ed. A. M. Granda and J. H. Maxwell. Plenum Press.

DeValois, R., and DeValois, K. (1975) Neural coding of color. In *Handbook of perception, vol. V: Seeing*, ed. E. C. Carterette and M. P. Friedman. Academic Press.

DeValois, R., and DeValois, K. (1988) *Spatial vision*. Oxford University Press.

De Yoe, E. A., and Van Essen, D. C. (1988) Concurrent processing streams in monkey visual cortex. *Trends in Neuroscience* 11: 219–226.

Drake, S. (1957) *Discoveries and opinions of Galileo*. Doubleday.

Durrer, H. (1986) Colouration. In *Biology of the integument, the skin of birds*, ed. J. Bereiter-Hahn, A. G. Matoltsy and K. S. Richards. Springer.

Dym, P., and McKean, S. (1975) *Fourier signals and integrals*. Academic Press.

D'Zmura, M., and Lennie, P. (1986) Mechanisms of color constancy. *Journal of the Optical Society of America A* 3: 1662–1672.

Emmerton, J. (1983) Pattern discrimination in the near-ultraviolet by pigeons. *Perception and Psychophysics* 34: 555–559.

Emmerton, J., and Delius, J. D. (1980) Wavelength discrimination in the "visible" and ultraviolet spectrum by pigeons. *Journal of Comparative Physiology A* 141: 47–52.

Freeman, W. (1975) *Mass action in the nervous system*. Academic Press.

Freeman, W., and Skarda, C. (1985) Spatial EEG patterns, nonlinear dynamics, and perception: The neo-Sherrington view. *Brain Research Reviews* 10: 145–175.

Gershon, R. (1987) The use of color in computational vision. *Technical Reports on Research in Biological and Computational Vision*: RBCV-TV-87-15. Department of Computer Science. University of Toronto.

Gibson, J. J. (1967) New reasons for realism. *Synthese* 17: 162–172.

Gibson, J. J. (1979) *The ecological approach to visual perception.* Houghton Mifflin Co.

Goldsmith, T. H. (1980) Hummingbirds see near ultraviolet light. *Science* 207: 786–788.

Goldsmith, T. H. (1990) Optimization, constraint, and history in the evolution of eyes. *Quarterly Review of Biology* 65: 281–322.

Goldsmith, T. H., Collins, J. S., and Licht, S. (1984) The cone oil droplets of avian retinas. *Vision Research* 24: 1661–1671.

Gouras, P. (1985) Color vision. In *Principles of neural science*, ed. E. R. Kandel and J. H. Schwartz. Elsevier.

Gouras, P., and Zrenner, E. (1981) Color vision: A review from a neurophysiological perspective. *Progress in Sensory Physiology* 1: 139–179.

Grossberg, S. (1984) *Studies in mind and brain.* D. Reidel.

Hailman, J. P. (1977) *Optical signals: Animal communication and light.* Indiana University Press.

Hardin, C. L. (1984) Are "scientific" objects coloured? *Mind* 93: 491–500.

Hardin, C. L. (1988) *Color for philosophers: Unweaving the rainbow.* Hackett.

Hardin, C. L. (1990) Why color? In Perceiving, measuring, and using color, ed. M. Brill. *Proceedings of SPIE* 1250: 293–300.

Harosi, F. I., and Hashimoto, Y. (1983) Ultraviolet visual pigment in a vertebrate: A tetrachromatic cone system in the dace. *Science* 222: 1021–1023.

Heider, E. R. (1972) Universals in color naming and memory. *Journal of Experimental Psychology* 93: 10–20.

Helson, H. (1938) Fundamental problem in color vision. I. The principles governing changes in hue, saturation, and lightness of nonselective samples in chromatic illumination. *Journal of Experimental Psychology* 23: 439–476.

Helson, H., and Jeffers, V. B. (1940) Fundamental problems in color vision. II. Hue, lightness, and saturation of selective samples in chromatic illumination. *Journal of Experimental Psychology* 26: 1–27.

Heywood, C. A., and Cowey, A. (1987) On the role of the cortical area V4 in the discrimination of hue and pattern in macaque monkeys. *Journal of Neuroscience* 7: 2601–2616.

Hilbert, D. R. (1987) *Color and color perception. A study in anthropocentric realism.* Stanford University: Center for the Study of Language and Information.

Hood, D. C., and Finkelstein, M. A. (1983) A case for the revision of textbook models of color vision: The detection and appearance of small brief lights. In *Colour vision: Physiology and psychophysics*, ed. J. D. Mollon and L. T. Sharpe. Academic Press.

Horn, B. K. P. (1974) Determining lightness from an image. *Computer Graphics and Image Processing* 3: 227–299.

Hudon, J., and Brush, H. A. (1989) Probable dietary basis of a color variant of the cedar waxwing. *Journal of Field Ornithology* 60(3): 361–368.

Humphrey, N. (1984) *Consciousness regained. Chapters in the development of mind.* Oxford University Press.

Hurlbert, A. (1986) Formal connections between lightness algorithms. *Journal of the Optical Society of America A* 3: 1684–1693.

Hurlbert, A. (1989) *The computation of color.* MIT AI Lab Technical Report 1154. Cambridge, MA.

Hurvich, L. M. (1981) *Color vision.* Sinnauer Associates, Inc.

Hurvich, L. M. (1985) Opponent-colours theory. In *Central and peripheral mechanisms of color vision,* ed. D. Ottoson and S. Zeki. Macmillan.

Hurvich, L. M., and Jameson, D. (1957) An opponent process theory of color vision. *Psychological Review* 64: 384–404.

Ingle, D. J. (1985) The goldfish as a retinex animal. *Science* 225: 651–653.

Ingling, C. R. Jr., and Tsou, B. H. P. (1977) Orthogonal combination of the three visual channels. *Vision Research* 17: 1075–1082.

Jackson, F. (1982) Epiphenomenal qualia. *Philosophical Quarterly* 32: 127–136.

Jacobs, G. H. (1981) *Comparative color vision.* Academic Press.

Jacobs, G. (1986) Color vision variations in non-human primates. *Trends in Neurosciences* 12: 320–323.

Jameson, D. (1985) Opponent-colours theory in the light of physiological findings. In *Central and peripheral mechanisms of colour vision,* ed. D. Ottoson and S. Zeki. Macmillan.

Jameson, D., and Hurvich, L. M. (1989) Essay concerning color constancy. *Annual Review of Psychology* 40: 1–22.

Jane, S. D., and Bowmaker, J. K. (1988) Tetrachromatic colour vision in the duck (*Anas platyrhynchos L.*): Microspectrophotometry of visual pigments and oil droplets. *Journal of Comparative Physiology A* 162: 225–235.

Judd, D. B. (1940) Hue, saturation, lightness of surface colors with chromatic illumination. *Journal of the Optical Society of America* 30: 2–32.

Kay, P., and McDaniel, C. K. (1978) The linguistic significance of the meaning of basic color terms. *Language* 54: 610–646.

Kelso, J. A. S., and Kay, B. A. (1987) Information and control: A macroscopic analysis of perception-action coupling. In *Perceptives on perception and action,* ed. H. Heuer and A. F. Sanders. Erlbaum.

Kitcher, P. (1988) Marr's computational theory of vision. *Philosophy of Science* 55: 1–25.

Land, E. H. (1977) The retinex theory of color vision. *Scientific American* 237: 108–128.

Land, E. H. (1978) Our "polar partnership" with the world around us. *Harvard Magazine* 80: 23–26.

Land, E. H. (1983) Recent advances in retinex theory and some implications for cortical computations: Color vision and the natural image. *Proceedings of the National Academy of Sciences U.S.A.* 80: 5163–5169.

Land, E. H. (1986) An alternative technique for the computation of the designator in the retinex theory of color vision. *Proceedings of the National Academy of Sciences U.S.A.* 83: 3078–3080.

Lennie, P. (1984) Recent developments in the physiology of color vision. *Trends in Neuroscience* 7: 243–248.

Lennie, P., Trevarthen, C., Van Essen, D., and Wässel, H. (1990) Parallel processing of visual information. In *Visual Perception. The neurophysiological foundations*, ed. L. Spillman and J. S. Werner. Academic Press.

Levine, J. S., and MacNichol, E. F. Jr. (1979) Visual pigments in teleost fishes: Effect of habitat, microhabitat and behavior on visual system evolution. *Sensory Processes* 3: 95–131.

Levine, J. S., and MacNichol, E. F. Jr. (1982) Color vision in fishes. *Scientific American* 246: 140–149.

Levins, J. S., and Lewontin, R. (1983) The organism as subject and object of evolution. *Scientia* 118: 63–82. Reprinted in Levins, R. and Lewontin, R. (1985) *The dialectical biologist*. Harvard University Press.

Levins, J. S., and Lewontin, R. (1985) Levins, R. and Lewontin, R. *The dialectical biologist*. Harvard University Press.

Livingstone, M. S., and Hubel, D. H. (1984) Anatomy and physiology of a color system in the primate visual cortex. *Journal of Neuroscience* 4: 309–356.

Livingstone, M. S., and Hubel, D. H. (1988) Segregation of color, movement, and depth: Anatomy, physiology, and perception. *Science* 240: 740–749.

Locke, J. (1690/1975) *An essay concerning human understanding*, ed. P. H. Nidditch. Oxford University Press.

Loew, E. R., and Lythgoe, J. N. (1978) The ecology of cone pigments in teleost fishes. *Vision Research* 18: 715–722.

Logothetis, N. K., Schiller, P. H., Charles, E. R., and Hurlbert, A. C. (1990) Perceptual deficits and the activity of the color-opponent and broad-band pathways at isoluminance. *Science* 247: 214–217.

Lythgoe, J. N. (1979) *The ecology of vision*. Oxford University Press.

Maldonado, P. E., Maturana, H., and Varela, F. J. (1988) Frontal and lateral visual systems in birds. *Brain, Behavior and Evolution* 32: 57–62.

Maloney, L. T. (1985) Computational approaches to color constancy. *Technical Report 1985–01*, Stanford University, Applied Psychological Laboratory.

Maloney, L. T., and Wandell, B. A. (1986) Color constancy: A method for recovering surface spectral reflectance. *Journal of the Optical Society of America A* 3(1): 29–33.

Marr, D. (1982) *Vision. A computational investigation into the human representation and processing of visual information*. W. H. Freeman.

Marr, D., and Poggio, T. (1977) From understanding neural computation to understanding neural circuitry. *Neuroscience Research Program Bulletin* 15: 470–488.

Martin, G. R. (1977) Absolute visual threshold and scotopic spectral sensitivity in the tawny owl (*Strix aluco*), *Nature* 268: 636–638.

Martin, G. R., and Lett, B. T. (1985) Formation of associations of coloured and flavoured food with induced sickness in five avian species. *Behavioral Neural Biology* 43: 223–237.

Matthen, M. (1988) Biological functions and perceptual content. *Journal of Philosophy* 85: 5–27.

Maturana, H. R., and Varela, F. J. (1980) *Autopoiesis and cognition: The realization of the living*. Boston Studies in the Philosophy of Science, vol. 42. D. Reidel.

Maturana, H. R., and Varela, F. J. (1982) Colour-opponent responses in the avian lateral geniculate: A case study in the quail. *Brain Research* 247: 227–241.

Maturana, H. R., and Varela, F. J. (1987) *The tree of knowledge. The biological roots of human understanding*. New Science Library.

McCann, J. J., McKee, S. P., and Taylor, T. H. (1976) Quantitative studies in retinex theory. *Vision Research* 16: 445–458.

Menzel, R. (1979) Spectral sensitivity and color vision in invertebrates. In *Comparative physiology and evolution of vision in invertebrates, handbook of sensory physiology*, vol. VII/6A, ed. H. Autrum. Springer-Verlag.

Menzel, R. (1989) Bienen sehen vieles anderes. Natürliches Farbsehsystem beschrieben. Forschung, *Mitteilungen der DFG* 2/89: 20–22.

Merleau-Ponty, M. (1964) *L'Oeil et L'esprit*. Gallimard.

Mollon, J. D. (1990) Neurobiology: The club-sandwich mystery. *Nature* 343: 16–17.

Mollon, J. D., and Sharpe, L. T. eds. (1983) *Color vision*. Academic Press.

Mollon, J. D., Bowmaker, J. K., and Jacobs, G. H. (1984) Variations of colour vision in a New World primate can be explained by polymorphism of retinal photopigments. Proceedings of the Royal Society B 222: 373–399.

Muntz, W. R. (1975) Behavioral studies of vision in a fish and possible relationships to the environment. In *Vision in fish*, ed. M. A. Ali. Plenum.

Muntz, W. R., and Mouat, G. S. (1984) Annual variation in the visual pigments of brown trout inhabiting lochs providing different light environments. *Vision Research* 24: 1575–1580.

Muntz, F, W., and McFarland, W. N. (1977) Evolutionary adaptations of fishes to the photopic environment. In *Handbook of sensory physiology*, vol. VII, ed. F. Crescitelli. Springer-Verlag.

Nagel, T. (1974/1980) What is it like to be a bat? In *Readings in the philosophy of psychology*, vol. 1, ed. Ned Block. Harvard University Press.

Nathans, J., Thomas, D., and Hogness, D. S. (1986) Molecular genetics of human color vision: The genes encoding blue, green, and red pigments. *Science* 232: 193–202.

Neitz, J., and Jacobs, G. H. (1986) Polymorphism of the long-wavelength cone in normal human color vision. *Nature* 323: 623–625.

Neumeyer, C. (1980) Simultaneous color contrast in the honeybee. Journal of *Comparative Physiology A* 139: 165–176.

Neumeyer, C. (1981) Chromatic adaptation in the honeybee: Successive color contrast and color constancy. *Journal of Comparative Physiology A* 144: 543–553.

Neumeyer, C. (1985) An ultraviolet receptor as a fourth receptor type in goldfish color vision. *Naturwissenschaften* 72: 162–163.

Neumeyer, C. (1986) Wavelength discrimination in the goldfish. *Journal of Comparative Physiology A* 158: 203–213.

Neumeyer, C. (1988) *Das Farbensehen des Goldfishes. Eine verhaltensphysiologische Analyse.* Thieme.

Neumeyer, C., and Arnold, K. (1989) Tetrachromatic color vision in the goldfish becomes trichromatic under white adaptation light of moderate intensity. *Vision Research* 29: 1719–1727.

Nuboer, J. F. W. (1986) A compartive view on color vision. *Netherlands Journal of Zoology* 36: 344–380.

Nuboer, J. F. W., and Wortel, J. (1987) Colour vision via the pigeon's red and yellow retinal fields. In *Seeing contour and colour,* ed. J. J. Kullkowski. Cambridge University Press.

Odling-Smee, F. J. (1988) Niche-constructing phenotypes. In *The role of behavior in evolution,* ed. H. C. Plotkin. The MIT Press/Bradford Books.

Ottoson, D., and Zeki, S., eds. (1985) *Central and pheripheral mechanisms of colour vision.* Macmillan.

Oyama, S. (1985) *The ontogeny of information: Developmental systems and evolution.* Cambridge University Press.

Palacios, A. (1991) La vision chromatique chez l'oiseau: Etude compartamentale. These de Doctorat. Université de Paris VI.

Palacios, A., and Varela, F. J. (1992) Color mixing in the pigeon. II: A psychophysical determination in the middle, short and near-UV (*Columbia livia*). range. *Vision Research* 32: 1947–1953.

Palacios, A., Bonnardel, V., and Varela, F. (1990a) Autoshaping as a method for the chromatic discrimination of the pigeon. *Comptes Rendues la Academic des Sciences (Paris), Sciences de la Vie* 331: 213–218.

Palacios, A. C., Martinoya, S., Bloch, S., and Varela, F. J. (1990b) Color mixing in the pigeon: A psychophysical determination in the longwave spectral range. *Vision Research* 30: 587–596.

Partridge, C., Shand, J., Archer, S. N., Lythgoe, J. N., and Groningen-Luyben, W. A. (1989) Interspecific variation in the visual pigments of the deep-sea fishes. *Journal of Comparative Physiology A* 164: 513–529.

Poggio, T., Torre, V., and Koch, C. (1985) Computational vision and regularization theory. *Nature* 317: 314–319.

Priest, G. (1989) Primary qualities are secondary qualities, too. *British Journal for the Philosophy of Science* 40: 29–37.

Ramachadran, V. S. (1985) The neurobiology of perception. *Perception* 14: 97–103.

Reeke, G. N., and Edelman, G. M. (1988) Real brains and artificial intelligence. *Daedelus* 117(1): 143–173.

Remy, M., and Emmerton, J. (1989) Behavioral spectral sensitivities of different retinal areas in pigeons. *Behavioral Neuroscience* 103: 170–177.

Robson, J. (1983) The morphology of cortico-fugal axons to the dorsal lateral geniculate nucleus. *Journal of Comparative Neurology* 216: 89–103.

Rosch, E. (1973) Natural categories. *Cognitive Psychology* 4: 328–350.

Rothschild, M. F. (1975) Remarks on carotenoids in the evolution of signals. *Coevolution of animals and plants*, ed. L. E. Gilbert and P. H. Raven. University of Texas.

Rowland, W. J. (1979) The use of color in intraspecific communication. In *The behavioral significance of color*, ed. E. H. Burtt Jr.

Rubin, J. M., and Richards, W. A. (1982) Color vision and image intensities: When are changes material? *Biological Cybernetics* 45: 215–226.

Rubin, J. M., and Richards, W. A. (1988) Color vision: Representing material categories. In *Natural computation*, ed. W. Richards. The MIT Press/Bradford Books.

Schiller, P. H., Logothetis, N. K., and Charles, E. R. (1990) Functions of the colour-opponent and broad-band channels of the visual system. *Nature* 343: 68–70.

Sejnowksi, T. J., Koch, C., and Churchland, P. S. (1988) *Computational neuroscience. Science* 241: 1299–1306.

Skarda, C., and Freeman, W. (1987) How brains make chaos in order to make sense of the world. *Behavioral and Brain Sciences* 10: 161–195.

Snodderly, D. M. (1979) Visual discrimination encountered in food foraging by a neotropical primate: Implications for the evolution of color vision. In: *The behavioral significance of color*, ed. E. H. Burtt Jr. Garland STPM Press.

Snow, D. W. (1971) Evolutionary aspects of fruit eating by birds. *Ibis* 113: 194–202.

Steriade, M., and Deschenes, M. (1985) The thalamus as a neuronal oscillator. *Brain Research Reviews* 18: 165–170.

Stroll, A. (1986) The role of surfaces in an ecological theory of perception. *Philosophy and Phenomenological Research* 46: 437–453.

Svaetichin, G., and MacNichol, E. F. (1958) Retinal mechanisms for chromatic and achromatic'vision. *Annals of the New York Academy of Sciences* 74: 385–404.

Teller, D. Y. (1984) Linking propositions. *Vision Research* 24: 1233–1246.

Teller, D. Y. (1990) The domain of visual science. In *Visual perception. The neurophysiological foundations*, ed. L. Spillman and J. S. Werner. Academic Press.

Teller, D. Y., and Pugh, E. N. Jr. (1983) Linking propositions in color vision. In *Colour vision: Physiology and Psychophysics*, ed. J. D. Mollon and L. T. Sharpe. Academic Press.

Thompson, E. (1989) Colour vision and the comparative argument: A case study in cognitive science and the philosophy of perception. Doctoral dissertation. Department of Philosophy, University of Toronto.

Turvey, M. T. (1977) Contrasting orientations to the theory of visual information processing. *Psychological Review* 84: 67–88.

Turvey, M. T., Shaw, R. E., Reed, E. S., and Mace, W. M. (1981) Ecological laws of perceiving and acting: In reply to Fodor and Pylyshyn. *Cognition* 9: 237–304.

Varela, F. J. (1979) *Principles of Biological Autonomy*. Elsevier North Holland.

Varela, F. J. (1984) Living ways of sense-making: A middle path for neuroscience. In *Disorder and order: Proceedings of the Stanford International Symposium*, ed. P. Livingston. Anma Libras.

Varela, F. J. (1989) *Connaitre: Les sciences cognitives, tendances et perspectives*. Editions du Seuil.

Varela, F. J. (1991a) Perception and the origin of cognition: A cartography of current ideas. In *Understanding origins; contemporary ideas on the origin of life, mind and society. Boston studies in the philosophy of science*, ed. F. Varela and J. P. Dupuy. Kluwer Associates.

Varela, F. J. (1991b) Organisms: A meshwork of selfless selves. In *Organism and the origin of the self*, ed. A Tauber. Kluwer Associates.

Varela, F., and Singer, W. (1987) Neuronal dynamics in the visual corticothalamic pathway as revealed through binocular rivalry. *Experimental Brain Research* 66: 10–20.

Varela, F. J., Thompson, E., and Rosch, E. (1991) *The embodied mind: Cognitive science and human experience*. The MIT Press.

Varela, F. J., Letelier, J. C., Marin, G., and Maturana, H. R. (1983) The neurophysiology of avian color vision. *Achivos de Biologia y Medicina Experimentales* 16: 291–303.

Wasserman, G. (1979) *Color vision: An historical introduction*. Academic Press.

Weedon, B. C. (1963) Occurrence. In *Carotenoids*, ed. O. Isler. Birkhauser Verlag.

Westphal, J. (1987) *Colour: Some philosophical problems from Wittgenstein*. Basil Blackwell.

Wheeler, T. G. (1982) Color vision and retinal chromatic information processing in teleost: A review. *Brain Research Reviews* 4: 177–235.

Whitmore, A. V., and Bowmaker, J. K. (1989) Seasonal variation in cone sensitivity and short-wave absorbing visual pigments in the rudd Scardinius erythrophthalmus. *Journal of Comparative Physiology A* 166: 103–115.

Wilson, M. (1987) Berkeley on the mind-dependence of colors. *Pacific Philosophical Quarterly* 68: 249–264.

Wright, A. (1972) The influence of ultraviolet radiation on the pigeon's color discrimination. *Journal of the Experimental Analysis of Behavior* 17: 325–337.

Wright, A. (1979) Color-vision psychophysics: A comparison of pigeon and human. In *Neural mechanisms of behavior in the pigeon*, ed. A. M. Granda and J. H. Maxwell. Plenum.

Wright, A., and Cummings, W. W. (1971) Color naming functions for the pigeon. *Journal of the Experimental Analysis of Behavior* 15: 7–17.

Wyszecki, G., and Stiles, W. S. (1982) *Color science: Concepts and methods, quantitative data and formulae*, 2nd ed. Wiley.

Yuille, A. (1984) A method for computing spectral reflectance. *AI Memo 752*. MIT AI Lab.

Zeki, S. (1980) The representation of colours in the cerebral cortex. *Nature* 284: 412–418.

Zeki, S. (1983) Colour coding in the cerebral cortex: The reaction of cells in monkey visual cortex to wavelengths and colours. *Neuroscience* 9: 741–765.

Zeki, S. (1985) Colour pathways and hierarchies in the cerebral cortex. In *Central and peripheral mechanisms of colour vision*, ed. D. Ottoson and S. Zeki. Macmillan.

16

Conscious Experience

Fred Dretske

There is a difference between hearing Clyde play the piano and seeing him play the piano. The difference consists in a difference in the kind of experience caused by Clyde's piano playing. Clyde's performance can also cause a belief—the belief that he is playing the piano. A perceptual belief that he is playing the piano must be distinguished from a perceptual experience of this same event. A person (or an animal, for that matter) can hear or see a piano being played without knowing, believing, or judging that a piano is being played. Conversely, a person (I do not know about animals) can come to believe that Clyde is playing the piano without seeing or hearing him do it—without experiencing the performance for themselves.

This distinction between a perceptual experience of x and a perceptual belief about x is, I hope, obvious enough. I will spend some time enlarging upon it, but only for the sake of sorting out relevant interconnections (or lack thereof). My primary interest is not in this distinction, but, rather, in what it reveals about the nature of conscious experience and, thus, consciousness itself. For unless one understands the difference between a consciousness of things (Clyde playing the piano) and a consciousness of facts (that he is playing the piano), and the way this difference depends, in turn, on a difference between a concept-free mental state (e.g., an experience) and a concept-charged mental state (e.g., a belief), one will fail to understand how one can have conscious experiences without being aware that one is having them. One will fail to understand, therefore, how an experience can be conscious without anyone—including the person having it—being conscious of having it. Failure to understand how this is possible constitutes a failure to understand what makes something conscious and, hence, what consciousness is.

The possibility of a person's having a conscious experience she is not conscious of having will certainly sound odd, perhaps even contradictory, to those philosophers who (consciously or not) embrace an inner spotlight view of consciousness according to which a mental state is conscious in so far as the light of consciousness shines *on* it—thus making one conscious *of* it.[1] It will also sound confused to those like Dennett (1991) who, though rejecting theatre metaphors (and the spotlight images they encourage), espouse a kind of first person operationalism about mental phenomena that links conscious mental states to those that can be reported and of which, therefore, the reporter is necessarily aware of having.

There is, however, nothing confused or contradictory about the idea of a conscious experience that one is not conscious of having. The first step in understanding the nature of conscious experience is understanding why this is so.

1   Awareness of Facts and Awareness of Things[2]

For purposes of this discussion I regard "conscious" and "aware" as synonyms. Being conscious of a thing (or fact) is being aware of it. Accordingly, "conscious awareness" and "consciously aware" are redundancies.

A. White (1964) describes interesting differences between the ordinary use of "aware" and "conscious." He also describes the different liaisons they have to noticing, attending, and realizing. Though my treatment of these expressions (for the purposes of this inquiry) as synonymous blurs some of these ordinary distinctions, even (occasionally) violating some of the strictures White records, nothing essential to my project is lost by ignoring the niceties. No useful theory of consciousness can hope (nor, I think, should it even aspire) to capture all the subtle nuances of ordinary usage.

By contrasting our awareness of things (x) with our awareness of facts (that P) I mean to be distinguishing particular (spatial) objects and (temporal) events[3] on the one hand from facts involving these things on the other. Clyde (a physical object), his piano (another object), and Clyde's playing his piano (an event) are all things as I am using the word "thing"; that he is playing his piano is a fact. Things are neither true nor false though, in the case of events, states of affairs, and conditions, we sometimes speak of them as what makes a statement true. Facts are what we express in making true statements about things. We describe our awareness of facts by using a factive complement, a that-clause, after the verb; we describe our awareness of things by using a (concrete) noun or noun phrase as direct object of the verb. We are aware of Clyde, his piano, and of Clyde's playing his piano (things); we are also aware that he is playing the piano (a fact).

Seeing, hearing, and smelling *x* are ways of being conscious of *x*.[4] Seeing a tree, smelling a rose, and feeling a wrinkle is to be (perceptually) aware (conscious) of the tree, the rose, and the wrinkle. There may be other ways of being conscious of objects and events. It may be that thinking or dreaming about Clyde is a way of being aware of Clyde without perceiving him.[5] I do not deny it (though I think it stretches usage). I affirm, only, the converse: that to see and feel a thing is to be (perceptually) conscious of it. And the same is true of facts: to see, smell, or feel that *P* is to be (or become) aware that *P*. Hence,

(1)   S sees (hears, etc.) *x* (or that *P*) $\Rightarrow$ S is conscious of *x* (that *P*)[6]

In this essay I shall be mainly concerned with *perceptual* forms of consciousness. So when I speak of S's being conscious (or aware) of something I will have in mind S's seeing, hearing, smelling, or in some way sensing a thing (or fact).

Consciousness of facts implies a deployment of concepts. If S is aware that *x* is *F*, then S has the concept *F* and uses (applies) it in his awareness of *x*.[7] If a person smells that the toast is burning, thus becoming aware that the toast is burning, this person applies the concept *burning* (perhaps also the concept *toast*) to what he smells. One cannot be conscious that the toast is burning unless one understands what toast is and what it means to burn—unless, that is, one has the concepts needed to classify objects and events in this way. I will follow the practice of supposing that our awareness of facts takes the form of a belief. Thus, to smell that the toast is burning is to be aware that the toast is burning is to believe that the toast is burning. It is conventional in epistemology to assume that when perceptual verbs take factive nominals as complements, what is being described is not just belief but knowledge. Seeing or smelling that the toast is burning is a way of coming to *know* (or, at least, verifying the knowledge) that the toast is burning. It will be enough for present purposes if we operate with a weaker claim: that perceptual awareness of facts is a mental state or attitude that involves the possession and use of concepts, the sort of cognitive or intellectual capacity involved in thought and belief. I will, for convenience, take belief (that *P*) as the normal realization of an awareness that *P*.

Perceptual awareness of facts has a close tie with behaviour—with, in particular (for those who have language), an ability to *say* what one is aware of. This is not so with a consciousness of things. One can smell or see (hence, be conscious of) burning toast while having little or no understanding of what toast is or what it means to burn. "What is that strange smell?" might well be the remark of someone who smells burning toast but is ignorant of what toast is or what it means to burn something. The cat can smell, and thus be aware of, burning toast as well as the cook, but only the cook will be aware that the toast is burning (or that it is the toast that is burning).

The first time I became aware of an armadillo (I saw it on a Texas road), I did not know what it was. I did not even know what armadillos were, much less what they looked like. My ignorance did not impair my eyesight, of course. I saw the animal. I was aware of it ahead of me on the road. That is why I swerved. Ignorance of what armadillos are or how they look can prevent someone from being conscious of certain facts (that the object crossing the road is an armadillo) without impairing in the slightest one's awareness of the things—the armadillos crossing roads—that (so to speak) constitute these facts. This suggests the following important result. For all things (as specified above) x and properties F,

(2)   S is conscious of $x \nRightarrow$ S is conscious that x is F.

Though (2) strikes me as self-evident, I have discovered, over the years, that it does not strike everyone that way. The reason it does not (I have also found) is usually connected with a failure to appreciate or apply one or more of the following distinctions. The first two are, I hope, more or less obvious. I will be brief. The third will take a little longer.

(a) *Not Implying vs. Implying Not.* There is a big difference between denying that A implies B and affirming that A implies not-B. (2) does not affirm, it denies, an implication. It does not say that one can only be aware of a thing by *not* being aware of what it is.

(b) *Implication vs. Implicature.* The implication (2) denies is a logical implication, not a Gricean (1989) implicature. *Saying* you are aware of an F (i.e., a thing, x, which is F) implies (as a conversational implication) that you are aware that x is F. Anyone who said he was conscious of (e.g., saw or smelled) an armadillo would (normally) imply that he thought it was an armadillo. This is true, but irrelevant.

(c) *Concrete Objects vs. Abstract Objects.* When perceptual verbs (including the generic "aware of" and "conscious of") are followed by abstract nouns (the difference, the number, the answer, the problem, the size, the colour) and interrogative nominals (where the cat is, who he is talking to, when they left), what is being described is normally an awareness of some (unspecified) fact. The abstract noun phrase or interrogative nominal stands in for some factive clause. Thus, seeing (being conscious of) the difference between A and B is to see (be conscious) *that* they differ. If the problem is the clogged drain, then to be aware of the problem is to be aware that the drain is clogged. To be aware of the problem it isn't enough to be aware of (e.g., to see) the thing that is the problem (the clogged drain). One has to see (the fact) *that* it is clogged. Until one becomes aware of this fact, one hasn't become aware of the problem. Likewise, to see where the cat is hiding is to see that it is hiding *there*, for some value of "there."

This can get tricky, and is often the source of confusion in discussing what can be observed. This is not the place for gory details, but I must mention one instance of this problem since it will come up again when we discuss which aspects of experience are conscious when we are perceiving a complicated scene. To use a traditional philosophical example, suppose S sees a speckled hen on which there are (on the facing side) 27 speckles. Each speckle is clearly visible. Not troubling to count, S does not realize that (hence, is not aware that) there are 27 speckles. Nonetheless, we assume that S looked long enough, and carefully enough, to see each speckle. In such a case, although S is aware of all 27 speckles (things), he is not aware of the number of speckles because being aware of the number of speckles requires being aware that there is that number of speckles (a fact), and S is not aware of this fact.[8] For epistemological purposes, abstract objects are disguised facts; you cannot be conscious of these objects without being conscious of a fact.

(2) is a thesis about concrete objects. The values of *x* are *things* as this was defined above. Abstract objects do not count as things for purposes of (2). Hence, even though one cannot see the difference between *A* and *B* without seeing that they differ, cannot be aware of the number of speckles on the hen without being aware that there are 27, and cannot be conscious of an object's irregular shape without being conscious that it has an irregular shape, this is irrelevant to the truth of (2).

As linguists (e.g., Lees, 1963, p. 14) observe, however, abstract nouns may appear in copula sentences opposite both factive (that) clauses and concrete nominals. We can say that the problem is *that his tonsils are inflamed* (a fact); but we can also say that the problem is, simply, *his* (inflamed) *tonsils* (a thing). This can give rise to an ambiguity when the abstract noun is the object of a perceptual verb. Though it is, I think normal to interpret the abstract noun as referring to a fact in perceptual contexts, there exists the possibility of interpreting it as referring to a thing. Thus, suppose that Tom at time t_1 differs (perceptibly) from Tom at t_2 only in having a moustache at t_2. S sees Tom at both times but does not notice the moustache—is not, therefore, aware that he has grown a moustache. Since, however, S spends twenty minutes talking to Tom in broad daylight, it is reasonable to say that although S did not notice the moustache, he (must) nonetheless have seen it.[9] If S did see Tom's moustache without (as we say) registering it at the time, can we describe S as seeing, and thus (in this sense) being aware of, a difference in Tom's appearance between t_1 and t_2? In the factive sense of awareness (the normal interpretation, I think), no; S was not aware that there was a difference. S was not aware at t_2 that Tom had a moustache. In the thing sense of awareness, however, the answer is: yes. S was aware of the moustache at t_2, something he was not aware of at t_1, and the moustache is a difference in Tom's appearance.

If, as in this example, "the difference between *A* and *B*" is taken to refer, not to the fact that *A* and *B* differ, but to a particular element or condition of *A* and *B* that constitutes their difference, then seeing the difference between *A* and *B* would be seeing this element or condition—a thing, not a fact. In this thing sense of "the difference" a person or animal who had not yet learned to discriminate (in any behaviourally relevant way) between (say) two forms might nonetheless be said to see (and in this sense be aware of) the difference between them if it saw the parts of one that distinguished it from the other. When two objects differ in this perceptible way, one can be conscious of the thing (speckle, line, star, stripe) that is the difference without being conscious of the difference (= conscious *that* they differ). In order to avoid confusion about this critical (for my purposes) point, I will, when speaking of our awareness or consciousness of something designated by an abstract noun or phrase (the colour, the size, the difference, the number, etc.), always specify whether I mean thing-awareness or fact-awareness. To be thing-aware of a difference is to be aware of the thing (some object, event, or condition, *x*) that makes the difference. To be fact-aware of the difference is to be aware of the fact that there is a difference (not necessarily the fact that *x* is the difference). In the above example, S was thing-aware, but not fact-aware, of the difference between Tom at t_1 and t_2. He was (at t_2) aware of the thing that made the difference, but not fact-aware (at t_2 or later) of this difference.

So much by way of clarifying (2). What can be said in its support? I have already given several examples of properties or kinds, *F*, which are such that one can be aware of a thing which is *F* without being aware that it is *F* (an armadillo, burning toast, a moustache). But (2) says something stronger. It says that there is no property *F* which is such that an awareness of a thing which is *F* requires an awareness of the fact that it is *F*. It may be felt that this is much too strong. One can, to be sure, see armadillos without seeing that they are armadillos, but perhaps one must, in order to see them, see that they are (say) animals of some sort. To see *x* (which is an animal) is to see that it is an animal. If this sounds implausible (one can surely mistake an animal for a rock or a bush) maybe one must, in seeing an object, at least see that it is an object of some sort. To be aware of a thing is at least be aware that it is . . . how shall we say it? . . . a thing. *Something or other*. Whether or not this is true depends, of course, on what is involved in being aware that a thing is a thing. Since we can certainly see a physical object without being aware that it is a physical object (we can think we are hallucinating), the required concept F (required to be aware that x is F) cannot be much of a concept. It seems most implausible to suppose infants and animals (presumably, conscious of things) have concepts of this sort. If the concept one must have to be aware of something is a concept that applies to *everything* one can be aware of, what is the point of insisting that one must have it to be aware?

I therefore conclude that awareness of things (x) requires no fact-awareness (that x is F, for any F) of those things.[10] Those who feel that this conclusion has too little support are welcome to substitute a weaker version of (2): namely, there is no *reasonably specific property* F which is such that awareness of a thing which is F requires fact-awareness that it is F. This will not affect my use of (2).

2   Conscious Beings and Conscious States

Agents are said to be conscious in an intransitive sense of this word (he regained consciousness) and in a transitive sense (he was conscious of her). I will follow Rosenthal (1990) and refer to both as *creature* consciousness. Creature consciousness (whether transitive or intransitive) is to be contrasted with what Rosenthal calls *state* consciousness—the (always intransitive) sense in which certain internal states, processes, events and attitudes (typically in or of conscious beings) are said to be conscious.

For purposes of being explicit about my own (standard, I hope) way of using these words, I assume that for any x and P,

(3)   S is conscious of x or that P ⇒ S is conscious (a conscious being).

That is, transitive (creature) consciousness implies intransitive (creature) consciousness. You cannot see or hear, taste or smell, a thing without (thereby) being conscious.[11] You cannot be aware that your cheque-book doesn't balance or conscious that you are late for an appointment (a fact) without being a conscious being.[12]

The converse of (3) is more problematic. Perhaps one can be conscious without being conscious of anything. Some philosophers think that during hallucination, for example, one might be fully conscious but (*qua* hallucinator) not conscious of any-thing. To suppose that hallucination (involving intransitive consciousness) is a consciousness of something would (or so it is feared) commit one to objectionable mental particulars—the sense data that one hallucinates. Whether or not this is so I will not try to say. I leave the issue open. (3) only endorses the innocent idea that beings who are conscious of something are conscious; it does not say that conscious beings must be conscious of something.

By way of interconnecting creature and state consciousness I also posit:

(4)   S is conscious of *x* or that *P* ⇒ S is in a conscious state of some sort.

Transitive creature consciousness requires state (of the creature) consciousness. S's consciousness of *x* or that *P* is a relational state of affairs; it involves both the agent, S, and the object (or fact) S is conscious of. The conscious state which (according to (4)) S must be in when he is conscious of *x* or that *P*, however, is not the sort of state the existence of which logically requires *x* or the condition described by *P*. Tokens of this state type may be caused by *x* or the condition described by "*P*" (and when they are, they may qualify as experiences of *x* or knowledge that *P*), but to qualify as a token of this type, *x* and the condition described by "*P*" are not necessary.

Thus, according to (4), when I see or hear Clyde playing the piano (or that he is playing the piano) and (thus) am conscious of him playing the piano (or that he is playing the piano), I am in a conscious state of some kind. When hallucinating (or simply when listening to a recording) I can be in the same kind of conscious state even if Clyde is not playing the piano (or I do not perceive him playing the piano). When Clyde is not playing the piano (or I am not perceiving him play the piano), we speak of the conscious state in question not as knowledge (that he is playing the piano) but as belief, not as perception (of Clyde playing the piano) but as halluci-nation (or perception of something *else*).[13]

I do not know how to argue for (4). I would like to say that it states the obvious and leave it at that. I know, however, that nothing is obvious in this area. Not even the obvious. (4) says that our perceptual awareness of both things (smelling the burning toast) and facts (becoming aware that it is burning) involves, in some essen-tial way, conscious subjective (i.e., non-relational and, in this sense, internal or subjective) states of the perceiver—beliefs (in the case of awareness of facts) and experiences (in the awareness of things). Not everything that happens in or to us when we become conscious of some external object or fact is conscious, of course.

Certain events, processes, and states involved in the processing of sensory information are presumably not conscious. But *something*, some state or other of S, either
an experience or a belief, has to be conscious in order for S to be made conscious
of the things and facts around him. If the state of S caused by x is not a conscious
state, then the causation will not make S conscious of x. This is why one can
contract poison ivy without ever becoming aware of the plant that poisons one.
The plant causes one to occupy an internal state of some sort, yes, but this internal
state is not a conscious state. Hence, one is not (at least not in contracting poison
ivy) conscious of the plant.

David Armstrong (1980, p. 59) has a favourite example that he uses to illustrate
differences in consciousness. Some may think it tells against (4). I think it does not.
Armstrong asks one to imagine a long-distance truck driver:

After driving for long periods of time, particularly at night, it is possible to "come to" and
realize that for some time past one has been driving without being aware of what one has
been doing. The coming-to is an alarming experience. It is natural to describe what went on
before one came to by saying that during that time one lacked consciousness. Yet it seems
clear that, in the two senses of the word that we have so far isolated, consciousness was
present. There was mental activity, and as part of that mental activity, there was perception.
That is to say, there was minimal consciousness and perceptual consciousness. If there is an
inclination to doubt this, then consider the extraordinary sophistication of the activities successfully undertaken during the period of "unconsciousness." (p. 59)

Armstrong thinks it plausible to say that the driver is conscious (perceptually) of
the road, the curves, the stop signs, etc. He *sees* the road. I agree. There is transitive creature consciousness of both things (the roads, the stop signs) and facts (that
the road curves left, that the stop sign is red, etc.). How else explain the extraordinary performance?

But does the driver thereby have, in accordance with (4), conscious experiences
of the road? Armstrong thinks there is a form of consciousness that the driver lacks.
I agree. He thinks what the driver lacks is an introspective awareness, a perception-
like awareness, of the current states and activities of his own mind. Once again, I
agree. The driver is neither thing-aware nor fact-aware of his own mental states
(including whatever experiences he is having of the road). I am not sure that normal
people have this in normal circumstances, but I'm certainly willing to agree that the
truck driver lacks it. But where does this leave us? Armstrong says (p. 61) that if
one is not introspectively aware of a mental state (e.g., an experience), then it (the
experience) is "in one good sense of the word" unconscious. I disagree. The only
sense in which it is unconscious is that the person whose state it is is not conscious

of having it. But from this it does not follow that the state itself is unconscious. Not unless one accepts a higher-order theory according to which state-consciousness is analysed in terms of creature-consciousness of the state. Such a theory may be true, but it is by no means obvious. I shall, in fact, argue that it is false. At any rate, such a theory cannot be invoked at this stage of the proceedings as an objection to (4). (4) is, as it should be, neutral about what makes the state of a person (who is transitively conscious of x or that P) a conscious state.

I therefore accept Armstrong's example, his description of what forms of consciousness the driver has, and the fact that the driver lacks an important type of higher level (introspective) consciousness of his own mental states. What we disagree about is whether any of this implies that the driver's experiences of the road (whatever it is *in* the driver that is required to make him conscious *of* the road) are themselves unconscious. We will return to that question in the final section.

Many investigators take perceptual experience and belief to be paradigmatic conscious phenomena.[14] *If* one chooses to talk about state consciousness (in addition to creature consciousness) at all, the clearest and most compelling instance of it is in the domain of sensory experience and belief. My present visual experience of the screen in front of me and my present perceptual beliefs about what is on that screen are internal states that deserve classification as conscious if anything does. (4) merely records a decision to regard such perceptual phenomena as central (but by no means the only) instances of conscious mental states.

Such is my justification for accepting (4). I will continue to refer to the conscious states associated with our consciousness of things (hearing Clyde playing the piano) as experiences and our consciousness of facts (that he is playing the piano) as beliefs. This is, I think, fairly standard usage. I have not, of course, said what an experience or a belief is. I won't try. That is not my project. I am trying to say what makes (or doesn't make) an experience conscious, not what makes it an experience.

Consciousness of things—e.g., seeing a stoplight turn green—requires a conscious experience of that thing. Consciousness of a fact—that the stop light is turning green—requires a conscious belief that this is a fact. And we can have the first without the second—an awareness of the stoplight's turning green without an awareness that it is turning green—hence a conscious experience (of the light's turning green) without a conscious belief (that it is turning green). Likewise, we can have the second without the first—a conscious belief about the stoplight, that it is turning green, without an experience of it. Someone I trust tells me (and I believe her) that the stoplight is turning green. So much by way of summary of the relationships between the forms of consciousness codified in (1) through (4).

We are, I think, now in a position to answer some preliminary questions. First: can one have conscious experiences without being conscious that one is having them? Can there, in other words, be conscious states without the person in whom they occur being fact-aware of their occurrence? Second: can there be conscious states in a person who is not thing-aware of them? These are important preliminary questions because important theories of what makes a mental state conscious, including what passes as orthodox theory today, depend on negative answers to one (or, in some cases both) of these questions. If, as I believe, the answers to both questions are affirmative, then these theories are simply wrong.

3   Experienced Differences Require Different Experiences

Glance at figure 16.1 long enough to assure yourself that you have seen all the elements composing constellation Alpha (on the left) and constellation Beta (on the right). It may be necessary to change fixation points in order to foveate (focus on the sensitive part of the retina) all parts of Alpha and Beta. If the figure is being held at arm's length, though, this should not be necessary though it may occur anyway via the frequent involuntary saccades the eyes make. A second or two should suffice.

During this brief interval some readers may have noticed the difference between Alpha and Beta. For expository purposes, I will assume no one did. The difference is indicated in figure 16.2. Call the spot, the one that occurs in Alpha but not Beta, Spot.

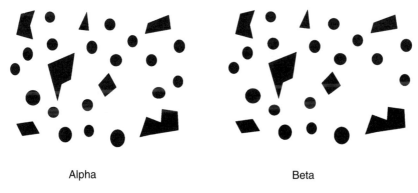

Alpha   Beta

Figure 16.1

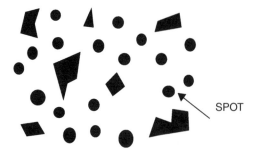

Figure 16.2

According to my assumptions, then, everyone (when looking at figure 16.1) saw Spot. Hence, according to (1), everyone was aware of the thing that constitutes the difference between Alpha and Beta. According to (4), then, everyone consciously experienced (i.e., had a conscious experience of) the thing that distinguishes Alpha from Beta. Everyone, therefore, was thing-aware, but not fact-aware, of the difference between Alpha and Beta. Spot, if you like, is Alpha's moustache.

Let E(Alpha) and E(Beta) stand for one's experience of Alpha and one's experience of Beta respectively. Alpha and Beta differ; Alpha has Spot as a part, Beta does not. E(Alpha) and E(Beta) must also differ. E(Alpha) has an element corresponding to (caused by) Spot. E(Beta) does not. E(Alpha) contains or embodies, as a part, an E(Spot), an experience of Spot, while E(Beta) does not. If it did not, then one's experience of Alpha would have been the same as one's experience of Beta and, hence, contrary to (4), one would not have seen Spot when looking at Alpha.[15]

One can, of course, be conscious of things that differ without one's experience of them differing in any intrinsic way. Think of seeing visually indistinguishable objects—similar looking thumb tacks, say. One sees (experiences) numerically different things, but one's experience of them is the same. Both experiences are conscious, and they are experiences of different things, but the differences in the experiences are not conscious differences. The differences are extrinsic to the experience itself. It is like having an experience in Chicago and another one in New York. The numerically different experiences may be qualitatively identical even though they have different (relational) properties—one occurs in Chicago, the other in New York. The perception of (visually) indistinguishable thumb tacks is like that.

The experiences of Alpha and Beta, however, are not like that. They are qualitatively different. They differ in their relational properties, yes, as all numerically different objects do, but they also differ in their intrinsic properties. These two experiences are not only experiences of qualitatively different objects (Alpha and Beta), they are experiences of the qualitative differences. The respects in which Alpha and Beta differ are not only visible, they are (by hypothesis) seen. One is, after all, thing-aware of Spot, the difference between Alpha and Beta. The experiences are not distinguished in terms of their intrinsic qualities by the person who has the experiences, of course, but that is merely to say that there is, on the part of this person, no fact-awareness of any differences in his experience of Alpha and his experience of Beta. That, though, is not the issue. The question is one about differences in a person's conscious experiences, not a question about a person's awareness of differences in his experiences. It is a question about *state* consciousness, not a question about *creature* consciousness.

Once one makes the distinction between state and creature consciousness and embraces the distinction between fact- and thing-awareness, there is no reason to suppose that a person must be able to distinguish (i.e., tell the difference between) his conscious experiences. Qualitative differences in conscious experiences are *state* differences; distinguishing these differences, on the other hand, is a fact about the *creature* consciousness of the person in whom these experiences occur.

The argument assumes, of course, that if one is thing-aware of the difference between Alpha and Beta (i.e., thing-aware of Spot), then E(Alpha) and E(Beta) must differ. It assumes, that is, that *experienced* differences require different experiences. What else could experienced differences be? The difference between E(Alpha) and E(Beta), then, is being taken to be the same as the difference between seeing, in broad daylight, directly in front of your eyes, one finger raised and two fingers raised. Seeing the two fingers is not like seeing a flock of geese (from a distance) where individual geese are "fused" into a whole and not seen. In the case of the fingers, one sees both the finger on the left and the finger on the right. Quite a different experience from seeing only the finger on the left. When the numbers get larger, as they do with Alpha and Beta, the experiences are no longer discernibly different to the person having them. Given that each spot is seen, however, the experiences *are*, nonetheless, different. Large numbers merely make it harder to achieve fact-awareness of the differences on the part of the person experiencing the differences. E(Spot) is really no different than the difference between experiencing one finger and two fingers in broad daylight. The only difference is that in the case of Alpha and Beta there is no fact-awareness of the thing that makes the difference.[16]

Since the point is critical to my argument, let me emphasize the last point. In speaking of conscious differences in experience it is important to remember that one need not be conscious of the difference (= conscious that such a difference exists) in order for such differences to exist. Readers who noticed a difference between Alpha and Beta were, thereby, fact-aware of the difference between Alpha and Beta. Such readers may also have become fact-aware (by inference?) of the difference between their experience of Alpha and their experience of Beta—i.e., the difference between E(Alpha) and E(Beta). But readers who were only thing-aware of the difference between Alpha and Beta were not fact-conscious of the difference between Alpha and Beta. They were not, therefore, fact-conscious of any difference between E(Alpha) and E(Beta)—their conscious experience of Alpha and Beta. These are conscious differences of which no one is conscious.

In saying that the reader was conscious of Spot—and, hence, in this sense, the difference between Alpha and Beta—without being conscious of the fact that they differed, we commit ourselves to the possibility of differences in conscious experience that are not reflected in conscious belief. Consciousness of Spot requires a conscious experience of Spot, a conscious E(Spot); yet, there is nothing in one's conscious beliefs—either about Spot, about the difference between Alpha and Beta, or about the difference between E(Alpha) and E(Beta)—that registers this difference. What we have in such cases is internal *state* consciousness with no corresponding (transitive) *creature* consciousness of the conscious state.[17] With no creature consciousness we lack any way of discovering, *even in our own case*, that there exists this difference in conscious state. To regard this as a contradiction is merely to confuse the way an internal state like an experience can be conscious with the way the person who is in that state can be, or fail to be, conscious of it.

It may be supposed that my conclusion rests on the special character of my example. Alpha contains a numerically distinct element, Spot, and our intuitions about what is required to see a (distinct) thing are, perhaps, shaping our intuitions about the character of the experience needed to see it. Let me, therefore, borrow an example from Irvin Rock (1983). Once again, the reader is asked to view figure 16.3 (after Rock 1983, p. 54) for a second and then say which, Alpha or Beta at the bottom, is the same as the figure shown at the top.

As closer inspection reveals, the upper left part of Alpha contains a few wiggles found in the original but not in Beta. Experimental subjects asked to identify which form it was they had seen did no better than chance. Many of them did not notice

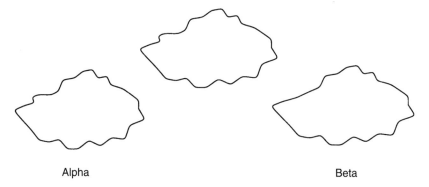

Alpha   Beta

Figure 16.3

that there were wiggles on the figure they were shown. At least they could not remember having seen them. As Rock (1983, p. 55) observes:

Taken together, these results imply that when a given region of a figure is a nonconsequential part of the whole, something is lacking in the perception of it, with the result that no adequate memory of it seems to be established.

No adequate *memory* of it is established because, I submit, at the time the figure is seen there is no fact-awareness of the wiggles. You cannot remember *that* there are wiggles on the left if you were never aware that there were wiggles on the left.[18] Subjects were (or may well have been) aware (thing-aware) of the wiggles (they saw them), but never became aware that they were there. The wiggles are what Spot (or Tom's moustache) is: a thing one is thing-aware of but never notices. What is lacking in the subject's perception of the figure, then, is an awareness of certain facts (that there are wiggles on the upper left), not (at least not necessarily) an awareness of the things (the wiggles) on the left.

In some minds the second example may suffer from the same defects as the first: it exploits subtle (at least not easily noticeable) differences in detail of the object being perceived. The differences are out there in the objects, yes, but who can say whether these differences are registered in here, in our experience of the objects? Perhaps our conviction (or *my* conviction) that we do see (and, hence, consciously experience) these points of detail, *despite* not noticing them, is simply a result of the fact that we see figures (Alpha and Beta, for instance) between which there are visible differences, differences that *could* be identified (noticed) by an appropriate shift of attention. But just because the details are visible does not mean that we see them or, if we do, that there must be some intrinsic (conscious) difference in the experience of the figures that differ in these points of detail.

This is a way of saying that conscious experiences, the sort of experiences you have when looking around the room, cannot differ unless one is consciously aware that they differ. Nothing mental is to count as conscious (no state consciousness) unless one is conscious of it (without creature consciousness). This objection smacks of verificationism, but calling it names does nothing to blunt its appeal. So I offer one final example. It will, of necessity, come at the same point in a more indirect way. I turn to perceptually salient conditions, conditions it is hard to believe are not consciously experienced. In order to break the connection between experience and belief, between thing-awareness and fact-awareness, then, I turn to creatures with a diminished capacity for fact-awareness.[19]

Eleanor Gibson (1969, p. 284), in reporting Kluver's studies with monkeys, describes a case in which the animals are trained to the larger of two rectangles. When the rectangles are altered in size, the monkeys continue to respond to the larger of the two—whatever their absolute size happens to be. In Kluver's words, they "abstract" the LARGER THAN relation. After they succeed in abstracting this relation, and when responding appropriately to the larger (A) of two presented rectangles (A and B), we can say that they are aware of A, aware of B (thing-awareness), and aware that A is larger than B (fact awareness). Some philosophers may be a little uncomfortable about assigning beliefs to monkeys in these situations, uncomfortable about saying that the monkey is aware *that* A is larger than B, but let that pass. The monkeys at least exhibit a differential response, and that is enough. How shall we describe the monkeys' perceptual situation *before* they learned to abstract this relation? Did the rectangles *look* different to the monkeys? Was there any difference in their experience of A and B *before* they became aware that A was larger than B? We can imagine the difference in size to be as great as we please. They were not fact-aware of the difference, not aware that A is larger than B, to be sure. But that isn't the question. The question is: were they conscious of the condition of A and B that, so to speak, makes it true that A is larger than B?[20] Does their experience of objects change when, presented with two objects the same size, one of these objects expands making it much larger than the other? If not, how could these animals ever learn to do what they are being trained to do—distinguish between A's being larger than B and A's not being larger than B?

It seems reasonable to suppose that, prior to learning, the monkeys were thing-aware of a difference which they only became fact-aware of after learning was complete. Their experience of A and B was different, consciously so, before they were capable of exhibiting this difference in behaviour. Learning of this sort is simply the development of fact-awareness from thing-awareness.

The situation becomes even more compelling if we present the monkeys with three rectangles and try to get them to abstract the INTERMEDIATE IN SIZE relation. This more difficult problem proves capable of solution by chimpanzees, but monkeys find it extremely difficult. Suppose monkey M cannot solve it. What shall we say about M's perceptual condition when he sees three rectangles, A, B and C of descending size. If we use behavioural criteria for what kind of facts M is conscious of and assume that M has already mastered the first abstraction (the LARGER THAN relation), M is aware of the three rectangles, A, B and C. M is also aware that A is larger than B, that B is larger than C, and that A is larger than C. M is not, however, aware that B is INTERMEDIATE IN SIZE even though this is logically implied by the facts he is aware of. Clearly, although M is not (and, apparently, cannot be made) aware of the fact that B is intermediate in size, he is nonetheless aware of the differences (A's being larger than B, B's being larger than C) that logically constitute the fact that he is not aware of. B's being intermediate in size is a condition the monkey is thing-aware of but cannot be made fact-aware of. There are conscious features of the animal's experiences that are not registered in the animal's fact-awareness and, hence, not evinced in the animal's deliberate behaviour.

4   What, Then, Makes Experiences Conscious?

We have just concluded that there can be conscious differences in a person's experience of the world—and, in this sense, conscious features of his experience—of which that person is not conscious. If this is true, then it cannot be a person's awareness of a mental state that makes that state conscious. E(Spot) is conscious, and it constitutes a conscious difference between E(Alpha) and E(Beta) even though no one, including the person in whom it occurs, being conscious of it. It follows, therefore, that what *makes* a mental state conscious cannot be our consciousness of it. If we have conscious experiences, beliefs, desires, and fears, it cannot be our introspective awareness of them that makes them conscious.

This conclusion is a bit premature. The argument mounted in §3 was primarily directed at higher-order-thought (HOT) theories that take an experience or a belief (mental states) to be conscious in virtue of their being the object of some higher-order-thought-like entity, a higher-order mental state that (like a thought) involves the deployment of concepts. My concern in §3, therefore, was to show that conscious experience required no fact-awareness—either of facts related to what one experiences (e.g., Spot) or of facts related to the experience itself (e.g., E(Spot). One does not have to be fact-aware of E(Spot)) in order for E(Spot) to be conscious.

This leaves the possibility, however, that in order for one's experience of Spot to be conscious, one must be thing-aware of it. Perhaps, that is, E(Spot) is conscious, not because there is some higher order *thought* (involving concepts) about E(Spot), but rather because there is a higher-order *experience* (a non-conceptual mental state) of E(Spot), something that makes one thing-aware of E(Spot) in the same way one is thing-aware (perceptually) of Spot. This is a form of the HOT theory that Lycan (1992, p. 216) describes as Locke's "inner sense" account of state-consciousness. What makes an experience conscious is not one's (fact) awareness that one is having it, but one's (thing) awareness of it.

To my mind, Rosenthal (1990, pp. 34ff.) makes a convincing case against this "inner sense" version of state consciousness. He points out, for example, that one of the respects in which experiences are unlike thoughts is in having a sensory quality to them. E(Alpha), for instance, has visual, not auditory or tactile qualities. If what made E(Alpha) into a conscious experience was some higher order experience of E(Alpha), one would expect some distinctive qualia of this higher-order experience to intrude. But all one finds are the qualia associated with E(Alpha), the lower-order experience. For this reason (among others) Rosenthal himself prefers a version of the inner spotlight theory of consciousness in which the spotlight is something in the nature of a fact-awareness, not thing-awareness, of the lower order mental state or activity.

Aside, though, from the merits of such specific objections, I think the "inner sense" approach loses all its attraction once the distinction between thing-awareness and fact-awareness is firmly in place. Notice, first, that if it is thing-awareness of a mental state that is supposed to make that mental state conscious, then the "inner sense" theory has no grounds for saying that E(Spot) is not conscious. For a person might well be thing-aware of E(Spot)—thus making E(Spot) conscious—just as he is thing-aware of Spot, without ever being fact-aware of it. So on this version of the spotlight theory, a failure to realize, a total unawareness of the fact *that* there is a difference between E(Alpha) and E(Beta), is irrelevant to whether there is a conscious difference between these two experiences. This being so, the "inner sense" theory of what makes a mental state conscious does nothing to *improve* one's epistemic access to one's own conscious states. *As far as one can tell*, E(Spot) (just like Spot) may as well not exist. What good is an inner spotlight, an introspective awareness of mental events, if it doesn't give one epistemic access to the events on which it shines? The "inner sense" theory does nothing to solve the problem of what makes E(Spot) conscious. On the contrary, it multiplies the problems by multiplying the facts of which we are not aware. We started with E(Spot) and gave arguments in support of the view that E(Spot) was conscious even though the person in whom it occurred was not fact-aware of it. We are now being asked to explain this fact by another fact of which we are not fact-aware: namely, the fact that we are thing-aware of E(Spot). Neither E(Spot) nor the thing-awareness of E(Spot) makes any *discernible* difference to the person in whom they occur. This, surely, is a job for Occam's Razor.

If we do not have to be conscious of a mental state (like an experience) for the mental state to be conscious, then, it seems, consciousness of something cannot be what it is that makes a thing conscious. Creature consciousness (of either the factive or thing form) is not necessary for state consciousness.[21] What, then, makes a mental state conscious? When S smells, and thereby becomes aware of, the burning toast, what makes his experience of the burning toast a conscious experience? When S becomes aware that the light has turned green, what makes his belief that the light has turned green a conscious belief?

This is the big question, of course, and I am not confronting it in this paper. I am concerned only with a preliminary issue—a question about the relationship (or lack thereof) between creature consciousness and state consciousness. For it is the absence of this relation (in the right form) that undermines the orthodox view that what makes certain mental states conscious is one's awareness of them. Nonetheless, though I lack the space (and, at this stage, the theory) to answer the big question, I would like to indicate, if only briefly, the direction in which these considerations lead.

What makes an internal state or process conscious is the role it plays in making one (intransitively) conscious—normally, the role it plays in making one (transitively) conscious of some thing or fact. An experience of x is conscious, not because one is aware of the experience, or aware that one is having it, but because, being a certain sort of representation, it makes one aware of the properties (of x) and objects (x itself) of which it is a (sensory) representation. My visual experience of a barn is conscious, not because I am introspectively aware of it (or introspectively aware that I am having it), but because it (when brought about in the right way) makes me aware of the barn. It enables me to perceive the barn. For the same reason, a certain belief is conscious, not because the believer is conscious of *it* (or conscious of having it[22]), but because it is a representation that makes one conscious of the fact (that *P*) that it is a belief about. Experiences and beliefs are conscious, not because you are conscious of them, but because, so to speak, you are conscious *with* them.

This is not to deny that one may, in fact, be conscious of one's own experiences in the way one is, in ordinary perception, conscious of barns and other people. Perhaps we are equipped with an introspective faculty, some special internal scanner, that takes as its objects (the *x*s it is an awareness of), one's experiences of barns and people. Perhaps this is so. Perhaps introspection is a form of meta-spectation—a sensing of one's own sensing of the world. I doubt this. I think introspection is best understood, not as thing-awareness, but as fact-awareness—an awareness that one has certain beliefs, thoughts, desires and experiences *without* a corresponding awareness of the things (the beliefs, thoughts, experiences and desires) themselves. Introspection is more like coming to know (be aware) that one has a virus than it is like coming to see, hear, or feel (i.e., be aware of) the virus (the thing) itself.

Whether these speculations on the nature of introspection are true or not, however, is, independent of the present thesis about consciousness. The claim is not that we are unaware of our own conscious beliefs and experiences (or unaware that we have them). It is, instead, that our being aware of them, or that we have them, is not what makes them conscious. What make them conscious is the way they make us conscious of something else—the world we live in and (in proprioception) the condition of our own bodies.

Saying just what the special status is that makes certain internal representations conscious while other internal states (lacking this status) remain unconscious is, of course, the job for a fully developed theory of consciousness. I haven't supplied that. All I have tried to do is to indicate where not to look for it.

Notes

I am grateful to Berent Enc, Güven Guzeldere, Lydia Sanchez, Ken Norman, David Robb and Bill Lycan for critical feedback. I would also like to thank the Editor and anonymous referees of *Mind* for a number of very helpful suggestions.

1. I am thinking here of those who subscribe to what are called higher order thought (HOT) theories of consciousness, theories that hold that what makes an experience conscious is its

being an object of some higher-order thought or experience. See Rosenthal (1986, 1990, 1991), Armstrong (1968, 1980, especially Ch. 4, "What is Consciousness?") and Lycan (1987, 1992). I return to these theories in section 4.

2. This section is a summary and minor extension of points I have made elsewhere; see especially Dretske 1969, 1978, 1979.

3. When I speak of events I should be understood to be including any of a large assortment of entities that occupy temporal positions (or duration): happenings, occurrences, states, states-of-affairs, processes, conditions, situations, and so on. In speaking of these as temporal entities, I do not mean to deny that they have spatial attributes—only that they do so in a way that is derived from the objects to which they happen. Games occur in stadiums because that is where the players are when they play the game. Movements (of a passenger, say) occur in a vehicle because that is where the person is when she moves.

4. White (1964, p. 42) calls "aware" a polymorphous concept (p. 6); it takes many forms. What it is to become or be aware of something depends on what one is aware of. To become aware of a perceptual object takes the form of seeing or hearing or smelling or tasting or feeling it.

5. One must distinguish Clyde from such things as Clyde's location, virtues, etc. One can be aware of Clyde's location and virtues without, at the time, perceiving them. But unlike Clyde, his virtues and location are not what I am calling things. See the discussion of abstract objects below.

6. I will not try to distinguish direct from indirect forms of perception (and, thus, awareness). We speak of seeing Michael Jordan on TV. If this counts as seeing Michael Jordan, then (for purposes of this essay), it also counts as being aware or conscious of Michael Jordan (on TV). Likewise, if one has philosophical scruples about saying one smells a rose or hears a bell—thinking, perhaps, that it is really only scents and sounds (not the objects that give off those scents or make those sounds) that one smells and hears—then, when I speak of being conscious of a flower (by smelling) or bell (by hearing), one can translate this as being indirectly conscious of the flower via its scent and the bell via the sound it makes.

7. Generally speaking, the concepts necessary for awareness of facts are those corresponding to terms occurring obliquely in the clause (the that-clause) describing the fact one is aware of.

8. I am here indebted to Perkins' (1983, pp. 295–305) insightful discussion.

9. If it helps, the reader may suppose that later, at t_3, S remembers having seen Tom's moustache at t_2 while being completely unaware at the time (i.e., at t_2) that Tom had a moustache. Such later memories are not essential (S may see the moustache and *never* realise he saw it), but they may, at this point in the discussion, help calm verificationists' anxieties about the example.

10. For further arguments see Dretske (1969, Ch. 2; 1979; 1981, Ch. 6; and my reply to Heil in McLaughlin, 1991, pp. 180–185).

11. White (1964, p. 59): "Being conscious or unconscious *of* so and so is not the same as simply being conscious or unconscious. If there is anything of which a man is conscious, it follows that he is conscious; to lose consciousness is to cease to be conscious of anything."

12. One might mention dreams as a possible exception to (3): one is (in a dream) aware of certain things (images?) while being asleep and, therefore, unconscious in the intransitive sense. I think this is not a genuine exception to (3), but since I do not want to get side-tracked arguing about it, I let the possibility stand as a "possible" exception. Nothing will depend on how the matter is decided.

13. For purposes of illustrating distinctions I use a simple causal theory of knowledge (to know that P is to be caused to believe that P by the fact that P) and perception (to perceive x is to be caused to have an experience by x). Though sympathetic to certain versions of these theories, I wish to remain neutral here.

14. E.g., Baars (1988), Velmans (1991), Humphrey (1992).

15. I do not think it necessary to speculate about how E(Spot) is realized or about its exact relation to E(Alpha). I certainly do not think E(Spot) must literally be a *spatial* part of E(Alpha) in the way Spot is a spatial part of Alpha. The argument is that there is an intrinsic *difference* between E(Alpha) and E(Beta). E(Spot) is just a convenient way of referring to this difference.

16. Speaking of large numbers, Elizabeth, a remarkable eidetiker (a person who can maintain visual images for a long time) studied by Stromeyer and Psotka (1970), was tested with computer-generated random-dot stereograms. She looked at a 10,000 dot pattern for one minute with one eye. Then she looked at another 10,000 dot pattern with the other eye. Some of the individual dots in the second pattern were systematically offset so that a figure in depth would emerge (as in using a stereoscope) if the patterns from the two eyes were fused. Elizabeth succeeded in superimposing the eidetic image that she retained from the first pattern over the second pattern. She saw the figure that normal subjects can only see by viewing the two patterns (one with each eye) simultaneously.

I note here that to fuse the two patterns the *individual dots* seen with one eye must somehow be paired with those retained by the brain (*not* the eye; this is not an after-image) from the other eye.

17. I return, in the next section, to the question of whether we might not have thing-awareness of E(Spot)—that is, the same kind of awareness of the difference between E(Alpha) and E(Beta) as we have of the difference between Alpha and Beta.

18. Though there may be other ways of remembering the wiggles. To use an earlier example, one might remember seeing Tom's moustache without (at the time) noticing it (being fact-aware of it). Even if one cannot remember *that* Tom had a moustache (since one never knew this), one can, I think, remember *seeing* Tom's moustache. This is the kind of memory (episodic vs. declarative) involved in a well-known example: remembering how many windows there are in a familiar house (e.g., the house one grew up in) by imagining oneself walking through the house and counting the windows. One does not, in this case, remember that there were 23 windows although one comes to know that there were 23 windows by using one's memory.

19. The following is an adaptation of the discussion in Dretske (1981, pp. 151–2).

20. *Conditions*, recall, are things in my sense of this word. One can be aware of an object's condition (its movement, for instance) without being aware that it is moving. This is what happens when one sees an adjacent vehicle's movement *as* one's own movement or an object's

movement as an expansion or contraction. It is also what occurs in infants and, perhaps, animals who do not have the concept of movement: they are aware of O's movement, but not aware that O is moving.

21. Neither is it sufficient. We are conscious of a great many internal states and activities that are not themselves conscious (heart beats, a loose tooth, hiccoughs of a fetus, a cinder in the eye).

22. If fact-awareness was what made a belief conscious, it would be very hard for young children (those under the age of 3 or 4 years, say) to have conscious beliefs. They don't yet have a firm grasp of the concept of a belief and are, therefore, unaware of the fact that they have beliefs. See Flavell (1988), Wellman (1990).

References

Armstrong, D. M. 1968: *A Materialist Theory of the Mind*. London: Routledge and Kegan Paul.

Armstrong, D. M. 1980: *The Nature of Mind and Other Essays*. Ithaca, New York: Cornell University Press.

Astington, J., P. Harris, and D. Olson, eds. 1988: *Developing Theories of the Mind*. New York: Cambridge University Press.

Baars, B. 1988: *A Cognitive Theory of Consciousness*. Cambridge: Cambridge University Press.

Dennett, D. C. 1991: *Consciousness Explained*. Boston: Little Brown.

Dretske, F. 1969: *Seeing and Knowing*. Chicago: University of Chicago Press.

———1978: "The role of the percept in visual cognition," in Savage 1978, pp. 107–127.

———1979: "Simple seeing", in Gustafson and Tapscott 1979, pp. 1–15.

———1981: *Knowledge and the Flow of Information*. Cambridge, Massachusetts: MIT Press/A Bradford Book.

———1990: "Seeing, believing and knowing," in Osherson, Kosslyn and Hollerbach 1990.

Favell, J. H. 1988: "The development of children's knowledge about the mind: From cognitive connections to mental representations," in Astington, Harris, and Olson 1988.

Gibson, E. 1969: *Principles of Perceptual Learning and Development*. New York: Appleton Century & Crofts.

Grice, P. 1989: *Studies in the Way of Words*. Cambridge, Massachusetts: Harvard University Press.

Gustafson, D. F. and B. L. Tapscott, eds. 1979: *Body, Mind and Method: Essays in Honor of Virgil Aldrich*. Dordrecht, Holland: Reidel.

Humphrey, N. 1992: *A History of the Mind: Evolution and the Birth of Consciousness*. New York: Simon and Schuster.

Lees, R. B. 1963: *The Grammar of English Nominalizations*. Bloomington, Indiana: Indiana University Press.

Lycan, W. 1987: *Consciousness*. Cambridge, Massachusetts: MIT Press.

Lycan, W. 1992: "Uncertain Materialism and Lockean introspection." *Behavioral and Brain Sciences* 15.2, pp. 216–217.

McLaughlin, B., ed. 1991: *Critical Essays on the Philosophy of Fred Dretske*. Oxford: Basil Blackwell.

Milner, A. D. and M. D. Rugg, eds. 1992: *The Neuropsychology of Consciousness*. London: Academic Press.

Osherson, D., S. Kosslyn and J. Hollerback, eds. 1990: *An Invitation to Cognitive Science, Volume 2, Visual Cognition and Action*. Cambridge, Massachusetts: MIT Press.

Perkins, M. 1983: *Sensing the World*. Indianapolis, Indiana: Hackett Publishing Company.

Rock, I. 1983: *The Logic of Perception*. Cambridge, Massachusetts: MIT Press/A Bradford Book.

Rosenthal, D. 1986: "Two concepts of consciousness." *Philosophical Studies* 94.3, pp. 329–359.

Rosenthal, D. 1990: "A theory of consciousness." Report No. 40, Research Group on Mind and Brain, ZiF, University of Bielefeld.

Rosenthal, D. 1991: "The independence of consciousness and sensory quality," in Villanueva (1991), pp. 15–36.

Savage, W., ed. 1978: *Minnesota Studies in the Philosophy of Science: Perception and Cognition*, Vol IX. Minneapolis, Minnesota: University of Minnesota Press.

Stromeyer, C. F. and J. Psotka 1970: "The detailed texture of eidetic images," *Nature*, 225, pp. 346–349.

Velmans, M. 1991: "Is human information processing conscious?" *Behavioral and Brain Sciences* 14.4, pp. 651–668.

Villanueva, E., ed. 1991: *Consciousness*. Atascadero, CA: Ridgeview Publishing Company.

Wellman, H. M. 1990: *The Child's Theory of the Mind*. Cambridge, Massachusetts; MIT Press/A Bradford Book.

White, A. R. 1964: *Attention*. Oxford: Basil Blackwell.

17

The Content of Perceptual Experience

John McDowell

1. Daniel Dennett's aim, in his richly suggestive paper "Toward a Cognitive Theory of Consciousness,"[1] is to represent the content with which we persons have conscious dealings as a selection from the content that would figure in a sub-personal, cognitive-scientific account of the operations of our internal machinery. What effects the selection, according to Dennett's suggestion, is the fact that some of that sub-personal content is available to an internal public-relations organization that accounts for our linguistic output—not that we actually state everything that is in our consciousness, but the idea is that we could do so.

What is in question is precisely access to content, rather than something we could without qualification conceive as access to content-bearers: for Dennett remarks (p. 159) that "we have no direct personal access to the *structure* of *content*ful events within us." The idea is that "events within us" are contentful *by virtue of* their structure: for the content possessed by an internal event or state is a function of its function in the organism, and this function "is—in the end, must be—a function of the *structure* of the state or event and the systems of which it is a part" (p. 163). But only some of the events and states within us that possess content in this way make available to *us* the content that their structurally determined role in the system confers on them (although they transmit content freely among themselves, unnoticed by us). And when they make their content available to us, the structure in virtue of which they have it does not figure in an accurate phenomenology of our consciousness; it remains a topic for theory, not mere introspective noticing.

I think it is phenomenologically acute of Dennett to deny that we have "direct personal access" to structure; the background thesis, that the content in question is possessed in virtue of structure, generates familiar temptations to suppose otherwise. Consider visual experience. The relevant internal event will be described, in the cognitive-scientific framework Dennett is working in, as something on the lines of a computation of a representation of part of the environment from a pair of arrays of intensities and wavelengths. The way information is contained in this base for computation is naturally described as imagistic. If we assume that the content-ful consciousness involved in a visual experience is a matter of access to such an event, it can be very tempting to equate the plain fact that our visual consciousness is of how things *look* to us with the theoretical idea (not a plain fact of conscious-ness at all) that what we have access to in this sort of consciousness is more than the contents of the computationally derived representations (at various levels: see pp. 157–8), and includes specifically the image-like character of the base of the com-putations—a matter of structure in Dennett's sense. But whatever may be true about the information-processing that takes place in the visual system, there are no images (two-dimensional arrays) in the phenomenology of vision: it is the relevant tract of the environment that is present to consciousness, not an image of it. It is to Dennett's credit that he resists this falsification of what visual consciousness is like.

2. Another thought of Dennett's seems less acute as phenomenology. Having introduced the notion of presentiments or premonitions by way of cases in which, for instance, one is struck, without knowing why, by the thought that someone is looking over one's shoulder as one writes (pp. 165–6), he goes on to apply the notion to ordinary visual experience (p. 166):

Right now it occurs to me that there are pages in front of me, a presentiment whose aetiol-ogy is not known directly by me, but which is, of course, perfectly obvious. It is my visual system that gives me this presentiment, along with a host of others.

The suggestion is that these perceptual "presentiments" are unlike, for instance, the presentiment that someone is looking over one's shoulder only in their con-nectedness with what precedes and follows them (which is presumably what makes the aetiology so obvious). They are like that sort of presentiment in that the aeti-ology, although obvious in this case, unlike that one, is, as we might say, phenom-enologically extrinsic ("not known directly by me").

This suggestion seems phenomenologically off key, perhaps especially about visual experience. What it seems to threaten is the presentness to one of the seen envi-ronment. On Dennett's suggestion, that a seen object is there before one is a mere premonition, something one finds oneself inclined to suppose, unaccountably so far as anything contained in the experience itself goes. Or perhaps we can change the aspect, and say that the presence of the object is a hypothesis, the obviously best explanation of the premonition; here the claim of obviousness cannot undo the damage done by the idea of a hypothesis—it cannot give us back the idea that the object itself is presented to one's awareness.

Consider a basic (demonstratively expressible) singular empirical judgement, say a judgement one might express, in a suitable perceptual situation, by saying "That cat is asleep." The content of such a judgement depends on the perceived presence of the cat itself. A premonition would at best yield content to the effect that a cat that is in a certain region (and has, no doubt, all manner of visible properties, but registering the richness of the available content does not help) is asleep. This lacks the particularity of the original judgement—its relating to a particular cat (*that* one, as one will be able to say if one is in the right perceptual situation); not just to some cat that satisfies a general specification, however rich. We might try to recapture particularity by making out that the thought is carried to the right object by the "obvious" hypothesis about the premonition's aetiology. But that is not how demonstratively expressible thought makes contact with its object. Such thought does not need to be 'carried to' its object by a hypothesis, because the object is directly there for the thinker.[2]

3. It may seem captious to complain about phenomenological niceties. But I think the off-key phenomenology reflects a serious epistemological difficulty.

Consider Kant's advance over Hume. Hume inherits from his predecessors a conception according to which no experience is in its very nature, intrinsically, an encounter with objects. What Kant takes from Hume is that there is no rationally satisfactory route from such a predicament to the epistemic position that we are in (obviously in, we might say). Transcendental synthesis (or whatever) is not supposed to be such a route: the whole point of its being transcendental, in this context, is that it is not supposed to be something that we, our familiar empirical selves, go in for. It would be a mistake to think we can domesticate Kant's point by detranscendentalizing the idea of synthesis, so as to suggest that the idea of encountering objects is put in place by interpretation of data, perhaps by inference to the best explanation, with the interpretation being something we do, or at least something that might figure in a "rational reconstruction" of our being in the epistemic position we are in. That would just be missing *Hume's* point. Kant does not miss Hume's point. He builds on it: since there is no rationally satisfactory route from experiences, conceived as, in general, less than encounters with objects, glimpses of objective reality, to the epistemic position we are manifestly in, experiences must be intrinsically encounters with objects. But how could they be that if their aetiology were phenomenologically extrinsic?

Dennett's idea of experiences as presentiments requires a pre-Humean epistemological optimism. Not that Dennett would dream of urging epistemologists to revert to such a stance: his attention is simply not fixed on epistemological considerations.

I think this sort of situation is not uncommon: we have a new-fangled move in the philosophy of mind, enmeshed in a quite old-fashioned philosophical difficulty, in a way that has no connection with the intentions of its proponents (who imagine that their questions and answers are simply insulated from that kind of thing).

Of course I am not suggesting that Dennett's conception of experiences as presentiments is the same as Hume's conception of experiences as impressions. But both conceive experiences as less than encounters with objects. Hume's good point, the one Kant builds on, generalizes beyond the specifics of his own picture, to warrant an epistemological pessimism about any such conception of experience.

4. I do not believe that the off-key phenomenology is just a gratuitous slip on Dennett's part.

Consider the framework role played in Dennett's thinking by the idea of what our visual systems tell us. His main aim is to capture the thought that *we* (and not just some sub-personal parts of us) are on the receiving end of this telling. I shall come back to that; but for present purposes, we need to focus rather on the content of the telling. What could our visual systems, conceived in the information-processing vein that Dennett is defending, tell us? (Or tell our brains, if one prefers something modelled on the original formula "what the frog's eye tells the frog's brain"?)

Here is a candidate for being a possible message to me, on occasion, from my visual system: that there is a cat, with such and such properties, at such and such a position in my egocentric space. The considerations in §3 above actually suggest that the framework undermines even this, since it undermines the possibility that experiences, as it conceives them, might possess objective content at all; but we can let that pass for now, in order to get the "presentiment" idea going. The relevant question at this point is rather this: could my visual system tell me, in addition, that a cat figures in the aetiology of the original message? How could my visual system, conceived as a sub-personal computing device, be in a position to tell me that? We are letting the visual system pass muster as capable of telling me about such things as the presence of cats with such and such properties, on the basis that it discriminates such circumstances more or less reliably. (Actually the truth is that it enables *me* to do that rather than that *it* does that, and this is crucial; but I am playing along with a different way of talking.) But my visual system is surely not a reliable discriminator of cases in which the input from which it starts has one kind of aetiology as against cases in which it has another. If, as a matter of routine, the visual system added a suitable message about aetiology to whatever it told me about the environment ("This message was caused by the fact it reports"), and if the visual system *is* a more or less reliable detector of features of the environment, the added message would be more or less reliably correct. But it would not be, as we are supposing the original message about the environment might be, a case of *informing* me of something. From the perspective, as it were, of the information-processing device, it would be more like an expression of blind faith: not the sort of thing that belongs in a sensible theory of the functioning of an information-processing device. (A routine additional message that might make a certain sense would be "This is your visual system speaking." This leaves Dennett's "presentiment" idea untouched: it merely registers that the presentiments can be distinctively visual.)

5. If I am right so far, Dennett's basic framework necessitates the "presentiment" idea: perceptual experiences as he conceives them would have to be presentiments. And the idea is deeply unsatisfactory, in a way that is not just a matter of phenomenological nuance. What has gone wrong?

To begin on a diagnosis, I want to turn away, for the moment, from Dennett's ultimate aim of accounting for personal-level psychological truth, and consider the perceptual lives of frogs. Dennett alludes to a famous paper called "What the Frog's Eye Tells the Frog's Brain,"[3] but he commends a suggestion, by Michael Arbib, that one might prefer the formula "What the frog's eye tells the frog" (p. 163). His point is that "sub-personal" content-ascription in the theory of frog perception is controlled by the requirements of a biological account whose topic is the life of *frogs* rather than the doings of their parts.

Still, the original formula "what the frog's eye (or visual system) tells the frog's brain" was not wrong. What it enables us to stress is that we understand the "sub-personal" metaphor of telling in terms of informational transactions between one part of an organism and *another part*. So if we want to talk of informational transactions between part of a creature and the *creature*, we cannot simply carry over the metaphor; we need to work for the extension. In the metaphor, our parts talk to one another; they do not, at least in general, talk to us. Dennett does a great deal of work at the necessary extending of the metaphor for the case of persons, making room for the idea of what our visual systems tell *us* (this is the main aim of his paper). But the point should hold for frogs too. In a "sub-personal" account of frog perception in which the frog's eye (or visual system) does some telling, say announcing that there is a bug-like object at such and such a position in the frog's motor space, what gets told of this will be another *part* of the frog, say one that the theorist labels "motor control." What entitles us to say, not just that the frog's visual system informs the frog's motor control of the presence of a bug-like object, but that it gets the message to the *frog*? It is part of Dennett's own point that there is no extra twist in the "sub-personal" account of what happens in frogs, analogous to the extra twist in the sub-personal account of our inner workings that is supposed to make room for *us* to have access to the content of our inner states and events. How, then, does the *frog* get into the act?

I suspect that this question—which is, I insist, a serious one—tends to be suppressed because of an unfortunate feature of the otherwise excellent distinction between the personal and the sub-personal. Theories of internal information-processing in frogs are at best "sub-personal" (I have needed the scare quotes at several points), not sub-personal, because there are no persons around in contrast with whom we can mark the standard distinction. It would be easy to think on these lines: the frog's being informed, by its visual system, of the presence of a bug-like object would certainly not be a personal-level involvement with content; so it is sub-personal; so why not simply *identify* it with the "sub-personal" content-involving transaction that we already have in our theoretical sights, the frog's motor control's being informed of that by its visual system? But this would be confused. The point of saying that the theory of internal information-processing in frogs is "sub-personal" is not that no persons are involved, something that is indeed equally true of talk whose subject is frogs themselves, but that the fundamental idea of such a theory is the idea of informational transactions between *parts* of frogs. If we speak in all seriousness (and why should we not?) of *frogs* learning about their environment through vision, what is in question is, by all means, not personal involvement with content. But it is *froggy* involvement with content, and it ought to be just as pressing to ask how this connects with sub-froggy informational transactions—how the frog gets into the act—as it is to ask how our personal involvement with content connects with sub-personal informational transactions within us.

What is more, if it were right to suppose that the personal-level involvement with content which we enjoy when we learn about the environment in (conscious) experience is a matter of access on our part to some of the sub-personally generated content that is being passed from part to part within us, it should be just as plausible to suppose that the involvement with content that is enjoyed by a frog when it learns about the environment in vision is to be understood in terms of access on the frog's part to its own interior. But this seems merely ludicrous. The frog's access in perception is, like ours, to the environment.

6. When we apply the idea that frogs learn, through vision, about features of their environment, we are subject to two controls. First, there is frog life, which, like all animal life, is a matter of more or less competently inhabiting an environment. In this context, we ask questions like the following: what features of the environment would a creature need to become informed of, in order to live in it with precisely the competence that frogs display? Second, there are the facts about frog perceptual equipment. Here we have questions like the following: is *this* the kind of thing that we can make sense of a creature's becoming informed of by the use of, say, eyes? Or, more specifically: can we understand how possession of a visual system that works like *this* makes it possible for a creature to become informed of just *these* features of its environment?

The specific questions that arise under the second head can be answered, in principle, by constructing characterizations of the relevant perceptual equipment as information-processing devices, which transmit their results to other (functionally specified) parts of the organism (for instance, "motor control"). There is an obvious interplay between the results of investigation here and the answers we give to questions under the first head. Casual observation of frog life might induce the provisional thought that frogs become informed, through vision, of the presence of bugs. Then it turns out that a good theory of the relevant perceptual equipment fails to support the view that the equipment processes information about arrays of light into information about the presence of bugs. The equipment hardly processes information at all (it is a limiting case of an information-processing device), but rather simply reacts to any small moving speck. It is better to view the informational transaction as the transmission, to "motor control," of information to the effect that a small moving speck is at such and such a point in motor space. So we recast our conception of what frogs become informed of: at best the presence of a bug-like object at a certain place. (Given the usual sort of environment that frogs inhabit, this is good enough for their somewhat low-grade competence.) Some may think even this goes too far; but it is hard to see how we could credit frogs with being less informed about their environment than this without representing them as not in touch with it at all—a position that has all the appearance of a philosophers' prejudice.

The fact that there is this perfectly intelligible interplay between what we decide we can correctly say, in content-involving terms, about frogs, on the one hand, and the detail of a content-involving (information-processing) account of the inner workings of the parts of frogs, on the other, is no reason to mix the two stories together.

In the account of inner workings, one sub-froggy part of a frog transmits information to another: the frog's eye talks to the frog's brain, not to the frog. In the sense
in which the frog's eye tells the frog's brain things, nothing tells the frog anything.
We may still want to say that the frog gets told things. But what does *this* telling is
not something in the frog's interior; that is what generated the idea that we could
attribute dealings with content to the *frog* only if we credited it with something like
introspection. Rather, what tells the frog things is the environment, making features
of itself apparent to the frog, equipped as it is with frog perceptual apparatus. This
is a different metaphor of telling, not in competition with the "sub-personal" one.
It is essential not to be misled by the enormous capacity for illumination that the
"sub-personal" account has (together, perhaps, with the true but irrelevant point
that frogs are not persons) into thinking that the "sub-personal" account exhausts
the content-involving truth in this area of biology. The second metaphor encapsu-
lates a whole extra field of truths. What is more, the involvement of content here,
and only here, is literal: underneath the metaphor of the environment telling the
frog things, we have the literal truth that the frog becomes informed of things.
Whereas the content-involving truth at the "sub-personal" level is irreducibly
metaphorical.

The "sub-personal" account of a sensory system, which treats it as an information-
processing device that transmits its informational results to something else inside an
animal, cannot adequately characterize what its sensory systems are for the animal
(as opposed to what they are, metaphorically speaking, for the internal parts that
receive the results of the information-processing): namely, modes of sensitivity or
openness to features of the environment—not processors of information, but
collectors of it.

It would be a confusion to think that the distinction I am making here is blurred
by the minimal extent of information-processing in frog vision in particular. What
the frog's eyes do for the frog is to put it in touch with moving specks in its spatial
environment: things that are in fact bugs, in the sort of case that is sufficiently
normal in frogs' lives. From the frog's point of view, its eyes enable it simply to pick
up the fact that there is a moving speck (with luck, a bug) out there. From the point
of view of the frog's "motor control" (to speak in the terms of the "sub-personal"
metaphor), the presence out there of a moving speck is rather (at most) the best
hypothesis the eyes (or, probably better in view of how little the eyes do, the whole
system) can come up with in order to account for the input of light (what is in fact
light, though the system does not even know this much) to the eyes. If all goes well,

the frog is in direct touch with a feature of its external environment; the internal information-processing system is in direct touch only with structural properties of the immediate inputs to it—which, in the metaphor, it interprets as clues to the nature of the external environment. (Of course the frog does no such thing.)

What could an internal information-processing device really tell an animal? To give a positive answer, we should need to deal satisfactorily with the question I am suppressing, about how to make sense of the frog's being on the receiving end of "sub-personal" telling; but my point now is not that we have no inkling how that might be done. What could an information-processing device *really* tell *anything* (including another component in a sub-personal of "sub-personal" informational system)? It is essential to realize that the answer to this question can be, in fact is, "Nothing," without the slightest threat being posed to the utility, or even the theoretical indispensability, of cognitive science.

A sub-personal or "sub-personal" informational system is a physical mechanism, connected to its surroundings by transducers that convert physical impacts from outside into events of the sort that the system can work on, and perhaps by transducers that convert the system's end-products into physical interventions in the exterior. The system knows nothing even about the character of the immediate physical impacts on the input transducers, or the immediate physical interventions in the exterior that result from its operations by way of the output transducers, let alone about the nature and layout of the distal environment. The operations of the system are determined by structures exemplified in the initial contributions of the transducers, and in intermediate events and states in the system, which have no meaning for the system. In short, in Dennett's own memorable and exactly right phrase, the system is a syntactic engine, not a semantic engine.[4] The same goes for its parts.

Animals, by contrast, are semantic engines. To stick with the present example, they become informed that . . . (say, that there is a bug-like object at such and such a position). The background against which this makes sense is their competent inhabiting of their environment. Now this competence would be quite mysterious if there were no interestingly structured machinery inside them, controlling their behaviour in a way that is responsive to impacts from the environment. We could not make sense of the competence that enables us to make sensible use of the claim that *animals* have dealings with content if we could find nothing inside them but, say, a completely homogeneous jelly. And nobody knows how to make sense of an animal's internal control mechanism, and connect it conceptually to the competence it is supposed to explain, except by describing it *as if* it were, what we know it is not really, a semantic engine, interpreting inputs as signs of environmental facts and, as output, directing behaviour so as to be suitable to those facts in the light of the animal's needs or goals. To insist that the attribution of content at this sub-personal or "sub-personal" level is "as if" talk is in no way to debunk it. The content-attribution is not, as it were, irresponsible: it is constrained by the physiological facts, in a way that is exemplified, on a small scale, by the discovery of how little interpretation ("as if" interpretation, we must say) can be credited to the visual systems of frogs. And it is surely clear, at least in a general way, how content-attribution that is only "as if" can even so pull its weight in addressing a genuine explanatory need: the question is what enables us animals to be the semantic engines we are.

It is crucial to see that the question about real content with which we are helped by the "as if" attribution of content to states and events in internal mechanisms is this causal or enabling question. One can easily fall into a temptation to suppose that the question is rather a constitutive one. If we could see dealings with content on the part of animals as somehow constitutively explained in terms of information-processing in their interiors, that might seem a protection against a metaphysical embarrassment. (After all, we might say to ourselves, cognitive science is science: maybe it is not quite clear that ecology and ethology are science.) But this temptation is disastrous: if we offer a constitutive explanation of genuine content in terms of a merely "as if" attribution of content, we make genuine content fragile and problematic.

Dennett's basic picture is that *our* dealings with content are nothing but our access to some of the content manipulated by our internal information-processing systems, and this seems to be a case of succumbing to the temptation. It flies in the face of the insight that the internal systems are only syntactic engines: access to our interiors cannot be what constitutes our dealings with content, since there is no content in there, although it is enormously useful to talk as if there were. Dennett writes ("Beyond Belief," pp. 26–7):

Somehow, the syntactical virtuosity of our brains permits us to be interpreted at another level as semantic engines—systems that (indirectly) discriminate the significance of the impingements on them.

The idea that our discrimination of the significance of the impingements on us is *indirect* reflects the idea that our becoming informed of environmental facts just is the upshot of the sort of computational process that we attribute to our perceptual systems—as if we were in the predicament of our nervous systems, blocked off from the environment by transducers rather than inhabiting it. No wonder our status as semantic engines becomes a mystery ("somehow"), and no wonder it is a comfort to make room for the suggestion that it is just a way of talking, not a fact (the syntactical virtuosity of our brains "permits us to be interpreted as" semantic engines, rather than just making it intelligible that we are such). If we drop the attempt to read the envisaged explanations constitutively, "permits" can take its proper significance: unmysteriously, the syntactic virtuosity of our brains enables us to relate to the environment in the direct way that is constitutive of our being the semantic engines we are.

7. Sidney Morgenbesser is said to have accused a cognitive-scientifically minded colleague of believing that our intelligence is Artificial Intelligence. We can now see a sense in which that ridiculous belief is almost correct: we ourselves have genuine intelligence, but there is Artificial Intelligence inside us—not in the sense of an artefact, but in the sense of an imitation or fake. That is to say: we have inside us something that is not intelligent at all (it knows nothing and understands nothing); even so, we can be enormously helped in finding it comprehensible how we can be intelligent, even though we are made of nothing but the stuff of which everything is made, including mere "stupid" *things* like sticks and stones, by seeing how this completely unintelligent internal equipment of ours can have imposed, on top of the truth about its mindless manipulations of structures that are meaningless to it, an "as if" description in terms of dealings with content. That makes it possible to understand how this mindless internal control system enables us to do what it takes to display genuine mindedness, namely to live competently in an environment.

"Display" may mislead here, encouraging the thought: maybe that is what it takes to *show* mindedness, but it can be there anyway, perhaps in a brain in a vat. I think we are now in a position to begin to see through this. I shall approach the point by way of another striking philosophical remark that we can now see in the proper light, namely John Searle's claim that we are brains in vats (vats of bone, not glass, with input and output linkages to the environment different from those in the standard mad-scientist fantasy; but vats none the less).[5] The truth is that our brains are indeed brains in vats, and that is exactly why we must not identify ourselves with them. To a brain it is all one whether its vat is glass or bone, and what, if anything, is outside its input and output transducers. To repeat, a brain knows nothing and understands nothing: all it does is to manipulate structures that have no meaning for it. That is not the truth about us. Without any threat at all to the enormous power of cognitive science to enable us to explain our mindedness (in one sense of "explain our mindedness"; not constitutive explanation), we ought to be able to see that the sheer fact that a brain is going through the motions that an embodied brain goes through when a person thinks or experiences is by itself no ground at all for supposing that there is a mind in there. (It may be a different matter if the mad scientist's vat contains what used to be an embodied brain; perhaps memory can give subjectivity a tenuous foothold there.)

There is a persisting inclination to suppose that this cannot be right: if the brain goes through the right paces, it must at least *seem* to it that it thinks or enjoys experience, and then even if we can make out a difference between having it seem to one that those things are so and their being so, the seeming is enough for subjectivity. Here it really is to the point to respond: you might as well suppose it seems to an electronic calculator that things are thus and so.

8. I have been urging, in effect, that we take Dennett's distinction between attributing content at the personal level and attributing it at the sub-personal level as a special case of a more general distinction, between content-attribution at the level of the animal and content-attribution at the level of its internal machinery. At the level of internal machinery, it is useful to talk of sensory systems as information-processing devices; but for the animal its sensory systems are modes of openness to features of its environment. Information-processing characterizations of the internal machinery figure in explanations of how it can be that animals are in touch with their environments. The "as if" content that is usefully deployed at the lower level helps make intelligible the genuine content that appears at the higher level by way of "enabling" explanations, not as somehow constituting that content. Since there is no getting around the fact that the internal machinery is really only a syntactic engine, the attempt to see a constitutive relation between the lower and the upper levels undermines our hold on the fact that animals are semantic engines.

It will not have escaped notice that my descriptions of what sensory systems are for an animal that possesses them are Gibsonian.[6] A proper understanding of the relation between the two levels should help us to see through some cross purposes in a familiar style of cognitive-scientific response to Gibson's claims.

Gibson himself sometimes seems to deny that the idea of processing information has any role in characterizations of the operations of sensory systems. This is fully intelligible, given the fundamental point that he wants to make: that perceiving (something that animals do) is not processing information, but simply taking it in. In fact that claim is, as should by now be clear, fully compatible with recognizing that it can be useful to characterize sensory systems, *not* from the animal's point of view, as information-processing devices. The claim gives the framework within which such characterizations have their explanatory point.

Some cognitive-scientific critics of Gibson, not equipped with the distinction of levels, read Gibsonian descriptions of the sensory systems as if they were meant to serve the intellectual function that their own theories serve. It is not surprising if that makes the Gibsonian descriptions seem idiotic. David Marr, for instance, in his brilliant and path-breaking information-processing approach to vision, cites Gibson only as a half-baked precursor. When Gibson resoundingly, and rightly, denies that perceiving is processing information, Marr can hear only a reflection of failure to understand what information-processing is. In this framework, Gibson's positive remarks about the sensory systems can indicate at best a massive under-estimation of how difficult the information-processing task, the task of extracting information about environmental invariants from "the flowing array of ambient energy," is.[7] And really this is an understatement: if we read Gibson as attempting to say something at the lower of the two levels, then given what is obvious about the physical impingements to which, say, visual systems are restricted, the idea of directly collecting information about "environmental invariants" through vision looks like an appeal to magic. As Dennett says, quite correctly given this reading of Gibson, and completely missing Gibson's point, Gibson represents the visual system as "a hunk of wonder tissue."[8]

9. The distinction of levels equips us to see that there is nothing unscientific, no mere know-nothing refusal to acknowledge the rich promise of cognitive science, in denying that dealings with content on the part of perceiving animals should be equated with computationally described goings-on in their interiors. Moving to personal dealings with content, such as the conscious perceptual experiences of adult human beings, makes all kinds of differences. But there is no reason to suppose that it makes any difference on this point: our dealings with content, in our consciously enjoyed perceptual experience, are no more a matter of access to our own interiors than a frog's dealings with content are.

Dennett offers a picture of our internal functional organization, in which perceptual systems process bare data into comparatively rich information about the environment, and their products (at various levels of processing) are stored in a special short-term buffer memory ("M"), which feeds into a system controlling speech. (There is more complexity besides: see p. 155.) About this picture, he floats (p. 165) "the bold hypothesis that you are a realization of this flow chart, and that it is in virtue of this fact that it seems—to us and to you—that there is something it is like to be you" (that is, that you are conscious). As far as anything I have said goes, this may well be right. The important point is that if it is right, it is right as a piece of cognitive science, with "in virtue of" receiving a causal reading, not a constitutive one. The suggestion has the same shape as one to the effect that it is in virtue of possessing perceptual equipment that admits of such and such an information-processing characterization that an animal can be in touch with such and such features of its environment.

One might put this by saying that consciousness itself escapes Dennett's cognitivistic net: he offers what may be an enabling explanation of consciousness, but not a constitutive one. In one sense, this leaves us without an account of consciousness. We lack an account of what it is, even if we have an account of what enables it to be present. It would be a mistake to think this makes consciousness a metaphysical embarrassment: as if, in denying that consciousness is a matter of configurations in the satisfyingly material medium of the nervous system, we were committed to regarding it as a matter of configurations in an immaterial medium instead. As I have insisted, there is nothing inherently mysterious in a frog's being in touch with its environment (of course not in a "personal" way); we take that idea in our stride, in the context of thinking about how the frog's life fits into the environment. There is no difficulty in principle, although all kinds of differences must be acknowledged, about extending this comprehension to our own case: our personal-level dealings with content are intelligible in the context of our distinctively human life.

One striking advantage to be derived from rejecting the idea that conscious perceptual experience is a special kind of access to content that is in the first instance sub-personal, i.e., to the content of events or states in our interiors, is that it enables us to repossess the phenomenology of perception. I have already said something about a phenomenological misrepresentation that Dennett is led to (see section 2). Let me give another example: discussing the richness of experience, Dennett writes (p. 170):

One experiences more at any time than one wants to say then. What fills the "periphery," adds detail to one's "percepts," inhabits "fringe consciousness," is, as phenomenologists have insisted, *there*. Where? In M [the special buffer memory]. No more mysterious process of presentation or apprehension of inhabitants of phenomenal space is needed.

Certainly no such thing is needed, but Dennett's alternative answer, 'In M," is surely quite wrong as phenomenology. The phenomenologically right answer—

which, once we have the status of sub-personal theorizing straight, we can recognize as the right answer, period—is: in the part of the world (ordinary objective space, "not phenomenal space") that lies open to view.

10. At one point (pp. 160–1) Dennett remarks, in passing, that his construction has a Kantian flavour: his flow chart diagrams how intuitions (the sub-personal, and hence certainly not conceptual, content of states or events that result from perceptual data-processing) are "knitted together" with concepts (which figure in the articulable shape that contents acquire when they are made available to the system that controls speech). I think the real lesson of Dennett's paper is this: a dualism of intuitions and concepts cannot be made safe by simply removing it from the sphere of the transcendental—by assigning the task of fitting intuitions and concepts together to something empirical, whether it is the empirical self (as in section 3) or, as here, an empirically postulated internal apparatus. In either case, just because the "synthesis" is not transcendental (nor therefore something that simply disappears if we attempt a domesticated formulation of what we can learn from Kant), there is an epistemological come-uppance. The great beauty of Dennett's paper is how rigorously he lets his theory control his phenomenological claims; their failure of fit can now emerge as a fault line along which the whole structure must break apart.

We must see our way to not needing to give an account of how concepts and intuitions are brought into alignment. Another way of saying the same thing would be that we cannot make use of the notion of an interface between mind (which inhabits the space of concepts) and world, where the world presents the mind with non-conceptual items for it to work into conceptual shape. Or (yet another formulation) we cannot make sense of the mind as a "black box" in the world. (Obviously we can make sense of an interface between nervous systems and the world outside them.)[9] This paper has been about perceptual connections between mind and world, but the point has obvious reverberations for how we think of action too: if seen objects (say) are not on the far side of an "input" interface between mind and world, there is, to say the least, no point in trying to represent objects acted on—which may, of course, be the same objects—as lying on the far side of an "output" interface.

Notes

1. In his *Brainstorms* (Hassocks: Harvester, 1978), pp. 149–73. Page references to Dennett, unless otherwise specified, are to this paper. Dennett has discussed issues about consciousness more recently, in *Consciousness Explained* (Boston, Toronto, London: Little, Brown and

Co., 1991). But I think the earlier work is still worth attention. Dennett (in conversation) has agreed that the book does not supersede what I take issue with in the paper.

2. Sce Gareth Evans, *The Varieties of Reference* (Oxford: Clarendon Press, 1982), especially ch. 6.

3. J. Y. Lettvin et al., *Journal of the Institute of Radio Engineers* (1959), pp. 1940–51.

4. The idea is implicit in his remarks about the role of structure in sub-personal content-attribution (p. 163). For the phrase itself, see "Beyond Belief," in Andrew Woodfield (ed.), *Thought and Object* (Oxford: Clarendon Press, 1982), pp. 1–95, at p. 26.

5. See *Intentionality* (Cambridge UP, 1983), p. 230.

6. See J. J. Gibson, *The Senses Considered as Perceptual Systems* (London: Allen & Unwin, 1968).

7. See Marr's *Vision* (New York: W. H. Freeman, 1982), pp. 29–30. At p. 3 of *The Senses Considered as Perceptual Systems*, Gibson writes: "The unanswered question of sense perception is how an observer, animal or human, can obtain constant perceptions in everyday life on the basis of . . . continually changing sensations." Marr misreads this. He takes Gibson to be acknowledging the urgency of that question, whereas Gibson is describing how the problems look in the approach that he is going to reject. See p. 2 ("The seemingly paradoxical assertion will be made that perception is not based on sensation"); p. 320 ("The puzzle of constant perception despite varying sensations disappears").

8. "Cognitive Wheels," in C. Hookway (ed.), *Minds, Machines and Evolution* (Cambridge UP, 1984), pp. 129–51, at pp. 149–50 (n. 21).

9. Searle, in *Intentionality*, has the "black box" picture of the mind firmly in place (we *are* brains in vats: see §7 above). This means that he cannot capitalize on what appears as an isolated insight, that perceptual experience is presentation, not representation (see p. 46). He tries to do better than Dennett's "premonition" idea by insisting that the aetiology of an experience enters into its conditions of satisfaction. But with the interface in place, it is merely mysterious how it can do so.

18

On the Function of Visual Representation

Dana H. Ballard

1 The Recent History of Visual Representation

Vision is our most elaborate sense, and as such has challenged philosophers over many centuries to explain the mystery of its functioning. However, the advent of computer science has allowed a new perspective, namely that of a *computational theory*. Grounded in information theory, a computational theory seeks to describe what information is extracted from the image, but perhaps more importantly, how that information is computed and used. The elements of such a theory may be more readily appreciated in comparison to what might be termed the last pre-computational theory. In a series of books, Gibson (1950; 1979) argued for *direct perception*. The nub of this theory was that the environment is the repository for information necessary to act. Its information is expressed in terms of invariants that are implicitly contained in the optical array. The best known example is that of optic flow, the velocity patterns induced on the optic array by motion of the observer. This special kind of time-varying image contains information about significant behavioural events, for example, parameters related to the time to collision. The optic flow invariants illustrate the two most important tenets of this theory, namely: (1) The world is the repository of the information needed to act. With respect to the observer, it is stored "out there," and by implication not represented internally in some mental state that exists separately from the stimulus. (2) The information needed to act is computed directly (direct perception).

In the light of later work that meticulously counts the computational overhead, the second tenet seems a controversial claim. As pointed out by Geoff Hinton, it is likely that Gibson was trying to distinguish between the sequential computational model advocated for logical reasoning and the computation involved in perception;

however, subsequent computational theories turn on the cost of computing these invariants.

Marr (1982) originated the first computational theory of vision. His emphasis focussed on representation of vision, or the data structures needed to support the information extraction process. Vision was the problem of determining "what is where." The what of vision was object-centered representations. These are useful, as object-centered descriptions are invariant with respect to the viewer. Finding out where objects are was judged to be difficult, as objects appear in viewer-centered co-ordinates. In other words, the object-centered and viewer-centered descriptions do not match. Thus computing such descriptions was claimed to be a very difficult task that could only be done in several stages. A series of representations was proposed, each with the objective of facilitating the computation of object-centered descriptions. These are summarized in table 18.1.

The table shows that photometric data is converted into physical data, but more importantly that most of the representations of vision are retinotopically indexed, that is, accessed by spatial co-ordinates in a retinal co-ordinate system. In neurological terms, the visual maps are retinotopically indexed. Transisting neurons within these maps produces responses whose predominant variation is in terms of the retinal effective stimulus. As the first computational theory of vision, it was enormously valuable in defining the principal issues. One of its major successes was the definition of the $2^1/2$ dimensional sketch, a representation that is used by what has been termed "early vision." The kinds of explicit features used in the retinotopic maps of early vision—optic flow, texture, colour and disparity—have been observed in monkey cortex.

Despite these and other successes, there were major issues not addressed in the theory. The most important may have been the exclusion of the effects of the perceiver's behavioural context. The theory was essentially about passive vision.

Table 18.1
Marr's Representational Structures

Data Structure	Index	Type
image	retinotopic	photometric features
primal sketch	retinotopic	photometric features
$2^1/2$-D sketch	retinotopic	physical properties
object-centered representations	object-centered	physical properties

Another thing Marr did not include was the special features of human vision, such as its elaborate gaze control system that includes saccades, and the fovea, with its greatly enhanced resolution near the optical axis. To understand these omissions from a single perspective, let us consider another of Marr's contributions. He defined three principal levels of analysis: the *task level*, which defines what is computed; the *algorithm level*, which defines how these things are computed; and the *implementation level*, which defines the machine-level details of the computation. In reality, however, the algorithm level interacts with the implementation level. In other words, the algorithms that are most efficient depend on the structure of the underlying machine. We argue that much of the work in vision has ignored a level of detail of the biological machine that has been termed the *embodiment* level (Ballard 1991a; Brooks 1986). Having a particular kind of body plays a major role in determining what is practical to compute. For example, without rapid eye movements, the retinal image becomes more valuable as a memory of the imaged scene, whereas with such movements it is far less useful.

Embodiment not only changes what is practical to compute but how the computation is done. The traditional view is that the products of vision are first computed and then used by cognition. The new view is that if the purpose of vision is the *sine qua non*, then even the earliest products of vision need be done only insofar as to subserve this purpose. The most radical view is that traditional image-like structures are never computed independently of a behavioural context.

In order to better understand these claims, we will discuss some of the issues arising from current computational vision models that seek to do without embodiment. Embodiment provides crucial context, so that doing without it leads to positing structures that represent information independently of context. This leads to what we term the *literalist view*. We will examine this view first from the point of internal consistencies. Next we will introduce a rival viewpoint, supported by embodiment: that of the *functional view*. We will attempt to show that functional explanations raise further difficulties for literalism.

2   The Literalist View

The main tenet of the literalist view is that much of the phenomena of vision result from *retinotopic* computations in the brain circuitry. In other words, the phenomena happen at the level of Marr's $2^{1}/_{2}$-D sketch. In its strongest form, namely that there is a picture in the head, it probably has no proponents, but by only weakening the statement a little there are many proponents. For example, there is substantial support for the fact that visual illusions are the direct product of retinotopic computations (Grossberg 1973; Ramachandran 1987). And the support is increased by weakening the tenet a bit further to encompass the notion that the retinotopic representations compute physical properties of the external world (Poggio et al. 1992). A way to remember this is as "You See What You Think You See," i.e., there are retinotopic representations in the brain that directly correspond to your conscious percept.

It is easy to see the attraction of such a view: there is extensive neurological evidence that there are retinotopic representations in the brain that seem to represent precisely the products that participate in the illusion. And there are psychological studies that point to the fact that humans behave *as if* they had access to a retinotopic map of visual information (Kosslyn 1992).

A couple of examples illustrate the strong form of the literalist view. One is from Yuille and Grzywacz (1988). Yuille models the observed phenomena of *motion capture*. In motion capture, random dots are "jiggled" against a background of a translating sine wave grating. The dots appear to move with the velocity of the grating and are thus said to be "captured" by the grating. To model this phenomenon, Yuille uses a retinotopic velocity space. The velocity of the dots in this space is ultimately made by his algorithm to conform to the velocity of the background. The point is that the velocity of the dots is explicitly represented in retinotopic space. From the literalist point of view, the dots are captured in our perception because they are captured in the representation. In a second example, vision in the blind spot of the retina has been studied by Ramachandran (1992). Subjects report being able to interpolate missing corners of squares when the missing corner interpenetrates the visual field of the blind spot. In other words, they see the figure as whole when the missing corner is invisible. How could they have this perception if there were not a retinotopic place in the cortex where this percept is explicitly created?

3   Problems with the Literalist View

While the idea of a retinotopic representation that looks like either the physics that we think we see or the way the world appears to be is appealing, problems start to arise when the details of this promise are confronted. As a case study in the difficulties with the literalist view, we will first turn to Churchland's stereo model (Churchland 1996). Next we will argue that there is insufficient time to accomplish extensive propagation of the retina, a feature of some models. Then there is the difficult issue of what constitutes a perception. The "Nina" experiments with visual search challenge the classical definitions. Do people really see what they think they see? Experiments by Grimes (1996) show that the amount of information captured during a fixation is much less than previously believed. Finally, we will conclude by offering a non-retinotopic version of "motion capture."

Case Study of Churchland's Stereo

The main point of this model is to suggest that previous models of stereo have failed to take into account that the measurements are referred to the fixation point (but see Ballard 1991a; Lehky and Sejnowski 1990). Churchland points out that the computations are naturally conducted in relative terms with the disparity in the horopter as a surface that moves with the fixation point. He constructs a connectionist model that learns the correct responses by enjoying some pre-wiring together with the backpropagation-training algorithm. Leaving aside the difficulties with backpropagation as a supervised algorithm, let us consider the main issues from the literalist perspective. In the first place, disparity is not the same as depth, which depends on the fixation point geometry. The solution to this is the construction of an auxiliary network, which corrects the measurements. The auxiliary network represents the literalist view. A percept is captured by explicit circuitry. This of course leads to the possibility of an explosion of circuits to capture every percept. Churchland (1996) seems to recognize this difficulty, but stops short of a solution:

> In the model, these determinations are made by a network auxiliary to the main one, a network whose inputs are the current pair-presentation, and whose six outputs are the absolute distances of each of the three external planes grasped by the three output layers, and the absolute width of an object one pixel across at each of those distances. There is no expectation that this auxiliary net has a structure corresponding to anything real in humans, but it does illustrate that the relevant computations can be quickly and easily performed by a feedforward system.

The difficulty with representing the percept veridically resurfaces in a discussion of the fact that the disparity code itself is not related to depth: "But something important is still missing. As described to this point, the network has no simultaneous representation of objects and their relative positions throughout a range of different depths. *One might even hold this capability to be definitive of true or full stereopsis* [emphasis mine]." The problem is: how can the model be a model of the percept if the internal representation is allowed to stray from a copy of the percept?

Here Churchland finally gives in to the wisdom of representing information that could support the behaviour rather than the percept itself.

A final problem and its solution will serve as a summary of the difficulties of literal representation. In matching gray levels in the stereo algorithm, there is the problem that large areas of uniform gray levels are reported as matches, thereby confounding the algorithm, which desires punctate matches. The solution, apparently also used by biology, which devotes a large percentage of circuitry to encoding edges, is to match points of photometric change or edges, rather than the gray levels themselves. Of course, now one is faced with the inevitable: this solution means that the internal depth map is incomplete, having values only at the matched points. What can be done? Here the literalist versus non-literalist are finally at odds. The literalist solution is to interpolate so that the representation looks like the precept. The non-literalist seeks to find ways to use the representation as is to model the external behaviour.

If Illusions Survive Eye Movements Then Either the Circuitry Is Very Fast or the Perception Is Non-retinotopic

One fact of primate vision is that of saccadic eye movements. The small size of the fovea places a premium on quickly placing the point of gaze on targets of interest. Probably as a consequence the primate visual system has a very fast, ballistic mechanism for moving the eyes quickly to targets. Speeds of up to 700°/second are reached, and as a consequence the visual input is extremely blurred during the movement. Under normal circumstances, fixation durations (the time between saccades when gaze is stabilized) are about 300 milliseconds. How do we account for illusions that survive saccadic eye movements? There are two possibilities. One is that there is sufficient time to perform the necessary computations to produce the illusion within each fixation. The other is that the retinotopic data is adjusted for the movements themselves (Anderson and Van Essen 1991; Duhamel et al. 1992). Both of these alternatives have potential difficulties. In the first, the best known algorithms require that the computations propagate over the retinotopic array. Given that normal cortical firing rates are about 10 hertz, there is only time for a single neuron to send 20 spikes during a fixation. Thus one cannot be confident that there is sufficient time for the information to propagate. In the second, there must be posited extensive machinery to handle the updating. As we will see in a moment, there are other complications.

Nina Searching—Do S's Have Perceptions or Don't They?

One subjective observation that fuels literalist intuitions is that of perception. Traditionally, visual perception has been given a primal status (Fodor 1983) in that, evoking Gibsonian terms, it seems immediate and cannot be overturned by our cognitive set. Hence the historical and persisting boundaries between perception and cognition. Recently, however, there have been several experiments that challenge both the sanctity of perception and the perceptual-cognitive dichotomy. We will present two examples here. In the first, we are able to catch the human system in an ambiguous state whereby according to its eye movements it is registering a stimulus; however, it cannot report a conscious percept. What is the status of the material that is on the retinal array but somehow not perceived by the subject? A special set of images is the "Nina" set. The face of a young woman is camouflaged by embedding it in a scene of comparable line drawings. Subjects are given the task of detecting the location of the Nina face in the figure and their eye movements are recorded. Analysis shows that subjects look at the correct location many times when they do not report it. From detection theory this is uninteresting: the subject did not have enough evidence to decide on the location of the face. Yet this scenario reveals a problem in separating the participation of the observer from the perception. Did the subjects have the perception of Nina or didn't they? If they did not, what grounds do we have for studying unconscious perception, since we can't really know when we are having one? Or alternatively, if we can't have perception without the background of mental set, then the presuppositions of most perception experiments could be called into question.

Grimes's Saccadic Experiments

The Nina experiments raise a fundamental scepticism about the boundary between perception and cognition that is supported by a second series of experiments by Grimes (1996). These experiments study integration across eye movements. Subjects were instructed to look for changes in images and push a button if they detected any change. The changes, in the cases where there were any, were introduced only during the transit of a saccade. The images were of visually rich natural scenes. Surprisingly, subjects ignored huge changes in the image structure under these conditions. For example, in one image a huge green parrot, which dominates the scene, changes color to crimson. About 30 percent of the subjects do not report this change. In another example a prominent bunch of bananas switches orientation from pointing right to pointing left. None of the subjects report this change. One interpretation of these studies is that the content of the image is extensively linked to a semantic description. Subjects are insensitive to changes that affect that description in the subsequent fixation. As a corollary these experiments cast doubt on models that place a premium on integrating the content of the retinotopic array across fixations (Anderson and Van Essen 1991; Duhamel et al. 1992). If there were machinery for integrating across saccades one would expect that gross changes in the scene as introduced in the Grimes paradigm would be straightforward to detect. In contrast, it appears that the retinotopic information is not important from one saccade to the other.

Motion Capture without Retinopathy: Subspaces

To conclude our criticism of literalism per se, we offer an alternative explanation of motion capture. To be fair to Yuille's account, his explanation is in the form of a detailed computer model whereas ours is in the form of a thought-experiment and therefore much weaker. Nonetheless, consider that the brain architecture need not represent the details of the motion in the image, but only the coarse details. In this case, at an abstract level there are representations that denote "moving dots" and "motion to the left." Faced only with this information, the perceptual apparatus is designed to report "dots moving to the left." The conclusion follows from the non-retinotopic information, rather than the retinotopic information. Note that if the retinotopic information was computed veridically, as in the literalist explanation, there would still have to be a parser that analyzes the resultant picture in the head to produce the same report, so the introduction of the reporting structure adds nothing extra to the account.

4   The Alternative to Literalism: Functionalism

At the other end of the spectrum from the literalist view is the *functionalist view*. To remember it, let us term it "You Don't See What You Think You See." The principal tenet is that the machinery of the brain has to be accountable to the observed external behaviour, and that there are many ways to do this other than positing literal data structures.

The functionalist view depends critically on levels of abstraction. We are very comfortable with having to deal with many different levels of abstraction in biological systems. Sejnowski and Churchland (1990) identify seven different levels used in the study of the brain in computational neuroscience. However, in our models of human intelligence, we have not always been able to appreciate the need for such a hierarchy of abstraction. One reason may have been that the early work in the field has been dominated by tenets of artificial intelligence. One of the most important of these is that intelligence can be described in purely computational terms without recourse to any particular embodiment. From this perspective, the special features of the human body and its particular ways of interacting in the world have been seen as secondary to the fundamental problems of intelligence.

That systems can appear dramatically different at different levels of abstraction can be best illustrated with an example from computer science. Consider the way virtual memory works on a conventional workstation. Virtual memory allows the applications programmer to write programs that are larger than the physical memory of the machine. What happens is that prior to the running of the program, it is broken up into smaller pages, and then at run-time the requisite pages are brought into the memory from peripheral storage as required. This strategy works largely because conventional sequential programs are designed to be executed sequentially, and the information required to interpret an instruction is usually very localized. Consider now two very different viewpoints. From the application programmer's viewpoint, it appears that a program of unlimited length can be written. But the system programmer's viewpoint is very different. The environment is very dynamic as individual pages are moved in and out of physical memory. This captures the difference between the cognitive level and the approach we are terming embodiment. At the symbolic level, which neglects the details of the machine, the world appears seamless and stable. It is only at the embodiment level that we find that this must be an illusion, as the human's real-time visuo-motor system has many creative ways to interact with the world in a timely manner.

Neural-level models of behaviour tend to make the opposite kind of error. These models offer a very concrete view of processing at very small spatial and temporal scales that obscure the coarser features of behaviour. For example, in vision, spatial scales of 20′ and temporal scales of 2 to 50 milliseconds are important, whereas at the level of eye and hand movements, time constants are about an order of magnitude larger (see table 18.2).

In contrast to both of the above views, our central thesis is that intelligence has to relate to interactions with the physical world, and that means that the particular form of the human body is an important constraint in delimiting the aspects of

Table 18.2
Different Spatio-Temporal Scales

Time, Milliseconds	Processing Feature
2	shortest interspike interval
40	average attentional search time for each item
300	average eye fixation time
400	shortest reaction time

intelligent behaviour. Thus embodiment is crucial and illuminating and, we argue, best handled by positing a distinct level of abstraction, as depicted in figure 18.1.

Embodiment models may be seen as a level of abstraction properly between cognitive models and neural models. Embodiment models differ from cognitive models by implicitly modelling time, as opposed to the explicit models used at the cognitive level (e.g., Alien and Hayes 1989). Embodiment is distinguished from neural levels by using deictic primitives, as opposed to neural levels, which capture the implementation details of deictic models. The embodiment level specifies how the constraints of the physical system interact with cognition. One example is the movements of the eyes during the co-ordination of the hand in problem-solving tasks. Our purpose is to show that important features of cognition can be traced to constraints that act at this level of abstraction, and more importantly, that these features challenge the usefulness of the literalist interpretation of visual perception.

5   Embodiment Model

The main visual behaviour that the human has is the ability to fixate an environmental point. By fixating an environmental point, humans can use a special frame of reference centered at that point to simplify the task. This turns out to have a profound effect on the original "what is where" formulation of vision proposed by Marr. Technically, the ability to use an external frame of reference centered at the fixation point leads to great simplifications in algorithmic complexity (Ballard 1989). (This is a very different assertion than that of Marr 1982, who emphasized that vision calculations were initially in viewer-centred co-ordinates.) The fixation frame allows for closed-loop behavioural strategies that do not require precise three-dimensional information. For example, in grasping an object, we can first fixate the object and then direct the hand to the centre of the retinal co-ordinate system. In depth, the hand can be controlled relative to the plane of fixation. Informally, we

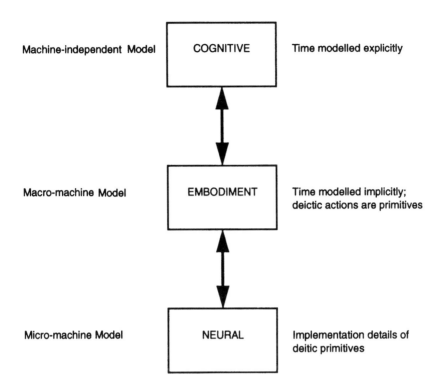

Machine-independent Model | COGNITIVE | Time modelled explicitly

Macro-machine Model | EMBODIMENT | Time modelled implicitly; deictic actions are primitives

Micro-machine Model | NEURAL | Implementation details of deitic primitives

Figure 18.1
Embodiment as an Intermediate Level of Machine Architecture.

refer to this behaviour as a "do-it-where-I'm-looking" strategy, but more technically it is referred to as a deictic strategy, after Agre and Chapman (1987).

The deictic strategy of using the perceptual system to actively control the point of action in the world has precisely the right kind of invariance for a large number of behaviours. One task that we have studied in detail (Ballard et al. 1992) is a block-copying task. In this task, subjects must copy a pattern of coloured blocks on a computer display by moving coloured blocks from a supply area with the computer mouse. By virtue of the fact that only one block can be moved at once, this task requires that the blocks be handled sequentially. However, our contention is that it can be further reduced to embodiment-level primitives. Let us consider the copying task at this more detailed level.

To copy the first block, its colour has to be determined. One way to do that is to fixate the block in question in the model area. Next a block of that colour has to be located and picked up in the source area. Finally that block has to be moved and

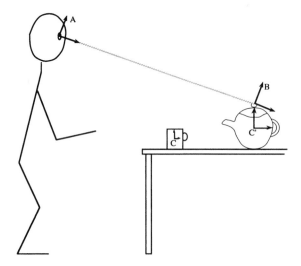

Figure 18.2
If vision is passive, computations must be performed in a viewer-centered frame (*A*). Instead, biological data argue for a world-centered frame (*B*). This frame is selected by the observer to suit information-gathering goals and is centered at the fixation point. The task of the observer is to relate information in the fixation point frame to object-centered frames (*C*), (*C'*).

dropped in the workspace. Subsequent block moves are more complicated, as the relationship of the new block with the model has to be determined and then replicated in the workspace. In rough outline a cognitive program for a block move looks like:

Repeat until {the pattern has been copied}:

Fixate(*A block in the model area with a given colour*)

Remember(The colour)

Fixate(A block in the source area with the same colour)

PickUp(The block currently fixated)

Fixate(*The appropriate location*)

Remember(location)

Fixate(Location in the workspace)

Move(The block to the fixated location)

PutDown(The block currently held at the current location)

In the model program, italics are used to denote a structure that has to be "bound" to the sensor data, whereas non-italicized arguments to the primitives denote structures that are already bound. Here binding is used in the same way as the value of a variable in a computer program is bound or assigned to that variable. These instructions make extensive use of deictic reference. It is assumed that the instruction *Fixate* will orient the centre of gaze to point to a place in the image with a feature appropriate to the argument of the function. If multiple instances of the feature are present, then some tie-breaking scheme must be used. The deictic nature of these instructions is illustrated by *PickUp*, *Move* and *PutDown* which are assumed to act at the centre of the fixation frame, irrespective of its specific location in three-dimensional space. Fixate is actually also a deictic instruction if we include a mechanism for target selection, such as a focus of attention. A focus of attention may be thought of as an electronic fovea, in terms of its ability to select target locations. Thus *Fixate* becomes two instructions:

AttendTo(*image-feature appropriate for target selection*)

Fixate(Attended location)

The exact behaviour of these instructions depends on the particular embodiment, but the assumption at this level of modelling is that they can be designed to perform as described. We have shown that similar albeit simpler problems can be learned by a computer using these instructions (Whitehead and Ballard 1990).

Somewhat surprisingly, the above program, with only minor modifications, has proven to be an accurate model of human performance (Ballard et al. 1992). The principal result of the block-copying tasks, which is also suggested by the model program, is that for manipulating individual blocks, colour and relative location are acquired *separately*, even though they are notionally associated with the same retinal location. If this is true, then what was the representational status of a block's colour and location before they were bound by the task context? From the Triesman experiments (1982), it is obvious that binding is a problem.

6   Functional Uses of Retinotopic Representations

To develop our earlier metaphor, the embodiment level may be thought of as the operating system level and the cognitive level as the user program level (Dennett 1991; Ballard 1991b). At the embodiment level, stability may not be the issue but rather the function of a sequential program dedicated to achieving current goals. To accomplish this the algorithms that use the retinotopic array may need to appropriate it in many ways that could be at odds with stability. To emphasize this point, the primitives are articulated into neural-level representations. The motivation for such primitives is economy. The simplification of active viewing can also be understood with reference to the problem of relating internal models to objects in the world. One interpretation of the need for sequential, problem-dependent eye-movements is that the general problem of associating many models to many parts of the image simultaneously is too hard. In order to make the computation tractable within a single fixation, it has to be simplified into either one of location (one internal model) or one of identification (one world-object). A location task is to find the image co-ordinates of a single model in the presence of many alternatives. In this task the image periphery must be searched and one can assume that the model has been chosen *a priori*. An identification task is to associate the foveated part of the image with one of many possible models. In this task one can assume that the location of the material to be identified is at the fixation point. This dichotomy is exactly equivalent to the WHERE/WHAT dichotomy seen in the parietal and infero-temporal areas of visual cortex (Mishkin et al. 1983). Swain and Ballard (1991) have shown that both identification and location behaviours are much simpler than their combination, which has been termed "image understanding." The simplification of separating location and identification tasks has recently been extended to shape models as well (Ballard and Wixson 1992).

Using Colour for Identification

Colour can solve both the what and where problems using the colour histogram (Swain 1990; Swain and Ballard 1990; 1991). For the problem of object identification, the use of histogram matching provides a very robust index that is insensitive to deformations of the object. A drawback of the matching process was sensitivity to lighting conditions, but recent extensions of this work by Funt and Finalyson (1991) have shown that a modified index is insensitive to such variations.

Using Colour for Location

For the problem of object location. Swain's algorithm uses feedback to the retinotopic representations of colour in the following way: the image colours are rated as to how helpful they are in selecting the current model. This rating is retinotopic and becomes a saliency map. Low-pass filtering of the saliency map followed by maximum detection is sufficient to locate the desired object.

Table 18.3
The Biological Organization of Cortex into WHAT/WHERE May Have a Basis in Computational Complexity. Trying to match a large number of image segments to a large number of models at once may be too difficult

		Models	
		One	Many
Image Parts	*One*	*Manipulation*: trying to do something with an object whose identity and location are known	*Identification*: trying to identify an object whose location can be fixated
	Many	*Location*: trying to find a known object that may not be in view	*Image Understanding*: trying to locate and identify all the structure in an image. Too Difficult?

Successful experiments have been conducted on a database of 70 articles of clothing. These are non-rigid and difficult to identify with current techniques. The experiments are preliminary and illustrate the concept of object location using top-down feedback. Interestingly, this is a very different proposal than that of Koch and Ullman (1985), who suggested a bottom-up technique that used coincidental feature alignment to define a salience measure. The main point, however, is that at the embodiment level the computation is dominated by the eye movement cycle. That cycle can be broken up into two kinds of tasks: (1) an identification task, whereby a property is extracted from the fixated location, and (2) a location task, whereby the eye is moved to a new location. Furthermore, as figure 18.3 implies, the natural mapping of these algorithms onto the known cortical architecture uses the same architecture in fundamentally different ways. Thus the state of the cortex, instead of representing visual invariants, will vary with the demands of the location/identification cycle.

7   Programs with Small Numbers of Variables

Robot-Learning Example

Work done with a particular exocentric model of the use of gaze, combined with the concept of deictic representations, suggested that it would be efficacious if the human visual system solved problems in a minimal way. To explore this possibility,

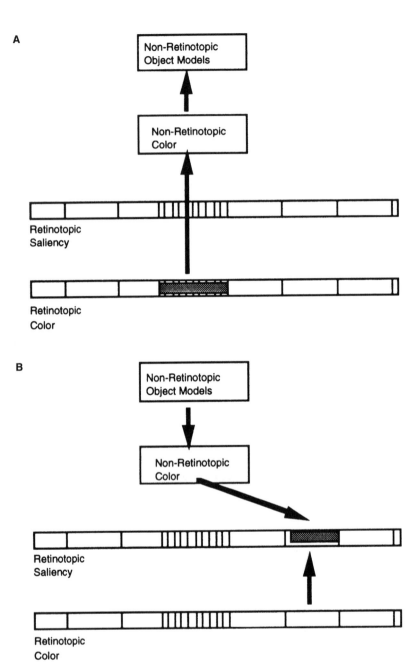

Figure 18.3
(A) Identification tasks can be modeled by using foveal features in a table-lookup scheme.
(B) Location tasks can be modeled by comparing model features and retinal features in a
saliency map. These two tasks use the same cortical architecture in different ways at different
times.

hand-eye co-ordination was studied for a sequential copying task. The strategy of memorizing the configuration to be copied in its entirety before moving blocks seemed to never be used. Instead, a variety of different programs were used to check the course of the copying task in the midst of moving individual blocks. These strategies point to the use of minimal memory solutions.

The main observation is that although eye movements are used for the terminal phase of hand movements, they are used for other tasks prior to that phase. This implies that the underlying decision process that moves the eyes leaves key decisions until just before they are required. The results are compatible with the standard model of the brain as having a limited capacity for short-term memory, but they suggest a new interpretation of that memory. Rather than focus on the small number of items themselves, think of the number of behavioural programs that can be constructed with a limited number of memory registers. The limited number need only be a handicap if the entire task is to be completed from memory; in that case the short-term memory system is overburdened. In the more natural case of performing the task with ongoing access to the visual world, the task is completed perfectly. Detailed analysis of this case suggests that the subjects are using an economical representation scheme to represent or remember information about the task just before it is required. We refer to this scheme as *just-in-time representation*.

One way to reduce the burden of representation to just that essential for the task is to use *markers*, temporary variables that record partial computational results. This notion of markers has been championed by Agre and Chapman as a general method of object-centered computation. The notion is that markers provide a local context to resolve reference ambiguity. Agre and Chapman's focus was routine activity. They sought to model behaviour in terms of ongoing activity. Responses to the activity were in the form of rules that were activated by local context. The key points were that in routine activity, long causal chains were not necessary. It turns out that the fixation point strategy can be thought of as a kind of marker that has the right kind of transfer for learning many tasks. In our laboratory, Steve Whitehead has studied learning using a reinforcement paradigm (Whitehead and Ballard 1990). Whitehead has been studying block-stacking tasks. On each trial, the system, which is an abstracted model of our robot, is presented with a pile of coloured blocks. A pile consists of any number of blocks arbitrarily arranged. Each block is uniformly coloured. The system can manipulate the pile by picking and placing objects. When the system arranges the blocks into a successful configuration, it receives a positive reward and the trial ends. For example, one extremely simple block-stacking task is for the system to learn to pick up a light gray block. In this case, the successful configurations consist just of those states where the system is holding a gray object. The system learns to arrange arbitrary configurations of blocks into successful configurations. The key point here is that the marker encoding obviates the need for explicit co-ordinates.

7 Plus or Minus 2

How many markers are needed? In a study of chess-playing, it was found that subjects needed Miller's limit of 7 plus or minus 2 (Chase and Simon 1973). However, our studies suggest that the normal limit in everyday tasks might not use the full capacity of short-term memory. Instead, human decision tasks have to consider the following two constraints. If too few variables are used then the decision function becomes ambiguous, as shown in figure 18.4. On the other hand, if too many variables are used, then the decision function becomes very difficult to learn, as its cost scales exponentially with the number of variables.

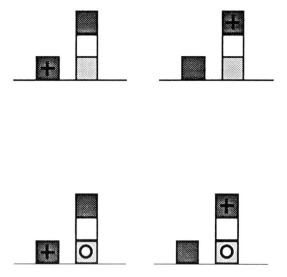

Figure 18.4
Encoding tasks with respect to deictic markers leads to ambiguities when the number of markers is too small. Here the task is to pick up the light gray block. On the top row the situation is ambiguous, with only one marker. On the left the desired action is to move the fixation frame to the light gray block (and then to the top), but in the right the desired action is to pick up the gray block. (Top) With only the context of a single marker, these two different situations cannot be disambiguated. (Bottom) An additional marker provides the context needed to disambiguate the situation.

Back to Grimes

The 7 plus or minus 2 limit allows a succinct explanation of the Grimes result. How could subjects misperceive huge visual features on their retinae? The answer is that they can only be aware of the items that they have explicitly kept track of, and this is a dynamic buffer of 7 plus or minus 2 variable bindings. If an image structure is, at the appropriate instant, not one of the bound variables, then no matter how salient it is, its changes will not be perceived.

Conclusion

A number of different avenues of investigation have suggested that much of the basic phenomenology of vision can be traced to "a picture in the head," retinotopic structures that represent phenomena of the world in a more or less veridical sense. While it is so far impossible to disprove this literal interpretation of experience, there are a variety of new results that challenge this literalism. These new results can be integrated under the heading of functionalism. Focussing on the tasks that humans have to do rather than subjective experiences, functionalism provides a new way of evaluating experimental data. In addition, the behaviour needs to be interpreted in terms of a human model that is both sufficiently abstract to suppress confounding neural-level detail, yet sufficiently concrete to include the crucial body mechanisms that mediate perception and action.

In regard to any dichotomy of putative brain function it is always possible that the brain can do both. In this case it is possible that the brain can simultaneously represent the visual invariants that correspond to the "perception" of seeing and the invariants that correspond to functional programs. However, the intent of this paper is to suggest that many of the phenomena that might have previously garnered a literal interpretation can be more succinctly explained by functional models, even though these functional models may challenge many of our intuitions about perception.

Acknowledgments

This research was supported in part by the Human Scientific Frontiers Program, the National Science Foundation (IRI-8903582) and the National Institutes of Health (1R24RRO6853).

References

Agre, P. E., and D. Chapman (1987). Pengi: An implementation of a theory of activity. *Proceedings, American Association for Artificial Intelligence (AAAI) 87.*

Allen, J. F., and P. J. Hayes (November 1989). Moments and points in an interval-based temporal logic. *Computational Intelligence* 5(4): 225–238.

Anderson, C. H., and D. C. Van Essen (1991). Dynamic neural routing circuits. In A. Gale and K. Carr (eds.), *Visual Search 2* (Proceedings, Second International Conference on Visual Search, Durham University, Sept. 1990). New York: Taylor and Francis.

Ballard, D. H. (1989). Reference frames for animate vision. *Proceedings, International Joint Conference on Artificial Intelligence*, Detroit, MI.

———(1991a). Animate vision. *Artificial Intelligence* 48: 57–86.

———(January 1991b). Sub-symbolic modeling of hand-eye coordination. *Proceedings, Wolfson Lecture Series*, Wolfson College, Oxford.

Ballard, D. H., M. M. Hayhoe, E. Li and S. D. Whitehead (March 1992). Hand-eye coordination during sequential tasks. *Proceedings, Philosophical Transactions of the Royal Society of London B*, London.

Ballard, D. H., and L. E. Wixson (October 1992). Object indexing. Working Paper, Computer Science Department, University of Rochester.

Brooks, R. A. (1986). A robust layered control system for a mobile robot. *IEEE Journal of Robotics and Automation* RA-2: 14–23.

Churchland, Paul (1996). A feedforward network for fast stereo vision with movable fusion plane. In K. Akins (ed.), *Perception*. Oxford: Oxford University Press.

Chase, W. G., and H. A. Simon (1973). Perception in chess. *Cognitive Psychology* 4: 55–81.

Dennett, D. C. (1991). *Consciousness Explained*. New York: Little Brown.

Duhamel, J.-R., C. L. Colby and M. E. Goldberg (3 January 1992). The updating of the representation of visual space in parietal cortex by intended eye movements. *Science* 255: 90–92.

Fodor, J. A. (1983). *The Modularity of Mind*. Cambridge, MA: MIT Press.

Funt, B. V., and G. D. Finalyson (October 1991). Color constant color indexing. CSS/LCCR TR91-09, Centre for Systems Science, Simon Fraser University.

Gibson, J. J. (1950). *The Perception of the Visual World*. Boston: Houghton Mifflin.

———(1979). *The Ecological Approach to Visual Perception*. Boston: Houghton Mifflin.

Grimes, J. (1996). On the failure to detect changes in scenes across saccades. In Akins, K (ed.), *Perception*. Oxford: Oxford University Press, 89–110.

Grossberg, S. (1973). Contour enhancement, short-term memory and constancies in reverberating neural networks. *Studies in Applied Mathematics* 52: 217–257.

Koch, C., and S. Ullman (1985). Shifts in selective visual attention: Towards the underlying neural circuitry. *Human Neurobiology* 4: 219–227.

Kosslyn, S. M. (1992). *Wet Mind: The New Cognitive Neuroscience*. New York: Maxwell Macmillan International.

Lehky, S. R., and T. J. Sejnowski (1990). Neural model of stereoacuity and depth interpolation based on a distributed representation of stereo disparity. *Journal of Neuroscience* 10(7): 2281–2289.

Marr, D. C. (1982). *Vision*. San Francisco: W. H. Freeman.

Mishkin, M., L. G. Ungerleider and K. A. Macko (1983). Object vision and spatial vision: Two cortical pathways. *Trends in Neuroscience* 6: 414–417.

Poggio, T., M. Fahle and S. Edelman (1992). Fast perceptual-learning in visual hyperacuity. *Science* 256(5059): 1018–1021.

Ramachandran, V. S. (September 1987). Interactions between motion, depth, color and form: The utilitarian theory of perception. *Proceedings, Conference on Visual Coding and Efficiency*.

——(1992). Perceptual filling in of the blind spot and of cortical and retinal scotomas. *Investigative Ophthalmology and Visual Science* 33(4): 1348.

Sejnowski, T. J., P. Churchland and C. Koch (1990). Computational neuroscience. *Science* 241(4871): 1299–1306.

Swain, M. J. (November 1990). Color indexing. Ph.D. thesis and TR 360, Computer Science Department, University of Rochester.

Swain, M. J., and D. H. Ballard (December 1990). Indexing via color histograms. *Proceedings, international Conference on Computer Vision*, Kyoto, Japan.

Swain, M. J., and D. H. Ballard (1991). Color indexing. *International Journal of Computer Vision* (Special Issue) 7(1): 11–32.

Triesman, A. (1982). The role of attention in object perception. *The Royal Society International Symposium on Physical and Biological Processing of Images*, London.

Whitehead, S. D., and D. H. Ballard (1990). Active perception and reinforcement learning. *Neural Computation* 2: 409–419.

Yuille, A. L., and N. M. Grzywacz (May 1988). A computational theory for the perception of coherent visual motion. *Nature* 333: 71–74.

19

Seeing Is Believing—Or Is It?

Daniel C. Dennett

We would all like to have a good theory of perception. Such a theory would account for all the known phenomena and predict novel phenomena, explaining everything in terms of processes occurring in nervous systems in accordance with the principles and laws already established by science: the principles of optics, physics, biochemistry and the like. Such a theory might come to exist without our ever having to answer the awkward "philosophical" question that arises:

What exactly is *the product* of a perceptual process?

There seems to be an innocuous—indeed trivial—answer:

The product of a perceptual process is *a perception*!

What could be more obvious? Some processes have products, and the products of perceptual processes are perceptions. But on reflection, is it so obvious? Do we have any idea what we might mean by this? What are perceptions? What manner of thing—state, event, entity, process—is a perception? It is merely a state of the brain, we may say (hastening to keep dualism at bay), but what could make a state of the brain a *perceptual* state as opposed to, say, merely a metabolic state, or—more to the point—a *pre*-perceptual state, or a *post*-perceptual state? For instance, the state of one's retinas at any moment is surely a state of the nervous system, but intuitively *it* is not a perception. It is something more like the raw material from which subsequent processes will eventually fashion a perception. And the state of one's motor cortex, as it triggers or controls the pressing of the YES button during a perceptual experiment is intuitively on the *other* side of the mysterious region, an effect of a perception, not a perception itself. Even the most doctrinaire behaviourist would be reluctant to identify the button-pressing behaviour of your finger as itself the perception; it is a response to . . . what? To a stimulus occurring on the retina, says the behaviourist. But now that behaviourism is history we are prepared to insist that this peripheral response is mediated by another, internal response: a perception is a response to a stimulus, and a behavioural reaction such as a button-press is a response to a perception. Or so it is natural to think.

Natural or not, such ways of thinking lead to riddles. For instance, in a so-called computer vision system does any internal state count as a perception? If so, what about a simpler device? Is a Geiger counter a perceiver—*any* sort of perceiver? Or, closer to home, is thermoregulation or electrolyte balance in our bodies accomplished by a *perceptual* process, or does such manifestly unconscious monitoring not count? If not, why not? What about "recognition" by the immune system? Should we reserve the term "perception" for processes with *conscious* products (whatever they might be), or is it a better idea to countenance not only unconscious perceptual processes but also processes with unconscious *perceptions* as their products?

I said at the outset that a good theory of perception *might* come into existence without our ever having to get clear about these awkward questions. We *might* achieve a theory of perception that answered all our detailed questions without ever tackling the big one: what is a perception? Such a state of affairs might confound the bystanders—or amuse or outrage them, but so what? Most biologists can get on with their work without getting absolutely straight about what life is, most physicists comfortably excuse themselves from the ticklish task of saying exactly what matter is. Why should perception theorists be embarrassed not to have achieved consensus on just what perception is?

"Who cares?" some may say. "Let the philosophers haggle over these stumpers, while we scientists get on with actually developing and testing theories of perception." I usually have some sympathy for this dismissive attitude, but I think that in this instance, it is a mistake. It leads to distortion and misperception of the very theories under development. A florid case of what I have in mind was recently given expression by Jerry Fodor (in a talk at MIT, November 19, 1991): "Cognitive Science is the art of pushing the soul into a smaller and smaller part of the playing field." If this is how you think—even if this is only how you think *in the back of your mind*— you are bound to keep forcing all the phenomena you study into the two varieties: pre-perceptual and post-perceptual, forever postponing a direct confrontation with the product at the presumed watershed, the perception or perceptual state itself. Whatever occupies this mysterious middle realm then becomes more and more unfathomable. Fodor, on the same occasion, went on to say in fact that there were two main mysteries in cognitive science: consciousness and the frame problem—and neither was soluble in his opinion. No wonder he thinks this, considering his vision of how Cognitive Science should proceed. This sort of reasoning leads to viewing the curving chain of causation that leads from pre-perceptual causes to post-perceptual effects as having not only a maximum but a pointed summit—with a sharp discontinuity just where the corner is turned. (As Marcel Kinsbourne has put it, people tend to imagine there is a gothic arch hidden in the mist; see figure 19.1.)

There is no question that the corner must be turned somehow. That's what perception is: responding to something "given" by *taking* it—by responding to it in one interpretive manner or another. On the traditional view, all the taking is *deferred* until the raw given, the raw materials of stimulation, have been processed in various ways. Once each bit is "finished" it can enter consciousness and be *appreciated* for the first time. As C.S. Sherrington put it: "The mental action lies buried in the brain, and in that part most deeply recessed from outside world that is furthest from input and output" (1934, p. 23).

I call the mythical place somewhere in the centre of the brain "where it all comes together" for consciousness the Cartesian Theater (Dennett 1991, Dennett and Kinsbourne 1992). All the work that has been dimly imagined to be done in the Cartesian Theater has to be done somewhere, and no doubt all the corner-turning happens in the brain. In the model that Kinsbourne and I recommend, the Multiple Drafts Model, this single, unified taking is broken up in cerebral space and real time. We suggest that the judgmental tasks are fragmented into many distributed moments of micro-taking (Kinsbourne 1988). There is actually very little controversy about the claim that there is no place in the brain where it all comes together. What people have a hard time recognizing—and we have a hard time describing—are the implications of this for other aspects of the traditional way of thinking.

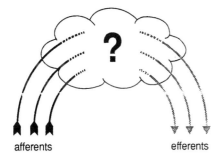

afferents   efferents

Figure 19.1

I want to concentrate here on just one aspect: the nature of "takings." An accompanying theme of Cartesian materialism, what with its sharp discontinuity at the summit, is the almost irresistible tendency to see a sharp distinction between, on the one hand, the items that presumably reside at the top, and, on the other hand, the various items that are their causes and effects. The basic idea is that until some content swims all the way up from the ears and retinas into this Theater, it is still just pre-conscious, pre-experienced. It has no moxie; it lacks the *je ne sais quoi* of conscious experience. And then, as the content completes its centripetal journey, it abruptly changes status, bursting into consciousness. Thereafter, the effects that flow, directly or indirectly, from the Audience Appreciation that mythically occurs in the Cartesian Theater count as post-conscious, and these effects, too, lack some special something.

Let's consider a garden variety case of this theme in slow motion, working backwards from peripheral behaviour to conscious perception. Suppose you tell me you believe in flying saucers. Let us further suppose that that behaviour—the telling— is an indirect effect of your once having been shown a highly detailed and realistic photograph of what purported to be a flying saucer. The behaviour of telling is itself an indirect effect of your belief that there are flying saucers—you are telling me what you actually believe. And that belief in turn is an effect of yet another prior belief: your belief that you were shown the photograph. And this belief that you were shown the photograph was originally supported by yet prior beliefs of yours about all the details in the photograph you were shown. Those beliefs about the particular details of the photograph and the immediate perceptual environment of your looking at it were themselves short-lived *effects*—effects of having seen the photograph. They may all have faded away into oblivion, but these *beliefs* had their onset in your memory at the very moment—or very shortly thereafter—that you had the conscious visual perception of the photograph. You believe you saw the photograph because you did see the photograph; it didn't just irradiate your retinas; you saw it, consciously, in a conscious experience.

It looks as if these perceptual beliefs are the most immediate effect of the perceptual state itself.[1] But they are not (it seems) the perception itself, because they are (it seems) *propositional*, not . . . um, *perceptual*. That at least is a common understanding of these terms. Propositional, or conceptual, representations are more abstract (in some hard-to-define way), and less, well, vivid and colourful. For instance, V. S. Ramachandran draws our attention to the way the brain seems to "fill in" the region of our blind spots in each eye, and contrasts our sense of what is in our blind spot with our sense of what objects are behind our heads: "For such objects, the brain creates what might be loosely called a logical inference. The distinction is not just semantic. Perceptual and conceptual representations are probably generated in separate regions of the brain and may be processed in very different ways" (Ramachandran 1992, 87). Just what contrast is there between perceptual and conceptual? Is it a difference in degree or kind, and is there a sharp discontinuity in the normal progression of perceptual processes? If there is, then one—and only one—of the following is the right thing to say. Which is it to be?

1. *Seeing is believing.* My belief that I see such-and-such details in the photograph in my hand is a perceptual state, not an inferential state. I do, after all, *see* those details to be there. A visually induced belief to the effect that all those details are there just *is* the perception!

2. *Seeing causes (or grounds) believing.* My belief that I see such-and-such details in the photograph in my hand is an inferential, non-perceptual state. It is, after all, merely a belief—a state that must be inferred from a perceptual state of actually seeing those details.

Neither, I will argue, is the right thing to say. To see why, we should consider a slightly different question, which Ramachandran goes on to ask: "How rich is the perceptual representation corresponding to the blind spot?" Answers to that eminently investigatable question are simply neutral with regard to the presumed controversy between *(1)* and *(2)*. One of the reasons people tend to see a contrast between *(1)* and *(2)* is that they tend to think of perceptual states as somehow much richer in content than mere belief states. (After all, perceptions are like pictures, beliefs are like sentences, and a picture's worth a thousand words.) But these are spurious connotations. *There is no upper bound on the richness of content of a proposition.* So it would be a confusion—a simple but ubiquitous confusion—to suppose that since a perceptual state has such-and-such richness, it cannot be a propositional state, but must be a perceptual state (whatever that might be) *instead*.

No sane participant in the debates would claim that the product of perception was either literally a picture in the head or literally a sentence in the head. Both ways of talking are reckoned as metaphors, with strengths and shortcomings. Speaking, as Kinsbourne and I have done, of the Multiple *Drafts* Model of consciousness leans in the direction of the sentence metaphor, in the direction of a language of thought. (After all, those drafts must all be *written*, mustn't they?) But our model could just as readily be cast in picture talk. In Hollywood, directors, pro-

ducers and stars fight fiercely over who has "final cut"—over who gets to author-
ize the canonical version of the film that will eventually be released to the public.
According to the Multiple Cuts Model, then, nobody at Psychomount Studios has
final cut; films are made, cut, edited, recut, re-edited, released, shelved indefinitely,
destroyed, spliced together, run backwards and forwards—and no privileged subset
of these processes counts as the Official Private Screening, relative to which any *subsequent* revisions count as unauthorized adulterations. Different versions exist
within the corridors and cutting rooms of Psychomount Studios at different times
and places, and no one of them counts as the definitive work.

In some regards the Multiple Cuts version is a more telling metaphor—especially
as an antidote to the Cartesian Theater. There are even some useful elaborations.
Imagine cutting a film into its individual frames, and then jumbling them all up—
losing track of the "correct" order of the frames. Now consider the task of "putting
them back in order." Numbering the frames in sequence would accomplish this,
provided that any process that needs access to sequencing information can then
extract that information by comparing frame numbers. There is no logical necessity actually to splice the frames in order, or line them up in spatial order on the
film library shelf. And there is certainly no need to "run" them through some pro-
jector in the chosen temporal order. The chosen order can be unequivocally secured
by the numbering all by itself. The counterpart in our model of consciousness is
that it *does not follow* from the fact that we are equipped to make sequence judgments about events in our experience that there is *any* occurrence in real time of a
sequence of neural representations of the events in the order judged. Sometimes
there *may* be such a sequence occurring in the brain, but this cannot be determined
simply by an analysis of the subjective content of experience; it is neither a necessary nor sufficient condition for a like-ordered subjective sequence.

In other regards, however, the Multiple Cuts version of our model is altogether
too vivid, what with its suggestions of elaborate *pictorial* renderings. We should be
leery of metaphor, but is there any alternative at this point? Are there any non-
metaphorical ways of talking that capture the points that need making? How about
the terms being popularized by the connectionists: "vector coding and vector completion"? This new way of talking about content in cognitive science is appealing
partly because whatever it is, vector coding is obviously neither pictures nor words,
and partly, I suspect, because none of the uninitiated dare to ask just what it means!

Let me tell you what it means, so far as I can tell. Think of an enormous multi-
dimensional hyperspace of possible contents—all the possible contents a particular

organism can discriminate. A vector, if I may indulge yet again in metaphor, can be considered a path leading into a particular quadrant or subspace in this hyperspace. Vector completion is just the process of pursuing a trajectory to an ultimate destination in that hyperspace. Most of the hyperspace is empty, unoccupied. When something (some *sort* of thing) has been encountered by an organism, it renders the relevant portion of the organism's hyperspace *occupied*; recognizing it again (or being reminded of it by another, similar one) is getting back to the same place, the same co-ordinates, by the same or a similar path. Vector completion creates a path to a location in content-hyperspace.

"Vector completion" talk is just as metaphorical as "language of thought" talk or "pictures in the head" talk; it is simply a *more abstract* metaphorical way of talking about content, a metaphor which neatly evades the talk of pictures versus sentences, while securing the essential informational point: to "discriminate" or "recognize" or "judge" or "turn the corner" is simply to determine some determinable aspect of content within a space of possibilities.

Vector-completion talk is thus like *possible-world semantics*; it is propositional without being sentential (see, e.g., Stalnaker 1984). It provides a way of asserting that a particular "world" or "set of worlds" has been singled out from all the possible worlds the organism might single out for one purpose or another. Acknowledging that perception or discrimination is a matter of vector completion is thus acknowledging something so uncontroversial as to be almost tautological. Vector completion is a cognitive process in the same way growing old is a biological process; short of dying, whatever you do counts.

Almost tautological, but not quite. What the connectionists argue is that as long as you have machinery that can traverse this huge statespace efficiently and appropriately (completing the vectors it *ought* to complete most of the time), you don't have to burden the system with extra machinery—scene-painting machinery *or* script-writing machinery. A highly particular content can be embodied in the state of a nervous system without having any such further properties—just so long as the right sort of transitions are supported by the machinery. Given the neutrality of vector-coding talk, there is no particular reason for the machinery described to be connectionist machinery. You could describe the most sentential and logistic of representation-systems in vector-coding terms if you wished. What you would lose would be the details of symbol-manipulation, lemma-proving, rule-consulting that carried the system down the path to completion—but if those features were deemed beneath the level of the intended model, so much the better. But—and here is the meat, at last—connectionist systems are particularly well-suited to a vector-coding description because of the way they actually accomplish state transitions. The connectionist systems created to date exhibit *fragments* of the appropriate transitional behaviour, and that's a promising sign. We just don't know, yet, whether whole cognitive systems, exhibiting all the sorts of state transitions exhibited by cognizing agents, can be stitched together from such fabrics.

One of the virtues of vector-coding talk, then, is its neutrality; it avoids the spurious connotations of pictures or sentences. But that very neutrality might actually prevent one from thinking vividly enough to dream up good experiments that reveal something about the actual machinery determining the contents. Ramachandran has conducted a series of ingenious experiments designed to shed light on the question of how rich perceptual representations are, and the metaphor of pictorial filling-in has apparently played a large role in guiding his imaginative transition from experiment to experiment (Ramachandran and Gregory 1991, Ramachandran forthcoming). I have been sharply critical of reliance on this "filling-in" metaphor, (Dennett 1991, 1992), but I must grant that any perspective on the issue that encourages dreaming these experiments up is valuable for just that reason, and should not be dismissed out of hand, even if in the end we have to fall back on some more neutral description of the phenomena.

One of the most dramatic of these experiments is Ramachandran and Gregory's "artificial scotoma" which the brain "fills in" with "twinkle." According to Ramachandran (1992), it can be reproduced at home, using an ordinary television set. (I must confess that my own efforts to achieve the effect at home have not been successful, but I do not doubt that it can be achieved under the right conditions.)

Choose an open channel so that the television produces "snow," a twinkling pattern of dots. Then stick a very tiny circular label in the middle of the screen. About eight centimeters from the label, tape on a square piece of gray paper whose whose sides are one centimeter and whose luminances roughly matches the gray in the snow. . . . If you gaze at the label very steadily for about 10 seconds, you will find that the square vanishes completely and gets "replaced" by the twinkling dots. . . . Recently we came up with an interesting variation of the original "twinkle" experiment. When a volunteer indicated that the square had been filled in with twinkling dots, we instructed the computer to make the screen uniformly gray. To our surprise, the volunteers reported that they saw a square patch of twinkling dots in the region where the original gray square had been filled in. They saw the patch for as long as 10 seconds. (Ramachandran 1992, 90)

In this new perceptual illusion, the illusory *content* is *that there is twinkling in the square.* But, one is tempted to ask, how is this content *rendered*? Is it a matter of the representation being composed of hundreds or thousands of individual illusory twinkles or is it a matter of there being, in effect, a label that just says "twinkling" attached to the representation of the square?

Can the brain represent twinkling, perceptually, without representing individual twinkles?

This is a good mind-opening question, I think. That is, if you ask yourself this question, you are apt to discover something about how you have been tacitly understanding the issues—and the terms—all along. Real twinkling—twinkling in the world—is composed of lots of individual twinkles, of course, happening at particular times and places. That's what twinkling is. But not all representations of twinkling are composed of lots of representations of individual twinkles, happening at particular times and places. For instance, this essay frequently represents twinkling, but never by representing individual twinkles. We know that during the induction phase of this experiment, over a large portion of your retina, there are individual twinkles doing their individual work of getting the twinkle-representation machinery going, by stimulating particular groups of cells at particular times and places. What we don't yet know is whether, when neurally represented twinkling "fills in" the neurally represented square area—an area whose counterpart on the retina has no individual twinkles, of course—this represented twinkling consists of individual representations of twinkles. This is part of what one might want to know, when the question one asks is: *how rich* is the neural representation? It is an empirical question, and not at all an obvious one. It does not follow from the fact that *we see the twinkling* that the individual twinkles are represented. They may be, but this has yet to be determined. The fact that the twinkling is remarkably vivid, subjectively, also settles nothing. There are equally stunning illusory effects that are *surely* not rendered in individual details.

When I first saw Bellotto's landscape painting of Dresden at the North Carolina Museum of Art in Raleigh, I marvelled at the gorgeously rendered details of all the various people walking in bright sunlight across the distant bridge, in their various costumes, with their differences in attitude and activity. (See figure 19.2.)

I remember having had a sense that the artist must have executed these delicate miniature figures with the aid of a magnifying glass. When I leaned close to the painting to examine the brushwork, I was astonished to find that all the little people were merely artfully positioned single blobs and daubs of paint—not a hand or foot or head or hat or shoulder to be discerned. (See figure 19.3.)

Nothing shaped remotely like a tiny person appears on the canvas, but there is no question that my brain represented those blobs *as* persons. Bellotto's deft

Figure 19.2

brushwork "suggests" people crossing the bridge, and my brain certainly took the "suggestion" to heart. But what did its *taking* the suggestion amount to? We may want to say, metaphorically, that my brain "filled in" all the details, or we may want to say—more abstractly, but still metaphorically—that my brain completed the vector: *a variety of different people in various costumes and attitudes*. What I doubt very much, however, is that any particular neural representations of hands or feet or hats or shoulders were created by my brain. (This, too, is an empirical question, of course, but I'll eat my hat if I'm wrong about this one!)

How can we tell, then, how rich the content of the neural representation actually is? As Ramachandran says, by doing more experiments. Consider for instance another of his embellishments on the artificial scotoma theme, in which the twinkling background is coloured pink, and there is a "conveyor belt" of spots coherently moving from left to right within the gray square region (Ramachandran 1992). As before, the square fades, replaced by pink, but the conveyor belt continues for awhile, before its coherent motion is replaced by the random jiggling of the rest of the background. Ramachandran concludes, correctly, that there must be two separate "fill in" events occurring in the brain; one for the background colour, one for the motion. But he goes on to draw a second conclusion that does not follow:

The visual system must be actually seeing pink—i.e., creating a visual representation of pink in the region of the scotoma, for if that were not true why would they actually see the spots moving against a pink background? If no actual filling in were taking place they would simply

Figure 19.3

have been unable to report what was immediately around the moving spots. (Ramachandran 1992)

Of course in some sense "the visual system must be actually seeing pink"—that is, the subject is actually seeing pink that isn't there. No doubt about it! But this does not mean the pink is represented by actually filling in between the moving spots on the conveyor belt—and Ramachandran has yet another experiment that shows this: when a "thin black ring" was suddenly introduced in the centre of the square, the background colour, yellow, "filled the interior of the ring as well; its spread was not 'blocked' by the ring." As he says,

This observation is especially interesting since it implies that the phrase "filling in" is merely a metaphor. If there had been an actual neural process that even remotely resembled "filling in" then one would have expected its progress to be blocked by the black ring but no such effect occurred. Therefore we would be better off saying that the visual system "assigns" the same color as the surround to the faded region. . . . (Ramachandran 1992)

In yet another experiment, Ramachandran had subjects look at a fixation point on a page of text which had a blank area off to the side. Subjects duly "filled in" the gap with text. But of course the words were not readable, the letters were not identifiable. As Ramachandran says: "It was as though what was filled in was the 'texture' of the letters rather than the letters themselves" (1992). No rendering of individual letters, in other words, but rather a representation *to the effect that* there was no gap in the text, but just more of the same—more 12-point Times Roman, or whatever. The effect is, of course, perceptual, but that does not mean it is not conceptual, not propositional. The content is actually *less rich* than it would have to be, if the gap were filled with particular letters spelling out particular words (or non-words).

Let's now return to the opening question: what is *the product* of perception? This question may have seemed at first like a good question to ask, but it gets one off on the wrong foot because it presupposes that perceptual processes have a single kind of product. To presuppose this, however, is already to commit oneself to the Cartesian Theater. There are in fact many different ways of turning the corner, or responding to the given, and only a few of them are "pictorial" (or for that matter "sentential") in any sense at all. For instance, when something looms swiftly in the visual field, one tends to duck. Ducking is one sort of taking. It itself is not remotely pictorial or propositional; the behaviour is not a speech act; it does not express a proposition. And there is no reason on earth to posit an intermediary state that "represents" in some "code" or "system of representation."

Suppose a picture of a cow is very briefly flashed in your visual field, and then masked. You might not be able to report it or draw it, but it might have the effect of making you more likely to say the word "milk" if asked to name a beverage. This is another sort of corner-turning; it is presumably accomplished by activating or sensitizing a particular semantic domain centered around cows, so your visual system must have done its interpretive work—must have completed the *cow* vector—but its only "product" on this occasion may be just to turn on the cow-neighbouring portion of your semantic network.

The magician moves his hand just so, misdirecting you. We know he succeeded, because you exhibit astonishment when he turns over the cup and the ball has vanished. What product did he produce by this manipulation of your visual system? Astonishment now, but that, like ducking, is not a speech act. The astonishment is caused by failed expectation; you had *expected* the ball to be under the cup. Now what sort of a "product" is this unarticulated expectation? Is it a sentence of mentalese, "The ball is under the cup" swiftly written in your belief-box, or is it a pictorial representation of the ball under the cup? It's something else, propositional only in the bland sense that it is content-specific; it is *about the ball being under the cup*, which is not the same thing as being *about the cup being on the table* or being *about the magician having moved his hands away from the cup*. Those are *different* products of visual perception, vectors into different regions of your content hyperspace.

This state that you have been put into not only grounds your astonishment if the magician now turns over the cup, but also influences how you will perceive the next move the magician makes if he doesn't turn over the cup. That is, this "product" of perception can immediately go on to influence the processes producing the *next* products of perception, and on and on. Ramachandran illustrates this point with an experiment in which a field of yellow rings is shown to subjects in such a way that one of the rings has its inner boundary obscured by the blind spot. (See figure 19.4.)

What will their brains do? "Fill in" with yet another ring, just like all the other rings, or "fill in" the center of the obscured ring with yellow, turning it into a yellow disk? The latter, it turns out; the solid yellow disk "pops out" as the exception in the field of yellow rings. But even this is not a demonstration of *actual* filling in; in this case, the brain has evidence that there is a yellow region with a circular perimeter, and it has no *local* evidence about whether or not the whole region is yellow. Not having any contrary evidence, it draws the inference that it must be "more of the same"—*more yellow*. This is a fine example of a micro-taking, for this "*conclusion*" amounts to the creation of the content *yellow disk*, which in turn becomes a *premise* of sorts: the odd-one-out in a field represented as consisting of yellow

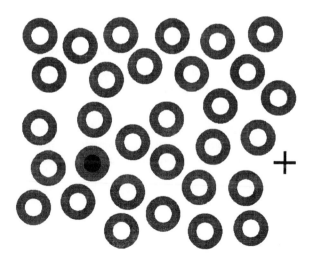

Figure 19.4

rings, which then triggers "pop out." It might have turned out otherwise; the micro-taking process first invoked for the blind-spot region might have had access to the global information about the multitude of rings, and treated this global content as evidence for a different inference: considered globally, "more of the same" is *more rings*. In that case there would have been no pop-out, and the field would have been seen, veridically, in fact, as a uniform field of rings. So the experiment very definitely shows us something about the order and access relations between a variety of micro-takings, but in neither case does the brain have to provide something in order to arrive at its initial judgment.

The creation of conscious experience is not a batch process but a continuous process. There is not one corner that is turned, once, but many. The order in which these determinations occur determines the order in which they can have effects (no backwards causation allowed!), but is strictly independent of the *order represented* in the contents thus determined. The micro-takings have to interact. A micro-taking, as a sort of judgment or decision, can't just be inscribed in the brain in isolation; it has to have its consequences—for guiding action and modulating further micro-judgments made "in its light." This interaction of micro-takings, however it is accomplished in particular cases, has the effect that a modicum of coherence is maintained, with discrepant elements dropping out of contention, and all without the assistance of a Master Judge. Since there is no Master Judge, there is no *further* process of being-appreciated-in-consciousness, so the question of *exactly* when a particular element was *consciously* (as opposed to unconsciously) taken admits no non-arbitrary answer. And since there is no privileged moment at which to measure richness of content, and since the richness of content of micro-takings waxes and wanes, the idea that we can identify *perceptual*—as opposed to conceptual—states by an evaluation of their contents turns out to be an illusion.

Note

1. This is what I called the β-manifold in "Two Approaches to Mental Images," in Dennett (1978).

References

Dennett, D. C. (1978). *Brainstorms*. Cambridge, MA: MIT Press.
——(1991). *Consciousness Explained*. Boston: Little, Brown.

———(1992). Filling in versus finding out: A ubiquitous confusion in cognitive science. In P. van den Broek, Herbert L. Pick, Jr., and D. Knill, (eds.). *Cognition: Conceptual and Methodological Issues*. Washington, DC: American Psychological Association.

Dennett, D. C., and M. Kinsbourne (1992). Time and the observer: the where and when of consciousness in the brain. *Behavioral and Brain Sciences*, 15, 2 (June): 183–201.

Kinsbourne, M. (1988). Integrated field theory of consciousness. In A.J. Marcel and E. Bisiach, (eds.). *Consciousness in Contemporary Sciencer*. Oxford: Oxford University Press.

Ramachandran, V. S. (1992). Blind spots. *Scientific American*, 266 (May): 86–91.

———(1992) "Filling in gaps in perception: Part I. *Psychological Science*, 1:199–205.

Ramachandran, V. S., and R. L. Gregory (1991). Perceptual filling in of artificially induced scotomas in human vision. *Nature* 350, 6320:699–702.

Sherrington, C. S. (1934) *The Brain and Its Mechanism*. Cambridge: Cambridge University Press.

Stalnaker, R. (1984). *Inquiry*. Cambridge, MA: MIT Press.

20

Sensory Substitution and Qualia

Paul Bach-y-Rita

I Introduction

A person who has suffered the total loss of a sensory modality has, indirectly, suffered a brain lesion. In the absence of a modality such as sight, behavior and neural function must be reorganized. However, blind persons have not necessarily lost the capacity to see (Bach-y-Rita 1972), since we do not see with the eyes, but with the brain. In normal sight, the optical image does not get beyond the retina. From the retina to the central perceptual structures, the image, now transformed into nerve pulses, is carried over nerve fibers. It is in the central nervous system that pulse-coded information is transformed into the subjective visual experience. It appears to be possible for the same subjective experience that is produced by a visual image on the retina to be produced by an optical image captured by an artificial eye (a TV camera), when a way is found to deliver the image from the camera to a sensory system that can carry it to the brain.

The rest of the process of vision substitution should then depend upon experience and training, and the ability of the subject to have the same control over the image capture as with eyes: thus, camera movement must be under the control of one of the subject's motor systems (hand, head movement, or any other). Indeed, we have shown that this is possible, once the blind person has learned the mechanics. This includes camera control: zooming, aperture and focus, and the correct interpretation of the effects of camera movement, such as occurs when the camera is moved from left to right and the image seems to move from right to left. Furthermore, many phenomena associated with vision have to be learned; for example, when viewing a person seated behind a desk, the partial image of the person must be correctly interpreted as a complete person with the image of the desk interposed, rather than perceiving just half a person. The subjective experience is comparable (if not qualitatively identical) to vision, including subjective spatial localization in the three-dimensional world. Even the visual illusions that have been tested (e.g., waterfall effect) are the same as vision.

However, in studies with congenitally blind adolescents and adults, the emotional content, or qualia (as the term will be used here) of the sensory experience appears to be missing. The apparent absence of qualia in our studies may be related to the few hours of practice that the subjects have had, or it may be related to more fundamental issues. Sensory substitution experience that starts in early childhood may have a different relation to qualia.

In our studies, tactile vision substitution has been a model of brain plasticity. The brain is a plastic organ, with various mechanisms of information transmission and mechanisms of compensation for damage and sensory loss. Reorganization of brain function is possible not only in early development, but throughout life, although after certain "critical periods," specific training or appropriate rehabilitation is necessary. However, conceptual models have limited the appreciation for the brain's capacity for functional reorganization, and knowledge of the most efficient rehabilitation procedures is limited by the paucity of well-planned, scientifically validated studies. The neuroscience data gathered over the last few decades is justifying the re-evaluation of the conceptual models that have served so well for the last 100 years. One result of the re-evaluation should be a concept of the therapeutic potential of long-term brain reorganization (e.g., after stroke) and for sensory substitution, such as following the loss of vision. In fact, our studies with congenitally blind persons have demonstrated that tactile vision substitution can compensate for certain aspects of blindness.

Conceptual models determine the therapy chosen for treatment and rehabilitation. In the case of brain rehabilitation, the procedures have been developed within the constraints of a conceptual model of brain function and recovery potential that has not reflected the high potential for late as well as early reorganization and recovery of function. Connectionist-localizationist models of the brain emphasize the representation of function, without adequately stimulating an understanding of brain plasticity. The effect has been that rehabilitation methods are aimed primarily at the early post-lesion stage, with intensive therapy during the first few months and little therapy thereafter. A conceptual model that includes the potential for early and late reorganization encourages the development of programs to obtain functional recovery even years after the damage. Comparably, a conceptual model of brain organization that includes late as well as early plasticity provides the base for developing sensory substitution-based therapy, such as following the loss of vision.

Following a brief discussion of brain plasticity, some historical aspects of the effect of the prevailing conceptual framework on rehabilitation will be noted. Studies of tactile vision substitution for blind persons will be noted, and studies of tactile vision substitution for blind persons will be summarized. I have discussed these subjects in a recent book (see Bach-y-Rita 1995), from which this paper is derived. This article will also explore some philosophical issues, in particular qualia, that are related to the development of tactile vision substitution in children, adolescents and adults.

II Sensory Substitution as a Model of Brain Plasticity

Our sensory substitution studies were initiated a number of years ago as models of brain plasticity; congenitally blind persons were considered a Jacksonian model (Hughlings Jackson emphasized the opportunities for discovery offered by the experiments made on the brain by disease [excerpts in Clarke and O'Malley, 1968]). The major source of afferent information had been eliminated before they had the opportunity to develop the mechanisms for the analysis of visual information. Thus, a thorough study of congenitally blind persons learning to use a vision substitution system, with the image from an artificial receptor delivered to the brain through sensory systems that have remained intact, offered several unique opportunities:

1. The ability to control and evaluate all aspects of an entirely novel perceptual learning experience, since no relevant visual learning could go on without the use of the substitute receptor system (TV camera and stimulus array).

2. The opportunity to evaluate central nervous system mechanisms involved in the perceptual development and sensory substitution process.

3. The opportunity to evaluate the interrelationships of relevant systems, such as the role of motor control (to move the camera), on spatial localization with a vision substitution system.

Our studies with the TVSS have been extensively described (e.g., Bach-y-Rita 1972; 1989; 1995; Bach-y-Rita et al. 1969; Bach-y-Rita and Hughes 1985; Bach-y-Rita and Sampaio 1995; Collins and Bach-y-Rita 1973; White et al. 1970). We developed tactile vision substitution systems (TVSS) to deliver visual information to the brain via arrays of stimulators in contact with the skin of one of several parts of the body (abdomen, back, thigh). Optical images picked up by a TV camera are transduced into a form of energy (vibratory or direct electrical stimulation) that can be mediated by the skin receptors. The visual information reaches the perceptual levels for analysis and interpretation via somatosensory pathways and structures. After sufficient training with the TVSS, our subjects reported experiencing the image in space, instead of on the skin. They learn to make perceptual judgments using visual means of analysis, such as perspective, parallax, looming and zooming, and depth judgments.

However, there are many practical limitations, such as the need to sweep an image with the camera, instead of picking up the whole image at once (as with the eyes), which results in increased time to make a correct identification, and the inability to deal with visual clutter, with shadows, and with fast movement, at least with the present low resolution systems. Also, there are many psychological issues that must be addressed before a system can be practical. Thus, exploring the face of one's loved-one can be very disappointing, since the emotional messages that the long experience with vision have provided have not been perceived with our TVSS (similar problems are confronted by congenitally blind persons who acquire sight through surgical correction of the cause, such as congenital cataracts, that had prevented vision).

A   Perceptual Studies

Once the subject has learned with one motor system (e.g., hand held camera, thus using the corresponding kinesthetic system), the camera can be switched to another system (e.g., mounted on the head), with no loss of perceptual capacity. And when the man-machine interface, the electro- or vibrotactile array, is moved from one area of skin to another (e.g., from the back to the abdomen or to the forehead), there is no loss of correct spatial localization, even when the array is switched from back to front, since the trained blind subject is not perceiving the image on the skin, but is locating it correctly in space. Similarly, a blind person using a long cane does not perceive the resulting stimulation as being in the hand, but correctly locates it on the ground being swept with the cane, and a person writing with a pen does not perceive the contact as being on the fingers, but rather locates it subjectively on the page.

Our data suggest that, at least initially, the blind subjects obtain the "visual" information primarily by an analysis of contours, although simultaneous analysis of the information is also used. Thus, artificial edge enhancement should produce improved performance in the early stages. Subjects using the TVSS learn to treat the information arriving at the skin in its proper context. Thus, at one moment the information arriving at the skin has been gathered by the TV camera, but at another it relates to the usual cutaneous information (pressure, tickle, wetness, etc.). The subject is not confused; when he/she scratches his/her back under the matrix nothing is "seen." Even during task performance with the sensory system, the subject can perceive purely tactile sensations when asked to concentrate on these sensations.

Two examples will be presented of complex "hand-eye" coordination tasks with the TVSS:

1. Batting a ball.

The perceptual task in catching an object is to pick up information about two components, the object to be caught and the catching body part or tool. Both may be moving and the catching person does not only need information about their continuously changing positions, but also about the direction of their motions in order to be able to make proper preparations for their encounter. The time available for this activity is often very short. Can tactile information obtained from a matrix of point stimuli replace visually obtained information in this situation?

An experiment with a stationary version of the TVSS displaying the tactile matrix on the subject's back (Jansson and Brabyn 1981) indicated that touch can replace vision to some extent in such a situation. The subject was seated in a chair with the tactile matrix (20 × 20 vibrators) on his back. In his hand he had a response bar with which he had to bat a ball rolling towards him. The only perceptual information about its motion was provided via the tactile matrix on his back which also contained information about the position of the response bat. The total time of approach was about 3.5 sec. The ball rolled off the table, but the subject did not know the position on the table edge that would be reached by the ball, since the trough could be moved from one side to another in front of the blind subject. Thus, the subject had to identify the rolling ball, calculate the time it would take to reach the edge of the table, calculate the position on the table (to his left or right or middle), identify the location in his "visual" field of the bat, and correctly time his movement of the bat in order to bat the ball.

The experimental result with two well trained blind subjects was that the mean of the performance was rather close to perfect, but there was a variability much greater than with visual guidance. It is thus possible to pick up information from a tactile display of the type used here and prepare and perform the appropriate movements in real-time, but it must be remembered that touch does not have the precision of vision (Jansson 1983).

2.   Electronic assembly and inspection.

A vocational test of the TVSS revealed its potential application to jobs presently reserved for sighted workers. A person totally blind since two months from birth spent three months on the miniature diode assembly line of an electronic manufacturer. During the assembly process, he received a frame containing 100 small glass cylinders with attached wires, as the frame emerged from an automatic filling machine that filled each cylinder with a small piece of solder. The automatic process was 95% efficient, and so approximately 5% of the cylinders remained unfilled. His first task after receiving each frame was to inspect each of the cylinders and to fill by hand those that remained unfilled. This was accomplished with a small TV camera mounted in a dissecting microscope, under which the blind worker passed the frame containing the cylinders. The information from the cylinders was passed through an electronic commutator, in order to transform it into a tactile image, and was delivered to the skin of the abdomen of the worker by means of 100 small vibrating rods in an array clipped to the workbench.

In order to receive the image, the blind worker had only to lean his abdomen against the array (without removing his shirt). He did not wear any special apparatus and his hands were left free to perform the inspection and assembly tasks under the microscope. He filled the empty cylinders by means of a modified injection needle attached to a vacuum: he placed the needle in a dish filled with small pieces of solder. The needle picked up only one piece, since the suction was then blocked. He then brought the needle with the solder into the "visual" field under the microscope, and by hand-eye coordination placed the needle in an empty cylinder, at which point he released the suction, and the solder dropped in. He repeated the process for each empty cylinder encountered, and then passed the frame to another loading machine where it was automatically filled with diode wafers. Again, the task was then to fill the approximately 5% of cylinders that did not have a diode wafer, which he did as above, except that this stage offered two extra problems: the wafers were very thin and flat and did not always fall flat into the cylinders. Sometimes they landed on edge. Furthermore, the wafers were gold on one side and silver on the other, and they had to be correctly oriented. He had the additional task of turning over 50% of the wafers. This task was accomplished by identifying the color on the basis of light reflectance, since the silver side reflected more light.

The blind worker was able to perform the tasks, but was much slower than the line worker, and became more fatigued than they did. Thus, he would not have been a competitive worker on that line. However, it did demonstrated the feasibility of developing jobs in an industrial setting in the future (Bach-y-Rita 1982).

B   Applications to the Education of Blind Children

We have demonstrated that it is possible to develop an understanding, in congenitally blind students, of the visual world including visual means of analysis (Miletic, Hughes, and Bach-y-Rita 1988). Children learn to understand and use visual means of analysis such as monocular cues of depth, and interposition; for the latter, one example of the training is to view three candles lined up one behind the other. Only one is perceived because the view of the others is blocked; the child then moves his/her head to see the three candles appearing as they are viewed from the side. For an additional rewarding learning experience with the candles, one is lit, and the child views the flame and blows on it to produce waving of the flame, which is perceived with interest and excitement. Comparable "visual" experiences have been explored and further applications are planned in regard to learning math and geometry and science, and in the development of a portable system for itinerant teachers of blind students.

C   Other Sensory Substitution Systems

1   Sign Language.   Very interesting clues to the brain's capacity to reorganize function can be obtained from an analysis of learning of sign language by deaf persons. Bellugi and Klima (1979) have extensively studied American Sign Language (ASL) development, which they consider to differ dramatically from English and other spoken languages; for example, the grammatical pattern and the modification of lexical units are entirely distinct, and it has its own rules of syntax. In spite of the enormous structural specialization for auditory-vocal speech, the brain is capable of developing a different language system based on hand movements and visual recognition. Their analysis of the mechanisms for the regular modification of the lexical units of ASL reveal that the processes operate as simultaneous (not linear sequential) changes on signs, and that these are essentially organized as simultaneously occurring components. This characteristic may reflect the different capacities of the perceptual systems involved; the auditory being essentially sequential, including its receptor characteristics, while the visual system (used in ASL) is essentially a parallel-input system (discussed in Bach-y-Rita 1980).

Bellugi and Klima (1979) suggest that right-handed deaf people whose major form of communication is ASL have the normal pattern of left hemisphere specialization for language, but that, in contrast to results with hearing subjects, the left hemisphere of signing deaf people is also specialized for a non-language task which has a strong visual-spatial component. They speculate that since spatial localization is an important aspect of the grammar of sign language, it may be adaptive to bring together these two functions within the same hemisphere. Further clues to this organization may be obtained from a case of a right-handed deaf person well-trained in ASL, who had a left hemisphere cerebral vascular accident with sign language aphasia.

2   Cutaneous Sensory Substitution Following Leprosy.   We undertook a preliminary study of cutaneous sensory substitution with persons who had lost hand sensation due to leprosy (Collins and Madey 1974). A special glove was fabricated with pressure and temperature transducers in the fingertips which relayed the pattern "felt" on the finger tips, to an area of skin on the forehead where sensation was intact. Subjects were able to distinguish rough from smooth surfaces, soft and hard objects, and the structure (curved; irregular, etc.) of the surface. A small crack in the table surface could be detected. A subject reported the pleasure of perceiving his light touch of his girlfriend without having to monitor it by sight, as he was accustomed to doing.

Under NASA sponsorship, we extended this work to the development of gloves for astronauts. Sensors were placed in the fingertips of gloves used in space walks, in order to compensate for the loss of tactile sensation, leading to the decrease in manual performance (Bach-y-Rita et al. 1987).

III   Philosophical Issues

Our principal work has been with congenitally blind persons. One of our congenitally blind research subjects, who wrote his Ph.D. dissertation (in the Department of Philosophy of New York University) on this subject, has presented a first-person account (Guarniero 1974, 1977).

In the Bach-y-Rita and Hughes (1985) report, we noted the following: "An understanding of the functional equivalence between visual and vibrotactile processing would have both basic scientific and practical implications, the former because it would bear on whether information for the various perceptual systems ought to be considered modality specific or amodal, and the latter because the data would suggest the possibilities and constraints for vision substitution and other prosthetic developments . . . Although the early system was termed a tactile vision substitution system, we have been reluctant to suggest that blind users of the device are actually seeing. Others (e.g., Heil 1983; Morgan 1977) have not been so reluctant, claiming that since blind subjects are being given similar information to that which causes the sighted to see and are capable of giving similar responses, one is left with little alternative but to admit that they are seeing (and not merely "seeing").

In *Molyneux's Question*, Morgan (1977) offers two basic arguments for this position. First, the structural nature of the perceptual system does not offer any criteria for distinguishing seeing from not seeing; e.g., the horseshoe crab is offered as an example of a biological system with fewer receptors than most mammals but which can nonetheless see. Second, Morgan addresses behavioral equivalence: if blind subjects receive (optical conversions of) optical information that would satisfy criteria for seeing in the sighted and respond in an indistinguishable manner, one might concede that the blind are "seeing."

We further noted that using a tactile vision substitution system (TVSS) is more like visual perception than typical tactile perception (for example, under normal ecologically valid conditions the tactile perceptual system usually involves concurrent kinesthetic information, which leads to designating it the "haptic" system). Are the systems the same? Clearly not on quantitative grounds, since the resolution of the TVSS is orders of magnitude less than the visual system, but one also might ask if the ways in which the systems differ are crucial. In any case, sighted persons still see, even under environmentally impoverished conditions such as fog or rain or at dusk, where shapes and patterns are difficult to distinguish, and a person with blurred tunnel vision is still using the remaining visual capacity to see.

For the perceptual regions of the brain, it is immaterial how the information enters the body as long is it is gathered by a perceptual organ with motor control and is received by a receptor matrix that can cope with the detail of the display. So long as the display presents the information reliably, the brain can apparently be trained to use the information from the TV camera as it uses the information from any of the intact sensory systems.

Blind subjects who have trained with the TVSS demonstrate perceptual equivalence between and across modalities. However, this is also frequently noted under other circumstances: Gibson (1966) noted that "fire" is the same whether the information has been obtained by hearing, feeling, looking, or smelling. There is a common aspect of perceptual activity that permits one to utilize information from several channels in such a way that invariant properties of objects are extracted.

As learning progresses, the information extraction processes become more and more automatic and unconscious. Miller (1956) considered that a "chunking" phenomena allows the number of bits per chunk to increase. A blind subject "looking" at a display of objects must initially consciously perceive each of the relative factors such as the perspective of the table, the precise contour of each object, the size and orientation of each object, and the relative position of parts of each object to others nearby. With experience, information regarding several of these factors is simultaneously gathered and evaluated. The increased information transfer through a sensory substitution system can be interpreted in terms of Miller's "chunking" model. The highly complex "visual" input can thus be reduced, by selective processes, to manageable proportions, allowing the input to be mediated by the somesthetic system or, in Gibsonian (1966) terms, the subject learns to extract the relevant information.

The development of the digital computer has led to an understanding of the ability to create complex images from a very small set of information units, in this case from strings of "on" and "off" signals, or bits. In reality, this had been known for a long time, since images, complex thoughts and emotions can be conveyed in written language merely by the differing combinations of 26 letters, and Beethoven's Fifth Symphony is a combination of a few basic notes. However, it is at least in part due to the development of the computer that scientists and philosophers have been able to conceptualize perceptual mechanisms that can be entirely based on combinations of bits of information. However, mechanistic comparisons, such as comparisons of the brain to a digital computer (it should be noted that previous technology advances such as the development of the telephone switchboard and of holography led to comparisons of the brain to those systems), are not tenable, especially in view of the nonsynaptic nature of much of the brain's information management (Bach-y-Rita, 1995). The human brain is much more technically sophisticated than any present or even presently forseeable electronic device. Even the nervous systems of insects, which allow highly developed functions such as the ability to identify and localize potential mates at great distances in moths, and the pattern perception and homing and complex motor behavior of Monarch butterflies, defy simulation on the most advanced computers.

Many relevant studies have been summarized in Dennett's 1991 book. He noted that "there are perceptual analysis tasks, such as speech perception, which would be beyond the physical limits of the brain's machinery if it didn't utilize ingeneous anticipatory strategies that feed on redundancies in the input" (144). He writes: "The world provides an inexhaustible deluge of information bombarding our senses, and when we concentrate on how much is coming in, or continuously available, we often succumb to the illusion that it all must be used, all the time. But our capacities to use information, and our epistemic appetites, are limited. If our brains can just satisfy all our particular epistemic hungers as they arise, . . . we will never be able to tell . . . that our brains are provisioning us with less than everything that is available in the world" (16). Writes Dennett: "A conscious mind is an observer, who takes in a limited subset of all the information . . . available at a particular . . . continuous sequence of times and places." He concludes: "All varieties of perception—indeed, all varieties of thought or mental activity—are accomplished in the brain by parallel, multitrack processes of interpretation and elaboration of sensory inputs . . . Feature detections or discriminations only have to be made once. That is, once a particular 'observation' of some feature has been made, by a specialized, localized portion of the brain, the information content thus fixed does not have to be sent somewhere else to be rediscriminated by some 'master' discriminator . . . discrimination does not lead to a representation of the already discriminated feature for the benefit of the audience in the Cartesian Theater—for there is no Cartesian Theater" (111–113).

Such comments aid in the understanding of the capacity of a poor resolution sensory substitution system to provide the information necessary for complex image interpretation. Furthermore, even the stated inadequacies of the skin (e.g., poor two-point resolution) do not appear as serious barriers to eventual high performance (e.g., such as when the presence of greatly improved techniques and devices are available, and when teaching methods improve. Even then, the information transmission capacities of sensory substitution systems may only be fully demonstrable under specific conditions, such as when they are available to a blind person starting from the first few months of life) when considered in the light of the material Dennett (1991) has synthesized. In fact, comparable defects can be described for mammalian eyes: O'Regan (1992) has noted that the design of the human eye is apparently illogical, with light passing through a dense tangle of neural matter and a web of blood vessels before reaching the sensory cells at the back of the retina, and with several other examples of apparent poor design such as the non-uniformity of the retina (even within the fovea) and the presence of the blind spot, and the further smearing and image displacement produced by the saccadic eye movements. "And yet," O'Regan notes, "despite all these defects, vision seems perfect to us. The deep . . . mystery of why we can see so well with such a terrible visual apparatus remains comparatively unfathomed" (463).

In O'Regan's view, the outside world is considered a form of ever-present external memory that can be sampled at leisure with eye movements, thus eliminating the requirements for a more perfect peripheral apparatus and central memory store, especially since there is no need to represent the image at any specific place in the brain. He concludes that "many problems in perception evaporate if we adopt the view that the brain need make no internal representation or replica or 'icon' of the outside world" (O'Regan 1992).

We are, of course, left with the problem that the actual neural structures and mechanisms have not been identified. At some level, all of the components of perception must be rooted in identifiable (eventually!) physico-chemical events. From the studies examined in the preceeding chapters, it is likely that nonsynaptic mechanisms play a role in widely dispersed transitory events related to most of perception, and in the data storage of the relatively small part of the information related to specific perceptual tasks.

Dennett has stated that "multiple functions . . . in nature . . . are everywhere. One of the reasons theorists have had such a hard time finding plausible designs for consciousness in the brain is that they have tended to think of brain elements as serving just one function each" (175). Yet there has been evidence since Flourens's (1842) time of overlapping function, and recent plasticity studies have emphasized the efficiency of the brain in developing multiple-use strategies. In one of the studies, Bach-y-Rita (1964) presented evidence for multisensory cells in the brainstem, and discussed the possible role of diffusion neurotransmission in the dynamic multiple-use role of those cells. Those studies reported in 1964 may also bear on the problem Dennett (1991) posed: "How, then, does the brain keep track of the temporal information that it needs?" (145).

A Sensory Overload

Normal sensory systems do not usually overload. The central nervous system is able to select only the information needed for any particular perceptual task. Twenty-five years ago we stated:

Many efforts at creating sensory aids set out to provide a set of maximally discriminable sensations. With this approach, one almost immediately encounters the problem of overload—a sharp limitation in the rate at which the person can cope with the incoming information.

It is the difference between landing an aircraft on the basis of a number of dials and pointers that provide readings on such things as airspeed, pitch, yaw, and roll, and landing a plane with a contact analog display. Visual perception thrives when it is flooded with information, when there is a whole page of prose before the eye, or a whole image of the environment; it falters when the input is diminished, when it is forced to read one word at a time, or when it must look at the world through a mailing tube. It would be rash to predict that the skin will be able to see all the things the eye can behold, but we would never have been able to say that it was possible to determine the identity and layout in three dimensions of a group of familiar objects if this system had been designed to deliver 400 maximally discriminable sensations to the skin. The perceptual systems of living organisms are the most remarkable information reduction machines known. They are not seriously embarrassed in situations where an enormous proportion of the input must be filtered out or ignored, but they are invariably handicapped when the input is drastically curtailed or artificially encoded. Some of the controversy about the necessity of preprocessing sensory information stems from disappointment in the rates at which human beings can cope with discrete sensory events. It is possible that such evidence of overload reflects more an inappropriate display than a limitation of the perceiver. Certainly the limitations of this system are as yet more attributable to the poverty of the display than to taxing the information handling capacities of the epidermis. (White et al. 1970, 26–27)

While there are definitely problems with the TVSS in the interpretation of objects in the presence of a cluttered background, they do not appear to be due to overload, but rather to be primarily due to the poverty of the display resulting from the low resolution of the present systems.

B   Qualia

Subjects trained with the tactile vision substitution system have noted the absence of qualia, which in a number of cases has been quite disturbing. Thus, well-trained subjects are deeply disappointed when they explore the face of a wife or girlfriend and discover that, although they can describe details, there is no emotional content to the image. In two cases, blind university students were presented *Playboy* centerfolds, and although they could describe details of the undressed women, it did not have the affective component that they knew (from conversations with their sighted classmates) that it had for sighted persons. Similar experiences have previously been noted by congenitally blind persons who acquire sight following surgery: colors have no affective qualities, and faces do not transmit emotional messages (e.g., Gregory and Wallace 1963).

The absence of qualia with substitute sight may be compared to the acquisition of a second language as an adult. The emotional aspects of the new language are often lacking, especially with emotionally charged words and expressions, such as curse words. It appears that both spoken language and other sensory messages require long experience within the context of other aspects of cultural and emotional development to be able to contain qualia.

In some sense, qualia have been evident in the tactile sensory substitution experience, but in a limited fashion. For example, school-age children perceiving the flame of a candle for the first time, are always pleased by the experience, especially when their actions influence the sensory message, such as when they blow gently on the candle and perceive the flickering flame. A university student who had just married showed great interest and pleasure in the exploration of typical kitchen instruments and activities, such as in the process of baking a cake. Another was delighted that the three-dimensional images helped her to understand the structure of a traffic intersection. A leprosy patient who had lost all sensation in his hands expressed great pleasure when he perceived the sensation of his active touch of his wife, using a glove with artificial tactile receptors that transmitted the information from active touch to the skin of the forehead where his sensation was intact.

However, these and similar reports of qualia are overshodowed by the more frequent reports of displeasure at the absence of qualia, noted above. It remains to be demonstrated, by appropriatly designed experiments, whether persons who begin to use vision sensory substitution as adolescents or adults will ever fully develop the qualia that are present with vision in persons sighted since birth. Will specific training be necessary? Will qualia develop with extended use of the substitution system?

Systems for blind babies (cf. Bach-y-Rita and Sampaio 1995) have already provided some suggestive evidence for the development of qualia, such as the infant's smile upon perceiving the mother's approach. Our working hypothesis is that when such systems are used from infancy, the qualia will develop, even if the system is not continuously in use. Thus, we expect that an hour a day or even less should be sufficient for the baby to grow with the contextual inclusion of the substitute sensory information. It would then be a part of the development of the entire personality, and when thus included as an integral part of the emotional development process, qualia comparable to those of sighted persons should be obtained. Improved systems for both babies and adults should provide experimental models for exploring the development of qualia with behavioral as well as brain imaging and electrical activity studies.

C Evidence in Support of Postulates

A number of questions that were posed in an earlier paper (Bach-y-Rita 1967) have been answered, at least in part, by our studies, and those of others. Among the questions were the following:

Is it possible to alter the central effects of afferent impulses from a circumscribed region? Central sensory representation, although to a degree phylogenetically determined, may possibly be modified if the functional roles of the particular "sensations" are modified. This concept can be submitted to test by increasing the functional demands from a cutaneous area which normally has a limited sensory role. This can be accomplished by presenting suitable coded "visual" information from an artificial receptor to a cutaneous area. A successful vision substitution system, producing high resolution "visual" (rather than the normal tactile) experiences on presentation of the optical images to the skin of the back, may produce measurable central effects.

D Other Sensory Substitution Systems

Two particularly successful sensory substitution system are sign language for deaf persons and Braille for blind persons. With both, the substitution can be accomplished in real-time. Thus, a sign language conversation can be held without a decoding delay, and a blind person can immediately perceive written material picked up with the finger tips. A consideration of the brain mechanisms in both of these sensory substitution systems leads to the conclusion that reading can be accomplished without direct input of the material read to the auditory cortex, and with sign language the auditory cortex is also by-passed, at least in the early stages of information arrival in the brain. Similarly, with TVSS, "visual" information first reaches the somatosensory cortex.

Therefore, sensory substitution in persons with congenital sensory loss, as well as in those with acquired loss, provides very interesting opportunities for studies of late brain reorganization. A few such behavioral and electrophysiological studies have been mentioned above, but many more are needed, as well as many other kinds, such as cerebral imaging experiments. Furthermore, many practical applications may be developed. Results to date have demonstrated limitations, at least with present equipment, but partial practical applications are certainly feasible at present. Thus, we have been exploring applications to visual concept development in congenitally blind school children. Studies with blind infants have shown promising results in regard to orienting to the parents and to objects in space, including reaching behavior (cf. Bach-y-Rita and Sampaio 1995). Under NIH sponsorship, we are also exploring the development of a haptic exploration system for access by blind persons to two- and three-dimensional computer graphics (Kaczmzrek, Tyler, and Bach-y-Rita 1994).

The technology developed for sensory substitution also has other applications. One such, astronaut gloves, was mentioned above. Another promising area is in Virtual Reality (Kaczmarek and Bach-y-Rita 1995). For a third application, we have proposed in a NIH grant submission the development of tri-sensory stimulation for learning disabilities. Improved man-machine interface technology will open up a vast array of applications, some of which we can only dream about today. And each new technological development that allows access to brain mechanisms not previously explored will pose a new set of philosophical issues.

Acknowledgement

Partial support from the National Institutes of Health, National Eye Institute Research Grant 1-RO1-EY 10019 is appreciated. Helpful comments and encouragement from George Adelman, Henning Henningsen and CUM Smith are gratefully acknowledged. Part of this book was written while I was a Visiting Scientist, Laboratoire de Psychologie Expérimentale, Université René Descartes (Paris V) and Chercheur Associé, Centre National de Recherche Scientifique, Paris. The warm hospitality of the Maison Suger, Maison des Sciences de L'Homme, Paris, is greatly appreciated.

References

Bach-y-Rita, P. (1964). Convergent and long latency unit responses in the reticular formation of the cat. *Exp. Neurol.*, *9*, 327–344.

Bach-y-Rita, P. (1967). Sensory plasticity: Applications to a vision substitution system. *Acta Neurol. Scand.*, *43*, 417–426.

Bach-y-Rita, P. (1972). *Brain Mechanisms in Sensory Substitution*. New York: Academic Press.

Bach-y-Rita, P. (1980). Brain plasticity as a basis for therapeutic procedures. In P. Bach-y-Rita (Eds.), *Recovery of Function: Theoretical Considerations for Brain Injury Rehabilitation* (pp. 225–263). Bern, Switzerland: H. Huber.

Bach-y-Rita, P. (1982). Sensory substitution in rehabilitation. In L. Illis, M. Sedgwick, and H. Granville (Eds.), *Rehabilitation of the Neurological Patient* (pp. 361–383). Oxford: Blackwell Scientific Publications.

Bach-y-Rita, P. (1989). Physiological considerations in sensory enhancement and substitution. *Europa Med. Phs.*, *25*, 107–128.

Bach-y-Rita, P. (1995). *Nonsynaptic Diffusion Neurotransmission and Late Brain Reorganization*. Demos, NY.

Bach-y-Rita, P., Collins, C. C., Saunders, F., White, B., and Scadden, L. (1969). Vision substitution by tactile image projection. *Nature*, *221*, 963–964.

Bach-y-Rita, P., and Hughes, B. (1985). Tactile vision substitution: Some instrumentation and perceptual considerations. In D. Warren and E. Strelow (Eds.), *Electronic Spatial Sensing for the Blind* (pp. 171–186). Dordrecht, the Netherlands: Martinus-Nijhoff.

Bach-y-Rita, P., and Sampaio, E. (1995). Substitution sensorielle chez les adultes et les enfants aveugles. In Y. Christen, M. Doly, and M.-T. Droy-Lefaix (Eds.), *Vision et adaptation* (pp. 108–116). Amsterdam: Elsevier.

Bach-y-Rita, P., Webster, J., Tompkins, W., and Crabb, T. (1987). Sensory substitution for space gloves and for space robots. In G. Rodriques (Ed.), *Proceedings of the Workshop on Space Robots*, Publication 87-13, vol. II (pp. 51–57). Pasadena, CA: Jet Propulsion Laboratories.

Bellugi, U., and Klima, E. (1979). Language: perspectives from another modality. In *Brain and Mind: CIBA Foundation Symposium No. 69* (pp. 99–117). Amsterdam: Exerpta Medica.

Clarke, E., and O'Malley, C. D. (1968). *The Human Brain and Spinal Cord*. Berkeley: University of California Press.

Collins, C. C., and Bach-y-Rita, P. (1973). Transmission of pictorial information through the skin. *Advan. Biologic. Med. Phys.*, *14*, 285–315.

Collins, C. C., and Madey, J. M. (1974). Tactile sensory replacement. *Proc. San Diego Biomed. Symp.*, *13*, 15–26.

Dennett, D. C. (1991). *Consciousness Explained*. London: Penguin Books.

Edelman, G. M. (1992). *Bright Air, Brilliant Fire*. New York: Basic Books.

Flourens, P. (1842). *Recherches Expérimentales sur les Propriétés et les Fonctions du système Nerveux Dans les Animaux* (2nd ed.). Paris: Ballière.

Gibson, J. J. (1966). *The Senses Considered as Perceptual Systems*. Boston: Houghton Mifflin.

Gregory, R. L., and Wallace, J. G. (1963). Recovery from early blindness: A case study. *Experimental Psychology Monograph* No. 2. Cambridge: Heffner & Sons.

Guarniero, G. (1974). Experience of tactile vision. *Percep.*, *3*, 101–104.

Guarniero, G. (1977). Tactile vision: A personal view. *Vis. Impairment and Blindness*, 125–130.

Heil, J. (1983). *Perception and Cognition*. Berkeley: University of California Press.

Jansson, G. (1983). Tactile guidance of movement. *Intern. J. Neuroscience*, *19*, 37–46.

Jansson, G., and Brabyn, L. (1981). *Tactually Guided Batting* No. 304). Uppsala University Psychological Reports.

Kaczmarek, K., and Bach-y-Rita, P. (1995). Tactile displays. In W. Barfield and T. Furness-Illrd (Eds.), *Advanced Interface Design and Virtual Environments*, (pp. 349–414). Oxford: Oxford University Press.

Kaczmarek, K., Tyler, M. E., and Bach-y-Rita, P. (1994). Electrotactile haptic display on the fingertips: Preliminary results. *Proc. 16th Annu. Int. Conf. IEEE Engineering in Med. Biol. Soc.*, *16*.

Miletic, G., Hughes, B., and Bach-y-Rita, P. (1988). Vibrotactile stimulation: An educational program for spatial concept development. *J. Vis. Impair. and Blindness* (November), 366–370.

Miller, G. A. (1956). The magical number seven, plus or minus two: Some limits on our capacity to process information. *Psychol. Rev., 63,* 81–97.

Morgan, M. J. (1977). *Molyneux's Question.* Cambridge: Cambridge University Press.

O'Regan, J. K. (1992). Solving the "real" mysteries of visual perception: The world as an outside memory. *Canad. J. Psychol., 46,* 461–488.

White, B. W., Saunders, F. A., Scadden, L., Bach-y-Rita, P., and Collins, C. C. (1970). Seeing with the skin. *Percep Psychophys, 7,* 23–27.

21

The Visual Brain in Action

A. David Milner and Melvyn A. Goodale

1   The Functions of Vision

Standard accounts of vision implicitly assume that the purpose of the visual system is to construct some sort of internal model of the world outside—a kind of simulacrum of the real thing, which can then serve as the perceptual foundation for all visually derived thought and action. The association of rich and distinctive conscious experiences with most of our perceptions gives credence to the idea that they must constitute a vital and necessary prerequisite for all of our visually based behavior.

But even though the perceptual representation of objects and events in the world is an important function of vision, it should not be forgotten that vision evolved in the first place, not to provide perception of the world per se, but to provide distal sensory control of the many different movements that organisms make. Many of the visual control systems for the different motor outputs evolved as relatively independent input-output modules. Thus, the different patterns of behavior exhibited by vertebrates, from catching prey to avoiding obstacles, can be shown to depend on independent pathways from the visual receptors through to the motor nuclei, each pathway processing a particular constellation of inputs and each evoking a particular combination of effector outputs.

Of course, the visually guided behavior of many animals, particularly complex animals such as humans, is not rigidly bound to a set of visuomotor modules, however subtle those mechanisms might be. Much of our behavior is quite arbitrary with respect to sensory input and is clearly mediated by some sort of internal model of the world in which we live. In other words, representational systems have evolved—systems that permit the brain to model the world, to identify objects and events, to attach meaning and significance to them, and to establish their causal relations. In humans and other primates, vision provides some of the most important inputs to these representational systems. Such systems are not linked directly to specific motor outputs but are linked instead to cognitive systems subserving memory, semantics, planning, and communication. Of course the ultimate function even of these higher-order systems has to be the production of adaptive behavior. The distinction between systems of this kind and the dedicated visuomotor modules described earlier is that the former enable us to select appropriate courses of action with respect to patterns of visual input, while the latter provide the immediate visual control required to execute those actions.

In our book *The Visual Brain in Action* (Milner and Goodale 1998), we argue that these two broad kinds of vision can be distinguished not only on functional grounds, but also by the fact that they are subserved by anatomically distinct substrates in the brain. Thus the distinction between vision for action and vision for perception helps us to understand the logic lying behind the organization of the visual pathways in the brain.

2   The Visual Brain

Evolution has provided primates with a complex patchwork of visual areas occupying the posterior 50% or so of the cerebral cortex (for review, see Zeki 1993). But despite the complexity of the interconnections between these different areas, two broad "streams" of projections have been identified in the macaque monkey brain, each originating from the primary visual area (V1): a ventral stream projecting eventually to the inferior temporal (IT) cortex, and a dorsal stream projecting to the posterior parietal (PP) cortex (Ungerleider and Mishkin 1982). Of course, these regions also receive inputs from a number of other subcortical visual structures, such as the superior colliculus (via the thalamus). These two pathways are illustrated schematically in figure 21.1. Although some caution must be exercised in generalizing from monkey to human, it seems likely that the visual projections from primary visual cortex to the temporal and parietal lobes in the human brain may involve a separation into ventral and dorsal streams similar to that seen in the monkey.

In 1982, Ungerleider and Mishkin argued that the two streams of visual processing play different but complementary roles in the perception of incoming visual information. According to their original account, the ventral stream plays a critical role in the identification and recognition of objects, while the dorsal stream medi-

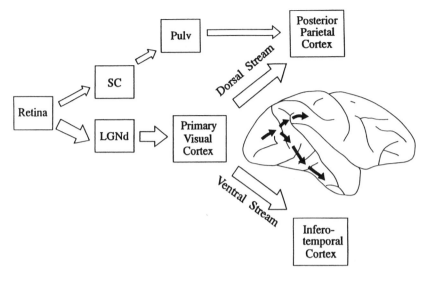

Figure 21.1
The major routes of visual input into the dorsal and ventral streams. The diagram of
the macaque brain on the right of the figure shows the approximate routes of the cortico-
cortical projections from the primary visual cortex of the posterior parietal and the
inferotemporal cortex, respectively. LGNd: lateral geniculate necleus, pars dorsalis; Pulv;
pulvinar; SC: superior coliculus.

ates the localization of those same objects. Some have referred to this distinction
in visual processing as one between object vision and spatial vision—"what" versus
"where." Apparent support for this idea came from work with monkeys. Lesions
of inferior temporal cortex produced deficits in the animal's ability to discriminate
between objects on the basis of their visual features but did not affect their performance on a spatially demanding "landmark" task. Conversely, lesions of the posterior parietal cortex produced deficits in performance on the landmark task but
did not affect object discrimination learning. Although the evidence available at the
time fitted well with Ungerleider and Mishkin's proposal, recent findings from a
broad range of studies in both humans and monkeys are more consistent with a distinction not between subdomains of perception, but between perception on the one
hand and the guidance of action on the other.

One source of evidence for the perception-action distinction comes from the study
of the visual properties of neurons in the ventral and dorsal streams. Neurons in
ventral stream areas such as IT are tuned to the features of objects, and many of

them show remarkable categorical specificity; some of these category-specific cells maintain their selectivity irrespective of viewpoint, retinal image size, and even color. They are little affected by the monkey's motor behavior, but many are modulated by how often the visual stimulus has been presented and others by whether or not it has been associated with reward. Such observations are consistent with the suggestion that the ventral stream is more concerned with the enduring characteristics and significance of objects than with moment-to-moment changes in the visual array.

Neurons in the dorsal stream show quite different properties from those in the ventral stream. In fact, the visual properties of neurons in this stream were discovered only when methodological advances permitted the experimenter to record from awake monkeys performing visuomotor tasks. Different subsets of neurons in PP cortex turned out to be activated by visual stimuli as a function of the different kinds of responses the monkey makes to those stimuli. For example, some cells respond when the stimulus is the target of an arm reach; others when it is the object of a grasp response; others when it is the target of a saccadic eye movement; others when the stimulus is moving and is followed by a slow pursuit eye movement; and still others when the stimulus is stationary and the object of an ocular fixation. In addition, of course, there are many cells in the dorsal stream, as there are in the ventral stream, that can be activated passively by visual stimuli—indeed logic requires that the visuomotor neurons must receive their visual inputs from visual cells that are not themselves visuomotor. These purely visual neurons are now known to include some that are selective for the orientation of a stimulus object. One important characteristic of many PP neurons is that they respond better to a visual stimulus when the monkey is attending to it, in readiness to make a saccadic or manual response. This phenomenon is known as neuronal enhancement.

The electrophysiology can readily explain why posterior parietal lesions impair landmark task performance: quite simply, the monkey fails to orient toward the landmark. Recent behavioral studies bear out this interpretation. The electrophysiology also explains one of the most obvious effects of PP lesions, namely the monkeys' inability to reach accurately to grasp a moving or stationary food morsel, and why they fail to shape and orient their hands and fingers appropriately to pick up the morsel. The most recent development in this area has been the elegant experiments of Gallese and his colleagues (1997). They have demonstrated that microinjections of a drug (muscimol) into a particular part of the PP cortex will cause a temporary impairment in hand shaping when the monkey reaches to grasp objects.

This fits well with the recent discovery of visually responsive cells within that same part of PP cortex, as well as in anatomically linked areas of premotor cortex, which respond selectively during the grasping of particular objects (Sakata et al. 1997; Rizzolatti et al. 1988). Such evidence is consistent with the proposal that visual networks in the dorsal stream compute more than just spatial location. Indeed, in agreement with the electrophysiology, the behavioral literature is fully consistent with the idea that the dorsal stream has a primary role in mediating the visual control and guidance of a wide range of behavioral acts (Milner and Goodale 1993). Furthermore, even though the egocentric locations of visual targets are indeed computed within the PP cortex, it has now been clearly shown that this is done separately for guiding movements of the eyes and for movements of the hands, both in the monkey brain (Snyder et al. 1997) and in the human brain (Kawashima et al. 1996).

While lesions of one system (the dorsal stream) can thus disrupt visuomotor control without affecting perception, the converse is also true. The classic studies of bilateral temporal lobe lesions in monkeys showed unequivocally that visual recognition was severely affected (Kluever and Bucy 1938), but the investigators noticed that the monkeys retained a wide range of visuomotor skills. For example, they observed that the lesioned monkeys did not bump into obstacles or misjudge distances when jumping. In a more recent study, IT-lesioned monkeys that had failed to learn a pattern discrimination despite many weeks of training, nevertheless remained highly adept at catching gnats flying within the cage room. In another study, inferotemporal monkeys were found able to track and seize a rapidly and erratically moving peanut. Thus the evidence from IT lesions allows us to delineate a range of residual visual skills that do not depend on the ventral stream.

The same dissociations following brain damage have been observed in humans. The first systematic description of a patient of bilateral posterior parietal damage was published by Balint (see Harvey 1995). Balint's patient had three major groups of symptoms: attentional (including a narrowing of visual attention), visuomotor (what Balint called optic ataxia), and oculomotor (fixed gaze). Optic ataxia was manifest as a difficulty in accurately reaching in space to pick up objects with the right hand. In many respects, these disorders closely resemble those seen in the PP-lesioned monkey. In both monkeys and humans, for example, optic ataxia appears to be visuomotor rather than purely visual or purely motor.

Accordingly, similar lesions in the superior parietal lobule and the neighboring intraparietal sulcus also cause difficulties in executing visually controlled saccadic eye movements in space. Furthermore, patients with optic ataxia not only fail to reach in the right direction but also have difficulty orienting their hand and forming their grasp appropriately with respect to target objects. For example, Perenin and Vighetto (1988) found that their optic ataxic subjects made errors in hand rotation as they tried to reach towards and into a large oriented slot. Often such patients are also unable to use visual information to form their grip as they reach towards an object. Although a normal individual opens the hand in anticipation of the target object, the maximum aperture being scaled in proportion to the size of the object, patients with lesions in the superior parietal cortex often show deficient grip scaling as they reach out to pick up an object (Jeannerod 1986). Yet despite the failure of these patients to orient their hands, to scale their grip appropriately, or to reach towards the right location, they have comparatively little difficulty in giving perceptual reports of the orientation and location of the very objects they fail to grasp.

On the other side of the equation, an impairment of ventral stream function seems to occur in humans who suffer from the condition known as visual form agnosia. The classic case of this disorder was described by Benson and Greenberg (1969). Their patient was not only unable to recognize faces or objects, he could not even reliably identify geometric shapes visually, nor distinguish reliably between a square and a rectangle with a $2:1$ aspect ratio. Yet the patient was certainly not cortically blind. Recently we have described a very similar patient, D.F. (Milner et al. 1991). We have examined her spared abilities to use visual information in a series of experimental studies. We have found that her attempts to make a perceptual report of the orientation of an oriented slot show little relationship to its actual orientation, whether her reports are made verbally or by manual means (see figure 21.2). However, when she was asked to insert her hand or a hand-held card into the slot, she shows no difficulty, moving her hand or the card towards the slot in the correct orientation and inserting it quite accurately (see figure 21.2). Videorecordings have shown that her hand begins to rotate in the appropriate direction as soon as it leaves the start position. In short, although she cannot report the orientation of the slot, she can insert her hand or post a card into it with considerable skill.

Similar dissociations between perceptual report and visuomotor control were also observed in D.F. when she was asked to deal with the intrinsic properties of objects such as their size and shape. Thus, she showed excellent visual control of anticipatory hand posture when she was asked to reach out to pick up blocks of different sizes that she could not distinguish perceptually. Just like normal subjects, D.F. adjusted her finger-thumb separation well in advance of her hand's arrival at the

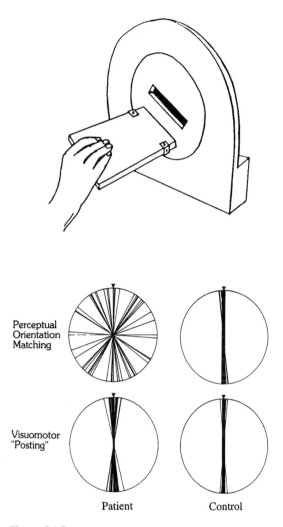

Perceptual Orientation Matching

Visuomotor "Posting"

Patient   Control

Figure 21.2
The diagram at the top of this figure illustrates the apparatus that was used to test sensitivity to orientation in the patient D.F. The slot could be placed in any one of a number of orientations around the clock. Subjects were required to either rotate a hand-held card to match the orientation of the slot or to "post" the card into the slot as shown in this figure. The polar plots at the right of the figure illustrate the orientation of the hand-held card on the perceptual matching task and the visuomotor posting task for D.F. and an age-matched control subject. The correct orientation on each trial has been rotated to vertical. Note that although D.F. was unable to match the orientation of the card to that of the slot in the perceptual matching card, she did rotate the card to the correct orientation as she attempted to insert it into the slot on the posting task.

object and scaled her grip size in a perfectly normal and linear fashion in relation to the target width (Goodale et al. 1991). Yet when she was asked to use her finger and thumb to make a perceptual judgement of the object's width on a separate series of trials, D.F.s' responses were unrelated to the actual stimulus dimensions, and showed high variation from trial to trial.

D.F.'s accurate calibration of grip size during reaching to grasp contrasts markedly with the poor performance of optic ataxic patients with occipitoparietal damage. D.F. is adept as normal subjects in many grasping tasks. In a recent study (Carey et al. 1996), for example, we have shown that when reaching to pick up rectangular shapes that varied in their orientation as well as their width, D.F. showed simultaneously both normal sensitivity to orientation and normal sensitivity to width. She is not entirely normal in dealing with complex shapes however. We found no evidence, for example, that she is able to deal with two different orientations present in a single target object, such as a cross, when reaching to grasp it. Yet, despite this difficulty with two oriented contours, we have found some evidence that the gross shape of an object can influence where D.F. places her fingers (Goodale et al. 1994b; Carey et al. 1996). For an example of D.F.'s sensitivity to shape see figure 21.3, which compares D.F.'s ability with that of a patient with posterior parietal damage.

If, then, we make the plausible assumption that the ventral stream is severely damaged and/or disconnected in D.F. (an assumption that is quite consistent with her pattern of brain damage), it is reasonable to infer that the calibration of these various residual visuomotor skills must depend on intact mechanisms within the dorsal stream. The visual inputs to this stream, which provide the necessary information for coding orientation, size, and shape, could possibly arise via V1, or via the collicular-thalamic route, or via both. Both routes would appear to be available to D.F., since MRI evidence indicates a substantial sparing of V1 in this patient, with no suggestion of collicular or thalamic damage. Patients with lesions of V1, however, although in some cases able to perform such visuomotor tasks at an above-chance level ("blindsight": Perenin and Rossetti 1996; Rossetti 1998), do so far less proficiently than D.F. We therefore believe that the collicular-pulvinar route alone cannot account for her preserved abilities.

Our various studies of D.F. show that she is able to govern many of her actions using visual information of which she has no awareness. But it is clear that this is only true of actions that are targeted directly at the visual stimulus. She cannot successfully use the same visual information to guide an identical but displaced response—a response using the same distal musculature but at another location.

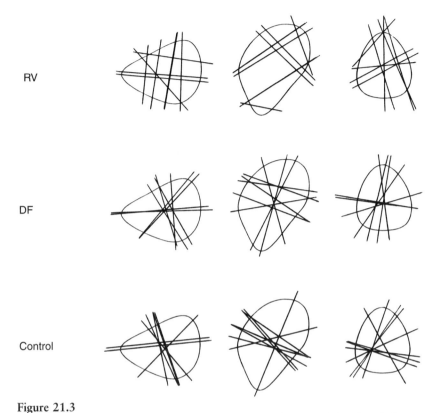

RV

DF

Control

Figure 21.3
The "grasp lines" (joining points where the index finger and the thumb first made contact with the shape) selected by a patient with optic ataxia (R.V.), a patient with visual form agnosia (D.F.), and the control subject when picking up three of twelve shapes that were presented to them. The four different orientations in which each shape was presented have been rotated so that they are aligned. No distinction is made between the points of contact for the thumb and finger in these plots. Notice that D.F.'s grasp lines do not differ from those of the control subject while R.V. often chose unstable grasp points that do not pass through the center of mass of the object.

Presumably the difference is that a response displaced in this way is necessarily an arbitrary or symbolic one—not one that would fall within the natural repertoire of a hard-wired visuomotor control system. Thus D.F. seems to be using a visual processing system dedicated for motor control, which will normally only come into play when she carries out natural goal-directed actions.

There are temporal as well as spatial limits on D.F.'s ability to drive her motor behavior visually. After showing her a rectangular block, Goodale et al. (1994a) asked D.F. to delay for either 2 or 30 seconds with eyes closed, before allowing her to reach out as if to grasp it. Even after a 30-second delay, the preparatory grip size of normal subjects still correlated well with object width. In D.F., however, all evidence of grip scaling during her reaches had evaporated after a delay of even 2 seconds. This failure was not due to a general impairment in short-term memory. Instead, it seems that a delayed reach is no longer a natural movement, and indeed this is so even for normal subjects. A detailed kinematic analysis of the control subjects showed that they moved their hand abnormally in the delay conditions, as if their apparently normal grip scaling was actually generated artificially by imagining the object and then "pantomiming" the grasp. This pantomiming strategy would not have been open to D.F., since she could not have generated a visual image of something that she failed to perceive in the first place. Presumably, the visual processing that is available to her has a very short time constant, because it is designed to deal with present or imminent states of the visual world, and to disregard past states that may no longer be relevant (for example, as a result of self-motion). Rossetti (1998) has recently described a similar loss of visuomotor control in the hemianopic field of a "blindsight" patient following a brief delay. Perhaps more surprisingly, we have recently observed a complementary improvement in visuomotor performance in a bilateral optic ataxic patient (A.T.) after a 5-second delay. Presumably in this case the patient was able to throw off the dominance of the dorsal stream under the delay condition, allowing her to make use of her better-preserved ventral system.

3 Visual Awareness

According to the present interpretation, D.F.'s brain damage has uncovered a visual processing system (specifically the human dorsal stream) that can operate in relative isolation within the domains of size, shape and orientation. D.F. has no explicit awareness of the shapes and sizes that she is able to grasp by virtue of her remaining visual apparatus. We suggest that like D.F., we too carry out these functions using visual information that is not present in our awareness. Indeed, we suggest that in providing visual guidance for our actions the dorsal stream acts in large part alone and independent of any acquired "knowledge base."

One of the ways in which the visual information used by the motor system can be shown to be quite different from that which we experience perceptually is through the study of visual illusions. Gregory (1997) has argued over many years that higher-level visual illusions, including geometric illusions, deceive the perceptual system because the system makes (false) assumptions about the structure of the world based on stored knowledge. These include, for example, assumptions about perceptual stability and spatial constancy. It seems that the dorsal system, by and large, is not deceived by such spatial illusions (Bridgeman et al. 1979, 1981; Wong and Mack 1981; Goodale et al. 1986), perhaps because evolution has taught it that a little "knowledge" can be quite literally a dangerous thing. Instead, the dorsal stream directs our saccadic eye movements and our hand movements to where a target really is, which is not always where our perceptual system tells us it is. Similarly, under appropriate circumstances geometric illusions can be seen to affect visually guided reaching (Gentilucci et al. 1996) and grasping (Aglioti et al. 1995; Brenner and Smeets 1996; Haffenden and Goodale 1998) far less than they affect our perceptual judgments. Thus, we may perceive an object as bigger than it really is, but we open our finger-thumb grip veridically when reaching for it.

We propose that the processing accomplished by the ventral stream both generates and is informed by stored abstract visual knowledge about objects and their spatial relationships. We further surmise that the particular kinds of coding that are necessary to achieve these ends coincide with those that render the representations accessible to our awareness. This would fit with the idea that coded descriptions of enduring object properties, rather than transitory egocentric views, are precisely what we need for mental manipulations such as those required for the planning of action sequences and the mental rehearsal of alternative courses of action.

But, of course, the mere fact that processing occurs in this generalized way in the ventral stream could not be a sufficient condition for its reaching visual awareness. For example, there are generally many items processed in parallel at any given time, most of which will be filtered out of awareness by the operation of selective attention. We have therefore proposed that it is only those items that receive more than a certain threshold level of relative activation—for example, through the sharpening effects of spatial gating processes known to be active during selective attention (e.g., Moran and Desimone 1985; Chelazzi et al. 1993)—that will reach awareness. That is, we are proposing a conjoint requirement for an item to attain visual awareness: (a) a certain kind of coding (one that is object-based and abstracted from the viewer-centerd and egocentric particulars of the visual stimulation that gives rise to it) and (b) a certain level of activation of these coding circuits above the background level of neighboring circuits.

We do not deny, then, that perception can proceed unconsciously under some circumstances, for example, when the stimuli are degraded by masking or short exposure, or when they are outside the current focus of selective attention. We believe that there is good empirical evidence for such "subliminal" perception of complex patterns, processing that is capable of activating semantic representations of certain kinds. Our assumption is that this form of unconscious perception arises through the partial or diffused activation of neuronal assemblies in the ventral stream, and that it does not reach awareness due to the fact that there is insufficient focusing of the activation above the noise of the surrounding assemblies. If this notion is correct, we would predict that such subconscious stimulation, although able to prime certain kinds of semantic decision tasks, would not provide usable inputs to the visuomotor system. Conversely, visual form information that can successfully guide action in a patient like D.F. should not be expected to have significant priming effects on semantic tasks—precisely because that visual processing is never available to conscious experience, even in the normal observer. In short, it may be the case that for an "undetected" visual stimulus to be able to prime decision tasks, it must at least in principle be accessible to consciousness.

4   The Visual Brain in Action

Although we have emphasized the separation of the dorsal and ventral streams, there are of course multiple connections between them, and indeed adaptive goal-directed behavior in humans and other primates must depend on a successful integration of their complementary contributions. Thus, the execution of a goal-directed action might depend on dedicated control systems in the dorsal stream, but the selection of appropriate goal objects and the action to be performed depends on the perceptual machinery of the ventral stream. One of the important questions that remains to be answered is how the two streams interact both with each other and with other brain regions in the production of purposive behavior.

At the level of visual processing, however, the visuomotor modules in the primate parietal lobe function quite independently from the occipitotemporal mechanisms generating perception-based knowledge of the world. Only this latter, perceptual, system can provide suitable raw materials for our thought processes to act upon. In contrast, the other is designed to guide actions purely in the "here and now," and its products are consequently useless for later reference. To put it another way, it is only through knowledge gained via the ventral stream that we can exercise insight, hindsight, and foresight about the visual world. The visuomotor system may be able to give us "blindsight," but in doing so can offer no direct input to our mental life (Weiskrantz 1997).

References

Aglioti, S., Goodale, M. A., and DeSouza, J. F. X. (1995). Size-contrast illusions deceive the eye but not the hand. *Current Biol., 5*, 679–685.

Badcock, C. (1994). *PsychoDarwinism: The new synthesis of Darwin and Freud.* London: HarperCollins.

Benson, D. F., and Greenberg, J. P. (1969). Visual form agnosia: A specific deficit in visual discrimination. *Arch. Neurol., 20*, 82–89.

Brenner, E., and Smeets, J. B. J. (1996). Size illusion influences how we lift but not how we grasp an object. *Experimental Brain Research, 111*, 473–476.

Bridgeman, B., Kirch, M., and Sperling, A. (1981). Segregation of cognitive and motor aspects of visual function using induced motion. *Perceptual Psychophysics, 29*, 336–342.

Bridgeman, B., Lewis, S., Heit, G., and Nagle, M. (1979). Relation between cognitive and motor-oriented systems of visual position perception. *Journal of Experimental Psychology (Human Perception), 5*, 692–700.

Carey, D. P., Harvey, M., and Milner, A. D. (1996). Visuomotor sensitivity for shape and orientation in a patient with visual form agnosia. *Neuropsychologia, 34*, 329–338.

Chelazzi, L., Miller, E. K., Duncan, J., and Desimone, R. (1993). A neural basis for visual search in inferior temporal cortex. *Nature, 363*, 345–347.

Gallese, V., Fadiga, L., Fogassi, L., Luppino, G., and Murata, A. (1997). A parietal-frontal circuit for hand grasping movements in the monkey: Evidence from reversible inactivation experiments. In P. Thier and H.-O. Karnath (Eds.), *Parietal lobe contributions to orientation in 3D-space* (pp. 255–270). Heidelberg: Springer-Verlag.

Gentilucci, M., Chieffi, S., Daprati, E., Saetti, M. C., and Toni, I. (1996). Visual illusion and action. *Neuropsychologia, 34*, 369–376.

Goodale, M. A., Pelisson, D., and Prablanc, C. (1986). Large adjustments in visually guided reaching do not depend on vision of the hand or perception of target displacement. *Nature, 320*, 748–750.

Goodale, M. A., Milner, A. D., Jakobson, L. S., and Carey, D. P. (1991). A neurological dissociation between perceiving objects and grasping them. *Nature, 349,* 154–156.

Goodale, M. A., Jakobson, L. S., and Keillor, J. M. (1994a). Differences in the visual control of pantomimed and natural grasping movements. *Neuropsychologia, 32,* 1159–1178.

Goodale, M. A., Meenan, J. P., Buelthoff, H. H., Nicolle, D. A., Murphy, K. J., and Racicot, C. I. (1994b). Separate neural pathways for the visual analysis of object shape in perception and prehension. *Current Biol., 4,* 604–610.

Gregory, R. (1997). Knowledge in perception and illusion. *Philosophical Transactions of the Royal Society of London B, 352,* 1121–1127.

Haffenden, A. M., and Goodale, M. A. (1998). The effect of pictorial illusion on prehension and perception. *Journal of Cognitive Neuroscience, 10,* 122–136.

Harvey, M. (1995). Translation of "Psychic paralysis of gaze, optic ataxia, and spatial disorder of attention" by Rudolph Balint. *Cognitive Neuropsychology, 12,* 261–282.

Jeannerod, M. (1986). The formation of finger grip during prehension: a cortically mediated visuomotor pattern. *Behavioral Brain Research, 19,* 99–116.

Kawashima, R., Naitoh, E., Matsumura, M., Itoh, H., Ono, S., Satoh, K., Gotoh, R., Koyama, M., Inoue, K., Yoshioka, S., and Fukuda, H. (1996). Topographic representation in human intraparietal sulcus of reaching and saccade. *Neuroreport, 7,* 1253–1256.

Kluever, H., and Bucy, P. C. (1938). An analysis of certain effects of bilateral temporal lobectomy in the rhesus monkey, with special reference to "psychic blindness." *Journal of Psychology, 5,* 33–54.

Milner, A. D., and Goodale, M. A. (1993). Visual pathways to perception and action. In T. P. Hicks, S. Molotchnikoff and T. Ono (Eds.), *Progress in Brain Research, Vol. 95* (pp. 317–337). Amsterdam: Elsevier.

Milner, A. D., and Goodale, M. A. (1998). *The visual brain in action.* Oxford Psychology Series, No. 27. Oxford: Oxford University Press.

Milner, A. D., Perrett, D. I., Johnston, R. S., Benson, P. J., Jordan, T. R., Heeley, D. W., Bettucci, D., Mortara, F., Mutani, R., Terazzi, E., and Davidson, D. L. W. (1991). Perception and action in visual form agnosia. *Brain, 114,* 405–428.

Moran, J., and Desimone, R. (1985). Selective attention gates visual processing in the extrastriate cortex. *Science, 229,* 782–784.

Perenin, M.-T., and Rossetti, Y. (1996). Grasping without form discrimination in a hemianopic field. *Neuroreport, 7,* 793–797.

Perenin, M.-T., and Vighetto, A. (1988). Optic ataxia: A specific disruption in visuomotor mechanisms. I. Different aspects of the deficit in reaching for objects. *Brain, 111,* 643–674.

Rizzolatti, G., Camarda, R., Fogassi, L., Gentilucci, M., Luppino, G., and Matelli, M. (1988). Functional organization of inferior area 6 in the macaque monkey. II. Area F5 and the control of distal movements. *Experimental Brain Research, 71,* 491–507.

Rossetti, Y. (1998). Implicit perception in action: short-lived motor representations of space. *Consciousness and Cognition, 7,* 520–558.

Sakata, H., Taira, M., Murata, A., Gallese, V., Tanaka, Y., Shikata, E., and Kusunoki, M. (1997). Parietal visual neurons coding 3-D characteristics of objects and their relation to hand action. In P. Thier and H.-O. Karnath (Eds.), *Parietal lobe contributions to orientation in 3D space* (pp. 237–254). Heidelberg: Springer-Verlag.

Snyder, L. H., Batista, A. P., and Andersen, R. A. (1997). Coding of intention in the posterior parietal cortex. *Nature, 386,* 167–170.

Ungerleider, L. G., and Mishkin, M. (1982). Two cortical visual systems. In D. J. Ingle, M. A. Goodale, and R. J. W. Mansfield (Eds.), *Analysis of visual behavior* (pp. 549–586). Cambridge, MA: The MIT Press.

Weiskrantz, L. (1997). *Consciousness lost and found.* Oxford: Oxford University Press.

Wong, E., and Mack, A. (1981). Saccadic programming and perceived location. *Acta Psychologica, 48,* 123–131.

Zeki, S. (1993). *A vision of the brain.* Oxford: Blackwell.

22

What Is a Neural Correlate of Consciousness?

David J. Chalmers

The search for neural correlates of consciousness (NCCs) is arguably the corner-stone of the recent resurgence of the science of consciousness. The search poses many difficult empirical problems, but it seems to be tractable in principle, and some ingenious studies in recent years have led to considerable progress. A number of proposals have been put forward concerning the nature and location of neural correlates of consciousness.

A few of these include 40-hertz oscillations in the cerebral cortex (Crick and Koch 1990), intralaminar nuclei in the thalamus (Bogen 1995), reentrant loops in thalamocortical systems (Edelman 1989), 40-hertz rhythmic activity in thalamocortical systems (Llinás et al. 1994), extended reticular-thalamic activation system (Newman and Baars 1993), neural assemblies bound by NMDA (Flohr 1995), certain neurochemical levels of activation (Hobson 1997), certain neurons in the inferior temporal cortex (Sheinberg and Logothetis 1997), neurons in the extrastriate visual cortex projecting to prefrontal areas (Crick and Koch 1995), and visual processing within the ventral stream (Milner and Goodale 1995). (A longer list can be found in Chalmers 1998. Review articles on neural correlates of consciousness, especially visual consciousness, can be found in Crick and Koch 1998 and Milner 1995.)

As the full title of T. Metzinger's book *Neural Correlates of Consciousness: Empirical and Conceptual Questions* (The MIT Press, 2000) suggests, all this activity raises a number of difficult conceptual and foundational issues. I can see at least five sorts of foundational questions: (1) What do we mean by "consciousness"? (2) What do we mean by "neural correlate of consciousness"? (3) How can we find the neural correlate(s) of consciousness? (4) What will a neural correlate of consciousness explain? (5) Is consciousness reducible to its neural correlate(s)?

The first two questions are conceptual questions, the third is an epistemological or methodological question, the fourth is an explanatory question, and the fifth is an ontological question. The first, fourth, and fifth are versions of general questions that philosophers have discussed for a long time (my own view on them is in Chalmers 1995; 1996). The second and third questions are more specific to the NCC investigation. I have discussed the third question in Chalmers (1998). Here I want to focus on the second question.

What does it mean to be a neural correlate of consciousness? At first glance, the answer might seem to be so obvious that the question is hardly worth asking. An NCC is a neural state that directly correlates with a conscious state, or that directly generates consciousness, or something like that. One has a simple image: When your NCC is active, perhaps your consciousness turns on in a corresponding way. But a moment's reflection suggests that the idea is not completely straightforward, and that the concept needs some clarification.

Here, I will attempt a little conceptual spadework in clarifying the concept of an NCC. I don't know that this is the deepest problem in the area, but it seems to me that if we are looking for an NCC, it makes sense to get clear on what we are looking for. On the way I will try to make contact with some of the empirical work in the area, and see what concept of NCC is at play in some of the central work in the field. I will also draw out some consequences for the methodology of empirical work in the search. Most of this is intended as a first step rather than a last word. Much of what I say will need to be refined, but I hope at least to draw attention to some interesting issues in the vicinity.

As a first pass, we can use the definition of a neural correlate of consciousness given in the program of the ASSC conference. This says a neural correlate of consciousness is a "specific system in the brain whose activity correlates directly with states of conscious experience." This yields something like the following:

A neural system N is an NCC if the state of N correlates directly with states of consciousness.

There are at least two things to get clear on here. First, what are the relevant "states of consciousness"? Second, what does it mean for a neural state to "correlate directly" with states of consciousness? I will look into both these things in turn.

States of Consciousness

I will take it that the states of consciousness we are concerned with here are states of subjective experience or, equivalently, states of phenomenal consciousness. But what *sorts* of states are relevant? In the NCC literature, I can see a few different classes of states that are sometimes considered.

Being Conscious

The first option is that the states in question are those of being conscious and of not being conscious. The corresponding notion of an NCC will be that of a neural system whose state directly correlates with whether a subject is conscious or not. If the NCC is in a particular state, the subject will be conscious. If the NCC is not in that state, the subject will not be conscious.

This is perhaps the idea that first comes to mind when we think about an NCC. We might think about it as the "neural correlate of creature consciousness," where creature consciousness is the property a creature has when it is conscious, and lacks when it is not conscious.

Although this is an interesting notion, it does not seem to capture the sort of NCC that most work in the area is aimed at. As we'll see, most current work is aimed at something more specific. There are, however, some ideas that can be taken as aiming at this notion at least in part. For example, the ideas of Bogen (1995) about the intralaminar nucleus seem to be directed at least in part at this sort of NCC.

Examining current work, it's interesting to note that insofar as there is any consensus at all about the location of this sort of NCC, the dominant view seems to be that it should be in or around the thalamus, or at least that it should involve interactions between the thalamic and cortical systems in a central role. Penfield (1937) argued that "the indispensable substratum of consciousness" lies outside the cerebral cortex, probably in the diencephalon (thalamus, hypothalamus, subthalamus, epithalamus). This theme has been taken up in recent years by Bogen, Newman and Baars (1993), and others.

Background State of Consciousness

A related idea is that of the neural correlate of what we might call the background state of consciousness. A background state is an overall state of consciousness such as being awake, being asleep, dreaming, being under hypnosis, and so on. Exactly what counts as a background state is not entirely clear, since one can divide things up in a number of ways, and with coarser or finer grains; but presumably the class will include a range of normal and of "altered" states.

We can think of this as a slightly finer-grained version of the previous idea. Creature consciousness is the coarsest-grained background state of consciousness:

it is just the state of being conscious. Background states will usually be finer-grained than this, but they still will not be defined in terms of specific contents or modalities.

A neural correlate of the background state of consciousness, then, will be a neural system N such that the state of N directly correlates with whether a subject is awake, dreaming, under hypnosis, and so on. If N is in state 1, the subject is awake; if N is in state 2, the subject is dreaming; if N is in state 3, the subject is under hypnosis; and so on.

It may well be that some of the thalamocortical proposals discussed above are intended as, or might be extended into, proposals about this sort of NCC. A more direct example is given by Hobson's (1997) ideas about neurochemical levels of activation. Hobson holds that these levels can be grouped into a three-dimensional state-space, and that different regions in this space correspond to different overall states of consciousness: wakefulness, REM sleep, non-REM sleep, and so on. When chemical levels are in a particular region in this space, the subject will be awake; when they are in another region, the subject will be in REM sleep; and so on. On this reading, one might see the neurochemical system as an NCC of the sort characterized above, with the different regions in state-space corresponding to correlates of the various specific background states.

Contents of Consciousness

There is much more to consciousness than the mere state of being conscious, or the background state of consciousness. Arguably the most interesting states of consciousness are *specific* states: the fine-grained states of subjective experience that one is in at any given time. Such states might include the experience of a particular visual image, of a particular sound pattern, of a detailed stream of conscious thought, and so on. A detailed visual experience, for example, might include the experience of certain shapes and colors in one's environment, of specific arrangements of objects, of various relative distances and depths, and so on.

Specific states like these are most often individuated by their *content*. Most conscious states seem to have some sort of specific content representing the world as being one way or another. Much of the specific nature of a visual experience, for example, can be characterized in terms of content. A visual experience typically represents the world as containing various shapes and colors, as containing certain objects standing in certain spatial relations, and so on. If the experience is veridical, the world will be the way the experience represents it as being. If the experience is an illusion or is otherwise misleading, the world will be other than the experience represents it. But either way, it seems that visual experiences typically have detailed representational content. The same goes for experiences in other sensory modalities, and arguably for many or most nonsensory experiences as well.

Much of the most interesting work on NCCs is concerned with states like these. This is work on the neural correlates of the contents of consciousness. Much work on the neural correlates of visual consciousness has this character, for example. This work is not concerned merely with the neural states that determine that one *has* visual consciousness; it is concerned with the neural states that determine the specific contents of visual consciousness.

A nice example is supplied by the work of Logothetis and colleagues on the NCC of visual consciousness in monkeys (Logothetis and Schall 1989; Leopold and Logothetis 1996; Sheinberg and Logothetis 1997). In this work, a monkey is trained to press various bars when it is confronted with various sorts of images: horizontal and vertical gratings, for example, or gratings drifting left and right, or faces and sunbursts (I will use horizontal and vertical gratings for the purposes of illustration). After training is complete, the monkey is presented with two stimuli at once, one to each eye. In humans, this usually produces binocular rivalry, with alternating periods of experiencing a definite image, and occasional partial overlap. The monkey responds by pressing bars, in effect "telling" the experimenter what it is seeing: a horizontal grating, or a vertical grating, or an interlocking grid.

At the same time, neurons in the monkey's cortex are being monitored by electrodes. It is first established that certain neurons respond to certain stimuli: to horizontal lines, for example, or to flowers. Then these neurons are monitored in the binocular rivalry situation, to see how well they correlate with what the monkey seems to be seeing. It turns out that cells in the primary visual cortex (V1) don't correlate well: When the monkey is stimulated with horizontal and vertical gratings but "sees" horizontal, a large number of "vertical" cells in V1 fire as well. At this point, most cells seem to correlate with retinal stimulus, not with visual percept. But farther into the visual system, the correlation increases, until in the inferior temporal (IT) cortex, there is a very strong correlation. When the monkey is stimulated with horizontal and vertical grating but "sees" horizontal, almost all of the relevant horizontal cells in IT fire, and almost none of the vertical cells do. When the monkey's response switches, indicating that it is now "seeing" vertical, the cell response switches accordingly.

These results naturally lend themselves to speculation about the location of a visual NCC. It seems that V1 is unlikely to be or to involve an NCC, for example, due to the failure of V1 cells to correlate with the contents of consciousness. Of course there are still the possibilities that some small subset of V1 is an NCC, or that V1 is a neural correlate of some aspects of visual consciousness but not of others, but I leave those aside for now. On the other hand, IT seems to be a natural candidate for the location of an NCC, due to the strong correlation of its cells with the content of consciousness. At least it is natural to suppose that IT is a "lower bound" on the location of a visual NCC (due to the failure of strong correlation before then), though the NCC itself may be farther in. None of this evidence is conclusive (and Logothetis and colleagues are appropriately cautious), but it is at least suggestive.

It is clear that this work is concerned with the neural correlates of the *contents* of visual consciousness. We are interested in finding cortical areas whose neural activity correlates with and predicts specific contents of consciousness, such as experiences of horizontal or vertical lines, or of flowers or sunbursts. The ideal is to find a neural system from whose activity we might determine the precise contents of a visual experience, or at least its contents in certain respects (shape, color, and the like).

Interestingly, it seems that in doing this we are crucially concerned with the representational contents of the neural systems themselves. In the Logothetis work, for example, it is important to determine the receptive fields of the cells (whether they respond to horizontal or vertical gratings, for example), in order to see whether the receptive fields of active cells match up with the apparent contents of visual consciousness. In essence, the receptive field is acting at least as a heuristic way of getting at representational content in the neurons in question. Then the crucial question is whether the representational content in the neural system matches up with the representational content in visual consciousness.

This suggests a natural definition of a neural correlate of the contents of consciousness:

A neural correlate of the contents of consciousness is a neural representational system N such that representation of a content in N directly correlates with representation of that content in consciousness.

Or, more briefly:

A content NCC is a neural representational system N such that the content of N directly correlates with the content of consciousness.

For example, the Logothetis work lends itself to the speculation that IT might contain a content NCC for visual consciousness, since the content of cells in IT seems to correlate directly (at least in these experiments) with the contents of visual consciousness. (Much more investigation is required to see whether this correlation holds across the board, of course.)

This definition requires that we have some way of defining the representational content of a neural system independent of the contents of consciousness. There are various ways to do this. Using a cell's receptive field to define its representational content is probably the simplest. A more refined definition might also give a role to a system's projective field, and to the sort of behavior which activity in that system typically leads to. And there may be still more complex notions of representational content, based on complex correlations with the environment, patterns of behavior, and activity in other cells. But even a crude definition of representational content (e.g., the receptive field definition) is good enough for many purposes, and can yield informative results about the visual NCC.

It is arguable that much work on the visual NCC tacitly invokes this sort of definition. Another example is Milner and Goodale's (1995) work on the two pathways of visual perception. They suggest that the ventral stream is largely for cognitive identification and decision, while the dorsal stream is largely for on-line motor response; and that visual consciousness correlates with activity in the ventral stream.

Much of the support for this work lies with patients who have dissociations between specific contents of conscious perception and the contents involved in motor response. For example, a subject with visual form agnosia (e.g., Milner and Goodale's patient D.F.) cannot consciously identify a vertical slot but can "post" an envelope through it without problem; subjects with optic ataxia (e.g., those with Balint's syndrome) can identify an object but cannot act appropriately toward it. The dissociations here appear to go along with damage to the ventral and dorsal pathways, respectively.

What seems to be going on, on a natural interpretation of these results and of Milner and Goodale's hypothesis, is that for these subjects, there is a dissociation between the contents represented in the ventral pathway and those represented in the dorsal pathway. In these cases, the character of a motor response appears to be determined by the contents represented in the dorsal pathway, but the character of conscious perception appears to be determined by the contents represented in the ventral pathway.

Thus one can see Milner and Goodale's hypothesis as involving the suggestion that the ventral stream contains the neural correlates of the contents of visual consciousness. The hypothesis is quite speculative, of course (though it is interesting to note that IT lies in the ventral stream), but it seems that the content-based analysis provides a natural interpretation of what the hypothesis is implicitly claiming in regard to the visual NCC, and of what may follow if the hypothesis turns out to be correct.

One could give a similar analysis of much or most work on the visual NCC. When Crick and Koch (1998) propose that the visual NCC lies outside V1, for example, much of the experimental evidence they appeal to involves cases where some content is represented in consciousness but not in V1, or vice versa. For example, Gur and Snodderly (1997) show that for some quickly alternating isoluminant color stimuli, color cells in V1 flicker back and forth even though a single fused color is consciously perceived. And results by He et al. (1996) suggest that orientation of a grating can fade from consciousness even though orientation cells in V1 carry the information. The results are not entirely conclusive, but they suggest a mismatch between the representational content in V1 and the content of consciousness.

One can apply this sort of analysis equally to NCCs in other sensory modalities. An NCC of auditory consciousness, for example, might be defined as a neural representational system whose contents correlate directly with the contents of auditory consciousness: loudness, direction, pitch, tone, and the like. The idea can arguably apply to defining the neural correlates of bodily sensations, of conscious mental imagery, and perhaps of conscious emotion and of the stream of conscious thought. All these aspects of consciousness can be naturally analyzed (at least in part) in terms of their content. In looking for their respective NCCs, we may ultimately be looking for neural systems whose content correlates with the contents of these aspects of consciousness.

Arbitrary Phenomenal Properties

(This section is more technical than those above, and may be skipped by those not interested in philosophical details.)

One might try to give a general definition of an NCC of various states of consciousness, of which each of the above would be a special case. To do this, one would need a general way of thinking about arbitrary states of consciousness. Perhaps the best way is to think in terms of arbitrary *phenomenal properties*. For any distinctive kind of conscious experience, there will be a corresponding phenomenal property: in essence, the property of having a conscious experience of that kind. For example, being in a hypnotic state of consciousness is a phenomenal property; having a visual experience of a horizontal line is a phenomenal property; feeling intense happiness is a phenomenal property; feeling a throbbing pain is a phenomenal property; being conscious is a phenomenal property. Phenomenal properties can be as coarse-grained or as fine-grained as you like, so long as they are wholly determined by the current conscious state of the subject.

With this notion in hand, one might try to define the neural correlate of an arbitrary phenomenal property P:

A state N1 of system N is a neural correlate of phenomenal property P if N's being in N1 directly correlates with the subject having P.

Note that we here talk of a *state* being an NCC. Given a *specific* phenomenal property—experiencing a horizontal line, for example—it is no longer clear that it makes sense to speak of a given system being the NCC of that property. Rather, it will be a particular state of that system. Neural firing in certain horizontal cells in IT (say) might be a neural correlate of seeing a horizontal line, for example; and having one's neurochemical system in a certain region of state-space might be a neural correlate of waking consciousness, on Hobson's hypothesis. These are specific states of the neural systems in question.

Most of the time, we are not concerned with neural correlates of single phenomenal properties, but of *families* of phenomenal properties. Hobson is concerned not just with the neural correlate of waking consciousness, for example, but with the neural correlate of the whole family of background states of consciousness. Work on the visual NCC is not concerned with just the neural correlate of horizontal experience, but with the neural correlates of the whole system of visual experiential contents.

We might say a *phenomenal family* is a set of mutually exclusive phenomenal properties that jointly partition the space of conscious experiences, or at least some subset of that space. That is, any subject having an experience (of a certain relevant kind) will have a phenomenal property in the family, and will not have more than one such property. Specific contents of visual consciousness make a phenomenal family, for example: Any visually conscious subject will have some specific visual content, and it will not have two contents at once (given that we are talking about *overall* visual content). The same goes for contents at a particular location in the visual field: Anyone with an experience of a certain location will have some specific content associated with that location (a red horizontal line, say), and not more than one. (Ambiguous experiences are not counterexamples here, as long as we include ambiguous contents as members of the family in question.) The same goes for color experience at any given location: There will be a phenomenal family (one property for each color quality) for any such location. And the same is true for background states of consciousness. All these sets of phenomenal properties make phenomenal families. We can then say:

A neural correlate of a phenomenal family S is a neural system N such that the state of N directly correlates with the subject's phenomenal property in S.

For any phenomenal family S, a subject will have at most one property in S (one background state, or one overall state of visual consciousness, or one color quality at a location). Neural system N will be an NCC of S when there are a corresponding number of states of N, one for every property in P, such that N's being in a given state directly correlates with the subject's having the corresponding phenomenal property. This template can be seen to apply to most of the definitions given above.

For the neural correlate of creature consciousness, we have a simple phenomenal family with two properties: being conscious and not being conscious. An NCC here will be a system with two states that correlate with these two properties.

For the neural correlate of a background state of consciousness, we have a phenomenal family with a few more properties: dreaming, being in an ordinary waking state, being under hypnosis, and so on. An NCC here will be a neural system with a few states that correlate directly with these properties. Hobson's neurochemical system would be an example.

For the neural correlate of contents of consciousness, one will have a much more complex phenomenal family (overall states of visual consciousness, or states of color consciousness at a location, or particular conscious occurrent thoughts), and a neural representational system to match. The state of the NCC will correlate directly with the specific phenomenal property.

Notice that in the content case, there is an extra strong requirement on the NCC. In the other cases, we have accepted an arbitrary match of neural states to phenomenal states—any state can serve as the neural correlate of a dreaming state of background consciousness, for example. But where content is concerned, not any neural state will do. We require that the *content* of the neural state in question match the content of consciousness. This is a much stronger requirement.

It is arguable that this requirement delivers much greater explanatory and predictive power in the case of neural correlates of conscious content. The systematicity in the correlation means that it can be extended to predict the presence or absence of phenomenal features that may not have been present in the initial empirical data set, for example. And it also will dovetail more nicely with finding a mechanism and a functional role for the NCC that match the role we associate with a given conscious state.

It is this systematicity in the correlation that makes the current work on the neural correlate of visual consciousness particularly interesting. Without it, things would be much more untidy. Imagine that we find arbitrary neural states which correlate directly with the experience of horizontal lines (for example) such that there is no corresponding representational content in the neural state. Instead, we match seemingly arbitrary states N1 with horizontal, N2 with vertical, and so on. Will we count this as a neural correlate of the contents of visual consciousness? If we do, it will be in a much weaker sense, and in a way that will lead to much less explanatory and predictive power.

One might then hope to extend this sort of systematicity to other, noncontent-involving phenomenal families. For example, one might find among background states of consciousness some pattern or some dimension along which they vary systematically (some sort of intensity dimension, for example, or a measure of alertness). If we could then find a neural system whose states do not arbitrarily correlate with the phenomenal states in question, but vary along a corresponding systematic dimension, then the NCC in question will have much greater potential explanatory and predictive power. So this sort of systematicity in phenomenal families is something we should look for, and something we should look to match in potential neural correlates.

Perhaps one could define a "systematic NCC" as a neural correlate of a phenomenal family such that states correlate with each other in some such systematic way. I will not try to give a general abstract definition here, since things are getting complex enough, but I think one can see a glimmer of how it might go. I will, however, keep using the neural correlate of the contents of consciousness (especially visual consciousness) as the paradigmatic example of an NCC, precisely because its definition builds in such a notion of systematicity, with the corresponding explanatory and predictive power.

Direct Correlation

The other thing that we need to clarify is the notion of "direct correlation." We have said that an NCC is a system whose state correlates directly with a state of consciousness, but what does direct correlation involve, exactly? Is it required that the neural system be necessary and sufficient for consciousness, for example, or merely sufficient? And over what range of cases must the correlation obtain for the system to count as an NCC? Any possible case? A relevantly constrained set of cases? And so on.

The paradigmatic case will involve a neural system N with states that correlate with states of consciousness. So we can say that

state of N---state of consciousness

and, specifically,

N is in state N1---subject has conscious state C.

In the case of the contents of consciousness, we have a system N such that representing a content in N directly correlates with representation in consciousness. So we can say

representing C in N---representing C in consciousness.

The question in all these cases concerns the nature of the required relation (represented here as "---"). How strong a relation is required here for N to be an NCC?

Necessity, Sufficiency?

The first question is whether the NCC state is required to be necessary and sufficient for the conscious state, merely sufficient, or something else in the vicinity.

Necessity and Sufficiency   The first possibility is that the state of N is necessary and sufficient for the corresponding state of consciousness. This is an attractive requirement for an NCC, but it is arguably too strong. It might turn out that there is more than one neural correlate of a given conscious state. For example, it may be there there are two systems, M and N, such that a certain state of M suffices for being in pain and a certain state of N also suffices for being in pain, where these two states are not themselves always correlated. In this case, it seems that we would likely say that both M and N (or their corresponding states) are neural correlates of pain. But it is not the case that activity in M is necessary and sufficient for pain (since it is not necessary), and the same goes for N. If both M and N are to count as NCCs here, we cannot require an NCC to be necessary *and* sufficient.

Sufficiency   From the above, it seems plausible that we require only that an NCC state be *sufficient* for the corresponding state of consciousness. But is any sufficient state an NCC? If it is, then it seems that the whole brain will count as an NCC of any state of consciousness. The whole brain will count as an NCC of pain, for example, since being in a certain total state of the whole brain will suffice for being in pain. Perhaps there is some very weak sense in which this makes sense, but it does not seem to capture what researchers in the field are after when looking for an NCC. So something more than mere sufficiency is required.

Minimal Sufficiency   The trouble with requiring mere sufficiency, intuitively, is that it allows irrelevant processes into an NCC. If N is an NCC, then the system obtained by conjoining N with a neighboring system M will also qualify as an NCC by the previous definition, since the state of N + M will suffice for the relevant states of consciousness.

The obvious remedy is to require that an NCC has to be a *minimal sufficient system*: that is, a *minimal* system whose state is sufficient for the corresponding conscious state. By this definition, N will be an NCC when (1) the states of N suffice for the corresponding states of consciousness, and (2) no proper part M of N is such that the states of M suffice for the corresponding states of consciousness. In this way, we pare down any potential NCC to its core: Any irrelevant material will be whittled away, and an NCC will be required to contain only the core processes that suffice for the conscious state in question.

Note that on this definition, there may be more than one NCC for a given conscious state. It may be that there is more than one minimal sufficient system for a given state, and all of these will count as a neural correlate of that state. The same goes for systems of phenomenal states. This seems to be the right result: We cannot know a priori that there will be only one NCC for a given state or system of states. Whether there will actually be one or more than one for any given state, however, is something that can be determined only empirically.

There is a technical problem for the minimality requirement. It may turn out that there is significant redundancy in a neural correlate of consciousness, such that, for example, a given conscious visual content is represented redundantly in many cells in a given area. If this is so, then that visual area as a whole might not qualify as a minimal sufficient system, since various smaller components of it might themselves correlate with the conscious state. In this case the definition above would imply that various such small components would each be an NCC. One could deal with this sort of case by noting that the problem arises only when the states of the various smaller systems are themselves wholly correlated with each other. (If their mutual correlation can be broken, so can their correlation with consciousness, so that the overall system or some key subsystem will again emerge as the true NCC). Given this, one could stipulate that where states of minimal sufficient systems are wholly correlated with each other, it is the union of the system that should be regarded as an NCC, rather than the individual systems. So an NCC would be a minimal system whose state is sufficient for a given conscious state and is not wholly correlated with the state of any other system. I will pass over this complication in what follows.

What Range of Cases?
An NCC will be a minimal neural system N such that the state of N is sufficient for a corresponding conscious state C. This is to say: If the system is in state N1, the subject will have conscious state C. But the question now arises: Over what range of cases must the correlation in question hold?

There is sometimes a temptation to say that this question does not need to be answered: All that is required is to say that *in this very case*, neural state N1 suffices for or correlates with conscious state C. But this does not really make sense. There is no such thing as a single-case correlation. Correlation is always defined with respect to a range of cases. The same goes for sufficiency. To say that neural state N1 suffices for conscious state C is to say that in a range of cases, neural state N1 will always be accompanied by conscious state C. But what is the range of cases?

Any Possible Case   It is momentarily tempting to suggest that the correlation should range across any possible case: If N is an NCC, it should be impossible to be in a relevant state of N without being in the corresponding state of consciousness. But a moment's reflection suggests that this is incompatible with the common usage in the field. NCCs are often supposed to be relatively limited systems, such as the inferior temporal cortex or the intralaminar nucleus. But nobody (or almost nobody) holds that if one excises the entire inferior temporal cortex or intralaminar nucleus and puts it in a jar, and puts the system into a relevant state, it will be accompanied by the corresponding state of consciousness.

That is to say, for a given NCC, it certainly seems *possible* that one can have the NCC state without the corresponding conscious state—for example, by performing sufficiently radical lesions. So we cannot require that the correlation range over all possible cases.

Of course, one could always insist that a *true* NCC must be such that it is impossible to have the NCC state without the corresponding conscious state. The consequence of this would be that an NCC would almost certainly be far larger than it is on any current hypothesis, since we would have to build in a large amount of the brain to make sure that all the background conditions are in place. Perhaps it would be some sort of wide-ranging although skeletal brain state, involving aspects of processes from a number of regions of the brain. This might be a valid usage, but it is clear that this is not what researchers in the field are getting at when they are talking about an NCC.

We might call the notion just defined a *total* NCC, since it builds in the totality of physical processes that are absolutely required for a given conscious state. The notion that is current in the field is more akin to that of a *core* NCC. (I adapt this terminology from Shoemaker's [1981] notion of a "total realization" and a "core realization" of a functional mental state.) A total NCC builds in everything and thus automatically suffices for the corresponding conscious states. A core NCC, on the other hand, contains only the "core" processes that correlate with consciousness. The rest of the total NCC will be relegated to some sort of background conditions required for the correct functioning of the core.

(Philosophical note: The sort of possibility being considered here is natural or nomological possibility, or possibility compatible with the laws of nature. If we required correlation across all *logically* possible cases, there might be no total NCC at all, since it is arguably logically possible, or coherently conceivable, to instantiate any physical process at all without consciousness. But it is probably not naturally possible. It is almost certainly naturally necessary that a being with my brain state will have the same sort of conscious state as I, for example. So natural possibility is the relevant sort for defining the correlation here.)

The question is, then, how to distinguish the core from the background. It seems that what is required for an NCC (in the "core" sense) is not that it correlate with consciousness across any possible conditions, but rather that it correlate across some constrained range of cases in which some aspects of normal brain functioning are held constant. The question then becomes What is to be held constant? Across just what constrained range of cases do we require that an NCC correlate with consciousness?

Ordinary Functioning Brain in Ordinary Environments One might take the moral of the above to be that one cannot require an NCC to correlate with consciousness in "unnatural" cases. What matters is that the NCC correlates with consciousness in "natural" cases, those which actually occur in the functioning of a normal brain.

The most conservative strategy would be to require correlation only across cases involving a normally functioning brain in a normal environment, receiving "ecologically valid" inputs of the sort received in a normal life.

The trouble with this criterion is that it seems too weak to narrow down the NCC. It may turn out that this way, we find NCCs at all stages of the visual system, for example. In the normal visual environment, we can expect that the contents of visual systems from V1 through IT will all correlate with the contents of visual consciousness, and that even the contents of the retina will do so to some extent. The reason is that in normal cases all these will be linked in a straightforward causal chain, and the systems in question will not be dissociated. But it seems wrong to say that merely because of this, all the systems (perhaps even the retina) should count as an NCC.

The moral of this is that we need a finer-grained criterion to dissociate these systems and to distinguish the core NCC from processes that are merely causally linked to it. To do this, we have to require correlation across a range of *unusual cases* as well as across normal cases, since it is these cases that yield interesting dissociations.

Normal Brain, Unusual Inputs   The next most conservative suggestion is that we still require a normal brain for our range of cases, but that we allow any possible inputs, including "ecologically invalid" inputs. This would cover the Logothetis experiments, for example. The inputs that evoke binocular rivalry are certainly unusual, and are not encountered in a normal environment. But it is precisely these that allow the experiments to make finer-grained distinctions than we normally can. The experiments suggest that IT is more likely than V1 to be an NCC, precisely because it correlates with consciousness across the wider range of cases. If states of V1 truly do not match up with states of consciousness in this situation, then it seems that V1 cannot be an NCC. If that reasoning is correct, then it seems that we require an NCC to correlate with consciousness across all unusual inputs, and not just across normal environments.

The extension of the correlation requirement from normal environments to unusual inputs is a relatively "safe" extension and seems a reasonable requirement, though those who place a high premium on ecological validity might contest it. But it is arguable that this is still too weak to do the fine-grained work in distinguishing an NCC from systems linked to it. Presumably unusual inputs will go only so far in yielding interesting dissociations, and some systems (particularly those well down the processing pathway) may well remain associated with each other on any unusual inputs. So it is arguable that we will need finer-grained tools to distinguish the NCC.

Normal Brain, Varying Brain Stimulation   The next possibility is to allow cases involving not just unusual inputs, but also direct stimulation of the brain. Such direct stimulation might include both electrode stimulation and transcranial magnetic stimulation. On this view, we will require that an NCC correlate with consciousness across all cases of brain stimulation, as well as normal functioning. So if we have a potential NCC state that does not correlate with consciousness in a brain stimulation condition, that state will not be a true NCC.

This requirement seems to fit some methods used in the field. Penfield (e.g., Penfield and Rasmussen 1950) pioneered the use of brain stimulation to draw conclusions about the neural bases of consciousness. Libet (1982) has also used brain stimulation to good effect, and more recently Newsome and colleagues (e.g., Salzman et al. 1990) have used brain stimulation to draw some conclusions about neural correlates of motion perception in monkeys. (See also Marge 1991 for a review of transcranial magnetic stimulation in vision.)

Clearly, brain stimulation can be used to produce dissociations that are finer-grained than can be produced with unusual inputs. One might be able to dissociate activity in any system from that in a preceding system by stimulating that system directly, for example, as long as there are not too many backward connections. Given a candidate NCC—inferior temporal cortex, say—one can test the hypothesis by stimulating an area immediately following the candidate in the processing pathway. If that yields a relevant conscious state without relevant activity in IT (say), that indicates that IT is probably not a true NCC after all. Rather, the NCC may lie in a system farther down the processing chain. (I leave aside the possibility that there might be two NCCs at different stages of the chain.)

This reasoning seems sound, suggesting that we may tacitly require an NCC to correlate with consciousness across brain stimulation conditions. There is no immediately obvious problem with the requirement, at least when the stimulation in question is relatively small and localized. If one allows arbitrarily large stimulation, there may be problems. For example, one presumably could use brain stimulation, at least in principle, to disable large areas of the brain (by over-stimulating them, for example) while leaving NCC activity intact. In this case, it is not implausible to expect that one will have the relevant NCC activity without the usual conscious state (just as in the case where one lesions the whole NCC and puts it in a jar), so the correlation will fail in this case. But intuitively, this does not seem to disprove the claim that the NCC in question is a true NCC, at least before the stimulation. If that is so, then we cannot allow unlimited brain stimulation in the range of cases relevant to the correlation; and, more generally, some of the problems with lesions (discussed below) may apply to reasoning that involves brain stimulation. Nevertheless, one might well require that an NCC correlate with consciousness at least across cases of limited stimulation, in the absence of strong reason to believe otherwise.

Abnormal Functioning Due to Lesions   In almost all of the cases above, we have retained a normally functioning brain; we have just stimulated it in unusual ways. The next logical step is to allow cases where the brain is not functioning normally, due to lesions in brain systems. Such lesions might be either natural (e.g., due to some sort of brain damage) or artificial (e.g., induced by surgery). On the latest view, we will require that an NCC correlate with states of consciousness not just over cases of normal functioning but over cases of abnormal functioning as well.

This certainly squares with common practice in the field. Lesion studies are often used to draw conclusions about the neural correlates of consciousness. In Milner and Goodale's (1995) work, for example, the fact that consciousness remains much the same following lesions to the dorsal stream but not to the ventral stream is used to support the conclusion that the NCC lies within the ventral stream. More generally, it is often assumed that if some aspect of consciousness survives relatively intact when a given brain area is damaged, then that brain area is unlikely to be or to contain an NCC.

The tacit premise in this research is that an NCC should correlate with consciousness, not just in cases of normal functioning but in cases of abnormal functioning as well. Given this premise, it follows that if we find an abnormal case in which neural system N is damaged but a previously corresponding conscious state C is preserved, then N is not a neural correlate of C. Without this premise, or a version of it, it is not clear that any such conclusion can be drawn from lesion studies.

The premise may sound reasonable, but we already have reason to be suspicious of it. We know that for any candidate NCC, sufficiently radical changes can destroy the correlation. Preserving merely system N, cut off from the rest of the brain, for example, is unlikely to yield a corresponding conscious state; but, intuitively, this does not imply that N was not an NCC in the original case.

Less radically, one can imagine placing lesions immediately downstream from a candidate NCC N, so that N's effects on the rest of the brain are significantly reduced. In such a case, it is probable that N can be active without the usual behavioral effects associated with consciousness, and quite plausibly without consciousness itself. It's not implausible that an NCC supports consciousness largely by virtue of playing the right functional role in the brain; by virtue of mediating global availability, for example (see Baars 1988 and Chalmers 1998). If that is so, then if the system is changed so that the NCC no longer plays that functional role, NCC activity will no longer correlate with consciousness. But the mere fact that correlation can be destroyed by this sort of lesion does not obviously imply that N is not an NCC in a normal brain. If that inference could be made, then almost any candidate NCC could be ruled out by the right sort of lesion.

It may be that even smaller lesions can destroy a correlation in this way. For example, it is not implausible that for any candidate NCC N, there is some other local system in the brain (perhaps a downstream area) whose proper functioning is required for activity in N to yield the usual effects that go with consciousness, and for N to yield consciousness itself. This second system might not itself be an NCC in any intuitive sense; it might merely play an enabling role, in the way that proper functioning of the heart plays an enabling role for functioning of the brain. If that is so, then if one lesions this single area downstream, activity in N will no longer correlate with consciousness. In this way, any potential NCC might be ruled out by a localized lesion elsewhere.

The trouble is that lesions change the architecture of the brain, and it's quite possible that changes to brain architecture can change the location of an NCC, so that a physical state which was an NCC in a normal brain will not be an NCC in the altered brain. Given this possibility, it seems too strong to require that an NCC correlate with consciousness across arbitrary lesions and changes in brain functioning. We should expect an NCC to be architecture-dependent, not architecture-independent.

So an NCC should not be expected to correlate with consciousness across arbitrary lesion cases. There are now two alternatives. Either we can require correlation across some more restricted range of lesion cases, or we can drop the requirement of correlation in abnormal cases altogether.

For the first alternative to work, we would have to find some way to distinguish "good" lesions from "bad" lesions. An NCC would be expected to correlate with consciousness across the good lesions but not the bad lesions. If one found a "good" lesion case where activity in system N was present without the corresponding conscious state, this would imply that N is not an NCC; but no such conclusion could be drawn from a "bad" lesion case.

The trouble is that it is not at all obvious that such a distinction can be drawn. It might be tempting to come up with an after-the-fact distinction, defined as the range of lesions in which correlation with a given NCC N is preserved, but this will not be helpful, since we are interested in the criterion that makes N qualify as an NCC in the first place. So a distinction will have to be drawn on relatively a priori grounds (it can then be used to determine whether a given correlation pattern qualifies an arbitrary system as an NCC or not). But it is not clear how to draw the distinction. One might suggest that correlation should be preserved across small lesions but not large ones; but we have seen above that even small lesions might destroy a potential NCC. Or one might suggest that lesions in downstream areas are illegitimate, but upstream and parallel lesions are legitimate. But even here, it is not clear that indirect interaction with an upstream or parallel area might be required to support proper functioning of an NCC. Perhaps with some ingenuity one might be able to come up with a criterion, but it is not at all obvious how.

The second alternative is to hold that correlation across cases of normal functioning (perhaps with unusual inputs and brain stimulation) is all that is required to be an NCC. If this is so, one can never infer directly from the fact that N fails to correlate with consciousness in a lesion to the conclusion that N is not an NCC. On this view, the location of an NCC is wholly architecture-dependent, or entirely dependent on the normal functioning of the brain. One cannot expect an NCC to correlate with consciousness in cases of abnormal functioning or different architecture, so no direct conclusion can be drawn from failure of correlation across lesion cases. Of course, one can still appeal to cases with unusual inputs and brain stimulation to make fine-grained distinctions among NCCs.

The main conceptual objection to the second alternative is that one might *need* lesion cases to make the finest-grained distinctions that are required. Consider a hypothetical case in which we have two linked systems N and M that correlate equally well with consciousness across all normal cases, including all unusual inputs and brain stimulation, but in almost all relevant lesion cases, consciousness correlates much better with N than with M. In this case, might we want to say that N rather than M is an NCC? If so, we have to build some allowance for abnormal cases into the definition of an NCC. An advocate of the second alternative might reply that such cases will be very unusual, and that if N and M are dissociable by lesions, there is likely to be some unusual brain stimulation that will bring out the dissociation as well. In the extreme case where no brain stimulation leads to dissociation, one might simply bite the bullet and say that both N and M are equally good NCCs.

Taking everything into consideration, I am inclined to think the second alternative is better than the first. It seems right to say that "core" NCC location depends on brain architecture and normal functioning, and it is unclear that correlation across abnormal cases should be required, especially given all the associated problems. A problem like the one just mentioned might provide some pressure to investigate the first alternative further, and I do not rule out the possibility that some way of distinguishing "good" from "bad" lesions might be found, but all in all it seems best to say that an NCC cannot be expected to correlate with consciousness across abnormal cases.

Of course this has an impact on the methodology of the search for an NCC. As we have seen, lesion studies are often used to draw conclusions about NCC location (as in the Milner and Goodale research, for example, and also in much research on blindsight), and failure of correlation in lesion cases is often taken to imply that a given system is not an NCC. But we have seen that the tacit premise of this sort of research—that an NCC must correlate across abnormal as well as normal cases— is difficult to support, and leads to significant problems. So it seems that lesion studies are methodologically dangerous here. One should be very cautious in using them to draw conclusions about NCC location.

This is not to say that lesion studies are irrelevant in the search for an NCC. Even if correlation across abnormal cases is not *required* for system N to be an NCC, it may be that correlation across abnormal cases can provide good *evidence* that N is an NCC, and that failure of such correlation in some cases provides good evidence that N is not an NCC. Say we take the second alternative above, and define an NCC as a system that correlates with consciousness across all normal cases (including unusual input and stimulation). It may nevertheless be the case that information about correlations across all these normal cases with unusual stimulation is difficult to come by (due to problems in monitoring brain systems at a fine grain, for example), and that information about correlation across lesion cases is easier to obtain. In this case, one might sometimes take correlation across abnormal cases as *evidence* that a system will correlate across the normal cases in question, and thus as evidence that the system is an NCC. Similarly, one might take failure of correlation across abnormal cases as evidence that a system will fail to correlate across certain normal cases, and thus as evidence that the system is not an NCC.

The question of whether a given lesion study can serve as evidence in this way needs to be taken on a case-by-case basis. It is clear that some lesion studies will not provide this sort of evidence, as witnessed by the cases of severe lesions and downstream lesions discussed earlier. In those cases, failure of correlation across abnormal cases provides no evidence of failure of correlation across normal cases. On the other hand, it does not seem unreasonable that the Milner and Goodale studies should be taken as evidence that even in normal cases, the ventral stream will correlate better with visual consciousness than the dorsal stream. Of course the real "proof" would come from a careful investigation of the relevant processes across a wide range of "normal" cases involving standard environments, unusual inputs, and brain stimulation; but in the absence of such a demonstration, the lesion cases at least provide suggestive evidence.

In any case, the moral is that one has to be very cautious when drawing conclusions about NCC location from lesion studies. At best these studies serve as indirect evidence rather than as direct criteria, and even as such there is a chance that the evidence can be misleading. One needs to consider the possibility that the lesion in question is changing brain architecture in such a fashion that what was once an NCC is no longer an NCC, and one needs to look very closely at what is going on to rule out the possibility. It may be that this can sometimes be done, but it is a nontrivial matter.

Overall Definition

With all this, we have come to a more detailed definition of an NCC. The general case is something like the following:

An NCC is a minimal neural system N such that there is a mapping from states of N to states of consciousness, where a given state of N is sufficient, under conditions C, for the corresponding state of consciousness.

The central case of the neural correlate of the content of consciousness can be put in more specific terms:

An NCC (for content) is a minimal neural representational system N such that representation of a content in N is sufficient, under conditions C, for representation of that content in consciousness.

One might also give a general definition of the NCC for an arbitrary phenomenal property or for a phenomenal family, but I will leave those aside here.

The "conditions C" clause here represents the relevant range of cases, as discussed above. If the reasoning above is on the right track, then conditions C might be seen as conditions involving normal brain functioning, allowing unusual inputs and limited brain stimulation, but not lesions or other changes in architecture. Of course the precise nature of conditions C is still debatable. Perhaps one could make a case for including a limited range of lesion cases in the definition. In the other direction, perhaps one might make a case that the requirement of correlation across brain stimulation or unusual inputs is too strong, due to the abnormality of those scenarios. But I think the conditions C proposed here are at least a reasonable first pass, pending further investigation.

Of course, to some extent, defining what "really" counts as an NCC is a terminological matter. One could quite reasonably say that there are multiple different notions of NCC, depending on just how one understands the relevant conditions C, or the matter of necessity and sufficiency, and so on; and not much really rests on which of these is the "right" definition. Still, we have seen that different definitions give very different results, and that many potential definitions have the consequence that systems which intuitively seem to qualify as an NCC do not qualify after all, and that NCC hypotheses put forward by researchers in the field could be ruled out on trivial a priori grounds. Those consequences seem undesirable. It makes sense to have a definition of NCC that fits the way the notion is generally used in the field, and that can make sense of empirical research in the area. At the same time we want a definition of NCC to be coherent and well-motivated in its own right, such that an NCC is something worth looking for, and such that the definition can itself be used to assess various hypotheses about the identity of an NCC. It seems to me that the definition I have given here is at least a first pass in this direction.

Methodological Consequences

The discussion so far has been somewhat abstract, and the definitions given above may look like mere words; but from these definitions and the reasoning that went into them, one can straightforwardly extract some concrete methodological recommendations for the NCC search. Many of these recommendations are plausible or obvious in their own right, but it is interesting to see them emerge from the analysis.

Lesion Studies Are Methodologically Dangerous

Lesion studies are often used to draw conclusions about neural correlates of consciousness, but we have seen that their use can be problematic. The identity of an NCC is arguably always relative to specific brain architecture and normal brain functioning, and correlation across abnormal cases should not generally be expected. In some cases, lesion studies can change brain architecture so that a system which was previously an NCC is no longer one. So one can never infer directly from failure of correlation between a system and consciousness in a lesion case to the conclusion that the system is an NCC. Sometimes one can infer this indirectly, by using the failure of correlation here as evidence for failure of correlation in normal cases, but one must be cautious.

There May Be Many NCCs

On the definition above, an NCC is a system whose activity is *sufficient* for certain states of consciousness. This allows for the possibility of multiple NCCs in at least two ways. First, different sorts of conscious states may have different corresponding NCCs; there may be different NCCs for visual and auditory consciousness, for example, and perhaps even for different aspects of visual consciousness. Second, even for a particular sort of conscious state (such as pain), we cannot rule out the possibility that there will be two different systems whose activity is sufficient to produce that state.

Of course it *could* turn out that there is only a small number of NCCs, or perhaps even one. For all that I have said here, it is possible that there is some central system which represents the contents of visual consciousness, auditory consciousness, emotional experience, the stream of conscious thought, the background state of consciousness, and so on. Such a system might be seen as a sort of "consciousness module," or perhaps as a "Cartesian theater" (Dennett 1991) or a "global workspace" (Baars 1988), depending on whether one is a foe or a friend of the idea (see Chalmers 1998 for some discussion). But it is by no means obvious that there will be such a system, and I think the empirical evidence so far is against it. In any case, the matter cannot be decided a priori, so our definition should be compatible with the existence of multiple NCCs.

Minimize Size of an NCC

We have seen that an NCC should be understood as a *minimal* neural system which correlates with consciousness. Given this, we should constrain the search for the

NCC by aiming to find a neural correlate that is as small as possible. Given a broad system that appears to correlate with consciousness, we need to isolate the core relevant parts and aspects of that system which underlie the correlation. And given the dual hypotheses that consciousness correlates with a broad system or with a narrower system contained within it, we might first investigate the "narrow" hypothesis, since if it correlates with consciousness, the broad system cannot be a true NCC.

So to some extent it makes sense to "start small" in the search for an NCC. This fits the working methodology proposed by Crick and Koch (1998). They suggest that an NCC may involve a very small number of neurons (perhaps in the thousands) with certain distinctive properties. There is no guarantee that this is correct (and my own money is against it), but it makes a good working hypothesis in the NCC search. Of course one should simultaneously investigate broad systems for correlation with consciousness, so that one can then focus on those areas and try to narrow things down.

Distinguish NCCs for Background State and for Content
We have seen that there may be different NCCs for different sorts of states of consciousness. An important distinction in this class is that between the neural correlate of background state of consciousness (wakefulness, dreaming, etc.) and the neural correlate of specific contents. It may be that these are quite different systems. It is not implausible, on current evidence, that an NCC for background state involves processes in the thalamus, or thalamocortical interactions, while an NCC for specific contents of consciousness involves processes in the cortex. These different sorts of NCC will require quite different methods for their investigation.

NCC Studies Need to Monitor Neural Representational Content
Arguably the most interesting part of the NCC search is the search for neural determinants of specific contents of consciousness, such as the contents of visual consciousness. We have seen that an NCC here will be a neural representational system whose contents are correlated with the contents of consciousness. To determine whether such a system is truly an NCC, then, we need methods that monitor the representational content of the system. This is just what we find in Logothetis's work, for example, where it is crucial to keep track of activity in neurons with known receptive fields.

This gets at a striking aspect of the NCC search in practice, which is that the most informative and useful results usually come from neuron-level studies on monkeys. Large claims are sometimes made for brain imaging in humans, but it is generally difficult to draw solid conclusions from such studies, especially where an NCC is concerned. We can trace the difference to the fact that neuron-level studies can monitor representational content in neural systems, whereas imaging studies cannot (or at least usually do not). The power of single-cell studies in the work of Logothetis, Andersen, Newsome and colleagues (e.g., the works of Logothetis and Newsome already cited, and Bradley et al. 1998) comes precisely from the way that cells can be monitored to keep track of the activity profile of neurons with known representational properties, such as receptive and projective fields. This allows us to track representational content in these neural systems and to correlate it with the apparent contents of consciousness. This is much harder to do in a coarse-grained brain-imaging study, which generally tells one that there is activity in a region while saying nothing about specific contents.

A moral is that it makes sense to concentrate on developing methods which can track neural representational content, especially in humans (where invasive studies are much more problematic, but where evidence for conscious content is much more straightforward). There has been some recent work on the use of imaging methods to get at certain aspects of the content of visual consciousness, such as colors and shapes in the visual field (e.g., Engel et al. 1997), and different sorts of objects that activate different brain areas (e.g., Tong et al. 1998). There is also some current work using invasive methods in neuro-surgery patients to monitor the activity of single cells. One can speculate that if a noninvasive method for monitoring single-cell activity in humans is ever developed, the search for an NCC (like most of neuroscience) will be transformed almost beyond recognition.

Correlation Across a Few Situations Is Limited Evidence

According to the definition above, an NCC is a system that correlates with consciousness across arbitrary cases of normal functioning, in any environment, with any unusual input or limited brain stimulation. In practice, though, evidence is far weaker than this. Typically one has a few cases, involving either a few subjects with different lesions, or a study in which subjects are given different stimuli and one notes an apparent correlation. This is to be expected, given the current technological and ethical constraints on experimental methods. But it does mean that the evidence which current methods give is quite weak. To truly demonstrate that a given system is an NCC, one would need to show correlation across a far wider range of cases than is currently feasible. Of course current methods may give good *negative* evidence about systems that fail to correlate and thus are not NCCs, but strong positive evidence is harder to find. Positive hypotheses based on current sorts of evidence should probably be considered suggestive but highly speculative.

We Need Good Criteria for the Ascription of Consciousness

To find an NCC, we need to find a neural system that correlates with certain conscious states. To do this, we first need a way to know when a system is in a given conscious state. This is famously problematic, given the privacy of consciousness and the philosophical problem of other minds. In general, we rely on indirect criteria for the ascription of consciousness. The most straightforward of these criteria is verbal report in humans, but other criteria are often required. Where nonhuman subjects are involved, one must rely on quite indirect behavioral signs (voluntary bar-pressing in Logothetis's monkeys, for example).

A deep problem for the field is that our ultimate criteria here are not experimentally testable, since the results of any experiment will require such criteria for their interpretation. (First-person experimentation on oneself may be an exception, but even this has limitations.) So any experimental work implicitly relies on preempirical principles (even "philosophical" principles) for its interpretation. Given this, it is vital to refine and justify these preempirical principles as well as we can. In the case of verbal report, we may be on relatively safe ground (though even here there may be some grounds for doubt, as witnessed in the debates over "subjective threshold" criteria in unconscious perception research; see, e.g., Merikle and Reingold 1992). In other cases, especially nonhuman cases, careful attention to the assumptions involved are required. I don't think this problem is insurmountable, but it deserves careful attention. Our conclusions about NCC location will be no better than the preexperimental assumptions that go into the search. (I consider this problem, and its consequences for the NCC search, in much more detail in Chalmers 1998.)

Methodological Summary

We can use all this to sketch a general methodology for the NCC search. First, we need methods for determining the contents of conscious experience in a subject, presumably by indirect behavioral criteria or by first-person phenomenology. Second, we need methods to monitor neural states in a subject, and in particular to monitor neural representational contents. Then we need to perform experiments in a variety of situations to determine which neural systems correlate with conscious states and which do not. Experiments involving normal brain functioning with unusual inputs and limited brain stimulation are particularly crucial here. Direct conclusions cannot be drawn from systems with lesions, but such systems can sometimes serve as indirect evidence. We need to consider multiple hypotheses in order to narrow down a set of minimal neural systems that correlate with consciousness across all relevant scenarios. We may well find many different NCCs in different modalities, and different NCCs for background state and conscious contents, although it is not out of the question that there will be only a small number. If all goes well, we might expect eventually to isolate systems that correlate strongly with consciousness across any normally functioning brain.

Should We Expect an NCC?

One might well ask: Given the notion of an NCC as I have defined it, is it guaranteed that there will *be* a neural correlate of consciousness?

In answering, I will assume that states of consciousness depend systematically in some way on overall states of the brain. If this assumption is false, as is held by some Cartesian dualists (e.g., Eccles 1994) and some phenomenal externalists (e.g., Dretske 1995), then there may be no NCC as defined here, since any given neural state might be instantiated without consciousness. (Even on these positions, an NCC *could* be possible, if it were held that brain states at least correlate with conscious states in ordinary cases). But if the assumption is true, then there will at least be some minimal correlation of neural states with consciousness.

Does it follow that there will be an NCC as defined here? This depends on whether we are talking about neural correlates of arbitrary conscious states or about the more constrained case of neural correlates of conscious contents. In the first case, it is guaranteed that the brain as a whole will be a neural system which has states that suffice for arbitrary conscious states. So the brain will be one system whose state is sufficient for a given conscious state; and given that there is at least one such system for a given state, there must be at least one such *minimal* system for that state. Such a system will be an NCC for that state. Of course this reasoning does not guarantee that there will be only one NCC for a given state, or that the NCC for one state will be the same as the NCC for another, or that an NCC will be simple, but we know that an NCC will exist.

In the case of neural correlates of the content of consciousness, things are more constrained, since a neural correlate is required not just to map to a corresponding state of consciousness, but to match it in *content*. This rules out the whole brain as even a nonminimal neural correlate, for example, since representing a content in the brain does not suffice to represent that content in consciousness (much of the brain's representational content is unconscious). Of course we may hope that there will be more constrained neural systems whose content systematically matches the contents of some aspect of consciousness. But one might argue that it is not obvious that such a system *must* exist. It might be held, for example, that the contents of consciousness are an emergent product of the contents of various neural systems, which together suffice for the conscious content in question, but none of which precisely mirrors it.

I think one can plausibly argue that there is reason to expect that conscious contents will be mirrored by the contents of a neural representational system at *some* level of abstraction. In creatures with language, for example, conscious contents correspond well with contents that are made directly available for verbal report; and in conscious creatures more generally, one can argue that the contents of consciousness correspond to contents which are made directly available for the global voluntary control of behavior (see, e.g., Chalmers 1998). So there is a correlation between the contents of consciousness and contents revealed or exhibited in certain functional roles within the system.

Given that these contents are revealed in verbal report and are exhibited in the control of behavior, there is reason to believe that they are represented at some point within the cognitive system. Of course this depends to some extent on just what "representation" comes to. On some highly constrained notions of representation— if it is held that the only true representation is symbolic representation, for example—then it is far from clear that the content revealed in behavior must be represented. But on less demanding notions of representation—on which, for example, systems are assigned representational content according to their functional role—then it will be natural to expect that the content revealed in a functional role will be represented in a system which plays that functional role.

This does not guarantee that there will be any single neural system whose content always matches the content of consciousness. It may be that the functional role in question is played by multiple systems, and that a given system may sometimes play the role, and sometimes not. If this is so, we may have to move to a higher level of abstraction. If there is no localizable neural system that qualifies as a correlate of conscious content, we may have to look at a more global system—the "global availability" system, for example, whereby contents are made available for report and global control—and argue that the contents of consciousness correspond to the contents made available in this system. If so, it could turn out that what we are left with is more like a "cognitive correlate of consciousness," since the system may not correspond to any neurobiological system whose nature and boundaries are independently carved out. But it can still function as a correlate in some useful sense.

In this context, it is important to note that an NCC need not be a specific anatomical area in the brain. Some of the existing proposals regarding NCCs involve less localized neurobiological properties. For example, Libet (1993) argues that the neural correlate of consciousness is temporally extended neural firing; Crick and Koch (1998) speculate that the NCC might involve a particular sort of cell throughout the cortex; Edelman (1989) suggests that the NCC might involve reentrant thalamocortical loops; and so on. In these cases, NCCs are individuated by temporal properties, or by physiological rather than anatomical properties, or by functional properties, among other possibilities. If that is the case, the "neural representational system" involved in defining a neural correlate of conscious content might also be individuated more abstractly: The relevant neural representational contents might be those represented by temporally extended firings, or by certain sorts of cells, or by reentrant loops, and so on. So abstractness and failure of localization are not in themselves bars to a system's qualifying as an NCC.

It seems, then, that there is a range of possibilities for the brain-based correlates of conscious states, ranging from specific anatomical areas, through more abstract neural systems, to purely "cognitive" correlates such as Baars's (1988) global workspace. Just how specific an NCC may turn out to be is an empirical question. One might reasonably expect that there will be some biological specificity. Within a given organism or species, one often finds a close match between specific functions and specific physiological systems, and it does not seem unlikely that particular neural systems and properties in the brain should be directly implicated in the mechanisms of availability for global control. If that is the case, then we may expect specific neural correlates even of conscious contents. If not, we may have to settle for more abstract correlates, individuated at least partly at the cognitive level, though even here one will expect that some neural systems will be much more heavily involved than others. In any case it seems reasonable to expect that we will find informative brain-based correlates of consciousness at some level of abstraction in cognitive neurobiology.

Some have argued that we should not expect neural correlates of consciousness. For example, in their discussion of neural "filling-in" in visual perception, Pessoa et al. (1998) argue against the necessity of what Teller and Pugh (1983) call a "bridge locus" for perception, which closely resembles the notion of a neural correlate of consciousness. Much of their argument is based on the requirement that such a locus must involve a spatiotemporal isomorphism between neural states and conscious states (so a conscious representation of a checkerboard would require a neural state in a checkerboard layout, for example). These arguments do not affect neural correlates of conscious contents as I have defined them, since a match between neural and conscious content does not require such a spatiotemporal correspondence (a neural representation of a shape need not itself have that shape). Pessoa et al. also argue more generally against a "uniformity of content" thesis, holding that one should not expect a match between the "personal" contents of consciousness and the "subpersonal" contents of neural systems. It is true that the existence of such a match is not automatic, but as before, the fact that conscious contents are mirrored in specific functional roles gives reason to believe that they will be subpersonally represented at least at some level of abstraction.

It has also been argued (e.g., by Güzeldere 1999) that there is probably no neural correlate of consciousness, since there is probably no area of the brain that is specifically dedicated to consciousness as opposed to vision, memory, learning, and so on. One may well agree that there is no such area, but it does not follow that there is no neural correlate of consciousness as defined here. An NCC (as defined here) requires only that a system be correlated with consciousness, not that it be dedicated solely or mainly to consciousness. Güzeldere's alternative conception of an NCC is much more demanding than the conception at issue in most empirical work on the subject, where it is often accepted that an NCC may be closely bound up with visual processing (e.g., Logothetis; Milner and Goodale), memory (e.g., Edelman), and other processes. This becomes particularly clear once one gives up on the requirement that there be a single NCC, and accepts that there may be multiple NCCs in multiple modalities.

Conclusion

The discussion in the previous section helps bring out what an NCC is not, or at least what it might turn out not to be. An NCC is defined to be a *correlate* of consciousness. From this, it does not automatically follow that an NCC will be a system solely or mainly dedicated to consciousness, or even that an NCC will be the brain system most responsible for the generation of consciousness. It certainly does not follow that an NCC will yield an explanation of consciousness, and it is not even guaranteed that identifying an NCC will be the key to understanding the processes underlying consciousness. If one were to define an NCC in these stronger terms, it would be far from obvious that there must be an NCC, and it would also be much less clear how to search for an NCC.

Defining an NCC solely in terms of correlation seems to capture standard usage best, and it also makes the search more clearly defined and the methodology clearer. Correlations are easy for science to study. It also means that the search for an NCC can be to a large extent theoretically neutral rather than theoretically loaded. Once we have found an NCC, one might hope that it will turn out to be a system dedicated to consciousness, or that it will turn out to yield an explanation of consciousness, but these are further questions. In the meantime the search for an NCC as defined poses a tractable empirical question with relatively clear parameters, one that researchers of widely different theoretical persuasions can engage in.

There are certain rewards of the search for an NCC that one might reasonably expect. For example, these systems might be used to monitor and predict the contents of consciousness in a range of novel situations. For example, we may be able to use them to help reach conclusions about conscious experience in patients under anesthesia, and in subjects with "locked-in syndrome" or in a coma. In cases where brain architecture differs significantly from the original cases (perhaps some coma cases, infants, and animals), the evidence will be quite imperfect, but it will at least be suggestive.

These systems might also serve as a crucial step toward a full science of consciousness. Once we know which systems are NCCs, we can investigate the mechanisms by which they work, and how they produce various characteristic functional effects. Just as isolating the DNA basis of the gene helped explain many of the functional phenomena of life, so isolating NCC systems may help explain many functional phenomena associated with consciousness. We might also systematize the relationship between NCCs and conscious states, and abstract general principles governing the relationship between them. In this way we might be led to a much greater theoretical understanding.

In the meantime, the search for a neural correlate of consciousness provides a project that is relatively tractable, clearly defined, and theoretically neutral, one whose goal seems to be visible somewhere in the middle distance. Because of this, the search makes an appropriate centerpiece for a developing science of consciousness, and is an important springboard in the quest for a general theory of the relationship between physical processes and conscious experience.

References

Anderson, R. A. 1997. Neural mechanisms in visual motion perception in primates. *Neuron* 18: 865–872.

Baars, B. J. 1988. *A Cognitive Theory of Consciousness.* Cambridge: Cambridge University Press.

Bogen, J. E. 1995. On the neurophysiology of consciousness, part I: An overview. *Consciousness and Cognition* 4: 52–62.

Bradley, D. C., Chang, G. C., and Andersen, R. A. 1998. Encoding of three-dimensional structure-from-motion by primate area MT neurons. *Nature* 392: 714–717.

Chalmers, D. J. 1995. Facing up to the problem of consciousness. *Journal of Consciousness Studies* 2: 200–219. Also in S. Hameroff, A. Kaszniak, and A. Scott, eds., 1996, *Toward a Science of Consciousness* (Cambridge, Mass.: MIT Press); and in J. Shear, ed., 1997, *Explaining Consciousness: The Hard Problem* (Cambridge, Mass.: MIT Press).

Chalmers, D. J. 1996. *The Conscious Mind: In Search of a Fundamental Theory.* New York: Oxford University Press.

Chalmers, D. J. 1998. On the search for the neural correlate of consciousness. In S. Hameroff, A. Kaszniak, and A. Scott, eds., *Toward a Science of Consciousness.* Cambridge, Mass.: MIT Press.

Crick, F., and Koch, C. 1990. Towards a neurobiological theory of consciousness. *Seminars in the Neurosciences* 2: 263–275.

Crick, F., and Koch, C. 1995. Are we aware of neural activity in primary visual cortex? *Nature* 375: 121–123.

Crick, F., and Koch, C. 1998. Consciousness and neuroscience. *Cerebral Cortex* 375: 121–123.

Dennett, D. C. 1991. *Consciousness Explained.* Boston: Little Brown.

Dretske, F. 1995. *Naturalizing the Mind.* Cambridge, Mass.: MIT Press.

Eccles, J. C. 1994. *How the Self Controls Its Brain.* New York: Springer-Verlag.

Edelman, G. M. 1989. *The Remembered Present: A Biological Theory of Consciousness.* New York: Basic Books.

Engel, S., Zhang, X., and Wandell, B. 1997. Colour tuning in human visual cortex measured with functional magnetic resonance imaging. *Nature* 388: 68–81.

Flohr, H. 1995. Sensations and brain processes. *Behavioral Brain Research* 71: 157–161.

Gur, M., and Snodderly, D. M. 1997. A dissociation between brain activity and perception: Chromatically active cortical neurons signal chromatic activity that is not perceived. *Vision Research* 37: 377–382.

Güzeldere, G. 1999. There is no neural correlate of consciousness. Paper presented at Toward a Science of Consciousness: Fundamental Approaches. Tokyo, May 25–28.

He, S., Cavanagh, P., and Intriligator, J. 1996. Attentional resolution and the locus of visual awareness. *Nature* 384: 334–337.

Hobson, J. A. 1997. Consciousness as a state-dependent phenomenon. In J. Cohen and J. Schooler, eds., *Scientific Approaches to Consciousness*. Hillsdale, NJ: Lawrence Erlbaum.

Leopold, D. A., and Logothetis, N. K. 1996. Activity changes in early visual cortex reflect monkeys' percepts during binocular rivalry. *Nature* 379: 549–553.

Libet, B. 1982. Brain stimulation in the study of neuronal functions for conscious sensory experiences. *Human Neurobiology* 1: 235–242.

Libet, B. (1993). The neural time factor in conscious and unconscious events. In *Experimental and Theoretical Studies of Consciousness* (Ciba Foundation Symposium 174). Wiley.

Llinás, R. R., Ribary, U., Joliot, M., and Wang, X.-J. 1994. Content and context in temporal thalamocortical binding. In G. Buzsaki, R. R. Llinas, and W. Singer, eds., *Temporal Coding in the Brain*. Berlin: Springer-Verlag.

Logothetis, N., and Schall, J. 1989. Neuronal correlates of subjective visual perception. *Science* 245: 761–763.

Marge, E. 1991. Magnetostimulation of vision: Direct noninvasive stimulation of the retina and the visual brain. *Optometry and Vision Science* 68: 427–440.

Merikle, P. M., and Reingold, E. M. 1992. Measuring unconscious processes. In R. Bornstein and T. Pittman, eds., *Perception Without Awareness*. New York: Guilford.

Milner, A. D. 1995. Cerebral correlates of visual awareness. *Neuropsychologia* 33: 1117–1130.

Milner, A. D., and Goodale, M. A. 1995. *The Visual Brain in Action*. Oxford: Oxford University Press.

Newman, J. B. 1997. Putting the puzzle together: Toward a general theory of the neural correlates of consciousness. *Journal of Consciousness Studies* 4: 47–66, 100–121.

Newman, J., and Baars, B. J. 1993. A neural attentional model of access to consciousness: A global workspace perspective. *Concepts in Neuroscience* 4: 255–290.

Penfield, W. 1937. The cerebral cortex and consciousness. In *The Harvey Lectures*. Reprinted in R. H. Wilkins, ed., *Neurosurgical Classics*. New York: Johnson Reprint Corp., 1965.

Penfield, W., and Rasmussen, T. 1950. *The Cerebral Cortex of Man: A Clinical Study of Localization of Function*. New York: Macmillan.

Pessoa, L., Thompson, E., and Noe, A. 1998. Finding out about filling in: A guide to perceptual completion for visual science and the philosophy of perception. *Behavioral and Brain Sciences* 21: 723–748.

Salzman, C. D., Britten, K. H., and Newsome, W. T. 1990. Cortical microstimulation influences perceptual judgments of motion direction. *Nature* 346: 174–187.

Sheinberg, D. L., and Logothetis, N. K. 1997. The role of temporal cortical areas in perceptual organization. *Proceedings of the National Academy of Sciences* 94: 3408–3413.

Shoemaker, S. 1981. Some varieties of functionalism. *Philosophical Topics* 12: 93–119. Reprinted in *Identity, Cause, and Mind.* Cambrioge: Cambridge University Press, 1984.

Teller, D. Y., and Pugh, E. N. 1983. Linking propositions in color vision. In J. D. Mollon and L. T. Sharpe, eds., *Color Vision: Physiology and Psychophysics.* London: Academic Press.

Tong, F., Nakayama, K., Vaughan, J. T., and Kanwisher, N. 1998. Binocular rivalry and visual awareness in human extrastriate cortex. *Neuron* 21: 753–759.

23

On the Brain-Basis of Visual Consciousness: A Sensorimotor Account

Alva Noë and J. Kevin O'Regan

1 Introduction: The Basic Argument

Much work on the brain basis of vision and visual consciousness rests on the idea that for every conscious state of seeing (for every visual experience), a neural substrate exists whose activation is sufficient to produce it. It is widely supposed, in addition, that the function of this neural substrate is to produce sensory experience by generating a "representation" of what is experienced (Chalmers 2000). On this way of thinking, then, vision is the process in the brain whereby such a representation is produced.

We propose a very different conception of what vision is and of the role of the brain in vision. This chapter is based on our previous work on what we call a "sensorimotor" approach to vision (O'Regan and Noë 2001, 2002; Noë and O'Regan 2000; Noë 2002a, b).

According to this view, vision is not a process in the brain. Though the brain is necessary for vision, neural processes are not, in themselves, sufficient to produce seeing. Instead, we claim that seeing is an exploratory activity mediated by the animal's mastery of sensorimotor contingencies. That is, seeing is a skill-based activity of environmental exploration. Visual experience is not something that happens *in* individuals. It is something they *do*.

Seeing, according to this theory, is comparable to dancing with a partner. Just as dancing consists in a delicate interaction between *two* partners, so seeing, we argue, depends on patterns of interaction between the perceiver and the environment. There is no doubt that neural activity is necessary to enable one's skillful participation in a dance, but it is unlikely that this neural activity is sufficient to give rise to the dancing. After all, the dance, with its weight changes, moments of disequilibrium, and rebounds, depends on the actions and reactions of the partner (not to mention the nonbrain body). For exactly similar reasons, we argue, neural activity is not sufficient to produce visual experience. Seeing does not consist in the activation of neural structures (even though it causally depends upon such activation).

A further consequence of this approach to seeing and visual experience—seeing is something individuals do, not something that takes place inside them—is that it allows us to develop a new framework for thinking about the *qualitative character of experience*. One of the chief advantages of this new framework, we argue, is that it enables one to overcome the problem of the explanatory gap (Levine 1983).

In sections 2–4, we lay out the basic approach. In sections 5–6, we explore the implications of this approach for problems in visual neuroscience.

2   The Nature of Vision and Visual Consciousness

2.1   Vision and the Laws of Sensorimotor Contingency

Consider a simple phototactic device such as one of Braitenberg's vehicles (Braitenberg 1984). The imagined vehicle is equipped with two light sensors positioned next to each other on the front of the wheeled vehicle. The left sensor is linked to the right rear wheel driving mechanism, and the right sensor is linked to the left rear wheel driving mechanism. As a result of this wiring, the vehicle will orient itself toward light sources and move toward them. Such a simple mechanism can track and hunt light sources. Suppose there is a light source on the left. This causes the vehicle to turn in the direction of the light source. Once the vehicle has so turned, the light source is no longer on the left. It now causes both the left and right wheel drive to activate at the same level, moving the vehicle toward the light source. In this way, what stimulation the system receives is dependent on what actions it performs, and what the system does is affected by what stimulation it receives. This vehicle is built in such a way as to embody, as it were, a set of rules of sensorimotor contingency (a set of rules of interdependence between stimulation and movement).

Now consider a more complicated device such as a missile guidance system. It pursues an airplane by making use of, for instance, visual information about the plane. Suppose the system is designed to speed up in response to the diminishing of the image of the airplane in its camera and to maintain speed if the size of the image is growing. Similarly, it is capable of modifying its behavior depending on whether the image of the plane shifts to the left or right, up or down. For example, the system might be designed to shift to the left when the image of the airplane shifts to the left in its viewfinder, thus bringing the image of the plane back into the center. The missile guidance system, one may say, *masters* the sensorimotor contingencies of airplane tracking; it is built in such a way as to exploit, in its tracking activities, the interdependence between the availability of sensory information and its motor behavior. The system is, in this sense, *attuned* to the structure of sensorimotor contingencies. It is *perceptually coupled* with its environment.

We propose that perceptual systems in animals be thought of along the lines of the sort of simple systems described here. A visual perceiver is familiar with (masters) the ways in which visual information changes as a function of movement of the perceiver with respect to the environment. Movement toward an object causes an expansion of the retinal projection. A flick of the eyes to the left causes a displacement of projected items to the right. Because of the curvature of the retina, the retinal projection of a straight line is deformed in a predictable manner as one directs one's eyes upward. In addition, perceivers are familiar with the ways in which changes in the position of the object relative to its environment give rise to new patterns of stimulation. A vast array of sensorimotor contingencies exists; to be a perceiver is, *at least*, to be the master of these regularities. (See O'Regan and Noë 2001, for more detailed exposition.)

Perceptual sensitivity, according to our theory, consists in the ability to explore the environment in ways mediated by implicit knowledge of the patterns of sensorimotor contingency that govern perceptual modes of exploration.

2.2 Beyond Visual Sensitivity: Visual Awareness

The simple systems we have described exhibit some measure of perceptual sensitivity. It would, however, be unreasonable to say that such a system is *aware* of that to which it is perceptually sensitive. Such a system does not *see*. However, we have described what we can think of as the ground of a system's more full-blooded perceptual awareness—namely, the perceptual coupling of animal and environment that consists in the animal's access to environmental detail thanks to its mastery of the relevant sensorimotor contingencies. For an animal to be, in addition, *perceptually aware* of that to which it is perceptually sensitive is not only for it to be appropriately coupled perceptually, but for it to integrate its coupling behavior with its broader capacities for thought and rationally guided action. The driver, for example, who fails to pay attention to what he or she is doing or to that to which he or she is responding is still able to exercise mastery of the sensorimotor contingencies needed to drive the car. Such a driver is, as it were, on "automatic pilot." When in addition the driver is able to make use of information not only about that to which he or she is perceptually sensitive, but also about the character of his or her perceptual tracking of the environment, we say the driver is *aware* of what he or she perceives.

So, for example, perceptual sensitivity gets one to detect the changing of the traffic light as one drives. An individual only *sees* the light (that is, become perceptually aware of it, in our sense), when he or she exerts control over coupling with the light and when he or she uses the information about the light this coupling affords. (We notice later, in section 3 that this way explaining matters fits very nicely with the findings of recent psychological studies.)

We contrast, then, two distinct levels of perceptual capacities. First, there is perceptually guided activity or perceptual coupling. This is basic perceptual sensitivity. Second, there is access to and control over information about that to which individuals are perceptually coupled. This is perceptual awareness.

2.3   Visual Consciousness

We have offered accounts of two levels of perceptual capacity: perceptual sensitivity and perceptual awareness. What, in our view, is visual consciousness? Visual consciousness, we argue, is simply what we have been calling visual awareness. More important, there is no need to think of visual consciousness as constituting a further third level of perceptual capacity.

To explain, let us distinguish two kinds of visual consciousness: (1) *transitive visual consciousness* or *consciousness of*, and (2) visual consciousness in general.

1. To be *transitively conscious* is to be conscious *of* a feature of a scene.[1] Consciousness, in this sense, is that we have called visual awareness. Thus, to say that one is transitively conscious of (say) the shape of a parked car in front of one is to say that one is, first, currently exercising mastery of the laws of sensorimotor contingency that pertain to information about the shape of the car; and second, that one is attending to this exercise, in the sense that one is integrating it into one's current planning, reasoning, and speech behavior.

Notice that when you are transitively conscious of the shape of the car, you may fail to attend to its color, or to the fact that the object in front of you *is* a car. As you shift your attention from aspect to aspect of the car, features of the car enter consciousness. What happens when you thus shift attention is that you draw into play different bits of implicit knowledge of the relevant sensorimotor contingencies.

2. *Visual consciousness in general*, on the other hand, is a higher-order capacity. To be visually conscious in general is *to be able* to become aware of a present feature

(that is, to become transitively conscious of it). In this sense of visual consciousness, one can contrast *being visually conscious* with being asleep or with being blind. Consciousness in this most general sense consists in one's possession of the ability to become *conscious of* aspects of a scene (that is, in one's ability to see, to explore aspects of the environment in a fashion mediated by the relevant sensorimotor contingencies).

2.4 What Is Visual Experience? A Temporally Extended Pattern of Skillful Activity

Implicit in this account is a somewhat unorthodox analysis of the nature of visual experience. We propose that visual experience is the activity of exploring the environment as mediated by mastery of appropriate patterns of sensorimotor contingency in ways that draw on broader capacities for action, thought, and (in humans) language use. More important, visual experience or conscious seeing, as opposed to the mere processing of visual information, is not something that occurs inside animals. It is something they do.

To understand the force of this claim, consider the experience of driving a particular kind of car, say a Porsche. In what does this experience consist? Notice that, in one sense, there is no *feeling of driving a Porsche*. That is, the character of Porsche driving does not consist in the occurrence of a special sort of momentary flutter or bodily sensation. What defines the character of driving a Porsche, rather, is *what a person does when he or she drives a Porsche*. There are characteristic ways in which the vehicle accelerates in response to pressure on the gas pedal. There are definite features of the way the car handles in turns, how smoothly the gears shift, and so on. What it is like to drive a Porsche is constituted by all these sensorimotor contingencies and by one's skillful mastery of them, one's confident knowledge of how the car will respond to manipulations of its instruments.

In one sense, then, there *is* no single experience of driving a Porsche. What it is like to drive a Porsche depends on these various activities. In another sense, however, one can speak of the experience of driving a Porsche, but this must be understood not in terms of the occurrence of defining sensations, but rather, in terms of one's comfortable exercise of one's knowledge of the sensorimotor contingencies governing the behavior of the car.

Seeing (having visual experiences), we argue, is like Porsche driving. It is not something that happens in individuals, but something they do. And the character of seeing, like that of driving, is constituted by the character of the various things one does when one sees (or when one drives).

Suppose you stand before a red wall. It fills up your field of view. What is it like for you to see this red wall? Try to describe the experience. How do you fulfill this instruction? One thing you might do is direct your attention to one aspect or another of the wall's redness. For example, you might focus on its hue, or its brightness. In this way you become transitively conscious of (that is to say, *aware of*) this or that aspect of the wall's color. How do you accomplish this? In what does your focusing on the red hue of the wall consist? It consist in the (implicit) knowledge associated with seeing redness: the knowledge that if you were to move your eyes, there would be changes in the incoming information that are typical of sampling with the eye or typical of the nonhomogeneous way the retina samples color; knowledge that if you were to move your head around, there might be changes in the incoming information typical of what happens when illumination is uneven, and so forth. Most important, there is not *one* thing in which the focusing of your attention on the hue (say) consists. Eye movements, shifts of attention, the application of understanding—seeing the red hue of the wall consists in all of this. There is no simple, unanalyzable core of the experience. There are just the different things you do when you interact with the redness of the wall.

Of course this is not to deny that vision may, under certain circumstances, involve feelings or sensations of a nonvisual nature. So, for example, if you are trying to track the movement of an object without moving your head, you may feel a certain distinctive eye strain. If you witness an explosion, you may feel dazzled in a way that causes definite sensations in the eyes. If vision is, as we have argued, a mode of activity, then there may be features of the activity that in this way contribute to its "felt character." And so, likewise, there may be sensations that occur when driving, for example, the press of the steering wheel on your hands. But crucially these are not *intrinsic* or *defining* properties of the experiencing. They are rather more or less accidental accompaniments of the activity of seeing on a particular occasion.

2.5   The Ineffability of the Qualitative Character of Experience

We have proposed that experience is a temporally extended activity of exploration as mediated by the perceiver's knowledge of sensorimotor contingencies. The differences in the qualitative character of perceptual experiences correspond to differences in the character of the relevant sensorimotor contingencies. Just as the difference between driving a Porsche and driving a tank consists in the different things one does in driving it—or in the different skill-based understanding of how to drive the vehicle—so the difference between seeing a red flower and smelling a red flower consists in the different patterns of sensorimotor contingency governing one's perceptual encounter with each. To experience a red object, or the feel of driving a Porsche, is to know such things as that if one changes the illumination in such and such ways (or presses down on the accelerator in such and such ways), it will produce such and such changes in the stimulation.

It follows, based on this approach, that to reflect on the character of one's experience is to reflect on the character of one's law-governed exploration of the environment, on what one does in seeing. Some of the sensorimotor contingencies governing vision are easily accessible to awareness. If one reflects on the character of one's visual experience of a colorful flower, for example, it is easy to comprehend the manner in which the appearance of the flower is a function of viewing angle and illumination. If one looks at a plate and turns it, one can become aware of the way its profile becomes elliptical. If one puts on inverting lenses, it is immediately apparent that eye and head movements produce surprising patterns, thus enabling one to direct one's attention to the disruption of familiar patterns of sensorimotor contingency. But though one has access to these aspects of the sensorimotor contingencies, there are other components of the sensorimotor contingencies that do not lend themselves easily to propositional description, and that are not so easily brought into consciousness: the exact laws that the flower's color obeys when one changes the illumination, the exact rule determining the modification of the plate's profile, the precise disruption caused by distorting lenses. Other examples that are even less accessible to consciousness are the particular way the macular pigment and the nonhomogeneity of retinal sampling affect sensory input when the eye moves, the optic flow that occurs when the head rotates, and so forth.

These considerations enable us to see clearly a feature of experience that has often puzzled scientists and philosophers, namely, its apparent ineffability. It is very difficult to describe everything one does when one sees, just as it is difficult to describe everything one does when one is engaged in other skillful activities such as athletic endeavors, playing an instrument, or speaking a language. A major portion of one's mastery of sensorimotor contingencies takes the form of practical know-how. When one attempts to inquire into the more subtle features of what goes on when one perceives, we immediately come up against the fact that it is very difficult to describe any but the most high-level, gross sensorimotor contingencies.

There is nothing mysterious about this inability. In general, the ability to know how to do something does not carry with it the ability to reflect on what it is one does when exercising the ability in question. The difficulty of describing the character of experience is not evidence of the special character of experience in the world order. But it does bring forcibly to mind the fact that experiences are exercisings of complicated capacities, not ongoing occurrences in the mind or brain.

2.6   What Are Sensory Modalities?

The approach to vision and visual experience developed here, according to which vision is a mode of exploration of the world that is mediated by knowledge of sensorimotor contingencies, offers a standpoint from which one can reconsider the question of the nature of sensory modalities. Not very much scientific investigation has addressed this kind of question. Most scientists seem satisfied with some variant of Müller's (1838) classic concept of "specific nerve energy." Müller's idea, in its modern form, amounts to the claim that what determines the particularly visual aspect of visual sensations is the fact that visual sensations are transmitted by particular nerve pathways (namely, those originating in the retina and not in the cochlea) that project to particular cerebral regions (essentially cortical area V1). It is certainly true that retinal influx comes together in relatively circumscribed areas of the brain and that this may provide an architectural advantage in the neural implementation of the calculations necessary to generate visual-type sensations. But what is it about these pathways that generates the different sensations? Surely the choice of a particular subset of neurons or particular cortical regions cannot, *in itself*, explain why one attributes visual rather than auditory qualities to this influx.

In our view, the differences between the sensory modalities are to be understood in terms of the different patterns of sensorimotor contingency governing perceptual exploration in the different modalities. To see a bottle, for example, is to explore visual-motor contingencies such as transformations in the appearance of the bottle as one moves in relation to it. To touch it, on the other hand, is to explore the structure of tactile-motor contingencies. The bottle impedes, guides, and informs tactile exploration of the bottle. The difference between seeing a bottle, and touching it, consists in just these sorts of facts about the active engagement the perceiver undertakes with the environment (see Noë 2001, 2002).

3   Is the Visual World a Grand Illusion?

3.1   An Important Empirical Upshot: Change Blindness

An important consequence of this account of visual consciousness is that individuals are not, in general, aware of all the details present before them in the environment. They do not, that is, experience everything in the visual field all at once. They only see that to which they are currently attending. This idea was the impetus for a number of surprising experiments performed by O'Regan, Rensink, and others (Rensink, O'Regan, and Clark 1997; O'Regan et al. 2000; O'Regan, Rensink, and Clark 1999). In these experiments, observers are shown displays of natural scenes and asked to detect cyclically repeated changes, such as a large object shifting, changing color, or appearing and disappearing. Under normal circumstances a change of this type would create a transient signal in the visual system that would be detected by low-level visual mechanisms. This transient would exogenously attract attention to the location of the change, and the change would therefore be immediately seen.

In these experiments, however, conditions were arranged such that the transient that would normally occur was prevented from playing its attention-grabbing role. This could be done in several ways. One method consisted in superimposing a very brief global flicker over the whole visual field at the moment of the change. This global flicker served to swamp the local transient caused by the change, preventing attention from being attracted to it. A similar purpose could be achieved by making the change coincide with an eye saccade, an eye blink, or a film cut in a film sequence (for a review, see Simons and Levin 1997; Simons 2000). In all these cases a brief global disturbance swamped the local transient and prevented it from attracting attention to the location of the change. Another method used to prevent the local transient from operating in the normal fashion was to create a small number of additional, extraneous transients distributed over the picture, somewhat like mud splashes on a car windscreen (cf. O'Regan, Rensink, and Clark 1999). These local transients acted as decoys and made it likely that attention would be attracted to an incorrect location instead of going to the true change location.

The results of the experiments showed that in many cases observers have great difficulty seeing changes, even though the changes are very large and occur in full view—they are perfectly visible to someone who knows what they are. In other experiments, O'Regan, Rensink, and Clark found that, in many cases, observers could be looking directly at the change at the moment the change occurred and still not see it.

These results are surprising if one supposes that individuals do in fact experience all the detail present in the environment, or if one subscribes to the view that the visual system builds up a detailed internal representation of the three-dimensional environment on the basis of successive snapshot-like fixations of the scene. But under the view that what one sees is the aspect of the scene to which one is attending—with which one is currently interacting—then it is not at all surprising that large changes might go completely unnoticed if they happen to correspond to parts of the scene that have not been attended to.

Other results showing that people can be looking directly at something and not see it had previously been obtained. Neisser and Becklen used a scenario that was a visual analogue of the "cocktail party" situation, where partygoers were able to attend to one of many superimposed voices. Neisser and Becklen (1975) visually superimposed two independent film sequences, demonstrating that observers were able to single out and follow one of the sequences, while being oblivious to the other. Simons and Chabris (1999) have recently replicated and extended these effects.

Finally Mack and Rock (1998) have conducted a number of experiments using their paradigm of "inattentional blindness." In this, subjects are engaged in an attention-intensive task such as determining which arm of a cross is longer. After a number of trials, an unexpected, perfectly visible, additional stimulus appears near the cross. The authors observe that on many occasions this extraneous stimulus is simply not noticed.[2]

3.2   The Grand Illusion Hypothesis

How can we reconcile these striking results with our impression that, when one sees, one is aware, as if all at once, of all the present environmental detail? Do phenomena such as change blindness and inattentional blindness demonstrate that visual consciousness is a grand illusion, as several authors have suggested (e.g., Blackmore et al. 1995; Dennett 1991, 1992, 1998; O'Regan 1992; Rensink, O'Regan, and Clark 1997)?

As pointed out by Noë, Pessoa, and Thompson (2000) and Noë (2002a), this "grand illusion hypothesis" rests on a mistaken account of the everyday phenomenology of perceptual experience. It is true that most perceivers will assent to the claim that, when they see, they see the whole scene, with all the detail. That is, it is true that normal perceivers take themselves to be aware of a detailed environment. They take themselves to learn that the environment is detailed thanks to their experience, and they are able, on the basis of their experience, to encounter each bit of (visible) detail. But there is no illusion in any of this. Perceivers are right to take themselves to have access to environmental detail and to learn that the environment is detailed. Moreover, the change blindness results are entirely compatible with this account of the character of our visual experience.

What is called into question by the change blindness results (and by the inattentional blindness results) is the idea that when one sees environmental detail, one has all of it in consciousness at once. What is challenged is the idea that all the detail is present in the head *now*. If *all* the detail were present in the head *now*, then surely one would not fall victim to change blindness.

But is there any reason to believe that normal perceivers are commited to this "details in the head" conception of visual consciousness? When normal perceivers assert that they take themselves to see the detailed environment, do they mean to say that they take themselves to have all the detail present to consciousness all at the same time? According to our theory, there is absolutely no reason to think that normal perceivers believe this.

Consider, for a moment, what your perceptual experience is actually like. You open your eyes and you take in all this detail. Does it really seem to you now as if all that detail is in your consciousness now, all at once? Does it seem to you as if you simultaneously attend to all the detail? No. It seems to you as if the detail is *there*, in front of you, in the world, and as if you have access to that detail by means of eye, head, and body movements.

Perceivers all know, whether they reflect on this or not, that visual exploration of the environment requires continuous adjustments. They squint, lean forward, reach for their glasses, tilt their reading material to the light, and casually walk to the window to get glimpses. They act as though they believe that the detail is there, in front of them, and that to acquire detail, to bring it into consciousness, they need to act.

It is of course true that people find the change blindness experiments very surprising. In addition, students are apt to find surprising familiar psychology demonstrations of their inability to tell the color of an object held in peripheral vision. It is sometimes suggested (e.g., by Dennett 1998, 2001) that this astonishment is evidence that they do tend to think of our experience along the lines of the "details in the head" conception. But there are other ways of explaining the astonishment. According to our theory, vision is a complicated skill-based activity. People tend to be unaware, when they are engaged in their perceptual lives, of the complicated things they do when they see. Just as dancers, musicians, or athletes are inattentive to the subtle modulations they undertake in the conduct of their activity, so perceivers fail for the most part to attend to the ways in which seeing depends on eye movements (as well as on head and body movements). The surprise one feels in demonstrations such as these is comparable to the surprise one feels when discovering how difficult it is to perform a manual task such as typing or driving with a cast on one's little finger. One is insensitive to the complexity of the things one does when one does things.

3.3   The World as an Outside Memory

The account of vision developed here enables one to understand how it is possible to enjoy a sense of perceptual awareness of the whole scene, even though one only sees that to which one directs one's attention. One's sense of the perceptual presence of the whole scene stems from the fact that one has continous *access* to the scene.

To explain this, consider that the environmental detail is present, lodged, as it is, right there before individuals and that they therefore have access to that detail by the mere movement of their eyes or bodies. According to the sensorimotor contingency view, perceivers are masters of the sensorimotor contingencies in virtue of which they can acquire perceptual information. This mastery consists not only in the possession of sensorimotor skills, but also—and this is hugely important—in the ability on the part of perceivers, to draw on those skills effortlessly as need arises. One way to capture the point we are trying to make is to note that one is seldom surprised by sensorimotor contingencies (as one would be, say, were one to put on inverting lenses). With the possession of skillful mastery of sensorimotor contingencies, then, there comes a readiness in the face of new experience. One might say, of this readiness, that it consists in the knowledge that the mere flick of an eye or turn of the head will make available currently unavailable information, but this would be somewhat misleading insofar as the sort of knowledge at play here is practical and nontheoretical.

On this analysis, there is no need for the brain to construct a detailed internal representation or model of the environment, since the environment is there to serve, in Brooks's (1991) phrase, as its own best model. As O'Regan (1992) has proposed, the environment serves as a kind of external memory store. Information is available in the environment to be sampled as needed, by the flick of the eye or the turn of the head.

This analysis of a perceiver's sense of contact with detail in terms of confident skill-based access to detail is relevant to an account of the visual phenomenon of "amodal completion."

Take, for example, the perceptual experience of partially occluded objects. When you see a cat through a picket fence, you take yourself to perceive a cat, even though, if the cat stands still, you only really see strips of the cat's surface through the slats of the fence. Crucially, there is a genuine sense in which you experience or perceive and do not merely surmise the strictly unseen portions of the cat. Your experienced relation to the unperceived portion of the cat is not at all like your relation to the hallway outside your door. The hallway is also felt to be present. But this feeling of presence is nonperceptual. The sensorimotor contingency theory offers an explanation of the difference between what is directly seen, what is amodally perceived, and what is merely "thought as present" but not perceived. First, as the perceiver of the cat, you "know," in a practical sense, that a step to the right will produce new cat-surface. It is the knowledge that movement or alteration of the sensory organ gives rise, in systematic and predictable ways, to new sensory data, which provides the sensory character of your contact with the cat. Second, it is precisely the absence of this sort of sensorimotor contingency in the case of the hallway outside your door, or the room behind your head, that makes these latter examples a "thought presence" but not an "experienced presence." Consider, for example, that if you blink, this has no affect on your feeling of the presence of the room behind the head. This goes a long way to showing that the felt presence of the room behind the head is not a *perceptual* presence.

4   Visual Consciousness Reconsidered

4.1   The Problem of Qualia

It may be argued that there is still something missing in our account of vision—namely, an explanation of the *qualitative character* of visual experience. Can the sensorimotor contingency theory in addition provide an explanation of what philosophers have called "the raw feel" or "qualia" of seeing?

As we understand it, the qualia debate rests on what Ryle (1949) called a category mistake. Qualia are meant to be properties of experiential states or events. But experiences, we have argued, are not states. They are ways of acting. They are things we do. There is no introspectibly available property determining the character of one's experiential states, for there are no such states. Hence, there are, in this sense at least, no (visual) qualia. Qualia are an illusion, and the famous explanatory gap (Levine 1983) is no real gap at all.

It is important to stress that in saying this we are not denying that experience has qualitative character. We have already said a good deal about the qualitative character of experience and how it is constituted by the character of the sensorimotor contingencies at play when we perceive. Our claim, rather, is that it is confused to think of the qualitative character of experience in terms of the *occurrence* of something (whether in the mind or brain). Experience is something one does, and its qualitative features are aspects of this activity.

What Gives Rise to the Illusion of Qualia?

Many philosophers, vision scientists, and laypeople will say that seeing always involves the occurrence of raw feels or qualia. If this view is mistaken, as we believe, then how can we explain its apparent plausibility to so many? In order to make our case convincing, we must address this question.

To appreciate one main source of the illusion of qualia, consider once again the phenomenon of change blindness. Many people say that they have the impression that when they see, the entire visual field is present to consciousness in all its nearly infinite detail. The change blindness results suggest that they do not have such detailed, picture-like awareness. What explains the conviction that they do? As we have discussed above, and as argued by O'Regan (1992; O'Regan, Rensink and Clark 1999), the explanation is that individuals have access to all the detail by means of the mere flick of an eye or turn of the head, and so it is *as if* they have everything in view all the time. The *feeling* of presence of the detail stems from their implicit knowledge of the ways in which movements of the eye and head gives rise to new detail and new information. It is significant that one can explain this feeling without supposing that all the detail is represented in consciousness.

In exactly this way when you see something red, you *feel* that the redness has a certain definite, sensation-like presence and immediacy. The explanation for this is that you have access to the redness by the most minute of eye movements or attentional shifts. The redness is there, in the environment. The slightest eye, head, or attention movement reveals further information about its character. Because you have continuous *access* to the redness in the environment, it may seem as if you are mentally in contact with it continuously. This leads you to say, mistakenly, that there is a feeling of redness (say) in your head all along.

We have already considered an important second source of the illusion of qualia. We tend to overlook the complexity and heterogeneity of experience, which makes it seem as if in experience there are *unified sensation-like* occurrences. Just as there is no single, unitary quality of driving a Porsche, so there are no single unitary visual *sensations*.

4.3 Is the Illusion of Qualia Really So Widespread?

Is the illusion of qualia really as widespread as it would seem? Perhaps not. If you ask what a person sees, he or she will not bring up visual experiences and their intrinsic features. In everyday life, discussions of what one sees are for the most part confined to discussions of things themselves (of the things one sees). Even when one is viewing a piece of art, when one may deliberately try to reflect on the way the work affects him or her visually, nonphilosophers will rarely confuse the question *What is it like to look at the piece?* (What it reminds one of, how it makes one feel, whether one finds it pleasant or not) with that favorite question of philosophers', namely, *What is it like to have an experience as of seeing a painting* (that is, what are the intrinsic, qualitative features of the visual experience)?

Another way to make this point is to say that qualia-based accounts of the phenomenology of experience actually misdescribe the phenomenological character of experience (what experience is like). Qualia talk, one might say, is theory driven and so the illusion of qualia is a theoretical illusion. Crucially, normal perceivers do not, by virtue of being normal perceivers, buy into the relevant theory.

4.4 Overcoming the Explanatory Gap (Or Why There Is No Gap)

The problem of the explanatory gap is that of explaining qualia in physical or biological terms. We believe that our view bridges this gap. More accurately, it demonstrates that the gap itself is an artifact of a certain—we believe mistaken—conception of experience. There is not really any gap at all.

Our claim, simply put, is this: There is no explanatory gap because there is nothing answering to the theorist's notion of qualia. That is, we reject the conception of experience that is presupposed by the problem of the explanatory gap. (Note that we can make this claim even though we do not, as we have been at pains to explain above, deny that there are experiences and that experience has qualitative character.)

To appreciate the structure of our claim, consider once again, very briefly, the Porsche-driving example. We have argued that the feeling of driving a Porsche is constituted by the different things one does when one drives a Porsche, and from our confident mastery of the relevant sensorimotor contingencies. We can now appreciate that there is no need to explain the physical or causal basis of the occurrence of the unitary Porsche-driving quality, for there is no such quality. And so, likewise, there is no need to seek a neural basis for the occurrence of visual qualia such as that of red, for, in the relevant sense, there are no such qualia.

Critics will object that it is no easier to see how possession and mastery of sensorimotor skill can bridge the explanatory gap than it is to see how different patterns of neural activity can accomplish the same feat. But this very question betrays a failure to understand our proposal. For our claim is *not* that knowledge and exercise of sensorimotor contingencies can solve the same feat. Our claim is that there is no feat to be accomplished and *therefore* no possible way in which neural activity can accomplish it. Let's return again to simple examples. You hold a bottle in your hand. You *feel* the whole bottle. But the differents parts of your hands make contact only with isolated parts of its surface. Nevertheless, don't you feel the whole bottle as present? That is, phenomenologically speaking, the feeling of presence of the bottle is not a *conjecture* or an *inference*. The feeling you have is the knowledge that movements of the hand open up and reveal new aspects of bottle surface. It feels to you as if there's stuff there to be touched by movement of the hands. That's what the feeling of the presence of the bottle consists in. But the basis of the feeling, then, is not something *occurring* now. The basis rather is your knowledge *now* as to what you can do.

5   Vision and Brain

5.1   Neural Correlates of Visual Consciousness?

A considerable amount of recent work in visual science and consciousness studies has been devoted to the quest for what has been called "neural correlates of consciousness" (Crick and Koch 1990, 1995, 1998); for an illuminating review, see Chalmers (2000). As an illustration of such work, we use the impressive studies of Logothetis and colleagues (Logothetis, Leopold, and Sheinberg 1996; Logothetis 1998; Leopold and Logothetis 1996, 1999) analyzing neural substrates of binocular rivalry in laboratory monkeys. In binocular rivalry each eye is presented with a different stimulus (e.g., a horizontal bar, a face). Under these conditions the observer experiences not both stimuli, or some amalgam of the two, but rather a sequence of alternating percepts corresponding roughly to one or the other of the two stimuli. When one stimulus is dominant, the other is not perceived. The perceptual reversals occur irregularly and at intervals of a few seconds. Logothetis and collaborators show that in tested visual areas (e.g., V1/V2, V4, MT, IT, STS), some neurons are unaffected by perceptual reversals. The activity of these neurons is driven by the stimulus patterns entering the eyes, which remain unchanged. The activity of other neurons, however, depends directly on the internally generated shifts in the percept.

The percentage of such percept-driven cells is substantially higher in IT and STS, where 90 percent of tested neurons correlate to percepts, than in other visual areas. (In V1/V2, for example, a much smaller percentage of neurons were percept-driven.) These data suggest (it is claimed) that neural activity in IT and STS forms the neural correlate of the experience.

Other kinds of neural representations or neural correlates of conscious perceptual experience arise in the context of perceptual completion phenomena. A classic example is the work of von der Heydt and his colleagues, who found neurons in V2 that fire for illusory contours similar to how they fire for real contours (von der Heydt, Peterhans, and Baumgartner 1984; von der Heydt and Peterhans 1989; Peterhans and van der Heydt 1989). A number of other examples involving perceptual completion have been reviewed by Pessoa, Thompson, and Noë (1998). (See also Thompson, Noë, and Pessoa 1999.)

Work like that described above has been received with enthusiasm: Researchers believe that the discovery of neural representations that correlate with perceptual experience brings us closer to understanding what gives rise to the perceptual experience. The underlying assumption is that if a set of neurons is found in the brain that correlates strongly with aware perceptual states, then, because these neurons are probably linked to the mechanisms that are generating awareness, one is likely to be able to explain perceptual awareness by appeal to this neural activity.

But this reasoning is unsound. Indeed, consider what would happen if one were actually to find a set of neurons that correlated *perfectly* with visual awareness. For the sake of illustration, suppose one were to discover that in the pineal gland of macaque monkeys there is a tiny projection room in which what is seen by the monkey is projected on an internal screen whose activity correlates perfectly with the monkey's visual awareness. On reflection it is clear that such a discovery (this would surely be the Holy Grail of a neural correlate of consciousness seeker!) would not bring us any closer to understanding how monkeys see. For one would still lack an explanation of how the image in the pineal gland *generates* seeing, that is, how it enables or controls or modulates the forms of activity in which seeing consists. One would certainly be entitled, on the basis of the strong correlation between features of what is seen and features of what is projected onto the pineal projection screen, to assume that this neural activity played some role in vision. But nothing more could be said about such a discovery.

Why do some researchers believe that to understand the nature of consciousness or vision it is necessary to track down the neural representations that correlate with conscious experience? One possible explanation is that these researchers are (perhaps unwittingly) committed to the idea that the discovery of *perfect* correlation would give one reason to believe that one had discovered *the* neural activity sufficient to produce the experience (as suggested by Chalmers 2000). Teller and Pugh (1983) call such a neural substrate of experience the bridge locus. In addition, thinkers may unwittingly subscribe to what Pessoa, Thompson, and Noë (1998) and Thompson, Noë, and Pessoa (1999) have called *analytic isomorphism*. This is the view that for every experience there will be a neural substrate whose activity is sufficient to produce that experience (a bridge locus) and that there will be an isomorphism (though not necessarily spatial or topographic) between features of the experience and features of the bridge locus. It is the existence of such an *isomorphism* that works to justify the claim that the discovery of such a neural substrate would *explain* the occurrence of the percept.

We believe that one must reject the metaphysical dogma of analytic isomorphism. As argued by Pessoa, Thompson, and Noë (1998), no neural state will be sufficient to produce experience. Just as mechanical activity in the engine of a car is not sufficient to guarantee driving activity (suppose the car is in a swamp, or suspended by a magnet), so neural activity alone is not sufficient to produce vision.

Note also that if this view is correct, then it is a mistake to expect to find neurons that *are* perfectly correlated with visual consciousness. Ultimately visual consciousness is not a single thing but rather a collection of task and environment-contingent capacities, each of which can be appropriately deployed when necessary. Furthermore, we expect that if neurophysiologists do find neurons that correlate strongly with awareness, then most likely this will only be for one or the other set of conditions or tasks.

5.2 There Is No Need for "Binding"

Neuroanatomists believe that the visual system is composed of numerous, more or less independent subsystems (or modules), which extract a variety of different attributes such as color, contrast, depth, orientation, and texture from the visual stimulus (e.g., De Yoe and van Essen 1988; Livingstone and Hubel 1988; Zeki 1993). The fact that these modules operate independently and are often localized in different cerebral regions raises the question of how the separate streams of information ultimately come together to give us a unified experience. One suggestion for solving this so-called binding problem was the idea of the "grandmother cell" in which single cells, or at least highly localized cerebral regions, combine information pertaining to specific precepts: for example, face-sensitive cells (Rolls 1992), place-sensitive cells (O'Keefe et al. 1998), or view-sensitive cells (Rolls and O'Mara 1995). A more recent idea that does not require bringing signals into a single brain location has also received support from neurophysiological evidence (cf. Brecht, Singer, and Engel 1998; Castelo-Branco, Neuenschwander, and Singer 1998; Abeles and Prut 1996; Llinas and Ribary 1993; Gray and Singer 1989). Under this view, separate cortical areas that are concurrently analyzing the different aspects of a stimulus might oscillate in synchrony, and it might be this synchrony that provides the unity of perceptual experience (as well as the perceptual experience of unity).

There are two motivations in the reasoning that underlies these types of investigations: One concerns temporal unity, and the other concerns "conceptual" unity. Certainly it is true that one has the impression that, when one recognizes an object, all its attributes are seen simultaneously at one "perceptual moment." This leads scientists to think that the objects' attributes must be bound together *synchronously* in the internal representation in order to provide the singleness of the perceptual moment. But this is a fallacy. Thinking that physical synchrony is necessary to have a synchronous experience is the same kind of fallacy as thinking that because we experience the world spatially, there must be topologically equivalent maps in the brain. Underlying this fallacy is the implicit assumption that the synchrony or coherence of perception requires presenting information in a synchronous or coherent way to an internal homunculus. In fact, just as the perception of the three-dimensional world does not require three-dimensional maps in the brain, subjective simultaneity does not require simultaneity of brain events.[3] This point has been made by Dennett and Kinsbourne (1992); see also O'Regan (1992) and Pessoa, Thompson, and Noë (1998). What explains the temporal unity of experience is the fact that experience is a thing one is doing, and one is doing it *now*.

Concerning the issue of "conceptual" coherence, a similar argument can be made: The fact that object attributes seem perceptually to be part of a single object does not require them to be "represented" in any unified kind of way: for example, at a single location in the brain or by a single process. They *may* be so represented, but there is no *logical necessity* for this. Furthermore, if they are represented in a spatially or temporally localized way, *the fact that they are so represented cannot in itself* be what explains the spatial, temporal, or conceptual phenomenology of perceptual coherence.[4] What explains the conceptual unity of experience is the fact that experience is a thing one is doing, and one is doing it with respect to a conceptually unified external object.

Earlier we noted that were researchers to discover pictures in the brain that correlated with the experience of seeing, one would still have moved very little closer toward an explanation of seeing. But once one recognizes this, then one further realizes that there is no reason to suppose that to explain seeing one should seek detailed internal pictures. There is no longer any rationale for supposing that there is a place in the brain where different streams of information are brought together and "unified" (whether conceptually or temporally). With the appreciation of this point, we can dismiss the problem of binding as, in essence, a pseudoproblem.

6   Toward a Sensorimotor Approach to Visual Neuroscience

6.1   Experience Does Not Derive from Brain Activity Alone

We have already taken steps toward a positive characterization of the role of the brain in vision in claiming that studies of the neural bases of vision must be framed by a consideration of the whole animal's broader behavioral and cognitive capacities. In the following sections, we try to extend these remarks.

Consider the missile guidance system discussed earlier. Suppose that at the present moment the target airplane happens to have gone out of the field of view of the missile. No information is coming into the missile's sights right now. Nevertheless, the missile guidance system has a certain potential: It "knows" that by making the appropriate change in its trajectory, it should be able to bring the missile back into view. Thus, even though at this particular moment the airplane is not visible and no visual information is coming in, it is still correct to say that the missile is currently tracking its target.

Exactly the same point, we argue, can be made about seeing and the sensorimotor contingencies governing seeing. When you make an eye saccade, the sensory stimulation provided by an object will change drastically due to very strong retinal smearing. At that very moment, you do not receive sensory input from the object. But there is no more reason to think that this interruption in stimulation leads to an interruption in seeing than to assume that the missile is no longer tracking the plane when the plane happens to go out of the missile's sights. The missile continues to track the plane, and the perceiver continues to see, because each is master of the relevant sensorimotor contingencies, and each is exercising those capacities in an appropriate manner. Seeing an object consists precisely in the knowledge of the relevant sensorimotor contingencies—in being able to exercise mastery of the fact that if, among other things, you make an eye movement, the stimulus will change in the particular way typical of what happens when you move your eyes. If the stimulation due to the object did not change in that way, then you would not be seeing the object—you might, for example, be hallucinating it.

These considerations call attention to the fact that interruptions and discontinuities in stimulation (owing to saccades, blinks, eye movements, chromatic aberrations, and other supposed defects of the visual apparatus) are in fact part of what seeing is. It is one's exercise of the mastery of just such regularities in sensorimotor contingencies in which seeing consists. What is striking for our purposes is that just as moments of stillness and inactivity may be essential to the performance of a dance, so moments of neural inactivity may be precisely what characterizes the exercise of sight. This is a fact that can only come into focus based on a conception of vision as a mode of activity such as that developed by the sensorimotor contingency theory.

Considerations such as these show further that although neural activity is necessary for vision, there need be no one-to-one mapping between seeing and occurrent neural states and processes. Vision requires all manner of neural events, but crucially, on our view, the experience of seeing itself cannot be equated with the simultaneous occurrence of any particular neural activity. This follows from the fact that, at any given moment, the brain may be inactive.

6.2   What Is the Function of the Brain in Vision?

What then is the function of the brain in vision? Very generally speaking, it is to enable the knowledge and exercise of sensorimotor contingencies. Seeing, we argue, is constituted by the brain's present attunement to the changes that would occur as a consequence of an action on the part of the perceiver. Visual experience is just the exercise of the mastery of relevant sensorimotor contingencies. An example may help make the point clearer. Your visual apprehension of the roundness of a plate consists in part in your knowledge that changes in your relation to the plate (movements relative to the plate) will induce changes in the plate's profile. That it looks round to you now, despite its elliptical profile, is constituted by your application, now, of skillful mastery of the appropriate rule of sensorimotor contingency. Other rules of sensorimotor contingency may be, as it were, more low-level. As you move your eye across a straight line, there is a characteristic pattern of transformation of the retinal stimulation. The brain is attuned to this pattern. One important function of the brain may thus consist in the testing of the appropriateness of the application of certain patterns of sensorimotor contingency.

An important advantage of this view is that it allows us to escape from the problem of having to explain how brain activity could give rise to experience. We escape from this problem because we propose that experience does *not* derive from brain activity. Experience is just the activity in which the exploring of the environment consists. The experience lies in the doing.

6.3   Strategies for Future Research

A good deal of recent neuroscientific research shows that to understand the role the brain plays in supporting perceptual and motor capacities, it is necessary to keep clearly in view the broader context of the animal's skillful task-oriented activity. Specific neural states cannot be perfectly correlated with specific perceptual states. You cannot understand the contribution of neural activity if you restrict yourself to a brain's-eye view. This fits with our model of vision and visual consciousness. Seeing is not a simple occurrence; it is a rich, exploratory activity within a certain environment and with a certain sensory apparatus, drawing on a number of heterogeneous capacities. Neural activity does not in itself produce experience. Neural activity contributes to experience only as enabling mastery and exercise of laws of sensorimotor contingency.

An exhaustive survey of this neuroscientific research goes beyond the scope of this discussion. Here we briefly indicate some examples.

6.3.1   Neural Plasticity and Sensory Substitution.   A currently active domain of investigation in neurophysiology concerns findings showing that cortical representations of visual or somatosensory information can change as a function of stimulation, use, or lesion. For example, Pascual-Leone et al. (1993) show that the sensorimotor representation of the reading finger in the cortex of proficient Braille readers becomes greatly developed at the expense of the representations of other fingers (cf. Sterr et al. 1998). Sadato et al. (1998) have suggested that in proficient Braille readers, tactile processing is "rerouted" to occipital visual cortex (cf. Cohen et al. 1999). The cortical representation of owl monkeys' fingertips become enlarged when the monkeys engage in haptic exploration training (Jenkins et al. 1990). Iriki, Tanaka, and Iwamura (1996) found that receptive fields of bimodal (somatosensory and visual) neurons in the caudal postcentral gyrus of macaque monkeys were altered during tool use "to include the entire length of the rake or to cover the expanded accessible space." Other examples include reorganization of cortical representations as a result of intracortical microstimulation, cortical lesions, digit

amputation or fusion (cf. Wall et al. 1986; Merzenich et al. 1984; Merzenich et al. 1987; Jenkins, Merzenich, and Recanzone 1990), as well as the work of von Melchner, Pallas, and Sur (2000) showing that auditory cortex of ferrets can be "rewired" to process visual information.

Perhaps the most exciting work in this area has been undertaken by Bach-y-Rita and his colleagues on tactile vision substitution systems (TVSS) (Bach-y-Rita 1972). In TVSS, optical images picked up by a camera (worn, say, on the head) are transduced in such a way as to activate an array of stimulators (vibrators or electrodes) in contact with the skin (on, e.g., the abdomen, back, or thigh). Optical images in this way produce a localized pattern of tactile sensation. After an initial period of training, congenitally blind subjects cease to experience tactile sensations when they use the TVSS device and report that they experience objects as arrayed before them in three-dimensional space, just as captured by the camera. As Bach-y-Rita observed, "They learn to make perceptual judgments using visual means of analysis such as perspective, parallax, looming and zooming, and depth judgments" (see chapter 20). Such tactile perception enables subjects to make judgments of shape, size, and number and also to perceive spatial relationships between things, of the sort normally made by vision. With sufficient practice, subjects are able to engage in tasks requiring skillful sensorimotor coordination, e.g., batting a ball or working on an assembly line. In addition, TVSS-aided perception is susceptible to familiar forms of visual distortion and illusion: for example, distant objects "look" small, objects can occlude each other, etc. Today, tactile vision is a very poor substitute for seeing (resolution is low, function diminishes in cluttered environments), but it is indeed a substitute.

6.3.2 Attention and Action. Rizzolatti and his colleagues have developed a "premotor theory of spatial attention" according to which, first, "conscious space perception results from the activity of several cortical and subcortical areas, each with its own neural space representation" (Rizzolatti, Riggio, and Sheliga 1994), and second, these "neural maps" directly function in the guidance of movement and action. There are not two systems, one for spatial attention and one for action. "The system that controls action is the same that controls what we call spatial attention" (256), write Rizzolatti, Riggio, and Sheliga. These claims dovetail with psychophysical, psychological, and neuroscientific evidence demonstrating linkages between perception and motor action. For example, Kustov and Robinson (1996) "studied superior colliculus in monkeys as they shifted their attention during different tasks, and found that each attentional shift is associated with eye-movement preparation" (p. 74). Another line of evidence linking spatial attention and motor activity comes from studies of neglect in animals and humans with damage to cortical motor areas (Kinsbourne 1987, 1995; Rizzolatti, Matelli, and Pavesi 1983). Neglect appears to be best understood as a difficulty in shifting attention to the affected part of the visual field. The fact that neglect should arise from damage to cortical areas serving motor activity further demonstrates the link between attention and motor activity.

6.3.3   Two Visual Systems: The What and the How.

In the last few years a very influential view of the structure of the visual brain has surfaced, according to which there are two streams of visual processing, a dorsal stream and a ventral stream. Opinions differ on the exact functions of the two systems, but Ungeleider and Mishkin (1992) distinguished between a dorsal "where" system devoted to localizing objects, and a ventral "what" system devoted to identifying them. A somewhat different classification was proposed by Goodale and Milner (1992) (cf. also Milner and Goodale 1995), who emphasized that the dorsal system is concerned with coordinating actions directed towards objects, whereas in the ventral system recognition and classification operations are performed that allow persons to memorize and reason about objects. Jeannerod (1997) refers to the dorsal stream as "pragmatic," in that it provides the ability to make the necessary transformations between visual input and motor output to locate an object with respect to the body and to grasp and manipulate it, and calls the ventral stream the "semantic" system. Evidence for this latter interpretation of the two-streams hypothesis comes from studies of the effects of lesions in humans (Milner and Goodale 1995). As they point out, damage to the dorsal stream is associated with impairments of visuomotor control such as optic ataxia (Harvey 1995) in the absence of impairments of the subject's ability to make verbal reports about the shape, features, and location of what is seen. Conversely, damage to the ventral stream produces visual agnosias (Benson and Greenberg 1969; Milner et al. 1991) without impairing visuomotor functioning.

From the standpoint of the sensorimotor contingency view we propose here, the possibility of this kind of double dissociation is not surprising. In our view, seeing is an activity that depends on a broad range of capacities, for example, capacities for bodily movement and guidance, on the one hand, and capacities for speech and rational thought, on the other. To the extent that these capacities are independent, it is not surprising that they can come apart in the manner described. It is not surprising, therefore, that the dorsal system can operate in relative isolation from the ventral system.

Our approach leads us to doubt, on certain interpretations at least, Milner and Goodale's claim that what the visual agnosia patient DF (who retains normal visuo-motor skill) lacks is *visual awareness* of what she sees. Milner and Goodale (1995) suggest that, like DF, normals carry out visually guided actions using information that is not present in awareness and say that only information in the ventral stream enters awareness. According to the view developed here (the sensorimotor contingency view), people are aware of what they see to the extent that they have control over that information for the purposes of guiding action and thought. Awareness is always, we argue, a matter of degree. Even the distracted driver is somewhat aware of what he sees, to the extent that, if we were to ask him, he would tell us what he is looking at. The case of DF is thus a case of what would seem to be partial awareness. She is unable to describe what she sees, but she is otherwise able to use it for the purpose of guiding action.

This may seem like a purely verbal dispute, but an important point is at stake here. What makes the information conscious or aware, in our view, cannot consist just in the activity or lack of activity in a certain brain region (e.g., the ventral stream). Consciousness or awareness is not a property that informational states of the brain can just come to have in that way. Rather, visual awareness is a fact at the level of the integrated behavior of the whole organism. Milner and Goodale (1995) suggest that damage to the ventral stream disrupts non-visuomotor aspects of seeing. This is an important finding. But it would be a mistake to infer from this that the ventral stream is therefore the place where visual awareness happens.

Apart from the above provisos, the "two visual systems" view fits well with the position we develop in this chapter. First, as expected from the sensorimotor contingency–based approach, at the neural level there is a tight connection between seeing and moving. Second, the two-systems approach provides evidence supporting a claim we have made at different stages in this chapter, namely, that seeing does not depend on the existence of unified representations of what is seen. On the two-systems approach, for example, there is not one single representation of space in the brain.

6.3.4 Downward Causation.   Considerable evidence exists that when neural correlates of consciousness have been found, these are sensitive to mood, attentional set, and task. Thompson and Varela (2001) have referred to the modulation of

individual neurons by patterns of activity of populations of neurons and also by the attitude or set of the whole animal as "downward causation." So, for example, as stressed by Varela (1984), Varela, Thompson, and Rosch (1991), Thompson (1995), Pessoa, Thompson, and Noë (1998), and Thompson and Varela (2001), responses in visual cells depend on behavioral factors, such as body tilt (Horn and Hill 1969), posture (Abeles and Prut 1996), and auditory stimulation (Morell 1972; Fishman and Michael 1973). Other studies show that attention and the relevance of a stimulus for the performance of a behavioral task can considerably modulate the responses of visual neurons (Moran and Desimone 1985; Haenny, Maunsell, and Schiller 1988; Chelazze et al. 1983; Treue and Maunsell 1996). Leopold and Logothetis (1999) write about binocular rivalry: "We propose that the perceptual changes are the accidental manifestation of a general mechanism that mediates a number of apparently different behaviors, including exploratory eye movements and shifts of attention. We also propose that while the different perceptions of ambiguous stimuli ultimately depend on activity in the 'sensory' visual areas, this activity is continually steered and modified by central brain structures involved in planning and generating behavioral actions" (p. 254). Leopold and Logothetis suggest that to understand perceptual reversals of the kind encountered when one views an ambiguous figure, or when one undergoes binocular rivalry, it is necessary to consider not only neural activity in visual cortex, but the animal's capacities for thought and action.

Work in these and other areas provides evidence in favor of ways of understanding the role of the brain in vision and consciousness that are different from the ideas in the neural correlate of consciousness and binding problem research programs. Like work in the fields of dynamic systems theory (e.g., Kelso and Kay 1987) and embodied cognition both in robots and in animals or humans (Brooks 1991; Ballard 1991; Clancey 1997; Aloimonos 1992; Cotterill 1995, 1997), this research suggests the importance of accounts of the brain as an element in a system and not, as it were, as the seat of vision and consciousness all by itself.

7   Conclusion

In this chapter we have targeted for criticism a widespread conception of vision as a process in the brain. We have proposed a very different conception of vision and visual consciousness, according to which vision is an activity of exploration of the environment drawing on the perceiver's understanding of the ways in which what individuals do (e.g., eye movements) affects the character of sensory input. According to this sensorimotor approach to vision, vision is a capacity not of the brain, but of the whole active, environmentally situated perceiver.

Our approach has important implications for the understanding of the brain basis of vision and visual experience. First, negatively, our view rejects the idea that neural activity could be sufficient, as a matter of law, to produce visual consciousness. For this reason, we think a good deal of research on the so-called neural correlates of visual consciousness is misdirected. Second, positively, our view leads to the conclusion that the role of the brain in producing vision is to enable active exploration based on implicit knowledge of sensorimotor contingencies. We have indicated, briefly, the ways our approach supports avenues of research into such phenomena as neural plasticity, sensory substitution, attention and action, and downward causation. Crucially, in our view, studies of the neural basis of vision must be framed by consideration of the whole animal's broader behavior and cognitive capacities. Finally, we believe that the approach taken here enables us to give an account of the qualitative character of perceptual experience that avoids the mysteries and pitfalls associated with other accounts.

Notes

1. The notion of transitive consciousness is due to David Rosenthal. The first use of the phrase in print is in Malcolm 1984.
2. In Noë and O'Regan (2000), we explore the philosophical significance of work on inattentional blindness.
3. See Dennett (1991) and Dennett and Kinsbourne (1992) for a similar point.
4. A similar point can be made in connection with the supposed phenomenon of neural "filling in." One doesn't experience a gap in the visual field corresponding to the blind spot. From this it cannot be deduced, as noticed by Dennett (1991, 1992), that there is a neural representation of the filled in blind spot. After all, the brain may simply ignore the absence of information corresponding to the blind spot. If it does, then there's no need for any neural process of filling in. But from this it follows, further, that if it were the case that the neural structures corresponding to our visual experience were spatially continuous and isomorphic to the content of our experience (as if "filling in" had occurred), this could not, in itself, explain one's failure to notice the blind spot! These points are explored in Pessoa, Thompson, and Noë (1998) and also in Thompson, Noë, and Pessoa (1999).

Works Cited

Abeles, M., and Y. Prut. 1996. Spatio-temporal firing patterns in the frontal cortex of behaving monkeys. *J Physiol Paris* 90(3–4): 249–250.

Aloimonos, Y. E. 1992. Purposive and qualitative active vision [Special issue]. *CVGIP: Image Understanding* 56(1).

Bach-y-Rita, P. 1972. *Brain mechanisms in sensory substitution*. New York: Academic Press.

Ballard, D. H. 1991. Animate vision. *Artificial Intelligence* 48: 57–86.

Benson, D. F., and J. P. Greenberg. 1969. Visual form agnosia: A specific deficit in visual discrimination. *Arch. Neurol.* 20: 82–89.

Blackmore, S. J., G. Brelstaff, K. Nelson, and T. Trpscoanko. 1995. Is the richness of our visual world an illusion? Transsaccadic memory for complex scenes. *Perception* 24: 1075–1081.

Braitenberg, V. 1984. *Vehicles*. Cambridge, MA: The MIT Press.

Brecht, M., W. Singer, and A. K. Engel. 1998. Correlation analysis of corticotectal interactions in the cat visual system. *J Neurophysiol* 79(5): 2394–2407.

Brooks, R. 1991. Intelligence without representation. *Artificial Intelligence* 47: 139–159.

Castelo-Branco, M., S. Neuenschwander, and W. Singer. 1998. Synchronization of visual responses between the cortex, lateral geniculate nucleus, and retina in the anesthetized cat. *J Neurosci* 18(16): 6395–6410.

Chalmers, D. J. 2000. What is a neural correlate of consciousness? In T. Metzinger, ed., *Neural Correlates of Consciousness: Empirical and Conceptual Questions*. Cambridge, MA: The MIT Press.

Chelazze, L., E. K. Miller, J. Duncan, and R. Desimone. 1983. A neural basis for visual search in inferior temporal cortex. *Nature* 363: 345–347.

Clancey, W. J. 1997. *Situated cognition: On human knowledge and computer representations*. Cambridge: Cambridge University Press.

Cohen, L. G., R. A. Weeks, N. Sadato, P. Celnik, K. Ishii, and M. Hallett. 1999. Period of susceptibility for cross-modal plasticity in the blind. *Ann Neurol* 45(4): 451–460.

Cotterill, R. M. J. 1995. On the unity of conscious experience. *Journal of Consciousness Studies* 2: 290–312.

Cotterill, R. M. J. 1997. On the mechanism of consciousness. *Journal of Consciousness Studies* 4: 231–247.

Crick, F., and C. Koch. 1990. Toward a neurobiological theory of consciousness. *Seminars in the Neurosciences* 2: 263–275.

Crick, F., and C. Koch. 1995. Are we aware of neural activity in primary visual cortex? *Nature* 375: 121–123.

Crick, F., and C. Koch. 1998. Consciousness and neuroscience. *Cerebral Cortex* 8: 97–107.

De Yoe, E. A., and D. C. van Essen. 1988. Concurrent processing streams in monkey visual cortex. *Trends in Neuroscience* 11: 219–226.

Dennett, D. C. 1991. *Consciousness Explained*. Boston: Little Brown.

Dennett, D. C. 1992. "Filling in" versus finding out: A ubiquitous confusion in cognitive science. In H. L. Pick Jr., P. van den Broek, and D. C. Knill, eds., *Cognition: Conceptual and Methodological Issues* 33–49. Washington, DC: American Psychological Association.

Dennett, D. C. 1998. No bridge over the stream of consciousness. *Behavioral and Brain Sciences* 21(6): 753–754.

Dennett, D. C. 2001. Surprise, surprise. [Comment on O'Regan and Noë 2001.] *Behavioral and Brain Sciences* 24(5).

Dennett, D. C., and M. Kinsbourne. 1992. Time and the observer: The where and when of consciousness in the brain. *Behavioral and Brain Sciences* 15: 183–247.

Fishman, M. C., and C. R. Michael. 1973. Integration of auditory information in cat's visual cortex. *Vision Research* 13: 1415.

Goodale, M. A., and A. D. Milner. 1992. Separate visual pathways for perception and action. *Trends in Neurosciences* 15(1): 20–25.

Gray, C. M., and W. Singer. 1989. Stimulus-specific neuronal oscillations in orientation columns of cat visual cortex. *Proc Natl Acad Sci USA* 86(5): 1698–1702.

Haenny, P. E., J. H. R. Maunsell, and P. H. Schiller. 1988. State dependent activity in monkey visual cortex. *Experimental Brain Research* 69: 245–259.

Harvey, M. 1995. Translation of "Psychic paralysis of gaze, optic ataxia, and spatial disorder of attention" by Rudolph Balint. *Cognitive Neuropsychology* 12: 261–282.

Horn, G., and R. M. Hill. 1969. Modifications of the receptive field of cells in the visual cortex occurring spontaneously and associated with bodily tilt. *Nature* 221: 185–187.

Iriki, A., M. Tanaka, and Y. Iwamura. 1996. Coding of modified body schema during tool use by macaque postcentral neurones. *Neuroreport* 7(14): 2325–2330.

Jeannerod, M. 1997. *The cognitive neuroscience of action*. Oxford, UK: Blackwell Publishers, Inc.

Jenkins, W. M., M. M. Merzenich, and G. Recanzone. 1990. Neocortical representational dynamics in adult primates: implications for neuropsychology. *Neuropsychologia* 28(6): 573–584.

Jenkins, W. M., M. M. Merzenich, M. T. Ochs, T. Allard, and E. Guic-Robles. 1990. Functional reorganization of primary somatosensory cortex in adult owl monkeys after behaviorally controlled tactile stimulation. *J Neurophysiol* 63(1): 82–104.

Kelso, J. A. S., and B. A. Kay. 1987. Information and control: A macroscopic analysis of perception-action coupling. In H. Heuer and A. F. Sanders, eds., *Perspectives on perception and action*. Hillsdale, NJ: Erlbaum.

Kinsbourne, M. 1987. Mechanisms of unilateral neglect. In M. Jeannerod, ed., *Neurophysiological and neuropsychological aspects of spatial neglect*, 69–86. Amsterdam: North-Holland.

Kinsbourne, M. 1995. Awareness of one's own body: An attentional theory of its nature, development and brain basis. In J. L. Bermudez, A. Marcel, and N. Eilan, eds., *The Body and the Self*, 205–223. Cambridge, MA: The MIT Press.

Kustov, A. A., and D. L. Robinson. 1996. Shared neural control of attentional shifts and eye movements. *Nature* 384: 74–77.

Leopold, D. A., and N. K. Logothetis. 1996. Activity changes in early visual cortex reflect monkeys' percepts during binocular rivalry. *Nature* 379(6565): 549–553.

Leopold, D. A., and N. K. Logothetis. 1999. Multistable phenomena: Changing views in perception. *Trends in Cognitive Studies* 3(7): 254–265.

Levine, J. 1983. Materialism and qualia: The explanatory gap. *Pacific Philosophical Quarterly* 64: 354–361.

Livingstone, M., and D. Hubel. 1988. Segregation of form, color, movement and depth: Anatomy, physiology and perception. *Nature* 240: 740–749.

Llinas, R., and U. Ribary. 1993. Coherent 40-Hz oscillation characterizes dream state in humans. *Proc Natl Acad Sci USA* 90(5): 2078–2081.

Logothetis, N. K. 1998. Single units and conscious vision. *Philos Trans R Soc Lond B Biol Sci* 353(1377): 1801–1818.

Logothetis, N. K., D. A. Leopold, and D. L. Sheinberg. 1996. What is rivalling during binocular rivalry? *Nature* 380(6575): 621–624.

Mack, A., and I. Rock. 1998. *Inattentional blindness*. Cambridge, MA: The MIT Press.

Malcolm, N. 1984. Consciousness and causality. In D. M. Armstrong and N. Malcolm, eds., *Consciousness and causality*. Oxford: Blackwell.

Merzenich, M. M., R. J. Nelson, J. H. Kaas, M. P. Stryker, W. M. Jenkins, J. M. Zook, M. S. Cynader, and A. Schoppmann. 1987. Variability in hand surface representations in areas 3b and 1 in adult owl and squirrel monkeys. *J Comp Neurol* 258(2): 281–296.

Merzenich, M. M., R. J. Nelson, M. P. Stryker, M. S. Cynader, A. Schoppmann, and J. M. Zook. 1984. Somatosensory cortical map changes following digit amputation in adult monkeys. *J Comp Neurol* 224(4): 591–605.

Milner, A. D., and M. A. Goodale. 1995. *The visual brain in action*. Oxford, UK: Oxford University Press.

Milner, A. D., D. I. Perrett, R. S. Johnston, P. J. Benson, T. R. Jordan, D. W. Heeley, et al. 1991. Perception and action in "visual form agnosia." *Brain* 114: 405–428.

Moran, J., and R. Desimone. 1985. Selective attention gates visual processing in extrastriate cortex. *Science* 229: 782–784.

Morell, F. 1972. Visual system's view of acoustic space. *Nature* 238: 44–46.

Müller, J. 1838. *Handbuch der Physiologie des Menschen*, vol. V. Coblenz: Hölscher.

Neisser, U., and R. Becklen. 1975. Selective looking: Attending to visually-specified events. *Cognitive Psychology* 7: 480–494.

Noë, A. 2002a. Experience and the active mind. *Synthese* 29: 41–60.

Noë, A. 2002b. On what we see. *Pacific Philosophical Quarterly* 83: 1.

Noë, A., and J. K. O'Regan. 2000. Perception, attention and the grand illusion. *Psyche* 6(15). Online. Available at <http://psyche.cs.monash.edu.au/v6/psyche-6-15-noe.html>.

Noë, A., L. Pessoa, and E. Thompson. 2000. Beyond the grand illusion: what change blindness really teaches us about vision. *Visual Cognition* 7: 93–106.

O'Keefe, J., N. Burgess, J. G. Donnett, K. J. Jeffery, and E. A. Maguire. 1998. Place cells, navigational accuracy, and the human hippocampus. *Philos Trans R Soc Lond B Biol Sci* 353(1373): 1333–1340.

O'Regan, J. K. 1992. Solving the "real" mysteries of visual perception: The world as an outside memory. *Canadian Journal of Psychology* 46: 461–488.

O'Regan, J. K., and A. Noë. 2001. A sensorimotor account of vision and visual consciousness. *Behavioral and Brain Sciences* 24(5).

O'Regan, J. K., and A. Noë. 2002. What it is like to see: A sensorimotor theory of perceptual experience. *Synthese* 29: 79–103.

O'Regan, J. K., H. Deubel, J. J. Clark, and R. A. Rensink. 2000. Picture changes during blinks: Looking without seeing and seeing without looking. *Visual Cognition* 7: 191–212.

O'Regan, J. K., R. A. Rensink, and J. J. Clark. 1999. Change-blindness as a result of "mudsplashes." *Nature* 398: 34.

Pascual-Leone, A., A. Cammarota, E. M. Wassermann, J. P. Brasil-Neto, L. G. Cohen, and M. Hallett. 1993. Modulation of motor cortical outputs to the reading hand of Braille readers. *Ann Neurol* 34(1): 33–37.

Pessoa, L., E. Thompson, A. Noë. 1998. Finding out about filling in: A guide to perceptual completion for visual science and the philosophy of mind. *Behavioral and Brain Sciences* 21(6): 723–802.

Peterhans, E., and R. von der Heydt. 1989. Mechanisms of contour perception in monkey visual cortex. II. Contours bridging gaps. *J Neurosci* 9(5): 1749–1763.

Rensink, R. A., J. K. O'Regan, and J. J. Clark. 1997. To see or not to see: The need for attention to perceive changes in scenes. *Psychological Science* 8(5): 368–373.

Rizzolatti, G., M. Matelli, and G. Pavesi. 1983. Deficit in attention and movement following the removal of postarctuate (area 6) and prearctuate (area 8) cortex in monkey. *Brain* 106: 655–673.

Rizzolatti, G., L. Riggio, and B. M. Sheliga. 1994. Space and selective attention. In C. Umilta and M. Moscovitch, eds., *Attention and Performance XV*, 231–265. Cambridge, MA.: The MIT Press.

Rolls, E. T. 1992. Neurophysiological mechanisms underlying face processing within and beyond the temporal cortical visual areas. *Philos Trans R Soc Lond B Biol Sci* 335(1273): 11–20; discussion 20–11.

Rolls, E. T., and S. M. O'Mara. 1995. View-responsive neurons in the primate hippocampal complex. *Hippocampus* 5(5): 409–424.

Ryle, G. 1949. *The concept of mind.* London: Penguin Books.

Sadato, N., A. Pascual-Leone, J. Grafman, M. P. Deiber, V. Ibanez, and M. Hallett. 1998. Neural networks for Braille reading by the blind. *Brain* 121(Pt 7): 1213–1229.

Simons, D. 2000. Current approaches to change blindness. *Visual Cognition* 7: 1–16.

Simons, D. J., and C. F. Chabris. 1999. Gorillas in our midst: Sustained inattentional blindness for dynamic events. *Perception* 28(9): 1059–1074.

Simons, D. J., and D. T. Levin. 1997. Change blindness. *Trends in Cognitive Sciences* 1(7): 261–267.

Sterr, A., M. M. Muller, T. Elbert, B. Rockstroh, C. Pantev, and E. Taub. 1998. Perceptual correlates of changes in cortical representation of fingers in blind multifinger Braille readers. *J Neurosci* 18(11): 4417–4423.

Teller, D. Y., and E. N. Pugh Jr. 1983. Linking propositions in color vision. In J. D. Mollon and L. T. Sharpe, eds., *Colour vision: Physiology and psychophysics*. London: Academic Press.

Thompson, E. 1995. *Colour vision*. London: Routledge.

Thompson, E., and F. J. Varela. 2001. Radical embodiment: Neural dynamics and consciousness. *Trends in Cognitive Sciences* 5(10): 418–425.

Thompson, E., A. Noë, and L. Pessoa. 1999. Perceptual completion: A case study in phenomenology and cognitive science. In J. Petitot, J.-M. Roy, B. Pachoud, and F. J. Varela, eds., *Naturalizing Phenomenology: Issues in Contemporary Phenomenology and Cognitive Science*. Stanford: Stanford University Press.

Treue, S., and J. H. R. Maunsell. 1996. Attentional modulation of visual motion processing in cortical areas MT and MST. *Nature* 382: 539–541.

Ungerleider, L. G., and M. Mishkin. 1992. Two cortical visual systems. In D. J. Ingle, M. A. Goodale, and R. J. W. Mansfield, eds., *Analysis of visual behavior*, 549–586. Cambridge, MA: The MIT Press.

Varela, F. J. 1984. Living ways of sense-making. A middle path for neuroscience. In P. Livingstone, ed., *Order and disorder: Proceeding of the Stanford International Symposium*, 208–224. Stanford: Anma Libri.

Varela, F. J., E. Thompson, and E. Rosch. 1991. *The embodied mind: Cognitive science and human experience*. Cambridge, MA: The MIT Press.

von der Heydt, R., and E. Peterhans. 1989. Mechanisms of contour perception in monkey visual cortex. I. Lines of pattern discontinuity. *J Neurosci* 9(5): 1731–1748.

von der Heydt, R., E. Peterhans, and G. Baumgartner. 1984. Illusory contours and cortical neuron responses. *Science* 224(4654): 1260–1262.

von Melchner, L., S. L. Pallas, and M. Sur. 2000. Visual behaviour mediated by retinal projections directed to the auditory pathway. *Nature* 404: 871–876.

Wall, J. T., J. H. Kaas, M. Sur, R. J. Nelson, D. J. Felleman, and M. M. Merzenich. 1986. Functional reorganization in somatosensory cortical areas 3b and 1 of adult monkeys after median nerve repair: possible relationships to sensory recovery in humans. *J Neurosci* 6(1): 218–233.

Index